The Talmud
of the
Land of Israel

Chicago Studies in the History of Judaism
Edited by Jacob Neusner
William Scott Green
Calvin Goldscheider

The University of Chicago Press
Chicago and London

The Talmud of the Land of Israel

A Preliminary Translation and Explanation

Volume 6   Terumot

Translated by   Alan J. Avery-Peck

ALAN J. AVERY-PECK is associate professor of classics and director of the Jewish Studies Program at Tulane University.

The University of Chicago Press, Chicago 60637
The University of Chicago Press, Ltd., London

© 1988 by The University of Chicago
All rights reserved. Published 1988
Printed in the United States of America

97 96 95 94 93 92 91 90 89 88   5 4 3 2 1

Library of Congress Cataloging-in-Publication Data

Talmud Yerushalmi. Terumot. English.
   Terumot.

   (The Talmud of the land of Israel; v. 6) (Chicago
studies in the history of Judaism)
   Bibliography: p. 551.
   Includes indexes.
   1. Talmud Yerushalmi. Terumot—Commentaries.
I. Avery-Peck, Alan J. (Alan Jeffery), 1953–   .
II. Title.   III. Series: Talmud Yerushalmi. English.
1982; v. 6.   IV. Series: Chicago studies in the history
of Judaism.

BM 498.5.E5   1982, vol. 6   296.1'2407 s   87–19068
[BM506.T6E5]   [296.1'24]
ISBN 0-226-57663-9

For Lisa

Contents

Preface

This translation and explanation of Tractate Terumot in *The Talmud of the Land of Israel* (the Yerushalmi, the Palestinian Talmud) is meant to facilitate study of the history and religion of the people of Israel in Palestine from the formation of the Mishnah (ca. 220 C.E.) to the fifth century C.E., when the Talmud itself was completed. Such study cannot be contemplated, let alone initiated, without a clear understanding of the principal document for the Judaism of that period, *The Talmud of the Land of Israel*. This translation of Tractate Terumot thus is intended as instrumental in the work of interpreting the Talmud and the Judaism which that document so richly reveals.

In light of its central purpose, the volume has two goals. The first is met in the translation itself, which for the first time produces Yerushalmi Terumot for an English-reading audience. The translation aims to render the Yerushalmi accessible even to individuals who are unaccustomed to the general character of Talmudic discourse and unfamiliar with the technical terms and concepts through which that discourse is expressed. To accomplish this I use the format of a running commentary. Using bracketed interpolations within the translation itself, I explain not only each of the Talmud's individual words and statements, but also the larger issues being addressed and the overall flow of each argument. This renders an extremely difficult text intelligible and available for use in historical and religio-historical studies.

Second, the volume's commentary points out the character of the Yerushalmi through an analysis of the relationship between its material and Mishnah Terumot. My theory in asking the limited question of the relationship between the Yerushalmi and the

Mishnah is that all use of the Talmud for historical study must begin with a clear conception of what the Yerushalmi is and of the goals that its authorities set for themselves in analyzing and discussing the Mishnah's material. My commentary therefore is designed to allow development of a typology of the Yerushalmi's materials and, on that basis, a characterization of this tractate as a whole.

The results of this study of the relationship between Yerushalmi Terumot and Mishnah Terumot appear in the introduction to this volume. There I detail the exact nature of Yerushalmi Terumot as a commentary to and expansion of Mishnah Terumot and propose a theory of the goal and purpose of the Yerushalmi's authorities, who determined the Talmud's character. The introduction also details the content and structure of Tractate Terumot, gives a full account of the methods used in the translation and commentary, and explains the theoretical considerations that determined those methods.

I am grateful to my teacher, Professor Jacob Neusner, who proposed this translation and commentary and under whose guidance the project was carried out. For his support and encouragement as a teacher and friend, both during my years at Brown University and since then, I thank him.

I further thank Professor Neusner for the opportunity to read the first three chapters of this translation in his graduate seminar at Brown University. In that seminar, Professor Roger Brooks, presently at Notre Dame University, and Professor Louis Newman of Carlton University, contributed important insights concerning both the overall mode of translation and the content and meaning of specific Talmudic discussions. As a result of their attention to my work, this translation and commentary is better than it otherwise could have been.

Over the past years, I have benefited from discussions with Professor Martin Jaffee of the University of Washington in Seattle. He kindly agreed to read a draft of the introduction and offered valuable aid in the rendering of several passages within the translation. I appreciate the time which he took to help me with my work.

Professor Gary Porton, the critical reader of this volume, suggested many corrections and improvements. Along with this, I thank him for the friendship and guidance that he has offered me since I first met him in 1973 when he was my undergraduate instructor at the University of Illinois in Urbana. In the years since then, his accomplishments have continued to serve as a model for me. I thank him for his guidance and continuing support.

I am grateful to the Max Richter Foundation for graciously helping to support publication of this volume. I am thankful as well for the support of the Harry Herman Memorial Fund, established by Helen and Shael Herman; Lisa and Mark Herman; Mollie and Avram Herman; and Morris Herman, all of New Orleans, Louisiana. Mr. Shael Herman also assisted in the arduous task of proofreading. I appreciate his good-natured assistance and the many improvements of style and content that he suggested.

Begun shortly before our wedding and completed on the eve of our first anniversary, this book is dedicated to my wife, Lisa J. Avery-Peck. Her support and boundless confidence assured that I would complete this volume. If it were not for her love and devotion, I could not even have begun it.

Introduction to Terumot

The Content of Mishnah Terumot

The topic of Tractate Terumot is heave-offering, one of the several agricultural gifts which the Mishnah requires Israelites to set aside from produce they grow upon the land of Israel.[1] The particular offering discussed here is designated for the use of the priests and their households. Yet the tractate's concern for this offering is not from the point of view of the priests. It does not answer the questions which they would ask, such as which priests deserve to receive the offering, the conditions under which members of their household may eat it, and how they might assure that Israelites pay the required share. The tractate, rather, takes the point of view of the Israelite householder who must set aside heave-offering. Tractate Terumot prescribes how Israelites are to designate a portion of their produce to be heave-offering, and it outlines their responsibility to protect the priest's due from common use until it is conveyed to the priest. In short, the tractate describes what it believes that all Israelites should know in order to properly pay one of their required agricultural dues.

Mishnah Terumot derives its concept of heave-offering from Scripture. Num. 18:8-13 delineates those offerings which the people of Israel contribute to the support of the Aaronide priesthood. After discussing Temple offerings, parts of which belong to the priests, it turns to agricultural dues. Verses 11-13 read:

> (11) This also is yours, the offering of their gift (*trwmt mtnm*), all of the wave offerings of the people of Israel; I have given them to

you, as a perpetual due; every one who is clean in your house
may eat of it. (12) All of the best of the oil, and all of the best of
the wine and of the grain, the first of them (r'šytm) which they
give to the Lord, I give to you. (13) The first ripe fruits (bkwry)
of all that is in their land, which they bring to the Lord, shall be
yours; every one who is clean in your house may eat of it.

It is difficult to determine the number and nature of the offerings
listed in these verses. "The offering of their gift," verse 11, appears to be a general term, referring to all agricultural dues
which are eaten by priests. These include the wave offerings
(vs. 11), the best of the oil, wine and grain (vs. 12), and the first
fruits (vs. 13). The people who stand behind Mishnah Terumot,
however, have read "the offering of their gift" in conjunction
with verse 12's "best of the oil, wine and grain, the first of
them." In this manner they identify a single agricultural offering
distinct from the "first fruits" of verse 13.[2] In the text before us
this due is called "heave-offering" (trwmh). It also is known by
the term "first," suggested by verse 12 (see M. Ter. 3:7).

The central facts which the Mishnah knows about heave-
offering are taken from this passage, namely, that heave-offering
is holy and the property of priests. In accordance with its sanctified status, it must be eaten in cultic cleanness and may be
eaten only by the priest and members of his household. These
facts, found in Scripture, are basic to everything the tractate
states about heave-offering. The Mishnah, moreover, completes
the Priestly Code's picture by taking up specific questions that
must be answered if the priests indeed are to be supported as
Scripture wishes. As I stated above, the Mishnah discusses how
Israelites are to separate and care for the required offering,
thereby assuring that the priest ultimately will receive and consume it.

This judgment about the relationship between Tractate Terumot and Scripture, however, is not entirely to the point. For the
tractate uses the framework which I have described to discuss a
question different from the simple one left open by Scripture—
how Israelites are to pay the priestly due. While dependent upon
the Hebrew Bible, the Mishnah develops this topic in a way
quite unforeseen in Scripture. Having learned from the Priestly
Code that heave-offering is holy and to be eaten only by priests,
the Mishnah's authorities take up the following very specific line
of questioning.

They want to know, first, how and why this agricultural tax,
comprised of produce grown on the land of Israel, comes to be

holy. Most produce of the land may be eaten or otherwise used by anyone, without restriction. How does certain food come to be different?

The second, closely related, issue is the effect this holy produce, heave-offering, has upon other, secular food with which it is mixed. Does the heave-offering's holiness contaminate the other food, so that it all must be deemed consecrated? This second issue is expanded to include other cases in which heave-offering is used as though it were secular, for instance, cases in which it is eaten by a nonpriest or planted as seed.

Finally, the authorities of Tractate Terumot discuss the circumstances under which heave-offering ceases to be holy, such that it again may be eaten or used by anyone, as is common produce. This is the end point of the process that began with the food's initial consecration as a priestly gift.

The tractate thus uses the laws governing the separation and disposition of heave-offering as a context in which to provide a larger picture of its notion of sanctification and of the safe conduct of the holy through the profane world. Mishnah Terumot does not dwell upon the priesthood and its needs, the central concern of Scripture. Rather, it presents a detailed theology of sanctification which explains how things become holy, what happens to them once they are holy, and how they ultimately cease to be holy.[3]

With the overarching topic of the tractate clear, we may turn to the specific theory of sanctification which the Mishnah's authorities express. The first issue is their notion of how heave-offering becomes holy in the first place. According to Tractate Terumot, this depends upon certain thoughts and deeds of the Israelite householder. That is to say, it is the common Israelite—the nonpriest—who, while forbidden to eat holy produce, has the power to cause the produce to be deemed holy. He does this by first formulating the intention to consecrate produce as a priestly due. Then he pronounces a formula by which he orally designates a portion of his produce to be heave-offering. Finally, he effects his intention by physically separating that portion of the produce from the rest of the batch. Through these thoughts and actions the common Israelite determines what produce, and how much of it, is to be holy.[4]

The point is that the Israelite householder is central to the process of sanctification. The holy heave-offering comes into being *only* if the Israelite properly formulates the intention to sanctify part of the produce of the land and indicates that intention through corresponding words and actions.[5] The tractate further suggests that once consecrated, the offering's holiness is maintained in the secular world only if the Israelite is intent upon preventing its misuse. That is to say, according to the tractate, the heave-offering cannot be profaned so long as the Israelite does not intend to use it incorrectly. In line with this, if an Israelite *unintentionally* eats the heave-offering, he does not cause the loss of the holy produce. He simply sanctifies more produce to replace the heave-offering which he inadvertently ate. If, by contrast, the nonpriest *intentionally* eats the heave-offering, he is culpable for destroying the holy thing.[6] He cannot replace the sanctified offering and, further, he is liable to extirpation. Only by his intention does the common Israelite encroach upon the holy, just as it is only through his intention that he designates produce to be holy in the first place.

Finally, the end of the tractate points out that heave-offering ceases to be holy at the point at which common Israelites no longer deem that produce worthy of a sanctified status.[7] This occurs if the produce is of an insignificant quantity or if it is not deemed desirable as food. In either case, what had been holy again may be used for the Israelite's own benefit, just like any other secular food.

The single message of Tractate Terumot is that the presence of holiness in this world depends upon the thoughts and deeds of common, nonpriestly, Israelites. Produce becomes holy because they wish it to be so. The holiness is maintained because these same people are intent upon protecting the sanctity. Heave-offering ceases to be holy when common Israelites no longer consider it fit for holy status. These central notions are developed through the tractate's diverse and sometimes arcane rules. They shine through the haze of details which Mishnah Terumot's authorities discuss and dispute.

As I noted at the outset, in discussing heave-offering, the authorities of Mishnah Terumot shifted from the focus of the Priestly Code, with its emphasis upon the priests' own powers and privileges. Instead they chose to speak of the centrality of the Israelite in the processes of the holy. The reason for this choice, made by the formulators of the Mishnah, is clear when we stop to recall the historical situation in which they did their work.

Along with the rest of the Mishnah, Tractate Terumot came into being in the land of Israel in the late second century. Its authorities faced the crisis caused by the destruction of the

Temple in Jerusalem, in 70 C.E., and the failed Bar Kokhba revolt of 135 C.E.[8] As part of the Mishnah as a whole, Tractate Terumot thus spoke to a time in which the Temple, the visible sign of God's presence and dominion, was gone. The cult, through which the people of Israel had acknowledged God's lordship and appealed to his mercies, had ceased. The land of Israel was now under the hand of foreigners, with little hope for its return to Israelite sovereignty. For these reasons, Israelites living in this time had good reason to believe that God's lordship over and concern for the people and land of Israel indeed had come to an end. All that Scripture had promised was lost.

In this sad period, the authorities of the Mishnah rehearsed and made explicit the scriptural requirement that all Israelites pay the priestly due. By doing this they put forward the powerful statement that the relationship between the people of Israel and God remained the same as it was before the wars with Rome. Events of history were to be ignored. Clearly, with the Temple in ruins, the priests no longer functioned in cultic service to God. Despite this loss of function, however, they still were to be treated as God's representatives on earth. For this reason they still were to receive the share which God mandated for them. This masks the deeper claim of the tractate. By acknowledging the continuing status and privileges of the priests, the rabbis of Mishnah Terumot affirmed that God remained owner of the land and Lord over the people of Israel. Only because God still was present and in control did his claim to the produce grown by the people of Israel remain in effect.

For the authorities of Mishnah Terumot, the priesthood thus served as a symbol evoking God's lordship and dominion. At the same time, for these rabbis, the priestly station could be nothing more than a symbol. For with the Temple and cult destroyed, the priests no longer played a concrete role in the sanctification of Israelite life. In light of this, in focusing upon a particular locus and means of sanctification to be operative in their day, the authorities of Tractate Terumot turned their attention away from the priests. They concentrated instead upon heave-offering, which Israelites themselves designate to be holy. In this offering the Mishnah's rabbis recognized a strong proof that the holiness they sought still abided in the world. If the people themselves declared things to be holy and maintained that holy status in a secular world, it meant that, even with the Temple gone, cultic sanctification still existed. The God who once moved in response to the priestly invocation at the altar continued to rule. With the

Temple gone, he moved in response to the intentions and perceptions of his common people, Israelites who separated and protected the offering which he mandated. The tractate's message is poignant. For as is clear, with the Temple destroyed and the land defiled, the intentions and perceptions of Israelites were all that remained to defy the events of history and to affirm God's presence and dominion.

The Structure of the Tractate

Tractate Terumot is carefully structured so as to detail the system of sanctification just described. It unfolds in three parts, each discussing one of the stages in the continuum through which Israelites (1) designate and separate heave-offering, (2) guard the offering against misuse while it is in their own, secular domain, and (3) either convey the offering to the priest or determine that it no longer has a sanctified status. The following outline depicts these three sections of the tractate in detail.[9] The comments at the end of each of these larger sections explain both what subjects have been covered and why they have been redacted in their present order.

I. How heave-offering is designated and separated. 1:1–4:6

A. *Improper ways of separating heave-offering.* 1:1–3:4

1. IMPROPER WAYS OF SEPARATING HEAVE-OFFERING WHICH YIELD HEAVE-OFFERING THAT IS NOT VALID. 1:1–5

1:1   Five sorts of people may not separate heave-offering; if they do so, it is not valid heave-offering.

1:2   Expansion of one item from 1:1's list.

1:3   Expansion of another item from 1:1's list.

1:4   They may not separate olives as heave-offering for wine, nor grapes for oil; if they do so: the Shammaites say, "It is valid"; the Hillelites say, "Not valid."

1:5   They may not separate heave-offering, plus list of ten categories of produce; if they do so, it is not valid.

2. IMPROPER WAYS OF SEPARATING HEAVE-OFFERING WHICH NEVERTHELESS YIELD VALID HEAVE-OFFERING. 1:6–2:3

1:6   Five sorts of people may not separate heave-offering; if they do so, it is valid heave-offering.

1:7   They may not separate heave-offering by measure, weight, or count (plus complementary rules).

1:8   They may not separate oil as heave-offering for crushed olives, nor wine for crushed grapes; if they did so, it is valid heave-offering.

1:9   Expansion of 1:8: They may separate oil as heave-offering for olives which have been preserved, etc.

1:10   Principle governing 1:8–9.

2:1   They may not separate clean produce as heave-offering for unclean; if they do so, it is valid heave-offering (Eliezer: they may do so de jure).

2:2   They may not separate unclean produce as heave-offering for clean; if one did so unintentionally, it is valid; intentionally, he has done nothing.

2:3   Two more examples of principle of 2:2.

3. SPECIAL PROBLEMS: HEAVE-OFFERING SEPARATED FROM ONE KIND OF PRODUCE FOR PRODUCE OF A DIFFERENT KIND. 2:4–6

2:4   They do not separate produce of one kind as heave-offering for produce of a different kind; if one did so, it is not valid.

2:5   Development of 2:4.

4. SPECIAL PROBLEMS: CASES OF DOUBT WHETHER OR NOT HEAVE-OFFERING WAS VALIDLY SEPARATED. 3:1–4

3:1   In cases of doubt the first separation is valid, but heave-offering must be separated a second time.

3:2   Continuation of 3:1.

3:3   Partners who both separated heave-offering from the same commonly owned batch of produce: Aqiba, sages, and Yose dispute.

The problem of this first section of the tractate is how the heave-offering required of the householder's produce is designated within that produce and then separated from it so that it can be given to a priest. These are the first human actions involving heave-offering; therefore they constitute the logical starting point for the tractate. The central point of this material is that, on the basis of certain thoughts and deeds, the Israelite householder determines both what produce and how much of it is to be deemed heave-offering.

The discussion takes place in two main parts. We begin by establishing who may separate heave-offering and what produce may be used for that offering (part A). This material is redacted first because it contains the facts that the householder will need to know when he undertakes the actual designation and separation of the offering. This is the subject of part B, which in turn details how the offering is designated, how much is designated, and when this is to be done.

II. The proper handling of heave-offering which has been separated but not yet given to the priest. 4:7–10:10

A. Heave-offering which is mixed with unconsecrated produce: Neutralization. 4:7–5:9

1. HOW HEAVE-OFFERING IS NEUTRALIZED. 4:7–13

4:7   Heave-offering is neutralized when mixed in 101 parts of unconsecrated produce, so Eliezer; Joshua: slightly more.

4:8   Joshua: Black figs neutralize white ones and vice versa (plus two more examples); Eliezer: they do not; Aqiba offers mediating position.

4:9   Explanation of Aqiba's view, 4:8.

4:10   Expansion of 4:8–9

4:11   Expansion of 4:8–9.

4:12   Two bins of unconsecrated produce into one of which heave-offering fell—the unconsecrated produce neutralizes the heave-offering.

4:13   Legal precedent involving Aqiba and Yose. Yose invokes principle of 4:12.

2. RULES REGARDING THE BATCH IN WHICH HEAVE-OFFERING
WAS NEUTRALIZED AND THE PRODUCE TAKEN TO REPLACE THE
LOST HEAVE-OFFERING. 5:1–9

5:1   Triplet: A *seah* of unclean heave-offering which fell into less than a hundred of unconsecrated produce—let it all rot. If the heave-offering was clean—sell the mixture to a priest. If the unconsecrated produce was unclean, the priest eats the mixture in small bits.

5:2   A *seah* of unclean heave-offering which fell into a hundred of clean unconsecrated produce—let a *seah* be raised up and burned, so Eliezer; sages: let it be eaten in small bits.

5:3   A *seah* of clean heave-offering which fell into a hundred of unclean unconsecrated produce—raise up and eat a *seah* of produce in small bits.

5:4   A *seah* of unclean heave-offering which fell into a hundred of clean heave-offering—Houses dispute.

5:5   Heave-offering which was neutralized and raised up and fell into other unconsecrated produce—Eliezer: it imparts the status of heave-offering like true heave-offering. Sages: it does not.

5:6   A *seah* of heave-offering which fell into less than a hundred of unconsecrated produce and some of the mixture fell into other unconsecrated produce—same dispute as at 5:5.

5:7   A *seah* of heave-offering which fell into a hundred of unconsecrated produce and one lifted it out and more heave-offering fell into the same unconsecrated produce—the unconsecrated produce remains permitted to nonpriests.

5:8   A *seah* of heave-offering which fell into a hundred of unconsecrated produce and was not lifted out before more heave-offering fell in—the batch now has the status of heave-offering; Simeon: it does not.

5:9   A mixture of heave-offering and unconsecrated food that is ground and the quantity of which diminishes—the proportion of heave-offering to unconsecrated produce remains the same.

B. *Heave-offering which is eaten by a nonpriest. 6:1–8:4*

1. UNINTENTIONAL CONSUMPTION: PAYMENT OF THE PRIN-
CIPAL AND ADDED FIFTH. 6:1–6

6:1   A nonpriest who unintentionally eats heave-offering pays the
priest the value of the heave-offering (principal) and an added
fifth.

6:2   The daughter of an Israelite who unintentionally ate heave-
offering and afterwards married a priest—to whom does she pay
the principal and added fifth?

6:3   One who unintentionally gives his workers or guests heave-
offering to eat—who pays the principal and added fifth? (Meir
and sages dispute.)

6:4   Triplet: One who steals heave-offering and does not eat it, etc.; if
he unintentionally ate it, etc.; if it was heave-offering dedicated
to the Temple, etc.

6:5   They do not pay the principal and added fifth (plus list of six
categories of produce), so Meir; sages disagree.

6:6   They pay the principal and added fifth for heave-offering of one
kind with produce of a different kind, so Eliezer; Meir: only
with the same kind (plus scriptural proof for each view).

2. INTENTIONAL CONSUMPTION: PAYMENT OF THE PRINCIPAL
BUT NOT THE ADDED FIFTH. 7:1–3

7:1   A nonpriest who intentionally eats heave-offering pays the principal but not the added fifth.

7:2   The daughter of a priest who married an Israelite and afterwards
ate heave-offering pays the principal but not the added fifth, so
Meir; sages: she pays both.

7:3   Triplet of cases in which the individual pays the principal but
not the added fifth. General rule summarizing laws for cases in
which nonpriests pay both principal and added fifth or pay principal but not added fifth.

3. CASES OF DOUBT CONCERNING A NONPRIEST'S CULPABILITY
FOR EATING HEAVE-OFFERING. 7:5–8:4

7:4–5   Two bins, one filled with heave-offering and one filled with unconsecrated produce—if heave-offering falls into one of them,

but it is not known which, we hold that it fell into heave-offering. Triplet: If a nonpriest ate the produce in one of the bins . . .

7:6   If produce from one bin fell into unconsecrated produce . . .

7:7   If produce from one bin was sown as seed . . .

8:1   The wife of a priest who was eating heave-offering and was told, "Your husband has died"—Eliezer: she is culpable for wrongly eating heave-offering as a nonpriest. Joshua exempts.

8:2   Same issue as 8:1

8:3   Same issue as 8:1.

8:4   Same issue as 8:1.

C. *The cultic contamination of heave-offering.* 8:5–10

8:5   Liquids that are left uncovered must be poured out for fear that a snake deposited venom in them.

8:6   For what quantity of liquid does 8:5 apply?

8:7   Foods that might contain snake venom are forbidden for consumption.

8:8   A jug of wine concerning which there arose a suspicion of uncleanness—Eliezer: one must still protect it in cleanness. Joshua: let him make it certainly unclean.

8:9   A jug of wine in the status of heave-offering which broke in the upper vat and the lower vat is unclean (plus expansions): Eliezer and Joshua, same dispute as at 8:8.

8:10   Women to whom gentiles said, "Give us one of your number so that we may rape her, or we will rape each of you," let them all be raped (= position of Eliezer, 8:8).

D. *Heave-offering planted as seed.* 9:1–8

9:1   The householder may not plow up heave-offering that he intentionally planted; unintentionally, he may plow it up.

9:2–3   Expansion of 9:1: a field planted with heave-offering is subject to offerings left for the poor.

9:4   Expansion of 9:1: the crop is subject to tithes.

9:5   What grows from heave-offering has the status of heave-offering (plus laws for the crops of seed in the status of seven other agricultural offerings).

9:6   Case of doubt concerning whether or not a field is planted with heave-offering: we rule according to whether or not the seed disintegrates.

9:7   Crop grown from untithed seed is subject to principle of 9:6 (plus other rules for untithed produce).

9:8   Continuation of 9:7: rules for untithed produce plus rule for fruit produced by saplings grown from seed in the status of heave-offering.

   E. *Heave-offering that is cooked or otherwise prepared with unconsecrated produce.* 10:1–10

10:1   That which is flavored by heave-offering takes on the status of heave-offering (Judah glosses).

10:2   Dough leavened with heave-offering takes on the status of heave-offering. Water tainted by barley in the status of heave-offering does not take on the status of heave-offering.

10:3   Unconsecrated bread which absorbs vapors from heave-offering wine—Meir: it has the status of heave-offering; Judah: it does not; Yose: mediating position.

10:4   Bread baked in an oven fired with heave-offering cumin remains unconsecrated.

10:5a   Rules regarding produce flavored with fenugreek in the status of heave-offering.

10:5b   Other rules for fenugreek.

10:6   Unconsecrated olives which are pickled with olives in the status of heave-offering—if they are flavored, they are forbidden.

10:7   Expansion of 10:6 for case of clean and unclean fish and locusts.

10:8   Only that which is pickled with leeks in the status of heave-offering is forbidden (vs. 10:6). Yose: only that which is boiled with beets is forbidden; Simeon: rule for cabbage; Aqiba: only that which is flavored by forbidden meat is forbidden (vs. 10:1–6)

10:9   Yohanan b. Nuri: rules for liver.

10:10   An egg spiced with forbidden spices is forbidden. Liquid in
         which heave-offering is cooked is forbidden.

Unit **II** discusses the householder's responsibility to protect
from loss heave-offering that he has separated but not yet given
to the priest. Since this heave-offering remains in the Israelite's
domain, it is in danger of being used as though it were his own
common produce. It might be mixed or cooked with common
food or eaten by the nonpriest. Such cases are of central interest
to the tractate, for they offer a context in which to explore what
happens when sanctified produce is used as though it were secular. This constitutes the major anomaly possible within the topic
of heave-offering. It is the point at which the desired barrier
between the holy and profane is broken. Its adjudication, accordingly, takes up the longest section of the tractate. This material endeavors to establish the effect that holy produce has upon
common food with which it is mixed: Does the mixture become
holy because of the presence of heave-offering in it? It further
outlines the householder's own culpability and concomitant responsibility to replace heave-offering which, through his fault,
is lost.

The discussion takes place in five parts. Each details rules for
a particular hazard that might befall heave-offering in an Israelite's domain. These parts have been ordered so as to form logical
transitions with the material of unit **I**, which precedes, and
unit **III**, which follows. We begin with the first problem the
householder might encounter after he designates and separates
heave-offering. This is the now-holy heave-offering's falling back
into the food from which it was separated. We progress through
three other potential problems: the heave-offering's being eaten
by the nonpriest, its being rendered unclean, and its being
planted as seed. The unit ends with cases in which heave-
offering is cooked or otherwise prepared with unconsecrated
produce. These belong at the end of this section in order to form
a transition to unit **III** which follows, for the topic of that unit is
the priest's own preparation and use of heave-offering.

III. The preparation and use of heave-offering by the priest.
11:1–7.

A. *The proper preparation of produce in the status of heave-offering.*
   11:1–3

11:1   Produce in the status of heave-offering must be prepared in the way that unconsecrated produce of its type normally is prepared.

11:2   Expansion of 11:1: culpability of nonpriest who eats heave-offering which was improperly prepared.

11:3   Expansion of theory of 11:1: (plus four rules on liquids made from agricultural offerings).

B. *Refuse from produce in the status of heave-offering.* 11:4–5

11:4   Refuse that has food value or which the priest wishes to eat retains the status of heave-offering.

11:5   A storage bin from which one emptied heave-offering—he need not sit and pick up every last kernel of grain. Same rule for a jug of oil in the status of heave-offering which one emptied.

C. *Heave-offering which is not fit as human food but has some other use.* 11:6–7

11:6   Vetches in the status of heave-offering are used to feed the priest's cattle.

11:7   Unclean oil in the status of heave-offering may be kindled in the priest's lamp.

The tractate concludes with rules for the final disposition of heave-offering. These rules make the point that the offering should be used to the purpose for which it was designated. That is, it must be eaten by a priest. This is the case so long as the priestly due is considered worthy as food. If it is not, it is no longer deemed to have a consecrated status. Then it also may be used by nonpriests, just like any other common produce. In light of this larger theory, the unit asks when produce is or is not deemed to be a food. It answers that this depends upon priests' and Israelites' own perceptions of what is edible. To expound this theory, the unit begins by discussing the normal preparation of food in the status of heave-offering (part A). The next topic is refuse from such food (part B). The final issue is what is done with heave-offering which, while not deemed a food, has some other customary use (part C).

The Content of Yerushalmi Terumot

The preceding description of the content and structure of Mishnah Terumot is essential for understanding Yerushalmi Terumot.
The Talmud's discussions, first, are based upon the Mishnah's
facts. The Yerushalmi, furthermore, is totally subservient to the
ordering of the Mishnah's materials. Yet, while necessary to
understanding the subject of this tractate of the Talmud, these
preceding analyses do not introduce Yerushalmi Terumot. This is
because, while wholly dependent upon the Mishnah for topic
and structure, the Talmud's authorities have an agenda of issues
and concerns quite foreign to those of the Mishnah. To explore
the character of the Talmud of the land of Israel in its own right,
we therefore must look at its own particular content and goals.
This requires, first, that we bear in mind some important facts
about the theological motives and pedagogical traits of Mishnah
Terumot. Then we may delineate the character of the Yerushalmi
as it is revealed through its relationship to the Mishnah.

Mishnah Terumot describes a system of holiness in full and
eloquent detail. At the hands of the Mishnah's final formulators,
the tractate's numerous laws come together to create a statement
of theology more powerful than any of its components alone
could communicate. Yet this same systemic character that gives
the Mishnah its power produces a statement that is flawed and
fragile. For when examined through its constituent parts, Mishnah Terumot is enigmatic. Outside of the context of the Mishnah's system of holiness, the tractate's discrete rules lose all
vestige of meaning and importance. They are perplexing, for the
Mishnah does not provide the facts necessary for understanding
them. Many are arcane, with no apparent application in the concrete world. Perhaps the deepest problem is that, while claiming
to speak of how things are and should be for the people of Israel
as a whole, the Mishnah suggests no proof of or basis for its
authority. Those who do not already concede the Mishnah's as-
cendancy need not be persuaded by Tractate Terumot's specific
directives.

In the centuries following the creation of the Mishnah, the
authorities of the Yerushalmi attempted to correct what they re-
garded as the weaknesses of Mishnah Terumot. They did this by
transforming the Mishnah's essay about the system of holiness
into a collection of distinct, individually accessible, legal statements. Each rule was to have its own, independent, meaning
which could be interpreted outside of the Mishnah's complex

system of laws. The Yerushalmi's authorities therefore provided the secondary interpretive structure that the Mishnah itself lacks. The practical applications that the Yerushalmi's masters ascribed to individual rules likewise needed to be shown for cases in which the Mishnah had its own, purely theoretical concerns. The Talmudic rabbis therefore indicated the concrete cases in which the tractate's rules would apply. Finally, by linking Mishnaic laws to specific scriptural passages, the Yerushalmi's authorities provided for the Mishnah's rules a basis of authority to which all Israelites would concede. In these ways, the Yerushalmi turned a closed and idiosyncratic network of interdependent rules into a compendium of discrete legal statements. Each was rendered accessible, intelligible, and manifestly significant.

The purpose of the Yerushalmi's masters is not far below the surface. For them the Mishnah constituted Torah. Its stature, perhaps, was only slightly below that of Scripture itself. For the Talmudic authorities, this meant that, ultimately, all of the people of Israel were to follow the Mishnah's law, under the guidance and rule of the rabbis themselves. The latter's work on Tractate Terumot, along with the rest of the Mishnah, was designed to facilitate their program. The Mishnah was to serve as a code of law and a basis for all legal decisions. The Talmudic masters therefore needed to make explicit the source of the Mishnah's authority. More than that they had to determine the exact details of its directives and to augment its corpus of laws. These tasks became the central focus of their work.

To prove these claims concerning the goal of the Yerushalmi's formulators, we must examine in detail the character of their work. After an overview of the Yerushalmi's approach to the Mishnah, we address specific questions concerning the sorts of issues raised by the Talmudic masters and the types of discussions they themselves provide.

The Yerushalmi is comprised of a line by line commentary to Mishnah Terumot. It takes up the Mishnah's individual rules and the statements of its several authorities in sequence. In this way it breaks the Mishnah down into a series of discrete sentences, analyzing each rule in its own right, without regard to the systemic context provided by Mishnah Terumot as a whole. What is striking, then, about the relationship between Yerushalmi Terumot and the Mishnah is what the Yerushalmi ignores. It ignores the most basic characteristic of the Mishnah, that it is a structured essay in which groups of legal statements make larger points and within which each topic follows logically from the preceding one.[10] Because the Talmud is a line by line, and often phrase by phrase, commentary, the student of the Yerushalmi is not permitted to perceive these facts. For the Talmud, for example, the authorities in a Mishnaic dispute do not necessarily argue a single proposition. Examined separately, each authority has his own perspective and concern, unrelated to that of the other. The views of each authority often are treated as equally valid, each to be applied in a specific case. For the Yerushalmi, moreover, groups of the Mishnah's parallel cases do not come together to establish a legal principle or ideal. Viewing each rule and statement separately, the Talmudic masters find only a maze of details to be enumerated, explained, and applied in a variety of cases often unknown to the Mishnah itself.

In its approach, accordingly, the Yerushalmi pays little or no attention to the overarching logic of the Mishnah's topic or to the structure of its presentation. The Yerushalmi's formulators thereby transformed an anthological essay into a collection of distinct rules and legal statements. As I have stated, the Yerushalmi is totally subservient to the Mishnah's structure, consistently following the order of Tractate Terumot's rules. This passivity, however, masks the Yerushalmi's innovation. By ignoring the importance of the Mishnah's larger structure, the Talmudic masters destroy the systemic power of the tractate. The Talmud reduces the Mishnah to a corpus of disjointed legal statements, each with its own meaning and practical application (albeit determined only by the Yerushalmi's own rabbis!), but with no contextual meaning.

Their atomistic approach points to the central concern of the Yerushalmi's framers. They were intent upon the meaning of individual rules, which could serve for the guidance of the Israelite community. Examination of the specific sorts of materials they created strengthens this impression of the goal of the Talmudic masters. To accomplish this analysis, I have broken Yerushalmi Terumot's discussions into three basic types, dividing each type in turn into its constituent categories. This summary of the content of Yerushalmi Terumot shows that the greatest portion of the Talmud is comprised of explanatory comments attached to the Mishnah's individual rules. Within this exegetical material, the Yerushalmi's authorities desire to know what the Mishnah's rules mean and work to tie them to specific statements of Scripture, from which they claim the rules derive. The second most prominent material in Yerushalmi Terumot contains supplementary rules and cases. These expand the Mishnah's laws so as to apply them in a wide variety of situations unforeseen within the Mishnah's own limited range of interests. They further contain a great number of rules which the Talmud's own authorities supplied, augmenting the Mishnah's corpus of law. Only a small percentage of the tractate's material falls outside of these first two areas. These materials are the synthetic discussions which examine the relationship among discrete rules and statements within the Mishnah, the Tosefta, and the Talmudic literature as a whole. These materials differ from the ones just described in that their primary focus is not the specific meaning and application of individual rules.

In the following, each of the units within Yerushalmi Terumot is listed under the applicable category.[11] In the first section, "Exegetical Material," I list all units which explain a statement or rule of the Mishnah. This includes pericopae which cite neither Scripture nor any Tannaitic text as the basis for their explanations (section 1), units in which there is an Amoraic dispute over a rule's meaning (section 2), and materials which claim that the Mishnah's rule, or a specific authority's opinion, derives from Scripture (section 3), the Tosefta (section 4), or from a different pericope within the Mishnah itself (section 5).

I. Exegetical Material

1. EXPLANATION BASED UPON LOGIC[12]

1:6 **I**   M. Ter. 1:6 explained (plus supplementary rules).

1:8 **III**   Conditions under which M. Ter. 1:8C–D applies.

2:1 **IV**   Meaning of M. Ter. 2:1C.

2:1 **V**   Logic of M. Ter. 2:1D–E.

2:1 **VI**   Logic of M. Ter. 2:1D–E.

2:1 **VII** Logic of M. Ter. 2:1.

2:1 **XIV** At M. Ter. 2:1, which authority's opinion is law?

2:2 **I**   Explanation of M. T.Y. 4:7.

2:2 **II**   Clarification of dispute at M. Ter. 2:2K–M + R.

2:3 **I**   M. Bes. 2:3 explained.

2:3 **III**   M. Ter. 2:3 explained.

2:4 **II**   Point of M. Ter. 2:4C made explicit.

2:5 **III**   Implications of M. Ter. 2:6V–W drawn out.

3:1 **I**   Analysis of M. Ter. 3:1 (plus implications for other rules).

3:1 **VII**   General principle: Which Tannaitic authority does the law follow?

3:3 **I**   Dispute at M. Ter. 3:3 explained.

3:3 **II**   Opinion of Aqiba, M. Ter. 3:3, explained (plus secondary issue).

3:3 **III**   Opinion of Yose, M. Ter. 3:3, explained.

3:4 **II**   M. Ter. 3:4N–P explained.

3:8 **II**   Dispute at M. Ter. 3:9E–F explained.

4:1 **II**   M. Ter. 4:1A–B vs. C explained.

4:1 **IV**   Statement of circumstances under which M. Ter. 4:1B–C applies.

4:3 **VI**   Circumstances under which M. Ter. 4:3H applies.

4:4 **I**   Circumstances under which M. Ter. 4:4 applies.

4:4 **II**   M. Ter. 4:4F explained.

4:8 **II**   M. Ter. 4:8A–B explained.

4:8 **III**   M. Hal. 1:4 explained.

4:8 **VII**   Circumstances under which M. Ter. 4:7 applies.

4:8 **VIII**   Circumstances under which M. Ter. 4:8 applies.

5:1 **V**   Circumstances under which M. Ter. 5:1E applies.

5:1 **VII**   Definition of term at M. Ter. 5:1I.

5:2 **II**   M. Ter. 5:2D–E explained.

5:2 **III**   Definition of term at M. Ter. 5:2D.

5:3 **I**   Clarification of M. Ter. 5:2 (plus expansion).

5:4 **I**   Clarification of M. Ter. 5:4N.

5:5 **II**   M. Ter. 5:5D explained.

5:7 **II**   M. Ter. 5:7E explained.

5:8 **I**   M. Ter. 5:8F–G + H explained.

5:9 **I**   Circumstances under which M. Ter. 5:9 applies.

6:1 **V**   M. Ter. 6:1E explained.

6:1 **VII**   Circumstances under which M. Ter. 6:1F applies.

6:4 **I**   M. Ter. 6:4E–F explained.

6:6 **V**   Implications of M. Ter. 6:6E drawn out.

7:1 **VII**   Implications of M. Meg. 1:5 (plus extended discussion).

7:1 **IX**   Clarification of facts of M. Ket. 3:1.

7:2 **I**   M. Ter. 7:2B explained.

7:6 **II**   Circumstances under which M. Ter. 7:6N–O applies.

7:7 **I**   Circumstances under which M. Ter. 7:7Y applies.

8:1 **I**   Factual basis of M. Ter. 8:1.

8:1 **II**   Reasoning of Eliezer, M. Ter. 8:1H, explained.

8:3 **I**   Nature of dispute at M. Ter. 8:1–2 explained.

8:3 **III**   Point of M. Ter. 8:2U expressed.

8:5 **XX**   Circumstances under which M. Ter. 8:4G applies.

8:6 **II**   Circumstances under which M. Ter. 8:5 applies.

8:8 **I**   Assumption behind M. Ter. 8:8 expressed.

8:9 **VIII**   Point of Eliezer, M. Ter. 8:9–11, indicated.

8:10 **I**   Circumstances under which M. Ter. 8:12 applies.

9:1 **I**   Point of M. Ter. 9:1 indicated.

9:1 **IV**   Implications of M. Ter. 9:1 expressed.

9:1 **V**   Reason for M. Ter. 9:1F–G given.

9:2–3 **III**   Meaning of M. Ter. 9:3N indicated.

9:4 **I**   Meaning of M. Ter. 9:3O expressed.

9:4 **III**   Meaning of M. Ter. 9:3S expressed.

2. AMORAIC DISPUTES OVER MEANING

1:4 **II**   Zeira disputes Yohanan's explanation of M. Ter. 1:4C.

1:5 **II**   Hezeqiah and Yohanan dispute meaning of M. Ter. 1:5.

3:1 **VI**   Dispute over Yohanan's explanation of T. Ter. 4:7G–H.

3:6 **III**   Hiyya bar Ba and Samuel b. Isaac dispute meaning of
M. Ter. 3:6.

3:8 **III**   Anonymous dispute over meaning of M. Ter. 3:9E–F.

4:1 **I**   Samuel and anonymous authority dispute meaning of
M. Ter. 4:1.

4:3 **VII**   Kahana and Yohanan dispute meaning of M. Ter. 4:3I–K.

4:5 **II**   Yohanan and Hezeqiah dispute meaning of M. Ter. 4:5A.

4:6 **I**   Huna and Hinena dispute meaning of M. Ter. 4:6C2.

4:8 **I**   Yohanan and Kahana dispute meaning of M. Ter. 4:8C.

4:8 **IV**   Rabbis and Bar Padiah dispute meaning of M. Ter. 4:8A–B.

5:1 **II**   Hezeqiah and Yohanan dispute meaning of M. Tem. 7:5.

5:1 **III**   Hezeqiah and Yohanan—continuation of previous statement.

5:6 **I**   Yose b. Hanina and Yohanan dispute meaning of M. Ter. 5:6G.

5:6 **II**   Hilpa and anonymous authorities dispute theory underlying
M. Ter. 5:5–6.

6:3 **I**   Yohanan, Simeon b. Laqish, and Yose b. Hanina dispute
M. Ter. 6:3.

6:5 **I**   Yohanan, Simeon b. Laqish, and anonymous authorities clarify
dispute at M. Ter. 6:5A–D + E.

6:6 **IV**   Abin and anonymous authorities dispute implications of
M. Ter. 6:6E.

7:3 **I**   Hiyya the elder and Yannai dispute case parallel to M. Ter. 7:3.

7:7 **II**   Yannai and Zeira dispute meaning of M. Ter. 9:6.

8:4 **II**   Anonymous authorities dispute meaning of M. Ter. 8:3X.

8:5 **XV**   Jeremiah and others dispute reasoning of rule at M. A.Z. 2:6.

10:7 **III**   Yose b. Hanina and Simeon bar Hiyya dispute meaning of M. Ter. 10:8F.

11:1 **III**   Eleazar and Yohanan dispute meaning of M. Ter. 11:1F–G.

11:4 **I**   Eleazar and Yohanan dispute meaning of M. Ter. 11:4B–D.

3. EXPLANATION FROM SCRIPTURE

1:1 **I**   M. Ter. 1:1 derived from Ex. 25:1–2.

1:1 **VII**   M. Ter. 1:1D derived from Num. 18:28.

1:1 **VIII**   M. Ter. 1:1F derived from Num. 18:28.

1:1 **II**   M. Hag. 1:1 derived from Dt. 31:12.

1:1 **I**   M. Ter. 1:5A–D derived from Dt. 14:28–29.

1:10 **I**   M. Ter. 10:10A–E derived from Num. 18:27.

2:1 **I**   M. Ter. 2:1A derived from Num. 18:27.

2:1 **II**   General principle: rules for heave-offering from Num. 18:27.

2:4 **I**   M. Ter. 2:4A derived from Num. 18:11.

2:5 **II**   M. Ter. 2:6T derived from Num. 18:32.

3:5 **III**   M. Ter. 3:5C derived from Num. 18:27–28.

3:6 **II**   M. Ter. 3:6B derived from Ex. 22:29.

3:7 **II**   M. Ter. 3:8 derived from Lev. 5:4.

4:3 **I**   M. Ter. 4:3 derived from Ez. 45:13 (= T. Ter. 5:8).

4:3 **II**   M. Ter. 4:3D derived from Num. 31:30 (= T. Ter. 5:8).

4:3 **III**   M. Ter. 4:3E derived from Ez. 45:13 (= T. Ter. 5:8).

4:3 **V**   M. Ter. 4:3F–G derived from Ez. 45:11.

4:5 **III**   M. Ter. 4:5E derived from Num. 18:12.

4:5 **IV**   M. Ter. 4:5F derived from Num. 16:21.

4:7 **I**   M. Ter. 4:7 derived from Num. 18:29.

6:1 **I**   Quantity of "added fifth" derived from Lev. 22:14.

6:1 **II**   M. Ter. 6:1 derived from Lev. 22:14.

6:4 **II**   M. Ter. 6:4E–G derived from Lev. 22:14.

6:4 **III**   M. Ter. 6:4G derived from Lev. 22:9 (= T. Ter. 7:8).

7:2 **II**   M. Ter. 7:2A–E derived from Lev. 21:9.

7:2 **III**   M. Ter. 7:2F–G derived from Lev. 21:9.

8:2 **I**   M. Ter. 8:1I–K derived from Dt. 26:3 and 33:11.

8:3 **II**   Lev. 11:20–23 is source for several rules for forbidden foods.

8:9 **VII**   M. Bek. 5:2 derived from Dt. 12:16.

9:4 **VI**   Dt. 25:4 source for rules concerning muzzling animals used in threshing.

11:2 **IV**   M. Ter. 11:2D, E–F derived from Lev. 11:23.

11:6 **I**   M. Ter. 11:9G derived from Lev. 22:11.

11:6 **II**   M. Ter. 11:9H derived from Lev. 22:11.

4. EXPLANATION FROM TOSEFTA

1:1 **V**   T. Ter. 1:3 explains M. Ter. 1:1C2.

1:2 **I**   T. Ber. 3:5 explains M. Ber. 2:3, M. Meg. 2:4.

1:8 **IV**   T. Ter. 3:4 clarifies M. Ter. 1:8.

2:3 **V**   T. Shab. 3:11 explains M. Ter. 2:3.

4:9 **I**   T. Ter. 5:10 explains M. Ter. 4:7A–C, 4:8.

6:6 **I**   T. Ter. 7:9 explains M. Ter. 6:6B.

9:4 **IV**   T. Ter. 8:3 explains M. Ter. 9:3T–U (plus Amoraic discussion).

11:4 **II**   T. Ter. 10:4 explains M. Ter. 11:5I–J.

5. EXPLANATION FROM MISHNAH

1:9 **I**   M. Ter. 1:10 clarifies M. Ter. 1:9.

1:9 **II**   M. Ma. 1:6 explains M. Ter. 1:9.

3:6 **I**   M. Ter. 3:6B explains M. Ter. 3:6C.

9:5 **I**   M. Ter. 9:5B explains M. Ter. 9:4B.

11:4 **IV**   M. Ed. 3:3 explains M. Ter. 11:4–5.

This material comprises 161 units out of a total of 349 found in Yerushalmi Terumot as a whole, that is, 46.13 percent of the total. Of this material, 71.43 percent, in turn, comprises the Yerushalmi's authorities' own line by line exegesis of the Mishnah (sections 1 and 2). They clarify the Mishnah's often abstruse language, define terms, and in the majority of cases, explain exactly what the Mishnah's rules prohibit and permit. Notably, only a relatively small percentage of these explanations (15.53 percent of the exegetical material as a whole) are under dispute by Amoraic authorities.

Of this exegetical material, 20.5 percent uses Scripture to derive and explain the Mishnah's rules. The claim in these discussions is that the Mishnah's own authorities only made explicit what Scripture itself requires of all Israelites. The Yerushalmi thus gives weight to the central rabbinic claim that the Mishnah comprises divine revelation. The assertion is proven by demonstrating that the Mishnah's rules correspond to those found in the document accepted by all Israelites as revealed. The meager amount of material in sections 4 and 5 indicates that the Yerushalmi's authorities did not consider the Mishnah and Tosefta themselves to be important sources for the interpretation of the Mishnah. Such interpretation was better based upon the authoritative Scripture or upon the Talmudic masters' own sense for the meaning the Mishnah's rules should have.

In their second major category of discussion, the "Supplementary Material," Yerushalmi's rabbis fill out the corpus of rules found in the Mishnah. They do this by citing the Tosefta's cognate material (section 1) as well as by reporting Tannaitic statements unknown in the Mishnah or the Tosefta (section 2). Yet more than this, the Talmudic authorities are themselves active in legislating rules unknown to the Mishnah (sections 3 and 4) and in developing the implications of the Mishnah's rules to show how they apply to new cases and problems unforeseen by the Mishnah (section 5). Finally, through stories and legal precedents, they indicate how the law functions in concrete, contemporary cases (section 6).

II. Supplementary Material

1. Rules cited from Tosefta

2:1 **III**   T. Ter. 3:19C–D supplements M. Ter. 2:1 (plus cognate rules).

2:1 **X**   T. Ter. 3:8C–H supplements M. Ter. 2:1 (plus anonymous explanation).

2:1 **XI**   T. Ter. 3:7A supplements M. Ter. 2:1 (plus Tannaitic and Amoraic discussion).

2:1 **XII**   T. Ter. 3:18 complements M. Ter. 2:1 (plus Amoraic explanation).

2:1 **XIII**   T. Ter. 3:7 complements M. Ter. 2:1 (plus Amoraic explanation).

2:3 **IV**   T. Shab. 3:5 complements M. Ter. 2:3 (plus Amoraic discussion and rules).

2:4 **III**   T. Ter. 4:1–2 supplements M. Ter. 2:4 (plus Amoraic discussion).

3:1 **III**   T. Ter. 4:5J–K supplements M. Ter. 3:1 (plus Amoraic explanation).

3:1 **IV**   T. Ter. 4:6A–D supplements M. Ter. 3:1 (plus Amoraic explanation).

3:4 **IV**   T. Ter. 3:12 supplements M. Ter. 3:4.

3:4 **V**   T. Ter. 3:13 supplements M. Ter. 3:4 (plus Amoraic discussion).

3:5 **V**   T. Ter. 4:9 supplements M. Ter. 3:5.

3:6 **V**   T. Ter. 4:10 supplements M. Ter. 3:5 (plus Amoraic discussion).

3:8 **I**   T. Ter. 4:13 complements M. Ter. 3:9.

4:3 **IV**   T. Ter. 5:3 supplements M. Ter. 4:3 (plus scriptural prooftext).

4:10 **I**   T. Ter. 5:11 supplements M. Ter. 4:10 (plus Amoraic discussion).

4:10 **II**   T. Ter. 5:11 supplements M. Ter. 4:10 (plus explanation).

4:12 **I**   T. Ter. 6:12 supplements M. Ter. 4:12 (plus Amoraic analysis).

4:12 **III**   T. Ter. 6:13 supplements M. Ter. 4:12 (plus Amoraic analysis).

5:3 **II**   T. Ter. 6:1 comlements M. Ter. 5:6E (plus Amoraic discussion).

5:9 **III**   T. Ter. 6:10 supplements M. Ter. 5:9.

6:1 **VI**   T. Ter. 8:2 supplements M. Ter. 6:1.

7:6   T. Ter. 6:16 supplements M. Ter. 7:6 (plus anonymous rules).

8:5 **IX**   T. Ter. 7:13 supplements M. Ter. 8:4.

8:5 **X**   T. Ter. 7:13 supplements M. Ter. 8:4.

8:5 **XI**   T. Ter. 7:13 supplements M. Ter. 8:4.

8:5 **XII**   T. Ter. 7:16 supplements M. Ter. 8:4.

8:5 **XIII**   T. Ter. 7:16 supplements M. Ter. 8:4.

8:5 **XVII**   T. Ter. 7:12 supplements M. Ter. 8:4 (plus Amoraic discussion).

8:6 **I**   T. Ter. 7:14–15 supplements M. Ter. 8:5.

8:10 **II**   T. Ter. 7:20 supplements M. Ter. 8:12.

9:4 **II**   T. Ter. 8:5–6 supplements M. Ter. 9:4C–E.

10:2 **II**   T. Ter. 8:9 supplements M. Ter. 10:2 (plus Amoraic discussion).

10:10 **II**   T. Ter. 9:5 supplements M. Ter. 10:12 (plus Amoraic rules).

10:10 **III**   T. Ter. 9:5 supplements M. Ter. 10:12 (plus Amoraic rules).

11:1 **I**   T. Ter. 9:7 supplements M. Ter. 11:1 (plus Amoraic discussion).

11:2 **II**   T. Ter. 9:8 supplements M. Ter. 11:2.

11:3 **II**   T. Ter. 9:9 supplements M. Ter. 11:3.

11:5 **IV**   T. Ter. 10:12 supplements M. Ter. 11:6–8.

11:7 **III**   T. Ter. 10:9 supplements M. Ter. 11:10 (plus Amoraic discussion).

11:7 **IV**   T. Ter. 10:9 supplements M. Ter. 11:10.

2. Tannaitic rules not found in Mishnah or Tosefta [13]

1:3 **I**   Meir supplements M. Ter. 1:3 (plus Amoraic discussion).

5:8 **II**   Supplement to rules of neutralization.

5:9 **II**   Supplement to rules of neutralization.

6:1 **VIII**   Supplement to M. Ter. 6:10

7:1 **V**   Supplement to M. Ter. 7:1.

8:7 **II**   Eliezer supplements M. Ter. 8:6.

9:8 **II**   Supplements M. Ter. 9:7H–J.

3. RULES IN NAMES OF AMORAIM

1:1 **IX**   Rule for agency, supplements M. Ter. 1:1D–F.

1:10 **II**   Amoraic supplement to M. Ter. 1:1C.

2:1 **IX**   Hiyya the elder expands M. Ter. 2:1D–E.

2:3 **II**   Hiyya bar Ashi: rule cognate to M. Ter. 2:3.

3:1 **II**   Yohanan supplements M. Ter. 3:1.

3:5 **IV**   Yohanan supplements M. Ter. 3:5.

3:5 **VI**   Yohanan and Simeon b. Laqish dispute rule cognate to M. Ter. 3:5.

3:5 **VII**   Hoshaya b. R. Shammai supplements M. Ter. 3:5.

4:3 **IX**   Simeon b. Laqish supplements M. Ter. 4:3 (plus discussion).

4:3 **X**   Yohanan supplements M. Ter. 4:3 (plus biblical prooftext).

4:8 **VI**   Simeon b. Laqish supplements M. Ter. 4:8 (= T. Ter. 5:10M–T).

4:12 **II**   Simeon supplements M. Ter. 4:12.

5:1 **I**   Hiyya paraphrases T. Ter. 6:1F–G.

5:9 **V**   Yohanan supplements M. Ter. 5:9.

5:9 **VI**   Rules on obligations of judge: several Amoraim.

6:1 **III**   Yohanan: rules cognate to M. Ter. 6:1C.

6:1 **IX**   Yohanan and Simeon b. Laqish dispute rule cognate to M. Ter. 6:1F.

7:1 **II**   Yohanan and Simeon b. Laqish: rules for punishments.

8:5 **I**   Jacob bar Aha, Simeon bar Ba and Yohanan supplement M. Ter. 8:4.

8:5 **II**   Several Amoraim supplement M. Ter. 8:4.

8:5 **III**   Abbahu supplements M. Ter. 8:4.

8:5 **IV**   Jacob bar Aha and Imi supplement M. Ter. 8:4 (plus incident).

8:5 **VII**   Hiyya bar Ba: rules concerning venom (plus incident).

8:5 **VIII**   Imi: folk health hints.

8:5 **XIX**   Jacob bar Aha supplements M. Ter. 8:4.

8:7 **III**   Jonah, Hezeqiah, and Tabbi supplement M. Ter. 8:6.

8:7 **IV**   Hiyya bar Ba supplements M. Ter. 8:6.

9:5 **III**   Yohanan supplements M. Ter. 9:4D–E.

9:8 **III**   Supplement to M. Ter. 9:7: Abbahu in the name of Yohanan.

10:4 **I**   Supplement to M. Ter. 10:4: Rav and Levi dispute.

10:4 **III**   Rav: rule cognate to statement immediately preceding.

10:7 **IV**   Rule cognate to 10:8–9: Ba bar Zabdah and Isaac.

10:9 **I**   Ba and Zeira supplement M. Ter. 10:11.

11:5 **III**   Rules loosely connected to M. Ter. 11:8H: Hilaphta b. Saul and Ba.

11:7 **VI**   Supplement to M. Ter. 11:10: Imi.

11:7 **VIII**   Supplement to M. Ter. 11:10: Yosa.

11:7 **XI**   Supplement to M. Ter. 11:10: house of Yannai.

4. RULES CITED ANONYMOUSLY

4:2 **II**   Supplement to M. Ter. 4:2.

6:1 **X**   Complements M. Ter. 6:1 (= T. Ter. 7:5).[14]

6:2 **I**   Complements M. Ter. 6:2.

6:6 **II**   Supplements M. Ter. 6:6A–B.

6:6 **III**   Supplements M. Ter. 6:6C.

7:4–5 **I**   Supplements M. Ter. 7:4 (plus expanded discussion).

5. MISHNAH'S RULES APPLIED TO NEW CASES

1:3 **II**   M. Ter. 1:3O serves as basis for set of rules concerning minor.

1:9 **III**   M. Ter. 1:9 supplemented with new cases.

3:2 **V**   M. Ter. 3:2O is basis for ruling in different case.

3:5 **II**   M. Ter. 3:5A–B applied to new situation (T. provides ruling).

3:6 **IV**   M. Ter. 3:6 applied to case suggested by M. Ter. 1:10.

4:1 **III** M. Ter. 4:1C applied to new case.

4:1 **V** M. Ter. 4:1A–C applied to new case.

4:3 **VIII** M. Ter. 4:3I–K + M serves to answer new legal question.

4:8 **V** M. Ter. 4:8 applied to new case.

4:12 **IV** M. Ter. 4:12 applied to new case.

4:12 **V** M. Ter. 4:12 applied to new case.

8:2 **II** M. Ter. 8:2K applied to new case.

8:2 **III** M. Ter. 8:1I applied to new case.

9:1 **II** M. Ter. 9:1 applied to new case.

9:1 **III** M. Ter. 9:1 applied to new case.

9:2–3 **I** M. Ter. 9:2 applied in new case.

9:2–3 **II** M. Ter. 9:2L–M applied in case of T. Toh 8:4.

9:6 **I** M. Ter. 9:5A–B applied to new case.

9:6 **II** M. Ter. 9:5 and 5:9 produce new situation.

10:3 **I** M. Ter. 10:3A–C analyzed within new situations.

10:3 **III** M. Ter. 10:3D–F applied to new cases.

10:4 **II** M. Ter. 10:2D–F applied to new cases.

10:5b **II** M. Ter. 10:6 applied to new case.

11:5 **II** M. Ter. 11:8G applied to new cases.

11:5 **V** Refinements of M. Ter. 11:8I–J.

6. Instantiation of Mishnah's rules

8:5 **V** Incident concerning improperly slaughtered meat.

8:5 **VI** Incident concerning uncovered wine.

8:5 **XIV** Incident concerning snake venom.

8:5 **XVI** Incident concerning snake venom.

5 **XVIII** Incident concerning snakes.

8:7 **V** Incident concerning snakes.

8:7 **VI**	Incident concerning snakes.
8:10 **III**	Supplement to M. Ter. 8:12.
8:10 **IV**	Supplement to M. Ter. 8:12.
8:10 **V**	Supplement to M. Ter. 8:12.
10:3 **II**	Supplement to M. Ter. 10:3C.
11:7 **V**	Supplement to M. Ter. 11:10.
11:7 **VII**	Supplement to M. Ter. 11:10.

Comprising 36.96 percent of the Yerushalmi's units, the complementary material takes up slightly less of the total than does the exegetical material (129 units in contrast to 161). Of these units, 37.21 percent consist of statements assigned to Tannaitic authorities (sections 1 and 2). These present rules which supplement those found in the Mishnah, and they usually include a short Amoraic gloss on their meaning. A further 28.68 percent of this material consists of rules suggested by Amoraim to round out the Mishnah's corpus of law (section 3). One central aspect of the Yerushalmi's work thus was to complete the task of legislation which its authorities see the Mishnah's masters as having begun.

Along these same lines, the Yerushalmi's rabbis devote a great deal of effort to defining the implications of the Mishnah's rules and applying them to cases unknown to the Mishnah. These units, listed in section 5, compose 19.38 percent of the present material. Section 6's discussions show how the Mishnah's rules served as a basis for behavior and legal decisions in the Yerushalmi's authorities' own lives. Not surprisingly, these cases concern the most practically applicable rules in the tractate, those concerning foods which might have been contaminated by snake venom. This material constitutes 10.08 percent of this category.

The final, and smallest, component of Talmudic material is designated as "Synthetic Materials." This refers to the treatment of issues which transcend individual laws and legal statements. These discussions compare and contrast rules taken from diverse contexts within the Mishnah, the rest of the Tannaitic literature, and in some cases, the Yerushalmi itself. They represent the attempt to find overarching principles informing discrete units of law, rather than entire tractates, which can guide legal decision-making. They also point out internal contradictions which might plague the corpus of law.

Alongside the discussion of contradictory rules (section 1) and correlated ones (section 2), I include in this section the Yerushalmi's units that discern which Mishnaic authority stands behind a rule stated anonymously in Mishnah Terumot (section 3). These discussions belong here because, just as in the treatment of apparently correlated rules, they point out agreements in the ideas of two or more discrete statements within the Mishnah. We also find a few cases in which an Amoraic exegesis of one pericope of the Mishnah is applied to some other one (section 4) or in which the Yerushalmi points out that an interpretation proposed for one Mishnaic rule is proven unviable by a different rule (section 5). In these several cases we see how the approach characteristic of the Synthetic Material's analysis of Mishnah Terumot might have been developed into a tertiary analysis of the Talmud's own discrete discussions and their relationship to the Mishnaic materials they claim to explain.

III. Synthetic Materials

1. DISCUSSION OF APPARENTLY CONTRADICTORY TANNAITIC STATEMENTS

1:1 **II**   M. Ter. 1:1 contradicts M. Makh. 6:1.

1:1 **III**   T. Ter. 1:1 contradicts M. Yeb. 14:1.

1:2 **III**   M. Ter. 1:2L contradicts M. Ter. 1:2H–J and M. Yeb. 12:4A–D.

1:4 **I**   M. Ter. 1:10 contradicts M. Ter. 1:4.

1:4 **III**   T. Ter. 3:19A contradicts M. Ter. 2:2K–N (expansion discusses M. Ter. 1:4).

1:7 **I**   M. Ter. 4:6 contradicts M. Ter. 1:7 (plus biblical prooftext).

1:8 **I**   M. Ter. 1:10 contradicts M. Ter. 1:8.

3:4 **III**   M. Ter. 3:4O–P contradicts M. Ter. 1:8.

4:4 **III**   M. Ter. 4:4F contradicts M. Ter. 4:4G.

4:4 **IV**   M. Me. 6:1 contradicts M. Ter. 4:4G.

4:11 **I**   M. Ter. 4:10N contradicts M. Ter. 4:11R–S.

4:13 **I**   T. Ter. 5:13E–F contradicts M. Ter. 4:13.

5:1 **IV**   M. Ter. 5:1E contradicts M. Ar. 6:5.

5:7 **I**   M. Ter. 5:9I–K contradicts M. Miq. 7:2.

6:1 **IV**   Anonymous Tannaitic statement contradicts T. Ter. 7:7C–D.

7:1 **I**   M. Mak. 3:1 contradicts M. Ket. 3:1.

7:1 **III**   M. Mak. 3:1 contradicts M. Ket. 3:1.

7:2 **IV**   M. Ter. 7:1A contradicts M. Ter. 8:1.

10:1 **VI**   M. M.S. 2:1 contradicts M. Ter. 10:1H.

10:2 **I**   M. Ter. 10:2A–C contradicts T. Ter. 8:9H.

10:7 **I**   T. Ter. 9:2C contradicts T. Ter. 9:2B.

10:10 **IV**   M. Ter. 10:12D contradicts M. Miq. 7:2.

11:3 **I**   M. Ter. 11:3E–F contradicts a Tannaitic teaching.

11:4 **III**   M. Ter. 11:4L contradicts a Tannaitic teaching.

11:5 **I**   M. B.B. 5:8 contradicts M. Ter. 11:8H.

2. DISCUSSION OF APPARENTLY CORRELATED TANNAITIC STATEMENTS

2:5 **V**   M. Ter. 2:6W–X = M. Kil. 1:2.

3:1 **V**   M. Ter. 3:1/M. Ter. 2:2 together point to overarching principle.

3:5 **I**   Simeon, M. Ter. 3:5B = Shammaites, M. Ter. 1:4C.

4:2 **I**   M. Ter. 4:2C = M. Dem. 7:3.

4:5 **I**   M. Ter. 4:5B = M. Ter. 1:4C.

5:2 **I**   M. Ter. 5:2C = M. Zeb. 8:5.

8:4 **I**   M. Ter. 8:3X = Tarfon, M. Ma. 3:9.

8:9 **I**   M. Ter. 8:8 + 9–11 = M. Pes. 1:7.

8:9 **II**   M. Ter. 8:8 + 9–11 = M. Pes. 1:7.

8:9 **IV**   M. Bek. 5:2 = M. Ter. 8:9–11.

8:9 **V**   M. Bek. 5:2 = M. Ter. 8:9–11.

8:9 **VI**   M. Bek. 5:2 = M. Ter. 8:8.

8:9 **IX**   M. Ter. 8:9 = M. Pes. 1:7.

9:8 **I**   Simeon, T. Dem. 5:9 = M. Ter. 9:7H–J.

3. WHICH TANNAITIC AUTHORITY?

1:1 **IV**   M. Ter. 1:1C1 does not accord with Judah.

1:1 **VI**   M. Ter. 1:1C3 does not accord with Judah.

2:5 **I**   M. Ter. 2:6O is the opinion of Judah.

2:5 **IV**   M. Ter. 2:6T is the opinion of Ishmael b. R. Yose (plus expansion).

3:7 **I**   M. Ter. 3:8: Hillelites or Shammaites?

5:9 **IV**   M. Ter. 5:9H is the opinion of Yose.

7:5 **III**   M. Ter. 7:6P is the opinion of Judah (plus expansion).

8:7 **I**   M. Ter. 8:6A–F is the opinion of Gamaliel.

11:1 **II**   M. Ter. 11:1C is the opinion of Rabbi (plus expansion).

4. EXEGESIS OF ONE RULE APPLIED TO A DIFFERENT RULE

1:8 **II**   Y. Ter. 1:4 **I** and Y. Ter. 1:8 **I** correlated for ambiguous case.

5:1 **VI**   Positions at Y. Ter. 2:1 **II** applied to M. Ter. 5:1G.

7:1 **VII**   Positions at Y. Ter. 7:1 **I.**H and S applied to new cases.

7:1 **VIII**   Positions at Y. Ter. 7:1 **I.**V–X and 7:1 **VII.**D–E and K–M in new cases.

8:9 **III**   Jeremiah misinterprets view of Meir, T. Pes. 3:10.

10:5a **I**   Y. Ter. 10:2 **II** applies to M. Ter. 10:5E–F.

10:6 **II**   Y. Ter. 10:2 **II** applied to M. Ter. 10:7.

5. EXEGESIS OF ONE RULE CONTRADICTED BY A DIFFERENT RULE

2:1 **VIII**   Yohanan, Y. Ter. 2:1 **I.**B–D, contradicts M. Ter. 2:1G.

3:4 **I**   Simeon b. Laqish's view contradicts M. Ter. 3:4K.

5:5 **I**   Yohanan's view contradicts M. Ter. 5:5D.

7:1 **IV**   Simeon b. Laqish's view contradicts M. Ter. 6:1.

As in the previous material, emphasis is upon those exegetical issues that play a central role in the development of a corpus of law and creation of a guide to legal decision making. Of this material, 66.1 percent concerns either the discovery of larger principles, upon the basis of which a wide variety of cases may be adjudicated,[15] or the suggestion that certain rules might be contradictory, posing a problem for the judging of specific cases (sections 1 and 2).[16]

Yerushalmi's masters are rather uninterested in the question of which Mishnaic authority stands behind a specific rule. This emphasizes the fact that the Yerushalmi's exegetical agenda is pointed to understanding practical and conceptual aspects of the Mishnah's rules. For this reason the role of individual Tannaitic authorities, section 3, is hardly of interest. It represents only 15.26 percent of the present material, 2.58 percent of the Yerushalmi as a whole. The question of the cogency of the Yerushalmi's own materials is only slightly developed, sections 4 and 5. It constitutes 18.64 percent of this material and 3.16 percent of the Yerushalmi as a whole.

By viewing all of the Yerushalmi's materials in synoptic form, we may draw a clear picture of the character of the Talmudic corpus and the overall goal of its formulators. Table 1 summarizes the results of the preceding discussions.

The synoptic table allows us to answer the question, what is Yerushalmi Terumot? As the preponderance of exegetical materials shows, it is primarily an explanatory commentary to Mishnah Terumot. It delineates the basic meaning and point of the Mishnah's rules and, in many cases, establishes their scriptural origins. The second major focus of Yerushalmi Terumot is upon development of the Mishnah's corpus of laws. The Yerushalmi cites, and often gives a short explanation of, supplementary rules found in the Tosefta. Viewed as a whole, however, the Yerushalmi's authorities' expansions of the Mishnah's corpus (**II**:3–6) take up the greatest portion of the "Supplementary Material." By far the least prominent aspect of the Yerushalmi is the correlation of diverse rules from the Mishnaic and Talmudic corpus as a whole. This synthetic material, a main component of later rabbinic exegesis, is only a minor facet of the Yerushalmi's discussion of this tractate.

Table 1   Synopsis of Yerushalmi Terumot

	Number of units	% of category	% of Yerushalmi Terumot
I. Exegetical Material			
1. Explanation based upon logic	90	55.90	25.79
2. Amoraic dispute over meaning	25	15.53	7.16
3. Explanation from Scripture	33	20.50	9.46
4. Explanation from Tosefta	8	4.97	2.29
5. Explanation from Mishnah	5	3.10	1.43
Totals	161	100.0	46.13
II. Supplementary Material			
1. Rules cited from Tosefta	41	31.78	11.75
2. Tannaitic rules not found in Mishnah or Tosefta	7	5.43	2.01
3. Rules cited in names of Amoraim	37	28.68	10.60
4. Rules cited anonymously	6	4.65	1.72
5. Mishnah's rules applied to new cases	25	19.38	7.16
6. Instantiation of Mishnah's rules	13	10.08	3.72
Totals	129	100.00	36.96
III. Synthetic Material			
1. Discussion of contradictory Tannaitic statements	25	42.37	7.16
2. Discussion of correlated Tannaitic statements	14	23.73	4.01
3. Which Tannaitic authority?	9	15.26	2.58
4. Exegesis of one rule applied to a different rule	7	11.86	2.01
5. Exegesis of one rule contradicted by a different rule	4	6.78	1.15
Totals	59	100.00	16.91
Final Totals	349		100.00

The atomistic mode of the Yerushalmi's commentary and the overall focus of its questions point to the purpose of those who created Yerushalmi Terumot. They sought to transform a systemic statement of theology into a compendium of legal rulings which could serve as a basis for legal decisions concerning a wide range of topics and issues. This accounts for the Yerushalmi's exegetical interests, as well as for its concern for augmenting the Mishnah's corpus of law. The "Synthetic Material," with its concern for the inner workings of the law code as a whole, is equally at home within such an enterprise. Accordingly, roughly 11 percent of the Talmudic discussions concern the locating of overarching principles and the delineation of rules which, while superficially contradictory, have their own distinct ranges of application.

What Yerushalmi masters did not do is as informative as what they did do. While the Yerushalmi is concerned with the Mishnah's individual rules, we have seen that it shows little interest in Mishnah Terumot as a whole. This is shown by its atomistic mode of commentary, as well as by its disregard of the Mishnah (or Tosefta) as a source of facts and principles that explain the Mishnah's own rules (I:4–5). Further, while the source of a rule in Scripture was of concern to the Talmudic authorities, the possibility that it was the view of a specific Mishnaic rabbi was not. Attributing rules to Tannaim did not meet the Talmud's goals of explaining the meaning of the law or of grounding it in the authoritative Scripture. Finally, the single-mindedness of the Yerushalmi's formulators bears noting. Nearly all of their material is dedicated to explaining and augmenting Mishnah Terumot. They stopped neither to tell us about the lives and character of the Yerushalmi's masters, nor to develop a history of the Mishnah's authorities and period. These issues were irrelevant in the creation of a compendium of rules intended to serve all ages. Such material therefore occurs only in the most modest amounts, in cases in which it is relevant to the understanding of a specific legal ruling or to that rule's application in a concrete case (II:6).

The Yerushalmi's attentiveness to the explanation and expansion of the Mishnah's individual rules reveals that its authorities viewed the Mishnah as the central law code of the people of Israel. As the chief interpreters of that code, the former would be the rightful leaders of the Israelite community. This vision shaped their overall approach to Mishnah Terumot. The questions they asked and the materials they themselves developed supply the key to understanding their vision of the Israelite people united under God's law—set out in the Mishnah and explained and interpreted by the Yerushalmi's own rabbis. The people of Israel were *not* to *believe* in the Mishnah's sophisticated theological views; they were to *perform* its rules and carry out its precepts.

Theory of Translation and Explanation

Conclusions regarding the history of Judaism in the land of Israel from the close of the Mishnah into the fifth century depend upon interpretation of the Talmud of the land of Israel, the primary source for Judaism in that period. For Tractate Terumot, this work of analysis is begun in the translation and explanation that follow. Let me specify the goals and method of this work, beginning first with the more central task of translation and turning afterwards to the commentary.

This translation aims to reproduce in colloquial American English the sense and flow of the Talmudic discussions found in Yerushalmi Terumot. My hope is to render the Talmud accessible even to individuals who are both unaccustomed to the general characteristics of Talmudic discourse and unfamiliar with the technical terms and concepts through which that discourse is expressed.

To meet this goal I make extensive use of interpolated comments, set off in brackets from the Talmud's own words. These bracketed materials serve three purposes. First, they allow me to transform the Talmud's abstruse and often fragmented clauses into complete English sentences. This creates intelligible prose. Second, they provide for the explanation, within the translation itself, of technical terms and legal concepts. Finally, interpolated explanations supply the logical links normally lacking from Talmudic discourse. At the beginning of each discussion a bracketed explanation introduces the issue of the unit. At each step in the argument such comments explain the present state of the discussion and indicate the direction it is about to take. In this way these comments create a running commentary to the text.[17] This allows readers to make sense of that text without constant reference to a set of disjointed footnotes or to a separate commentary.

To increase intelligibility, the text is broken up into its smallest component parts. These are the individual sentences or thoughts from which the larger discussions are created. This facilitates study by allowing the reader to examine independently each stage in the Talmud's discourse. Designation of these components by letter allows for easy reference to any of the lines of text.

Along with this division into individually lettered stichs, the Talmud's discussions are broken into their smallest complete units of discourse. Designated by roman numerals, these units are the shortest elements of Talmudic discussion which address and resolve a single issue and which are substantively independent of the material that precedes and follows.[18] Dividing the text into these units facilitates study by isolating the proper focus of study, the individual *sugya*. It further aids in the creation of a typology of the Yerushalmi's materials by allowing the determination of the relationship between each of the Talmud's discussions and the pericope of the Mishnah upon which it is based.

This same goal of creating a typology is met by the utilization, within the translation, of three type styles. Pericopae of the Mishnah appear in oblique type. Citations, or near citations, of Tosefta are in boldface type. The Talmud's own words, and my bracketed comments, are in roman type.[19] This use of different type styles clearly highlights the points at which the Talmud cites and explains antecedent materials or otherwise makes use of those materials.

The overall goal of this translation thus is to render both the Talmud's individual words and terms, and its larger meaning, in intelligible English. It does this without resorting to a separate commentary or set of footnotes. Certain disadvantages of this mode of translation deserve noting. The first is that the use of interpolated language sometimes obscures the exact wording and sentence structure of the Hebrew and Aramaic original. Maintaining the exact linguistic structure of the text would have facilitated study of the Talmud's use of stereotyped language and linguistic constructions. Such analysis has proven imperative for the proper understanding of the Mishnah.[20] Unlike the Mishnah, however, the present document is not characterized by a high degree of formulaic language and set linguistic forms. I, therefore, believe that, rather than highlighting linguistic construction, the proper goal of the translation is to provide extreme clarity in the rendering of an excessively difficult text.

The second problem is that the mode of translation I have chosen might prevent the reader from struggling with the text in its unembellished form before turning to and evaluating my interpretation of that text. Yet the approach I have chosen appears to me preferable to an unaugmented translation. Because of the Yerushalmi's extreme economy of language, a word-for-word translation would not facilitate interpretation. The reader still would depend upon my own explanation, contained perhaps in separate comments. This would have the disadvantage of being cumbersome and inexact. Instead I have chosen the straightforward approach of a running commentary. It remains possible to read through any section of the translation while ignoring my interpolations. This presents an accurate picture of what the original text says and allows readers to formulate their own opinions as to possible meanings other than the ones I suggest.[21]

The form and goal of the translation have determined the content of the commentary. Since a running explanation is incorporated into the translation itself, the comments that follow each unit of Talmudic discourse serve a different purpose. They provide an overview of the point of the Yerushalmi's discussion and outline the relationship between the Talmudic material and the pericope of the Mishnah to which that material is related.[22] My theory in asking the limited question of the relationship between the Mishnah and the Talmud is that all use of the Yerushalmi for historical study must begin with a clear conception of what the Yerushalmi is and of the goal that its authors set for themselves in creating this document. My own analysis of these issues, presented in the first sections of this introduction, depends upon the reading of the Yerushalmi's individual units presented in my commentary.

The Yerushalmi's several units pertinent to a single pericope of the Mishnah are introduced with a translation to and explanation of that pericope. The explanation points out the issues in the Mishnah that are addressed by the Talmud and provides an overview of the Yerushalmi's discussion. These explanations, further, detail which aspect of the Mishnah pericope is dealt with in each of the Yerushalmi's units. They serve to substantiate the contention made earlier in this introduction that the Yerushalmi consists, for the most part, of a line-by-line explanation of and supplement to Mishnah Terumot.

To summarize, the translation and commentary are in four parts: (1) the Yerushalmi's materials are introduced in the comments to the pertinent pericope of the Mishnah; (2) the Talmud's individual discussions are rendered accessible to the English reader in a translation that makes use of interpolated language so as to

provide a running commentary; (3) the comments that follow
each unit explain the relationship between that unit and the material in the Mishnah, and (4) the analysis already presented in
this introduction summarizes the results of this study and provides a preliminary description of the character of Yerushalmi
Terumot and its relationship to Mishnah Terumot.

Manuscripts and Editions

The translation is based upon the Leiden manuscript (hereafter:
L) and is corrected and notated to indicate varients from the *editio princeps* (hereafter: V), the Rome manuscript (hereafter: R)
and standard printed editions (hereafter: P).[23] I also collate readings and corrections suggested by PM, GRA, and the other
commentaries referred to in the bibliography. Within the manuscripts and editions that I cite only a small range of textual variation exists. As a result, a reader easily can make use of this
translation while following the original text given in the most
commonly available editions of the Yerushalmi, P and V.

I number the pericopae of the Yerushalmi according to L
(= V). This same enumeration generally accords with that given
by PM, as well as with the numbering of Mishnah pericopae
found in standard editions. The few divergences from the usual
numbering of Mishnah Terumot, as well as the consistently different numbering of P, are noted. The page and column designations found in V are given in brackets, within the translation.

The translation diverges from L in two minor ways. First,
I translate the pertinent pericope of Mishnah Terumot at the
head of each numbered section of the Yerushalmi. This differs
from L, in which the complete chapter of the Mishnah is found
at the head of the Talmudic discussion of that chapter. I have
made this change, comparable to PM's presentation of the text,
in order to facilitate explanation of those specific rules of the
Mishnah addressed by the Yerushalmi. This also eases analysis of
the relationship between each unit of the Yerushalmi and the
pericope of the Mishnah upon which it depends.

Second, in cases in which the wording of a pericope found in
manuscripts of the Tosefta is different from and more intelligible
than the wording found in the Yerushalmi, I follow the Tosefta's
version. This renders the discussion as a whole clearer. I follow
this same method when a parallel passage from elsewhere in the
Talmud makes better sense than the wording in Yerushalmi

Terumot. In both such cases, the source of and reason for the correction is indicated. If there is a significant question of meaning, the wording found in Yerushalmi Terumot is given either in parentheses within the translation, or in the notes. This allows the reader to determine the text that was before me in L and the reason for my particular choice of reading. The same procedure is followed when there are other textual problems.

Conclusion

Through reference to the most important manuscripts and editions, attention to the available commentaries, and use of the parallels found elsewhere in the Talmudic literature, I make every effort to locate and treat problems of text and interpretation. Still, this volume rightly is designated "preliminary," in accordance with the title Dr. Jacob Neusner has used for this 35-volume translation of *The Talmud of the Land of Israel*.[24] My work is preliminary because, whatever attempts I have made, a firm and final text for translation is not yet in hand. I have not been able to collate and analyze all of the available readings for every pericope. The complex task of lower criticism of the Yerushalmi's text still stands before us. My own concern for textual problems and variants is only a first and provisional attempt to pick out from a complex literary tradition readings that, on the surface, appear correct. When a complete study of the textual history of Tractate Terumot, along with the Yerushalmi as a whole, has been completed, this work will need to be redone.

Second, since we do not yet have a philological study or modern dictionary for the Talmud of the land of Israel, the meanings that I have imputed to the many obscure Hebrew and Aramaic words and phrases in this tractate are only a first step, to be retraced when the proper lexicographical tools are available.

Third, until the first two needs are met, a modern philological and *halakhic* commentary to the Yerushalmi is impossible. Until such a commentary is in hand, my interpretations of the Yerushalmi's materials must be deemed provisional.

Despite these problems, I believe that a viable translation of the Talmud of the land of Israel is both feasible and a present scholarly need. For it is unlikely that the several difficulties I have noted will be corrected within this century.[25] Until they are, the present translation and explanation should meet the purpose to which they are dedicated. This is to provide the foundation for the study of the formation of Judaism in the land of Israel in the third through fifth centuries. Such historical and religio-historical work cannot be contemplated, let alone initiated, without access to the primary document upon which such study depends, the Talmud of the land of Israel. The translation of Tractate Terumot which follows thus is intended as instrumental in the work of interpreting the Talmud of the land of Israel and the form and the history of the Judaism which that document so richly reveals.

I Yerushalmi Terumot
Chapter One

1:1

[A] *Five [sorts of people] may not separate heave-offering,*

[B] *and if they separated heave-offering, that which they have separated is not [valid] heave-offering:*

[C] *(1) a deaf-mute, (2) imbecile, (3) minor,*

[D] *and (4) one who separates heave-offering from [produce] which is not his own.*

[E] *A gentile who separated heave-offering from [the produce of] an Israelite,*

[F] even with permission—

[G] that which he has separated is not [valid] heave-offering.

Since the deaf-mute, imbecile and minor, C, do not understand the implications of their actions, they may not validly separate heave-offering. They do not have the power of intention required to set aside produce as a consecrated priestly gift. D and E–G are separate. Unless he has been designated as an agent, a person is not able to impart a status of sanctification to that which belongs to someone else (M. Kil. 7:4–5). This accounts for D. E–G points out that a gentile may not even act as the agent of an Israelite so as to validly separate heave-offering from that Israelite's produce.

The Yerushalmi addresses the two parts of this pericope, A–C and D + E–G, in turn. Unit **I** explains A–C from Scripture, while units **II–III** go on to describe qualifying circum-

stances. Units **IV** and **VI** determine which Tannaitic authority
stands behind the inclusion here of the deaf-mute and minor.
Unit **V** details the characteristics of an imbecile. The
Yerushalmi's second section (units **VIII–IX**) explains first D and
then E–F on the basis of Scripture.

[**I**.A]   [40a] *Five may not separate heave-offering* [M. Ter. 1:1A].

[B]   R. Samuel bar Nahman derived[1] [reasons for the inclusion of]
each [of the five individuals] from this [verse, Ex. 25:1–2]:

[C]   "[The Lord said to Moses], 'Speak to the people of Israel[2] that
they may take for me an offering (*trwmh*; i.e., heave-offering).'
This [reference to the people of Israel] excludes gentiles [from
separating heave-offering].

[D][3]   "'From every man [whose heart makes him willing you shall receive the offering for me].' This excludes minors [from separating heave-offering].

[E]   "'Whose heart makes him willing.' This excludes deaf-mutes
and imbeciles.

[F]   "'And this is the offering which you shall receive from them.'
This excludes [from separating the offering] one who separates
[produce] that belongs to someone else."

Only E and F require explanation. Deaf-mutes and imbeciles, E,
are deemed to have no understanding (see Y. Ter. 1:1 **II**). They
therefore cannot have the desire Ex. 25:2 requires of those who
separate the offering. "From them," F, is taken to mean "from
that which belongs to them."

[**II**.A]   Now the deed [of a deaf-mute, imbecile, or minor who separates
heave-offering] should indicate that he gave [proper] thought [to
separating it, so that the separation is valid, contrary to M. Ter.
1:1B].

[B]   [That this should be the case is proven] by what we have learned
there [in the Mishnah]: *[If] a deaf-mute, imbecile, or minor
brought [produce] up [to the roof to keep it free of maggots],*

even though he gave thought that dew should fall on it—it is not under the law, if water be put.

[C]   *For these individuals have the power of deed, but not the power of intention* [M. Makh. 6:1E–G; i.e., as A states, their deed is efficacious, even though their intentions are not].

[D]   What deed of theirs [would indicate that the deaf-mute, imbecile, or minor indeed gave thought to the water]?

[E]   R. Huna said,[4] "If he [physically] placed [the produce] in dew."

[F]   And so we learned there [in the Mishnah, another passage which supports A's contention]: *If a deaf-mute, imbecile or minor brought [a beast down to the water to drink], even though he gave thought that its hooves should be rinsed off, [water which is splashed by the hooves] is not under the law, if water be put. For these individuals have the power of deed, but not the power of intention* [M. Makh. 3:8H–I].

[G]   What deed of theirs [would indicate that the deaf-mute, imbecile, or minor gave thought to the water]?

[H]   Said R. Huna, "If he scrubbed [the cattle's] hooves in the water."

[I]   So you also should say here [in the case of heave-offering], let their deed [in physically separating the heave-offering] indicate their intention [to separate the offering, such that their separation is valid, as A suggested it should be].

[J]   R. Samuel, R. Abbahu in the name of R. Yohanan, R. Zeira in the name of our rabbis [stated why the proposition of A–I is unacceptable]:

[K]   "[Scripture states], 'And your offering (*trwmtkm;* i.e., heave-offering) shall be reckoned (*nhšb*) to you' (Num. 18:27).

[L]   "In the case of matters concerning which intention (*mhšbh*) is [specifically] mentioned [in Scripture], one's deed is not sufficient to indicate that intention.

[M]   "But in a case in which intention is not [specifically] mentioned, one's deed is sufficient to indicate one's intention.

[N]   "And here [in the case of heave-offering], since intention is [specifically] mentioned [at Num. 18:27: And your offering shall be reckoned (*nhšb*) to you . . .], one's deeds are not sufficient to indicate one's intention. [Thus the reasoning of A–I is unacceptable]."

[O]   R. Yose stated a contradiction before Samuel, "Lo, in the case of a writ of divorce, intention is not [specifically] mentioned [in Scripture], yet [in that case] one's deeds [still] are not sufficient to indicate one's intention,

[P]   "as we have learned [in the Mishnah]: *All are fit to [act as a scribe in the] writing of a writ of divorce, even⁵ a deaf-mute, imbecile, or minor* [M. Git. 2:5A].

[Q]   "Said R. Huna, 'This is the case only if an adult of sound mind stands at his shoulder [to supervise; the deed of these individuals alone is not enough]!" [Yose, O–P, cites Huna, Q, to prove that the case of the writing of a writ of divorce presents an exception to the principle of L–N. In this case, Scripture does not mention intention. Even so, as Huna states, the deed of the deaf-mute, imbecile, or minor is not efficacious. This is proven by the fact that they must be supervised, Q. The weight of this is to show that the principle of L–N does not hold.]

[R]   [In order to prove that Huna, Q, is wrong] R. Yohanan asked, "[How can it be that the deaf-mute, imbecile, or minor who acts as a scribe in the writing of a writ of divorce need be supervised by another individual? If the validity of the writ depends on this other person] would [the actions of the deaf-mute, etc., in doing the writing fulfill the requirement that the scribe] write [the writ] specifically for her [i.e., for the woman being divorced]?" [No, for if the validity of the writ depends on the other individual, the scribe himself did not write it for the specific woman. It thus is clear that when M. Git. 2:5A states that a deaf-mute, imbecile, or minor may write a writ of divorce, it means that he may do so unaided. Yose is wrong. The case of a writ of divorce, which he cites, does not contradict the principle of L–M.]

[S]   R. Yose went and stated⁶ [why Yohanan, R, is wrong and Huna's statement, Q, stands], "There [in the case of the writ of divorce], this one [i.e., the deaf-mute, imbecile, or minor] does the writing, while this one [i.e., the husband] does the divorcing." [Since the deaf-mute, etc., may not act as an agent of the husband, a fit adult plays that role. But the validity of the writing of the writ for the specific woman depends only on the actions of the deaf-mute, etc. Yose's original statement, O, stands. In the case of a writ of divorce, intention is not specifically mentioned; yet unsupervised, a deaf-mute, imbecile, or minor may not write a writ.]

[T]   (Delete: But here the same person who gives thought [to the deed actually] separates the heave-offering.)[7]

[U]   R. Jacob bar Aha said, "In light [of what Yose says, S] if [a deaf-mute, imbecile, or minor] wrote [the writ of divorce] and [also] divorced [with it his own wife], it would be a [valid] writ of divorce, [for no other individual would be needed to act as an agent].

[V]   "But here [in the case of heave-offering even though the deaf-mute, imbecile, and minor both] give thought and separate the heave-offering, [that which they separate is not valid heave-offering]." [Jacob bar Aha's point is that if we examine comparable cases, we see that in writing a writ of divorce the actions of the deaf-mute, etc., are efficacious, while in separating heave-offering they are not. The reason for the difference is as stated at L–M. The separation of heave-offering requires intention. Writing a writ of divorce does not. Yose's objection, O–Q, does not stand.]

[W]   R. Jacob bar Aha [and] R. Hiyya in the name of R. Yohanan disagree with this teaching [of Huna, Q, that under supervision deaf-mutes, etc., write writs of divorce for others (so PM; cf. GRA). Contrary to Huna, Yohanan, R, states that writs of divorce which these individuals write while supervised are not valid.]

[X]   What is the reason [Yohanan disagrees]?

[Y]   R. Yohanan's opinion concerning heave-offering [i.e., that if supervised, a deaf-mute, imbecile, or minor may validly separate this offering] accords with [the teaching of] R. Ishmael the son of R. Yohanan b. Beroqah regarding the mixing of the ash of the red heifer with water [below, BB].

[Z][8]   And R. Yohanan's statement concerning writs of divorce [R] is in accordance with [the teaching of] our rabbis concerning the mixing of the ash of the red heifer with water [below, AA].

[AA]   For it is taught:[9] [Concerning] a deaf-mute, imbecile, or minor—acts of mixing the ash of the red heifer with water which they perform are not valid [see T. Par. 5:7A. No allowance is made for cases in which the individuals are supervised. In the same way, Yohanan does not allow these individuals to write a writ of divorce under supervision.][10]

[BB]   [Qualifying AA] R. Ishmael the son of R. Yohanan b. Beroqah says, "[If they mix the water and ash] unaided, it is not [40b] valid. [If they do it] with supervision, it is valid." [See T. Par. 5:7C. In accordance with this view, Yohanan states that if a deaf-mute, imbecile, or minor separates heave-offering under supervision, the separation is valid.]

The premise that underlies the unit as a whole is that the deaf-mute, imbecile, and minor may not separate heave-offering because it is uncertain whether or not they are capable of giving requisite thought to the performance of that action.[11] With this as the basic supposition, the problem is to delineate why such an inability precludes these individuals from separating the offering. The issue is addressed in two primary segments of the unit. A–I poses the question just stated. J–N + O–V answers it. W–BB is secondary, relating to an apparent inconsistency in the position of Yohanan, an authority central in the preceding exposition.

[**III.A**]   It is taught: A deaf-mute who separates heave-offering, that which he separates is not [valid] heave-offering.

[B]   **Rabban Simeon b. Gamaliel says, "In what case does this apply? If he was a deaf-mute from birth. But if he was of sound mind and became a deaf-mute, he may write [indicating his intention to separate heave-offering], and others may validate [the document] for him"** [T. Ter. 1:1].

[C]   (Delete: One who hears but does not speak, lo, he is equivalent to a person of sound mind [see T. Ter. 1:2].)[12]

[D]   R. Jacob bar Aha [and] R. Hiyya in the name of R. Yohanan disagree with this teaching [of Simeon b. Gamaliel].

[E]   They say, "For this teaching of our Mishnah is contrary: *[If a man of sound senses] became a deaf-mute or an imbecile, he may never put away [his wife through divorce;* M. Yeb. 14:1J].

[F]   "Now [if it is as Simeon b. Gamaliel states, that people who become deaf-mutes may indicate their intention through writing],
let the individual [referred to at M. Yeb 14 : 1J] write, and let
others validate [the document, such that he may divorce his
wife]!'"

[G]   [The solution to the contradiction posed by D–F is to] apply
[the statement of M. Yeb. 14 : 1J] only in a case in which [the
deaf-mute] does not know how to write. [If he does know how to
write, he may give written instructions regarding the divorce of
his wife.]

[H]   Replied R. Ba bar Mamel [to G], "But a teaching is at variance
[with the notion that written instructions ever are acceptable in
the case of a writ of divorce]: **Lo, if [a husband] wrote in his
own hand and said to the scribe, 'Write,' and to the witnesses,
'Sign,' even though they wrote it and signed it and gave it to
him and he gave it to her, it is not a [valid] writ of divorce** [T.
Git. 2 : 8A–B. G, therefore, must be wrong.]"

[I]   Said R. Yosa, "Cite the end of this [i.e., H's] teaching [and you
will see that] it is not contrary [to the notion that written instructions are acceptable for the writing of a writ of divorce]: **It
is not a [valid] writ of divorce unless [the scribe and wit-
nesses] hear his [i.e., the husband's] voice saying to the scribe,
'Write,' and to the witnesses, 'Sign'** [T. Git. 2 : 8C].

[J][13] "Is [the scribe's and witnesses'] only acceptable instruction hearing his voice?

[K]   "No, [in special cases, such as that of mutes (M. Git. 7 : 1D–F),
it is sufficient indication of his intent to divorce his wife] even if
he [simply] nods his head.[14]

[L]   "[Just as] you say that [the requirement that the scribe and witnesses hear his voice (I)] does not apply [in the case of certain
individuals, i.e., mutes],

[M]   "so here [the prohibition against written instructions, H] does
not apply [in the case of certain individuals, i.e., deaf-mutes. As
G states, then, a deaf-mute who can write may divorce his wife.
Ba bar Mamel, H, was wrong.]"[15]

[N]   Said R. Mana, "[Contrary to what Yosa says, L–M, the prohibition against writing cited at H] does apply [to a deaf-mute, so
that, as Ba bar Mamel said, G is unacceptable].

[O]   "[Yosa's analogy is unacceptable, since whereas] raising one's
voice [so as to be heard by the scribe and witnesses] is equivalent
to nodding one's head, [writing is not equivalent to raising one's
voice]." [The weight of this is that Ba bar Mamel, H, is right in
stating that written instructions never are acceptable in the writing of a writ of divorce. This being the case, G, which suggests
that a deaf-mute may give written instructions, is unacceptable,
and the contradiction originally posed at A–F stands.]

[P]   [Ezra objects to Mana's claim, O, that raising one's voice and
nodding are equivalent.] R. Ezra[16] asked R. Mana, "[If it is as
you say that raising one's voice and nodding one's head are
equivalent], then just as he must nod his head three times,[17] [as
M. Git. 7:1D–F requires of a mute], so they would need to
hear his voice three times." [Since they do not, it is clear that
there is no specific similarity between raising one's voice and
nodding. We therefore need not expect a similarity between
writing and raising one's voice. The net result is that Mana's
criticism of Yosa does not hold. Yosa is right and, therefore,
so is G's solution to the contradiction posed by A–F.]

[Q]   [Rejecting P, Mana] said to him, "As regards raising one's
voice—one time is sufficient; however, nodding the head requires three times. [Thus your criticism (P) of my statement
(N–O) is not to the point. As I concluded, raising the voice is
comparable to nodding; but writing is not comparable to speaking. Therefore it is clear that a deaf-mute may not give written
instructions regarding the divorce of his wife. The contradiction
posed at A–F stands]."

[R]   [Taking a different approach to solving A–F's contradiction] R.
Yudan said, "[The case of the separation of heave-offering and
that of the writing of a writ of divorce are not comparable since]
there [in the case of heave-offering the deaf-mute simply] signifies [that] 'Such and so[18] I [already] have done.' Here [in the
case of a writ of divorce he must] indicate [to the scribe and
witnesses] 'Such and so you must do.'"

[S]   R. Benjamin bar Levi[19] asked, "[Why should this matter? If] he
has powers of intention concerning the past [in that he may validly indicate in writing, 'Such and so I already have done,'] he
[must also have] them concerning the future [and may validly
indicate in writing, 'Such and so you must do.'] If he does not
have powers of intention concerning the past, he does not have

them concerning the future." [20] [Yudan's distinction between the two cases is unacceptable and does not solve the contradiction posed by A–F].

[T]   [In clarification of Yudan's point] said R. Abudimi (Y. Git. 7:1 and R read: Abba Mari), "[The individual who M. Yeb. 14:1J states never may divorce his wife] is a deaf-mute and [the reason he may not divorce his wife is not that written instructions are not acceptable, but because] a deaf-mute may not designate an agent, [which is what he would be doing by writing 'Such and so you must do']." [The deaf-mute, referred to at A–F, cannot divorce his wife because he may not appoint an agent, not because written instructions are unacceptable. The rule of agency accounts for the difference between the law governing the separation of heave-offering and that for the writing of a writ of divorce. The contradiction posed at A–F is resolved.]

[U]   [This explains why a mute must nod his head three times while, as Mana states, Q, a single spoken instruction would be sufficient.] Said R. Yose b. R. Bun, "[M. Git. 7:1, which requires three nods of the head], refers to a healthy person [who became a mute. And why is a writ of divorce [that he wrote before he became a mute] not valid [until, through three nods of the head, he indicates his intention to divorce his wife]? I might say that, [at the point at which he became a mute], he had been working on his deeds [and when questioned might initially nod his head in reference to the wrong document. After three nods of the head, the questioners may be sure that he is nodding about the writ of divorce.]

[V]   "And a Tannaitic teaching concurs with this: To what case [does the rule of M. Git. 7:1D–F] apply? To a case [in which he was pushed] into a cistern [see M. Git. 6:6] and came out as a mute.

[W]   "But if he became a mute because of disease, it is sufficient [validation of his writ of divorce] even if he nods his head only once [for in this case we need not assume that, at the moment he lost his voice, he had in mind any other document]."

Simeon b. Gamaliel states that a person of sound mind who becomes a deaf-mute may give written indication of his intention to separate heave-offering. On this basis, heave-offering he separates is valid. This rule contradicts M. Yeb. 14:1J, which states that a person who becomes a deaf-mute never may divorce his wife. We should expect that, as in the case of heave-offering, the individual may give written instructions regarding the divorce of his wife. This contradiction, posed at A–F, is followed by two independent attempts at harmonization. G's solution is debated and rejected at H–Q. R + S + T solves the problem. U–W is secondary, on a problem internal to P–Q. While in form U appears to be a response to T, in substance it can only refer back to Q, explaining why three nods of the head are required for validation of a mute's writ of divorce.[21]

[IV.A]   Which authority [stands behind M. Ter. 1:1C's rule regarding] the deaf-mute?

[B]   [The rule] is not in accordance with [the teaching of] R. Judah.

[C]   For it is taught: [**R. Judah says, "A deaf-mute who separated heave-offering—that which he has separated is (valid) heave-offering."**] Said **R. Judah, "Mᶜśh b: All of the sons of R. Yohanan b. Gudgada were deaf-mutes and, in Jerusalem, all of the foods requiring preparation in purity were prepared under their supervision."**

[D]   **They said to him, "[That was possible] because foods requiring preparation in purity do not require intention and [therefore] may be prepared under the supervision of a deaf-mute, imbecile, or minor. But [the separation of] heave-offering and tithes requires intention [and therefore may not be carried out by these individuals";** T. Ter. 1:1A–C].

[E]   But are [foods requiring preparation in purity] not invalidated through inattention?

[F]   R. Yose in the name of Rabbi[22] [said], "No! Intention is not mentioned in their regard. Supervision is mentioned in their regard."

As is usual in this form,[23] A's question is not answered. Instead it introduces a Tannaitic statement that proves that the law is not in accordance with the position of some specific authority. In this case, that authority is Judah, B–C. D + E–F is extrinsic to the form at A–C. It simply continues the Yerushalmi's treatment of

the Toseftan pericope introduced at C. E–F gives the reason for
D. Foods requiring preparation in purity need not be prepared
by people with powers of intention. This is because regarding
such foods, Scripture refers to supervision (šmyrh), but not to
intention. The pertinent verse is Lev. 22:9: '[The Aaronide
priests] shall therefore keep (šmrw) my charge (mšmrty).' In the
Yerushalmi's understanding the verse adjures the priests to protect (ŠMR) the holy foods referred to in Lev. 22:1–8 (PM).

[V.A]   [These are] the traits of an imbecile: (1) **One who goes out
[alone] at night, (2) who sleeps in a graveyard, (3) who rips his
clothing and (4) who loses what is given him** [T. Ter. 1:3A–B].

[B]   Said R. Huna, "[An imbecile is] a person who evidences all [of
the four traits listed at A]. For otherwise I might claim that one
who goes out [alone] at night is [not an imbecile, but simply] a
lycanthrope (Jastrow, p. 1341, s.v., qndrwpws), one who sleeps
in a graveyard offers incense to spirits [but is not an imbecile],
one who rips his clothing sees visions (so PM; Jastrow, p. 620,
s.v., kwlykws: is melancholy), and one who loses what is given
him [is not an imbecile, but simply] is delirious (qwrdyyqws; Jastrow, p. 1341)."

[C][24]   R. Yohanan said, "[A means that a person is deemed an im-
becile] even if he has only one of these [traits]."

[D]   Said R. Bun, "R. Yohanan's statement, that [he is an imbecile]
even if he has only one of these [traits] is logical,

[E]   "provided that, [in the case of a person who loses what is given
him, he loses everything that is given him. For although people
in general lose things that are given to them], even the greatest of
imbeciles does not lose everything given him." [If this individual
does, it may be certain that he is an imbecile (PM) and not an
average person who happens to have lost something.]

[F]   A delirious[25] person does not evidence any of these [four traits
listed at A, yet still is deemed an imbecile].

[G][26]   What is the meaning of delirious? Said R. Yose, "Confused in
mind."

[H]   A case came before R. Yose regarding a man from Tarsus [who
was delirious]. They would give him red meat after dark wine

and he would cease raving and dark wine after red meat and he would cease raving.

[I]   [R. Yose] said, "This is a delirious person, regarding whom sages said: '[If he is] at times an imbecile [and] at times lucid,

[J][27]   (Delete following T. Ter. 1:3: lo, he is [deemed] of sound mind in every respect.)

[K]   "'whenever he is an imbecile, lo, he is [deemed] an imbecile in every respect. But whenever he is sane, lo, he is equivalent to a person of sound mind in every respect'" [T. Ter. 1:3C–E].

[L]   The case [of a delirious person who wished to divorce his wife] came before Samuel. He said, "When he is sane let him give [his wife] a writ of divorce."

[M]   And [in this ruling] Samuel agrees with Simeon b. Laqish,[28] for R. Simeon b. Laqish said, "[Let a delirious person give his wife a writ of divorce] when he is quiet." [This is comparable to Samuel's statement, L, that when the man is sane, he may divorce his wife.]

[N]   [No, Samuel and Simeon's opinions are not equivalent.] Samuel's [opinion] is more stringent than that of R. Simeon b. Laqish, for [Samuel] said, "When he is sane (ḥlym) [i.e., fully cured] let him give her a writ of divorce." [Simeon b. Laqish, by contrast, requires only "quiet," that is, temporary relief. This is a less stringent position.]

[O]   [That by "sane" (ḥlym) Samuel refers to someone who is cured is proven by the verse:] 'Restore me to health (tḥlymyny) and make me live' [Is. 38:16; Samuel's term "sane" is equivalent to "restore me to health" in the cited verse. As the verse indicates, to restore to health means to rehabilitate, i.e., "to make live."]

The Yerushalmi cites and analyzes T. Ter. 1:3A–B in order to define the imbecile referred to at M. Ter. 1:1B. The discussion takes place in two parts, B versus C + D–E and F–G + H–O. The dispute, B versus C, is odd, since C neither refutes B nor offers support for its own claim. The opinions of the two authorities appear to have been artificially juxtaposed at the redactional level.

[VI.A] Who is the authority [behind M. 1 : 1's rule which states that heave-offering separated by a] minor [is not valid]?

[B]   It is not R. Judah.

[C]   For it is taught: [**R. Judah says, "As to] a minor whose father placed him in a cucumber field and who separates heave-offering while his father speaks (read: *mdbr*) at his side [indicating approval]—that which he separates is [valid] heave-offering."**

[D]   **[They said to him,] "It is not he [i.e., the minor] who separated heave-offering, but his father who confirmed [it] after him"** [T. Ter. 1 : 4, with slight variations].

[E]   When his father comes and confirms [the designation of heave-offering] is [the produce the son separated deemed to have had the status of] heave-offering from the time it first was separated, or [only] from the time [of the confirmation] and onward?

[F]   Said R. Shimi, "Let us answer this question on the basis of this [teaching]: **When the householder came and found someone standing in his [field, separating heave-offering without permission, so that the heave-offering was not valid, and] said to him, 'Pick for yourself this fine [produce]'—if there was fine produce, [the householder meant what he said and thus] he is not apprehensive of robbery [i.e., he agrees to the other person's actions, such that the produce which that person separates is valid heave-offering]. But if not [i.e., if there is no fine produce]—this one is apprehensive of robbery [and his comment was a cynical one. He does not agree to what the other person is doing, and the produce that person separates is not valid heave-offering.] And if [the householder] should pick [produce] and give it to him, either way [i.e., whether or not there was fine produce], he is not apprehensive of robbery [and the produce the other person has separated is valid heave-offering; T. Ter. 1 : 5F–I].**

[G]   "Should you say that, [in cases in which the owner of the produce shows that he agrees to the other's actions,] from the time [the produce] was separated it is deemed [valid] heave-offering? No! [It is heave-offering] from the time [that the owner's agreement is made known] and onward.

[H][29]   "And so here [in the case of the minor, D] it is heave-offering
from the time [of the father's actions] and onward."

The important issue, stated at E + F–H, is at what point
produce separated by one person, but approved by another, is
deemed to have the status of heave-offering. If the act of separating the heave-offering is definitive, we may deem the produce to
be heave-offering from the point at which it is separated. The
alternative is that the approval given by the owner of the produce
is probative. If this is so, the produce may not be deemed heave-
offering until this approval is given. Shimi, F–H, states that the
latter is the case. The validity of the separation of heave-offering
depends upon the approval of the person who owns the produce.
Until this approval is given, the produce does not have the status
of heave-offering (G + H). It is not however clear how Shimi
derives this view from F.

[VII.A]   "So shall you [Levites] also present an offering to the Lord"
[Num. 18:28]: (1) [This means that] "You" [shall present the
offering] but not your partners [on your behalf]; (2) "you," but
not your executors, [who are in charge of your estate]; (3) "you,"
*but not a person who separates heave-offering from [produce]
which does not belong to him* [M. Ter. 1:1D].[30]

[B]   (1) [How can Num. 18:28 mean] "you," but not your partners
[should separate heave-offering]? For [the contrary] we have
learned [in the Mishnah]: *Partners who separated heave-offering
[from the same commonly owned produce] one after the other—
R. Aqiba says, "That which each of them separates is [valid]
heave-offering"* [M. Ter. 3:3A–B].

[C]   [There is no contradiction between the exegesis of Num. 18:28,
which states that partners may not separate heave-offering, and
Aqiba, who says that they may, since] this [i.e., Aqiba] refers to
the great heave-offering, [which Israelite householders separate],
and this [exegesis] refers to heave-offering of the tithe, [which
Levites separate. Since the two rules refer to different offerings,
they are not contradictory.]

[D]   But did they not derive the [laws of the] great heave-offering
from [those of] heave-offering of the tithe, [such that C's distinction between the two offerings is not acceptable]?

[E]   [Yes, C is wrong.] Rather, [solve the contradiction between the exegesis of Num. 18:28 and the statement of Aqiba by saying that] this [exegesis] is the theory of the law (*hlkh*); [but] this [Mishnaic statement] is actual practice (*m*ʿ*śh*).

[F]   (2) [How can Num. 18:28 mean] "you," but not your executors [must separate heave-offering]? For [the contrary] we have learned: **Orphans who were supported by a householder, or [orphans] whose father designated for them executors—[the householder or executor] is required to tithe the orphan's produce** [T. Ter. 1:12A, with changes].

[G]   Associates say, "[There is no contradiction between the exegesis which states that executors may not separate heave-offering and the teaching which states that they may.] This [teaching, F] refers to permanent executors. This [verse, Num. 18:28] refers to temporary executors. [Since the passages refer to different types of executors, they are not contradictory]."

[H]   R. Yose asked, "[How can this solution to the contradiction be correct? For] if this [i.e., T. Ter. 1:12A] concerns permanent executors, [why did] we learn [concerning them: 'Executors] may sell movable property to [derive funds] to feed orphans but may not [sell] landed property [for that purpose]'? [If they may not sell landed property, then these individuals, referred to at T. Ter. 1:12A, clearly are not permanent executors, contrary to what G claims.]

[I]   "Rather, [the reason for the contradictory rulings is this]: This [exegesis] refers to an adult orphan, [who may tithe his own food]. This [teaching] refers to an orphan who is a minor [and may not tithe his own food (M. Ter. 1:1C)]." [In the case of the former there is no need for the executor to tithe, and he may not do so. In the latter case, the orphan cannot tithe for himself, and therefore the executor is allowed to do so for him.]

[J]   (3) "You," excludes *one who separates heave-offering from [produce] which does not belong to him* [M. Ter. 1:1D]. What is the reason that you deem [as invalid heave-offering a person separates from produce that is not his own (GRA)]? Is it because [the produce from which this person] separates heave-offering does not belong to him, or is it because [that produce] belongs to his fellow [i.e., someone else]?

[K]   Let us learn [the correct reason] from this [case]: If one re-
nounced ownership of his pile of [harvested, unprocessed] produce, smoothed it over [at which point the produce becomes
subject to the separation of tithes], and [then] went back and
took it again as his own, [is his separation of heave-offering from
that pile valid]?

[L]   If you deem [the reason for M. Ter. 1:1D, cited at J, to be that
one may not separate heave-offering from] produce which does
not belong to him, heave-offering [separated by this person] is
not valid, [for the produce did not belong to him at the point at
which it became subject to the separation of heave-offering].

[M]   But if you deem [the reason for M. Ter. 1:1D to be that one may
not separate heave-offering from] produce which belongs to his
fellow, that which [this individual] separates is [valid] heave-
offering, [for the produce from which he separated it did not belong to anyone else. No choice is made between the two possibilities. Instead, a second paradigmatic case is suggested to answer
the question of why a person may not separate heave-offering
from produce which does not belong to him.]

[N]   Let us learn [the reason that a person may not separate heave-
offering from produce which does not belong to him] from this:
*If one stole heave-offering which was dedicated [to the Temple]
and [unintentionally] ate it, he pays as restitution two added
fifths, [one for eating heave-offering and the other for eating produce dedicated to the Temple], and one principal, [to replace the
produce he ate. But he need not pay two principals, usually required in the case of theft (Ex. 22:7)], for the payment of twofold restitution is not applicable in [the case of the theft of] items
dedicated [to the Temple; M. Ter. 6:4E–G].*

[O]   Who had separated the heave-offering [from the produce dedicated to the Temple]? Was it not the treasurer [of the Temple]?

[P]   [Yes, it was.] Lo, he separates heave-offering from produce
which is not his own, [for it belongs to the Temple], but you say
that the heave-offering he separates is valid!

[Q]   [Thus it is clear that] the reasoning [which stands behind the
rule of M. Ter. 1:1D] is that a person [may not] separate heave-
offering from produce which belongs to his fellow. [In the case of
the treasurer, the produce belonged to the Temple, not his fellow. The heave-offering the treasurer separated therefore was

valid. Likewise, heave-offering separated from unowned produce
by the person at K is valid, for the produce did not belong to his
fellow.]

[R]   Or [in answer to the question of O] should we say, who separated
the heave-offering [which was dedicated to the Temple]? It was a
Levite (GRA: priest), who had dedicated [to the Temple] heave-
offering [given to him by an Israelite]. [If this is the case, there
is no evidence that the treasurer may separate heave-offering
from produce that belongs to the Temple. The weight of this is
that Q's reasoning, that one may not separate heave-offering from
produce which belongs to his fellow, but may separate it from
produce which does not belong to anyone else, is unproven.]

[S]   And [as proof that the rule regarding theft, cited at N, may apply to the case of produce in the status of heave-offering which
was dedicated to the Temple and not to heave-offering separated
by the treasurer from untithed produce which belonged to the
Temple], did not R. Hoshaya teach: The same rule applies to
one who dedicates untithed produce [to the Temple] and to one
who dedicated heave-offering? [In either case, if the produce
later is eaten by a non-priest, payment of two added fifths applies. The case of N thus may be one in which produce already
in the status of heave-offering was dedicated to the Temple. Conclusions, as at Q, based on the assumption that the treasurer of
the Temple separated the offering do not hold. This means that
Q's larger contention, that heave-offering may be separated by a
person who does not own the produce, so long as his fellow does
not own it, is unproven].

[T]   Said R. Idi, "[Contrary to this present discussion, it is the case
that the treasurer may separate heave-offering from produce that
belongs to the Temple, for] the treasurer is treated as though he
were one of [the produce's] owners." [This upholds Q. Just as in
the case of the treasurer of the Temple, a person may separate
heave-offering from produce which does not belong to him, so
long as that produce does not belong to his fellow.]

[U]   But this is not in accordance with the teaching of R. Yose, for R.
Yose says, "The treasurer is deemed a third party, [not equivalent to the owners of the produce. He therefore may not separate
heave-offering from it.]" [Yose rejects T and holds that a person
may not separate heave-offering from produce he does not own,
even if the produce does not belong to his fellow.]

B–E, F–I, and J–U analyze the tripartite exegesis of Num.
18:28 given at A. B–E and F–I are parallel. Each questions the
validity of A's exegesis by adducing a Tannaitic statement which
contradicts it. Each then suggests the reason for the apparent
contradiction. J–U is placed here because of A's citation of M.
Ter. 1:1D. Its point however is unrelated to A and the prior
discussions. It does not question A's exegesis of Num. 18:28,
but simply asks the meaning of M. Ter. 1:1D's rule.

[VIII.A] R. Zeira, R. Aha, R. Yosa, and R. Yohanan in the name of R.
Yannai:

[B] "[Scripture states] 'You, also you, [shall make an offering to the
Lord'; Num. 18:28]. This [repetition of the word 'you' is in
order] to include [your] agent [as someone who may separate
heave-offering on your behalf].

[C] "[But] just as you are sons of the covenant [i.e., Israelites], so
your agent must be a son of the covenant.

[D] "[This means that] you [Israelites] may be designated agents, but
a gentile may not be designated as an agent."

[E]³¹ R. Yose proposed, "[The point of this is that, for purposes of
separating heave-offering], a gentile may not be designated the
agent of another gentile, his fellow. But he may be designated an
agent of an Israelite."

[F]³² [40c] Said to him R. Zeira, "From the same verse [cited at B we
learn the correct rule for a gentile. The verse says that] 'you'
may be designated an agent. [Does the word 'you' in this verse]
not refer to an Israelite? [Yes, it does.] And so the point is that a
gentile may not be designated an agent, even of an Israelite,
[contrary to what Yose claimed, E]."

[G] Replied R. Hoshaya [to Zeira], "But, lo, a Tannaitic teaching
supports R. Yohanan's [position, as reasoned by Yose, E, that a
gentile may act as the agent of an Israelite (PM)]: **Said Rabban
Simeon b. Gamaliel, 'Now if a gentile [for whom an Israelite
sharecrops] does not wish [for the Israelite] to separate heave-
offering [from the gentile's portion of the produce, the Israel-
ite] does not separate heave-offering [on his behalf;'** T. Dem.
6:1B].

[H]   "[From this we may conclude that] if [the gentile] wished [for
the Israelite to do so, the Israelite] may separate heave-offering
[on the gentile's behalf]." [The Israelite may act as the agent of a
gentile and separate heave-offering for him. Hoshaya's point is
that the converse also is true, that a gentile may be designated
the agent of an Israelite, just as Yose, E, suggested.]

[I]   [In response to Hoshaya's claim that the Israelite acts as the
agent of the gentile], R. Abba says, "[Heave-offering separated
by the Israelite for the gentile, H, is valid only] if [the gentile]
confirms [the Israelite's separation of heave-offering] on his behalf." [In the case Hoshaya cites, the Israelite is not acting as the
agent of the gentile, for the validity of the heave-offering depends solely upon the gentile's confirmation. Abba's point is
that, failing to prove that an Israelite may act as the agent of a
gentile, Hoshaya likewise has not shown that a gentile may act as
the agent of an Israelite. Zeira's contention (F) stands, that contrary to what Yose, E, said, a gentile may not act as the agent of
an Israelite.]

The redundant occurrence of the word "you" at Num. 18:28
means that agents may be designated to separate heave-offering
on behalf of the owner of produce (B). The question is whether
or not gentiles, who may separate heave-offering (M. Ter. 3:9),
also may act as agents and do so for Israelites. The conclusion is
that they may not, just as M. Ter. 1:1E–F states.

[IX.A]   R. Yohanan in the name of R. Yannai [said, "Consider the case
of] an Israelite who said to a Levite, 'I have for you a *kor* of
[first] tithe,' and [before the Israelite actually gave him the tithe]
that Levite went and designated it to be the heave-offering of the
tithe required of a different batch [of first tithe which he had]. If
the Israelite then went and gave [the first tithe] to a different
Levite, [the first Levite] can do nothing more than complain
against him, [for he has no legal claim over the first tithe he
originally was assigned, and his designation of that first tithe to
be heave-offering of the tithe is not valid]."

[B]   [A is criticized.] Now you should say [that the Levite has no
legal claim only] if this [Israelite] gave [the tithe to a different

Levite] before this [first Levite] designated it [to be heave-offering of the tithe for a different batch].

[C]   But if this [first Levite, who was assigned the tithe], designated it [heave-offering of the tithe for a different batch] before this [Israelite] gave it [to the other Levite, A's rule does] not [apply; i.e., the designation of the Levite who was first assigned the tithe is valid, and that Levite has a legal claim to recover the offering, in order to give it to a priest].

[D]   [For] this is just like [the rule] we have learned in our Mishnah: *[If a man who had given another permission to separate heave-offering for him] retracted [the permission]—if he retracted it before [the other individual actually] separated heave-offering, that which [the other] separated is not [valid] heave-offering, [for it was separated without permission of the owner of the produce (M. Ter. 1:1D)]. But if he retracted [permission] after [the other individual] separated heave-offering, that which he separated is [valid] heave-offering, [for it was separated with the permission of the owner of the produce; M. Ter. 3:4K–M].*

[E]   Now the entire rule [regarding the validity of the designation of heave-offering of the tithe by the Levite, B–C] is derived from this [Mishnaic teaching, as follows]: From the point at which [the Israelite] said to [the Levite,] "I have a *kor* of [first] tithe for you,"[33] [that Levite] was made [the Israelite's] agent, [to do with the tithe whatever he pleased].

[F]   The result is that [when the Levite designated the heave-offering of the tithe, he did so] as one who designates (lit.: separates) the offering with the permission of the Israelite[-owner of the produce. This being the case, if the Levite designated the heave-offering of the tithe before the Israelite had given the first tithe to someone else, the designation was valid. It was performed with permission. The Israelite's later actions do not change that fact. But if the Israelite gave away the tithe, and thereby voided the Levite's agency before the designation was made, that designation is not valid. It was not made with permission. This is just as B–C suggests.]

[G]   [The following assumes a criticism of the above reasoning. Since the Israelite is not himself responsible for designating heave-offering of the tithe, he should not have the power to assign a

Levite to act as his agent in designating that offering (PM). If this indeed is the case, the conclusion reached above, at F, is unacceptable, for it is based on the claim that the Levite acts as the agent of the Israelite. G answers this criticism of F by explaining that Israelites may separate heave-offering of the tithe. They therefore also have the right to assign agents to designate that offering for them.] Resolve [the criticism just described] in accordance with [the teaching of] R. Yose. For: **R. Yose said, "[As to an Israelite] householder who separated heave-offering of the tithe—that which he has done is done [and valid; T. Ter. 1 : 9]."** [Since an Israelite may separate heave-offering of the tithe, he also may designate a Levite to be his agent in doing so. The reasoning of F holds.]

[H]   R. Yohanan in the name of R. Yannai [stated a new case, independent of the foregoing], "[As to] an Israelite who said to a Levite, 'I have a *kor* of [first] tithe for you, but, here, I give you its value [in money and will keep the tithe for myself'—the Levite] must be concerned about the heave-offering of the tithe which is in [the first tithe and which Levites normally are responsible for separating]." [This Levite therefore must designate produce to be the heave-offering of the tithe required of the first tithe, the value of which he was given.]

[I]   [This is] as [in the case of] a certain [Israelite named] Aliposa,[34] who gave [first] tithe to R. Simeon b. Abba. [Aliposa] said to him, "[The tithe] has been set right [i.e., heave-offering of the tithe already has been removed from it, and you therefore need not worry about removing it again]." [Simeon b. Abba] came and asked R. Yohanan [whether Aliposa was to be trusted, and Yohanan] said to him, "Aliposa, our brother, is trusted [regarding the separation of heave-offering of the tithe]."

[J]   R. Isa[35] raised a question in the presence of R. Yohanan, "In accordance with whose authority [did you rule that an Israelite is trusted to separate heave-offering of the tithe]? Was it in accordance with R. Yose? For: **R. Yose said, '[As to an Israelite] householder who separated heave-offering of the tithe—that which he has done is done [and valid;' T. Ter. 1 : 9]."**

[K]   [Yohanan] said to him, "Indeed, Babylonian, I based it on his [ruling]."

We continue to consider problems of agency, a topic suggested by M. Ter. 1 : 1D–F and introduced explicitly at Y. Ter. 1 : 1 **VIII.** The question of what happens if an individual initially extends permission for another to separate heave-offering as his agent, but later withdraws that permission, is phrased clearly at A. The proper rule is given at B–C + D–F + G.

H–K is substantively autonomous of the preceding, for its issue is not agency. It is placed here because it develops the question of an Israelite's right to separate heave-offering of the tithe, introduced at G.

1 : 2   [P: 1 : 1b]

[H] *A heresh (normally: deaf-mute)*

[I] *who speaks but does not hear*

[J] *may not separate heave-offering.*

[K] *But if he separated heave-offering, that which he has separated is [valid] heave-offering.*

[L] *The heresh of whom sages spoke under all circumstances, [such as above at M. 1 : 1B], is a person who neither hears nor speaks. [Heave-offering which such an individual separates is never valid.]*

The present pericope develops the idea introduced at M. Ter. 1 : 1. It is lettered accordingly. A person who speaks but does not hear (H–I) is deemed to be of sound mind, just like a hearing person. For this reason heave-offering he separates is valid (K). He may not however separate heave-offering de jure, H, for he cannot hear the blessing that he must recite upon separating the offering (B. Ber. 15a; see also T. Ter. 3 : 1–3). This underlying assumption of the Mishnah, that, to be valid, a blessing must be heard by the one who recites it, is analyzed in the Yerushalmi's first unit.[36] It asks which Tannaitic authority stands behind that particular view. The materials that follow in units **II** and **III** take up the claim of M. Ter. 1 : 2L, that the term *heresh* always refers to a deaf-mute. Several statements from the Mishnah are cited to prove that this is not the case.

[I.A]   (Supply following Y. Ber. 2 : 4: It is taught: **[If] one recited the prayer [i.e., the Eighteen Benedictions] but did not articulate [the words so as] to hear [what he said] he has [in any event] fulfilled his obligation [to recite this portion of the liturgy; T. Ber. 3 : 5].**)

[B]   [To clarify the teaching of] which [Tannaitic authority] does this rule need [to be stated]?

[C]   [To clarify the position] of R. Yose.

[D]   Which R. Yose?

[E]   That [R. Yose whose teaching] we learned [in the following Mishnaic passage]: *One who reads the* Shema *but does not articulate [the words so as] to hear [what he says] has [in any event] fulfilled his obligation [to read the* Shema*]. R. Yose says, "He has not fulfilled his obligation [unless he hears the words which he recites;"* M. Ber. 2 : 3]. [The point is that the rule for the Eighteen Benedictions, A, had to be stated explicitly in order to indicate that Yose agrees that these benedictions need not be recited aloud. Had that rule not been recorded, we would have assumed the opposite, that just as he holds for the *Shema,* Yose believes that to be valid the Eighteen Benedictions must be recited out loud (PM). The fact that he does not dispute A indicates that this is not the case.]

[F]   [Turning to a new issue, we refer to M. Meg. 2 : 4: All (people) are fit to (act as the agent of the community in) reading the Scroll of Esther (in public, on the festival of Purim), except for someone who is deaf, an imbecile, or a minor.] R. Matenah said, "[This rule, that a deaf-person may not read the scroll, is the teaching] of R. Yose." [As in the case of the *Shema,* M. Ber. 2 : 3. Yose holds that a person fulfills the obligation of reciting only if he hears what he says. Sages disagree.]

[G]   Said R. Yose, [an Amora], "[If Matenah had not stated that this exclusion of the deaf-person, M. Meg. 2 : 4, is the view of Yose alone], we would have reasoned: Why do Yose and sages disagree concerning the law of the *Shema?*

[H]   "It is because [concerning the *Shema*] the following is written [in Scripture, Dt. 6 : 4]: 'Hear.' [We would assume that Yose takes this literally, to mean that to fulfill the obligation to recite this particular passage, one must hear it. Sages, on the other hand, do not take the command 'Hear' literally. They therefore do not require that one recite the *Shema* out loud.]

[I]   "And [having found a reason for their disagreement concerning the recitation of the *Shema*, we would have thought that Yose and sages do] not [disagree concerning] all other commandments [involving recitation. Concerning these other commandments, Scripture does not specifically say, 'Hear.' In these cases, therefore, Yose can agree with sages that one need not hear the recitation.]

[J]   "[But] since R. Matenah said [that the exclusion of the deafperson from reading the Scroll of Esther] is [the position of] Yose [alone, we see that the disagreement between Yose and sages concerns] all of the other commandments in the Torah [involving recitation]."

[K]   What is the scriptural basis for R. Yose's [position, that in all cases a person must hear what he recites? It is Ex. 15:26, which states]: 'And you shall heed (lit.: listen to) his commandments in order to keep all his statutes.'[37] [This means that] your ears must hear what your mouth speaks [in order to fulfill God's commandments].

[L]   [To reject all that precedes] said R. Hisda, "[The list of categories of individuals who may not read the Scroll of Esther, M. Meg. 2:4] should not include the deaf person.

[M]   "[The deaf person is listed in] that teaching through a slip of the tongue." [Since the word "deaf person" normally occurs with imbeciles and minors, it was added in M. Meg. 2:4. This is in error. Hisda disagrees with Yose, the Amora, G, who holds that M. Meg. 2:4 is the teaching of the Tanna Yose alone. Hisda therefore rejects the conclusion based on this claim, J, that Yose holds that a person who does not hear cannot fulfill any commandment involving recitation. Hisda, rather, holds that the dispute between Yose and sages is specific to the case of the recitation of the *Shema*. This is contrary to the conclusion Yose, the Amora, reached at J.]

[N]   [In reaction to Hisda's statement, L–M] said R. Yose [the Amora], "It is reasonable [to assume] that [even] R. Hisda will concede that the law of heave-offering, [which states that since a deaf person does not hear the blessing he may not separate heave-offering, M. Ter. 1:2], is [the opinion of] R. Yose, [but

not of sages]." [If this is so we must conclude that in general
Yose holds that a blessing must be heard to be valid but that
sages hold that it need not be.]

[O] Said R. Yose b. R. Bun (P: R. Bun), "[We may indeed assume
that even Hisda will agree because, as I will now prove], you
have no [logical] choice other than to say that this rule [i.e., M.
Ter. 1:2] is [the opinion exclusively] of R. Yose.

[P] "For we learned [at M. Ter. 1:1] the rule for the first five [sorts
of people who may not separate heave-offering], and [a deaf per-
son] was not listed with them. And is this not because that which
[the individuals listed at M. Ter. 1:1] separate is not valid heave-
offering? [Yes, what they separate is not valid heave-offering.
What the deaf person separates is valid heave-offering. Therefore
the deaf person was not listed at M. Ter. 1:1.]

[Q] "But, lo, [at M. Ter. 1:6] we learn [about] a different five sorts
of individuals [who may not separate heave-offering]. Now [the
deaf person] is not listed with them [even though, like them,
heave-offering he separates is valid, *post facto*].

[R] "Thus the conclusion you must reach is that this rule, [which states
that de jure a deaf person should not separate heave-offering], is
[the opinion] of R. Yose." [It was taught separately from the list
of comparable individuals at M. Ter. 1:6 because it is the view of
Yose alone. As in the case of the *Shema*, Yose holds that the
person must hear the blessing he recites for that blessing to be
valid. Sages disagree and hold, as they do for the *Shema*, that
the person need not hear. They therefore would hold that a deaf
person even may separate heave-offering de jure.] [38]

Yose holds that to fulfill the requirement of reciting the *Shema*
an individual must hear what he reads. Anonymous authorities
hold that this is not the case but that even if the individual does
not hear what he recites, his obligation is fulfilled (M. Ber. 2:4).
The question is whether or not Yose and the anonymous sages
have this same disagreement in the case of other recitations. We
wish to know, that is, whether Yose holds in all cases that an
individual must hear what he recites, or whether he claims that
this is so only for the *Shema*. A–E introduces this question and
provides one answer. The long debate at F–R offers a second

solution and introduces the case of the blessing recited upon the separation of heave-offering. This accounts for the placement of the unit in this tractate.

[II.A]   We have learned there [in the Mishnah]: *All are obligated to bring the appearance offering [to the Temple, on the occasion of the pilgrimage festivals] except for a* heresh, *imbecile, and minor* [M. Hag. 1:1].

[B]   Associates in the name of R. Eleazar [explained the exclusion of a *heresh*, that is, someone who speaks but does not hear, or someone who hears but does not speak, on the basis of Dt. 31:12, which reads: 'Assemble the people, men, women, and little ones, and the sojourner within your towns], that they may hear, and that they may learn [to fear the Lord your God].'

[C]   [How the verse, B, explains Mishnah's rule, A, is unclear, for] on the basis [of the verse we can explain only why] someone who speaks but does not hear [need not appear at the Temple. It is because the appearance at the Temple is in order "to hear," as Dt. 31:12 states. This person does not hear and so need not appear.]

[D]   [But what is the reason that] someone who hears but does not speak [is excluded from appearing? Dt. 31:12 does not seem to require the ability to speak.]

[E]   R. Hila in the name of R. Eleazar [explained the reason on the basis of the statement in Scripture], 'That they may learn (*ylmdwn*).' [He said that this means], "And that they may teach (*ylmdwn;* so PM)." [Since those who do not speak cannot teach, they are excluded from appearing at the Temple.]

The unit is placed here because, like M. Ter. 1:2, it refers to a *heresh* who speaks but does not hear. It is unrelated to the larger set of concerns of the tractate.

[III.A]   [The following refers to M. Ter. 1:2L, which states that the term *heresh* always indicates a person who neither speaks nor hears.] Said R. Jonah, "This [Mishnaic passage which follows] proves that [rules such as M. Ter. 1:2L] which Rabbi [Judah the Patriarch states] as general principles [in fact] are not general principles, [for they do not apply in all cases].

[B]   "For we have learned: *A heresh*[39] *who speaks but does not hear should not separate heave-offering* [M. Ter. 1:2H–J].

[C]   "[Now this reference to a *heresh* who speaks but does not hear] leads us to reason that a person who hears but does not speak is [called] a *heresh*, [and that] one who speaks but does not hear [likewise] is called a *heresh*." [This is contrary to the principle given at M. Ter. 1:2L, that the term *heresh* always refers to a person who neither speaks nor hears. We conclude with A that such Mishnaic statements are not really general principles, for they do not apply in all cases.]

[D]   And have we not learned [in the Mishnah, another rule which contradicts the general principle that a *heresh* is a deaf-mute]: *A heresh-boy with whom the rite of removing the shoe was carried out,*[40] *a heresh-girl who performed the rite of removing the shoe [and] she who performs the rite of removing the shoe with a minor—her performance of the rite of removing the shoe is invalid* [M. Yeb. 12:4A–D]?

[E]   Now R. Yohanan stated [the reason that this contradicts the notion that a *heresh* is a deaf-mute], "[The rite of the *heresh* is invalid] if [the *heresh*] is unable to recite [the passage from Scripture (Dt. 25:7–8) which begins], 'And [the dead husband's brother] says [concerning his brother's wife, 'I do not wish to take her,'] and [if the wife is unable to recite the passage beginning] 'and [the wife] says, ['My dead husband's brother refuses to perpetuate his brother's name in Israel'].'" [Yohanan's point is that the individuals called by the term *heresh* at M. Yeb. 12:4 are mutes. They are not necessarily deaf.]

[F]   But this [contradicts what] we have learned in the Mishnah: *The heresh concerning whom sages spoke under all circumstances is one who neither hears nor speaks;* [M. Ter. 1:2L].

[G]   [The presence of] this [contradiction] supports the contention of R. Jonah, for R. Jonah said, "This proves that [rules such as M. 1:2L] which Rabbi [states] as general principles [in fact] are not general principles, [for they do not apply in all cases]."

Jonah contends that statements in the Mishnah that are formulated as general principles do not in fact apply in all cases. This is proven by reference to M. Ter. 1:2L, which claims that the term *heresh* always means deaf-mute. Two distinct examples, A–C and D–H, prove that the Mishnah's claim is incorrect. Each cites a passage in the Mishnah in which the term *heresh* refers to an individual who, while deaf or mute, is not a deaf-mute.

1:3 [P: 1:1c]

[M]   *A minor who has not produced two [pubic] hairs—*

[N]   *R. Judah says, "That which he separates is [valid] heave-offering."*

[O]   *R. Yose says, "If [he separated heave-offering] before he reached the age of vows [= majority], that which he has separated is not [valid] heave-offering.*

[P]   *"But if he separated heave-offering] after he reached the age of vows, that which he has separated is [valid] heave-offering."*

The dispute concerns the issue already settled at M. Ter. 1:1B, whether or not heave-offering separated by a minor is valid. Judah, N, states that it is, contrary to M. Ter. 1:1B. Yose disagrees, consistent with that other ruling. Yose also makes the further point that for purposes of separating heave-offering, whether or not a person is a minor is determined solely on chronological grounds. Once a child has reached the age of majority, vows he makes are binding. At this same age he may separate heave-offering. This is the case even if he has not yet produced two pubic hairs, the physical sign of majority. Before the chronological age of majority, heave-offering separated by a youth in no event is valid, even if he already has produced the physical signs of majority. The Yerushalmi's first unit explores the legal relationship between the age of majority and the physical signs of majority. The second unit concentrates on the laws concerning minors. It asks whether or not minors validly may perform certain duties besides separating heave-offering.

[I.A]   It is taught in the name of R. Meir, "Under no circumstances is heave-offering separated by [a minor deemed valid] heave-offering, unless [this person, who chronologically is a minor] has produced two pubic hairs, [the sign of majority]."

[B]⁴¹ R. Abin Kahana in the name of R. Hila [suggested the reason for Meir's view, that heave-offering separated by a minor who has not produced two pubic hairs is not valid], "[Num. 18:32 states concerning agricultural offerings], 'Bear no sin by reason of it.' [This means that] a person who [is subject to the laws of the Torah, such that he] bears sin, may separate heave-offering. [A minor who has not produced two pubic hairs and] who [therefore is not subject to the laws of the Torah] does not bear sin [and, concomitantly], may not separate heave-offering."

[C] [To indicate why B's reasoning is unacceptable] they replied, "Lo, a gentile [is not subject to the law and so] does not bear sin. Yet he may separate heave-offering." [See M. Ter. 3:9. It thus is clear that whether or not a person is subject to the laws of the Torah is not a factor in determining if heave-offering he separates is valid, contrary to the claim of B.]

[D] R. Yose in the name of R. Hila [suggested a different reason for Meir's view, that one who has not produced two pubic hairs may not separate heave-offering]: "[The reason is that Num. 18:27 states], 'And your offering shall be reckoned (nḥšb) to you.' [This means that] a person concerning whom the power of intention (mḥšbh) is mentioned may separate heave-offering. [A person such as a minor who has not produced two pubic hairs], concerning whom the power of intention is not mentioned, may not separate heave-offering."

[E] [Indicating why this reasoning is unacceptable] they replied, "Lo, the power of intention is mentioned with reference to a gentile, yet [a gentile] may separate heave-offering (M. Ter. 3:9). [It thus is clear that lack of power of intention is not the reason that a minor who has not produced two pubic hairs may not separate heave-offering.]⁴²

[F] "[The following statement proves that gentiles do not have the power of intention]: For did R. Hoshaya not teach, 'Gentiles do not have the power of intention, [neither] there [in the case of M. Makh.], to impart [to foodstuffs] susceptibility to uncleanness [by intentionally wetting them down, nor] here, to separate heave-offering'?"

The Yerushalmi supplements M. Ter. 1:3 by providing the opinion of yet another Tannaitic authority, Meir, A. He holds that once a minor has produced two pubic hairs, his separations of heave-offering are valid, even if he has not yet reached the age of majority. Meir thus takes the position opposite of Yose, M. Ter. 1:3O–P, that the age of majority is determinative. Two parallel units, B + C and D + E–F attempt to uncover the basis for Meir's view. Both attempts fail, and the reason for Meir's perspective is left unexplained.

[II.A]   R. Aha [and][43] R. Hinena in the name of R. Kahana [say], "In the opinion of one [such as Yose, M. Ter. 1:3O] who states that [a minor] may not separate heave-offering, [a minor also] may not dedicate [produce to the Temple]."

[B]   But why not say [the converse], that in the opinion of one[44] who holds that [a minor] may separate heave-offering, [a minor also] may dedicate [produce to the Temple]?

[C]   This is because R. Judah [could not agree to that claim], for [contrary to what is proposed at B], R. Judah says, "[A minor] may separate heave-offering [see M. Ter. 1:3N] but may not dedicate [produce to the Temple]." [No reason for Judah's view is given.]

[D]   Now [in disagreement with A's claim that one who holds that a minor may not separate heave-offering also holds that he may not dedicate produce to the Temple] R. Yohanan said, "Even [in the opinion] of one who holds that [a minor] may not separate heave-offering, [a minor] may dedicate [produce to the Temple]."

[E]   And what may [a minor] dedicate [to the Temple]? A burnt offering or peace offering, [both of which may be brought voluntarily, by anyone].

[F]   [A minor] may not bring a sin offering of the fat parts, for he is not subject to the sin offering of the fat parts [which is brought only by one who has sinned. A minor is not culpable under the law and therefore has no sin.]

[G]   [A minor] may not bring a sin offering of blood, for he is not subject to the sin offering of blood, [just as at F].

(1) [H]   What is the law [regarding whether or not a minor who has suf-
          fered a flux or sign of leprosy] may bring the offering [required
          for the purification] of one who has suffered a flux (*zybh*) or sign
          of leprosy?

[I]   [Is it the case that] since [either of these] is an obligatory offer-
          ing, [to which minors normally are not liable], that he may not
          bring it?

[J]   Or [is it the case that] since [a minor] may become unclean through
          [a flux (M. Zab. 2 : 1) or sign of leprosy (M. Neg. 3 : 1)] that he
          may bring [these offerings]?[45]

[K]   It is obvious that he may bring [these offerings, since, as J states,
          he is subject to them].

(2) [L]   What is the rule [regarding whether or not a minor] may be des-
          ignated the agent [of another for the bringing of these offerings]?

[M]   [Is it the case that] since [the minor] himself may become un-
          clean through [a flux or leprosy, such that he is subject to the
          offerings], that he [also] may be designated an agent [to bring]
          these [offerings for others]?

[N]   Or [is it the case that] since, in general, [a minor] may not be
          designated an agent, that he may not be designated an agent [to
          bring] these [offerings on the behalf of another]?

[O]   [In answer to the question posed at L + M−N] replied R. Yudan,
          "Lo, in accordance with the Torah produce [owned by a minor]
          is subject to the separation of tithes. [Yet even so] in accordance
          with the Torah [a minor may not separate heave-offering and
          tithes and thereby] exempt his produce [from those offerings].

[P]   "[Analogously] here [in the case of his bringing offerings for
          others] even though he is made unclean through [a flux or sign]
          of leprosy and may bring his own offerings], he may not be des-
          ignated an agent [to bring these offerings for others]." [Yudan's
          point is that the fact that a minor is subject to some obligation
          does not signify that he may carry out all of the responsibilities
          related to that obligation.]

(3) [Q]   What is the rule [regarding whether or not a minor] may bring
          first fruits [to the priests in the Temple]?

[R]   [If the rule is] in accordance with [the opinion of] R. Judah, who says, "They deemed [first fruits] to be equivalent to holy things of the provinces," [which are consumed outside of the Temple and which a minor may not bring (see M. Bik. 3:12 and M. Hal. 4:9), then, a minor] may not bring [first fruits].

[S]   [But if the rule is] in accordance with [the opinion of] rabbis [M. Bik. 3:12, M. Hal. 4:9], who say, "They deemed [first fruits] equivalent to holy things of the sanctuary," [which, as we saw at E and K, a minor may bring, then, a minor] may bring [first fruits]. [No choice is made between the two possibilities. We turn to a new question.]

(4) [T]   What is the rule [regarding whether or not a minor may bring the festal offering [brought by visitors to the Temple on the occasion of a pilgrimage festival]?

[U]   [Is it the case that] since this is an obligatory offering, [for which minors are not liable], that he may not bring it?

[V]   Or [is it the case that] since he may change its [i.e., the offering's] designation to that of a peace offering [M. Hag, 1:4, which a minor may bring, as above, E] that he may bring [the offering]? [Again, no answer is given. We turn to a new question.]

(5) [W]   What is the rule [regarding whether or not a minor] may bring a paschal lamb [to be sacrificed in the Temple on Passover]?

[X]   [Is it the case that], since this is an obligatory offering, [a minor] may not bring it?

[Y]   Or [is it the case that] since, as Simeon b. Laqish in the name of R. Yudan the Patriarch said, "A person may bring a paschal lamb on every day of the year other than [Passover] and change its designation to that of a peace offering," [which a minor may bring, that in this same way, a minor] may bring[46] [a paschal lamb on Passover]? [No answer is given. We turn to a new question.]

(6) [Z]   What is the rule [regarding whether or not a minor] may set aside the tithe of cattle [Lev. 27:32]?

[AA]   Now, if one explains it (supply with Y. Yeb. 13:3, PM: as does) R. Meir, for R. Meir says, "[Num. 18:29, which reads], 'From all your tithes,' [means that] they have deemed all tithes to be equivalent one to another," [then,] just as [a minor] may (read with Y. Yeb. 13:3, PM, GRA: not) set aside the tithe of grain [i.e., heave-offering and agricultural tithes], so he may (supply, as above: not) set aside the tithe of cattle.

(7) [BB]⁴⁷   What is the rule [regarding whether or not a minor validly] designates a substitute? [Reference is to a declaration that one animal set aside as an offering is to be exchanged by a different animal (Lev. 27:10). If the declaration is valid, both the original offering and the replacement are deemed sanctified.]

[CC]   If one reasons (supply, as above: as does) R. Meir, who says, "They deemed all tithes to be equivalent one to another," [then,] just as [a minor] may (supply: not) set aside the tithe of grain, so he may (supply: not) set aside the tithe of cattle. Just as he may (supply: not) set aside the tithe of cattle, so he may not designate a substitute [for the tithe of cattle].

[DD]   Or [to take CC's logic one step further] one may reason as does R. Simeon, for R. Simeon says, "[The rule that a minor may not designate a substitute for the] tithe of cattle teaches [the rule for whether or not a minor may designate] a substitute for any [other] holy thing.

[EE]   "Thus just as [a minor] may (supply, as above: not) set aside the tithe of grain, so he may (supply: not) set aside the tithe of cattle. And just as he may (supply: not) set aside the tithe of cattle, so he may not designate a substitute [for the tithe of cattle]. And just as he may not designate a substitute for it [i.e., the tithe of cattle], so he may not designate a substitute for any [other] holy thing."

(8) [FF]   What is the rule [whether or not priests who sacrifice] a holy thing [designated by a minor] are culpable [for doing so improperly by sacrificing it] outside [of the boundaries of the altar]?

[GG]   Kahana says, "They are not culpable [for sacrificing the minor's] holy thing outside [of the boundaries of the altar, for the holy thing designated by the minor is not deemed a true holy thing]."

[HH]⁴⁸   R. Yohanan and R. Simeon b. Laqish say, "They are culpable for [sacrificing] his holy thing outside [of the boundaries of the altar, for the holy thing designated by a minor is deemed a true holy thing]."

[II]   Now this [opinion] of Kahana, [GG], is contrary [40d] to [the view of] R. Judah, [M. Ter. 1:3N], for R. Judah [states that] in accordance with [the laws of] the Torah, [a minor] may [separate heave-offering and agricultural tithes and thereby] exempt his produce from [a further requirement of] the separation of tithes. [In light of Judah's claim, that the minor's designation of heave-offering is valid], how can you, [Kahana], say this [i.e., that offerings he brings to the Temple are not really valid, such that priests are not culpable for sacrificing them improperly]?

[JJ]   [Kahana's position is] in accordance with [the opinion of] one who says, "Of their own [volition] have [minors who separate heave-offering and tithes] accepted [the responsibility to separate these] tithes." [But according to the laws of Torah, they are not subject to this obligation, such that heave-offering and tithes that they separate are not true heave-offering and tithes. In the same way, their offerings are not true offerings, such that priests are not culpable for sacrificing them improperly].

The unit outlines the considerations that determine whether or not minors may validly perform ritual actions such as designating agricultural tithes or animal offerings. The central fact is that minors may not carry out actions that are done solely in fulfillment of obligations of the Torah, F. Minors are not subject to these obligations and therefore may not carry them out. Minors may, however, perform actions that are voluntary. Just as any person may give a free-will offering, so a minor may designate agricultural offerings and Temple sacrifices that are not obligatory (E). With this as its basic theory, the pericope analyzes several ritual actions in order to determine whether or not they are to be deemed obligatory. If they are, a minor may not perform them. If they are not, he may. In several of the examples given, this very issue of whether the rites are obligatory is under dispute, such that the question of whether or not a minor may perform those rites never is answered. This indicates that the central concern of the pericope is the delineation of a theory that governs the rights of a minor. The concern is not the final adjudication of specific cases.

1:4 [P: 1:2]

[A]   *They may not separate olives as heave-offering for [olive] oil, nor grapes [as heave-offering] for wine.*

[B]   *And if they separated [either olives as heave-offering for both
olives and oil, or grapes as heave-offering for both grapes and
wine]—*

[C]   *the House of Shammai say, "[The grapes' or olives'] own heave-
offering is in it [i.e., in that which they have separated; but that
which they separated for the wine or oil is not valid heave-
offering]."*

[D]   *But the House of Hillel say, "That which they have separated is
not [valid] heave-offering [in any respect]."*

A's rule depends on M. Ter. 1:10. Heave-offering may not be
separated from produce the processing of which is not completed
(e.g., olives, grapes) on behalf of produce the processing of which
is completed (oil, wine). The Houses dispute the status of heave-
offering separated contrary to this rule. The Shammaites state
that the designation of heave-offering from grapes for wine or
olives for oil is not valid. They claim, however, that by his actions the householder has separated heave-offering for olives or
grapes he owns. The Shammaites do not mind that the man's
original intention was not acceptable. They take into account only
his actions. The Hillelites, on the other hand, take seriously the individual's improper intention to separate heave-offering. He did
not fulfill his original intention. Therefore the separation is in no
way valid.

The Yerushalmi's discussion moves from concerns intrinsic to
the pericope before us to larger issues the pericope generates.
Unit I addresses a general problem concerning the Houses' positions here. Both Houses contradict M. Ter. 1:10's rule that, *post
facto,* separations of heave-offering such as those described here
are valid. Why do the Houses deem olives and grapes to be a
special case? Unit II moves from this general question to a specific one, the basis for the Shammaite's view. The final unit takes
up an issue outside of the range of questions pertinent to the
positions of the Houses. It considers a Toseftan pericope attributed to Yose. On the basis of the Tosefta's rule it asks how
Yose would rule in the case of M. Ter. 1:4B.

[I.A]   We have learned there [M. Ter. 1:10]: *They may not separate
heave-offering from produce the preparation [for consumption]*

of which is completed on behalf of produce the preparation of
which is not completed, [nor from produce (such as olives or
grapes) the preparation of which is not completed on behalf of
produce (such as oil or wine) the preparation of which is com-
pleted . . . But if one separated heave-offering (in either of these
ways), that which he has separated is (valid) heave-offering.]

[B]   But here you state this? [According to both Houses, M. Ter. 1:4,
even *post facto*, the man's separation of heave-offering from olives
on behalf of oil, or grapes on behalf of wine is not valid. This
contradicts M. Ter. 1:10, cited above, which states that *post facto*
such a separation is valid.]

[C]   R. Ila in the name of Yohanan [stated the reason that the Houses
ruled as they did, contrary to the law of M. Ter. 1:10], "[The
Houses ruled as they did] because [having heave-offering separated from olives instead of oil, or grapes instead of wine would
be tantamount to] stealing from the tribe [of priests]."

[D]   In what way would this be stealing from the tribe?

[E]   Said R. Hanania, "[It is stealing from the tribe] inasmuch as [it
forces the priest to do] the labor [involved in processing the
grapes and olives; this is labor the householder himself should
perform]."

[F]   [The following indicates why, for the case of olives and grapes,
the Houses take into account the consideration of labor, whereas,
for the case of other types of produce, they agree with M. Ter.
1:10, that *post facto* a separation of heave-offering is valid even
if it means that the priest himself will have to prepare the produce.] Imagine that it was panicles of rice [which the householder gave to the priest, instead of prepared rice]. It is an easy
thing for a man to crush any amount [of this produce in order to
prepare it for consumption]. [Priests therefore do not mind receiving as their share unprepared rice. This is not the case with
olives and grapes, which are difficult to process.]

[G]   [In order to prove that E–F is unacceptable and that olives and
grapes do not have a different rule because they are difficult to
process, the following discusses a type of produce which, like
olives and grapes, requires much processing.] "Imagine that it
was ears of grain [which the householder gave to the priest as
heave-offering instead of threshed grain. While, as with grapes
and olives, processing the ears is difficult, the Houses do not

state that unthreshed ears may not be given as heave-offering for threshed ones]"—this is the contradiction that R. Hanina [posed to the notion that the Houses are opposed to the householder's giving unprocessed olives or grapes because of the great amount of work this would force the priest to do. This cannot be the reason, since the Houses do not disapprove in a different case in which the same objection could be raised.]

[H]⁴⁹   [The previous explanation proving unacceptable, we have a different suggestion of why the Houses object to the separation of grapes as heave-offering for wine, or olives for oil.] R. Mana [said], "[Stealing from the tribe] means nothing other than that [a householder] who should (*mbqš*) separate an amount of produce [i.e., olives] commensurate with the quantity of oil [he owns, instead] separates an amount commensurate with the quantity of olives." [Since, by volume, olives contain a proportionately smaller quantity of oil, the priest in this case would receive less produce than is his rightful share. Mana claims that this is the reason the Houses do not permit the householder to separate heave-offering from olives instead of oil or from grapes on behalf of wine.]

[I]   [This explanation of the Houses position is unacceptable, since one can] imagine that the individual [will, in fact], separate as heave-offering [a quantity of olives] commensurate with the oil [which he has; i.e., there is no reason to assume, as H does, that the householder will separate too few olives or grapes].

[J]   [No! Even though it is possible that] this one time [the householder] does so [i.e., separates a sufficient quantity of olives as heave-offering for his oil], some other time he may not do so. [In order to prevent this occurrence, the Houses ruled that in no event may a householder separate heave-offering from olives for oil, or, for the same reason, from grapes on behalf of wine.]

[K]   And this [likelihood that, from time to time, the individual would separate too little heave-offering] is not the only [reason that the Houses do not allow individuals to separate olives as heave-offering on behalf of olive oil, or grapes on behalf of wine. Another reason is that] the fellow [of a person who correctly separates heave-offering in such a way, by taking for the priest an added quantity of olives or grapes], might see him [separating this extra share] and would say, "This person [is taking an extra share for the priest simply because he] intends [to separate] more [heave-offering than is required]. But [since] I do not intend [to separate] more [heave-offering than is required, I may go ahead and separate olives for oil or grapes for wine without separating an extra share]." [This misunderstanding would result in the second person's separating too little heave-offering. In order to prevent this, the Houses ruled that no person may separate heave-offering from grapes on behalf of wine, or olives on behalf of oil.]

[L]   [The following is separate.] Hezeqiah says, "[The Houses did] not teach [that a person may not separate heave-offering from unprocessed produce on behalf of processed produce], except in the case of olives [separated as heave-offering] on behalf of oil and grapes on behalf of wine.

[M]   "But in the case of all other types of produce, [they] did not [teach, for the Houses agree with M. Ter. 1:10 that *post facto* the separation is valid]."

[N]   [Contrary to L–M] said R. Yohanan, "[The Houses] taught [explicitly] concerning only olives [separated as heave-offering] on behalf of oil, and grapes [separated] on behalf of wine.

[O]   "But lo, [contrary to M. Ter. 1:10, they agree that this same rule] applies in the case of all other kinds of produce [as well, so that even *post facto* the separation of heave-offering is not valid]."

The contradiction between M. Ter. 1:10 and the position of the Houses, M. Ter. 1:4, is posed at A–B and explained at C. Ila in the name of Yohanan states that olives and grapes are a special case. By separating olives as heave-offering for oil, or grapes for wine, the householder steals from the priest. The question D–K, is in what way this constitutes stealing. E–F's suggestion is rejected, G. H provides a second possibility. This is upheld over I's criticism, at J and K.

L–M + N–O is separate and, indeed, logically prior to A–K. It asks whether the Houses in fact deem olives and grapes to be a special case. The alternative is that for all types of produce they disagree with the rule of M. Ter. 1:10. Hezeqiah, L–M, takes the position basic at A–K, that olives and grapes are a special case. Yohanan, N–O, takes the opposite view. Yohanan thus should reject the whole of A–K's exercise. In light of this, Ila's statement in Yohanan's name, C, is troublesome.

[**II.A**]   Associates in the name of R.[50] Yohanan [said], "[The Shammaites' opinion at M. Ter. 1 : 4, that heave-offering designated
from grapes on behalf of both grapes and wine is deemed valid
for the grapes, holds] even if [the designation for both grapes
and wine was made] at one [and the same] time" [i.e., in a single
designation].

[B]   R. Hanania and R. Imi in the name of R. Yohanan[51] [explained
why this is the case], "According to the House of Shammai [the
man] is treated as if he said [in two distinct designations], 'Lo,
this [produce in my hand] is [designated] heave-offering for itself and for that produce which is below it [in the vat].'" [Even
though stated at once, we deem the designation to be of two
distinct parts. Therefore one part of it, for the grapes, may be
deemed valid, and the other part, for the wine, invalid.]

[C]   R. Hanania reasoned, "[This is possible so long as the produce in
his hand is of the] same kind [as the produce below, in the vat]."

[D]   [Rejecting B] R. Zeira said to him [i.e., to Hanania], "Do not accept this reasoning [that the designation is valid for grapes, even
though it is not valid for wine, because it is deemed to be in two distinct parts. For] as soon as [the man] would say, 'Lo, these [grapes
in my hand are designated heave-offering for all the grapes I
own,' those grapes] in his hand would be rendered exempt [from
further designation as heave-offering], and the rest [of the grapes
that he owns] would be unconsecrated food [and likewise exempt
from designation as heave-offering]. Now [through a separate
designation] could this [tithed], unconsecrated food render exempt [from the separation of heave-offering] the untithed [wine]
which is below [in the tank]?" [It cannot, for what is exempt
may not be used as heave-offering for what is subject to the offering, M. Ter. 1 : 5. Thus the reasoning that the designation is in
two parts is not acceptable. If it were in two parts, the second
part in no event could be valid].

[E]   [In reply to Zeira, D] said R. Hanania the son of R. Hillel, "[The
suggestion that the designation is treated as if it were in two
parts is acceptable, for it is as if the two designations were made]
at one [and the same] time, [such that heave-offering is designated at once for all of the produce together].

[F]   "At the point at which he said, 'Lo, this [is heave-offering both
for itself and for what is below,' both] the produce in his hand

and that which is below [in the vat] would [at the same time] be rendered exempt [from the separation of heave-offering]." [Both parts of such a designation could be deemed valid. In this specific case, we therefore may deem only the second part of it valid, as the Shammaites claim, M. Ter. 1:4.]

[G]   [The following is separate. The issue is whether the Shammaite view, that one may attempt to designate heave-offering for both grapes and wine or olives and oil, applies only to heave-offering, or to heave-offering of tithe as well.] Said R. Hanina, "This view [of the Shammaites] seems reasonable for [the case of] the great heave-offering, [which householders separate], for this [offering must be separated from produce that is in a single batch, [a condition met by olives or grapes and the oil or wine below them in the vat].

[H]   "But for the case of heave-offering of the tithe [it is not reasonable], since [this offering] must be separated in a precise quantity, either by volume, weight, or number [of pieces of produce. These methods of calculation are not possible if some of the produce is in liquid and some in solid form.]"

B gives the reason for the Shammaites' position that a designation of grapes as heave-offering for wine is valid for grapes. B's reasoning prevails, E–F, over the objection of D. C appears irrelevant to this dispute as a whole. G–H is redacted here because, like the rest of the unit, it treats in a general way the position of the House of Shammai, M. Ter. 1:4C.

[III.A][52]   We have learned there [at M. Ter. 2:2K–N]: *They may not separate heave-offering from [produce] which is unclean on behalf of that which is clean. [And if he separated heave-offering (in that manner—if he did it) unintentionally, that which he has separated is (valid) heave-offering. (But if he did it) intentionally, he has not done anything.]*

[B]   [Contrary to the preceding rule] it is taught in the name of R. Yose, **"And if one separated heave-offering from [produce] which is unclean on behalf of that which is clean, whether he did this unintentionally or intentionally, that which he has done is done [and valid;"** T. Ter. 3:19A].

[C]   [Yose thus holds that *post facto* the wrong separation of heave-offering described at M. Ter. 2 : 2 is valid.] What [would] R. Yose say [concerning] this [separation of heave-offering from grapes for wine, described at M. Ter. 1 : 4? Would he also hold here that *post facto* the wrong separation of heave-offering is valid?]

[D]   [The answer is determined by the following reasoning]: Now if there [at M. Ter. 2 : 2, in a case in which] all [of the heave-offering is taken from unclean produce and so] is lost to the priest, [who may not eat unclean heave-offering], you [i.e., Yose] say that what [the householder] has done is done [and valid],

[E]   here [at M. Ter. 1 : 4, in the case of grapes given as heave-offering for wine, in which case] all [of the heave-offering] is not lost to the priest, [for the priest may eat what is given him], should [Yose not rule] in the same way, [that the separation is valid, *post facto?* It appears that he should.]

[F]   [This conclusion is shown to be wrong for] a Tannaitic teaching is found in the name of R. Yose, "*They may not separate olives as heave-offering on behalf of oil, nor grapes as heave-offering on behalf of wine. And if he separated heave-offering [in this way], the House of Shammai say, 'The heave-offering required of the [grapes or olives] themselves is in it.' But the House of Hillel say, 'That which they have separated is not [valid] heave-offering [in any way'"*; M. Ter. 1 : 4. Since Yose transmits M.'s dispute, we assume that he has the position of the Hillelites (PM), that the heave-offering is not valid. This is the opposite of the opinion which, according to D–E, Yose should hold.]

[G]   [It thus is clear that] the opinions[53] of R. Yose are reversed!

[H]   There, [for the case of unclean produce separated as heave-offering for what is clean], he said, "What the householder has done is done, [and valid]."

[I]   But here, [for the case of grapes or olives separated as heave-offering for wine or oil], he said, "That which he has separated is not [valid] heave-offering."

[J]   [The reason that Yose deems one separation valid but the other not is as follows:] There [regarding the separation of unclean produce as heave-offering for clean, Yose reasons that] it is not common for food to be unclean. Further, people do not [normally] err by thinking that they may separate heave-offering or tithes from one [i.e., unclean produce] on behalf of the other [i.e., clean produce. Since, in all, it is unlikely that people ever will separate unclean produce as heave-offering for clean, Yose says that, if this should occur, *post facto* the separation is valid.]

[K]   But [Yose reasons that] it is common [for people to separate] olives [as heave-offering] for oil and grapes for wine.

[L]   Therefore [he is concerned that] if you say this [i.e., that *post facto* such a separation of heave-offering is valid] people [ultimately] would think that it also is permitted [de jure] to separate olives as heave-offering for oil or grapes as heave-offering for wine. [To prevent this from happening, Yose rules that even *post facto* such a separation is not valid, as M. Ter. 1:4D states.]

An apparent inconsistency in the view of Yose is identified, A–I, and explained, J–L. Yose deems the separation of unclean produce as heave-offering for clean food to be valid *post facto*. Yose takes this position because, J, it will not have the undesired effect of causing people to think that they also may separate heave-offering in this fashion de jure. This is not so in the case of olives or grapes separated as heave-offering for oil or wine, M. Ter. 1:4. If this separation is deemed valid *post facto*, people also will think that it is permissible de jure, L. Yose therefore deems it invalid, even *post facto*.

1:5 [P: 1:3]

[A]   *They do not separate heave-offering*

[B]   *(1) from gleanings, or (2) from forgotten sheaves, or (3) from [produce growing in the] corner of a field [which is left for the poor], or (4) from ownerless produce;*

[C]   *and (5) not from first tithe from which heave-offering [of the tithe] has been removed;*

[D]   *and (6) not from second tithe or [produce] dedicated [to the Temple] which have been redeemed;*

[E]   *and (7) not from that which is subject [to the separation of heave-offering] on behalf of that which is exempt;*

[F]   and not from that which is exempt on behalf of that which is subject;

[G]   and (8) not from that which is picked on behalf of that which is not picked;

[H]   and not from that which is not picked on behalf of that which is picked;

[I]   and (9) not from that which is new [i.e., produce of the present year] on behalf of that which is old [i.e., produce left over from a previous year (see T. Ter. 2:6)];

[J]   and not from that which is old on behalf of that which is new;

[K]   and (10) not from produce of the land [of Israel] on behalf of produce from outside of the land [of Israel];

[L]   and not from produce from outside of the land on behalf of produce of the land.

[M]   And if they separated heave-offering [from any of the types of produce listed at B–D, or in any of the fashions described at E–L]—

[N]   that which they have separated is not [valid] heave-offering.

Heave-offering may not be separated from, or on behalf of, produce that is not subject to the separation of heave-offering. The Yerushalmi's first unit asks why this larger point, established clearly through the examples at B, needed to be stated explicitly at E–F. The Yerushalmi thus accounts for what on the surface is a redundancy in the Mishnah. The second, and final, unit turns to the pericope's concluding rule, M. Ter. 1:5M–N.

[I.A] R. Yohanan in the name of R. Yannai [said], "This [rule, at M. 1:5A–B, concerning what produce is not subject to the separation of heave-offering, is based on] one of the three [rabbinic interpretations] of Scripture that are clearly supported by [the literal sense of] the Torah.

[B]   "[The rule is based on Dt. 14:28–29, which states: 'At the end of every three years you shall bring forth all of the tithe of the produce of the same year, and lay it up within your towns.] And the Levite, because he has no portion or inheritance with you, shall come [and eat and be filled].'

[C]   "[This means that] from [produce in] which you have [a portion] but [in] which he does not have [a portion], you are obligated to give him [tithe].

[D]   "This excludes [from the separation of tithes] ownerless produce [M. 1:5B4], to which you and he have an equal right.

[E]   "Gleanings, forgotten sheaves, and [produce that grows in the] corner [of a field and is left for the poor] are like ownerless produce [and therefore also are not subject to tithes, M. Ter. 1:5B1–3]."

[F]   [If, as Yohanan says, the point of M. Ter. 1:5A–B is that the produce listed there is exempt from the separation of heave-offering, why does M. Ter. 1:5E–F have to state explicitly that heave-offering may not be separated from what is exempt?] Are not all of those [things which are exempt] already mentioned [at M. Ter. 1:5B]?

[G]   This is [the point] the Mishnah [wished to make by stating explicitly that heave-offering may not be separated from what is exempt]: And [they may not separate heave-offering] from what has reached one third of its growth [and so is subject to heave-offering] on behalf of what has not reached a third of its growth [and is not subject. Since this particular case is not listed explicitly, a general rule which would cover it needed to be stated.]

A–E's explanation of M. Ter. 1:5B reveals a redundancy in the Mishnah, pointed out at F. The Mishnah's purpose in giving a general rule is explained, G.

[II.A]   And if they separated heave-offering [in the ways described at M. Ter. 1:5]—that which he[54] has separated is [valid] heave-offering [cf., M. Ter. 1:5M–N].

[B]   According to Hezeqiah, [this rule, A] is under dispute.

[C]   According to R. Yohanan, [this rule is] the opinion of all [authorities].

Since neither Hezeqiah's nor Yohanan's view is explained, the
unit is enigmatic.

1:6 [P: 1:4a]

[A]   *Five [sorts of people] may not separate heave-offering,*

[B]   *but if they separated heave-offering, that which they have separated is [valid] heave-offering:*

[C]   *(1) a mute, (2) drunkard, (3) naked person, (4) blind person,
and (5) a person who has had a nocturnal emission*

[D]   *may not separate heave-offering.*

[E]   *But if they separated heave-offering, that which they have separated is [valid] heave-offering.*

The individuals listed here may not separate heave-offering either because they may not recite the blessing which accompanies
the separation (C1, 3, 5), or because they are not capable of
choosing the best of the produce for designation as the priestly
gift (C2, 4; see M. Ter. 2:6). This is pointed out in the Yerushalmi's one-unit discussion of this pericope. These people do
have requisite intention, such that heave-offering they separate is
valid *post facto*, E.

[I.A]   Some of these [individuals listed at M. Ter. 1:6 may not separate
heave-offering] because [they are not permitted to recite] the
blessing [which accompanies the separation of heave-offering;
see T. Ter. 3:3, T. Ber. 6:14].

[B]   And some of them [may not separate heave-offering] because
they are not able to [distinguish between produce of better and
worse quality in order to] separate heave-offering from the best
[of their produce, as required by M. Ter. 2:4].

[C]   A mute, a naked person, and one who has had a nocturnal emission [may not separate heave-offering] because [they may not re-
cite] the blessing. [For the case of the one who has had a nocturnal emission, see M. Ber. 3:4; for the naked person, see M.
Ber. 3:5 and T. Ber. 2:15.]

[D] A blind person[55] and a drunkard [may not separate heave-offering] because they are unable to [distinguish between produce of better and worse quality in order to] separate heave-offering from the best [of their produce].

[E] [The following is separate.] Abba bar R. Huna says, "An intoxicated person should not pray. But if he prays, his prayer is deemed a [valid] supplication [of God].

[F] "A drunkard should not pray. And if he prays, his prayer is deemed blasphemy."

[G] Who is [called] intoxicated? Anyone who has drunk a quarter-*log*.

[H] [Who is called] a drunkard? One who drank more[56] than that.

[I] There [in Babylonia] they say [a drunkard is] anyone who is unable to speak before the king [i.e., who lacks the requisite presence of mind].

[J] R. Zeira asked in the presence of R. Isi, "[As to] a drunkard—what is the rule regarding whether or not he may recite the grace [after meals]?"

[K] [Isi] said to him, "[Dt. 8:10] states, 'And you shall eat and be full and you shall bless [the Lord your God].' [This means] that even [if a man is so drunk as to be] unable [properly] to speak, [he must bless, for he has eaten and become full]."

[L] [The answer to the question concerning the grace after meals thus is obvious.] The only question which [need be asked] is whether or not [a drunkard] may recite the *Shema*. [This question is not answered. We turn to a different issue.]

[M] Said Abba bar Abin, "A certain pious one asked Elijah, may his memory be for good, '[As for] a naked person—what is the rule whether or not he may recite the *Shema?*' [Elijah] said to him, '[Dt. 23:14 states], "That [the Lord] may not see anything (*dbr*) indecent of you." [This means that he should not see you] speaking (*dybwr*) in indecency [i.e., in nakedness. Thus a naked person may not recite the *Shema*.]'"

[N] Taught Hezeqiah, "[This means that a naked person may] neither recite [the *Shema*] nor say the grace [after meals]."

The discussion of why the individuals listed at M. Ter. 1:6 may not separate heave-offering introduces the secondary matter at E–N. This concerns the specific rules for the drunkard and naked person and their right to recite blessings and to pray.

1:7 [P: 1:4b]

[A]   *They do not separate heave-offering by (1) a measure [of volume], or by (2) weight, or by (3) a count [of the number of pieces of produce being designated heave-offering].*

[B]   *But one may separate heave-offering on behalf of [produce] which (1) has been measured, (2) which has been weighed, (3) or which has been counted.*

[C]   *They may not separate heave-offering in a basket or in a vessel which [holds a known] measure, [for this would constitute separating heave-offering by volume, contrary to A].*

[D]   *But one may separate heave-offering in them [if they are] one-half or one-third part [filled, for in this case the heave-offering is not deemed measured out].*

[E]   *He may not separate heave-offering in [a basket which, when full, holds one] seah,[even if it is only] one half part [filled with produce to be designated heave-offering],*

[F]   *since its half-full mark is a [known] measure.*

The point is made through the contrast between the formal opposites, A and B. Produce to be heave-offering is chosen randomly, not through the deliberate actions of a householder who measures out the offering (A). This is common to the designation of all holy things. While the person may not measure out the heave-offering, he may determine the quantity of produce from which that offering is being taken. This allows him accurately to estimate the required quantity of heave-offering (M. Ter. 4:3) and assures that the priest receive his proper share. The Yerushalmi's one unit concentrates upon the dichotomy of A + B in order to determine the difference between separating heave-offering by a fixed measure and separating it from a batch of produce the quantity of which is known.

[**I.**A] There [at M. Ter. 4:6] we have learned: *One who [in separating heave-offering] counts [the produce] is praiseworthy, and one who measures [the volume of the produce] is more praiseworthy than he. But one who weighs [the produce] is the most praiseworthy of the three.*

[B] But here [at M. Ter. 1:7] you say this [i.e., the opposite, that heave-offering may not be separated by volume, weight, or count]!

[C] [To resolve the contradiction] said R. Joshua b. Levi, "This [rule, M. Ter. 1:7] applies to the great heave-offering, [which householders designate and which must be separated through estimation]. This [rule, M. Ter. 4:6] applies to heave-offering of the tithe, [which Levites separate]." [Heave-offering of the tithe must be exactly one-tenth of first tithe and therefore is separated by an exact measure. The distinct requirements of these two offerings account for the difference between the rules of M. Ter. 1:7 and M. Ter. 4:6.]

[D] But [contrary to the distinction made at C between the great heave-offering and heave-offering of the tithe] so taught a Tannaitic authority:

[E] Eliezer b. Gimel says, "From what [verse of Scripture do we learn] that they may not separate heave-offering by volume, weight, or a count [of the number of pieces of produce]? Scripture states, 'And your offering shall be reckoned to you' [Num. 18:27. This means that] through reckoning [i.e., estimation] you should separate heave-offering. But you may not separate heave-offering by volume, weight, or number.

[F] "[And, contrary to C,] just as the great heave-offering is separated through reckoning, so heave-offering of the tithe[57] is separated through reckoning. [Since the same rule applies to both of these offerings, C is unacceptable and the contradiction between M. Ter. 1:7 and M. Ter. 4:6 has not been resolved.]

[G] "But rather, [to solve that contradiction], so we have learned [M. Ter. 1:7B]: *But one may separate heave-offering from [produce] the volume of which has been calculated, which has been weighed, or which has been counted.*" [Just as at M. Ter. 1:7B, the point of M. Ter. 4:6 is that the householder may determine the quantity of produce from which heave-offering is being separated. He does this in order accurately to estimate the amount of heave-offering he must designate. As M. Ter. 1:7A states, how-

ever, he may not actually separate the heave-offering by a set
quantity.]

[H]   [In accord with G] said R. Eleazar, "This is the meaning of Mishnah [Ter. 4 : 6]: **A man may measure [the volume of] his untithed produce and bring [the produce] into his house, provided that he does not separate heave-offering according to a
[fixed] measure. A man may weigh his untithed produce and
bring it into his house, provided that he does not separate
heave-offering**[58] **according to a [fixed] weight. A man may count
his untithed produce and bring it into his house, provided that
he does not separate heave-offering according to a [fixed]
count**" [T. Ter. 3 : 4A]. [M. Ter. 4 : 6 thus agrees with M. Ter.
1 : 7A, which states simply that a man may not separate heave-
offering according to a fixed measure.]

A–B notes an apparent contradiction between M. Ter. 4 : 6 and
M. Ter. 1 : 7. C suggests one resolution, which is rejected at D–F.
G's explanation is supported, at H, on the basis of a Toseftan
pericope. A person may determine for how much produce heave-
offering is to be separated. The actual separation of heave-offering,
however, must be by estimation. This is just as M. Ter. 1 : 7 states.

1:8 [P: 1 : 5a]

[A]   *They may not separate oil as heave-offering on behalf of olives
that have been crushed [but the processing of which has not yet
been completed],*

[B]   *nor wine [as heave-offering] on behalf of grapes that have been
trampled [but the processing of which has not yet been completed, for, as M. Ter. 1 : 10 states, heave-offering may not be
separated from produce the processing of which is completed on
behalf of produce the processing of which is not completed].*

[C]   *But if he separated heave-offering [in either of these ways]—*

[D]   *that which he has separated is [valid] heave-offering.*

[E]   *But he must separate heave-offering again [from the wine or oil
which the grapes or olives eventually produce. This assures that
the priest receive as his share sufficient heave-offering.]*

[F]   *The first [produce separated as heave-offering] imposes the status of heave-offering [upon other produce with which it is mixed] by itself [i.e., even if it alone is mixed into other produce. Cf. M. Ter. 3:1.]*

[G]   *[And nonpriests who unintentionally eat it] are liable to [pay] the added fifth on its account.*

[H]   *But this is not the case for the second [produce separated as heave-offering; i.e., it is not subject to the added fifth and does not impose the status of heave-offering upon unconsecrated produce with which it is mixed].*

In the first separation, A–B, the individual takes sufficient heave-offering only for the wine or oil that the initial pressing of the grapes or olives produced. He therefore must separate heave-offering a second time, when the processing is completed, E. This assures that the priest receives his due share of all of the oil or wine which the householder has. F–H makes clear that in the second separation, the householder designates heave-offering from produce from which that offering already was validly separated. This second heave-offering thus cannot have the status of a true priestly gift. It is, simply, a gift of produce to the priest.

The Yerushalmi's four units have two distinct concerns. The first, at units **I–II,** is the reason that in this particular case heave-offering must be separated a second time. The Yerushalmi notes that in other comparable situations, this is not the case. Units **III–IV** turn to specific issues concerning the two separations of heave-offering. First we ask whether or not the man always must separate heave-offering twice. Then, ignoring what is explicit at M. Ter. 1:8D + F–G, the Yerushalmi asks whether or not the first separation indeed produces true heave-offering.

[I.A]   There [at M. Ter. 1:10] we have learned: *They may not separate heave-offering from produce the processing of which is completed [i.e., oil, wine] on behalf of produce the processing of which is not completed [i.e., olives, grapes]. [But if they separated heave-offering in this fashion, that which they have separated is valid heave-offering.]*

[B]   But [unlike that rule] here [at M. Ter. 1:8] you teach this, [that while the separation is valid, the individual must separate heave-offering a second time]!

[C]   [Said] R. Hila[59] in the name of R. Yohanan, "[They require the individual to go back and separate heave-offering a second time from the oil or wine] because of the requirement of purification water. [By forcing him to be sprinkled a second time in order to separate heave-offering from these liquids in cleanness, they assure] that the [laws of the] water of purification will not be nullified [through disuse]." [This consideration applies in the case of liquids, such as wine and oil (M. Ter. 1:8), which are susceptible to uncleanness. We assume that M. Ter. 1:10 refers to dry produce, which is not susceptible to uncleanness, such that the householder need not be in a state of cleanness when he separates heave-offering from it. Since he would not need to use the purification water, at M. Ter. 1:10 what the householder separates is deemed valid, and he is not required to separate heave-offering a second time.]

Hila, C, resolves the contradiction between M. Ter. 1:8 and M. Ter. 1:10, raised at A–B. The man is required to separate heave-offering a second time in order to force him again to attain a state of cultic cleanness. The concern of M. Ter. 1:8 thus is not the priests' receiving their due share. Rather, it is that common Israelites grow accustomed to being in a state of cultic cleanness.

[II.A]   [The concern is a separation of heave-offering that causes both loss to the priests (Y. Ter. 1:4 I) and the possibility of the purification water's falling into disuse (Y. Ter. 1:8 I). In determining the validity of such a separation of heave-offering], which takes precedence, [preventing] theft from the tribe [of priests, such that the separation is not deemed valid at all, as at Y. Ter. 1:4 I], or [preventing] the water of purification from falling into disuse, [such that the separation is deemed valid, but the individual is required to separate heave-offering a second time, as above, at Y. Ter. 1:8 I]?

[B]   Let us learn [which takes precedence] from this [case: **One who separates] olives [as heave-offering] on behalf of olives that are**

going to be crushed, or grapes [as heave-offering] for grapes
that are going to be trampled—[that which he has separated is
valid] heave-offering, but he must separate heave-offering
again, [when the processing of the grapes or olives is completed; T. Ter. 3:14M–P].

[C]   Lo, [in this case the consideration of] theft from the tribe applies, [insomuch as the original separation gives the priest produce that he will have to process]. And [so does the consideration
of] the prevention of the purification water's falling into disuse
[apply, since the original separation of heave-offering from olives
or grapes did not require the householder to attain a state of
cleanness, whereas a second separation, from oil or wine, would].

[D]   Yet [even though both of these considerations apply], it is taught
concerning this [case: **That which he has separated is valid]
heave-offering, but he must separate heave-offering again,
[from the wine or oil].**

[E]   This teaches that the consideration of the purification water's
falling into disuse takes precedence over the consideration of
theft from the tribe. [If the latter took precedence, the separation would not have been deemed valid at all, as at Y. Ter. 1:4 **I.**]

[F]   Which [consideration] would R. Yose say [takes precedence]
here?

[G]   Now if R. Meir, who rules leniently in cases of theft from the
tribe [and holds that the separation of heave-offering is valid],
rules stringently in cases of the prevention of purification water's
falling into disuse [and holds that the person must separate heave-
offering a second time, as below at I],

[H]   R. Yose, who rules stringently in the case of theft from the tribe
[and holds that such separations of heave-offering are not valid,
Y. Ter. 1:4 **III**]—is it not obvious that he [also] will rule stringently in cases of the prevention of purification water's falling
into disuse [and rule in such cases that heave-offering must be
separated a second time]?

[I]   There is a teaching in the name of R. Yose [which answers H's
question]: "They may not separate olives as heave-offering for
oil, nor grapes as heave-offering for wine. And if they separated
heave-offering [in these ways], that which he has separated is
[valid] heave-offering, but he must (follow GRA and delete: not)

separate heave-offering a second time"—the words of R. Meir. [As G claims, Meir rules strictly, in order to force the person to separate heave-offering a second time, in a state of cleanness.]

[J]   **R. Yose says, "The House of Shammai say, 'They may separate heave-offering [in these ways].' But the House of Hillel say, 'They may not separate heave-offering [in these ways].' And they agree that if he separated heave-offering [in either of these ways], that he need not separate heave-offering a second time"** [T. Ter. 3 : 14J–L. Yose's position, represented by both Houses, is that the man need not separate heave-offering a second time. Contrary to H, Yose is not concerned that individuals separate heave-offering in a state of cleanness so as to prevent the purification water from falling into disuse.]

[K]   [To summarize:] This [i.e., I–J] indicates the [two authorities'] opinions:

[L]   R. Meir rules leniently in the case of theft from the tribe, but he rules stringently in the case of the prevention of the purification water's falling into disuse.

[M]   R. Yose rules stringently in the case of theft from the tribe, but rules leniently in the case of the purification water's falling into disuse.

[N]   [N–Q proves that, contrary to J + M, just as in the case of theft from the tribe, so in the case of the purification water's falling into disuse, Yose rules stringently.] [41a] [60] There we have learned [M. Ed. 5 : 2]: *R. Yose says, "[There are] six cases in which the House of Shammai rule leniently and the House of Hillel rule stringently. (1) Fowl may be served upon a dining table together with cheese, but may not be eaten [with cheese], in accordance with the words of the House of Shammai. But the House of Hillel say, 'It neither may be served [with cheese] nor eaten [with it].' (2) They may separate olives as heave-offering on behalf of oil, or grapes [as heave-offering] on behalf of wine, in accordance with the words of the House of Shammai. But the House of Hillel say, 'They may not separate heave-offering [in either of these manners].'"*

[O]   Said R. Mana, "[The above dispute is reported incorrectly. The Houses did] not [disagree concerning] olives [separated as heave-offering] on behalf of oil.

[P]   "Rather, [they disputed concerning] oil [separated as heave-offering] on behalf of olives.

[Q]   "For this [is the case to] which R. Yose [referred]. For R. Yose says, '[The Houses agree that if one separated oil as heave-offering for olives], that which he has separated is [valid] heave-offering, but he must separate heave-offering again [from the oil which the olives will produce].'" [Mana's point is that Yose indeed wishes to prevent the purification water from falling into disuse. Yose therefore requires the man to separate heave-offering a second time from oil. This forces the man once again to use purification water to attain a state of cleanness. The conclusion at M, that Yose is not concerned about the purification water, is unacceptable. It is based on an incorrect citation of the Houses' position. The original reasoning, G–H, that Yose is concerned about the purification water, is correct.]

The rule of Y. Ter. 1:8 **I** is correlated with that of Y. Ter. 1:4 **I**, at A–E. According to Y. Ter. 1:4, a separation of heave-offering which does not provide sufficient produce for the priest is not valid at all. On the other hand Y. Ter. 1:8 states that in cases that require the householder's use of purification water, the separation is deemed valid, but the individual is required to separate heave-offering a second time. The question here is what happens in a case in which both factors are present. According to E the concern for the water of purification takes precedence. The initial separation is deemed valid, but the person is required to separate heave-offering a second time. Notably, the discussion as a whole is purely theoretical. The result would be the same whether the man separated heave-offering a second time or started from the beginning with a fresh separation of heave-offering. In either case the priest ultimately receives his proper share of the offering, and the individual carries out a correct separation of the priestly gift in a state of cultic cleanness. The Yerushalmi's concern here is the logic of the law, not the practical consequences of its ruling.

F–Q is secondary, on whether or not Yose can agree to the conclusion just drawn. Contrary to J + M, N–Q proves that he can agree with this conclusion. While the point of the unit is clear, the specifics of F–M are not. In no case known to us does Meir rule that a separation of heave-offering which does not pro-

vide the priest with sufficient produce is valid, G + I. There is
no basis in Tannaitic literature for the comparison between the
views of Yose and Meir.

[**III.A**][61]   [The following refers to M. Ter. 1:8C–E: *If a person separates
oil as heave-offering for olives, or wine as heave-offering for
grapes, that which he has separated is valid heave-offering, but
he must separate heave-offering again, from the oil or wine which
the olives or grapes later will produce.*] [This is the case] if, [at
the point at which he presses the olives into oil or the grapes into
wine, the heave-offering that he] originally [separated] no longer
exists.

[B]   But if the original heave-offering still exists, the individual may
orally designate it [to be the heave-offering required of the wine
or oil which was produced], and this is sufficient.

If the heave-offering originally separated for olives or grapes had
not yet been eaten by the priest, it may serve as heave-offering
for the oil or wine. It simply is orally designated to be such, B.
If that heave-offering already had been eaten, a second separation
must be performed on behalf of the wine or oil that the householder just had produced, A. The theory of the unit thus is that
oil and wine are distinct from the olives or grapes from which
they were produced. Even if heave-offering had been separated
from those olives and grapes, it must be separated, or at least
designated, again specifically for the oil or the wine which is
produced. In this, the unit disagrees with what has preceded. If
the second separation of heave-offering is intended to accustom
the individual to use the purification water, Y. Ter. 1:8 I–II, it
should be of no concern whether or not, at the time of that separation, the original heave-offering has been eaten.

[**IV.A**]   It is taught [T. Ter. 3:14I]: **The second produce [separated as
heave-offering in a case such as that of M. Ter. 1:8, in which
heave-offering must be separated twice] may not be eaten [by
a priest] until he separates from it heave-offering and tithes.**

[B]   [Concerning] the first produce separated as heave-offering—what
is its rule [i.e., need heave-offering and tithes be separated from it]?

[C]   [We may deduce the rule] on the basis of what we have learned
      [T. Ter. 3:14V–Y]: **[If the householder] went and pressed the**
      original olives [that he had separated as heave-offering] into
      oil, or the original grapes [that he had separated as heave-
      offering] into wine, he orally designates [the produce to be
      heave-offering] and need not separate heave-offering a sec-
      ond time.

[D]   This teaches that he need not[62] designate tithes for this [first
      produce separated as heave-offering].

      The theory is that of the preceding unit. The first heave-offering
      the man separated is true heave-offering, as proven by C. It
      therefore is not subject to the separation of tithes, D, even though
      it needs to be designated a second time.

      1:9 [P: 1:5b]

[A]   *But they may separate oil as heave-offering for olives that have*
      been preserved,

[B]   *and wine [as heave-offering] for grapes that are being made into*
      raisins, [for in these cases the processing both of the heave-
      offering and the produce for which it is separated is complete].

[C]   *Lo, if he separated oil as heave-offering for olives intended for*
      eating [i.e., the preparation of which is complete],

[D]   *or olives [as heave-offering] for olives intended for eating,*

[E]   *or wine [as heave-offering] for grapes intended for eating,*

[F]   *or grapes [as heave-offering] for grapes intended for eating,*

[G]   *but [afterwards] decided [instead] to press them [i.e., any of the*
      produce that he originally intended for consumption as foods],

[H]   *he need not separate heave-offering [a second time from the oil*
      or wine which is produced. Since his original separation was
      valid de jure, the man's later actions in processing the produce
      are not of consequence.]

Since the processing of all the produce is complete, A–B, the separation of heave-offering is valid, and the offering need not be separated a second time. This is the case even if the householder decides to further process the produce on behalf of which the original offering was taken. His initial intention is determinative. The Yerushalmi concentrates on what is striking about M.'s rule. Namely, heave-offering may be separated from one form of a genus of produce (e.g., oil) on behalf of a different form of that same genus (e.g., pickled olives). Units **I–II** suggest two different explanations of this rule. The final question is more general and practical, how should the individual who separates heave-offering as at A–B determine the correct quantity of the offering to separate?

[I.A]   We have learned in the following [pericope, M. Ter. 1:10]: *They may not separate heave-offering from produce the processing of which is completed on behalf of produce the processing of which is not completed. [But if they separated heave-offering in that manner, that which they have separated is valid heave-offering.]*

[B]   [On the basis of A's rule we should assume that heave-offering may be separated from oil, the processing of which *is* completed, for pickled olives, the processing of which *is* completed. Why then need the rule that heave-offering may be separated from oil or wine for pickled olives or raisins be stated explicitly, M. Ter. 1:9A–B? The reason is that we might think that just as at M. Ter. 1:10, where the separation is deemed valid *post facto*, so in the case of M. Ter. 1:9 a separation of heave-offering from one form of a genus of produce on behalf of a different form of that same genus only is valid] *post facto*, but is not [valid] *de jure*.

[C]   [Thus the rule of M. Ter. 1:9A–B must be stated explicitly to indicate that] even *de jure* [heave-offering may be separated from oil or wine on behalf of pickled olives or raisins].

The unit makes sense on the basis of the long interpolation at B, suggested by PM.

[II.A][63]   If you claim that this [produce, pickled olives or raisins, M. Ter. 1:9A–B] is different from produce the processing of which is completed [i.e., is like produce that is not fully processed, such that heave-offering should not be separated on its behalf from produce the processing of which is completed],

[B]   then [the reason that such a separation of heave-offering is valid, as M. Ter. 1:9A–B states, is] as we have learned [at M. Ma. 1:6]: *Dried pomegranates, raisins, and carobs [are subject to the separation of heave-offering and tithes] from the time that they have been formed into a pile, [even though they are not yet completely dried and ready for consumption].* [The point is that certain types of produce are subject to heave-offering before their processing is completed. This explains why heave-offering validly may be separated for pickled olives or raisins which, A suggests, are not considered fully processed.]

[C]   [In support of B's reasoning said] R. Yose b. Yose in the name of R. Isaac b. Eleazar, "The prohibition against [separating heave-offering from] produce the processing of which is completed on behalf of produce the processing of which is not completed [= M. Ter. 1:10] applies only to [produce processed on] the threshing floor and [in] the wine vat." [It does not apply to the items listed at M. Ma. 1:6 or to pickled olives or raisins, M. Ter. 1: 9A–B. Even if the processing of these things is not completed, heave-offering separated on their behalf from fully processed produce is valid.]

The Yerushalmi shifts its grounds of understanding and thereby presents a different interpretation of M. Ter. 1:9A–B. Even if we deem the processing of the pickled olives or of the grapes being made into raisins not to be complete, heave-offering may be separated on their behalf. The reason is given at B, and supported by C, where Yose b. Yose limits the applicability of the rules of M. Ter. 1:10 to wine, oil, and grain.

[**III**.A]   [If a person separates oil as heave-offering for olives], according to what [measure] does he separate the heave-offering? [Is it] in accordance with [the quantity of] oil [the olives are fit to produce] or in accordance with [the quantity of] food they [contain]?

[B]   Said R. Yohanan, "There is a dispute [concerning this question].

[C]   "Rabbi says, '[They separate as heave-offering a quantity of oil proper] for the amount of oil [64] [the olives are fit to produce].'

[D]   "Rabban Simeon b. Gamaliel says, [65] '[They separate as heave-offering a quantity of oil proper] for the edible produce which is in [the olives], but not for the pits.'

[E]   "And they agree that in the case of hard olives [which produce no oil when pressed] that they separate heave-offering for the edible produce which is in them, but not for the pits" [T. Ter. 3:15].

[F]   Hanania asked, "Is the same [issue under dispute] as regards [how we determine whether or not someone who carries olives on] the Sabbath [carries so much produce as to be culpable for carrying on the holy day]?"

[G]   [Yes it is. For] so do we find it taught: Rabbi says, "[A person who carries olives on the Sabbath is culpable if he carries so much as would produce] a quarter-*log* [of oil, the quantity of liquid which one is culpable for carrying on the holy day, M. Shab. 8:1]."

[H]   Rabban Simeon b. Gamaliel says, "[They determine culpability] as if it were figs [e.g., in accordance with the quantity of food which the person carries, M. Shab. 7:4]."

[I]   Said R. Hanania in the name of R. Hillel, "We also have learned this [following rule, T. Ter. 3:14M–P] which supports that view of Rabbi (follow PM and delete: Hoshaya): **[One who separates] olives [as heave-offering] on behalf of olives that are going to be crushed [for oil], or grapes [as heave-offering] on behalf of grapes that are going to be trampled [for wine—that which he has separated is valid] heave-offering. But he must separate heave-offering again [from the oil or wine which is produced]."** [Heave-offering must be separated a second time because, in the first separation, the individual took a quantity of the offering appropriate for the edible produce of the olives and not the liquid they are capable of producing. This is like the position of Rabbi, C, who wants the offering to be separated in accordance with the quantity of oil the olives will produce.]

[J]   So we have learned [at M. Ter. 1:9C–H, another rule which accords with the position of Rabbi]: *One who separated oil as heave-offering for olives intended for eating [i.e., the processing*

of which is complete], or olives [as heave-offering] for olives in-
tended for eating, or wine [as heave-offering] for grapes intended
for eating, or grapes [as heave-offering] for grapes intended for
eating, but [afterwards] decided [instead] to press them [i.e.,
any of the produce which he originally intended for consump-
tion as food], he need not separate heave-offering a second time,
[from the oil or wine which is produced].

[K]   [The man need not separate heave-offering a second time] because [even though] he [later] changed his mind, [at the time
of the first separation he did not intend to further process the
grapes or olives for which he separated heave-offering].

[L]   [This means that] if he did not change his mind [but, rather,
intended all along to continue the processing of the produce, he
would need to] separate heave-offering a second time, [in accordance with the quantity of liquids the grapes or olives produce.
This is like the position of Rabbi, C, who wants heave-offering
separated in accordance with the quantity of oil or wine the olives
or grapes can produce.]

A's question introduces the disputes, B–E and F–H. Rabbi, C
and G, always treats olives and grapes as liquids, for this is the
form in which they normally are consumed (see M. Ter. 11:3
and T. Ter. 9:9). Simeon b. Gamaliel, D and H, takes into account the actual use to which the specific produce will be put. It
will be eaten and therefore is treated as a food. I and J–L claim
to support the position of Rabbi, as my interpolations indicate.
Yet the materials cited from the Mishnah and the Tosefta actually
concur with Simeon b. Gamaliel, not with Rabbi. They state that
the use to which the produce will be put determines whether it
is treated as a liquid or a food. The Amoraic authority who composed this pericope apparently wished to show the superiority of
the view of Rabbi over that of Simeon b. Gamaliel even though
the Tannaitic materials he employed did not fit his purposes.

1:10 [P: 1:5c]

[A]   *They may not separate heave-offering*

[B]   *from (1) produce the preparation [for consumption] of which is completed on behalf of produce the preparation of which is not completed;*

[C]   *nor from (2) produce the preparation of which is not completed on behalf of produce the preparation of which is completed;*

[D]   *nor from (3) produce the preparation of which is not completed for produce the preparation of which is not completed.*

[E]   *But if he separated heave-offering [in any of these ways]—*

[F]   *that which he has separated is [valid] heave-offering.*

Unprocessed produce is not deemed food and so is exempt from the separation of heave-offering. Heave-offering may not be separated from it or on its behalf (A–D). Yet the produce ultimately will become subject to the separation of heave-offering. If the separation is carried out anyway, it therefore is valid. What will be required in the future is treated as though it is already necessary (E–F). The Yerushalmi sets out to discover why only fully processed produce should be given as heave-offering. Its first unit provides a reason derived from Scripture. The second unit builds upon the first but is only tangentially related to the issue of M. Ter. 1 : 10.

[I.A]   R. Imi in the name of R. Simeon b. Laqish [said], "[The basis for the rule of M. Ter. 1 : 10A–D is Num. 18 : 27], 'Your [i.e., the Levites'] offering [i.e., heave-offering of the tithe, given to the priests from first tithe] shall be reckoned to you as the grain of the threshing floor [i.e., it is to be given of produce the processing of which is completed].'

[B]   "In light of the fact that he [i.e., God] commands the Levites to separate heave-offering [of the tithe] from produce the processing of which is completed, you may reason that it is forbidden [for Israelites] to give [the Levite first tithe in the form of unthreshed] stalks. [They must, rather, give the Levite fully processed produce from which the Levite in turn will separate heave-offering of the tithe. By extension, the heave-offering that Israelites give the priest must also be of produce the processing of which is completed, as M. Ter. 1 : 10A–D states.]"

A–B finds a reason in Scripture that a householder must give the
Levite as first tithe fully processed produce. The implication is
that the rule for heave-offering should be the same.

[II.A]   Hiyya bar Ada in the name of R. Simeon b. Laqish [says], "[As
for] first tithe which [a householder] went ahead and separated
from stalks of grain, [from which heave-offering had not yet
been separated—the Levite] is forbidden to eat of [this tithe] as
a chance meal [i.e., without first separating heave-offering of the
tithe for the priest]." [This is the case even though, in its unprocessed form, the stalks usually should not be subject to the
separation of heave-offering, which normally is separated before
first tithe.]

[B]   What is the scriptural basis?

[C]   [The rule is based upon Num. 18:32, which states], 'You [Le-
vites] shall not profane the holy things [i.e., heave-offering] of
the people of Israel, lest you die.' [The Levites are not to eat
produce that contains the heave-offering that Israelites should
have separated. They must separate this offering in the form of
their own heave-offering of the tithe.]

[D]   What is the rule of the Torah concerning [whether or not a Levite
who transgresses the rule of A by eating first tithe from which]
heave-offering has not been separated is subject to [the forty]
stripes [inflicted upon a person who wrongly eats a holy thing,
such as heave-offering]?

[E]   R. Ashian in the name of R. Jonah [says], "The Mishnah states
that according to the Torah they do not receive stripes for [eating
first tithe] from which heave-offering was not separated.

[F]   "This is in accordance with what we learn there [M. Bik. 2:5]:
*Heave-offering of the tithe is like first fruits in two ways and like
heave-offering in two ways. It may be separated from clean produce on behalf of unclean produce and may be separated from
produce which is not in its same batch, like first fruits. But [until it
is separated] it renders forbidden [for consumption the other
produce] on the threshing floor and has a set measure, like heave-
offering.*

[G]   "You must reason: Does '[heave-offering] renders forbidden [for
consumption the other produce] on the threshing floor' not mean

[that it renders forbidden] only after [the pile of grain on the threshing floor has been] smoothed over, [signifying the completion of its processing]?

[H]   "[Yes, it does.] Thus you must say that according to the Torah, [Levites] do not receive [forty] stripes [for eating first tithe] from which heave-offering was not separated, [if the first tithe came from unprocessed produce]." [This is because, as M. Bik. 2 : 5 shows, the stringencies of heave-offering of the tithe, like those of heave-offering, do not apply until after the produce is fully processed.]

In place of the Israelite, the Levite, A, must separate heave-offering from his first tithe. D addresses the next logical question—what happens if the Levite does not separate the offering? In answer, E–H notes that the produce from which the Levite's first tithe was taken was not actually subject to the separation of heave-offering. While the Levite should not eat such produce without separating the priest's share, if he does, he is not held culpable (H).

2:1

[A] *They may not separate heave-offering from [produce] which is clean for that which is unclean.*

[B] *But if they separated heave-offering [in that manner], that which they have separated is [valid] heave-offering.*

[C] *Truly,*

[D] *[as regards] a circle of pressed figs, a portion of which became unclean—*

[E] *he may separate heave-offering from the clean [produce] which is in it on behalf of the unclean [produce] which is in it;*

[F] *and so [in the case of] a bunch of greens;*

[G] *and so [in the case of] a heap [of produce].*

[H] *[If] there were two circles [of pressed figs], two bunches [of greens], two heaps [of produce], one of which was unclean and one of which was clean—*

[I] *he may not separate heave-offering from [the clean produce in] one on behalf of [the unclean produce in] the other.*

[J] *R. Eliezer says, "They may separate heave-offering from that which is clean for that which is unclean."*

The Yerushalmi's long discussion of this pericope centers upon two questions: (1) why heave-offering may not be separated from clean produce on behalf of unclean produce (unit **I**, which intro-

duces its own secondary materials at units **II–III**); and (2) why
the items at M. Ter. 2:1F–H have the special rule that, in their
case, heave-offering may be separated from clean produce on behalf of unclean (units **V–XIII**). This latter discussion is introduced by unit **IV**, on the meaning of the term "truly," here at C.
The Yerushalmi's concluding unit contains a dispute concerning
which view is authoritative, that of Eliezer, J, or the anonymous
rule of A–B.

[**I.A**]   [41b] *They may not separate heave-offering from [produce] which*
is clean on behalf of that which is unclean [M. Ter. 2:1A].

[B]¹   R. Yohanan in the name of R. Yannai [derived this rule from
Num. 18:27]: "'And your offering shall be reckoned to you
as the grain of the threshing floor and the fullness of the wine
press.'

[C]   "[We derive M. Ter. 2:1A from that verse by the following reasoning:] In the case of [grain piled on] the threshing floor or
[wine in] the vat, is it possible for a portion of the produce to be
unclean and a portion clean? [No, it is not possible, for if part
becomes unclean, all will be rendered unclean.]

[D]   "Now even though [in other cases] it is possible [that some produce in a single batch might be clean and some unclean, such
that the householder would want to separate heave-offering from
the one for the other], we learn [whether or not he may do so in
such cases], in which it is possible, from [the paradigmatic cases
of the threshing floor and wine press], in which it is impossible." [I.e., in the paradigmatic cases of the wine vat and threshing floor there can be no separation of clean produce as heave-
offering for what is unclean, as C proves. That sort of separation
therefore is ruled out in all cases.]

[E]   On this basis [we must reason that even *post facto* if a person
separates heave-offering from clean produce on behalf of un-
clean], that which he has separated is not [valid] heave-offering.
[Yet this cannot be the case, for it is contrary to M. Ter. 2:1B,
which states that *post facto* a separation of clean produce as heave-
offering for unclean produce is valid.]

[F]   [The reason that contrary to what logic would tell us, the separation is valid *post facto* is that, at Num. 18:26], '[You shall present

an offering] from it [to the Lord]' is written. [Thus, so long as the offering is taken from its same batch of produce, it is valid. This is the case even if the offering is clean and the produce on behalf of which it is taken is unclean.]

The discussion in Num. 18:26–27 of heave-offering of the tithe (Scripture's "tithe of the tithe") serves as the basis for the rules of M. Ter. 2:1A–B.

[**II.A**]   All [scriptural] passages teach [the law for the specific topic about which they speak] and [further] instruct [concerning other comparable matters].

[B]   [Yet while Scripture's discussion of] heave-offering of the tithe instructs [concerning the great heave-offering, which Israelite householders separate], it does not teach [the law for heave-offering of the tithe itself].

[C]   [This is proven by the fact that Scripture's rule for] heave-offering of the tithe instructed concerning the great heave-offering, that it may not be taken from clean produce on behalf of unclean produce [as we saw at Y. 2:1 **I**].

[D]   Yet [heave-offering of the tithe itself] may be taken from clean produce on behalf of unclean produce.

[E]   What is the scriptural basis [for this rule, that heave-offering of the tithe may be separated from clean produce on behalf of unclean produce]?

[F]   R. Yose in the name of Hezeqiah [and] R. Jonah in the name of R. Yannai [say], "[Num. 18:28 states], 'And from it [i.e., first tithe] you [Levites] shall give the Lord's offering [i.e., heave-offering of the tithe] to Aaron the priest.'

[G]   "[This means that Levites] must give to Aaron the priest what is befitting his priestly status [i.e., clean produce, which priests may eat]."

[H]   [Suggesting a different proof that heave-offering of the tithe may be separated from clean produce on behalf of unclean produce] Kahana said, "[Num. 18:29 states that heave-offering of the tithe must be separated], 'From all the best of them [i.e., of the

tithes the Levites receive, such that the Levites may] give the
hallowed parts from them.'

[I]   "[This means that the Levite must] take [heave-offering of the
tithe] from the hallowed [i.e., clean] portion of [his tithe]."

[J][2]   [We turn to another example of B.] [Scripture's discussion of]
heave-offering of the tithe instructed concerning the great heave-
offering that it must be taken on behalf of produce which is in
its same batch [above, Y. Ter. 2:1 I.F].

[K]   Yet [heave-offering of the tithe itself] may be taken [from one
batch of first tithe on behalf of tithe] which is in a different batch.

[L]   What is the scriptural basis [for the rule that heave-offering of
the tithe may be separated from tithe in one batch on behalf of
tithe in a different batch]?

[M]   [Num. 18:29 states that Levites are to separate heave-offering of
the tithe] 'From *all* of your [i.e., Levites'] tithes.'

[N]   [This means that Levites may separate heave-offering of the tithe
from one batch for another even if] one [batch] is in Judah and
the other is in Galilee.[3]

[O]   [In this third case, the rules for the great heave-offering and for
heave-offering of the tithe are the same.] [Scripture's discussion
of] heave-offering of the tithe instructed concerning the great
heave-offering that it may only be separated from [produce] the
processing of which is completed [i.e., grain on the threshing
floor and wine in the press, Num. 18:27].

[P]   And [heave-offering of the tithe] also is separated [only] from
[produce] the processing of which is completed.

A answers the question left open by unit I, why Scripture's discussion of heave-offering of the tithe may be used to derive rules
for heave-offering. A's claim is illustrated at O–P, where the
rules for heave-offering of the tithe teach both about that offering separated by Levites and about the great heave-offering which
Israelites separate. B, exemplified at C–I and J–N, interrupts,
pointing out anomalous cases in which Scripture's discussion of
heave-offering of the tithe indicates the rule for the great heave-
offering but not for heave-offering of the tithe itself.

[**III.A**]   **Heave-offering of the tithe may be taken from clean [first tithe] on behalf of [other] clean [first tithe],**

[B]   **from unclean [first tithe] on behalf of [other] unclean [first tithe],**

[C]   **and⁴ from clean [first tithe] on behalf of unclean [first tithe].**

[D]   **But it may not be taken from unclean [first tithe] on behalf of clean [first tithe, for in this case the Levite cheats the priest out of produce which the priest may eat; T. Ter. 3:19C–D].**

[E]   R. Nehemiah says, "Just as [heave-offering of the tithe] may not be taken from unclean [first tithe] on behalf of clean [first tithe], so it may not be taken from unclean [first tithe] on behalf of [other] unclean [first tithe, for in this case also, the priest is given produce he may not eat]."

[F]   But R. Nehemiah concedes in the case of first tithe taken from produce about which there is a doubt whether or not it already had been tithed, [that heave-offering of the tithe for such first tithe may be taken from unclean produce. Since the priest might already have received his share, we permit the Levite to give him produce he may not eat; see T. Ter. 3:19E.]

[G]   Up to here [we have heard Nehemiah's opinion only for a case in which a Levite who has unclean first tithe also] has [clean first tithe] of the same kind. [In such a case Nehemiah, E, rules that the Levite should separate heave-offering of the tithe from the clean first tithe on behalf of the unclean, and not from unclean on behalf of unclean.]

[H]   [How would Nehemiah rule if the Levite] did not have [clean first tithe] of the same kind [so that he could use it as heave-offering of the tithe for the unclean first tithe? Since it is forbidden to separate heave-offering from one kind of produce on behalf of a different kind, in this case Nehemiah must hold either that the Levite should separate heave-offering of the tithe from the unclean first tithe, or that he should wait until he acquires clean first tithe of the same kind. The issue is which of these two views he holds.]

[I]   Let us learn the rule from the following:

[J]   R. Hanina of Ein Tuna went with R. Zeira to the hot springs at Geder.⁵ [Hanina] bought him [i.e., Zeira] eating olives [which had prepared in a state of cleanness, but from which heave-offering and tithes had not yet been separated]. [Zeira] wished [to put aside some of the clean olives for use] in tithing [unclean produce that he might purchase] in the coming days. [In this way he could avoid separating unclean produce as heave-offering, even for unclean produce. This is in line with the opinion of Nehemiah, E.]

[K]   [Hanina] said to him, "We need not be concerned for the [opinion of] a single authority [i.e., Nehemiah, for he alone holds that heave-offering may not be taken from unclean produce on behalf of other unclean produce. His view therefore is not authoritative.]"

[L]   Thus you must say [that Nehemiah's view holds] only if [the Levite] had [clean first tithe] of the same kind [as the unclean. In that case he should separate heave-offering of the tithe from the clean first tithe. If he has no clean first tithe, he may separate heave-offering of the tithe from the unclean.]

The Tosefta's materials on the separation of heave-offering of the tithe, cited at A–D and (in the Yerushalmi's own version) E–F, complement M. Ter. 2:1's discussion of the separation of heave-offering from clean and unclean produce. The Yerushalmi, for its part, takes up a problem internal to the position of Nehemiah, E–F. The Yerushalmi's question, phrased at G–H, is answered, L, on the basis of the legal precedent, J–K. Yet J–K deals with heave-offering, not heave-offering of the tithe. Furthermore, it suggests that Nehemiah's minority position in no event need be followed (K). The precedent thus is hardly so pertinent an answer to the Yerushalmi's particular question as its use here suggests.

[**IV.A**]   *Truly* [M. Ter. 2:1C].

[B]   Said R. Eliezer, "Anywhere [in Mishnah] that we teach [i.e., introduce a law with the term] 'Truly' it is a rule [given] to Moses [by God, in the revelation] at Sinai."

The contrast drawn at B is to rules that the Mishnaic authorities themselves derived through interpretation of the law revealed at Sinai and explicitly contained in the written Torah.

[V.A]   *[As regards] a circle of pressed figs a portion of which became unclean—[he may separate heave-offering from the clean produce which is in it on behalf of the unclean produce which is in it (M. Ter. 2:1D–E)].*

[B]   [How is it possible for a portion of a circle of pressed figs to be clean and a portion unclean], for as soon as one part of it is made unclean does not all of it become unclean [through contact with the unclean portion]?

[C]   [It is possible since] the Mishnah's [rule] refers to a case in which [the figs] are stuck together with fruit juice, [which does not serve as a connector for the conveyance of uncleanness].

M. 2:1D–E is introduced with the most obvious question, B, and answer, C.

[VI.A]   [The question is why it is permitted to separate heave-offering from the clean figs in a circle of pressed figs on behalf of the unclean ones, M. Ter. 2:1D–E. Even though the figs presently are all in a single batch], will they not ultimately be divided into two segments, [one clean and one unclean? Since the batch ultimately will be divided, we should expect it to be treated from the start as if it were in two distinct parts, in which case heave-offering may not be separated from the clean figs on behalf of the unclean ones.]

[B]   Solve the problem [of why, contrary to A's reasoning, M. Ter. 2:1D–E deems the separation valid, by stating that the case is one in which the householder] designated [clean figs in the circle to be heave-offering for unclean ones] while [all of the figs in the circle] still were joined together. [At the time of the designation all of the figs comprised a single batch. The designation therefore was valid. The fact that the batch later will be divided is irrelevant.]

[C]   *And so in the case of a bunch of greens* [heave-offering may be separated from clean produce for unclean produce within the bunch; M. Ter. 2:1F].

[D]   [As in the case of the circle of pressed figs] the Mishnah refers to a case in which [some of the greens in the bunch] were made unclean while [all the greens] were tied together [as a single batch].

[E]   But if [some single] stalks became unclean [and the householder then] bound them [together with clean stalks], in this case [it is] not [permitted to separate clean produce in the bunch as heave-offering for unclean produce, since here the clean and unclean are not deemed a single batch].

[F]   [Still, why should it be permitted to separate heave-offering from the clean greens on behalf of the unclean ones in a single bunch? Even though all the greens presently are in a single bunch], will they not ultimately be divided into two bunches, [one clean and one unclean? Since the batch ultimately will be divided, we should expect it to be treated from the start as if it were in two distinct parts, such that heave-offering may not be separated from one part for the other.]

[G]   Solve the problem [of why, contrary to F's reasoning, M. Ter. 2:1 deems the separation valid by stating that the case is one in which the householder] designated [clean greens in the bunch as heave-offering on behalf of unclean ones] while [all of the greens] still were joined together [as a single batch. Since the original designation is valid, the fact that the greens later will be split into distinct batches is irrelevant.]

[H]   [As for] a bunch [of greens a portion of] which became unclean and which one [then] unbound and rebound, what [is the rule whether or not heave-offering may be separated from the clean greens in the bunch on behalf of the unclean ones? If the greens' status as a single batch is determined by the fact that they were bound together at the point at which a portion became unclean, heave-offering may be separated in that way. But if the house-holder's actions in unbinding the bunch are determinative, heave-offering may not be separated from the clean produce for the unclean, for the produce is deemed to comprise two distinct batches. The question is not answered.]

The Yerushalmi defines the conditions under which clean and unclean produce are deemed to be in a single batch, such that the clean may be separated as heave-offering on behalf of the unclean (M. Ter. 2:1E–F). The parallel materials, A–B and F–G, make the point: Clean and unclean produce are deemed a

single batch if they are together at the point at which heave-
offering is separated. The fact that the clean and unclean later
will be eaten separately is of no concern. Contrary to the common theme in the Mishnah, the Yerushalmi holds that we need
not treat what ultimately will be as though it already were. While
distinct from the doublet at A–B + F–G, C–E adds an important point. To be deemed a single batch, clean and unclean produce must have been together at the point at which some of the
produce became unclean. That is, the batch must have been
formed while all of the produce still was clean. Once produce is
unclean, the householder may not himself join it into a single
batch with clean produce. The larger point is that man's actions,
either in joining the clean and unclean produce, or ultimately in
detaching it, do not determine whether or not the produce is a
single batch. This is determined only through circumstance,
i.e., the fact that a portion of a batch of produce should become
unclean and that the batch still is intact at the moment heave-
offering is separated. In light of this the ambiguity of H's case is
apparent. The clean and unclean produce initially constituted a
single batch. The householder then took the batch apart and re-
assembled it. If the original status of the batch is probative, the
clean produce within it may be designated heave-offering on behalf of the unclean. Or perhaps the householder's actions should
be determinative. If this is the case, the clean food could not be
separated as heave-offering on behalf of the unclean. Which alternative applies is not indicated.

[VII.A]   [The question is why M. Ter. 2:1 needs to state explicitly that
            not only in the case of a circle of pressed figs, but also in the
            cases of a bunch of greens and a heap of produce, heave-offering
            may be separated from what is clean for what is unclean. Would
            it not have been sufficient to] teach [this rule] for the circle [of
            pressed figs], but not to teach it for the bunch of greens; [or to]
            teach [the rule] for [the case of] the bunch [of greens], but not
            for a heap [of produce]?

[B]   [The reason that the bunch of greens needed to be mentioned
            along with the circle of pressed figs is that] if we had taught [the
            case of] a circle of pressed figs, but had not taught [the case of]
            a bunch [of greens], we would have reasoned that [in the case of]
            the circle of pressed figs, in which all [of the figs comprise] a

single entity, one may separate heave-offering [from clean produce in the circle on behalf of the unclean; but to the contrary
we would have thought that in the case of] a bunch [of greens] in
which all [of the produce] is not a single entity, one may not
separate heave-offering [from clean greens on behalf of unclean
ones. In order to correct this wrong impression, M. Ter. 2:1]
needed to teach [the case of] a bunch [of greens].

[C]   [The reason that M. Ter. 2:1 needed to mention a heap of produce as well as a bunch of greens is that] if it had taught concerning the bunch [of greens] but had not taught concerning the
heap [of produce], we would have reasoned that [in the case of] a
bunch [of greens], in which all of the produce is in a single,
circumscribed batch one may separate heave-offering [from clean
greens for unclean ones]; but [we would have reasoned], in the
case of a heap [of produce], in which all of the produce is not
in a single circumscribed batch, one may not separate heave-
offering [from clean produce on behalf of unclean produce. To
correct this unacceptable reasoning, the Mishnah needed to
teach explicitly that also in the case of a heap of produce heave-
offering may be separated from clean food on behalf of that which is
unclean.]

[D]   [Thus we have established that M. Ter. 2:1] needed [explicitly]
to teach concerning a circle [of pressed figs] and needed to teach
concerning a bunch [of greens] and needed to teach concerning a
heap [of produce].

The Yerushalmi explains why M. Ter. 2:1 needed to list more
than one example of a case in which clean produce may be separated as heave-offering for unclean produce.

[VIII.A]   Since [M. Ter. 2:1] teaches [explicitly: *If] there were two circles
[of pressed figs], two bunches [of greens], two heaps [of produce, one unclean and one clean—he may not separate heave-
offering from the clean produce in one on behalf of the unclean
produce in the other]*, why do we need the statement of R. Yohanan
in the name of R. Yannai [which proves on the basis of the verse],
'And your offering shall be reckoned to you as the grain [of the
threshing floor and the fullness of the wine press' (Num. 18:27)
that heave-offering may not be separated from clean produce on
behalf of unclean produce; above Y. Yer. 2:1 I.B–D? As we re-

call, Yohanan claims that it is impossible for a portion of a heap of produce on the threshing floor to be unclean and a portion clean. Yet in mentioning a heap of produce, M. Ter. 2:1G + H–I is clear that a heap of produce may be partially clean and partially unclean. How do we account for the contradiction?]

[B]   Said R. Hiyya bar Adda, "Mishnah refers to a heap of cucumbers or chatemelons." [A portion of such a heap may become unclean while a different portion remains clean. Yohanan refers to a heap of grain, part of which cannot be clean and part unclean. Since Yohanan and M. Ter. 2:1 refer to different sorts of produce, their statements are not contradictory.]

We turn to M. Ter. 2:1G, which appears to contradict the statement of Yohanan, Y. Ter. 2:1 I.B–D. That the two passages are not contradictory is shown at B.

[IX.A]   [If] there were two circles [of pressed figs], a portion of one which was unclean, and a portion of the other which was clean—what [is the rule whether or not] one may separate heave-offering from [the figs in] one [circle] on behalf of [the figs in] the other [circle]? [If we hold that, since the two rings are of similar composition, they comprise a single batch, this is permitted, just as at M. Ter. 2:1D–E. If we deem the figs to be contained in distinct batches, this is forbidden, as at M. Ter. 2:1A.]

[B]   [Which alternative applies] may be determined by the following [parallel] case:

[C]   If there were before him two piles of produce, from one of which he [already] had separated a portion of the [required] heave-offering and tithes and from the other of which he [already] had separated a portion of[6] the required heave-offering and tithes—what [is the rule whether or not] he may [subsequently] separate heave-offering from this [partially tithed batch] on behalf of the other [partially tithed batch]? [If we assume that it is a single batch, he may separate heave-offering in this way, as at M. Ter. 4:1A–B. If it is two distinct batches, he may not do so; see M. Ter. 4:1C, where we take into account the possibility that either the produce separated as heave-offering, or that on behalf of which it is designated may already be fully tithed. The question is essentially the same as at A.]

[D]   [Concerning this case] the disciples of R. Hiyya the elder[7] asked
       R. Hiyya the elder. Now he answered them [with Eccles. 4 : 5],
       "The fool folds his hands and eats his own flesh." [That is,
       someone who has been so foolish as to separate only a portion of
       the required heave-offering and tithes has made it impossible
       thereafter to separate from a single batch the agricultural gifts
       required of all his produce.]

[E]   [Claiming that Hiyya answered the question explicitly, said] R.
       Eleazar in the name of R. Hiyya the elder, "They may not sepa-
       rate heave-offering or tithes from one [partially tithed batch] on
       behalf of another." [By extension, in the case of two batches,
       each composed part of clean and part of unclean produce (above,
       A), heave-offering may not be separated from one on behalf of
       the other.]

       The Yerushalmi proposes a subtle expansion of M. Ter. 2 : 1D–E's
       rule that clean produce may be separated as heave-offering for
       unclean produce within its same batch. The Yerushalmi's ques-
       tion (at A, and again at C) is whether or not quantities of pro-
       duce which, while physically distinct, are of similar composi-
       tion may be deemed a single batch. If they are, the clean produce
       found in one quantity may be separated as heave-offering for the
       unclean produce in the other, as A suggests. The question is
       answered on the basis of Hiyya's ruling in a parallel case. So long
       as quantities of produce are physically distinct, they may not be
       deemed a single batch and heave-offering may not be separated
       from one on behalf of the other. This is quite different from the
       notion of the following units, which do not consider physical
       proximity a defining characteristic of a batch of produce.

[X.A] **Lo, if he placed many different kinds [of produce] together [in
       a single container]—if there was cabbage on top and cabbage
       on the bottom, but a different kind [of produce] was in the
       middle, he may not separate heave-offering or tithes from that
       [cabbage on top] on behalf of that [which is on the bottom, for
       the two batches of cabbage are distinct one from the other; T.
       Ter. 3 : 8C–H].**

[B][8] That which you have said applies if there is no space [between
       the two quantities of cabbage, but only the other kind of pro-

duce. In such a case heave-offering may not be separated from the cabbage on the bottom for that which is on top.]

[C]   But if there is an empty space [and no other produce to intervene between the two quantities of cabbage], one may separate heave-offering and tithes from this [cabbage on the bottom] on behalf of that [which is on top. They are deemed a single batch.]

The Yerushalmi continues to refine the definition of a single batch of produce. The claim now is that so long as there is clear access between two distinct quantities of produce, they are deemed a single batch, such that heave-offering may be separated from one on behalf of the other.

[XI.A]   **All [of the wine in] a wine-press room constitutes a single batch [such that heave-offering may be separated from one quantity of wine within the room on behalf of a different quantity; T. Ter. 3:7A].**

[B]   [In the same manner] all figs contained in a fig storage room constitute a single batch [for purpose of the separation of heave-offering].

[C]   It is taught: Said R. Judah, "This is the case when the majority of the produce from the threshing floor is in the middle [indicating that all of the produce in the room indeed constitutes a single, large batch]."

[D]   According to [Judah's view] if it is grain [on the threshing floor, then it will be deemed a single batch] even if [the produce in the middle is a byproduct of the grain, e.g.], straw or even stubble, [for these things are not considered a different kind of produce].

[E]   [To carry this reasoning forward] R. Haggai asked before R. Yose, "If there is unclean produce in the middle of [the threshing floor is all of the produce still deemed a single batch for purposes of separating heave-offering]?" [The alternative is that the unclean produce is deemed a different kind, which divides the rest of the produce into two separate batches, such that heave-offering may not be separated from one for another.]

[F]   [Yose] answered him, "Does [the unclean produce] touch⁹ the [produce] around it?" [It does not, for if it did, it would render unclean all of the produce on the threshing floor. Since it thus is distinct from the produce around it, it divides the produce on the threshing floor into autonomous batches, and heave-offering may not be separated from one on behalf of another.]

[G]   [Following the same line of reasoning] associates asked before R. Yose, "If there was a piece of cloth in the middle of [the threshing floor, does this divide the produce into distinct batches]?"

[H]   [Yose] said to them, "[This case which you describe] is like [the case in which there are] five sacks [of produce] on the threshing floor. [These sacks are deemed distinct from each other and therefore] they may not separate heave-offering and tithes [from the produce in] one [sack] on behalf of [the produce in] another." [Thus if there is a piece of cloth dividing the produce on the threshing floor, heave-offering may not be taken from one pile of produce on the floor on behalf of a different pile.]

The problem is the same as at Y. Ter. 2 : 1 **IX–X**, namely, the circumstances under which distinct quantities of produce are deemed a single batch for purposes of the separation of heave-offering. As at Y. Ter. 2 : 1 **X**, the theory here is that all of the produce must be of a single kind (D versus E + F) and may not be divided by a physical barrier (G + H). F assumes that the produce is susceptible to uncleanness.

[XII.A]   It is taught [T. Ter. 3 : 18H – K]: **R. Ilai says in the name of R. Eliezer, "They separate heave-offering from that which is clean for that which is unclean even in [the case of] wet [produce]. How [is this possible, for when the wet produce is brought together to form a single batch for purposes of the separation of heave-offering, the unclean produce will render unclean the clean produce? In order to form a single batch without rendering the clean produce unclean] one who pickled [his] olives in a state of uncleanness but wished to separate heave-offering from them in cleanness brings a funnel the [smaller] opening of which does not hold an egg's bulk [and which, therefore, does not convey uncleanness] and rests it in the opening of the jug [of unclean, pickled olives]. He brings clean olives** [10] **and places them in it [i.e., the funnel, and separates heave-offering (from these clean olives on behalf of the** unclean olives in the jug)]. **The result is that he [separates heave-offering from that which is clean for that which is unclean, and] separates from a single batch [as required by M. 2:1D–E]."**

[B]   [The Talmud interjects:] Why need [the smaller opening of the funnel] be smaller than an egg's bulk? Even if it were the size of an egg's bulk [the pickled olives in which it is inserted would] not [convey uncleanness to the clean olives contained in the funnel. This is because the unclean olives] are in small pieces, none [of which alone is of an egg's bulk such that it may impart uncleanness].

[C]   [The reason is that, to the contrary, the unclean olives do join together to form the quantity of food which conveys uncleanness (so M. Toh. 8:8, cited by PM). Therefore the opening of the funnel must be smaller than the size of an egg's bulk] so that [the unclean olives] do not render unclean the many [other] olives [in the top of the funnel, from which the heave-offering is to be separated].

[D]   [The following continues T. Ter. 3:18 and the issue of whether or not heave-offering may be separated from clean produce on behalf of unclean produce in the case of produce that is wet.] **They said to him [i.e., to Ilai, who spoke in the name of Eliezer, above, A], "Only to the case of wine and oil [i.e., liquids] is the term 'wet' applicable."** [Since the method Ilai suggests will not work for these things, he has not proven that in the case of wet produce heave-offering may be separated from what is clean on behalf of what is unclean.]

The Yerushalmi cites the material from the Tosefta relevant to M. Ter. 2:1's problem, A + D. B–C explains A. My translation of the Tosefta follows the superior version of the pericope found in MSS. of the Tosefta.

[**XIII.**A]   [The unit interprets T. Ter. 3:7: **All (of the wine in) a wine-press room constitutes a single batch (such that heave-offering may be separated from clean wine within the room on behalf of unclean wine).**]

[B]   How is this so?

[C]   **[If there was] one press [served] by two tanks, two presses [served] by one tank [or two presses (served) by two tanks, heave-offering may be separated from (the clean wine in) one of the tanks on behalf of the (unclean wine in) the other tank; T. Ter. 3:7C–D].**

[D]   This is reasonable [if there is] one press for two vats, [for then wine pressed in cleanness may be stored in one of the vats, and wine pressed in uncleanness in the other. In this case the clean wine could be used as heave-offering for the unclean.]

[E]   But [if there are] two presses for a single vat, it is not [reasonable to suggest that clean wine in the press-room may be used as heave-offering for unclean wine]. For once a portion [of the wine being pressed] becomes unclean, all of the wine will be rendered unclean, [for it is stored together in the single vat. Thus in the case of such a wine-press-room, there is no possibility of separating clean wine as heave-offering for unclean wine.]

[F]   R. La in the name of R. Eleazar [said], "Solve [the problem of what C means by assuming] that [the rule applies to a case in which the individual originally] intended [to store the wine from the two presses] in a single batch [i.e., vat], but changed his mind [and decided] to make two batches [i.e., to store the clean wine in one vat and the unclean in a different vat]." [If this is the case, the point of T. Ter. 3:7, cited at C, is that even though the wine ultimately is stored in distinct vats, since it originally was intended for a single vat, it is deemed a single batch. Heave-offering therefore may be separated from the clean wine for the unclean.]

[G]   [Carrying forward F] said R. Yose b. R. Bun, "That which you have said, [that heave-offering may be separated from the clean wine on behalf of the unclean, applies only] in a case in which [the wine] became unclean after [the householder] had filled [the vat with it] and skimmed [it], such that it became subject to the separation of heave-offering while it still was in a state of cleanness.

[H]   "But if [the wine] became unclean before it had been placed in the vat and skimmed, [it may] not [be deemed a single batch with clean wine]." [This is because at the point at which it became subject to the separation of heave-offering, the unclean wine already had become unclean and could not have been formed into a single batch with the clean wine.]

The discussion of the conditions under which clean and unclean produce are deemed to be in a single batch yields the conclusion at F + G–H. A single batch is created when the householder intends all of the wine to be in a single vat. The wine's status as a single batch is maintained even if he ultimately places the wine in different vats. G–H is familiar from Y. Ter. 2:1 **VI**. If clean and unclean wine are to be deemed a single batch, they must have been together in one vat while both were in a state of cleanness and already were subject to the separation of heave-offering. If they never could physically have been together in one vat, the householder's intention to deem the clean and unclean wine a single batch is null.

[**XIV**.A]   R. Tabbi [in the name of] R. Yoshiah b. R. Yannai [says], "The law is in accordance with [the opinion of] R. Eliezer, M. Ter. 2:1J, that clean produce may be separated as heave-offering on behalf of unclean produce]."

[B]   R. Isaac b. Nahman in the name of R. Hoshaya [says], "The law is in accordance with [the statement of] R. Eliezer."

[C]   R. Huna [in the name of]¹¹ R. Hanania says, "The law is not in accordance with [the statement of] R. Eliezer."

[D]   R. Yose b. R. Bun [and] R. Judah in the name of Samuel [say], "The law is not in accordance with [the statement of] R. Eliezer."

[E]   A case came before R. Imi [in which he had to rule whether or not clean produce may be separated as heave-offering on behalf of unclean produce]. He did not rule [in accordance with the opinion of R. Eliezer, that it may be. He ruled that it may not be.]

[F]   [To explain his position] he said, "[In the evaluation of Eliezer's position] there are two [authorities, i.e., Yoshiah b. R. Yannai, A, and Hoshaya, B] against two [authorities, i.e., Hanania, C, and Samuel, D]." [Since there is not a majority in favor of Eliezer's view, Imi ruled against it.]

[G]   [To refute Imi's justification] they said to him, "But R. Isaac b. Nahman ruled [in accordance with the opinion of Eliezer]."

[H]   Even so [Imi] did not rule [in accordance with the position of Eliezer].

Imi, E–F, counts two Amoraim in favor of Eliezer's view and two against. He therefore does not accept Eliezer's position as law. G claims that the view of Isaac b. Nahman carries special weight.

2:2 [P: 2:1b]

[K]   *They may not separate heave-offering from [produce] which is unclean on behalf of that which is clean.*

[L]   *And if he separated heave-offering [in that manner]—*

[M]   *[if he did it] unintentionally, that which he has separated is [valid] heave-offering;*

[N]   *[but if he did it] intentionally, he has not done anything [i.e., the separation is not valid].*

[O]   *And so [in the case of] a Levite who had [unclean first] tithe from which heave-offering [of the tithe] had not been separated.*

[P]   *[If he] was saving it for designation [as heave-offering of the tithe for other, clean first tithe which came into his possession]—*

[Q]   *[if he did this] unintentionally, that which he has done is done [and valid]; [but if he did it] intentionally, he has not done anything.*

[R]   *R. Judah says, "If he knew about it [i.e., that the produce was unclean] from the beginning, even though [he forgot, such that his later actions were unintentional], he has not done anything."*

The discussion begun at M. Ter. 2:1 continues here. A householder, K, or Levite, O, may not give the priest unclean produce, which the latter may not eat, instead of clean. If one did separate heave-offering in this improper manner, the validity of the separation depends upon the intention with which he carried it out. If he purposely separated produce that the priest may not eat (N, P), the separation is not valid. It was not performed with the proper intention to give the priest his share. Yet if the householder or Levite inadvertently separated unclean produce instead of clean, the separation is valid. The fact that the individual separated the offering with proper intention takes precedence over the fact that the priest will not be able to eat the produce he is given.

The Yerushalmi's first unit is an exegesis of M. T.Y. 4:7, placed
here because M. Ter. 2:2K occurs in the course of its discussion.
The second unit turns to the opinion of Judah, M. Ter. 2:2R,
and asks to what extent Judah disagrees with the rule of M. Ter.
2:2K–M.

[I.A]   [41c] There [at M. T.Y. 4:7] we have learned: *[In the case of] one
who separates the heave-offering required of a vat [of wine or oil]
and says, "Lo, this [produce] is [designated] heave-offering on
the condition that it comes up [from the vat] safely"—[we assume that he means] "safe from [the ladle's] breaking," or "safe
from [the wine or oil's] being spilled [back into the vat"; namely
we assume that the man wishes to prevent a situation in which
wine or oil he has designated to be heave-offering will spill and
be mixed with unconsecrated wine, imparting to all the wine or
oil in the vat the status of heave-offering]. But [we assume that
there was] no [condition that wine must come up safe] from
uncleanness. R. Simeon says, "[We] also [assume that the man
imposed the condition that the wine come up safe] from uncleanness, [such that if it turns out to be unclean, it is not valid
heave-offering]."*

[B]   Said R. Yose b. Hanina, "[Simeon's statement in] the Mishnah
refers to the uncleanness imparted by one who was unclean and
had immersed on that selfsame day [and awaits sunset, which
marks the conclusion of the process of purification; it is against
the touch of such a person which the householder who makes
the stated condition wishes to protect the wine or oil he separates
as heave-offering]."

[C]   [To explain why such a person is of particular concern,] said
R. Ila, "[Such a condition is made] because [priests] who have
immersed on the selfsame day often are found among the wine
vats, [waiting for sunset, at which time they may collect heave-
offering; PM]."

[D]   [Arguing that Simeon's concern cannot be the uncleanness imparted by one who has immersed on the selfsame day,] R. Yose
said, "The touch of one who has immersed on the selfsame day
has no effect upon untithed produce." [That is, one who has
immersed on the selfsame day does not impart uncleanness to
untithed produce he touches. A condition that wine or oil be

designated heave-offering only if it comes up from the vat safe
from the touch of such a person therefore is meaningless. So long as
the oil or wine has not reached the status of heave-offering, the
person who has immersed on the selfsame day has no effect upon
it. Only once it actually is heave-offering does the touch of such
a person render it unclean. Yet at that point it is too late for the
householder's condition to apply. Yose, B, thus is wrong. Simeon
does not refer to uncleanness imparted by one who has immersed
on the selfsame day.]

[E]   [In qualification of the original rule stating that the condition
that wine or oil be brought up from the vat safely means that the
ladle not break nor the wine or oil spill,] it is taught: Said R.
Yudan, "In what case [do we define 'safely' as being that the
ladle not break nor the wine or oil spill]? In the case of [the
separation of] the great heave-offering, for it must be separated
from one batch of produce [on behalf of that same batch]. [If
some of the wine or oil being separated as heave-offering should
spill, the householder would have to take an additional amount
of wine or oil from a different, as yet untithed, batch. Since in
the case of the great heave-offering this is not permitted, the one
who separates the offering imposes the condition that if something happens such that he does not separate sufficient produce,
the separation is not valid at all.]

[F]   "But in the case of heave-offering of the tithe, [if the ladle breaks or
some of the wine or oil spills] as well as any other mishap, [the
wine or oil still is said to have come up] in safety [and the separation is valid. If he needs to, the Levite may go ahead and take
additional heave-offering of the tithe from a different batch.]"

[G]   [This following rule derives from Yudan's reasoning:] If one was
separating heave-offering and heave-offering of the tithe at one
and the same time, [with the condition that the designation be
valid only if the wine or oil come up from the vat safely, the sepa-
ration] would not [be deemed to have been performed] safely [if the
ladle broke or some of the wine or oil spilled; that is, we would
impose the stringencies that apply in the case of the separation
of the great heave-offering].

[H]   Judah the son of Rabbi[12] explains [why this is the case], "It
never entered this man's mind to transgress the words of the
Torah by separating heave-offering of the tithe before the great
heave-offering." [Therefore he must impose conditions to assure

that the separation of heave-offering will be valid, with enough
of the offering separated.]

[I] [The following argues that whether or not the man wished to
transgress is not an acceptable criterion by which to judge the
validity of his actions.] Replied R. Ba bar Mamel, "But so we
have learned [at M. Ter. 2:2]: *They may not separate heave-
offering from [produce] which is unclean on behalf of that which
is clean.* [13] *[If he separated heave-offering in that manner—if he
did it unintentionally, that which he has separated is valid heave-
offering.]* Imagine that one separated heave-offering [from unclean produce on behalf of clean, and did so unintentionally,
such that the separation should be valid], but said that he did
not wish to transgress the words of Torah, [which state that
heave-offering may not be separated from unclean produce]."
[By H's reasoning, since the person did not wish to transgress,
the separation is not valid. Yet this cannot be the case, for M.
Ter. 2:2 states explicitly that the separation is valid. This proves
that whether or not the individual intended to transgress is irrelevant in determining the validity of his actions.]

[J] [Continuing his thought,] said R. Ba bar Mamel, "If you say
this, [that since the individual did not wish to transgress, his
separation of unclean produce as heave-offering on behalf of
clean produce is not valid], you cause the individual to advance
from a [potential] minor offense to a major one.

[K] "[That is, if his separation of heave-offering is not valid, the man
might eat] untithed produce, [and eating such produce is] a capital offense.

[L] "[But if the separation is valid, at worst this will result in] the
clean [priest's] eating the unclean [offering, which is a transgression of] a positive commandment [but not a capital offense]."

Careful exegesis of M. T.Y. 4:7 introduces M. Ter. 2:2A–C,
which accounts for the placement of the pericope in this context.
That a householder may himself separate heave-offering of the
tithe, in place of the Levite, G, is indicated at T. Ter. 1:9.

[II.A] It is taught in the name of R. Yose [T. Ter. 3:19A: **If one separated unclean produce as heave-offering on behalf of clean**

produce, whether [he did so] unintentionally or intentionally, that which he has done is done [and valid].

[B]   [Yose's position is evaluated in light of that of Judah, M. Ter. 2:2R, as follows:] R. Pinhas asked in the presence of R. Yosa, "Up to now [we have understood Judah's view to apply only] in a case in which [someone forgot that his produce was unclean, such that when he designated it heave-offering for clean produce] he thought that it was clean. [Judah states that such a case is adjudicated just as though the person knows that the produce being designated as heave-offering is unclean. The designation is not valid. In this Judah disagrees both with Yose, A, and with the anonymous rule of M. Ter. 2:2K, which states that an inadvertent separation of unclean produce as heave-offering for clean produce is valid.]

[C]   "[Would this same disagreement between Judah and the anonymous rule apply in a case in which] the person knew that the produce was unclean, [but forgot the rule of M. Ter. 2:2K], such that he believed that it is permitted to separate unclean produce as heave-offering on behalf of clean produce?" [Judah surely would deem the separation of heave-offering invalid, for he takes no account of forgetfulness. The question is whether the authorities behind M. Ter. 2:2K would agree with Judah or whether they again would deem this a case of inadvertence, such that the separation is valid.]

[D]   [Yosa] answered him [i.e., Pinhas], "It would have been proper had Rabbi [Judah the Patriarch, the presumed authority behind M. Ter. 2:2K–M] agreed with R. Judah. But [he did not, for] the law is according to the view of R. Yose [as given at A] both there [in the case described at B] and here [in the case detailed at C.]"

The question, B–C, is whether the anonymous rule of M. Ter. 2:2K–M ever agrees with Judah in disallowing forgetfulness as the basis for a claim of inadvertence. Yosa, D, states that, in all cases, M. Ter. 2:2K–M disagrees with Judah. It rules that separations of heave-offering carried out wrongly because the householder forgot the law are treated as unintentional. They therefore are valid. What confuses matters is the inclusion here of the opinion of Yose, A and D. Yose claims that a separation of unclean produce as heave-offering on behalf of clean produce is valid, whether or not it was performed unintentionally. Despite the claim of D, this opinion differs both from that of Judah and from the anonymous rule of M. Ter. 2:2K–M.

2:3 [P: 2:1C]

[S]   (1) *One who immerses [unclean] utensils on the Sabbath [in order to render them cultically clean]—*

[T]   *[if he does this] unintentionally, he may use them.*

[U]   *[But if he does so] intentionally he may not use them.*

[V]   *(2) One who tithes [his produce], or who cooks on the Sabbath—*

[W]   *[if he does this] unintentionally, he may eat [the food he has prepared].*

[X]   *[But if he does so] intentionally, he may not eat [the food].*

[Y]   *(3) One who plants [a tree] on the Sabbath—*

[Z]   *[if he does this] unintentionally, he may leave it [to grow].*

[AA]   *[But if he does so] intentionally, he must uproot [it].*

[BB]   *But in the seventh year [of the Sabbatical cycle], whether [he has planted the tree] unintentionally or intentionally, he must uproot [it].*

A person infringes upon the restrictions of the Sabbath by performing forbidden work. Just as in the preceding pericope, if he transgresses intentionally, he may not benefit from the actions. But if he does so unintentionally, his actions are not deemed a transgression, and he may benefit. The case of the tree planted in the Sabbatical year is different. The continued growth of the tree impinges upon the restrictions of that year. Even if the planting was unintentional, the person therefore must uproot the tree.

The Yerushalmi's materials concern in a general way the performance of forbidden work on the Sabbath. Only in unit **III** do we turn to the specific concern of this pericope, asking how the individual came inadvertently to perform forbidden work on the Sabbath. Unit **IV** answers the next logical question: When may the person who unintentionally transgresses eat the food he cooked, on the Sabbath itself, or only afterwards? We conclude with the Mishnah's last case, asking why the rule for a tree planted in the seventh year is different from that governing the planting of a tree on the Sabbath.

[I.A]   [The following refers to M. Bes. 2:3, where the Houses of Hillel and Shammai agree that people may not immerse vessels on the Sabbath in order to render them cultically clean. Y. asks to what sort of vessels the Houses refer.] [At] Mishnah [Bes. 2:3, the Houses refer] to large vessels, [which are not used to draw water].

[B]   But in the case of small vessels, [which are used to draw water, the Houses agree that the person may draw water in them and, in that way,] circumvent [14] [the law, since by drawing water] he immerses them [against their previous uncleanness (PM, QE)].

[C] [15]   So taught R. Hoshaya, "[On the Sabbath] a man may fill an unclean vessel [with water] from a well [so as to draw water] and [in that way] may circumvent [the law, since by drawing the water] he immerses the vessel [against its previous uncleanness]."

[D]   It is taught: [On the Sabbath, if] his [unclean] bucket or utensil fell into a well, he may circumvent [the law by using that opportunity to] immerse them [against their uncleanness].

[E]   [The question is the level of uncleanness of the vessels which the Houses agree may, through artifice, be immersed on the Sabbath.] [There are] two Amoraic authorities.

[F]   One states [that the Houses refer to vessels] rendered unclean even by a Father of Uncleanness.

[G]   But the other states [that the Houses refer to vessels] rendered unclean only by an Offspring of Uncleanness.

[H]   The one who claims [that they refer to vessels rendered unclean only by] an Offspring of Uncleanness replied to the one who states [that they refer to vessels rendered unclean even by] a Father of Uncleanness, "[If indeed the reference is to a vessel rendered unclean by a Father of Uncleanness, why should the Houses permit the person to circumvent the law and immerse it on the Sabbath? The fact is that the man will not be able to use such a vessel on the Sabbath anyway since], even [if it were immersed] on a weekday, [such a vessel] would have to await the

setting of the sun, [which marks the conclusion of its process of
purification]." [Since the man cannot use the vessel on the Sabbath, he should not be allowed to immerse it on that day. A vessel rendered unclean by an Offspring of Uncleanness, by contrast, may be used immediately after it is immersed. The Houses
allow the person to immerse it on the Sabbath, so that he may
use it on that same day.]

[I]   Said to him [the one who claims that the Houses refer as well to
a vessel which was rendered unclean by a Father of Unclean-
ness], "The case is one in which [the individual] wishes to use
[the vessel] for unconsecrated foods prepared in a state of cleanness, [but not for heave-offering or other Holy Things]." [For
such use the vessel rendered unclean by the Father of Uncleanness and then immersed need not await the setting of the sun. It
may be used immediately. The Houses have good reason to allow
the person to immerse this vessel on the Sabbath, so as to use it
on that same day.]

Primary at Y. Bes. 2:3, the pericope is found here because it
concerns the immersing of vessels on the Sabbath. This is the
topic of M. Ter. 2:3S–U. The unit treats two specific issues, the
sort of vessel that may be immersed on the Sabbath, A–D, and
its level of uncleanness, disputed at E–I.

[II.A]   [The following depends upon the rule found at B. Shab. 95a
(PM): They may rinse off drinking cups, dishes, and trays from
the evening of the Sabbath until the morning, that is, from Friday
night until Saturday morning. This allows people to do the dinner
dishes and ready them for Sabbath lunch. Dishes may not be
washed later on Saturday. Nor may other housework be done.

[B]   R. Jeremiah [and] R. Zeira in the name of R. Hiyya bar Ashi
[say], "[On Friday night or early Saturday morning] a smart
woman rinses a cup here, [in one part of her house], and a plate
there, [in another part], and a tray elsewhere, [in a different
part]. She winds up wetting down [16] [the dirt floor of] her house
on the Sabbath, [which, while desirable, normally is forbidden]."

The pericope continues the theme of the preceding, methods of performing on the Sabbath work which normally is forbidden on that day.

[**III.**A] [17]   R. Samuel in the name of R. Abbahu [says], "[The cases to which M. Ter. 2:3 refers are ones] in which [the person who tithes knows that it is the Sabbath, but] forgets the prohibition [against tithing on that day, in which case of inadvertence he may eat what he tithes; or] in which [the person both knows that it is the Sabbath and] knows the prohibition [against tithing on that day, in which case he may not eat what he tithes]." [In a case in which the person remembers the prohibition, but forgets that it is the Sabbath, he may not eat what he tithes. Forgetting that it is the Sabbath is not grounds for claiming inadvertence.]

[B]   [To show that what Samuel says is obvious,] said R. Yose, "Mishnah states this [explicitly]: *One who tithes [his produce] or who cooks on the Sabbath—[if he does so] unintentionally, he may eat [the food]. [But if he does so] intentionally, he may not eat [the food].*

[C]   "[By including together the rule for cooking with the one for tithing, the Mishnah indicated that it refers to a case] in which [the person knew that it was the Sabbath but] forgot the prohibition [against cooking or tithing on that day or] in which [the person both knew that it was the Sabbath and] knew the prohibition [against tithing or cooking on that day but went ahead and did so anyway.]" [It is not a case in which the person remembers the prohibition but forgets that it is the Sabbath, just as Samuel said.]

We turn to M. 2:3's middle case, in which a person transgresses by tithing or cooking on the Sabbath. Samuel explains M. Ter. 2:3V–X, stating that these actions are deemed unintentional only if the person forgets that it is not permitted to do these things on the holy day. Conversely, if he remembers the laws, but forgets that it is the Sabbath, the actions are deemed intentional. Forgetting the Sabbath is not grounds for claiming inadvertence. In this case the person may not eat the food which he has prepared. Yose, B–C, claims that what Samuel states is obvious from the Mishnah. The point of the proof is not clear.

[**IV.**A]   It is taught [T. Shab. 3:5]: "**One who cooks on the Sabbath—** [if he does so] unintentionally he may [immediately] eat [the food]. But if he does so intentionally he may not eat the food [until after the Sabbath]"—the words of R. Meir.

[B]   R. Judah says, "[If he does it] unintentionally he may eat [the food] after the Sabbath. [If he does it] intentionally, he never[18] may eat [the food]."

[C]   R. Yohanan, the sandal-maker, says, "[If he does so] unintentionally, after the Sabbath the food may be served to other people, but not to him [who wrongly prepared it on the Sabbath. If he did so] intentionally, it may [never] be served either to him or to others."

[D]   Samuel agreed with R. Yohanan, the sandal-maker.

[E]   [As for] Rab—when he would instruct among the associates, he would teach in accordance with [the opinion of] R. Meir. [But] in public [he would teach] according to [the stricter opinion of] R. Yohanan, the sandal-maker.

[F]   [Claiming that E is wrong], said R. Simeon bar Barsana, "[Rab] instructed us according to [the opinion of] R. Ishmael the son of R. Yohanan b. Beroqah.

[G]   "For R. Ishmael the son of R. Yohanan b. Beroqah taught, '[In the case of] any transgression (*dbr*) for the willful commission of which one is subject to extirpation, and for the inadvertent commission of which one is subject to a sin offering, and which one committed on the Sabbath—whether he did it intentionally or unintentionally (delete: it is forbidden), neither he nor others [ever] may eat of it.

[H]   "'But [in the case of] any transgression for the willful commission of which one is not subject to extirpation, and for the inadvertent commission of which [one is not subject to] a sin offering, and which one committed on the Sabbath—if he did this unintentionally, after the Sabbath [the food] may be served to others, but not to him. [But if he did it] intentionally, it [never] may be served either to him or to others'" [T. Shab. 3:6].

[I]   They asked in the presence of R. Yohanan, "[As for] you, what do you say [that the law is]?"

[J]   He said to them, "[As for] me, I know [to be law] only [what it says in] the Mishnah[19] [Ter. 2:3]: 'One who tithes [his produce], or who cooks on the Sabbath—[if he did this] unintentionally, he may eat [the food he has prepared. But if he does this] intentionally, he may not eat [the food].'" [This is the same as the position of Meir, above, A.]

[K]   R. Hisda heard [Yohanan's opinion, that the law follows the anonymous statement in M. 2:3, which allows one who inadvertently cooks on the Sabbath to benefit from his misdeed during that same Sabbath. Hisda] said, "Is it true that the laws [regulating labor] on the Sabbath have been repealed?!

[L]   "[To the contrary] did not R. Huna in the name of Rab say [the following]: And so taught R. Hiyya: At first [sages] ruled, 'One who forgets his stew [cooking] on his stove [such that it continues to simmer] on the Sabbath—if he does this unintentionally, he may eat [the stew on the Sabbath. But if he does this] intentionally, he may not eat the stew.' [Later, people] were suspected purposely of leaving [the food on the stove] and of saying, 'We forgot [about it,' so that they would be able to use the food which cooked on the Sabbath]. And [as a result, sages reverted] and forbade [for consumption on the Sabbath food] that had been forgotten [and unintentionally left on the stove].

[M]   "Yet you, [Yohanan], say in this case [that what the person unintentionally cooks on the Sabbath] is fit [for use on the Sabbath]!" [That cannot be so, for it is contrary to the Tannaitic statement just cited.]

[N]   [To explain Yohanan's position] said R. Hila, "[People] were suspected of [purposely] leaving [food on the stove] but were not suspected of [purposely] cooking [on the Sabbath. Therefore] they penalized [those who] left [food on the stove, ruling that even if they claimed to have done so unintentionally, they may not eat the food], but did not penalize those who cooked [on the Sabbath]." [In the case of these people, if they claim to have done so unintentionally, they are allowed to eat the food, as Yohanan states.]

[O]   [The sages of L] reverted to say, "Any stew [the flavor of which] is improved by being boiled down is forbidden [for consumption if it is left to boil on the Sabbath. But if] being boiled ruins it[s flavor] it is permitted [to eat it, even if it has been left to cook on the Sabbath]."

[P]   Which sorts of stews are improved by being boiled down? Cabbage, bean, and chopped (*trwp*) meat.

[Q]   Said R. Tanhum bar Ila, "Also: [as for] turnip heads and heads of leeks—they deemed them a kind of stew which is improved by being boiled down."

[R]   Eggs—what is their rule [whether or not boiling improves their flavor]?

[S]   R. Yose in the name of R. Ishmael, R. Jeremiah, R. Haninah in the name of R. Ishmael the son of R. Yose: "Father went into his house [on the Sabbath] and found there eggs [being boiled], and he forbade them [for consumption. He also found] warm [eggs, which were left on the stove, but not boiled (PM)] and permitted [them for consumption on the Sabbath]."

[T]   [In answer to the same question of R] R. Samuel bar Nathan in the name of R. Hamah bar Hanina [said], "Father and I went up to the springs at Geder, and [on the Sabbath] they served us eggs as small as crab apples, and their flavor was as good as that of apricots." [Presumably the eggs had been left to boil on the Sabbath. Contrary to Yose, S, Samuel claims such eggs are permitted.]

[U]   [Turning to a new question of whether food cooked on the Sabbath is permitted for consumption] it is taught [T. Shab. 3:13]: **A woman may not fill a pot with peas or leeks and put them in the oven on Sabbath eve at sunset, [for if she does, the food will cook on the Sabbath]. But if she [did this and] placed them [in the oven] they may not be eaten [the next day], after the Sabbath, until [they have remained in the oven after the Sabbath] long enough to cook [in the span of time since the Sabbath. Then we may deem the food to have cooked after the Sabbath, not on the holy day.]**

[V]   R. Aha says, "[The case at U is one in which the woman cooked the food on the Sabbath] intentionally, [and the ruling, that she may not eat the food until after the Sabbath, is] in accordance with [the opinion of] R. Meir [above, A]." [Meir holds that one who intentionally cooks on the Sabbath may not eat the food until after the Sabbath.]

[W]   [Disagreeing] R. Yose says, "[The case is one in which the woman cooked the food on the Sabbath] unintentionally, [and the ruling, that she may not eat it until after the Sabbath, is] in accordance with [the position of] R. Judah [above, B]." [Judah holds that one who unintentionally cooks on the Sabbath may not eat the food until after the Sabbath.]

[X]   Said R. Mana, "Correctly has R. Yose stated [that the case at U is one in which the woman unintentionally cooks on the Sabbath and that the rule that she may not eat the food until after the Sabbath follows the view of R. Judah. We know this from the following, T. Shab. 3:11]: **One who plants [a tree] on the Sabbath—[if he did so] unintentionally, he may leave [it to grow. But if he did so] intentionally, he must uproot [it]. In the seventh year [of the Sabbatical cycle], whether [he planted the tree] unintentionally or intentionally, he must uproot [it].**

[Y]   **"R. Judah said, 'The rules are reversed. [If he planted it] in the seventh year [of the Sabbatical cycle—if he did so] unintentionally, he may leave it [to grow. If he did so] intentionally, he must uproot [it. And if he planted the tree] on the Sabbath—whether he did so unintentionally or intentionally, he must uproot [it], lest he benefit [from the forbidden work he did on the Sabbath].'**

[Z]   "Now here [in the case of cooking, U,] so long as you say [that one must] wait after the Sabbath enough time for the [food] to cook, it is like [the case of] a person who in no way benefits from [work done on] the Sabbath." [Yose, W, thus is correct that the case of U conforms to Judah's view. Even one who unintentionally transgresses the rules of the Sabbath may in no way benefit from that transgression.]

The Yerushalmi's discussion of M. Ter. 2:3V–X is an elaboration of T. Shab.'s parallel materials. These materials introduce each of the unit's two sections, A–O and U–Z. In the first, the discussion of whether or not foods cooked on the Sabbath may be eaten on that same day leads to a minor digression, P–T. This concerns whether or not certain foods are improved through overcooking. The problem of the second part is to discern which of A–B's authorities stands behind the rule stated anonymously at U.

[V.A]   What is the reason that rabbis, [M. 2 : 3, stated that, while one who unintentionally plants a tree on the Sabbath may let it grow, one who does so in the Sabbatical year must uproot it]?

[B]   [The reason they made the distinction is that Israelites] **are suspected of [transgressing the laws of] the Sabbatical year [by lying and claiming that they unintentionally performed prohibited labor]. But they are not suspected of [transgressing the laws of] the Sabbath [by making such false claims].**

[C]   **Another reason is that they count [the years of] the Sabbatical cycle, [such that people always will know that a certain tree was planted in the seventh year], but they do not count Sabbaths.** [Therefore if a tree planted on the Sabbath is left to grow, people soon will forget. The presence of such a tree will not taint the field; T. Shab. 2 : 21].

[D]   How [do these two explanations] work [when applied to a concrete case]?

[E]   [If one inadvertently planted] a sapling fewer than thirty days before [the start of] the Sabbatical year, [in which case the seventh year is deemed to be the sapling's first year of growth (M. Sheb. 2 : 6)], and the sapling continued to grow in the seventh year itself—[what is the law whether or not the sapling must be uprooted]?

[F]   If you say [that sages required saplings planted in the seventh year to be uprooted because Israelites are] suspected [of lying in order to transgress the rules of the seventh year, then in this case the tree may be left to grow. Since the tree was not actually planted in the seventh year] there is here no [reason for] suspicion.

[G]   If you say [that the basis for M. 2 : 3's rule is that the years of the Sabbatical cycle are] counted, [such that it always will be known that a certain tree was planted in the seventh year, then in this case the tree must be uprooted. Since its first year of growth is counted as the seventh year], there is here [concern for] counting.

[H]   [We have a different case in which the consideration of suspicion or that of counting might apply. If one planted] a sapling fewer than thirty days before the end of[20] the Sabbatical year, [so that its first year of growth is deemed to be the first year of the new Sabbatical cycle] and [the sapling] continued to grow in the eighth [i.e., first] year—[what is the rule whether or not it must be uprooted]?

[I]   (Supply following T. Shab. 2:21)[21] If you say [that the reason sap-
       lings planted in the seventh year must be uprooted is that] they
       count [the years of the Sabbatical cycle, in this case the tree need
       not be uprooted, for] there is no [issue of] counting. [The tree's
       growth is from the first year of the Sabbatical cycle.]

[J]   [But] if you say [that the reason is that Israelites are] suspected
       [of lying in order to transgress the law, then in this case the tree
       must be uprooted, for] there is here [reason for] suspicion. [This
       is because, in actuality, the tree was planted in the seventh year.
       The cases suggested at E and H thus are inconclusive in indicat-
       ing which reason accounts for the rule of M. Ter. 2:3. The mat-
       ter can go either way.]

[K]   Still [the reason trees inadvertently planted in the seventh year
       must be uprooted] is that suggested by the one who says, "It is
       because they count [the years of the Sabbatical cycle]."

[L]   [We know that this is so] for as for the one who says [the reason
       is that Israelites are] suspected [of lying in order to circumvent the
       rules of the Sabbatical year], is it possible that [rabbis would]
       punish [those who] inadvertently [transgress the law] on account
       of [those who] intentionally [do so? No, this is not possible.
       Therefore we know that suspicion is not the reason. Counting
       the years must be.]

       Two possible reasons for the rule of M. Ter. 2:3Y–BB are tested
       by means of concrete cases, E–G and H–J. This proves incon-
       clusive, such that we must turn to logic, K–L. All people should
       not be punished on account of the suspected sins of a few, L.
       From this reasoning the conclusion of the unit, K, is derived.

       2:4 [P: 2:2; M. Ter. 2:4–5]

[A]   *They may not separate heave-offering from [produce of one]
       kind on behalf of [produce] which is not of its same kind.*

[B]   *And if he separated heave-offering [in this way]—that which he
       has separated is not [valid] heave-offering.*

[C]   *All kinds of wheat are [considered] one [species];*

[D]   *all kinds of figs, dried figs and [circles of] pressed figs are [con-
       sidered] one [species]—*

[E]   *so he separates heave-offering from one [species of wheat or figs]*
       on behalf of a different [species].

[F]   *Wherever there is a priest [to receive the heave-offering at once, the*
       householder] separates heave-offering from the choicest [produce].

[G]   *Wherever there is not a priest [to receive the heave-offering im-*
       mediately], he separates heave-offering from that which keeps
       [without spoiling].

[H]   *R. Judah says, "He always should separate heave-offering from*
       the choicest [produce]."

[I]   *[2:5] They separate a whole small onion as heave-offering [for*
       other produce], but not half of a large onion.

[J]   *R. Judah says, "No, rather, they separate half of a large onion as*
       heave-offering [for other produce]."

[K]   *And so would R. Judah say, "They separate onions from large*
       towns as heave-offering for [onions] from villages, but not [onions]
       from villages [as heave-offering] for [onions] from large towns,

[L]   *"since they [i.e., the onions grown in large towns] are the food*
       of city people [and therefore are of higher quality]."

The Yerushalmi's attention is on M. Ter. 2:4A–E, the rule that
heave-offering may not be separated from produce of one kind
on behalf of produce of a different kind. Its first unit suggests
the scriptural basis for this rule. Unit **II** provides a light gloss of
C, explaining the larger, though obvious, implications of that
rule. The final unit moves outside of the framework of the Mishnah. It cites the Tosefta's supplementary materials and examines
them in light of a variety of parallel rules found elsewhere in the
Mishnah. Surprisingly the Yerushalmi ignores M. Ter. 2:4F–H
and all of M. Ter. 2:5I–L, a fact for which I cannot account.

[I.A]   R. Yohanan in the name of R. Yanani [said], "[M. Ter. 2:4A
        derives from] one of three[22] [rabbinic] interpretations of Scrip-
        ture which are clearly intended by the Torah [itself; cf., Y. Ter.
        1:5 I].

[B]   "[For Scripture states that the following sorts of food should go
        to the priest as heave-offering:] 'All the best of the oil and all the

best of the wine and the grain' (Num. 18:11)." [The fact that
Scripture refers separately to the best of the oil and the best of
the wine indicates that each of these must be given as heave-
offering unto itself and not on behalf of some different kind of
produce.]

[C]   [It is now suggested that matters are not so simple as A–B implies.] [Yet] how do we interpret [the passage, for it refers to
wine and grain as one but does not mention explicitly "the best
of the grain"]?

[D]   Perhaps it teaches that [whereas one may not separate oil as heave-
offering on behalf of wine], they may separate wine as heave-
offering for grain, or grain [as heave-offering] for wine.

[E]   [Indicating how we know that D is wrong,] they replied, "Lo,
wine and oil, lo, these [each derive from the fruit of] a kind
of tree; yet [even so] they may not[23] separate heave-offering or
tithes from one on behalf of the other. [Grain does not come
from a sort of tree and, indeed, has nothing in common with
wine or oil. It therefore is obvious that it may not be designated
heave-offering on behalf of oil or wine, nor oil or wine on its
behalf.]

[F]   "Moreover you must state: 'If [in the case of] wine and oil, which
have in common that both [derive from the fruit of] kinds of
trees [which are not Diverse Kinds, B. Bek. 54a], they may not
separate heave-offering and tithes from one for the other, [41d]
[then] certainly I must include [in this rule] two kinds of grain,
or two kinds of produce [distinct species of which are Diverse
Kinds. Therefore I must rule] that they may not separate heave-
offering or tithes from one [such species] on behalf of another.'"

Yohanan, A–B, suggests that an exegesis of Scripture is the basis
for M. Ter. 2:4A. C–D is a good criticism of his claim, for it
suggests an interpretation consistent with the whole of Scripture's verse. E answers C–D, but only when supplied with the
long interpolation suggested by PM. F, then, depends upon E
but does not carry forward E's problem exactly. The former
wants to know the rule for two kinds of grain, not grain and
wine or oil. The unit thus is a poor composite, the interpretation
of which is only conjectural.

[II.A]   *All kinds of wheat are [deemed] one [kind]* [M. Ter. 2:4C].

[B]   [This rule] needed to be taught in order to indicate the following:

[C]   [They may] even [separate heave-offering] from light-colored wheat on behalf of dark-colored wheat or from dark-colored wheat on behalf of light-colored wheat.

B–C suggests the point of M. Ter. 2:4C, cited at A.

[III.A]   *All kinds of [figs, whether fresh] figs, dried figs, or [rings of] pressed figs, are [considered] one [species], so one may separate heave-offering from one on behalf of another* [M. Ter. 2:4D–E].

[B]   It is taught: **They separate [fresh] figs [which are plump and large] as heave-offering on behalf of dried figs²⁴ [which are small] according to number, and dried figs [as heave-offering] on behalf of [fresh] figs according to volume, [in order to give the priest an enhanced quantity of produce]. But [they do] not [separate fresh] figs [as heave-offering] on behalf of dried figs according to volume, nor dried figs [as heave-offering] on behalf of [fresh] figs according to number, [since either of these methods would give the priest a smaller quantity of produce than he would otherwise receive].**

[C]²⁵   **Rabban Simeon b. Gamaliel says, "Baskets of [fresh] figs and baskets of dried figs are all equal. They separate heave-offering and remove tithes from one on behalf of the other."**

[D]   **Said R. Ishmael b. R. Yose, "Father would take ten dried figs from the drying place [as heave-offering and tithes] for ninety figs which were in the basket"** [T. Ter. 4:1–2].

[E]   [Explaining the statement of Simeon b. Gamaliel, C (PM)] R. Jeremiah reasoned, "[To separate fresh figs as heave-offering for dried ones] you treat the dried [figs] as if they are swollen [to their original size] and take [as heave-offering for them] baskets of [fresh] figs in accordance with this [measure]."

[F]   [To show that Jeremiah is wrong] R. Jonah and R. Yose, two Amoraim, [say], "It is normal for what is swollen to become compressed, but not for what is compressed to swell up. [Therefore it is not acceptable to treat dried figs as if they were their original size.]

[G]   "[Rather] let him take [as heave-offering] for [fresh] figs large baskets [of dried figs, so that the priest will receive a sufficient quantity of the smaller produce]."

[H]   R. Aha said to them [i.e., Jonah and Yose], "So would R. Ila, your teacher, criticize [Jeremiah's view, on the basis of the following]:

[I]   "There [at M. Toh. 3:4] we have learned [in the Mishnah's complete version]: *[As to] an egg's bulk of [unclean] foodstuff, [which is the minimum quantity that contracts uncleanness], which one left out in the sun such that it shrank [to less than an egg's bulk], and so an olive's bulk of corpse matter, an olive's bulk of carrion, a lentil's bulk of dead, creeping insect or an olive's bulk of Refuse, Remnant, or Forbidden Fat, [each of these likewise having shrunk to a quantity less than that which contracts uncleanness or imposes liability for a transgression]—lo, these things are now deemed clean, [since they are of less volume than the minimum or, [in the case of Refuse, Remnant, and Forbidden Fat, people who eat them] do not become subject by reason of them for transgressing the laws of Refuse, Remnant, or Forbidden Fat.*

[J]   "[If] one placed these things in the rain so that they swelled up [to greater than the minimum volume in which they contract uncleanness], they are unclean." [The point is that contrary to Jeremiah's claim, E, food is subject to all laws in accordance with its present size, not its original volume.]

[K]   [Disagreeing with the conclusion reached at J] the Daromeans say, "[Food which is left out in the rain and swells to greater than the minimum volume may contract uncleanness] only if it was an olive's bulk [i.e., the minimum] from the start." [That is, if an olive's bulk of food was left in the sun, shrank to less than an olive's bulk, and then, because of the rain, swelled up again, it contracts uncleanness. If food never had been an olive's bulk, but swelled up, it does not contract uncleanness.]

[L]   [To the contrary] both R. Yohanan and R. Simeon b. Laqish say, "[Once the food swells to greater than the minimum, it contracts uncleanness], even if it was not an olive's bulk [i.e., the minimum] from the start."

[M]   [We turn to a new case that illustrates the same issue:] There [at M. Men. 5:1] we have learned: *[All meal offerings are brought unleavened, except for the leavened thank offering and the two loaves of shew bread, which are leavened.]*

[N]   *[R. Meir says, "The leaven for them is taken from their own (dough) and (with this) they are leavened."]*

[O]   *[R. Judah says, "Indeed: this would not be the best (leaven for the purpose). Rather, one brings (high-quality) leaven and places it in the measure and then fills the measure with meal. (In this way one is assured of having sufficient dough for the offering.)"]*

[P]   *They said to him, "Even [an offering prepared] this [way] may contain too little or too much [dough]."*

[Q]   Who [stands behind the statement introduced] "They said to him"?

[R]   R. Meir, [N].

[S]   [Meir's point is that] sometimes the leaven [that Judah would have the person bring] would be of good [quality] and would rise. Now [in this case] the meal might be of too little volume, but because of the high-quality leaven, it swells up. You [therefore] must judge the leavened [dough] as if it was compressed [to the original volume of the meal]. Thus it turns out that there is too little [meal in the offering].

[T]   And sometimes the leaven [that Judah would have the person bring] would be of low [quality], such that it would contract. Now [in this case], the meal might be of sufficient quantity, but because of the low-[quality] leaven, it would fall [and appear to be of too little volume]. You [therefore] must judge [the dough] as if it had risen. Thus it turns out that there is more than enough [meal in the offering]. [The point is that by adding leaven to the meal, as Judah suggests, O, one never can tell whether the dough contains the proper quantity of meal for the offering. To avoid this problem, Meir, N, holds that one allows the meal to be leavened with leaven created from the dough itself. This way we know exactly the quantity of the offering, and whether it rises or not is irrelevant.]

[U]   [M–T is ignored. A–L is summarized.] As for the opinions of R. Jeremiah [E] (delete: the Daromeans), R. Yohanan and R. Simeon b. Laqish [L]—the three of them state the same thing regarding [a case in which the food] has swelled up [i.e., that you take heed of the increased size of the food, not its original quantity].

[V]   As for the opinions of (supply: the Daromeans) [K], R. Yonah and R. Yose [F]—all three of them state the same thing regarding [a case in which] the food is compressed[26] [i.e., we judge that which has swelled up as though it were its original size].

[W]   [This illustrates V.] Residents of Bar Patai cooked rice, forgetting to [first] tithe it.

[X]   [When asked whether the rice should be tithed in accordance with its increased, cooked volume, or its uncooked volume] associates reasoned, "Take [as tithes] fresh [uncooked] rice [in a quantity] commensurate [with the amount of fresh rice in] the cooked rice."

[Y]   Said to them R. Yose, "I also would rule thus.

[Z]   "Why?

[AA]   "Because [when it is cooked, the rice] swells up." [Yose therefore wants it to be treated as though it were its original size, his view at F, summarized at V.]

The Yerushalmi cites and, in a loose way, discusses the Tosefta's supplement to M. Ter. 2:4. The Tosefta's point, B, is that when one separates produce of one sort as heave-offering for produce of a different kind, he must assure that the priest receives sufficient food. For instance, when figs are dried, they shrivel and become smaller than fresh figs. If a householder separates by count dried figs as heave-offering for the other figs, the priest will receive a much smaller volume of produce than would otherwise be his share. For this reason, the householder who wishes to separate dried figs as heave-offering for fresh ones must do so by giving the priest a percentage of the volume of the produce. Conversely figs that are not dried are separated by number as heave-offering for dried figs, thereby providing the priest with an enhanced volume of produce. If, in such a case, heave-offering were separated by volume, the priest would receive fewer pieces of fruit than he would otherwise be given. Simeon b. Gamaliel, C, rejects the notion that heave-offering must be separated in the manners suggested at B. Jeremiah's interpretation of what Simeon b. Gamaliel means, E, is disputed, F–J versus K–L. Within that discussion, I–L forms an autonomous unit on M. Toh. 3:4. M–T likewise is autonomous, included here because it coincides topically with what precedes. Indeed, M–T is ignored by U–V, which summarizes the positions taken at A–L. W–AA illustrates V.

2:5 [P: 2:3; M. Ter. 2:6]

[M]   *And they separate olives [meant to be pressed] for oil as heave-offering on behalf of olives [intended] for pickling;*

[N]   *but not olives for pickling [as heave-offering] on behalf of olives for oil.*

[O]   *And [they separate] wine that has not been boiled [as heave-offering] for that which has been boiled,*

[P]   *but not that which has been boiled [as heave-offering] for that which has not been boiled.*

[Q]   *This is the general principle:*

[R]   *[in the case of] any [produce] that is a Diverse Kind in relation to another [type of produce]—he may not separate heave-offering from one on behalf of the other, even from the more choice [as heave-offering] for the less choice.*

[S]   *But [in the case of] any [produce] that is not a Diverse Kind in relation to other [produce]—he separates heave-offering from the more choice on behalf of the less choice, but not from the less choice on behalf of the more choice.*

[T]   *But if he separated heave-offering from the less choice for the more choice, that which he has separated is [valid] heave-offering.*

[U]   *Except in the case of rye-grass [separated as heave-offering] for wheat,*

[V]   *since it [i.e., rye-grass] is not a food.*

[W]   *Cucumber and squash are a single kind.*

[X]   *R. Judah says, "[They are] two [different] kinds."*

The general rule, R–T, makes the point originally introduced at
M. Ter. 2:4A. Heave-offering must be separated from one sort
of produce on behalf of produce of its same kind. This pericope
adds that within this single kind, heave-offering should be separated from the choicest produce. The Yerushalmi's discussion of
this principle is brief and diverse. Unit **I** indicates that Judah
stands behind M. Ter. 2:6O–P and goes on to discuss that fact.
Units **II** and **IV** refer to M. Ter. 2:6T, first finding the basis for
the rule in Scripture and then indicating from which Tannaitic
authority it derives. Unit **III** intervenes between these two related exercises. Drawing out the implications of U–X, it would
be better placed after unit **II** + **IV**'s discussion of T and before
unit **V**, which lightly glosses W–X.

[I.A]   Said R. Yohanan, "[The statement that wine that has not been
        boiled may be separated as heave-offering on behalf of wine which
        has been boiled, M. 2:6O] is the opinion of R. Judah." [Judah
        wants heave-offering to be separated from the unboiled wine, for
        it is of better quality (see M. 2:4H).]

[B]   [The problem is that M. Ter. 11:1 G–I states: *They may not boil
        wine in the status of heave-offering, since this diminishes it.] But
        R. Judah permits [one to boil wine which is heave-offering], for
        this improves it.*

[C]   Said R. Yohanan, "The opinions of R. Judah are contradictory.
        [At M. Ter. 2:6 he holds that unboiled wine is more choice and
        at M. Ter. 11:1 he states that boiled wine is better.]"

[D]   R. Eleazar says, "They are not contradictory.

[E]   "There [where Judah allows boiling wine, it is wine already in
        the status of heave-offering and the boiling is done] by the priest.
        [Judah allows him to boil heave-offering wine in order to protect
        it from spoiling. For that purpose boiled wine is better.]

[F]   "Here [where Judah prefers unboiled wine] the reference is to
        householders." [Judah states that they should separate as heave-
        offering unboiled wine, which is of better quality].

[G][27] [We turn to a new question, to be answered on the basis of the
        information given at C–F. The problem is what M. Ter. 11:1,
        cited above at B, means by "diminishes."] R. Eleazar and R.
        Yohanan—one states that [according to M. Ter. 11:1 people may

not boil wine in the status of heave-offering] because it diminishes its [desirability to wine] drinkers. But the other says it is
because it diminishes its quantity.

[H]   And we do not know which [authority] holds which position.

[I]   [We may derive the answer] from R. Yohanan's statement that
the positions of Judah are contradictory [above, C] and from
Eleazar's statement [D–F] that they are not contradictory, since
there [at M. Ter. 11:1] the reference is to the priest and here [at
M. Ter. 2:6] reference is to householders.

[J]   [Examination of these views shows that] it is R. Yohanan who
holds that [by "diminishes" M. Ter. 11:1 means that boiling
wine] diminishes its [desirability to wine] drinkers. [Yohanan
holds that the meaning of M. Ter. 11:1G is that boiling the wine
ruins (i.e., diminishes) its taste. Judah's disputing opinion, M.
Ter. 11:1H–I, must be that boiling the wine improves its flavor.
Yohanan therefore holds that Judah's opinion at M. Ter. 11:1
contradicts what he says at M. Ter. 2:6. Eleazar, on the other
hand, sees the issue at M. Ter. 11:1 as quantity. This is quite
independent of the issue of M. Ter. 2:6, which is taste. Eleazar
therefore sees no contradiction between the two views of Judah.]

[K]   [Agreeing with Yohanan's explanation of M. Ter. 11:1] R. Judah
b. R. Imi in the name of Resh Laqish [said], "[The meaning of
M. Ter. 11:1G] is that [boiling wine] diminishes its [desirability
to wine] drinkers.

[L]   A Tannaitic teaching is at variance with [the view of] R. Yohanan
[that boiling wine ruins its flavor. T. Ter. 4:4 states:] *[They may
separate wine] that has not been boiled [as heave-offering] for
that which has been boiled* [M. Ter. 2:6C] . . . **[Rabban Simeon b.
Gamaliel says],** "So much the more so **[they may separate wine]
that has been boiled [as heave-offering] for [wine] that has not
been boiled."** [Contrary to Yohanan, the implication of Simeon's
view is that the boiled wine is more desirable.]

[M]   Said R. Imi, "R. Yohanan did not teach [i.e., know] that Tannaitic statement."

Only A–F belong with M. Ter. 2:6. G–J and K–L are placed
here because they depend upon A–F. They concern the meaning
of M. Ter. 11:1.

[II.A] [The issue is why a separation of less choice produce as heave-offering for better produce is valid. We might think it should be invalid.] Said R. Bun bar Kahana in the name of Rabbi, "[The reason is that, when referring to the separation of heave-offering, Num. 18:32 states], 'And you shall bear no sin by reason of it, when you have offered the best of it [i.e., of your produce].' [The implication is that, if you do not separate the best, you have committed a sin.]

[B] "Since [a person who improperly separates heave-offering] has sinned, you know that his actions [in separating the offering] are deemed valid." [PM: If the actions were simply void, the individual could not be said to have sinned.]

Bun bar Kahana states that M. Ter. 2:6T derives from Scripture.

[III.A] [The reference is to M. Ter. 2:6U–V: rye-grass, which is *not* edible, may not be separated as heave-offering on behalf of wheat.] This means that anything which *is* edible, [no matter how low in quality], may be [separated as heave-offering on behalf of wheat, and the separation is valid].

The implication of M. Ter. 2:6U–V is drawn out.

[IV.A] Mishnah [Ter. 2:6T's rule, that if one separates produce of low quality as heave-offering for produce of better quality, the separation is valid], is the opinion of R. Ishmael b. R. Yose.

[B] For **R. Ishmael b. R. Yose said in the name of his father, "They may separate wine as heave-offering on behalf of vinegar, [which is of lower quality], but not vinegar [as heave-offering] on behalf of wine** [T. Ter. 4:6E].

[C] "If one transgressed and separated [vinegar as heave-offering for wine], that which he has separated is [valid] heave-offering, [just as M. Ter. 2:6T states]."

[D] [Disagreeing,] **Rabbi says, "Wine and vinegar are two distinct kinds** [of produce, such that] they may not separate heave-offering or tithes from one on behalf of the other." [And if one did so, the separation is not valid, contrary to M. Ter. 2:6T. See T. Ter. 4:7G.]

[E] Said R. Joshua b. Levi, "It is reasonable to assume that Rabbi agrees that, according to the Torah, [wine and vinegar are a single kind, such that a separation of heave-offering from one on behalf of the other should be valid].

[F] "What is the reason that Rabbi [states that they are two kinds, and that the separation is not valid at all]?

[G] "[The reason is] that, if you say [they are one kind, such that] it is permitted to separate wine as heave-offering on behalf of vinegar, someone might think that it also is permitted to separate vinegar as heave-offering on behalf of wine [de jure, which all agree one may not do]."

A + B–C is complete in itself. D + E–G is attached, as a dispute, because of its common issue, separating heave-offering from wine on behalf of vinegar or vice versa.

[V.A] *Cucumber and squash are a single kind.*

[B] *R. Judah says, "[They are] two [different] kinds"* [M. Ter. 2:6W–X].

[C] R. Judah's view is in accordance with the position he holds [elsewhere], and the rabbis' [anonymous] view is in accordance with the position they hold [elsewhere].

[D] For we have learned [M. Kil. 1:2]: *Cucumber and squash are not Diverse Kinds. [Therefore they may be planted together in a field].*

[E] *R. Judah says, "They are Diverse Kinds."*

The unit points out a correlation between the opinions of Judah and "sages" in two different contexts in M. Ter. 2:6W–X and M. Kil. 1:2.

3 Yerushalmi Terumot
Chapter Three

[A] *One who separates a chatemelon as heave-offering [for other chatemelons] and it is found to be bitter,*

[B] *[or who separates] a watermelon [as heave-offering for other watermelons] and it is found to be rotten—*

[C] *[that which he has separated is valid] heave-offering.*

[D] *But he must separate heave-offering again.*

[E] *One who separates a keg of wine as heave-offering [for other wine] and it is found to be vinegar—*

[F] *if it was known before he separated it as heave-offering that it was vinegar, [that which he has separated is] not [valid] heave-offering.*

[G] *But if it turned into vinegar after he separated it as heave-offering, lo, this is [valid] heave-offering.*

[H] *And if there is a doubt [whether or not it was vinegar when it was designated heave-offering, that which he has separated is valid] heave-offering.*

[I] *But he must separate heave-offering again.*

[J] *The first [produce separated as heave-offering at A–D and E + H–I] does not impose the status of heave-offering [upon other unconsecrated produce with which it is mixed] by itself [i.e., if it alone is mixed with other such produce].*

[K] *And [nonpriests who unintentionally eat it] are not required to pay back [its value and the added] fifth.*

[L]   *And so [is the case for] the second [produce separated as heave-offering].*

Produce separated as heave-offering turns out to be inedible. If it was inedible before it was designated the priest's due, the separation is not valid (F). The produce was not food and could not take on the status of heave-offering. If the produce went bad after it was designated heave-offering, however, the designation is valid (G). The priest bears the loss, for the produce already was his when it spoiled. The cases which are of interest in the Yerushalmi are those that involve a doubt, A–D and E + H–I. In such an instance, we must assume that the designation was valid. This is in case the food did not go bad until after it was separated as heave-offering. It might have gone bad before, however, and therefore the householder is required to separate heave-offering a second time (C–D, H–I). The Yerushalmi begins by asking why, for the case of the chatemelon, the first separation is valid. Since the chatemelon probably was bitter all along, it should not be. Unit **II** carries this forward. Units **III, IV,** and **VI** + **VII** work with the Tosefta's relevant materials. Unit **V** interrupts. Perhaps the most interesting of the present materials, it compares the rule of M. Ter. 3:1 with that of M. Ter. 2:2.

[**I.A**] [42a]   *One who separates a chatemelon as heave-offering [for other chatemelons] and it is found to be bitter—[that which he has separated is valid heave-offering, but he must separate heave-offering again; M. Ter. 3:1A].*

[B]   It makes sense [to say that if] a watermelon [is separated as heave-offering for other watermelons] and turns out to be rotten [that, while the person must separate heave-offering again, the original separation is valid, as M. Ter. 3:1C states. This is because we may assume that the watermelon did not become rotten until after it was designated heave-offering.]

[C]   But [in the case of] a chatemelon [separated as heave-offering for other chatemelons] which is found to be bitter, [it makes] no [sense to state that the separation is valid].

[D]   [It makes no sense, for] was [the chatemelon] not bitter [and so invalid for separation as heave-offering] from the start?

[E] [To explain M. Ter. 3:1C's rule,] said R. Yohanan, "They treat [the bitter chatemelon] as though it might be food." [Because of its ambiguous character, the chatemelon may validly be designated heave-offering, even though heave-offering will need to be separated a second time.]

[F] R. Jonah asked, "Do they deem all things [such as bitter chatemelons] possibly to be food [such that]: (1) they are rendered unclean like edibles, (2) [if they are rendered unclean and they are in the status of heave-offering] they must be burned, (3) [if they are heave-offering, a nonpriest who unintentionally eats them must pay their value plus] an added fifth, (4) [if they are in the status of second tithe] one receives [forty] stripes [for eating them] outside of the walls [of Jerusalem], and (5) if one makes an *erub* of them [it is a doubtful *erub* such that the person] becomes [like] one who drives an ass and a camel [at the same time; see M. Erub. 3:4]?" [Jonah's question is not answered.]

The problem posed by B–D is solved by Yohanan, E. Since the chatemelon might be a food, a designation of it to be heave-offering always is valid. This is the case even though heave-offering will need to be separated a second time, as M. Ter. 3:1D states. Jonah's question, F, is tacked on because, like Yohanan, he talks about produce that may or may not be edible. The issue is the restrictions which do, or do not, apply to that questionable food. But the relationship between E and F is tenuous and, indeed, Jonah's question is not answered. The problem of an *erub* the validity of which is in doubt (F5) is as follows. If the *erub* is valid, the man has acquired the right to move two thousand cubits in any direction from the point at which the *erub* was established. If the *erub* is not valid, he may move only within two thousand cubits of his home. If the validity of an *erub* established just beyond the Sabbath limit of the man's house is in doubt, the person cannot move at all, for by going either forward or back he is in danger of violating the restriction which limits movement on the holy day. In not being able to move at all, he is comparable to one who drives an ass and a camel at the same time. Since the ass will move only if urged from behind and the camel only if led, the individual will not be able to proceed at all.

[II.A]   There [we have learned]: Said R. Yohanan, "[As for] a loaf [of bread] about which there is a doubt whether or not it became unclean in private domain, [in which case the question of doubt is resolved stringently, and the bread is deemed unclean], and which one touched[1] in the public domain—[the person is deemed] unclean.

[B]   "But here [in a case in which we deal with a bitter chatemelon, or other things which, since they might not be edible, might not be subject to uncleanness at all], the person is deemed clean,

[C]   "for there are two questions of doubt [i.e., whether or not the food is susceptible to uncleanness, B, and, if it is, whether or not it actually was rendered unclean, A]."

If I have read the unit correctly (B), it is here because it refers to produce about which there is a doubt whether or not it is edible. This topic was introduced at unit I. Without the interpolation, required by context, the pericope makes no sense.

[III.A]   It is taught in the name of R. Yose [T. Ter. 4:5J–K]: **"You find nothing bitter in a chatemelon except for its inner part.** [The rest of the chatemelon is edible, such that it validly may be designated heave-offering.]

[B]   "What should [the householder] do [in order to make up for the inedible core of the chatemelon, which does not take on the status of heave-offering]?

[C]   **"He adds [other produce] to its outer part [to compensate for the bitter produce] and separates [i.e., designates, this additional food as heave-offering for the chatemelon]."**

[D]   R. Benjamin bar Levi asked, "[In the case of a question, such as whether or not the whole chatemelon is bitter], which it is possible to answer through a concrete test [i.e., taste], is it possible that sages [i.e., the anonymous authorities of M. Ter. 3:1A–B] would disagree with [Yose, by claiming that the whole melon is inedible? No, there is no disagreement over that question, which could be answered by tasting the chatemelon.]

[E]   "Rather, [Yose and sages] disagree concerning the need to examine [i.e., taste, each and every chatemelon]." [Yose holds that

chatemelons are assumed to be edible, and bitter only inside.
Sages rule that if the chatemelon is to be deemed edible at all, it
must be tasted.]

The material from the Tosefta relevant to M. Ter. 3:1A–D is
subject to analysis, D–E. The point is to discern the relationship between Yose's position and that of the Mishnah's anonymous authorities.

[IV.A] **If one separated a keg of wine as heave-offering [for other
wine] and it is found to have been left uncovered [such that it
might contain snake venom and is not fit for consumption,
M. Ter. 8:4], [or if one separated] a watermelon [as heave-
offering for other watermelons] and it is found to be punctured [with what might be teeth marks of snakes, such that the
watermelon may not be eaten, M. Ter. 8:6]—that which he
has separated is valid heave-offering, but he must separate
heave-offering again [T. Ter. 4:6A–D].**

[B] R. Yudan bar Pazzai [and] R. Simeon in the name of R. Joshua b.
Levi [say], "They did not state[2] [that what is designated heave-
offering is valid heave-offering] except [in a case in which the
produce is found to be] punctured [only after it was designated
heave-offering].

[C] "But de jure it is not permitted to separate as heave-offering
[watermelons that have puncture marks]."

[D] R. Jacob the Daromean asked in the presence of R. Yose, "Does
it not make sense [to state that the rule that de jure a person may
not separate as heave-offering a watermelon with puncture marks
applies only if] the person [actually] saw [a snake] biting [the
watermelon, such that he knows for certain that the punctures
are snake bites]?"

[E] [Yose] said to him, "[Even if the person sees the snake] does he
know whether or not [the snake] deposited venom [in the melon]?"
[Of course not. Therefore the person's seeing the snake does not
change anything. The same question of doubt about whether or
not there is venom in the watermelon arises without regard to
the person's seeing the snake. For this reason, as D suggests, a

punctured melon may not be designated heave-offering, even if
no one saw for certain that a snake made the marks.]

Interpretation of the Tosefta's material continues. B–C claims
that T. Ter. 4:6A–D makes the same point as M. Ter. 3:1E–I.
Since food that is suspected of containing snake venom may not be
eaten, a designation of it to be heave-offering is not valid, C. But
once produce has been designated validly, the fact that it is rendered forbidden for consumption does not void its status as heave-
offering, B. Jacob's criticism of B–C is countered by Yose, E.

[V.A]   Associates asked in the presence of R. Yose, "What is the difference between the present case, [M. Ter. 3:1, in which heave-
offering must be separated a second time] and that [of M. Ter.
2:2, in which a person separates] unclean [produce as heave-
offering for clean produce]?" [In that case the separation is valid
and heave-offering need not be separated a second time.]

[B]   He said to them, "[In the case of] unclean produce, the fact that
[the produce] is unclean prevents it [from being eaten, for a
priest may not eat unclean heave-offering. But the food is edible,
such that it may rightly have the status of heave-offering (GRA).]

[C]   "But here [in the case of produce that turns out to be bitter or
rotten, the food is comparable to] dust [which is not edible at
all]." [What is not edible may not be deemed heave-offering. For
this reason, the person must separate heave-offering again.]

The Yerushalmi analyzes seemingly comparable cases to discern
the theory that accounts for their different rules. This theory,
pointed out in the contrast between B and C, is that only what is
edible may have the status of heave-offering. A separation of
produce that is not edible, as at M. Ter. 3:1, does not yield a
valid priestly gift. The individual therefore must separate heave-
offering a second time.

[VI.A]   [Reference is to T. Ter. 4:7G–H. Rabbi holds that wine and vinegar are two distinct kinds of produce, such that heave-offering
may not be separated from one on behalf of the other. Sages

hold that they are one kind.] R. Jacob bar Aha in the name of
R. Yohanan [says], "The law follows the opinion of Rabbi."

[B]   [Claiming that Jacob bar Aha incorrectly transmits Yohanan's
statement,] R. Hiyya in the name of R. Yohanan [says], "[The
rule that vinegar may not be separated as heave-offering on behalf of wine, M. Ter. 3:1E–H] is the opinion of Rabbi." [But
Yohanan never explicitly stated that the law at T. Ter. 4:7G–H
follows the view of Rabbi.]

[C]   [Agreeing with B,] R. Ba bar Kohen asked in the presence of R.
Yose, "[Why should Yohanan have needed to state that the law
follows the opinion of Rabbi?] Has R. Hiyya not already stated
in the name of R. Yohanan, '[In a dispute between] Rabbi and
his associates, the law follows the opinion of Rabbi.'?" [Thus
Hiyya, B, must be right. Yohanan would not have made the obvious statement Jacob bar Aha attributes to him, A.]

[D]   [To support the contention of C] said R. Jonah, "Even [if Rabbi
is in dispute] with R. Eleazar b. R. Simeon [the law follows the
opinion of Rabbi]." [Therefore one never need state that the law
follows Rabbi.]

[E]   [Yose] said to him [i.e., Ba bar Kohen], "[Just as Jacob bar Aha
reports, A, Yohanan needed to state explicitly that the law follows the opinion of Rabbi. This is] because [the same rule concerning wine and vinegar] is taught by R. Ishmael b. R. Yose in
the name of his father, [T. Ter. 4:6E–G. Contrary to Rabbi,
Yose, Ishmael's father, holds that wine and vinegar are a single
kind.]

[F]   "Now [the fact is that] R. Yose [a different Amora from the one
speaking here at E–G] said in the name of R. Yohanan, '[In a
dispute between] R. Yose, [Ishmael's father], and his associates,
the law accords with the opinion of R. Yose, [Ishmael's father].'

[G]   "[This being the case] in order that you not think that even here
[concerning the law for wine and vinegar, A, the law follows the
opinion of R. Yose, Ishmael's father, Yohanan] needed to state
[explicitly] that the law accords with the opinion of Rabbi."
[Thus Jacob bar Aha, A, correctly reports this tradition in the
name of Yohanan.]

The Yerushalmi clarifies what Yohanan really said, A or B, by establishing what we logically could expect him to say, C–D vs. E–G. The assumption is that Yohanan would not state something that people could derive for themselves.

[VII.A]   R. Zeira [and] R. Jacob bar Idi in the name of R. Yohanan [say], "[In a dispute between] R. Meir and R. Simeon, the law follows the opinion of R. Simeon.

[B]   "[In a dispute between] R. Simeon and R. Judah, the law follows the opinion of R. Judah.

[C]   "[Thus] it is obvious [that in the case of a dispute between] R. Meir and R. Judah, the law follows the opinion of R. Judah."

[D]   R. Ba [and] R. Jacob bar Idi[3] in the name of R. Jonathan [say], "[In a dispute between] R. Meir and R. Simeon, the law follows the opinion of R. Simeon.

[E]   "[In a dispute between] R. Simeon and R. Judah, the law follows the opinion of R. Judah.

[F]   "And [thus] it is obvious [that in a dispute between] R. Meir, R. Judah, and R. Simeon, the law follows the opinion of R. Judah.

[G]   "And from this [conclusion, reached at F], you learn that [in the case of a dispute between] R. Judah and R. Simeon, the law follows the opinion of R. Judah [= E]."

Unit VI.C, D, and E spawn this pericope, which is irrelevant to the issues before us in M. Ter. 3:1. The unit consists of two versions of the same thing, A–C and D–F + G. PM resolves the redundancy of G and E by reading, at G, Meir instead of Simeon. This is hardly much of an improvement and has no support in editions and manuscripts.

3:2 [P: 3:1b]

[M]   *[If] one of them [i.e., of the quantities of produce separated as heave-offering at M. Ter. 3:1A–D or E + H–I] fell into unconsecrated produce, it does not impose the status of heave-offering [upon that produce (see M. Ter. 4:7)].*

[N]   *[If] the second [produce separated as heave-offering] fell else-*
       where, [i.e., into a different batch of unconsecrated produce], it
       does not impose the status of heave-offering [upon the mixture].

[O]   [But if] the two [quantities of produce separated as heave-offering]
       fell into the same place, [i.e., into the same batch of unconse-
       crated produce], they impose the status of heave-offering [upon
       that produce] in accordance with [the bulk of] the smaller of the
       two [quantities of produce separated as heave-offering].

The individual at M. Ter. 3:1 A–D separated two quantities of
heave-offering. This pericope establishes how the rules governing the disposition of heave-offering affect these two quantities
in a case in which they are mixed with unconsecrated produce.
True heave-offering imposes its own status upon unconsecrated
produce with which it is mixed (M. Ter. 4:7). The fact taken
into consideration here at M + N versus O is that both of the
quantities of produce the householder at M. Ter. 3:1 separated
cannot be true heave-offering.

The Yerushalmi, for its part, ignores the issue before us. It
asks a practical question, left open by the Mishnah, concerning
the disposition of the two quantities of heave-offering the householder separates. This problem is the procedure employed in
giving these two quantities of heave-offering to the priest.

[I.A]   What does [someone who, in accordance with the rule of M.
         3:1A–D, has separated heave-offering twice] do [with the two
         quantities of heave-offering]?

[B]   He gives both of them to a priest, and the priest pays him the
       value of one of them.

[C]   For which of them does the priest give the value, the larger or
       the smaller [quantity of heave-offering]?[4]

[D]   [We know the answer] from what is taught [at M. 3:2O: *If the*
       two quantities of heave-offering fell into the same batch of un-
       consecrated produce], they impose the status of heave-offering
       [upon that unconsecrated produce] in accordance with [the bulk
       of] the smaller of the two [quantities of produce separated as
       heave-offering].

[E]   This indicates that [the priest] pays him the value of the larger quantity of heave-offering. [As in the case at D, the smaller one is treated as true heave-offering, for which the priest does not pay.]

M. Ter. 3:2O, cited at D, provides an answer to the question left open by M. Ter. 3:1A–D. We assume that the smaller of the two batches of produce is true heave-offering. The priest must be given the larger quantity of produce as well, in case it is heave-offering. But since it might not be, he pays the householder for it, E.

3:3 [P: 3:2a]

[A]   *Partners who separated heave-offering [from the same commonly owned produce] one after the other—*

[B]   *R. Aqiba says, "That which was separated by both of them is [valid] heave-offering."*

[C]   But sages say, "[Only] that which was separated by the first is [valid] heave-offering."

[D]   *R. Yose says, "If the first [partner] separated the required measure [of heave-offering; see M. Ter. 4:3], that which was separated by the second [partner] is not [valid] heave-offering.*

[E]   *"But if the first [partner] did not separate the required measure [of heave-offering], that which was separated by the second [partner] is [also valid] heave-offering."*

The issue is the meaning of joint ownership. Aqiba holds that each partner has full ownership in one half of the produce. The first partner therefore validly separates heave-offering from his half alone (as unit **II** points out). The second partner may do the same. Sages have a different theory. They claim that the partners jointly own the whole batch. Either one of them may validly separate the heave-offering required of all of the produce. Once he does so, moreover, the batch is exempt from the further separation of the priestly gift. Since heave-offering may not be separated twice from the same batch, the second partner's separation is not valid. Yose, D–E, qualifies this view. He holds that if the

first partner separated less than the normal amount, the batch
still is susceptible to the separation of heave-offering. In this case
what the second parnter separates is valid heave-offering.

The Yerushalmi is unusually aware of the basic issue suggested by the Mishnah. This is indicated by the way in which its
materials are set out. We begin, unit **I**, with the central dispute
between Aqiba and the sages. Unit **II** describes the implications
of Aqiba's theory that each partner separates heave-offering only
for that portion of the produce over which he has full ownership.
The final unit turns to Yose's view and analyzes its relationship to
the position of sages. As my own interpretation indicates, it is
exactly in the context of the sages' opinion that Yose's statement
makes sense.

[I.A]   What [case] are we talking about [at M. Ter. 3:3, in which Aqiba
and sages disagree whether or not both partners' separations of
heave-offering are valid]?

[B]   If it is [a case of partners who are] careful (*mmḥyn*, so PM) [about
their joint ventures, it is obvious that they would not intend both
to separate heave-offering from the same produce. The dispute
cannot concern this case, for here] even R. Aqiba would agree
[with the sages, that if they both should separate heave-offering,
only the separation of the first is valid. The separation of the
second was in error and not valid.]

[C]   [But] if it is [a case of partners who are] not careful [about coor-
dinating their activities, they probably do not object to both separating heave-offering from the same batch. The dispute of M.
Ter. 3:3 cannot concern this case, for here] even the sages would
agree [with Aqiba that both of their separations of heave-offering
are valid].

[D]   Rather, we are talking about [a case of] average [partners. In the
case of such partners, Aqiba and the sages disagree.]

[E]   R. Aqiba [M. Ter. 3:3B] holds that average [partners] are not
careful [in their dealings with one another. He therefore claims
that if both separate heave-offering from the same produce, both
separations are valid, as above at C.]

[F]   But sages [M. Ter. 3:3C] hold that average [partners] are careful
[and would not desire both to separate heave-offering from the

same produce, as above at B. If they do, only that which the first separates is valid heave-offering.]

The Yerushalmi's theory is that both separations of heave-offering will or will not be valid depending upon what the partners had hoped to separate as heave-offering. If it is clear that they do not mind having heave-offering separated twice from the same produce, then both separations are valid, C. But if they desired to have heave-offering separated only once, then as soon as this is accomplished, the separation performed by the second partner cannot be valid, B. These facts, according to the Yerushalmi, are clear both to Aqiba and the sages, M. Ter. 3:3B + C. Their dispute refers to a case of partners who have not explicitly established whether or not they will permit heave-offering to be separated twice from their commonly owned produce, D. Aqiba holds that the case of such partners is to be adjudicated as at C. Sages state that they are like the individuals at B. The Yerushalmi thus claims that Aqiba and the sages do not disagree concerning the character of the law but only as regards its application in a case of ambiguity.

[II.A]   [The Yerushalmi explains that when Aqiba states that both partners' separations of heave-offering are valid, he means that each partner validly has separated heave-offering for that half of the commonly owned produce he rightfully can claim as his. Thus only half of what he separates has the status of true heave-offering.] In the opinion of R. Aqiba, the *seah* [of heave-offering separated] by the first [partner is composed] half of unconsecrated, untithed produce and half of produce in the status of heave-offering that [nonetheless] is subject to the separation of tithes. [PM: it is subject to tithes because it is much less than the minimum required quantity of heave-offering (M. Ter. 4:3). Therefore it is not treated as true heave-offering, which is not subject to tithes.]

[B]   The *seah* [of heave-offering separated] by the second [partner is composed] half of produce in the status of heave-offering and half of unconsecrated, untithed produce that is subject to the separation of all [of the agricultural offerings. The half in the status of heave-offering is not subject to tithes for, together with the first partner's heave-offering, it constitutes all of the priestly gift required of the produce.]

[C]   This [analysis of Aqiba's position is obvious and] needs [to be stated] only [to serve as the basis for the following question]:

[D]   [As for] the half *seah* [of produce validly separated as heave-offering] by the second [partner]—what is the rule [whether or not] it serves as the heave-offering required of the half *seah* [of produce separated] by the first [partner, which is subject to the separation of heave-offering? That is, does the heave-offering separated by the second partner comprise the priestly gift required of the untithed produce the first partner separated from the batch but which retained its untithed, unconsecrated status?]

[E]   Let us answer [this question] on the basis of the following:

[F]   Ariston brought out produce [to tithe it] and, having [unintentionally] left some of it in the sack, separated heave-offering [only from the produce he removed from the sack].

[G]   The case came before R. Yose, [to rule whether or not the produce designated as heave-offering serves also as the heave-offering required of the fruit that was left in the sack]. And he said, "The assumption is that he separated heave-offering on behalf of all[5] [of the produce, including that which he had forgotten in the sack]." [The implication is that also in the case of the two partners, that which the second separates as heave-offering serves as the priestly due required of the produce separated from the batch by the first partner, but which still is in an untithed state. Even though this produce was not physically present in the batch, we assume that the second partner intended to separate heave-offering on behalf of all of the untithed produce he jointly owned.]

The implications of Aqiba's view, M. Ter. 3:3B, are drawn out, A–B. C + D–G introduce and answer a secondary question left open by A–B.

[III.A]   [Yose, M. Ter. 3:3D, states that the second partner's separation is not valid if the first partner already had separated the required measure of heave-offering.] What [does Yose mean by "required measure"]?

[B]   [Does he mean] the measure established by the Torah [i.e., one-fiftieth of the batch; see M. Ter. 4:3D and T. Ter. 5:8A–G]?

[C]   Or [does he mean] the measure usually separated by this person's associates [i.e., him and his partner]?

[D]   If we say [that Yose means] the measure established by Torah, then Yose's [reason for claiming that only the first partner's separation of heave-offering is valid] is not the same as the rabbis' [reason for stating the same thing, M. Ter. 3:3C. Yose's reason is that after the first person separates heave-offering, no more of the batch has the potential, upon designation, of taking on the status of heave-offering.[6] The rabbis' reason is that each partner individually controls the whole batch. Once either of the partners separates heave-offering in any amount, he has exempted the whole batch from the further separation of heave-offering. This is the case even though the partner has designated so little heave-offering that, theoretically, more of the priestly gift could be designated from that same batch. See M. Ter. 4:3I–K.]

[E]   If we say [that Yose means] the measure normally separated by the person's associates, the opinion of R. Yose is the same as that of the rabbis. [If this is the case, Yose, like the rabbis, M. Ter. 3:3C, holds simply that each partner controls the whole batch. Once the partner separates heave-offering in any quantity usual for him, he exempts the whole batch from the further separation of heave-offering. Now the second partner cannot go back and separate heave-offering again. Which alternative is correct, D or E, is not indicated.]

A–C describes the possible meanings of Yose's position, M. Ter. 3:3D. D–E goes on to indicate the logical relationships between the views of Yose and the sages (M. Ter. 3:3C) that B–C's alternatives would suggest. The question of what Yose's view really means remains unanswered.

3:4 [P: 3:2b]

[F]   *In which case does the opinion [of Aqiba, M. Ter. 3:3B, that both partners' separations of heave-offering are valid] apply?*

[G]   *[It applies in a case] in which neither [of the partners] conferred [with the other. Since they had made no provision to have only one of them separate heave-offering, both of them may do so validly.]*

[H]   *But:*

[I]   *[In a case in which one] gave permission to a member of his household, to his slave, or to his maidservant to separate heave-offering—*

[J]   *that which that individual separates is [valid] heave-offering.*

[K]   *[If he] retracted [the permission]—*

[L]   *if he retracted it before [the other individual] separated heave-offering—that which [that individual] has separated is not [valid] heave-offering.*

[M]   *But if he retracted [it] after [the other person] separated heave-offering—that which [that individual] has separated is [valid] heave-offering.*

[N]   *Workers do not [automatically] have permission to separate heave-offering [from a householder's produce with which they are working],*

[O]   *except for those who tread [the grapes or olives in the tank],*

[P]   *for they at once impart to the tank [susceptibility to] unclean-ness. [The desire is to separate heave-offering before the wine in the tank actually becomes unclean.]*

The Yerushalmi concentrates upon I–P, the simple point of which is that a person may designate an agent to separate heave-offering on his behalf (I–J). This designation may be revoked, so long as this is done before the heave-offering actually is separated, K–M. Once the separation is validly performed, it may not retroactively be deemed invalid. Finally, N–P, certain work-ers are presumed to have permission from their employer to sepa-rate heave-offering on his behalf. This is so in a case in which the normal accomplishment of their task necessitates the separa-tion of heave-offering, for example, if they will render unclean the produce with which they work, P.

The Yerushalmi's first question is how one revokes the designa-tion of an agent. The other four units deal with the circumstances under which workers may and may not separate heave-offering on behalf of their employer. On the whole, these units constitute an extended commentary to those materials in Tosefta Terumot which correspond to this pericope of the Mishnah.

[**I.A**]   Now does this [rule, M. Ter. 3:4K, which states that a house-holder may nullify the permission he gave to another to separate heave-offering on his behalf,] not disagree with the opinion of Resh Laqish?[7]

[B]   For Resh Laqish says, "Through words a person may not void [his assignment of another to be] his agent."

[C]   Resolve the [apparent] contradiction by [claiming that M. Ter. 3:4K refers to a case in which the householder] told the [agent], "Go designate [heave-offering] in the northern portion [of the heap of produce]," but [instead the agent] went and designated it in the southern portion. [The agent's own actions caused his appointment to be canceled. Resh Laqish agrees with M. Ter. 3:4K that in this manner the householder's appointment of an agent is nullified.]

The inconsistency pointed out at A–B is resolved at C. The agent's separation is not valid, for he did not carry out the terms of his agency. The householder did not need to say anything in order to revoke the appointment of the agent.

[**II.A**]   [To explain why M. Ter. 3:4N–P states that workers may separate the heave-offering required of a vat of wine,] said R. Yohanan, "[As for] those who tread [the grapes]—once they have tread them warp and woof, they forthwith render [the grapes] unclean." [The workers are allowed to separate heave-offering on behalf of the householder so that the priestly gift will be separated before the wine is rendered unclean.]

We assume that the householder desires to have heave-offering separated from clean produce. His workers therefore are presumed to have his permission to separate heave-offering on his behalf before they render the wine unclean. For purposes of this separation of heave-offering they are deemed their employer's agents.

[**III.A**]   [M. Ter. 3:4O–P states that workers may separate heave-offering from the vat because, once they start treading, the produce becomes susceptible to uncleanness.] But is not [the contrary] taught [at T. Ter. 1 : 8]: **Workers who separated the heave-offering of the vat—that which they separate is not [valid] heave-offering.**

[B]   **But if it was a small vat, or if other householders would touch it [and render it unclean]—that which they separate is** (delete: not)[8] **[valid] heave-offering.**

[C]   Lo, [the workers' separation of heave-offering is valid] if others would touch [the vat so as to render it unclean].

[D]   [If] others do not touch [the vat], that which [the workers] separate is not [valid] heave-offering. [This is contrary to M. Ter. 3 : 4O–P, which states that workers may always separate heave-offering from the vat.]

[E]   What accounts for the difference [between the two rulings]?

[F]   This [rule, at M. Ter. 3 : 4O–P, where the workers are always allowed to separate heave-offering for the householder, refers] to [a vat of] wine.

[G]   This [rule, at T. Ter. 1 : 8, which states that workers do not automatically have permission to separate heave-offering, refers] to [a vat of] oil.

[H]   Are not [the rules for the separation of heave-offering from] wine and oil the same?

[I]   [No.] Wine is likely to be made unclean, [for people stand around the vat testing the vintage].

[J]   Oil is not likely to be made unclean, [for people do not normally stand around the vat. In the case of oil, therefore, even though the produce in the tank becomes susceptible to uncleanness, workers may not separate heave-offering for the householder, for there is little likelihood that the oil, while susceptible to uncleanness, will actually be rendered unclean.]

A contradiction between the Mishnah and the Tosefta is pointed out, A–D, and resolved, E + F–G. Since wine is likely to be rendered unclean, I, workers may separate heave-offering from it on behalf of the householder, M. Ter. 3 : 4O–P. Since oil is not likely to be rendered unclean, J, there is no need for the workers to separate heave-offering from it. Therefore they may not do so, T. Ter. 1:8. The only exception is a case in which there is some special concern for the cleanness of the oil, for example, if many people make use of the same vat, B.

[IV.A]   It is taught [T. Ter. 3:12]: **As of when may they separate the heave-offering required of the grapes in [the vat]?**

[B]   **From the time that they have trampled them warp and woof.** [At this point the processing of the wine is considered sufficiently complete. See M. Ter. 1:10.]

[C]   **As of when may they render it [i.e., the wine in the vat] unclean?**

[D]   **The House of Shammai say, "After second' tithe has been removed."** [The Shammaites hold that second tithe must be separated from clean produce.]

[E]   **The House of Hillel say, "After first tithe has been removed."** [Second tithe may be separated in uncleanness.]

[F]   **Said R. Yose** [T. Ter. 3:12: Judah], **"The law is according to the opinion of the House of Shammai, but the majority of people behave according to the opinion of the House of Hillel."**

[G]   Said R. Simeon, "The opinion of the House of Shammai appears [correct] for the period in which the Temple [still stood. Since second tithe was to be eaten in cleanness in Jerusalem, it should have been separated in cleanness.] But the opinion of the House of Hillel appears [correct] for the present time." [After the destruction of the Temple, second tithe is separated but may not be eaten at all. It therefore is of no concern that it is separated from unclean produce, E.]

[H]   **But sages say, "[The law]** does not follow the opinion of this one or that one [i.e., neither the Hillelites or the Shammaites]. Rather, **one separates heave-offering and heave-offering of the tithe and forthwith renders the vat unclean."**

Yerushalmi's contribution to Tosefta's discussion is at G. The material develops the preceding discussions.

[V.A] **As of when may they separate the heave-offering required of olives**[10] [T. Ter. 3:13]?

[B] There are those who teach, **"From the time that they have been ground"** [= Simeon, T. Ter. 3:13].

[C] And there are those who teach, **"From the time that they have been pressed, [an earlier stage in their processing";** T. Ter. 3:13].

[D] [The opinion of] the one who says, "From the time they have been pressed," is logical, [for according to it heave-offering should be separated early in the olives' processing, before they might be rendered unclean].

[E] [42b] [But] as for the one who said, "From the time they are ground"—[his view is unacceptable. For] did not R. Yohanan say, "[As for] those who tread [the produce in the vat]—once they have trodden warp and woof, forthwith they render [the produce in] the vat unclean?" [According to the one who says, "Ground," the heave-offering thus is separated improperly, from unclean produce.]

[F] Rather, [contrary to E, the opinion of the one who says, "Ground," B, is logical. For while] this [statement of Yohanan] refers to wine, [which is rendered unclean early in its processing], this [one who says, "Ground,"] refers to oil, [which, as we shall now see, is not rendered unclean early in its processing].

[G] Are not [the rules for separating heave-offering from] wine and oil the same?

[H] What is the difference whether it is wine or oil?

[I] [As for] wine—it is likely that it will be rendered unclean. [Therefore, heave-offering is separated from it early in its processing and, as Yohanan says, forthwith the wine in the vat may be rendered unclean.]

[J] [As for] oil—it is not likely that it will be rendered unclean, [as above Y. Ter. 3:4 **III**. Therefore the workers themselves do not render the oil unclean, and heave-offering is separated from it at a late stage in its processing.]

[K] Said R. Hiyya bar Adda, "In both [the case of wine and oil] it is likely that the produce will be rendered unclean."

[L]   "But it is more likely that the wine will be rendered unclean than that the oil will be."

[M]   [The following is a second dispute on when heave-offering is separated from olives. Yose, M, agrees with C, above, that it is separated early in the olives' processing. N–P indicates why he is wrong and argues that, as B and J state, it must be taken at a late stage in their processing.] It is taught [T. Ter. 3:13]: **R. Yose b. R. Judah says, "If one wishes, he brings olives [in a basket] and places them in the press and presses them warp and woof [and forthwith separates heave-offering from them]."**

[N]   **[To indicate why this is impossible,] they said to him: "[The law for] olives is not like that for grapes.**

[O]   **"Grapes are soft and let their wine ooze out [easily].** [Therefore heave-offering may be separated from them early on.]

[P]   **"Olives are hard and do not let their oil ooze out [easily]."** [For this reason the householder must wait until a late stage in their processing to separate heave-offering from them.]

At D–J + K–L, the Yerushalmi explains the reason for the two different opinions cited at T. Ter. 3:13, given here at A–C. Heave-offering may be separated from olives at a late stage in their processing, since they are not likely to be rendered unclean. In this way they differ from wine. M–P cites the Tosefta to suggest a quite different reason that heave-offering is separated from olives at a late stage in their processing. The reason is that, unlike grapes, the preparation of olives may not be considered complete until late in the process of pressing.

3:5 [P: 3:3a]

[A]   *[As for] one who says, "The heave-offering [required] of this heap [of produce] is within it," or "Its tithes are within it," [or] "Its heave-offering of the tithe is within it"—*

[B]   *R. Simeon says, "He has [validly] designated [these agricultural offerings]."*

[C]   *But sages say, "[He has not validly designated these things] unless he says '[They are] in its [i.e., the heap's] northern portion,' or '[They are] in its southern portion.'"*

[D]   R. Eleazar Hisma says, "One who says, 'The heave-offering of
this heap [is separated] from it, for it' has [validly] designated
[the heave-offering]."

[E]   R. Eliezer b. Jacob says, "One who says, 'A tenth of this [first]
tithe is made heave-offering of the tithe for it [i.e., for all of the
first tithe]' has [validly] designated it."

Before he actually separates heave-offering, the individual must
indicate where in the batch the offering is located. This act of
designation concentrates the holy offering, previously spread
evenly throughout the produce, into one particular area so that it
may be physically separated. Simeon and the sages dispute the
requirements of a valid designation. Simeon says it is sufficient
for the individual to state that the heave-offering is found within
one batch of produce and not in some other. In his physical act
of separating the offering he will indicate exactly what produce is
the priestly gift. Sages hold that the designation must be more
specific, accomplishing the purpose which Simeon reserves for
the physical separation. Eleazar Hisma and Eliezer b. Jacob
agree with Simeon and simply offer slight variations in what the
individual may say validly to designate heave-offering or heave-
offering of the tithe. The Yerushalmi ignores their views.
    Unit I gives the Yerushalmi's interpretation of Simeon's view.
It claims that, according to Simeon, the designation is valid but
that it causes the whole batch of produce to become a mixture
of heave-offering and unconsecrated produce. Unit II quibbles
about the meaning of Simeon's view. After dealing with the sages'
opinion, unit III, we turn again to that of Simeon units IV–VII.
His position is illustrated through cases in which the individual
does not know, or forgets, where he designated heave-offering.

[I.A]   R. Yose b. R. Bun in the name of R. Yohanan [said], "R. Simeon's
[opinion at M. Ter. 3:5B, that one validly designates heave-
offering and tithes simply by stating that they are within the
batch of produce] is just like [the opinion of] the House of Shammai.

[B]   "For [11] [at M. Ter. 1:4] the House of Shammai say [that if one
separates olives as heave-offering for olive oil, the heave-offering
required of the olives themselves is in that which he has separated, but that which was separated for the oil is not valid heave-

offering, such that as a result, what the person has designated as] the holy [heave-offering] is a mixture of heave-offering and unconsecrated produce.

[C]   "In the same way R. Simeon holds [that an individual who states that the heave-offering required of a batch of produce is within that produce renders] the holy [heave-offering] a mixture of heave-offering and unconsecrated produce." [Since the individual did not indicate where in the batch the heave-offering is located, all of the batch is a mixture of heave-offering and unconsecrated produce.]

The Yerushalmi suggests a unity between the legal principle of Simeon, M. Ter. 3:5B, and the Shammaites, M. Ter. 1:4C.

[II.A]   Up to now [we have assumed that Simeon, M. Ter. 3:5A–B, intends that a person validly designates heave-offering only] if he states [that the offering is] *within* [the heap].

[B]   [If the individual] says [simply that the offering is] *in* [the heap], what [would Simeon hold, that he had or had not validly designated the offering]?

[C]   Let us learn [the answer] from the following [T. M.S. 3:17]:

[D]   **[If a person said], "The second tithe which is *in* this produce is exchanged for these coins, [such that the coins take on the status of second tithe, and the requirement that second tithe be separated from the produce is fulfilled]," but did not designate [the second tithe to be in a particular place within the produce]—**

[E]   **R. Simeon says, "He [validly] has designated [the second tithe within the produce and, at the same time, has effected the exchange, such that the coins now are in the status of second tithe]."**

[F]   **But sages say, "His statement is null, unless he indicates [that the second tithe the status of which he desires to transfer to coins] is located [specifically] in the northern or southern section [of the heap]."**

[G]   This indicates that [according to Simeon] it is all the same [whether one says] "within," [as at A] or "in," [as at D. In either case the designation is valid.]

[H]   (Delete: The words of sages.)

The secondary question concerning Simeon's position, A–B, is answered on the basis of T. M.S. 3:17, C + D–E. F is irrelevant in the present context.

[III.A]   R. Zeira[12] in the name of R. Abudimi of Haifa in the name of R. Simeon b. Laqish [derived from Num. 18:27–28 the rule that, to be valid, a designation of heave-offering must indicate precisely where in the heap of produce the offering is located]: "'And your offering shall be reckoned to you' . . . 'and you shall separate [a gift to the Lord].'

[B]   "Just as 'reckoning' implies a specific [location], so 'separating' implies a specific [location]."

Zeira claims that the view of the sages, M. Ter. 3:5C, derives from Scripture.

[IV.A]   [If] he said, "The heave-offering required of this and that [heap of produce] is in this [heap]"—

[B]   Said R. Yohanan, "Wherever he designates the heave-offering of the one heap, there is located the heave-offering of the other [heap, even though he does not specifically say where the heave-offering of the second heap is located]."

[C]   R. Isaac bar R. Eleazar asked, "[In light of what you have said, is it the case that if] a *seah* of heave-offering fell into a heap of produce [containing more than one hundred *seahs*, such that the heave-offering simply is removed from the heap (see M. Ter. 4:7),] and one said, 'The heave-offering [required] of this heap is within it' [but did not specify where], that wherever the first heave-offering had fallen, there is located as well the heave-offering required of the heap, [which he orally designated]?" [The question is not answered.]

This secondary problem assumes the validity of Simeon's position, M. Ter. 3:5B, that a designation of heave-offering is valid even if it does not indicate precisely where in the batch the heave-offering is located.

[V.A]   **[If] a person said, "The heave-offering required of this heap [of produce] is [located] in its northern section"—**

[B]   **"The half of it [i.e., of the heap] on the northern side is a mixture of heave-offering and unconsecrated produce"—the words of Rabbi.**

[C]   [According to Rabbi] let [the man] take [as heave-offering] half [of the heap].

[D]   **"But sages say, "He marks it [i.e., the heap] out in the form of [the Greek letter] *Chi* [i.e., an '*X*']."**

[E]   [According to sages he must take as heave-offering] one-fourth [of the batch].

[F]   **Rabban Simeon b. Gamaliel says, "He takes the heave-offering from its most northern part" [T. Ter. 4:9].**

[G]   [This means that he takes as heave-offering] one-eighth.

The Tosefta's issue is the effect of a householder's statement that the heave-offering required of a batch is located in the batch's northern portion (= sages, M. Ter. 3:5C). How much of the batch must now be deemed to have the status of heave-offering? The Yerushalmi interprets the positions of the cited authorities as forming a numerical progression, with Rabbi's one-half followed by the sages' one-fourth and Simeon b. Gamaliel's one-eighth.

[VI.A]   [As for one who designated the heave-offering required of] two heaps [of produce] in one [of the heaps, but it is not known in which]—what [is the law]?

[B]   R. Yohanan says, "[That which he has designated to be] the holy [heave-offering] is a mixture of heave-offering and unconsecrated produce." [Since we do not know where in the two batches the

heave-offering is located, we must treat all of the produce as a
mixture of heave-offering and unconsecrated produce.]

[C]   R. Simeon b. Laqish says, "[That which he has designated] the
holy [heave-offering] is not a mixture of heave-offering and unconsecrated produce." [The reason is that, for the case of each
heap, we may claim that the heave-offering is in the other heap.
Therefore neither alone need be treated as a mixture of heave-
offering and unconsecrated produce; see M. Ter. 3:1-2].

The issue again is the effect of an ambiguous designation of heave-
offering, a topic suggested by the Mishnah.

[VII.A]   Said R. Hoshaya b. R. Shammai, "[If] there were before him
two *seahs* [of produce] and one heap [of produce] and he said,
'One of these [two] *seahs* of produce is designated heave-offering
on behalf of [the produce in] the heap,' he has sanctified [both
of] them [to be heave-offering], but he does not know which of
them [is the heave-offering].

[B]   "[If] there were before him two heaps [of produce] and a single
seah [of produce] and he said, 'Lo, this [*seah* of produce] is designated heave-offering on behalf of [one of] the heaps,' [one of
the heaps] has been set right [i.e., heave-offering has been designated on its behalf], but he does not know which one."

A's case is like those which have preceded but is adjudicated according to a different theory. It deems the ambiguous designation to have been valid for all of the questionable produce. This
differs from previous cases in which the ambiguous designation
created a mixture of heave-offering and unconsecrated produce
(cf., Y. Ter. 3:5 VI). B, the converse of A, leaves a doubt as to
which batch has had its heave-offering separated.

3:6 [P: 3:3b; M. Ter. 3:6-7]

[A]   *[As for] one who separates (1) heave-offering before first fruits,
(2) first tithe before heave-offering, (3) or second tithe before
first [tithe],*

[B]   *even though he transgresses a negative commandment,*

[C]   *that which he has done is done [and valid];*

[D]   *as it is written, 'You shall not delay to offer from the fullness of your harvest and from the outflow of your presses' [Ex. 22:29].*

[E]¹³   *And from where [do we know] that first fruits should be separated before heave-offering,*

[F]   *for this [i.e., heave-offering] is called "heave-offering" [Num. 18:11] and "first" [Num. 18:12],*

[G]   *and this [i.e., first fruits] is called "heave-offering" [Dt. 12:6] and "first" [Ex. 23:19].*

[H]   *Still, first fruits should be separated first, for they are the first fruits of all [produce].*

[I]   *And [they should separate] heave-offering before first [tithe],*

[J]   *since it [i.e., heave-offering] is called "first."*

[K]   *And [they should separate] first tithe before second [tithe],*

[L]   *since it [i.e., first tithe] has in it [an offering called] "first" [i.e., heave-offering of the tithe].*

The householder must separate agricultural offerings in a set order: first fruits, heave-offering, first tithe, second tithe. The reason is that if he does not, but separates for instance first tithe before heave-offering, the first tithe still will be subject to the separation of heave-offering and not yet fit for consumption by a Levite. This confusing state of affairs is to be avoided. If the householder disregards the correct order, however, his separations are valid, C, for validity depends upon the proper separation of each gift and not upon the order in which the gifts are separated.

The central issues for the Yerushalmi are, unit **I**, why the individual's separation is deemed valid, and, unit **II**, what is his punishment for transgressing? Unit **III** asks at what point in the sequence of separating the offerings is the individual deemed to have transgressed, a question which follows logically from unit **II**. Units **IV** and **V** turn to secondary matters, first an ambiguous case and then a discussion of the pertinent materials in the Tosefta.

[I.A]   R. Hamma bar Uqbah in the name of R. Yose b. R. Hanina
[says], "From the fact that [one who separates agricultural offerings in the wrong order is deemed to have] transgressed a negative commandment [M. Ter. 3:6B], you know that his actions [in
separating the offerings improperly] are valid [as M. Ter. 3:6C
states]." [If the actions were null, the individual could not be
deemed to have transgressed.]

[B]   [Continuing his thought] R. Hamma bar Uqbah in the name of
R. Yose b. R. Hanina says, "[For his transgression, the individ-
ual] receives the [forty] stripes."

[C]   [Suggesting that Hamma is wrong about the stripes,] said R.
Zeira, "They asked [about this] in the presence of R. Yohanan
and he was silent, [suggesting that the stripes are not inflicted]."

At A, Hamma bar Uqbah explains M. Ter. 3:6C on the basis
of M. Ter. 3:6B. B–C is loosely related. In light of B's attribution to A's authority, I assume that it is intended as the conclusion of this unit. It introduces the materials which follow in the
Yerushalmi.

[II.A]   What is the transgression [referred to at M. Ter. 3:6B]?

[B]   [Is it one for which] he receives [the forty] stripes, or for which
he does not receive the [forty] stripes?

[C]   R. Jacob bar Aha in the name of R. Yohanan came [and said],
"He does not receive stripes."

[D]   [Yohanan, C, holds that no stripes are inflicted because he does
not believe that the point of Ex. 22:29 is that one who separates
agricultural offerings in the wrong order has transgressed, contrary to M. Ter. 3:6B–D.] How [then] does R. Yohanan interpret [the verse], 'You shall not delay to offer from the fullness of
your harvest and from the outflow of your presses?'

[E]   He says it refers [not to the order in which agricultural offerings
are to be separated but] to the removal [from the householder's
domain of all tithes he has separated; see Dt. 26:12–15 and M.
M.S. 5:6–15]. [Yohanan holds that the verse adjures people to
carry out the removal at its proper time, not to separate the offerings in any set order. He therefore does not believe that one

who separates the offerings in the wrong order has transgressed
and is subject to stripes, as C says.]

Yohanan's position is given, C, and explained, D–E.

[III.A]   At what point [in an individual's separating agricultural offerings
in the wrong order] is he deemed to have transgressed?

[B]   R. Hiyya bar Ba says, "From the beginning [i.e., as soon as he
separates heave-offering without first having designated first
fruits]."

[C]   R. Samuel bar R. Isaac says, "At the end [i.e., only after the
person separates all of the offerings, and does so in the wrong
order, is he deemed to have transgressed]."

[D]   What [case might occur which would be adjudicated in] different [ways, depending upon which of] these [views, B or C, one
holds]?

[E]   These [views lead to] distinct [results] in [a case in which, for
example, an individual separates heave-offering first, but before
he separates first fruits] the produce burns up.

[F]   In the opinion of R. Hiyya bar Ba, [in such a case] the individual has transgressed, [for he already has separated one offering at
the wrong time, as at B].

[G]   In the opinion of R. Samuel bar R. Isaac, [in such a case] the
individual has not transgressed, [since he has not yet reached the
end of the sequence in which offerings are separated, C].

D + E–G indicates the practical implications of the different
explanations of M. Ter. 3:6 recorded at A + B–C. Neither view
derives from an exegesis of the Mishnah.

[IV.[14]A]   R. Samuel bar Abba asked, "[As for] first tithe which they went
ahead and separated while the produce still was [unprocessed]
in stalks, [such that it was not yet subject to the separation of
heave-offering at all, M. Ter. 1:10]—

[B]   has the person who did this transgressed [by separating agricultural offerings in the wrong order] or has he not transgressed?
[The question is not answered.]

The case covers a gray area in the law. The individual separates
first tithe before heave-offering. Yet at the point at which he does
so, the produce is not yet subject to the priestly gift. The question of whether or not this constitutes separating agricultural
offerings in the wrong order is not answered.

[V.A]   They taught in the presence of R. Abbahu, "**[The separation
of] heave-offering does not hinder [i.e., prevent] the [subse-
quent separation of] first fruits**" [T. Ter. 4:10F].

[B]   He said to them, "[This statement derives] from Abba Penimon."

[C]   R. Yose asked, "What [is the case] of which Abba Penimon
[spoke]?"

[D]   Said to him R. Mana, "I heard [my] father teach, '[If one had
separated heave-offering and first fruits at one and the same
time, such that] he had first fruits in his right hand and heave-
offering in his left, [what is the law]?

[E]   "'There are those who teach that he has transgressed, [since he
did not designate first fruits before he separated heave-offering].

[F]   "'[And] there are those who teach that he has not transgressed,
[since the heave-offering was not separated before the first fruits
were designated].

[G]   "'The ones who say he has transgressed are the rabbis.

[H]   "'The one who says that he has not transgressed is Abba
Penimon.'"

The unit is intended as an exegesis of T. Ter. 4:10F, cited at A.
But I do not see how the statement attributed to Abba Penimon
at F + H explains the view attributed to him at A–B. A–B and
D–H appear to be separate units, artificially joined by C.

3:7 [P: 3:4; M. Ter. 3:8]

[A]   *(1) One who [in designating agricultural gifts] intends to say, "Heave-offering," but says, "Tithe," [or intends to say] "Tithe," but says, "Heave-offering;"*

[B]   *(2) [or who, in designating a sacrifice intends to say], "Burnt-offering," but says, "Peace-offering," [or, intends to say] "Peace-offering," but says, "Burnt-offering;"*

[C]   *(3) [or who, in making a vow, intends to say], "That I will not enter this house," but says, "That house," [or intends to say] "That I will not derive benefit from this one," but says, "From that one,"*

[D]   *has not said anything,*

[E]   *until his mouth and heart agree.*

A person must say what he means in order for his words or thoughts to carry legal weight. Neither unexpressed intention nor an unwitting designation is valid. This point is examined in each of the Yerushalmi's two units to this pericope.

[I.A]   There we have learned [M. Naz. 5:1A]: *The House of Shammai says, "[An act of] consecration done in error is binding."*

[B]   Now said R. Jeremiah, "[According to the House of Shammai, even if] he intended to say [that an animal is] unconsecrated but, [through a slip of the tongue], said [that it is] a burnt-offering, he has consecrated it [as burnt offering]."

[C]   [Disagreeing with Jeremiah,] said R. Yose, "[The position of the House of Shammai] applies [only] if, [from the start], the individual had intended to consecrate [an animal to be some sacrifice] and, [while correctly indicating which sacrifice he intended], had erred in some [secondary] matter [e.g., he said, 'The black ox which goes out of my house first is consecrated,' and a white ox went out, M. Naz. 5:1D]."

[D]   As for the present [pericope of] Mishnah [i.e., M. Ter. 3:8B + D]—whose [opinion] is it, [that of the House of Shammai, who state that an act of consecration done in error is binding, or that of the House of Hillel, M. Naz. 5:1B, who state that an act of consecration done in error is not binding]?

[E]   In the opinion of R. Jeremiah, [above, B, M. Ter. 3:8B + D] is under dispute [by the Houses of Hillel and Shammai]. [The Hillelites, like M. Ter. 3:8D, hold that the act of consecration is not valid. The Shammaites hold that even though it was carried out in error, the act of consecration is valid.]

[F]   But in the opinion of R. Yose [above, C], both [Houses agree with M. Ter. 3:8D that the act of consecration is not valid]. [The Shammaites agree because the error did not concern a secondary matter. Rather it involved the very question of what offering the food was to be. As Yose, C, claims, in such a case, the Shammaites rule the act of consecration to be invalid.]

The unit begins as an exegesis of M. Naz. 5:1, A–C. At D–F it turns to the question of which of M. Naz. 5:1's authorities stand behind M. Ter. 3:8's rule. This accounts for its inclusion here.

[II.A]   It is taught: '[If anyone utters] with his lips [a rash oath . . . he shall be guilty' (Lev. 5:4); i.e., the oath is valid].

[B]   Now [this does] not [apply if he only contemplates the oath] in his heart [without pronouncing it orally. In such a case the oath is not valid.]

[C]   Is it possible that I should include [under the category of one who has made a valid oath] one who determines in his heart [to make the oath, but never orally pronounces it]?

[D]   [I should not, for] the Torah [A] states [specifically], "Utters," [meaning that, to be valid, the oath must be said out loud, as B has concluded].

[E]   And [in agreement] Samuel says, "One who determines in his heart [to make an oath] is not subject [to that oath] until he pronounces it [orally], with his lips."

[F]   But [to the contrary,] is this not taught: [To help in building the tent of meeting] 'All who were of willing heart [brought brooches and earrings . . . every man dedicating an offering of gold to the Lord;' Ex. 35:22]?

[G]   This refers to someone who determines in his heart [to give the contribution, without making an oral pronouncement]. [Yet even so, the people were bound to give the contributions. This is contrary to the preceding, which says that to be binding the vow must be stated out loud.]

[H]   [Thus we must ask, which sort of oath is to be deemed valid?] Do you say that it is even that [oath] which is determined in the heart [but not orally pronounced], or is it only that [oath] which one pronounces with the lips?

[I]   When [Scripture] states, 'You shall be careful to perform that which has passed your lips' [Dt. 23:23], lo, it means, "That which has passed your lips [is a valid oath." What simply is contemplated in the heart is not valid, contrary to F + G.]

[J]   If that is so, how do I understand [Ex. 35:22's reference to] 'All who were of willing heart,' which [means], "What one contemplates in his heart, [but does not orally pronounce, is valid]?"

[K]   That which Samuel [E] said, [that an oath which one contemplates in his heart is not valid, applies only to one who contemplates designating] a sacrifice. [Such a designation is valid only if said out loud. But other oaths, such as to contribute gifts for the building of the tent of meeting, are valid even if not accompanied by an oral pronouncement. This is the distinction between Ex. 35:22, F + G, and Lev. 5:4, A–E (PM).]

This legal *midrash* locates in Scripture the basis for the rule of M. Ter 3:8, that heave-offering must be orally designated. F–G presents a second statement of Scripture which, on the surface, contradicts A–E's claim. That the two verses speak of different sorts of designations, and so are not contradictory, is shown at K.

3:8 [P: 3:5; M. Ter. 3:9]

[A]   *[As to] a gentile and a Samaritan—*

[B]   *(1) that which they separate is [valid] heave-offering, (2) and that which they take as tithes is [valid] as tithes, (3) and that which they dedicate [to the Temple] is [validly] dedicated.*

[C]   *R. Judah says, "A gentile's vineyard is not subject to the [restrictions of] the fourth year [Lev. 19:24]."*

[D]   *But sages say, "It is."*

[E]   *Heave-offering separated by a gentile imposes the status of heave-offering [upon unconsecrated produce with which it is mixed], and [nonpriests who unintentionally eat it] are liable on its account to [pay back its value and] an [additional] fifth [Lev. 22:14].*

[F]   *But R. Simeon exempts [heave-offering separated by a gentile from these stringencies].*

The Yerushalmi ignores the deeper issue of whether or not, for purposes of the laws of agriculture, a gentile is like an Israelite. Unit **I** simply cites and lightly glosses the Tosefta's materials on M. Ter. 3:9A–B. Unit **II** assumes that a gentile may validly separate heave-offering and looks for a different reason for the dispute between E and F. The final unit settles an unclarity in the Mishnah, whether or not Simeon, F, exempts heave-offering separated by a gentile from all of E's stringencies, or only from the added fifth. C–D is ignored.

[I.A]   **"[If a gentile] brought heave-offering from within his house, they treat it like untithed produce [mixed] with the great heave-offering"—the words of Rabbi.**

[B]   **Rabban Simeon b. Gamaliel says, "They treat it like valid heave-offering."**

[C]   **"[If the gentile] took first tithe from within his house, they treat it like untithed produce [mixed] with first tithe"—the words of Rabbi.**

[D]   **Rabban Simeon b. Gamaliel says, "He need not separate [from it any additional offerings, for it is] first tithe alone" [see Lieberman, *TK*, II, p. 351].**

[E][15]   **"[If] he took second tithe from within his house—**

[F]   **"[If he said, 'It has been redeemed (by coins and therefore no longer is consecrated as second tithe),' he has not said anything.]**

[G]   **"[(But if he said), 'Redeem it yourselves],' they treat it like untithed produce [mixed] with second tithe"—the words of Rabbi.**

[H]   **Rabban Simeon b. Gamaliel says, "He need not separate [from it any additional offerings, for it is] second tithe alone"** [see Lieberman, *TK*, II, p. 351; T. Ter. 4:13].

[I]   [To account for the disputing opinions] said R. Yose b. R. Bun, "Rabbi [A, C and E–G] is concerned [that the gentile] separated the offering from produce of one kind on behalf of produce of a different kind.

[J]   "Rabban Simeon b. Gamaliel [B, D, H] is concerned that [the gentile] separated the offerings in the wrong order."

The Yerushalmi's contribution, I–J, is confusing. A separation of heave-offering from produce of one kind on behalf of produce of a different kind is not valid at all, M. Ter. 2:4. Contrary to I, such a separation would not result in a mixture of heave-offering and unconsecrated food. This therefore cannot be Rabbi's concern, A, C, and E–G. Simeon b. Gamaliel, B, D, and H, simply holds that the gentile's separation of agricultural offerings is valid. Whether or not the gentile separated the offerings in the correct order is irrelevant to understanding this view, unlike what J claims.

Penei Moshe's solution to these problems is not convincing. He states that, according to I, Rabbi holds there is a doubt whether or not the separation performed by the gentile is valid. Because of the doubt Rabbi holds the offering is to be treated as though it were mixed with unconsecrated food. The problem with Penei Moshe's claim is that this is not the normal fashion in which doubtful agricultural offerings would be treated (see, e.g., M. Ter. 3:1–2). As for J, Penei Moshe notes that even if the several offerings are separated in the wrong order, they are valid. While this is compatible with Simeon's position that the gentile's separations are valid, it does not explain why we should think that Simeon b. Gamaliel is concerned about the order of the separations.

[**II.A**]   *Heave-offering separated by a gentile imposes the status of heave-offering upon unconsecrated produce with which it is mixed, and [nonpriests who unintentionally eat it] are liable on its account to [pay back its value and] an [added] fifth. But R. Simeon exempts [M. Ter. 3:9E–F].*

[B]   Said R. Zeira, "This was said in the presence of R. Abbahu in
the name of R. Yohanan: 'Concerning what [case] did [Simeon
and the anonymous authority] disagree?

[C]   "'Concerning [the case of] heave-offering [that the gentile] separated from [produce on] his own threshing floor. [This produce
was grown by the gentile on property he purchased in the land
of Israel. The anonymous authorities of the Mishnah hold that a
field owned by a gentile in the land of Israel is just like land
owned by Israelites. The produce that grows on it is fully subject
to the separation of heave-offering and tithes. Therefore what
the gentile separates is valid heave-offering. But Simeon holds
that once the gentile purchases the field, it no longer is like the
rest of the land of Israel. Produce that grows on it is not subject
to agricultural offerings. Therefore what the gentile separates is
not true heave-offering and is not subject to the stringencies
which pertain to that offering.]

[D]   "'But [in the case of] a gentile who purchased some produce
[grown on the land of Israel by an] Israelite, even R. Simeon
agrees [that the heave-offering separated by the gentile is subject
to the stringencies which pertain to heave-offering separated by
Israelites, for the produce from which the gentile separated the
offering was subject to the separation of agricultural gifts].'"

[E]   [Zeira continues:] "Said to them R. Abbahu in the name of R.
Yohanan, '[You have cited Yohanan incorrectly, for Yohanan holds
that the very case in which the gentile purchases produce from
an Israelite] is under dispute.

[F]   "'[And, indeed, there is a problem here, for] there is an inconsistency in R. Simeon's [position. Simeon agrees that] according
to the Torah [the gentile's separation is valid, so as to] exempt
[his produce from the further separation of heave-offering]. Yet
[contrary to that fact], you [Simeon] say this, [that the heave-
offering he separates is not true heave-offering, inasmuch as it
is not subject to the stringencies which normally apply to that
offering! Since what he separates exempts his produce from the
further separation of heave-offering, it must be a true priestly
gift. Therefore your position that it is not is untenable.]'"

[G]   [Y. points out that Simeon takes the same position elsewhere.]
Now, is not the designation of sacrifices [by gentiles] imposed by
the Torah? [Certainly it is.] Yet [even so] R. Simeon exempts

[sacrifices designated by gentiles from the stringencies accorded sacrifices designated by Israelites. This is indicated in] what we have learned there [at M. Zeb. 4:5, following M.'s version]: *"Holy Things designated by gentiles are not subject to the restrictions of Refuse, Remnant, or uncleanness"—the words of R. Simeon* (alt.: Meir). *But R. Yose declares them subject.*

The issue of M. Ter. 3:9E–F is not the gentile's ability to designate agricultural offerings, but whether or not the produce from which he separates these offerings was subject to them in the first place. So A–D. E states that this is wrong. The issue is as phrased in the Mishnah, whether or not a gentile's separation yields a true priestly gift. F claims that Simeon's view in the Mishnah is not tenable. G repeats Simeon's position for a different case but does not counter F's contention. The point is simply that Simeon treats gentiles as a special case.

[**III**.A] They reasoned, "Concerning what do [Simeon and the anonymous authorities at M. Ter. 3:9E–F] disagree?

[B] "[They disagree] concerning [whether or not a nonpriest who unintentionally eats heave-offering designated by a gentile must pay the added] fifth.

[C] "But concerning [whether or not such heave-offering, when mixed in sufficient quantity with unconsecrated food], imposes the status of heave-offering upon that unconsecrated food, [they did] not [disagree. Simeon agrees that it does.]"

[D] [Contrary to A–C,] there is a Tannaitic teaching [which states], "Just as [Simeon disagrees concerning] this [i.e., the added fifth], so [he disagrees concerning] this [i.e., the power of heave-offering separated by a gentile to impose its own status upon unconsecrated produce with which it is mixed]."

The basis for neither view, C nor D, is indicated.

4 Yerushalmi Terumot Chapter Four

[A] *One who separates a portion of the heave-offering and tithes [required of a batch of produce]*

[B] *[subsequently] may remove [more] heave-offering from that [same] batch on behalf of that [same] batch.*

[C] *But [he may] not [separate heave-offering or tithes] from that batch [from which he already has separated some agricultural offerings] for a different batch.*

[D] *R. Meir says, "Also: he may remove heave-offering and tithes [from that batch from which he already has separated some agricultural gifts] on behalf of a different batch."*

A–C holds that the batch is not divisible. The person's proportional separation of agricultural offerings leaves all of the produce in the batch partially exempt from the separation of these gifts. This partially exempt produce may not now be used as heave-offering and tithes for other, fully subject, produce. Meir, D, states that the batch is divisible. When the householder separates some of the heave-offering and tithes, a portion of the produce is rendered fully exempt and the rest remains fully subject. The fully subject produce may still be used as heave-offering and tithes for a different batch. The Yerushalmi begins with central questions. Under what circumstances is the partial separation of agricultural offerings deemed valid (unit I), and why is there a distinction between separating heave-offering from one batch on behalf of that same batch, and from one batch on behalf of a dif-

ferent batch (unit **II**)? The rest is on secondary concerns. Unit **III**
asks of the application of B–C's rule to a different, comparable
case; the specifics of M. Ter. 4:1A–C's case are argued (unit
IV); and, in unit **V**, the opinion of a third authority is added to
the Mishnah's dispute.

[**I.A**]   [42c] *One who separates a portion of the heave-offering and*
      tithes [required of a batch of produce. . . . M. Ter. 4:1A].

[B]   [The issue is under what circumstances this partial separation of
      heave-offering is deemed valid.] Mishnah [speaks of a case] in
      which at the time at which the individual separated [the small
      portion of the required offerings] he intended to separate [more
      offerings, in order to fill out the required amounts. If he did not
      intend to separate the remaining quantities of required offerings,
      his initial, partial, separation would not be deemed valid.]

[C]   [Disagreeing with B] R. Samuel in the name of R. Zeira [says],
      "Mishnah [refers even to a case in which the individual] has not
      established [whether or not he will separate the rest of the re-
      quired offerings]." [Even though it is not clear that the individ-
      ual will fulfill the rest of his obligation, what he initially has
      done is valid.]

[D]   Said R. Mana in the presence of R. Yudan, "What is the [exact
      nature of the] dispute [between Samuel and B]?"

[E]   [Yudan] said to him, "[Samuel holds that even in the case of an
      individual who] has not [explicitly] established [whether or not
      he ultimately will separate the required quantities of agricultural
      offerings, we assume that] at the time the individual removes
      [the first portion of heave-offering] he intends to separate [the
      rest of the required amount]." [Even though he has not been ex-
      plicit concerning this, his initial separation therefore is deemed
      valid. A, on the contrary, holds that the individual must be ex-
      plicit. If he is not, his initial separation is not valid. The dispute
      between B and C thus does not concern whether or not the indi-
      vidual ultimately must separate all of the required offerings. All
      agree that he must. At issue rather is whether we assume that
      people are going to do this. Samuel states that we do; B, that we
      do not.]

B holds that to be valid, a person's intention must be explicitly expressed. Samuel, C, explained at E, holds that even if the person's plans remain unstated, we assume that he intends to do the right thing.

[**II.A**]   What is the difference between [the case of an individual who] takes [heave-offering] from a batch [of partially tithed produce] on behalf of that [same] batch [of produce, such that the separation is valid, M. Ter. 4:1A–B], and [the case of an individual who] takes [heave-offering] from one [partially tithed] batch [of produce] on behalf of [fully tithed produce] in a different batch, [such that the separation is not valid, M. Ter. 4:1C? That is, why do we distinguish between these two cases?]

[B]   [The difference is that] when he takes [heave-offering] from a batch [of partially tithed produce] on behalf of that [same] batch [of produce], only [fully] untithed, unconsecrated produce comes up in his hand [to be designated heave-offering for that same batch. This unconsecrated, untithed produce may be deemed heave-offering, as M. Ter. 4:1B states.]

[C]   But if he takes [heave-offering] from this batch [of partially tithed produce] on behalf of a different batch [of fully untithed produce], both [tithed and untithed produce from the partially tithed batch] will come up in his hand [to be designated heave-offering. This separation is not valid, M. Ter. 4:1C, because the already tithed produce that comes up in his hand may not be deemed heave-offering.]

[D]   [Y. now suggests that B–C's reasoning is unacceptable. This is clear because the following case presents] a difficulty [which B–C's logic leaves unresolved]:

[E]   [According to B, if] one took [produce from a partially tithed batch] in order to separate [heave-offering] from that batch on behalf of that [same] batch, only untithed, unconsecrated produce will go up into his hand.

[F]   [If] he then changes his mind and decides to separate [i.e., designate, the heave-offering he has separated from the partially tithed batch] on behalf of a different [untithed batch, can we now go back and, as required by C, state that] both [tithed and untithed produce] are in his hand? [Obviously not, for we already concluded, E, that only fully untithed produce is in his hand. Thus B–C's reasoning is not acceptable. The same point is made a second time in what follows.]

[G]   [According to C, if] he took [produce from the partially tithed batch] in order to separate [heave-offering] from that batch on behalf of a different [fully untithed batch], both [tithed and untithed produce] come up in his hand [and the separation is not valid].

[H]   [If] he now changes his mind and decides to separate [i.e., to designate the produce from the partially tithed batch as heave-offering] on behalf of the [same partially tithed batch], is it possible to say, [as B requires, that] only untithed produce came up in his hand? [Of course not, for according to G, he already has a mixture of tithed and untithed produce in his hand. Again we see that B–C is unacceptable.]

[I]¹   [I–J argues that B–C is unacceptable for a different reason. In line with B it would appear that when, in the first place, the individual] separated [from his produce] only a portion [of the required heave-offering], all of the [available] unconsecrated, untithed produce [in the batch] came up in his hand [and became heave-offering, leaving the rest of the batch fully exempt from the further separation of that offering. But this is impossible, for M. Ter. 4:2 requires the individual who separates a portion of the required heave-offering to separate heave-offering again, from the same batch. B therefore is unacceptable, since its logic leads to a wrong conclusion.]

[J]   [In the same way, according to C, if an individual] separates more [than the required quantity of heave-offering], both [tithed and untithed produce] comes up in his hand [and the separation therefore will not be valid. Yet this is not the case, for according to M. Ter. 4:5 a householder may validly separate a large percentage of his produce to be heave-offering. So again we see that C is not acceptable.]

B–C suggests why M. Ter. 4:1 must distinguish between a case in which the individual separates heave-offering from a partially tithed batch on behalf of that same batch and one in which he separates the heave-offering on behalf of a different batch. While

the rejection of B–C's reasoning is clear, D–H + I–J, B–C itself never is explained. The larger flow of the pericope therefore
is apparent; but its main point, expressed at B–C, is not.

[III.A] [Does M. 4:1C apply] also [in a case in which an individual]
errs [in separating heave-offering, so that if the person separates
more heave-offering than he needs to, he may not designate a
portion of what was separated as heave-offering for a different
batch? The following answers this question:]

[B] [If] one thought that he was obligated to separate two *seahs* of
heave-offering, but [it turns out that] he needed to separate only
one² [*seah*]—

[C] R. Imi in the name of R. Simeon b. Laqish [says], "He should
designate that extra *seah* [of heave-offering] which he separated
to be the heave-offering required of a different [batch of pro-
duce]." [Simeon b. Laqish holds that in this case, even though
some heave-offering has been taken from the batch, other heave-
offering, i.e., the second *seah*, may be designated on behalf of a
different batch. M. Ter. 4:1C does not apply.]

[D] [But Simeon b. Laqish must be wrong, for] have we not learned
[M. Ter. 4:1C: As for a batch of produce from which some of
the required heave-offering has been taken, heave-offering] *may
not [be separated from that batch] on behalf of a different batch?*
[The claim is that M. Ter. 4:1C does apply in the case of B and
that Simeon b. Laqish, C, is wrong.]

[E] Solve [the problem of how Simeon b. Laqish can hold his position by assuming that he refers to the case of] a person who
[habitually] separates much³ heave-offering, [M. Ter. 4:5. In the
case of such a person, both *seahs* are true heave-offering, and the
extra one may be designated on behalf of a different batch, as
Simeon b. Laqish suggests.]

[F] [Simeon's position] makes sense for the case of a person who
[habitually] separates much heave-offering.

[G] But [what] of [a person who, in the way suggested at B, accidentally separates more than the required quantity of] tithes? [The
additional tithes are not valid, M. Dem. 5:2, and therefore may
not be designated on behalf of a different batch. This appears to

invalidate Simeon b. Laqish's judgment, C, that a person who in error takes too much agricultural offering may designate a portion of what he separates on behalf of a different batch.]

[H]   R. Simeon b. Laqish has not taught [how it can be that if in error the person separates too much] tithes [he may go back and designate the extra amount on behalf of a different batch. It therefore appears that, contrary to Simeon b. Laqish's view, C, the rule of M. Ter. 4:1B–C does apply in a case such as is described at B.]

[I]   [No. Simeon's contention, C, is correct. The problem is that E does not rightly record his reasoning. He does not support his opinion by noting that one who habitually separates more than the required quantity of heave-offering validly has separated the offering.] Rather Simeon b. Laqish's reasoning [in holding that the person who accidentally separates too much offering may designate the extra quantity on behalf of a different batch] is that once you say that [when he separated heave-offering] all of the untithed, unconsecrated food came up in his hand [and became heave-offering, leaving the rest of the batch fully tithed], what difference does it make [whether he later designates all of the produce in his hand as heave-offering] for the same batch or [designates a portion of it] on behalf of a different batch?

The question is whether or not M. Ter. 4:1A–C's rule applies in a case in which the individual separates too much heave-offering.[4] Simeon b. Laqish, C, holds that it does not. A person who separates too much heave-offering may designate a portion of that which he separates to be the priestly gift required of a different batch. The issue is why this should be the case. E's explanation failing, F–H, I suggests a different reason: that *it makes no difference* whether the individual designates the heave-offering he separated all for the same batch or whether he assigns a portion of it to a different batch.

[IV.A]   What is the case [in which M. Ter. 4:1B–C holds that heave-offering may not be separated from a partially tithed batch on behalf of a different, untithed batch]?

[B]   It is one in which [the person] had separated heave-offering and tithes for the majority of the produce in the heap.

[C]⁵   [What is the rule if] he did not [yet] separate heave-offering and tithes from the majority of produce in the heap? [In such a case may he go ahead and separate from that batch agricultural gifts on behalf of different produce, or does the rule of M. Ter. 4:1B–C still apply?]

[D]   This is disputed by Hezeqiah and R. Yohanan.

[E]   [Hezeqiah holds that M. Ter. 4:1B–C applies only if the majority of the required heave-offering and tithes already has been separated from the heap. The reason is as follows:] For said Resh Laqish in the name of Hezeqiah, "Untithed produce disappears in a [batch which contains] a majority [of tithed produce]." [That is, the untithed produce is deemed insignificant and may be ignored. Since the whole batch is deemed exempt from the separation of heave-offering and tithes, agricultural gifts may not be separated from it on behalf of a different batch. This is not so in a case such as C. There the produce remains subject to the separation of heave-offering and tithes, such that these offerings may be separated from the batch on behalf of a different batch.]

[F]   But R. Yohanan says, "Untithed produce does not disappear in a majority [of tithed produce]. [Thus it is irrelevant to the law of M. Ter. 4:1B–C whether or not the individual has separated heave-offering and tithes sufficient for most of the produce in the batch. In neither case may the householder go back and take more heave-offering and tithes from that batch on behalf of a different batch.]

[G]   "[The reason the untithed produce does not disappear is that] when [the householder] sets his mind upon separating [heave-offering and tithes] the position [within the batch] of each stalk of grain is established." [The untithed stalks always remain distinct and so retain their untithed status. Which view is correct, E or F, is not indicated.]

The unit is a composite. The dispute at E–G is placed here to answer the question posed at A–C. Yet E–G is complete in itself and covers its own separate problem. This is whether or not a householder may ignore a small quantity of untithed produce located in a batch of tithed food. Only through the elaborate interpolations that I have supplied (following PM) is E–G made to answer A–C. While this may represent what was intended by the redactor of the unit, it should not obscure the artificial nature of this literary creation.

[V.A]   There are those who wish to reason according to that which R. Eliezer b. Jacob taught. For R. Eliezer b. Jacob taught [contrary to M. Ter. 4:1A–C and D: "Once a person has separated a portion of the heave-offering and tithes required of a batch of produce] he may not separate [the additional offerings that are required] either [from that batch] on behalf of that [same] batch or [from that batch] on behalf of a different batch."

[B]   Up to now [we assume that this applies only in the case of one who] has (follow GRA and delete: not) separated heave-offering and tithes from the majority of [produce in] the heap. [See Y. Ter. 4:1 **IV**.E. In this case the batch as a whole is deemed no longer subject to the separation of agricultural offerings. Therefore no additional offerings may be separated from it, even on its own behalf.]

[C]   [If] he has (supply: not) [yet] designated the heave-offering and tithes required of the majority [of produce] in the heap, [such that the heap still is subject to the separation of these things, will Eliezer b. Jacob still hold as he does at A]?

[D]   The rule is in accordance with the following [= Y. Ter. 2:1 **IX**]:

[E]   If there were before him two piles of produce, from one of which he [already] had separated a portion of the [required] heave-offering and tithes and from the other of which [42d] he [already] had separated a portion of the [required] heave-offering and tithes— what is the rule [whether or not] he [subsequently] may separate heave-offering from this [partially tithed batch] on behalf of the other [partially tithed batch]?

[F]   [Concerning this case] the disciples of R. Hiyya the elder asked R. Hiyya the elder. Now he answered them [with Eccles. 4:5], 'The fool folds his hands and eats his own flesh.' [That is, someone who has been so foolish as to separate only a portion of the heave-offering and tithes required of his produce has made it impossible later to separate from one of the partially tithed batches the agricultural gifts required of all the produce.]

[G]   [Claiming that Hiyya answered the question explicitly,] said R. Eleazar in the name of R. Hiyya the elder, "They may not sepa-

rate heave-offering or tithes from one [partially tithed batch] on
behalf of another."

Like the previous unit, this one is problematic. The main difficulty is that E–H in no way responds to A–C. GRA solves the
problem by deleting D and calling E–H a separate pericope.
Since, in its own right, E–H is pertinent to M. Ter. 4:1, this
solution has merit. But it is not supported by textual evidence
and should be considered only as provisional. The second difficulty is B–C. The distinction between produce from which the
majority of agricultural gifts has been taken and that from which
only some of these have been removed is significant to Hezeqiah,
Y. Ter. 4:1 **IV**. He states that a small quantity of untithed produce within the batch is ignored. Thus the view given here at A
logically might apply if the majority of agricultural offerings has
not been removed from the batch, as GRA corrects B to read.
Along these same lines, I have corrected C. As before, however,
there is no evidence in MSS. or in editions of the Yerushalmi to
support these readings. They are suggested as provisional.

4:2

[A] *"One whose produce [from which heave-offering already had
been separated] was in a storeroom and who gave a seah [of pro-
duce] to a Levite [as first tithe] and a seah [of produce] to a poor
person [as poor man's tithe]*

[B] *"may take another eight seahs [of produce] and eat them [without
further tithing]"—the words of R. Meir.*

[C] *But sages say, "He does not take produce [to eat] except in accordance with a calculation [of the percentage of tithes which
remain to be separated from the batch as a whole]."*

The positions are the same as at M. Ter. 4:1. Meir holds that the
tithes that were separated apply to some specific portion of the
batch. The householder may go ahead and eat this portion. The
sages, by contrast, state that what the man already has separated
applies to the batch as a whole. To eat any portion of the batch,
he must separate from that portion the quantity of tithes to which it
still is subject. Y. Ter. 4:1 **I** locates in M. Dem. 7:3 the basis for

the sages' position. Unit **II** cites materials from the Yerushalmi
which belong with that pericope of the Mishnah. These are
found here because of unit **I**'s reference.

[**I.**A]   R. Eleazar in the name of R. Hoshaya [says], "[Sages, M. Ter.
4:2C, state that the man separates tithes for that portion of the
batch which he eats because] they deemed him to be like a worker
who does not trust [his employer], the householder, [properly to
tithe produce, M. Dem. 7:3]." [Such a worker is allowed to
separate whatever tithes are required for that portion of the householder's produce he eats. M. Ter. 4:2C is comparable, for sages
have the person separate tithes for that portion which he eats.]

The Yerushalmi discerns a parallel between M. Ter. 4:2C and
M. Dem. 7:3.

[**II.**A]   The following is obvious:

[B]   [A person has separated heave-offering but not yet given it to
a priest.] If the unconsecrated produce, [for which the heave-
offering was separated], should burn up, that which was separated as heave-offering reverts to its unconsecrated state (so Y.
Dem. 7:3: *tybwlh*; Y. Ter. reads: *btylh*).[6]

[C]   [The problem is how to adjudicate a case in which] the *heave-
offering* burns up [before it is given to a priest. Must heave-
offering be separated from the produce again?]

[D]   [PM: One need not separate heave-offering again, for] when
the produce is eaten the heave-offering is retroactively deemed
sanctified.

D assumes that heave-offering does not take on a consecrated
status until the produce on behalf of which it was separated is
eaten. I do not see how this notion, foreign to the Mishnah,
answers the question posed at C.

4:3

[A] *[This is] the [required] measure of heave-offering:*

[B] *[If a person is] generous, [he separates] one-fortieth [of his produce].*

[C] *The House of Shammai say, "One-thirtieth."*

[D] *And [if he is] average, [he separates] one-fiftieth [of his produce].*

[E] *And [if he is] miserly, [he separates] one-sixtieth [of his produce].*

[F] *[If] he separated heave-offering and there came up in his hand one-sixtieth [of the produce]—[that which he has separated is valid] heave-offering.*

[G] *And he need not separate heave-offering again.*

[H] *If he [anyway separated] more [heave-offering, the additional produce separated as heave-offering] is subject to the separation of tithes [i.e., it is not true heave-offering].*

[I] *[If he separated heave-offering and] there came up in his hand one-sixty-first [of the produce—that which he has separated is valid] heave-offering.*

[J] *But he must separate heave-offering again,*

[K] *[in order to derive] the quantity [of heave-offering] he is used [to separating].*

[L] *[And he may separate the additional heave-offering] by measure [of volume], by weight or by a count [of the number of pieces of produce being separated as heave-offering].*

[M] *R. Judah says, "Also: [he may separate the additional quantity of heave-offering] from [produce] which is not in the same batch."*

The quantity of heave-offering contained in a batch of produce is determined by the householder himself. The more generous the person, the larger the percentage of the batch he is expected to separate for the priest. But there is a fixed minimum, one-sixtieth, which must in all cases be separated, F–H. If the person separates less than this quantity, he must separate heave-offering again in order to make up the prescribed amount.

The first part of the Yerushalmi's treatment provides the scrip-

tural basis for the Mishnah's rules. Units **I–III** explain from
Scripture the quantities listed at B, D, and E. Unit **IV** follows
logically, citing and explaining from Scripture the view of the
House of Shammai, which, M. Ter. 4:3B and T. Ter. 5:8, has a
different set of figures. Y. 4:3 **V–X** turns from Scripture to logic
in order to interpret the second section of this pericope, M. Ter.
4:3F–M.

[I.A]   **[How do we know that if one separated heave-offering and
there arose in his hand one-sixtieth (of the produce) that that
which he has separated is (valid) heave-offering?]**

[B]   **As it is written, '[This is the offering which you shall make:]
one-sixth of an *ephah* from each *homer* [= ten *ephahs*] of wheat
and one-sixth of an *ephah* from each *homer* of barley' [Ez.
45:13, cited at T. Ter. 5:8].**

[C]   Is it possible [that Scripture means that one should] separate
one-thirtieth [= two-sixths of an *ephah* for each *homer*] of wheat
and one sixtieth [= one sixth of an *ephah* for each *homer*] of
barley?

[D]   [No, for] Scripture states, 'Every offering' [Ez. 44:30, meaning]
that the same [percentage] of heave-offering [should be taken
from] every [sort of produce].

[E]   [The minimum required quantity of heave-offering, one-sixtieth,
is derived from Ex. 45:13, as shown at A–B. Samuel now indicates how that same verse may be used to derive the generous
quantity, one-fortieth.] Samuel says, "Add one-sixth [of an *ephah*]
to a sixth [of a sixth of an *ephah*] and the result is that one separates as heave-offering one-fortieth [of his produce: 1/6 + 1/12 =
1/4 *ephah per homer*, which is one-fortieth of the produce.]

B appears to be a citation of the Tosefta, which I have filled out
at A. Ez. 45:13 describes an offering of one-sixtieth of the produce. This accounts for M. Ter. 4:3's minimum figure. C–D
clarifies B's exegesis. E then draws a different conclusion from
the same verse. Giving the scriptural basis for the percentage
which the Mishnah calls generous, it introduces Y. Ter. 4:3
II–III, which will explain the figures the Mishnah gives for average and miserly individuals.

[**II.A**]   *[And if he is] average, [he separates] one-fiftieth [of his produce;* M. Ter. 4:3D].

[B]   Said R. Levi, "It is written: '**And from the people of Israel's half you shall take one drawn out of every fifty**[7] **[. . . and give them to the Levites who have charge of the tabernacle of the Lord;' Num. 31:30].**

[C]   "**Whatever [percentage] you took in a different context, lo, such is the proper [percentage] here.**

[D]   "**Just as [the percentage stated] there [at Num. 31:30] is one-fiftieth, so [the percentage] here is one-fiftieth.**"

The Yerushalmi cites T. Ter. 5:8, the version of which I translate at D.

[**III.A**][8]   *And [if he is] miserly, [he separates] one-sixtieth [of his produce;* M. Ter. 4:3E].

[B]   **[We know this] from what is written [Ez. 45:13: 'This is the offering which you shall make, one-sixth of an *ephah* from each *homer* (= ten *ephahs*) of wheat and] one-sixth of an *ephah* from each *homer* of barley' [T. Ter. 5:8].**

T. Ter. 5:8's exegesis of Ex. 45:13, cited at Y. Ter. 4:3 **I**, is repeated.

[**IV.A**]   **The House of Shammai say, "[If a man is generous he separates as heave-offering one-]thirtieth [of his produce"; T. Ter. 5:3B].**

[B]   [The Shammaites derive this from Ez. 45:13: 'This is the offering which you shall make: one-sixth of an *ephah* from each *homer* of wheat] and one-sixth of an *ephah* from each *homer* of barley.' [The Shammaites add together the two offerings of one-sixth. Thus they require the person to separate one-third *ephah per homer,* which is one-thirtieth of the produce.]

[C]   "**[And if he is] average, [he separates] one-fortieth [of his produce"; T. Ter. 5:3B].**

[D]⁹   [The Shammaites derived this percentage] from that [statement] of Samuel [above, Y. Ter. 4:3 I.E].

[E]   **"And [if he is] miserly, [he separates] one-fiftieth ¹⁰ [of his produce"; T. Ter. 5:3B].**

[F]   [The Shammaites derive this figure] from that [statement] of R. Levi [above, Y. Ter. 4:3 **II**].

[G]   [The following is separate:] For said R. Levi bar Hina, "Anyone who separates tithes as is required has not suffered any loss." [That is, whatever it costs in produce is compensated by heavenly reward.]

The view of the House of Shammai and its basis in Scripture are given, A–F. G is tacked on because of relevance of topic and, I suspect, the recurrence in it of the name of Levi. But unlike what the joining language "for" implies, G does not explain that which precedes.

[**V.A**]   What is the meaning of [the verse]: 'One tenth of a *homer* shall be an *ephah;* the *homer* shall be the standard measure' [Ez. 45:11]?

[B]   It is needed only to prove that which we learn [M. Ter. 4:3F–G]: *[If] he separated heave-offering and there came up in his hand one-sixtieth ¹¹ [of the produce, that which he has separated is valid] heave-offering, and he need not separate heave-offering [a second time].* [Ez. 45:13 states that heave-offering constitutes one-sixth of an *ephah* per *homer* of produce. Ez. 45:11, cited at A, indicates that an *ephah* is one-tenth of a *homer*. Therefore we know that a separation of one-sixtieth of the batch is valid and sufficient, as M. Ter. 4:3F–G states.]

[C]   Yet the House of Shammai say, "If he separated heave-offering and there came up in his hand one-fiftieth [of the produce, that which he has separated is valid] heave-offering, and he need not separate heave-offering [a second time]." [As at T. Ter. 5:3 the Shammaites hold that the minimum is one-fiftieth, separated by miserly people.]

[D]   [Giving a different minimum figure,] said R. Hanina bar Isi,¹² 'Bar Qappara taught only [as follows: 'If] he separated heave-offering and there came up in his hand between one-fiftieth and one-sixtieth [of the produce, that which he has separated is valid] heave-offering, and he need not separate heave-offering [a second time].'"

B answers A's question, essentially repeating the exegesis of Y. Ter. 4:3 I and **III**. C and D are independent of A–B and each other. They are placed here because they dispute the rule of M. Ter. 4:3F–G, cited at B. Since they do not respond to A's question, they must be deemed secondary.

[**VI**.A]   [The following refers to M. Ter. 4:3H. Once a person has separated the minimum required quantity of heave-offering, one-sixtieth, he need not separate heave-offering again. If he does so anyway, that which he separates is subject to tithes.] R. Isi in the name of R. Yohanan [says], "This [rule, that the additional produce is subject to tithes], applies only if, [by separating heave-offering again], the individual intended[13] to exempt the batch [from the separation of heave-offering]. [Since the batch already was rendered exempt by the initial separation, this intention is null. As a result, the produce that the person separates the second time is not true heave-offering and is subject to tithes.]

[B]   "But if, [through the additional separation], he did not intend to exempt the batch [from the separation of heave-offering, he may even separate] again as much [as he already separated]." [In this case the produce he separates is true heave-offering and is not subject to tithes. The reason is that the second separation is considered a part of the first one. The person simply wishes to separate much heave-offering, which is permitted, not to separate heave-offering twice, which is not.]

The Yerushalmi indicates the circumstances under which the rule of M. Ter. 4:3H applies. Yohanan's point is made explicit in my interpolations, at A versus B.

[**VII**.A]   [According to M. Ter. 4:3I–K, a person who separates as heave-offering less than one-sixtieth of the batch must separate heave-offering again in order to derive the quantity of heave-offering he is used to separating. The issue is what the Mishnah means

when it states: *The quantity which he is used to separating.*]
Kahana says, "[In the additional separation of heave-offering he
only may take enough produce to derive] *the quantity [of heave-
offering] he is used to separating.*" [He may not take more than
this amount.]

[B]   [Disagreeing] R. Yohanan says, "[He may *even* [separate] again
as much [as he separated the first time, with the result that he
will separate much more than he normally does].

[C]   "[We know this from the following reasoning:] For [the statement at M. Ter. 4:3K, that] he should separate the quantity that
he is used to separating indicates [14] [only] that he may not [sepa-
rate as heave-offering] less [than this amount. But he may separate more.]"

[D]   [Claiming that Yohanan is wrong,] said R. Eleazar, "[M. Ter.
4:3L states that one who takes additional heave-offering in order
to separate] *the quantity he is used [to separating may perform
this separation] by a measure [of the volume of produce* he is
separating as heave-offering. This normally is forbidden, M.
Ter. 1:7.]

[E]   "If, [as you say, the person referred to in this rule] intentionally
separates more heave-offering [than he normally would separate,
in which case the usual rules for the separation of heave-offering
should apply], how can it be that he even may perform this separation by a measure of volume?!" [It cannot be, since one who
separates much heave-offering may not do so by a measure of
volume. Therefore it is clear that Yohanan, B–C, is wrong. According to M. Ter. 4:3I–K, a person who separates additional
heave-offering may separate no more than he is used to separating, as Kahana, A, said.]

The meaning of M. Ter. 4:3I–K is under dispute between Kahana, A, and Yohanan, B–C. Eleazar, D–E, proves that Yohanan
is wrong.

[**VIII**.A]   R. Jonah says, "R. Simeon b. Laqish asked in the presence of R.
Yohanan, '[As for] the additional quantity of heave-offering
[which a householder who separated less than the required one-

sixtieth of the batch must go back and separate, M. Ter. 4:3I–K]—what is the rule [whether or not it is subject to the separation of tithes]?'

[B]   "[Yohanan] said to him, 'I have learned this rule in accordance with a minority opinion.'"

[C]   What [did Yohanan mean, that the produce] is subject [to the separation of tithes], or that it is exempt?

[D]   It is reasonable to assume that [he meant] it is subject [to tithes]. [The minority opinion he follows is that of Judah, M. Ter. 4:3M, who states that the additional quantity of heave-offering may be separated from a different batch altogether. This means that it is not true heave-offering and is subject to tithes.]

[E]   [But] if [contrary to D], you claim that [Yohanan thinks that the produce taken in the second separation] is exempt [from tithes], what [could Yohanan have meant by saying that he follows Judah's minority opinion]?

[F]   For if [contrary to D] R. Judah's [view], that [the second separation of heave-offering may be] from a different batch of produce, [means that the heave-offering taken in this separation is like true heave-offering and is] exempt [from the separation of tithes], is it not obvious that rabbis [i.e., the anonymous authorities of M. Ter. 4:3I–J], who do not allow the second heave-offering to be separated from a different batch, likewise hold that it is [true heave-offering and] exempt from tithes? [Yes. If Judah, who rules leniently concerning the second separation of heave-offering, holds that the produce derived from this separation is subject to tithes, then rabbis, who rule stringently concerning the separation, certainly hold that the produce is subject to tithes. Thus the *minority* opinion which Yohanan holds cannot be that the second heave-offering is not subject to tithes. This would not be a minority view. If Judah accepts it, so do all authorities. Therefore it is clear that D is correct. Yohanan's view, which follows Judah, is that the additional quantity of heave-offering is subject to the separation of tithes. It is not true heave-offering.]

The Yerushalmi fills out what the Mishnah leaves ambiguous. According to Yohanan the produce taken in the additional separation of heave-offering is subject to the separation of tithes.

[**IX**.A]   R. Yose came [and said], "R. Isi in the name of R. Simeon b. Laqish [said], 'The additional quantity of heave-offering [separated by a householder who does not designate sufficient heave-offering in his first separation, M. Ter. 4:3I–K] is subject to the separation of tithes.'"

[B]   [Amazed] said R. Yose, "Does the Mishnah say this?!" [It does not appear to.]

[C]   Said R. Zeira to R. Isi, "Which [statement in] the Mishnah [indicates whether or not the additional quantity of heave-offering is subject to tithes]?"

[D]   Now [Isi] did not answer him.

[E]   [Zeira himself answers the question, proving A to be unacceptable. Zeira] said to him [i.e., Isi], "Perhaps it is this statement which we learn [from the Mishnah] which makes the point: *[If] he separated heave-offering and there came up in his hand one-sixty-first [of the batch, that which he has separated is valid] heave-offering, but he must separate heave-offering [a second time; M. Ter. 4:3I–J]*.

[F]   "Now concerning this rule it is not taught: *When he goes back and separates more heave-offering, [that which he separates] is subject to [the separation of] tithes*" [M. Ter. 4:3H. That is, the Mishnah is explicit concerning the case in which it requires the householder to separate tithes from produce which he has designated as heave-offering. In the case of M. Ter. 4:3I–K no mention is made of separating tithes. We therefore know that tithes need not be separated. Simeon b. Laqish, cited by Isi at A, is wrong.]

The question is the same as at Y. Ter. 4:3 **VIII,** but the conclusion is the opposite. Unit **VIII** proves that, in Yohanan's view, the produce taken in a householder's second separation of heave-offering is subject to tithes. Zeira here claims that it is not. Since the two units do not speak to one another, it is impossible to determine what the Yerushalmi's own answer to this question might be.

[X.A]   According to the Torah how much [heave-offering need a person separate from his produce] in order to fulfill the obligation?

[B][15]   R. Yohanan says, "[He must separate as heave-offering] one-hundredth [of the batch], the same quantity as heave-offering of the tithe, [the biblical tithe of the tithe, Num. 18:25–32]."

[C]   [Yohanan now responds to a statement which is lacking from the text.] Said to him R. Yohanan, "From whom did you hear this?"

[D]   He said to him [i.e., to Yohanan], "I heard in a discussion among the associates that which R. Yannai said: '[One has fulfilled the obligation to separate heave-offering] even [if he separates] one-thousandth [of the batch].'"

[E]   [Giving a different answer to A,] said R. Mana, "There is no set measure [according to Torah]. For it is written, 'The best of your grain, wine, and oil,' [Num. 18:12. 'The best'] can be any amount, however [small]."

The Yerushalmi claims that the quantities of heave-offering listed in the Mishnah are not those demanded by the Torah, A. We recall, however, that the Yerushalmi itself holds that M. Ter. 4:3's laws are based on Scripture (Y. Ter. 4:3 I–IV). This epitomizes a dichotomy internal to the Yerushalmi. For the Yerushalmi, Scripture functions as a holy book, which supports all that the Mishnah states. But Scripture also can be made to forward those claims important to the Yerushalmi's own authorities, however much these diverge from the Mishnah's point of view. The result of this in the present pericope is to neutralize the Mishnah's statement of law and to replace it with the Yerushalmi's own picture. The Yerushalmi claims that Israelite householders fulfill the agricultural laws by giving up a much smaller percentage of their food than that required by the Mishnah. This reduced emphasis on the maintenance of the priestly class makes good sense in the Yerushalmi's time, long after the destruction of the Temple, when little hope remained for the renewed cultic functioning of the priests.

4:4

[A] *One who says to his agent, "Go and separate heave-offering [for me]"—*

[B] *[the agent] separates heave-offering in accordance with the disposition of the householder [i.e., he separates however much the householder normally separates].*

[C] *[But] if he does not know the disposition of the householder,*

[D] *he separates the average amount,*

[E] *one-fiftieth.*

[F] *[If the agent at A–B or C–D unintentionally] separated one-tenth less or more [than he should have]—that which he has separated is [valid] heave-offering.*

[G] *If he purposely added even one-hundredth—that which he has separated is not [valid] heave-offering.*

An agent must separate the quantity of heave-offering desired by the householder, A–E. If he purposely breaks this condition of his appointment, he does not act as an agent. The separation of heave-offering performed on behalf of the owner of the produce therefore is not valid, G. So long as the agent intended to carry out the will of the householder, a misestimation in the physical separation is of no concern. That which the agent separates is valid heave-offering, F.

The Yerushalmi covers each of the Mishnah's points in turn. Unit I is a close exegesis of A–E, asking under what circumstances the agent must separate heave-offering according to the disposition of the householder and when he simply may separate the average amount. The meaning of "one-tenth more or less heave-offering," F, is explained next. Unit III follows, indicating why the rule of M. Ter. 4:4F differs from that at G. The final pericope elucidates the larger theory of agency operative here. It does this by introducing M. Me. 6:1 and contrasting the rule for agency found there with that of the present unit. The theory that emerges is that when an agent does what the householder wishes, it is as though the householder himself performed the action. If the agent does not fulfill his assigned task, he alone is responsible for his deed.

[**I.**A]   Up to this point [we know only that M. Ter. 4:4A–B applies in a case] in which [the householder explicitly] said to him [i.e., the agent], "Go and separate heave-offering [for me] according to my disposition [i.e., separating the quantity I normally separate]."

[B]   [What if the agent] knows the disposition of the householder, but [the householder] does not [explicitly] say to him, "Go and separate heave-offering according to my disposition?" [In this case do we apply the rule of M. Ter. 4:4A–B and say that the agent must separate the quantity of heave-offering he knows the householder would separate? Or do we rule that since he was not requested specifically to do so, he does not separate heave-offering according to the householder's disposition, but rather separates the average amount, M. Ter. 4:4C–D?]

[C]   Let us learn [the correct rule] from this [M. Ter. 4:4C–D]: *If [the agent] does not know the disposition of the householder, [he separates the average amount].*

[D]   [Mishnah's point is that only] because he does not know the disposition of the householder [does he go ahead and separate the average amount].

[E]   This means that if he does know [the householder's disposition], even though [the householder] did not tell him [explicitly to separate heave-offering according to that disposition, the case is treated] as one in which he did tell him, [such that the agent is expected to separate the quantity the householder normally would separate].

So long as the agent knows how much heave-offering the householder normally separates he must designate that same amount. This is so even if the householder did not tell him specifically, "Separate the quantity I normally separate."

[**II.**A]   Said R. Bun bar Kahana, "[M. Ter. 4:4F means that an agent] who separates one-tenth [*seah*] less heave-offering [than he should, i.e., who separates nine-tenths *seah* instead of a full *seah*—that which he has separated is valid] heave-offering.

[B]   "And [an agent] who separates one-tenth [*seah*] more heave-offering [than he should, i.e., who separates a *seah* and one-

tenth instead of only a *seah*—that which he has separated is
valid] heave-offering.

[C]   "But [the separation is] not valid [if he separates one-tenth more or
less] of the unconsecrated produce [i.e., if he takes one-fortieth or
one-sixtieth instead of one-fiftieth; so GRA].

[D]   "For [in the case of C] the deficit [i.e., the amount of heave-
offering the agent may validly refrain from separating] does not
equal the additional [quantity of heave-offering that an agent
who separates too much validly may include in his separation]."

[E]   How [does this work in a concrete case]?

[F]   It is so in the case of [a householder who usually] separates one-
fiftieth [of his produce].

[G]   If [the agent] separates one-fortieth, he diminishes [the quantity
of produce the householder keeps] by six-fourths [of a *qab* =
one and one-half *qab* = one-quarter *seah*. (There are six *qabs* in
a *seah*.) This is as follows: He separates heave-offering from fifty
seahs of produce. The one-fiftheth which normally is separated
would yield one *seah* of heave-offering. If the agent separates
one-fortieth instead, he takes as heave-offering a *seah* and a quarter
(i.e., six-fourths of a *qab*). This leaves a quarter *seah* less unconsecrated produce than the householder normally would retain.]

[H]   But if he separates one-sixtieth [of the fifty *seahs* of produce, the
householder] profits by four-fourths [of a *qab* = one *qab*, or a
sixth of a *seah*. This is because the agent separated only five-
sixths of a *seah* instead of the full *seah* he would have separated
had he taken one-fiftieth of the batch.]

The underlying assumption is that an agent must be allowed the
same leeway in separating too little heave-offering as he is in separating too much heave-offering, D. This being the case, M. Ter.
4:4F's "one-tenth more or less heave-offering" must refer to the
specific amount of heave-offering the agent takes, not to the percentage of the batch he separates. D is explained at F–H.

[**III. A**] [16]   Here [at M. Ter. 4:4F] you state that [if the agent separates a
tenth less heave-offering than he should], that which he separates
is valid heave-offering.

[B]   But here [at M. Ter. 4:4G] you state that [if he separates even one-hundredth too much], that which he separates is not valid heave-offering. [What accounts for the different rules?]

[C]   Said R. Hanina the son of R. Hillel, "Here [at M. Ter. 4:4F, the agent] intended [to separate] too little heave-offering. [Since the householder should not object to having this quantity of produce in the status of heave-offering, the separation is valid.]

[D]   "[But] here [at M. Ter. 4:4G, the agent] intentionally separated too much heave-offering." [The householder will not agree to this. Therefore the separation is not valid.]

The Yerushalmi explains the distinction between M. Ter. 4:4F and G. At F the agent separates too little heave-offering. The Yerushalmi states that since the householder himself intended everything the agent separated to be heave-offering, the agent's separation is valid. At M. Ter. 4:4G the agent separates too much heave-offering. Since he will have separated produce that the householder did not intend to be a priestly gift, the Yerushalmi holds that the separation is not valid. Yet in suggesting this interpretation of the Mishnah, the Yerushalmi ignores the fact that, at M. Ter. 4:4F, a separation of too much heave-offering (as well as of too little) is deemed valid. The distinction the Yerushalmi draws therefore does not hold.

[IV.A]¹⁷   [The problem is that M. Me. 6:1 seems to contradict M. Ter. 4:4G.] R. Haggai asked in the presence of R. Yose, "There [at M. Me. 6:1] we learn: *[(If) an agent carries out the terms of his appointment (and in doing so commits an act of sacrilege, that is, puts a consecrated object to secular use), the householder (who appointed him) is guilty of the sacrilege (and the agent is not). (But) if the agent does not meet the terms of his appointment (and commits an act of sacrilege), he, (and not the householder), is guilty of the sacrilege, (for in committing the transgression he acted as his own person). How so? If (the householder) told him, 'Give (consecrated) meat to my guests,' but he gave them (consecrated) liver (instead), or (if) he told him, 'Give (consecrated) liver (to my guests),' and he gave them (consecrated) meat (instead), the agent has committed sacrilege. (Even though the householder intended to transgress, he is not culpable, for his wishes were not carried out.)]*

[B]   "*[If the householder] told him [i.e., the agent], 'Give them each one piece [of consecrated meat],' and [the agent] told them, 'Take two pieces each,' [by which statement he validly carries out the householder's will and adds his own stipulation], and they then went and took three pieces [of consecrated meat] each, [such that they both fulfilled the agent's stipulation and committed their own transgression]—all of them have committed sacrilege.*

[C]   [Haggai now asks his question:] "[Why is it] that [contrary to the theory of this rule] here [at M. Ter. 4:4G] you say this, [that if the agent purposely separates an additional quantity of heave-offering, his separation is in no way valid]?" [On the paradigm of M. Me. 6:1, we should treat the quantity of heave-offering that the householder told the agent to separate to be valid and only the additional quantity, separated by the agent without the house-holder's permission, as not valid. That is, by part of his actions the agent fulfills the terms of his appointment, just as at M. Me. 6:1. The rest of his actions are to be judged independently.]

[D]   [Yose] answered him, "[The two cases are not comparable.] There [at M. Me. 6:1], as soon as [the guests take] the first piece of meat, [the agent's] responsibility to the householder has been fulfilled. [The householder is culpable for that action, for it fol-lowed his instructions. Anything which happens afterwards is separate.]

[E]   "But here [at M. Ter. 4:4G] the responsibility [of the agent to] the householder is not fulfilled until each and every piece of wheat [has been designated heave-offering]." [Since the designa-tion of all of the wheat to be heave-offering occurs at one and the same time, the designation cannot be treated as if it were in two distinct parts. If the agent takes too much heave-offering, he has not done what the householder wished, and his separation is not valid at all.]

[F]   What in practice is the difference between the two different rules, [M. Me. 6:1 and M. Ter. 4:4G? The following is a case involving heave-offering in which M. Me. 6:1's theory of agency applies.]

[G]   [The householder tells his agent to separate heave-offering from one specific batch of produce. If] there were before him [i.e., the agent] two batches, and he separated heave-offering from one of them according to the wishes [of the householder] and separated heave-offering from the other against the wishes [of the house-holder, the first separation of heave-offering is deemed valid. It conforms to the wishes of the householder. Only the second separation is not valid, for the agent did not have permission to perform it.]

Yose, D–E, shows that the cases of M. Me. 6:1 and M. Ter. 4:4 are not comparable. F is misleading. What follows does not answer its question, which would require a delineation of the different legal rulings that would result from the application to the same case of M. Me. 6:1 first and then M. Ter. 4:4. G simply provides a situation in which the first part of the agent's actions fulfills the terms of his appointment. In the present case this means that, while this first separation of heave-offering is deemed valid, the subsequent one may not be. In this way the case is comparable to that referred to at M. Me. 6:1.

4:5 [P: 4:4b]

[A]   *One who separates much heave-offering:*

[B]   *R. Eliezer says, "[He may separate as much as] one-tenth [of his batch],*

[C]   *"[an amount] equal to [that separated as] heave-offering of the tithe.*

[D]   *"[If he wishes to separate] more than this, let him designate it [i.e., the surplus] heave-offering of the tithe for a different batch [of produce]."*

[E]   *R. Ishmael says, "[He may separate so much as to render] half [of the batch] unconsecrated produce and half [of the batch] heave-offering."*

[F]   *R. Tarfon and R. Aqiba say, "[He may separate as much heave-offering as he wishes] provided that he leaves there [some] unconsecrated produce, [however small an amount]."*

The issue is what percentage of the batch has the potential, upon the designation of the householder, of taking on the status of heave-offering. The three answers given, Eliezer's (B–D), Ishmael's (E), and Tarfon and Aqiba's (F), are analyzed in turn, units **I–II, III,** and **IV.**

[I.A]   R. Jeremiah in the name of R. Yohanan,[18] [and] R. Jacob bar
        Aha in the name of R. Simeon b. Laqish [say], "The opinion of
        R. Eliezer [M. Ter. 4:5B, that a person may only designate as
        heave-offering one-tenth of the batch], accords with the view of
        the House of Shammai [M. Ter. 1:4].

[B]   "For the House of Shammai hold that [if a householder separates
        as heave-offering some produce which rightly can have that status
        and some which cannot, the separation is valid, but that, as a
        result, what the house-holder has designated to be the] holy
        [heave-offering] is a mixture of heave-offering and unconsecrated
        produce.

[C][19] "In the same way R. Eliezer says, '[If the householder separates
        more than one-tenth of the batch, that which he has separated as
        the] holy [heave-offering] is a mixture of heave-offering and un-
        consecrated produce.'"

The Yerushalmi claims a correlation between two seemingly un-
connected rules of the tractate. Its notion that C is the view of
Eliezer, however, appears arbitrary. The same view may as well
be assigned to Ishmael, M. Ter. 4:5E. In light of this, the unit is
perplexing.

[II.A] [The question is how Yohanan and Hezeqiah understand the
        view of Eliezer, M. Ter. 4:5B. We recall that Yohanan, Y. Ter. 4:1
        IV, holds that a small quantity of untithed produce does not dis-
        appear in a majority of tithed produce. This is because once the
        heave-offering is designated, each and every stalk in the batch is
        established as either being heave-offering or being exempt from
        the separation of heave-offering. No confusion exists concerning
        which stalks are which. As we shall see, Hezeqiah, F–H, has
        the opposite view.] According to the opinion of R. Yohanan [as
        just described] it makes sense [to state as Eliezer does, that one
        who wishes to separate more than one-tenth of a batch must des-
        ignate additional produce to be heave-offering of the tithe for a
        different batch].

[B]   [The reason is as follows: According to Yohanan, once the house-
        holder] designates one-tenth [of the batch] as heave-offering, this
        leaves one out of every ten [stalks of grain or pieces of produce]

in the status of heave-offering and [renders] the rest [of the batch] exempt from the separation of heave-offering and subject only to the separation of tithes.

[C]   For this reason, [that the batch no longer is subject to the separation of heave-offering], you must state [along with Eliezer, M. Ter. 4:5D] that *[if he wishes to separate] more than this, let him designate it heave-offering of the tithe on behalf of a different batch [of produce* (M. Ter. 4:5D)].

[D]   But according to Hezeqiah [Y. Ter. 4:1 **IV,** who, it appears, holds that once heave-offering is separated from a batch of produce, the batch still remains subject to the separation of more heave-offering, Eliezer's view] is not logical. [In Hezeqiah's view the householder may designate additional produce to be heave-offering of the tithe for that same batch, as we shall now see.]

[E]   [Once one] designates one-tenth [of the batch] as heave-offering, does this leave one-tenth [of the batch to be heave-offering? The exact meaning of the question is not clear. The point is in the following:]

[F]   [In Hezeqiah's view, even after one-tenth of the batch has been separated as heave-offering] the rest [of the produce in the batch] still is subject to the separation of all [agricultural gifts, tithes as well as heave-offering].

[G]   Yet, [Hezeqiah may ask, why] should we learn this: *[Let the householder] designate additional [heave-offering]* as heave-offering of the tithe for a different batch [M. Ter. 4:5D]?

[H]   [In Hezeqiah's view, this makes no sense. Since, as F indicates, the batch still is subject to the separation of heave-offering] let him designate [the additional produce he wishes to give the priest] heave-offering of the tithe for that (read: same) batch [from which he already separated heave-offering]!

[I]   [The following seems to indicate that Hezeqiah did not follow the view H attributes to him. But the point is not entirely clear.] Hezeqiah's view follows that which R. Hiyya taught. For R. Hiyya taught, "[If the householder wishes to separate as heave-offering more than one-tenth of the batch,] let him designate the additional [amount] to be heave-offering of the tithe for a different batch."

The issue is the logic of the view of Eliezer, M. Ter. 4:5B. This
is analyzed in light of statements made previously by Yohanan
and Hezeqiah. The translation of E–I is provisional because of
unsolved questions of interpretation, E and I, and problems of
text, G–H. As found in P, V, and L, H repeats G, possibly a
case of dittography. H is lacking entirely from R. I have solved
the problem through the emendation at H. Alternatively, PM
reads "the same batch" at G and "a different batch" at H. He
thus assumes that the Yerushalmi has a different reading of M.
Ter. 4:5D than has been preserved in MSS. of that document.

[**III.**A]   What is the scriptural basis for the opinion of R. Ishmael [M.
Ter. 4:5E, that only half of a batch of produce may be designated heave-offering]?

[B]   [Num. 18:12 refers to] 'The best of your grain.'

[C]   The [quantity which is] the best of the grain can be only as much
as [the quantity of] the [remainder of] the grain [that is not the
best].

Only half of a batch of produce can be "the best" of that produce. This accounts for Ishmael's view, M. Ter. 4:5E.

[**IV.**A]   What is the scriptural basis [for the view of Tarfon and Aqiba,
M. Ter. 4:5F] that one has not validly separated heave-offering
unless he leaves behind some [unconsecrated produce]?

[B]   Scripture states, 'From the first of your coarse meal [you shall
give an offering to the Lord,' Num. 15:21].

[C]   [This means that the offering must be] 'from' the first [of the
coarse meal] and not be *all* of the first [of the coarse meal].

Like that of Ishmael, Y. Ter. 4:5 **III,** the view of Tarfon and
Aqiba derives from Scripture.

4:6 [P: 4:5]

[A]   *At three times [in the year] do they calculate [the quantity of
produce in] the [storage] basket [in order to allow the separation
of the proper quantity of heave-offering]:*

[B]   *(1) at [the time of] the first ripe fruits, (2) [at the time of] the
late summer fruits, and (3) in the middle of the summer.*

[C]   *(1) One who counts [the produce in order accurately to estimate
the quantity he must separate as heave-offering] is praiseworthy,
and (2) one who measures [the volume of the produce] is more
praiseworthy than he; but (3) one who weighs [the produce] is
the most praiseworthy of the three.*

Low-quality produce picked at the beginning and end of the harvest should not be designated heave-offering for the better produce that ripens and is picked in the middle of the summer,
A–B (see M. Ter. 2:6S). C is familiar from M. Ter. 1:7. The
householder may not measure out as heave-offering a set quantity of produce. But he may calculate the quantity of produce
from which the offering is to be separated. This allows him to
accurately estimate how much produce he should set aside as the
priest's gift. The Yerushalmi's one unit questions the meaning of
C and asks whether or not one may separate heave-offering simply by estimating how much produce is contained in the batch.

[I.A]   More praiseworthy than whom is the one [who measures the
quantity of produce from which he is going to separate heave-
offering, M. Ter. 4:6C2]?

[B]   Said R. Huna, "He is more praiseworthy than one who separates
heave-offering from [produce the quantity of which has been]
estimated [but the quantity of which has not been determined by
count, volume, or weight]." [Huna's point is that measuring the
quantity of the produce is not more praiseworthy than counting,
M. Ter. 4:6C1. It is more praiseworthy than simply estimating.]

[C]   Said R. Hanina the son of R. Hillel, "Mishnah [Ter. 4:6C] says
this explicitly.

[D]   "[M. Ter. 4:6C3 says:] *But one who weighs [the produce] is more praiseworthy than the [other] three."* [Read this way, the Mishnah implies that besides calculating volume, counting and weighing produce, referred to specifically at M. Ter. 4:6C, there is an additional method by which to separate heave-offering. This is simply to estimate how much food is in the batch, the method which Huna, B, adduces.]

[E]   [Disagreeing with B–D] said R. Hinena, "Interpret [M. Ter. 4:6C3] to mean: *[One who weighs the produce is the most praiseworthy] of the three* [i.e., of those who count, calculate the volume of, or weigh their produce].

[F]   "Now [if this is the meaning], you cannot learn from the verse anything [about separating heave-offering from produce the quantity of which only has been estimated]." [Unlike what Huna, B, and Hanina, C, claim, M. Ter. 4:6C knows nothing of the separation of heave-offering from produce which has not been counted, weighed, or had its volume calculated. The Mishnah refers only to these three.]

A's question is answered at B + C–D, with E–F providing a divergent view. The unit focuses on the interpretation of M. Ter. 4:6C3, disputed specifically at D versus E + F.

4:7 [P: 4:6]

[A]   *R. Eliezer says, "Heave-offering is neutralized [i.e., takes on the status of unconsecrated food, when one part of heave-offering is mixed] in [a total of] a hundred and one [parts of produce]."*

[B]   *R. Joshua says, "[It is neutralized when there is one part of heave-offering] in a hundred [parts of produce] plus [a bit] more.*

[C]   *"And this [bit] more has no [fixed] measure."*

[D]   *R. Yose b. Meshullam says, "[This bit more is] an additional qab per hundred seahs [i.e., 1/600 of the batch],*

[E]   *"[which equals] one-sixth of [the seah of] heave-offering [which is neutralized] in the mixture [of slightly more than one hundred seahs of produce]."*

If heave-offering constitutes less than approximately one percent
of a mixture with unconsecrated produce, it loses its sanctified
status. When this happens it may be eaten as common food, by
a nonpriest. The exact proportions under which heave-offering
is neutralized are disputed here. The Yerushalmi provides the
scriptural basis for the theory that underlies this pericope: If
much heave-offering is mixed with unconsecrated food, it imparts
its own consecrated status to that food. This accomplished, the
Yerushalmi simply repeats in its own words the present dispute.

[I.A] From what verse do we know that [heave-offering which is mixed
with unconsecrated produce] is not[20] [necessarily] neutralized
[but may, if it is of sufficient quantity, impart the status of heave-
offering to the whole batch]?

[B] Said R. Jonah, "[We know it because] it is written [in Scripture]:
'[Out of all the gifts to you (Levites), you shall present every
offering due to the Lord], from all the best of them, giving the
hallowed part from them' [Num. 18 : 29].

[C] "In the case of any [offering] that is lifted up 'from them'—if
[that offering] falls back 'into them' [i.e., into the produce from
which it was separated], it [imparts to that produce] its holy
status."

[D] And how much [heave-offering need there be in the batch such
that it imparts to that batch its own consecrated status]?

[E] [There must be at least] one [*seah* of heave-offering] in [a total
of] a hundred [*seahs* of produce].

[F] R. Eliezer [M. Ter. 4 : 7A] says [43a], "If one adds [to this hundred *seahs*] another *seah* [of unconsecrated produce, such that
the heave-offering constitutes one part in a hundred and one, the
heave-offering] is neutralized."

[G] R. Joshua [M. Ter. 4 : 7B–C] says, "[If one] adds any small amount
[of unconsecrated produce, the heave-offering] is neutralized."

[H] *R. Yose b. Meshullam says, "This additional amount [referred
to by Joshua] is one qab per hundred seahs, [which equals] one-
sixth of [the seah] of heave-offering which is neutralized in a
mixture [of slightly more than one hundred seahs of produce"*;
M. Ter. 4 : 7D–E].

[I]   And the law follows [Yose b. Meshullam's] view.

The first of the pericope's two units (A–C + D–E) provides a fact central to understanding M. Ter. 4:7. Under certain circumstances heave-offering imparts its own consecrated status to common food with which it is mixed. By now it is commonplace that such a law concerning heave-offering may be deduced from a scriptural statement about the tithe of the tithe, given the priest by the Levite. F–H rehearses the Mishnah's dispute concerning when heave-offering is neutralized. The Yerushalmi's contribution is at I.

4:8 [P: 4:7a]

[A]   *R. Joshua says, "[Unconsecrated] black figs serve to neutralize white figs [in the status of heave-offering with which they are mixed], and [unconsecrated] white figs serve to neutralize black figs [in the status of heave-offering].*

[B]   *"[And in the case of] cakes of pressed figs—(1) [unconsecrated] large ones serve to neutralize small ones [in the status of heave-offering], and [unconsecrated] small ones serve to neutralize large ones [in the status of heave-offering]; (2) [unconsecrated] round ones serve to neutralize square ones [in the status of heave-offering], and [unconsecrated] square ones serve to neutralize round ones [in the status of heave-offering]."*

[C]   *R. Eliezer deems [heave-offering mixed with such different types of its same genus of produce to remain] forbidden [for consumption by a nonpriest. The heave-offering is not neutralized.]*

[D]   *R. Aqiba says, "If it is known which [type of produce in the status of heave-offering] fell into the unconsecrated produce, the two different types] do not serve to neutralize the heave-offering in conjunction with one another.*

[E]   *"But if it is not known which [type of produce in the status of heave-offering] fell [into the unconsecrated produce, the two different types of produce] do serve to neutralize the heave-offering in conjunction with one another."*

Distinguishing features such as color and size of produce are irrelevant in determining whether or not heave-offering is neutralized. So Joshua, A–B. Eliezer disagrees, C. In a mixture of
unconsecrated white figs and black figs in the status of heave-
offering, for instance, the heave-offering can be distinguished
and so may be removed from the mixture. Since the priestly gift
is not lost, Eliezer says that it is not neutralized. Aqiba's view,
D–E, is in essential agreement with Eliezer. If the householder
knows which produce is heave-offering, it is not neutralized.

The Yerushalmi begins by explaining the nature of the dispute
between Joshua and Eliezer, unit I. At units II–IV it looks specifically at Joshua's view, asking how it is that heave-offering is neutralized in a batch from which it could be recovered and given to the
priest. This exercise is continued in the final unit, VIII, which
thus appears out of place. Units V–VII intervene, giving the law
of neutralization for ambiguous cases, namely, if it is not certain
that heave-offering was mixed with unconsecrated produce or if
there is a doubt whether or not the produce in the mixture actually has the consecrated status of a priestly gift. Since such secondary questions normally conclude the Yerushalmi's discussion,
the position of unit VIII is all the more perplexing.

[I.A]   [The question is why Eliezer, M. Ter. 4:8C, rules that white figs do
not serve to neutralize black ones in the status of heave-offering.]
R. Isi in the name of R. Yohanan [says], "R. Eliezer reasons that
[if] black figs [in the status of heave-offering] fall into [a batch of
unconsecrated] white figs, one may eat the white figs [which it is
known are not in the status of heave-offering and leave behind
the black ones, which are known to be heave-offering].

[B]   "Yet [even though this is the case, Joshua, M. Ter. 4:8A–B,
claims that] white figs serve to neutralize black figs?" [For the
reason given at A, this clearly is unreasonable.]

[C]   Said R. Eleazar,[21] "With this argument [given at A], R. Eliezer
would respond to R. Joshua's claim that [unconsecrated] white figs
serve to neutralize black figs [in the status of heave-offering]."

[D]   [From this] statement, [A, that Eliezer used to counter Joshua's
view, it is clear that Joshua] holds that [even] in a case in which
it is known what fell [i.e., that the black figs are in the status of
heave-offering and the white ones are unconsecrated], they neutralize the heave-offering in conjunction with one another.

[E]   [Disagreeing with D] Kahana says, "[Joshua holds that if it is known which figs are the heave-offering, the white and black figs] do not neutralize [the heave-offering in conjunction with one another]."

[F]   In the view of Kahana [that Joshua believes that unconsecrated white figs serve to neutralize black figs in the status of heave-offering only if the householder does not know which figs actually are in the status of heave-offering], what is the difference between the view of R. Joshua and that of R. Aqiba [M. Ter. 4:8D–E, who appears to hold that same view]?

[G]   [According to Kahana, their opinions differ] in the case of one who knew [which figs have the status of heave-offering] but forgot.

[H]   [In such a case, says Kahana], in the opinion of R. Joshua, [the white and black figs] serve to neutralize the [heave-offering in conjunction with one another, as though it never was known which are heave-offering].

[I]   [But] in the opinion of R. Aqiba, [in this case the white and black figs] do not serve to neutralize [the heave-offering in conjunction with one another. The case is treated as though the individual still knows which figs are heave-offering.]

A–C + D gives the issue underlying the dispute between Eliezer and Joshua, M. Ter. 4:8A–C. Eliezer states that the heave-offering may be retrieved from the mixture and therefore is not neutralized, A. Joshua, B + D, holds that neutralization occurs anyway. E suggests a different interpretation, which states that Joshua agrees to Eliezer's principle. The former disagrees with the latter only for the specific case in which the householder does not know which figs are heave-offering. In such a case the heave-offering cannot be recovered and so, Joshua says, is deemed neutralized. F–I explains how, in this view, Joshua's opinion differs from that of Aqiba, M. Ter. 4:7D–E.

[II.A]   [The following assumes that Joshua's view is that white figs serve to neutralize black ones even if it is known that the black ones, but not the white, are heave-offering. It describes a case in which the householder has many black and white figs. Only some of the black ones are in the status of heave-offering, and it is not known which.] Simeon bar Ba in the name of R. Yohanan [says], "[Joshua's opinion, M. Ter. 4:8A–B] applies only if one black fig [about which there is a question whether or not it is heave-offering] fell into two white figs [which are not heave-offering], such that [the black fig, which might be heave-offering,] is an insignificant portion [of the mixture]."

[B]   [Carrying forward the logic of A,] R. Zeira asked in the presence of R. Mana, "Does it not make sense that [the black fig which might be heave-offering must fall] into three [white figs which certainly are not heave-offering]?[22]

[C]   "Thus if one of them [i.e., of the white figs] is lost, there still will be two [white figs, as required by A]."

[D]   [Mana] said to him, "I also think that [is the case]."

[E]   [The following suggests a different interpretation of how unconsecrated white figs serve to neutralize black figs in the status of heave-offering.] Bar Padiah says, "One grinds [together all of the figs], and [as a result the vast majority of unconsecrated produce in the mixture] renders [the small quantity of heave-offering] permitted [for consumption by a nonpriest]." [The reason is that once all the produce is ground, the white and black figs cannot be separated from one another.]

[F]   And even though Bar Padiah said, "[One food] is not swallowed up [by a different food], except in the case of wine and oil [which, since they are liquids, cannot be separated once they are mixed]," he agrees in this case that [the consecrated black olives] are swallowed up [and so neutralized by the unconsecrated white olives with which they are ground].

[G]   The view of the rabbis disagrees [with that of Bar Padiah; see below, Y. Ter. 4:8 **IV**].

A, developed at B–C, gives one interpretation of Joshua's view that unconsecrated white figs serve to neutralize black ones in the status of heave-offering. It claims that, in Joshua's view, this occurs only if there is a vast majority of unconsecrated white figs. E–F suggests a different interpretation. Yet in E–F's view, Joshua's position is just like the one, in the Mishnah, held by Eliezer.[23] If heave-offering is to be neutralized, it must be inextricably mixed with unconsecrated produce. This is accomplished if the black and white figs are ground up together.

[III.A]   [The following refers to M. Hal. 1:4, which states that dough offering need not be separated from dough that had been unconsecrated, but which took on the status of heave-offering through being mixed with more than one-percent of that offering.] Kahana asked Samuel, "[Is it not so that] this [rule] we learn here [M. Hal. 1:4], that a mixture of heave-offering and unconsecrated produce [is not subject to the separation of dough offering], is not reasonable [except in a case] in which the mixture is composed of more than half of heave-offering [and less than half of unconsecrated dough]?" [If the mixture is mostly unconsecrated dough, however, it is logical that it is subject to dough offering, contrary to M. Hal. 1:4.]

[B]   [Samuel] said to him, "I also think so.

[C]   "But [to find out for sure] go to the land of Israel and ask."

[D]   [Kahana finds that his reasoning at A is not correct.] When [Kahana] went [to the land of Israel], he heard this which R. Yose in the name of R. Yohanan said, "Even if [only] one *seah* [of heave-offering] fell into [so much as] ninety-nine [*seahs* of] unconsecrated [dough, the mixture, which takes on the status of heave-offering, is not subject to dough offering, just as M. Hal. 1:4 states]."

[E]   Said R. Abbahu, "Thus did R. Simeon b. Laqish reply to [the statement of] Yohanan [D]: '[You are wrong!] How can a single *seah* [of dough in the status of heave-offering] exempt [from the separation of dough offering] all the rest [of the unconsecrated dough in the mixture]?'" [It is not reasonable to claim it does. A appears correct.]

[F]   [Yohanan answers Simeon b. Laqish], "Is it not so that in the case of a [large] cake of pressed figs [in the status of heave-offering, which is mixed] with [small unconsecrated] cakes of pressed figs, [that the mixture does not take on the status of heave-offering, since] it is certain that [the householder can identify which cake is] heave-offering and can remove it from the mixture?

[G]   "You say that this [exception to the rule which says that mixtures of heave-offering and unconsecrated produce take on the status of heave-offering] is a lenient ruling.

[H]   "So this [M. Hal. 1:4] is a leniency, [and even though the vast majority of the batch originally was subject to the separation of dough offering, once a little heave-offering is mixed in, the batch is exempt, as M. Hal. 1:4 states.]"

The unit explores the logic of M. Hal. 1:4. It appears here because Yohanan, F–H, refers to M. Ter. 4:8. But the issue is primary in the context of Y. Hal. 1:3 and not here. Indeed the unit intrudes between Y. Ter. 4:8 **II** and **IV**, which belong together.[24]

[**IV**.A]   [The following contains the rabbis' reply to Bar Padiah, who, Y. Ter. 4:8 **II**, states that if black figs in the status of heave-offering are mixed with unconsecrated white figs, the heave-offering is neutralized only if all of the produce in the mixture is ground up. Rabbis say that this is not always the case.] [Rabbis] answered him [i.e., Bar Padiah], "The law is different in the case of cakes [of pressed figs, consecrated large ones of which are mixed with unconsecrated small ones. In this case the heave-offering is neutralized even if all the figs are not ground up], for [the figs in the status of heave-offering], already lost [their consecrated status when they first were mixed with the large quantity of unconsecrated figs]."

[B]   [The following disagrees with A and agrees with Bar Padiah in that to be neutralized heave-offering must always be thoroughly ground up with the unconsecrated produce.] R. Jonah and R. Yose, the two of them in the name of R. Zeira [say], "Even if wheat [in the status of heave-offering] is mixed with [more than a hundred times its quantity in unconsecrated wheat], one must grind [the whole mixture in order] to render [the heave-offering] permitted [for common consumption]."

This continues Y. Ter. 4:8 **II**'s discussion of how different forms of the same kind of produce can join together to neutralize heave-offering. Rabbis, A, disagree with Bar Padiah, Y. Ter. 4:8 **II**. B argues in Bar Padiah's favor. Its notion is unknown to the Mishnah.

[**V.**A]   There were before him twenty [unconsecrated] figs and one fig
[in the status of heave-offering] fell into them, [imparting to the
whole batch the status of heave-offering]. Then one of the figs
[from the mixture] was lost [but it was not known whether or
not it was the one in the status of heave-offering],[25] and one more
[fig in the status of heave-offering fell] into [the mixture]. Again,
one of the [figs in the mixture] was lost [but it was not known
whether or not it was in the status of heave-offering. The result
is that there may be no figs in the status of heave-offering in the
batch, or there may be as many as two. Do we deem the batch to
have the status of heave-offering?]

[B]   R. Simeon b. Laqish says, "This case of doubt is adjudicated as
though [the status of heave-offering] was voided by the larger
number [of unconsecrated figs with which the figs in the status of
heave-offering were mixed]." [In essence, we assume that each
fig that fell from the batch was in the status of heave-offering.]

[C]   [Disagreeing,] R. Yohanan says, "Is there proof that in each case
[the fig in the status of heave-offering was lost]?" [No! It is more
likely that unconsecrated figs were lost. The batch as a whole
therefore must be deemed a mixture of heave-offering and unconsecrated produce, such that it is treated like heave-offering.]

[D]   R. Yohanan concedes that if one took heave-offering on their behalf [i.e., to replace the lost figs in the status of heave-offering]
from a different batch, or if [in separating heave-offering] from a
different batch one took much [heave-offering in order to make
up for the heave-offering figs lost in the unconsecrated figs], the
case is adjudicated as though the heave-offering was voided in
the larger quantity [of unconsecrated figs]. [That is, in order to
impart to the doubtful mixture the status of unconsecrated figs,
the householder simply may replace the heave-offering lost in
that mixture.]

How to adjudicate this case of doubt is disputed, B versus C + D.

[**VI.**A]   [The point is that of T. Ter. 5 : 10N – T. Consecrated and unconsecrated wine in sealed jugs are not deemed mixed together. Therefore the consecrated, heave-offering wine is not neutralized.
Once the jugs are opened, however, we deem the heave-offering

and unconsecrated wine to be mixed. If there is sufficient unconsecrated wine, the heave-offering is neutralized.] R. Simeon b.
Laqish in the name of R. Hoshaya [says], "[If] there were before
him one hundred and fifty [sealed] jugs [of wine, one of which
contains wine in the status of heave-offering, but it is not known
which], and a hundred of [the jugs] were [then] opened—[the wine
in] these hundred is permitted [for consumption by nonpriests].

[B]   "But [the wine in] the other fifty is forbidden [for consumption
by nonpriests]. [These jugs are not deemed mixed with the others. Any of them might contain heave-offering and therefore all
are forbidden to nonpriests.]

[C]   "But when these other fifty jugs are opened [the wine in them
too is deemed] permitted [for consumption by nonpriests]."
[Now all of the jugs are considered party to the mixture, and the
heave-offering is neutralized among all of them.]

[D]   [In qualification of A–C] said R. Zeira, "This applies [only] if
[the jugs] should happen to be opened. But de jure it is forbidden [purposely to open them in order to cause the heave-offering
to be neutralized]."

A jug of wine in the status of heave-offering is lost among jugs of
unconsecrated wine. The wine in the status of heave-offering is
deemed mixed with, and so neutralized by, unconsecrated wine
in jugs that are not sealed. The same point is made at T. Ter.
5:10N–T, a pericope that is not cited here.

[VII.A]   R. Zeira in the name of R. Padiah [says], "That which certainly
is in the status of heave-offering renders forbidden [up to] a hundred [times its quantity in unconsecrated produce with which it
is mixed]. [If the heave-offering is a smaller percentage than one-
hundredth of the batch, it is neutralized, as M. Ter. 4:7 states.]

[B]   "But if there is a doubt [whether or not produce is in the status
of heave-offering, it renders forbidden for consumption by a
nonpriest only up to] fifty [times its quantity in unconsecrated
produce with which it is mixed]." [In a proportion of less than
one to fifty, such questionable heave-offering is neutralized.]

[C]   [Zeira's statement is challenged. If we deem the doubtful heave-

offering to have the status of heave-offering so as to render forbidden fifty times its quantity of unconsecrated produce], why
[does it not have the same effect upon] sixty [times its quantity
in unconsecrated produce, and upon] seventy [times its quantity
in unconsecrated produce]? [That is, if you claim that produce
about which there is a doubt whether or not it is heave-offering
is in *some* respects like true heave-offering, you logically must
state that it is in *all* respects like true heave-offering. Thus it will
impart its own status to up to one hundred times its quantity in
unconsecrated produce.]

[D]   [C's challenge is answered through a qualification of the point of
B. Just as C suggests, doubtful heave-offering, like true heave-
offering, imparts its own status to up to one hundred times its
own quantity in unconsecrated produce. Further, if the doubtful
heave-offering falls into] up to fifty [times its own volume in unconsecrated produce] one may not (so GRA)[26] [render the mixture unconsecrated by taking] much [heave-offering from a different batch in order to make up for the heave-offering lost in
this mixture (see Y. Ter. 4:8 **V**.D). This is also the case for true
heave-offering.]

[E]   [Doubtful heave-offering differs from true heave-offering only in
that if the mixture has in it] a higher percentage [of unconsecrated produce] than this [i.e., one in fifty], one may (so GRA)
[render it unconsecrated by taking] much [heave-offering from a
different batch in order to compensate for the doubtful heave-
offering lost in the mixture. One may not do this in the case of
true heave-offering.]

The issue is whether or not produce about which there is a doubt
whether or not it is in the status of heave-offering is subject to
the same rules as produce that certainly is heave-offering. Zeira
says that it is not, A–B. It is neutralized under more lenient
circumstances than what certainly is heave-offering. C challenges
this contention, leading to the revision of A–B, at D–E.

[**VIII**.A]   Said R. Huna, "This is the meaning of Mishnah [Ter. 4:8B1]:
*[In the case of] cakes of pressed figs—[unconsecrated] large ones
serve to neutralize small ones [in the status of heave-offering]—*

[this is so] if [the large cakes] weigh [more than a hundred times what the small ones in the status of heave-offering weigh. We do not require that there be a hundred large unconsecrated cakes to neutralize one small cake in the status of heave-offering.]

[B]   *"And [unconsecrated] small [cakes of pressed figs] serve to neutralize large ones [in the status of heave-offering]—*[if there is a hundred times the quantity of consecrated cakes] by number." [The small unconsecrated cakes need not constitute one hundred times the weight or volume of the heave-offering in order to neutralize it.]

Huna resolves an ambiguity left open by M. Ter. 4:8. Produce of one size is in the status of heave-offering. Unconsecrated produce with which it is mixed is a different size. How do we determine whether or not this unconsecrated produce comprises a sufficient quantity to neutralize the heave-offering? Huna applies the standard that makes it most likely that the heave-offering will be neutralized. This puts the householder at an advantage, making it less likely that he will have to sell all of his contaminated produce to the priest at the low value of heave-offering.

4:9 [P: 4:7b]

[F]   *"How so? [The question is what Aqiba, M. Ter. 4:8D–E, means.]*

[G]   *"[If there were] fifty [unconsecrated] white figs and fifty [unconsecrated] black figs [together in a basket]—*

[H]   *"[if] a black fig [in the status of heave-offering] fell into the basket, the black figs are forbidden [for consumption as unconsecrated food, since any one of them might be heave-offering], but the white figs remain permitted [for consumption as unconsecrated food. It is clear that no white fig is heave-offering.]*

[I]   *"[If] a white fig [which was heave-offering] fell [into the basket], the white figs are forbidden [for consumption as unconsecrated produce], and the black figs remain permitted [for consumption as unconsecrated produce, just as at H].*

[J]   *"But if one does not know what [color fig in the status of heave-offering] fell [into the basket, the white and black figs join to-*

*gether and] serve to neutralize the heave-offering in conjunction
with one another, [such that all the figs in the basket remain
permitted for consumption]."*

[K] *And in this [rule at M. Ter. 4:8A–C], R. Eliezer rules stringently, [for he says that foods of differing colors, sizes, and shapes
do not join together to neutralize heave-offering], and R. Joshua
rules leniently, [stating that they do serve to neutralize heave-
offering in conjunction with one another].*

M. Ter. 4:9 explains the circumstances under which Aqiba, M.
Ter. 4:8D–E, holds that produce of different sizes or colors
joins together to neutralize heave-offering. Aqiba says that this
happens only if the householder does not know which produce is
the heave-offering. The Yerushalmi's one unit refers back to the
dispute between Eliezer and Joshua, M. Ter. 4:8A–C, and asks
whether either of these authorities holds this same view. This
acute reading of the dispute between Eliezer and Joshua in light
of Aqiba's particular concern is not, however, the work of the
Yerushalmi. This reading already exists in the Tosefta, which is
cited at length.

[I.A] *And in this [rule at M. Ter. 4:8A–C] R. Eliezer rules stringently
[for he states that foods of differing colors, sizes, and shapes do
not join together to neutralize heave-offering], and R. Joshua
rules leniently, [holding that they do; M. Ter. 4:9K].*

[B] [Yohanan now introduces two different versions of the dispute
between Eliezer and Joshua, M. Ter. 4:8A–C. One version, C,
is cited in the name of Meir. The other derives from Judah, D.]
Said R. Yohanan, "These Tannaitic authorities [i.e., Meir and
Judah, say the following]:

[C] **"When you reason, you can state [as follows]: '"If [the house-
holder] knows [which color figs are heave-offering, the black
and white figs do] not [join together to] neutralize [that heave-
offering]. If [the householder] does not know [which color fig
is the heave-offering, the black and white figs] do [join together to] neutralize [the heave-offering]"—the words of R.
Eliezer. R. Joshua says, "Whether or not [the householder]
knows [which color fig is in the status of heave-offering, the**

black and white figs join together to] neutralize [the heave-
offering]"'—the words of R. Meir.

[D]   "R. Judah says, '"Whether or not one knows [which color fig
is in the status of heave-offering, the black and white figs] do
not [join together to] neutralize [the heave-offering]"—the
words of R. Eliezer.[27] R. Joshua says, "Whether or not one
knows [which color fig is in the status of heave-offering, the
white and black figs] do [join together to] neutralize [the heave-
offering].""

[E][28]   "[We conclude with the view of Aqiba, M. Ter. 4:8D–E.] And
R. Aqiba says, 'If it is known which [color figs are in the status of
heave-offering, black and white figs] do not [join together to]
neutralize [the heave-offering]. But if it is not known [which
color figs are in the status of heave-offering, black and white
figs] do [join together to neutralize [the heave-offering'"; T.
Ter. 5:10].

The pericope interprets M. Ter. 4:8A–C through reference to
the Tosefta's supplementary discussion. A cites M. Ter. 4:9K
and accounts for the placement of the unit here, with M. Ter.
4:9. Yohanan then cites T. Ter. 5:10, which gives two versions
of the dispute between Eliezer and Joshua, M. Ter. 4:8A–C.
Meir, C, attributes to Eliezer the position held by Aqiba at M.
Ter. 4:8D–E. As my comment to that pericope indicated, this is
logical, making explicit the fundamental agreement between the
views of these two authorities. Meir cites in Joshua's name the
opposite of the opinion that authority holds in the Mishnah. I
cannot account for this.[29] Judah, D–E, simply repeats the substance of the opinions of each of M. Ter. 4:8's authorities.

4:10 [P: 4:7c]

[L]   *But in this [case] R. Eliezer is lenient and R. Joshua rules
stringently.*

[M]   *In [a case in which] one stuffed a* litra *of dried figs [in the status
of heave-offering] into the mouth of a jar [filled] with [a hundred
litras of] unconsecrated [dried figs], but does not know which
[jar he so stuffed]—*

[N]   R. Eliezer says, "They regard them as if they were loose figs,
and the ones at the bottom [of the jar] serve to neutralize the
ones at the top."

[O]   R. Joshua says, "[The heave-offering] will not be neutralized unless a hundred jars are there."

Even though the heave-offering in the mouth of the jar can be
recovered, it is neutralized. So Eliezer, N. This position previously was held by Joshua, a fact of which L is well aware. Joshua
holds that the heave-offering remains distinct from the unconsecrated produce and therefore is not neutralized. It loses its consecrated status only if the jar in which it is found is mixed among
a hundred other such jars, O. Then the heave-offering truly is
lost within a hundred times its quantity in unconsecrated produce. The Yerushalmi's comments, devoted to the pericope of
the Tosefta that supplements M. Ter. 4:10, are appropriate, for
the Tosefta's purpose is to clarify the principle that informs the
position of each of the Mishnah's authorities.

[I.A]   "A litra of dried figs [in the status of heave-offering] which one
stuffed into the mouth of a jar [filled with unconsecrated dried
figs], but does not know in which [jar] he stuffed them [M. Ter.
4:10M, with slight variation]; [or which one stuffed] into a
beehive [filled with dried figs], but does not know into which
beehive he stuffed them; [or which] one pressed on a circle of
pressed figs, but does not know on which circle of pressed figs
he pressed them—[30]

[B]   "R. Eliezer says, 'They regard the [figs on] top [of the jar, beehive, or ring of pressed figs] as if they are loose [and therefore
are mixed with the rest of the figs].[31] If there are there [in the
jar, etc.] a hundred and one litras [of produce, the one litra of
heave-offering] is neutralized. But if not, it is not neutralized.'

[C]   "R. Joshua says, 'If there are there a hundred mouths [of jars,
etc., the heave-offering] is neutralized. But if not, [produce in]
the mouths [of the jars, etc.] is forbidden, [since it might be
heave-offering] and [produce in] the bottoms [of the jars, etc.]
is permitted, [i.e., retains the status of unconsecrated food,
since it surely is not heave-offering]'"—the words of R. Meir
(so T.; Y.: R. Judah).

[D]   **R. Judah (so T.; Y.: Meir) says, "R. Eliezer says, 'If there are there a hundred mouths [of jars, etc., the heave-offering] is neutralized. But if not, [produce in] the mouths [of the jars, etc.] is forbidden and [produce in] the bottoms [of the jars, etc.] is permitted.'**

[E]   **"R. Joshua says, 'Even if there are there three hundred mouths [of jars, etc., the heave-offering] is not neutralized [for heave-offering in one jar is not neutralized by unconsecrated produce found in a different jar'"; T. Ter. 5:11].**

[F]   [The preceding] indicates that they treat jars (lit.: mouths) as a commodity that one [sells by a] count. [If they were treated as something normally sold by weight, it would be irrelevant how many jugs were present. What would matter simply would be the weight of unconsecrated produce and the weight of heave-offering mixed with that produce.]

[G]   This [fact, that T. Ter. 5:11 reports two different understandings of the dispute between Joshua and Eliezer,] supports [the contention of] R. Yohanan, who said [above, Y. Ter. 4:9 I.B], "These [two] Tannaitic authorities, [i.e., Judah and Meir, disagree concerning the issue between Joshua and Eliezer]."

[H][32]   This [fact, that Meir agrees, F, that even in the case of objects which are sold by a count, the objects become consecrated through being mixed with heave-offering] supports [the contention of] the one who claims that, in the opinion of R. Meir, everything [which is sanctified] has the power to impose its holy status [upon other things. This understanding of the position of Meir at M. Or. 3:7 is given by Simeon b. Laqish, Y. Or. 3:3. Yohanan there takes the opposite view, that in Meir's view, only certain sanctified things have the power to impose their own status on other, unconsecrated objects.]

[I]   This [fact, that T. Ter. 5:11 reports two different understandings of the dispute between Joshua and Eliezer], supports [the contention of] one who says, "These [two] Tannaitic authorities [disagree concerning the issue under dispute by Eliezer and Joshua]." [The reference here is unclear. GRA and RiDBaZ delete this stich. PM states that it refers to an (undisclosed) passage in Y. Or., chapter 3.]

[J]   This [claim, of Aqiba, M. Or. 3:7, that gourds, as well as six other types of food that are *orlah*, render forbidden other produce with which they are mixed] means that even [if the gourd is] one part in a hundred [in the mixture] it renders forbidden [the other produce with which it is mixed].

The Yerushalmi cites the Tosefta, A–E, and indicates its implications, F and G–J. A–C gives Meir's greatly expanded version of M. Ter. 4:10's dispute between Eliezer and Joshua. The two additional examples given at A do not change the case from what it is in the Mishnah. Although expanded in language, the opinions of Eliezer (B) and Joshua (C) likewise remain exactly as they were in the Mishnah. Judah, D–E, offers a different version of the argument. He attributes to Eliezer, D, the opinion held by Joshua in the Mishnah. At E Judah has Joshua reject the notion that heave-offering in the mouth of one jar can be neutralized by produce in the mouths of other jars. This leaves Joshua in the same position as Eliezer holds in the Mishnah. Judah's point, presumably, is to render the opinions of these authorities at M. Ter. 4:10 consistent with their positions at M. Ter. 4:8.[33]

Of the Yerushalmi's discussion, only F is pertinent within the present context. It gives a conclusion reached on the basis of the cited passage of the Tosefta and intrinsic to our understanding of M. Ter. 4:10. G refers back to Y. Ter. 4:9 I. H clarifies the larger principle of Meir. I probably should be deleted, and J is irrelevant to Y. Ter.

[II.A]   **If he pressed it [i.e., a *litra* of dried figs in the status of heave-offering] upon a circle of pressed figs but does not know where [on the circle] he pressed it, all [i.e., Eliezer and Joshua, M. Ter. 4:10] agree that it is neutralized [T. Ter. 5:11F, in the name of Judah].**

[B]   Said R. Abin, "But each [of the cakes of pressed figs upon which the heave-offering might have been pressed] must be comprised of [at least] two *litras* and a little more [of unconsecrated produce],

[C]   "so that [the heave-offering] will be nullified by being mixed with a much greater quantity [of unconsecrated produce]."

Abin's consideration is that introduced above, Y. Ter. 4:8
II.A–C.

4:11   [P: 4:8a]

[P]   *A seah of heave-offering which fell into the mouth of a store-jar,*

[Q]   *and one skimmed it off—*

[R]   *R. Eliezer says, "If in the layer removed were a hundred* seahs,

[S]   *"[the heave-offering] is neutralized in a hundred and one [parts of produce]."*

[T]   *But R. Joshua says, "[The heave-offering] is not neutralized."*

[U]   *A seah of heave-offering which fell into the mouth of a store-jar—he should skim it off.*

[V]   *But if so, why did they say heave-offering is neutralized in a hundred and one [parts of produce]? [That is the case only] if he does not know whether or not it [i.e., the produce which is heave-offering] is mixed up [with the unconsecrated produce] or where [in the unconsecrated produce] it fell.*

The Yerushalmi's one unit questions the consistency of the views ascribed to Eliezer here and in the preceding pericope, M. Ter. 4:10.

[I.A.]   The views [assigned to] R. Eliezer are contradictory.

[B]   There [at M. Ter. 4:10N] he states [that if figs in the status of heave-offering are on top of unconsecrated figs, they regard them all as loose figs and] *the [unconsecrated] bottom ones serve to neutralize the top ones [which are in the status of heave-offering].*

[C]   But here [at M. Ter. 4:11, he holds that the produce on the bottom does not serve to neutralize that which is on the top. Rather, the top of the batch is skimmed off, and only] *if there is in the layer that is removed* [one hundred and one parts of produce is the heave-offering neutralized].

[D]   [This means that in this case, Eliezer holds that the produce on the top and bottom of the batch] is not mixed up. [This is the opposite of what he holds at M. Ter. 4:10, cited at A.]

[E]   [The following explains why Eliezer's position at M. Ter. 4:11 is different from the one he holds at M. 4:10.] R. Jeremiah, R. Hiyya in the name of R. Yohanan, Simeon bar Ba in the name of Kahana, "[Eliezer indeed holds here, as at M. 4:10, that the heave-offering on the top of the bin is deemed mixed with the unconsecrated produce at the bottom. The heave-offering therefore is neutralized.] According to R. Eliezer, they [thus] treat the individual [who skimmed the produce off the top of the batch] as though he [simply needed to remove from the batch one *seah* of produce, equal to the heave-offering which originally fell in, but instead] intentionally [removed] much produce." [Eliezer's point is that in doing this the person creates a new mixture of unconsecrated produce and one *seah* of produce which is treated as heave-offering. If this heave-offering is to be neutralized, the mixture must contain a total of one hundred and one parts of produce.]

[F]   [The same explanation now is repeated in different words.] R. Ila [and] R. Asi in the name of R. Yohanan [say], "According to R. Eliezer, they treat it [i.e., the new mixture created when the person removes the upper layer of produce] as [one in which] the *seah* [of heave-offering, contained in that mixture,] is neutralized [if it is mixed] in a hundred [parts of unconsecrated produce]."

[G]   [What is the difference between the expressions of Eliezer's position at E and that at F?] In the opinion of R. Asi, [F, Eliezer holds that] it is permitted [in removing heave-offering from a batch in which it was neutralized] to separate much [heave-offering to give to the priest. This does not cause a new mixture. Thus in Asi's understanding, E is not an acceptable explanation of Eliezer's view.]

[H]   In the opinion of Kahana, [E, Eliezer holds that] it is forbidden [for the one who removes the heave-offering from a batch in which it was neutralized] to separate much [heave-offering. Therefore, as E explains, an individual who does so invariably will have created a new mixture of heave-offering and unconsecrated produce.]

[I]   [E and F also disagree in the case of one who] skimmed [the heave-offering off the top of the batch but, not having taken a hundred and one parts of produce], skimmed [some more produce off the top of the batch in order to neutralize the heave-offering].

[J]   In the opinion of R. Asi, this is permitted, [for it simply is a case of taking much heave-offering, which Asi, G, permits].

[K]   In the opinion of Kahana this is not permitted [just as at H].

[L]   In the opinion of R. Asi, [the person may go ahead and skim off more and more produce], even if [ultimately] he leaves no produce [in the storage bin].

[M]   In the opinion of Kahana, [if the heave-offering is to be neutralized, when the individual skims the produce from the storage bin] he must leave some [produce] behind [in the bin].

Yohanan explains that Eliezer's views at M. Ter. 4:10 and 4:11 are consistent. Since Yohanan's statement is transmitted in two different wordings, E and F, the implications of the two different traditions must be delineated, G + H, I–K, and L–M. It is not clear how the Yerushalmi deduces L–M from the materials given at E + F.

4:12 [P: 4:8b]

[A]   *(1) Two bins [the combined content of which is a hundred seahs of unconsecrated produce], or (2) two storage jars [the combined content of which is a hundred seahs of unconsecrated produce]*

[B]   *into one of which fell a seah of heave-offering,*

[C]   *and it is not known into which of them it fell—*

[D]   *[the produce in the bins or storage jars] serves to neutralize [the heave-offering] in conjunction with one another [i.e., we deem the heave-offering to have fallen into a single batch of a hundred seahs of produce].*

[E]   *R. Simeon says, "Even if they [i.e., the two baskets or storage jars] are in two [different] cities, [the produce in] them serves to neutralize the heave-offering in conjunction with one another."*

A *seah* of heave-offering is lost within a hundred *seahs* of unconsecrated produce. It is not known where. Even though the unconsecrated produce is divided between two containers, the heave-offering is neutralized, A–D. Simeon adds that the rule of D applies even if the containers are in different cities. In all events there are a hundred *seahs* of unconsecrated produce within which only one *seah* of heave-offering has been mixed. The Yerushalmi's discussion is framed (units **I** + **V**) by consideration of the question of the applicability of Simeon's view in cases of specific sorts of containers. Yet more than an exegesis of the Mishnah, in which the Yerushalmi shows little interest, this material interprets T. Ter. 6:12. The intervening units, **II–IV**, likewise have little interest in the specifics of this pericope. Instead they refer to secondary problems and ambiguous cases, constituting for the most part an analysis of the Tosefta's supplementary materials.

[I.A]   [T. Ter. 6:12A–B is subject to analysis:] **[If there were] (1) two bins [each containing less than a hundred *seahs* of unconsecrated produce, one each] in two [different] attics, [or there were] two [such] storage vessels in a single attic, lo, these [bins or storage vessels join together to create the quantity of unconsecrated produce needed to neutralize a *seah* of heave-offering which falls into one of the bins or vessels].**

[B]   [The question is why, if there are] two storage vessels in two [different] attics, in this case [the produce in them does] not [combine to create the quantity needed to neutralize heave-offering which falls into one of them].

[C]   What is the difference between a bin and a storage vessel, [such that bins in separate attics join together but storage jars do not]?

[D]   It is usual to move bins around, [such that even if presently they are in two different attics one could imagine their being moved to a single room]. It is not usual to move around storage vessels [and therefore, if they are located in different places, we in no event treat them as if they were in the same place].

The Yerushalmi's version of T. Ter. 6:12, A, fails to state that produce in two storage jars in two different attics combines to neutralize heave-offering. Why storage jars constitute a special case therefore requires explanation, B + C–D.

[II.A]   R. Zeira [and] R. Hiyya in the name of R. Simeon [say], "If there were before him two bins, each of which contained fifty *seahs* [of unconsecrated produce], and a *seah* of heave-offering fell into one of them, but it is not known which, [the produce in the two bins joins together to form the quantity needed to neutralize the heave-offering].

[B]   "[Now when the householder goes to take from the mixture a *seah* of produce to give to the priest as his share, if] he wishes to take it [all] up from this [or that bin], he may do so. Or he may take half [of the required *seah*] from each [of the two bins].

[C]   "And so in the case of two immersion pools, each of which contains twenty *seahs* [of rain water], and three *logs* of drawn water fall into one of the pools, but it is not known which—[the water in the two pools combines to create the quantity of water which counteracts the invalidating effect of the drawn water].

[D]   "[If] he wishes to remove the invalid [drawn] water [by taking three *logs*] from this pool, he may do so. [Or, if he wished to take it] from the other pool, he does so.[34] [And if he wishes to take] half from each pool, he may do so."

The unit answers a practical question. Heave-offering is neutralized within two separate containers. From which does the householder take the produce which must be given to the priest in place of the lost heave-offering? The answer is predictable. Since the two vessels are considered one, the householder may take the replacement offering from whichever he wishes, or even may separate half from each container. C–D provides a parallel case.

[III.A]   R. Simon[35] in the name of R. Padiah [says], "**There were before him two bins, this one containing fifty *seahs* [of unconsecrated produce] and this one containing fifty *seahs* [of unconsecrated produce], and a *seah* of heave-offering fell into one of them, and it is known into which of them it fell [such that that bin now is filled with produce deemed to be in the status of heave-offering]. Then a second [*seah* of heave-offering] fell [into one of the bins] but he does not know into which of them it fell. [In adjudicating the matter] he may say, 'Into the bin in which** the first *seah* of heave-offering fell, there the second fell [as well'; T. Ter. 6:13, with slight variations].

[B]³⁶   "Why [may he deem the second *seah* of heave-offering to have fallen where the first already fell]?

[C]   "For they may attribute an impairment in status to that the status of which already is impaired.

[D]   "[If] more [unconsecrated produce fell into the bin in which] it was known [that the first *seah* of heave-offering fell], such that [now there is sufficient unconsecrated produce to] void [i.e., neutralize, that one *seah* of heave-offering—if this happened] unintentionally, [that one *seah* of heave-offering] is neutralized, and [the batch of produce again] is permitted [for consumption by a nonpriest. See M. Ter. 5:9I–K.]

[E]   "And as for the second [fifty *seahs* of unconsecrated produce], they revert to a status of doubt [whether or not the second *seah* of heave-offering fell into them or into the other batch. Because of this doubt, as at Y. Ter. 4:12 I.A, the produce in the two bins combines to form the quantity needed to neutralize the second *seah* of heave-offering].

[F]   [43b] "The result is that two *seahs* [of heave-offering] were neutralized in [a total of] a hundred and fifty *seahs* [of unconsecrated produce].

[G]   "But [if there were] two bins, in this one fifty *seahs* [of unconsecrated produce] and in this [second] one fifty *seahs* [of unconsecrated produce], and a *seah* of heave-offering fell into one of them, but it is not known into which of them it fell, and afterwards a second [*seah* of heave-offering] fell [into one of them] and it is known into which of them it fell, he may not say, 'Into the place into which the second [*seah* of heave-offering] fell, there the first fell [as well'; T. Ter. 6:13E–F, with slight variation]. [The second mishap does not alter the status of doubt that pertains to both bins as soon as the first *seah* of heave-offering falls into one of them.]

[H]   "[If] more [unconsecrated produce was added] to one of them [i.e., the bins] such that [there is sufficient produce to] void [i.e., neutralize, one *seah* of heave-offering—if this happened] unintentionally, [the heave-offering is neutralized and that batch] is permitted [for consumption by nonpriests].

[I]   "And the other [bin] remains forbidden [for consumption by
       nonpriests] until more [unconsecrated produce] unintentionally
       [is added to it as well]."

The Yerushalmi explains and analyzes the Tosefta's cases in which
heave-offering is mixed in one of two separate containers of unconsecrated produce. While related to M. Ter. 4:12 in this general way, the material does not shed light on the Mishnah's specific issue or principle.

[IV.A]   [A *seah* of heave-offering falls into less than a hundred *seahs* of
          unconsecrated produce. We should expect the whole batch to
          take on the status of heave-offering. The question is whether or
          not one can prevent that from happening by making the follow-
          ing sorts of statements: If] he said, "That [produce] on the bot-
          tom [of the bin] is deemed to have the status of heave-offering,
          and what is on the top [of the bin] is unconsecrated," [or] "What
          is on the bottom [of the bin] is unconsecrated, and what is on the
          top is in the status of heave-offering"—[are these statements
          valid]?

[B]   [No. The statement is ineffectual, for] is the question [of where
       in the batch the heave-offering is located] determined by his
       will? [It certainly is not.]

[C]   And so is the case for an immersion pool [filled with less rain-
       water than is needed to neutralize drawn water which falls into
       the pool].

[D]   [If drawn water fell into the pool and] he said, "[The increased
       volume of water] at the bottom [of the pool] is made up of fit,
       [i.e., not drawn water, and the increased volume of water] at the
       top [of the pool] is made up of the unfit [drawn water," or, "The
       increased volume of water] at the bottom [of the pool] is made
       up of unfit [drawn water, and the increased volume of water] at
       the top [of the pool] is made up of fit [rainwater"—is the state-
       ment valid]?

[E]   [No. The statement is void, for] is the question [of where in the
       pool the drawn water is located] determined by his will? [It is not.]

The Yerushalmi poses a question left open by M. Ter. 4 : 12, which states that under certain circumstances two distinct batches may be treated as one. The Yerushalmi asks about the reverse, whether or not the householder may treat one batch as if it were two. The answer, B and E, is that he may not. Through their will people cannot divide one physical unit into separate parts. This constitutes a subtle clarification of the Mishnah's principle. The creation and dissolution of batches of produce is not a function of human will. It depends upon physical proximity, as in the present cases, or upon the overriding factor of doubt which unifies all of the suspect produce, as at M. Ter. 4 : 12. Through their will, however, people do not determine what constitutes a batch.

[V.A] You say [above, Y. Ter. 4 : 12 I] that [the produce in two] bins [located in different attics combines to form the quantity needed] to neutralize [heave-offering which falls into one of them], but that [produce in two] storage vessels [located in different attics does not combine to] neutralize [heave-offering which falls into one of them].

[B] What are the implications [of this fact in a concrete case]?

[C] [If there were] two storage vessels in two [different] attics and a *seah* of heave-offering fell into one of them, [but it is not known into which of them it fell, the produce in] both of them is deemed forbidden [for consumption by nonpriests].

[D] [If] more [unconsecrated produce] was placed in one of them such that [now that vessel contains sufficient unconsecrated produce to] void, [i.e., neutralize, the heave-offering—if this happened] unintentionally, [the heave-offering which might be in that storage vessel is deemed] neutralized and [the produce in the container now] is permitted [for consumption by a nonpriest].

[E] And as for the second [storage vessel], if more [unconsecrated produce] unintentionally is placed in it, it [too] is permitted [for consumption by a nonpriest].

[F] But the replacement *seah* of heave-offering [to be given to the priest as his share] need not be taken from the second [storage vessel], for [replacement] heave-offering already will have been taken [from the first storage vessel, when the produce in it became permitted].

Heave-offering falls into one of two separate batches, but it is not
known which, C–F. Since the batches do not combine (A), the
condition of doubt concerning each of them is treated separately.
Even when the produce in one of them is rendered permitted,
the other remains forbidden. It might contain the heave-
offering. It is subject to this doubt until it too is supplied with
sufficient produce to neutralize the heave-offering it might contain. F is not surprising. There was only one *seah* of heave-
offering to start out with, and that is all the produce that the
priest is to receive.

4:13 [P: 4:8c]

[A]   *Said R. Yose, "A case came before R. Aqiba concerning fifty
bundles of vegetables, among which had fallen a similar bundle,
half of which was heave-offering.*

[B]   *"And I said before him, '[The heave-offering] is neutralized.'*

[C]   *"Not that heave-offering is neutralized in [a mixture of one part
heave-offering in a total of] fifty-one [parts of produce but],
rather, because there were there a hundred and two half [bundles,
only one of which was heave-offering]."*

C makes the point, parallel to that of M. 4:12. Since all of the
produce is in doubt whether or not it is the heave-offering, it is
deemed to constitute a single batch. The Yerushalmi's one unit
questions the cogency of Yose's view here and that assigned to
him at T. Ter. 5:13. In order to resolve the apparent contradiction between the two statements in the name of Yose, the Yerushalmi proposes a larger principle which, it suggests, accounts
both for the Tosefta's and the Mishnah's rules.

[I.A]   It is taught [T. Ter. 5:13E–F: **R. Yose says**], "**If heave-offering is
mixed up [in a hundred and one parts of unconsecrated pro-
duce], it is neutralized. And [if it falls into the unconsecrated
produce but] is not mixed up [with it], it is not neutralized.**"

[B]   Yet [to the contrary] we learn [M. Ter. 4:13]: *Said R. Yose, "A
case came before R. Aqiba concerning fifty bundles of vegetables, among which had fallen a similar bundle, half of which*

was heave-offering. And I said before him, '[The heave-offering] is neutralized.'"

[C]   [In M. Ter. 4:13's case the heave-offering] was not mixed up [in the unconsecrated produce], yet even so [Yose states that] it is neutralized. [In light of A, why should that be?]

[D]   We must reason [that Yose's opinion is as follows:] As for any [produce] which one is careful to keep separate, [so long as it is separate] it is not neutralized. [This accounts for the rule at A.]

[E]   But [anything which] one is not careful to keep separate is neutralized, [even if it is not actually lost in the unconsecrated produce. This accounts for the rule at M. Ter. 4:13, cited at B.]

[F]   What are the implications [of E for a concrete case]?

[G][37]   [As for] an unclean chatemelon [in the status of heave-offering] which fell into a hundred clean, [unconsecrated] chatemelons, [which are not susceptible to uncleanness, not yet having been wet down]—

[H]   since he [is not concerned that the unclean chatemelon, which is heave-offering, will render the others unclean, and so] would not [normally] be careful to keep [that unclean melon] separate, it is neutralized.

[I]   [If the unconsecrated chatemelons] are rendered susceptible to uncleanness [by being wet down], since he [now] would be careful to keep [the unclean melon] separate, [that melon, which is in the status of heave-offering,] is not neutralized.

The Yerushalmi suggests an overarching legal principle to account for the two different views of Yose, A–B + D–E. F–I indicates how the principle works in concrete cases.

5:1

[A]   A seah *of unclean heave-offering which fell into less than a hun-dred [seahs] of unconsecrated produce,*

[B]   *or [which fell] into first tithe, or second tithe, or [produce] dedi-cated [to the Temple],*

[C]   *whether these things are clean or unclean—*

[D]   *let [all of the produce in the mixture] rot.*

[E]   *But if that seah [of heave-offering which fell into the other pro-duce] was clean—let [all of the produce in the mixture] be sold to priests, at the [low] value of heave-offering,*

[F]   *less the value of that same seah [of heave-offering which fell into the other produce and which already belongs to the priest].*

[G]   *And if it fell into first tithe—let him designate [the mixture, which is in the status of tithe and heave-offering], to be heave-offering of the tithe.*

[H]   *And if it fell into second tithe or [produce] dedicated [to the Temple]—lo, these may be redeemed.*

[I]   *And if the unconsecrated produce [into which the heave-offering fell] was unclean—let [all of the produce in the mixture] be eaten in small bits, or roasted, or kneaded with fruit juice, or divided into [little] lumps [of dough],*

[J]   *such that there will not be in a single place an egg's bulk [of produce, the smallest quantity that conveys uncleanness].*

What happens if some of the produce in a mixture of heave-offering and unconsecrated produce is unclean? The answer given here is that we adjudicate the case on the basis of the status of cleanness of the heave-offering. If the heave-offering is unclean, A–D, none of the produce is eaten. All is left to rot. If the heave-offering is clean, E–H and I–J, it must be eaten by a priest. How this is done depends upon the status of cleanness of the unconsecrated produce with which it is mixed. If that produce is clean, the mixture is sold to the priest, who may then eat it as he would any other heave-offering. But if the unconsecrated produce is unclean, the priest must eat the mixture in a special way. He prepares the food in a manner that prevents the unclean produce it contains either from imparting uncleanness to himself or to the heave-offering in the mixture.

The Yerushalmi's discussion is long, but begins to interpret the materials before us only at unit **III**. The first unit is generally related, talking about mixtures of heave-offering and produce subject to other agricultural restrictions. This complements M. Ter. 5:1B. Unit **II** introduces facts necessary for the discussion at unit **III**, itself pertinent to M. Ter. 5:1A–D. The question there is whether or not a mixture of unclean heave-offering and unclean, unconsecrated produce should be burned, rather than left to rot as D requires. Units **IV–VI** refer to E–G, explaining the meaning of "the [low] value of heave-offering" and delimiting the cases in which the householder is permitted to sell agricultural offerings to a priest. The final pericope answers the question, left open by I–J, of exactly how much produce comprises "less than an egg's bulk."

[I.A]   *A seah of unclean heave-offering which fell.* . . . [M. Ter. 5:1A.]

[B]   Taught R. Hiyya: [Even if the produce into which heave-offering falls is unconsecrated but] subject to tithes, [the heave-offering] is neutralized.

[C]   And [even if the produce is] aftergrowths of the seventh year [of the Sabbatical cycle, which belong to all people, the heave-offering] is neutralized.

[D]   [The problem is how in these cases the priest is to eat his share, which is subject to these other restrictions.] Untithed produce neutralizes [heave-offering which is mixed with it], and [in order to render fit for consumption the *seah* which is lifted out of the mixture for the priest], one designates[1] the [required] tithes. [Now what previously was untithed may be treated like fully tithed produce. The produce may be eaten by a priest without concern for the first or second tithe that it previously contained. See T. Ter. 6 : 1F–G.]

[E]   Aftergrowths of the seventh year neutralize [heave-offering], and [the produce that is taken from the batch to replace the lost heave-offering] is given [freely—as required in the case of after-growths—] to those who can eat it [i.e., priests].

[F]   Said R. Yose, "The Mishnah stated this [explicitly: As for] a *seah* of heave-offering which fell into less than a hundred [*seahs* of unconsecrated produce], it is (read: not) neutralized.

[G]   Because it fell into less than a hundred [*seahs* of unconsecrated produce, it is not neutralized].

[H]   Lo, if it fell into a hundred [*seahs* of produce], surely[2] it is neutralized. [This is the case no matter what other restrictions apply to the produce with which it is mixed.]

[I]   And [the produce taken from the batch to replace the heave-offering that was lost] is not [deemed] untithed.

The citation from M. Ter. 5 : 1 which introduces this material, A, is irrelevant to it, since we do not here even deal with unclean heave-offering. The unit instead paraphrases and explains T. Ter. 6 : 1F–G, referred to at B–D. The rule Yose refers to as "Mishnah," F–H, appears nowhere in the Tannaitic literature. The point of I is unclear.

[**II.A**]   There we have learned [M. Tem. 7 : 5]: *They may kindle [a lamp] with [unclean] bread or oil in the status of heave-offering.*

[B]   Hezeqiah says, "They mentioned only bread and oil. Therefore [43c] all other [unclean things in the status of heave-offering may] not [be used for kindling]."

[C]   R. Yohanan says, "It is all the same whether it is [unclean] bread, oil, or any other [produce in the status of heave-offering. All may be used for kindling.]"

[D]   [Questioning Hezeqiah's view,] R. Yudan of Cappadocia asked, "Is wheat like bread and olives like oil [such that, if these things are in the status of heave-offering and unclean, they may be used for kindling]?" [The question is not answered.]

[E]   R. Samuel bar Nahman in the name of R. Yohanan [says], "[As for] one who uses [clean (PM)] bread or oil in the status of heave-offering for kindling—let them burn his bones."

[F]   R. Samuel bar Nahman asked in the presence of R. Yohanan, "What is the law [whether or not one may] use for kindling [unclean produce in the status of heave-offering other than bread and oil (GRA)]?"

[G]   [Yohanan] said to him, "I would kindle with it, for such [produce as heave-offering] which was given for [the use of] your tribe, [the priests], was given to you, [to use as you wish]."

[H]   All agree in the case of [unclean] oil [in the status of heave-offering], that it is permitted [to use it for kindling].

[I]   [The following proves from Scripture that H is permitted.] For said R. Ba bar Hiyya in the name of R. Yohanan, "[Num. 18:8 states], 'I have given them [i.e., the consecrated things of the people of Israel] to you, as a consecrated portion.'

[J]   "'As a consecrated portion' [means] for use in [anointing individuals] for high office.

[K]   "'As a consecrated portion' [means] for use as an unguent.

[L]   "'As a consecrated portion' [means] for use in kindling." [All of these are permitted uses of oil in the status of heave-offering.]

A series of generally relevant, but logically unrelated, statements, D–L, expands A–C's dispute over the meaning of M. Tem. 7:5. I–L links H to Scripture. While primary to Y. Tem., the reason for the placement of the unit here becomes apparent as we turn to the following pericope of the Yerushalmi.

[III.A]   It is logical that [if unclean heave-offering imparts its own status to] clean, [unconsecrated produce, all of the produce in the mixture] should be left to rot [but may not be burned, just as M. Ter. 5:1D states. This is because, were it not for the presence of the unclean heave-offering, the clean, unconsecrated produce could be eaten. Since it is edible, it may not be burned.]

[B]³   [But] does it make sense that [if the unclean heave-offering imparts its own status to] unclean, [unconsecrated produce, all of the produce likewise] should be left to rot? [Since none of the produce in the mixture is edible, should not all of it rather be burned, contrary to M. Ter. 5:1D?]

[C]   In the opinion of Hezeqiah, it is logical [that the mixture] be left to rot, [as required by M. Ter. 5:1D. PM: This is in line with Hezeqiah's view at Y. Ter. 5:1 II.B. Except for bread and oil, unclean produce in the status of heave-offering should not be burned. This applies as well in the case of unclean mixtures of heave-offering and unconsecrated produce.]

[D]   [But] in the opinion of R. Yohanan, [that all unclean produce in the status of heave-offering may be used for kindling, Y. Ter. 5:1 II.C], let [the mixture] be used for kindling.

[E]   [In this] R. Yohanan follows the view of R. Yose b. Hanina, [that the heave-offering should be burned] lest [more unconsecrated produce is added to the mixture so that the unclean heave-offering is neutralized and] lifted out [of the mixture. In such a case we fear that it might accidentally be eaten by a priest. To prevent this from occurring, the mixture should be burned right away, and not left to rot.]

[F]   [This consideration, E,] would apply in the case [of heave-offering] of a sort [of produce] that is not [normally allowed to be] mixed up in other produce. [Such heave-offering is not neutralized, Y. Ter. 4:13 I. To assure that a priest does not eat it, Yohanan wants it to be burned.]

[G]   And [Yohanan's view applies as well] in the case of a sort [of produce in the status of heave-offering] that [normally is allowed to be] mixed up [in other produce and which therefore is neutralized, Y. Ter. 4:13 I].

[H]   [Even though the heave-offering is neutralized, Yohanan desires the unclean mixture of heave-offering and unconsecrated food to be burned], lest there be some mishap, [and a priest accidentally eats the unclean mixture].

A–B's proposition is analyzed in light of the positions of Hezeqiah and Yohanan, given at unit **II**. E–G expands Yohanan's position, again in light of considerations presented earlier.

[**IV**.A]   [The question is why a mixture of clean heave-offering and unconsecrated produce is sold to the priest at the low value of
heave-offering, M. Ter. 5 : 1E. Why may it not be sold to the
priest for however much the priest is willing to pay, even if this
is more or less than the usual value of the offering? We should
think that the householder may take as much as the priest is
willing to pay] since have we not reasoned, *the value of a sanctified object is determined [on the basis of the market] at the
[particular] time and place*[4] *[of the sale; M. Ar. 6 : 5]*? [What
then does M. Ter. 5 : 1E mean when it refers to the set value of
heave-offering?]

[B]   Said R. Hanina, "Solve the problem [of interpreting M. Ter.
5 : 1E] by assuming that [it refers to a case in which] the town [in
which the person with the heave-offering to sell is located] had
been destroyed, [leaving no priests to pay for the heave-offer-
ing]. As a result [the householder] cannot find [anyone to whom]
to sell [the mixture], even at the [low] value it would have were it
kindling." [PM: M. Ter. 5 : 1E's point is that the individual need
not go ahead and sell the mixture for such a low price. He may
wait until he finds a buyer to purchase the mixture at the usual
value of heave-offering.]

The Yerushalmi explains M. Ter. 5 : 1E through reference to M.
Ar. 6 : 5.

[**V**.A]   [Reference is to M. Ter. 5 : 1E: *But if the seah of heave-offering
which fell into the other produce was clean . . .*] This is to say
[that the rules given at M. Ter. 5 : 1E–H apply only if a *seah* of]
clean [heave-offering fell into less than a hundred *seahs* of] clean
[unconsecrated produce].

[B]   But if a clean [*seah* of heave-offering fell] into [less than a hundred *seahs* of] unclean [unconsecrated produce], then the law is
in accordance with what we learned in the Mishnah: *If the un-*

consecrated produce [into which the heave-offering fell] was
unclean. . . . [M. Ter. 5 : 1I–J].

The Yerushalmi repeats in its own terms what is explicit in the
Mishnah. The rule that the mixture containing heave-offering is
sold to the priest, M. Ter. 5 : 1E–H, applies only if clean heave-
offering falls into clean unconsecrated produce (A). The case for
clean heave-offering that falls into unclean unconsecrated produce has its own rule, given at M. Ter. 5 : 1I–J, referred to
here at B.

[VI.A]   [The unit assumes the following understanding of M. Ter. 5 : 1G:
         If heave-offering imparts to first tithe the status of heave-offering,
         one designates the mixture, which now has the status of heave-
         offering and first tithe, to be heave-offering of the tithe. The
         Mishnah does not state that any part of this mixture may be sold
         to the priest at the value of heave-offering. Therefore it is clear
         that all of the produce is given to the priest for free.] In the
         opinion of R. Yose this makes sense. For R. Yose in the name of
         Hezeqiah and R. Jonah in the name of R. Yannai [say (above, Y.
         Ter. 2 : 1 **II.** F–G)], "[Num. 18 : 28 states,] 'And from it [i.e.,
         first tithe] you [Levites] shall give the Lord's offering [i.e.,
         heave-offering of the tithe] to Aaron the priest.'

[B]   "[This means that one] must give Aaron the priest [without com-
         pensation] all that is befitting his priestly status, [including the
         mixture of heave-offering and first tithe that has the status of
         heave-offering of the tithe]."

[C]   [But] in the opinion of Kahana, who said [above, Y. Ter. 2 : 1 **II.**
         H–I], "Take [and give to the priest as heave-offering of the
         tithe] the hallowed portion [of first tithe]," M. Ter. 5 : 1G makes
         no sense].

[D]   [In this case as well, Kahana] should say, "Take [and give the
         priest for free only] the hallowed portion [of the tithe. The per-
         son need not give the priest without compensation the mixture,
         only part of which actually is consecrated.]

[E]   [The following explains that Kahana actually agrees with the in-
         terpretation of M. Ter. 5 : 1G given at A.] Now even though there

[at Y. Ter. 2 : 1 **II**] Kahana said, "Take [and give the priest for free only] the hallowed part [of first tithe]," he concedes [that in this case, the householder must give the priest for free the mixture of heave-offering and first tithe.]

[F]   For [Kahana's view is that] in all cases of something that [the householder] is required to give to the priest, [he must give it for free].

The Yerushalmi shows that positions cited in the names of Yose and Kahana at Y. Ter. 2 : 1 **II** are consistent with the rule of M. Ter. 5 : 1G. This is accomplished at A–B, for the case of Yose, and at C–D + E–F, for the view of Kahana.

[**VII**.A]   These *small bits* [in which size a mixture of clean heave-offering and unclean unconsecrated produce is to be eaten, M. Ter. 5 : 1I] comprise the quantity of a half egg's bulk.

The Yerushalmi provides a specific figure for the Mishnah's "less than an egg's bulk."

5:2 [P: 5 : 1b]

[A]   *[As to] a seah of unclean heave-offering that fell into a hundred [seahs] of clean unconsecrated produce [and so is neutralized]—*

[B]   *R. Eliezer says, "Let it be lifted out [of the mixture] and burned.*

[C]   *"For I say, 'The seah that fell [into the unconsecrated produce] is the [same] seah that is raised up [and is unclean.]'"*

[D]   *But sages say, "[The heave-offering] is raised up [out of the mixture] and is eaten dry, roasted, kneaded with fruit juice, or divided into lumps [of dough],*

[E]   *"so that there is not in a single place so much as an egg's bulk [of produce]."*

Eliezer's view is explained by C. Sages, D–E, hold that when it is neutralized, the heave-offering diffuses throughout the batch. The *seah* that is lifted out thus comprises a mixture of some small amount of unclean, and much clean, produce. As with other such mixtures (M. Ter. 5:1I–J) the produce is eaten in a way which prevents the unclean produce from imparting uncleanness either to the clean produce or to the priest.

The Yerushalmi points in turn to the central issues of Eliezer's and the sages' positions. Does Eliezer really believe that the *seah* of heave-offering that is lifted out of the batch is the same as that which fell in? Unit **I** addresses this question. Unit **II** confronts the logic of the sages' view, asking why the sages allow what originally was unclean heave-offering to be eaten at all. The final pericope is tacked on, repeating Y. Ter. 5:1 **VII,** just as M. Ter. 5:2D–E repeats M. Ter. 5:1I–J.

[I.A]   Said R. Simon, "R. Eliezer's [statement, M. Ter. 5:2C, that the *seah* of heave-offering which fell into the unconsecrated produce is the same *seah* that is lifted out] accords with his opinion there [at M. Zeb. 8:5, that if limbs of unblemished whole offerings are mixed with the limb of a blemished beast and one of the limbs is accidentally offered, one may then go ahead and offer the rest of the limbs. The assumption is that] the blemished [limb which fell into the valid ones] came up in his hand [and was offered first. This leaves no doubt but that the other limbs are from the unblemished animal.]

[B]   "In the same way [Eliezer] states here, [in the case of heave-offering, that] all of the unclean produce came up in his hand." [Since it is unclean heave-offering, it must be burned, as Eliezer states, M. Ter. 5:2B. We do not suppose that some of it is clean produce, which is not burned.]

[C]   [Suggesting a different interpretation of Eliezer's view,] R. Zeira asked, "Perhaps we should say that Eliezer [holds that the heave-offering that is raised up is burned not because it is the same that fell in, but] because [he wishes to build] a fence [around the law]. [So as to avoid the possibility that a priest will eat unclean heave-offering, Eliezer states that what comes up from the batch must be burned. He says this even though he does not believe that it is the same unclean heave-offering which originally fell into the unconsecrated produce.]

[D]   "[Proof that Eliezer wishes the *seah* of produce burned simply as a precautionary measure is in the following:] Is it not so that Eliezer agrees that one must designate tithes on behalf of a *seah* [of heave-offering] that one raised up from [a hundred *seahs*] of unconsecrated, untithed produce [in which the heave-offering was neutralized]?

[E]   "If you say that the *seah* [of produce] which fell [into the unconsecrated produce] is the same *seah* as is raised [out of that produce], then [that *seah* certainly is in the status of heave-offering] and one need not designate tithes on its behalf."

[F]   Said R. Mana, "Correctly has R. Zeira stated matters.

[G]   "For in the pericope of the Mishnah following [the one under discussion] we learn: [*As to*] *a seah of clean heave-offering which fell into a hundred* [seahs] *of unclean unconsecrated produce* [*let it be raised up and eaten dry, etc.* (M. Ter. 5:2F–G). Now in this case] R. Eliezer does not disagree." [He does not say that the *seah* of heave-offering which fell into the mixture is the same one that came out, such that it need not be treated as a mixture of clean and unclean produce. It thus is clear that Eliezer does not follow the principle that what falls into a mixture is what comes out. Zeira, C, is correct. Simon, A–B, is wrong.]

[H]   [Disagreeing with Mana, F–G], associates said in the presence of R. Yose, "Correctly has R. Simon stated [matters].

[I]   "For is it the case [as Zeira would have it, C] that they burn heave-offering [simply] as a precautionary measure, [lest priests come to transgress]?" [They certainly do not. Rather, they only burn heave-offering if it certainly is unclean. Eliezer's view, M. Ter. 5:2B, therefore must be that the *seah* of unclean heave-offering that fell into the unconsecrated produce is the exact same *seah* which was lifted out of that produce. It is unclean.]

[J]   [Rejecting associates' reasoning, Yose] said to them, "Is it not so that the six cases of doubt [concerning the status of cleanness of heave-offering] which we have learned [at M. Toh. 4:5] are cases [in which heave-offering] is to be burned [simply] as a precautionary measure? [Yes. In those cases the heave-offering is burned simply because it might be unclean. This is as a precaution, lest a priest accidentally eat the heave-offering.]

[K]   "And is it not so that here also [Eliezer holds that the heave-offering] must be burned simply as a precautionary measure, [and not because he believes that the produce which came up from the batch is the exact same as that which fell in]?" [On the basis of J, this appears to be the case. Thus Zeira, C–D, is correct, and Simon, A–B, is wrong. Eliezer does not hold that the *seah* of produce which is lifted out of the mixture for the priest is the same *seah* of unclean heave-offering which fell into the mixture. Yet as a precautionary measure, he holds that the *seah* which is lifted out must be burned.]

The theory underlying Eliezer's view is under dispute. Perhaps Eliezer does not hold that the *seah* that is lifted out of the mixture is the same as that which fell in. He might hold instead that the replacement offering is burned as a precautionary measure, lest it consist of unclean produce. Notably, this view, which prevails at J–K, ignores what M. Ter. 5:2C makes explicit. Eliezer holds that the *seah* which is lifted out of the mixture is the same as that which fell in.

[II.A] Associates (follow GRA, cited by RiDBaZ, and delete: say) asked in the presence of R. Yose, "[Why do sages, M. Ter. 5:2D–E, insist that the heave-offering taken to replace the lost offering be eaten in small quantities which do not convey uncleanness?] Why should this be a concern?

[B] "[For] if it is the unclean heave-offering [which originally fell into the batch that was raised out again] it should be burned [and not eaten at all].

[C] "[And] if it [mostly] is unconsecrated produce [that was lifted out of the mixture], what difference does it make that it should be rendered unclean [by the small amount of unclean heave-offering in the mixture]?"

[D] [Yose] answered them, "[The precautions suggested by sages must be taken for], is [the *seah* of produce removed from the mixture] not being eaten [by the priest] as heave-offering? Is it so that only clean heave-offering may be eaten?[5] And perhaps unclean [heave-offering] may (not) [be eaten]?

[E] [Yose now must prove that under certain circumstances, unclean heave-offering is not to be burned.] "Do you not agree that if there arises a doubt whether or not heave-offering is unclean while the heave-offering remains in its place, [i.e., is not mixed with unclean produce,] that it may not be burned? [All will accept this fact. Only heave-offering which certainly is unclean may be burned.]

[F]   "What difference does it make if the suspicion of uncleanness arises as a result of [the heave-offering's falling into] a different batch, or if the suspicion of uncleanness arises while the heave-offering remains in its place? [It makes no difference. Therefore it is clear that unlike what associates suggest, B, that which is raised out of the mixture may not be burned. Likewise, since it might be heave-offering, it may not be rendered certainly unclean, contrary to what associates allow at C. Thus, unlike what associates claim, the position of the sages, M. Ter. 5:2D–E, is logical.]

[G]   "Rather, if you [associates] wish to pose your objection [stated above at A–C], apply it to that which R. Hoshaya taught.

[H]   "For R. Hoshaya taught, '[As for] a *seah* of clean heave-offering which fell into a hundred *seahs* of unclean heave-offering—[let one *seah* be raised up and eaten in small pieces which do not convey uncleanness].'" [Associates' questions are well asked of this ruling. PM: If we deem the *seah* that is removed to be the same clean *seah* as fell in, it may be eaten as clean heave-offering and requires no special preparation. But if it is deemed to be unclean heave-offering that is taken from the mixture, it should not be eaten at all. In no event is the special preparation required by sages needed.]

A–C's question concerning the position of sages, M. Ter. 5:2D–E, is answered at D–F. G–H indicates that the associates' criticism of the sages would make sense, if applied to a case slightly different from the one given at M. Ter. 5:2.

[III.A]   These *small bits* [in which size a mixture of clean heave-offering and unconsecrated produce is to be eaten, M. Ter. 5:2D] comprise the quantity of a half egg's bulk.[6]

The unit repeats Y. Ter. 5:1 **VI**.

5:3 [P: 5:1c]

[F]   *A seah of clean heave-offering which fell into a hundred [seahs]*
       of unclean unconsecrated produce [and so was neutralized]—

[G]   *let it be raised up and eaten dry, roasted, kneaded with fruit*
       juice, or divided into lumps [of dough],

[H]   *such that there is not in a single place so much as an egg's bulk*
       [of produce].

The understanding is that of the sages, M. Ter. 5:2D–E. When
heave-offering is neutralized, it is dispersed throughout the
batch. The replacement offering therefore comprises a mixture
of clean and unclean produce, to be treated as G–H indicates.
Neither of the Yerushalmi's two units is pertinent specifically to
this pericope. The first, the longest and most complex pericope
we have seen in this tractate, pertains in a general way to the
rules of M. Ter. 5:1–3. This probably accounts for its placement here, at the end of that unit. Unit **II** does not belong here
at all. It deals in broad terms with the rules for a batch of produce to which heave-offering has imparted its own sanctified
status. It should be positioned either with M. Ter. 4:7, which
introduces the rules for mixtures, or with M. Ter. 5:6, which is
explicitly cited in the unit.

[I.A]   Hezeqiah says, "[In a case in which a *seah* of unclean heave-
        offering is neutralized in a hundred *seahs* of clean unconsecrated
        grain (M. Ter. 5:2)] even the unconsecrated [grain] which is left
        [after a *seah* is removed from the batch for the priest] may only
        [be prepared and] eaten in small lumps [of less than an egg's
        bulk],

[B]   "because of the dough offering [the unconsecrated grain] con-
        tains, [which must not be rendered unclean during the prepara-
        tion of the dough]."

[C]   This statement [of Hezeqiah] indicates that the prohibition
        against [the consumption of heave-offering] by nonpriests is nul-
        lified [when heave-offering is neutralized; i.e., a nonpriest may
        eat what once was heave-offering].

[D] But the prohibition of unclean produce is not nullified, [with the result that even after the unclean produce in the status of heave-offering is neutralized, some unknown portion of the batch is deemed unclean. The batch therefore must be prepared in small bits, so that this unclean produce does not render unclean the clean produce in the batch, and with it, the dough offering which eventually will be separated.]

[E] The views assigned to Hezeqiah [here and elsewhere] are contradictory.

[F] For there [in an undisclosed source] it says: [In a case such as that at A, in which there is one part unclean flour in a hundred and one parts clean flour], how large may each lump of dough be such that one [still] may prepare it in a state of cleanness, [without worrying that there is sufficient unclean flour in the lump to impart uncleanness to the clean flour in it]?

[G] Hezeqiah says, "(Follow GRA's correction:) One-sixth *qab* plus four *qabs*."[7] [This works as follows: The batch as a whole is 1/101 unclean. This means that lumps smaller than a hundred and one eggs' bulks in quantity do not contain the one egg's bulk of unclean produce which constitutes the minimum quantity that conveys uncleanness. Four and a sixth *qab* equals a hundred eggs' bulks. As Hezeqiah states, this amount may be kneaded as a single lump of dough, without fear that unclean flour in the lump will render unclean the clean flour. The lump would not contain a sufficient quantity of unclean flour (one egg's bulk) for that to happen.]

[H] Yet here [at A] he states this, [that to be prepared in cleanness the dough must be in lumps of less than an egg's bulk! This contradicts G, which states that they may be so large as a hundred eggs' bulk.]

[I] [To explain the apparent inconsistency,] said R. Yose "[The rule] there [F–G] applies in the case of one who first kneads [together the clean and unclean dough] and then separates dough offering. [In this case the clean and unclean flour are deemed evenly mixed together. Each lump of dough contains 1/101 unclean dough.]

[J] "But [the rule] here [at A] is for the case in which one separates [dough offering] and then kneads the dough." [At the time the offering is separated from the lump of dough, the clean and unclean produce has not been mixed together. Any lump of dough, however small, may contain all of the unclean produce. Therefore lumps must be kept to less than an egg's bulk, which will not render unclean whatever they touch.]

[K] [Referring back to G] said R. Abbahu, "All of our days we attempted aimlessly [to understand that statement of Hezeqiah], as though we were following the cane [which] a blind person [moves from side to side, never knowing exactly where it is going]. Finally we explained it through *Gematria* [i.e., an interpretation based on the numerical value of letters].

[L] "How many [eggs' bulk] are there in a *qab?*

[M] Twenty-four eggs' bulk. [*Qab* = four *log; log* = six eggs' bulk.]

[N] "How many [eggs' bulk] are there in a *seah?*

[O] "Ninety-six [8] eggs' bulk. [This assumes a *seah* to be four *qabs*. Normally a *seah* is reckoned at six *qabs*.]

[P] "A sixth of this is sixteen eggs' bulk.

[Q] "Now if one kneads [twenty-four eggs' bulk of dough (PM) in] six [separate lumps of four eggs' bulk, each] might contain so much as an egg's bulk of unclean [dough].

[R] "But if one kneads [this amount of dough in] four [separate lumps, each of six eggs' bulk], one does not have any [dough] left over.

[S] "What should one do?

[T] "Let him knead the dough in five [lumps, four of which contain five eggs' bulk, and one of which contains four eggs' bulk (PM)], and [let him] take [the required dough offering from the lump containing] four [eggs' bulk]."

[U] Hezeqiah's view is that one should not allow an egg's bulk of unclean [dough] to touch the kneading trough.

[V] The view of R. Yohanan is that an egg's bulk of unclean [dough may touch the kneading trough], just that [it] may not [9] touch [clean] dough.

[W] Said R. Yose to R. Jeremiah, "What Hezeqiah says, [that the unclean dough may not be allowed to touch the trough,] makes sense only if [what Hezeqiah means is that] de jure [the dough should not touch the trough, but if it does, it does not render it unclean].

[X]   "What R. Yohanan said, [that the unclean dough may touch the trough, makes sense only if he meant this to apply only] post facto." [If it touches, it does not render the trough unclean. But one in all events should try to prevent it from touching.]

[Y]   Said to him [Jeremiah], "I also think so."

[Z]   In the opinion of R. Yohanan, [in what case does the rule he gives regarding] a kneading trough apply?

[AA]   [Said] R. Yose b. R. Bun in the name of R. Jonah,[10] "Solve the problem [of under what circumstances Yohanan holds that the dough should not touch the kneading trough by stating that it is] the case in which one kneads a lump of dough in the size of seventeen eggs' bulk. This is the case in which [the total quantity of] dough is two hundred eggs' bulk.

[BB]   [We revert to question Hezeqiah's original proposition, A.] R. Ba bar Mamel asked, "But does [Hezeqiah's notion that the heave-offering neutralized in the mixture leaves the whole batch in a state of questionable cleanness] not contradict what R. Yose bar Hanina said?

[CC]   "For R. Yose bar Hanina said, "Carrion [i.e., improperly slaughtered meat, which may not be consumed and which is deemed unclean] is neutralized when it is mixed [in small proportions] with properly slaughtered meat.

[DD]   "It is neutralized so as not to impart uncleanness [to one who] touches [it].

[EE]   "But as for imparting uncleanness to one who moves it—in this respect it is not deemed neutralized, [but, rather, still has the power of carrion to impart uncleanness to one who moves it].

[FF]   "[The reason that the carrion is neutralized] is that the properly slaughtered meat [with which it is mixed] cannot take on the status of carrion." [Since this is the case, we hold that the carrion does not render unclean the mixture in which it is neutralized. In the same way, heave-offering should not render unclean the mixture in which it is neutralized, contrary to Hezeqiah, A.]

[GG]   [The reason that FF is unacceptable is now explained.] Said R. Yose, "There [as regards carrion] the properly slaughtered meat cannot take on the status of carrion [and therefore, the carrion does not render unclean the mixture in which it is neutralized].

[HH] "But here [as regards heave-offering] it is possible for unconsecrated produce to take on the status of heave-offering." [Therefore it also is possible for the unconsecrated produce to be rendered unclean by the heave-offering which is neutralized in it. This is as Hezeqiah, A, has claimed.]

[II] Said R. Hezeqiah, "It is R. Simon who posed the problem [at BB–FF, not Bar bar Mamel].

[JJ] "And [it is] R. Ba bar Mamel who solved [the problem, GG–HH, and not Yose]."

Hezeqiah makes an important point relevant to M. Ter. 5:1–3. The Mishnah states that the heave-offering taken from the batch in which it was neutralized is a mixture of clean and unclean produce. Hezeqiah notes that, if this is the case, then the rest of the batch left after the replacement offering is removed likewise is a mixture of clean and unclean produce. As such, it requires special treatment so that the dough offering, yet to be separated from it, is not rendered unclean. Hezeqiah's view is subject to careful scrutiny, with an apparent contradiction posed, E–H, and solved, I–J. A second problem is posed and then resolved at BB–FF + GG–JJ. These materials pose no problems of interpretation. The meaning of K–AA, however, is unclear.

[II.A] It is taught [T. Ter. 6:1]: *A seah of heave-offering which fell into less than a hundred* [seahs *of unconsecrated produce;* = M. Ter. 5:6E]—

[B] lo, it [i.e., all of the produce] takes on the status of heave-offering.

[C][11] [One who eats it unintentionally] is not [however] liable to repay its value and the added fifth [see M. Ter. 6:1].

[D] And they do not use it to repay the value and added fifth for another batch [of heave-offering which accidentally was eaten by a nonpriest], except in accordance with a calculation [of the quantity of unconsecrated produce in the mixture].

[E]   [This rule applies] in the case of a kind of produce that is not totally lost, [so as to be indiscernible within the mixture. Since the heave-offering can be distinguished in the batch, we do not deem the rest of the produce to be subject to all the stringencies normally accorded that offering. We know that that other produce is not actually true heave-offering.]

[F]   But in the case of a kind of produce that is totally lost [within the batch, as in the case of unconsecrated wine mixed with wine in the status of heave-offering (PM), the rule of A–D does not necessarily apply].

[G]   [Rather, in this case the batch is treated as heave-offering or unconsecrated produce] according to which is in the majority.

[H]   If the majority of the produce [in the mixture] is heave-offering, [the entire batch is treated as] heave-offering.

[I]   But if the majority of the batch is unconsecrated produce, [for purposes of the laws of consumption of heave-offering by a nonpriest, the batch is treated as] unconsecrated produce, [such that the nonpriest need pay back to a priest only that proportion of the produce he ate that was heave-offering].

The Yerushalmi suggests general criteria for determining whether or not a mixture of heave-offering and unconsecrated produce is treated as true heave-offering.

5:4 [P: 5:2a]

[I]   *A seah of unclean heave-offering which fell into a hundred [seahs] of clean heave-offering—*

[J]   *the House of Shammai declare [the mixture] forbidden [for consumption by a priest, as though it were unclean].*

[K]   *But the House of Hillel permit [the mixture to a priest, deeming it to be clean].*

[L]   *Said the House of Hillel to the House of Shammai, "Since clean [heave-offering] is forbidden to nonpriests, and unclean [heave-offering] is forbidden to priests, if clean [heave-offering] can be neutralized, so unclean [heave-offering] can be neutralized [when it is mixed with clean heave-offering]."*

[M]   *Said to them the House of Shammai, "No! If unconsecrated pro-*
        duce, to which leniency applies and which is permitted to non-
        priests, neutralizes clean [heave-offering], should heave-offering,
        to which stringency applies and which is forbidden to non-
        priests, [have the same power and] neutralize unclean [heave-
        offering]?"

[N]   *After they had agreed:*

[O]   *R. Eliezer says, "Let [the seah of unclean heave-offering] be*
        raised up [out of the mixture] and burned." [The rest is eaten by
        a priest.]

[P]   *But sages say, "It has been lost through its scantiness." [It need*
        not be removed from the mixture, which is deemed clean and
        may be eaten by a priest.]

Unclean heave-offering may not be eaten by a priest. The Mishnah asks whether or not such heave-offering becomes permitted
for consumption when it is mixed with a great quantity of clean
heave-offering, just as heave-offering mixed with unconsecrated
produce is neutralized and may be eaten by a nonpriest. The
House of Shammai state that it does not and so prohibit I's mixture from consumption by a priest. The Hillelites state that the
small quantity of unclean heave-offering may be disregarded and
the batch eaten by a priest. The issue is debated, L–M. The
Yerushalmi's problem is who conceded to whom in order to reach
the agreement to which N refers.

[I.A]   R. Yudan bar Pazzai and R. Aibo bar Nagri were sitting [to-
        gether]. They said, "We have learned [M. Ter. 5:4N]: *After [the*
        Houses of Hillel and Shammai] agreed. . . .

[B]   [Now, in order to reach this agreement], who conceded to whom,
        the House of Shammai to the House of Hillel, or the House of
        Hillel to the House of Shammai?"

[C]   [Yudan and Aibo] said, "Let us go out [to speak to other author-
        ities] so that we may learn [who conceded to whom]."

[D]   They went out and heard R. Hezeqiah [and] R. Aha in the name
        of R. Judah bar Hanina [say], "We find that in this issue alone

[i.e., that of M. Ter. 5:4] the House of Shammai [12] conceded to the House of Hillel."

[E]   R. Jonah in the name of R. Abaye derived the answer to [B's question] from this [M. T.Y. 2:7]: *[In the case of] a person who is pouring [liquid in the status of heave-offering] from one vessel to another, and one who, having immersed on the selfsame day, awaits the setting of the sun [which signifies the completion of his process of purification] touched the stream of liquid [joining the two vessels, the unclean liquid in the stream, which falls into the lower vessel], is neutralized in a hundred and one parts* [i.e., as the House of Hillel say at M. Ter. 5:4, the unclean heave-offering is neutralized in the clean heave-offering in the lower vessel.]

[F]   "Now if you say that [at M. Ter. 5:4] the House of Hillel concede to the House of Shammai, [that unclean heave-offering] is not neutralized [in clean heave-offering], then who stands behind this [rule of M. T.Y. 2:7] that it is neutralized?

[G]   "It could not be the House of Shammai, [who hold that unclean heave-offering is not neutralized in clean heave-offering].

[H]   "And it could not be the House of Hillel [13] [who, in F's suggestion, agree with the House of Shammai]." [Since the opposite is not tenable, it is clear that, as D claims, the Hillelites maintained their position. The Shammaites conceded to them that unclean heave-offering is neutralized in clean heave-offering.]

[I]   [This shows that it is possible that the Hillelites conceded to the Shammaites.] Said R. Hanina the son of R. Hillel, "Let us suppose that the House of Hillel taught this rule [found at M. T.Y. 2:7] and only later [changed their mind and] conceded to the House of Shammai."

[J]   Said R. Yose, "The Mishnah itself states [that, as D and H suggest, the Shammaites conceded to the House of Hillel]: *After they had agreed, R. Eliezer said, "Let [the seah of unclean heave-offering] be raised up out of the mixture and burned.* [Eliezer thus takes the Hillelite position, that the unclean heave-offering is neutralized, such that it may simply be removed from the mixture and the rest of the produce is deemed clean.]

[K]   "Now was R. Eliezer not [himself] a Shammaite?" [Yes he was. The fact that he takes the Hillelite position thus proves that, as D and H suggest, the Shammaites conceded to the Hillelites.]

[L]   [Another way we know that the House of Shammai conceded to
the Hillelites follows.] Said R. Hinena, "A Tannaitic teaching
explicitly states this, [that the Shammaites agreed to the Hillel-
ites]: After this [group] had conceded to the other [group, they
ruled] that [the unclean heave-offering] is neutralized [in the
clean, i.e., the Hillelite position]."

[M]   [The Yerushalmi indicates that on the basis of the dispute at M.
Ter. 5:4, it appears unlikely that the Shammaites would have
conceded to the Hillelites, contrary to D, H, J–K and L. At M.
Ter. 5:4] the House of Shammai overcame [43d] their, [i.e., the
House of Hillel's argument, for the Shammaites have the last
word in the dispute]. Yet [you would claim that] they [i.e., the
House of Shammai] conceded to them [i.e., the Hillelites!? The
claim is not reasonable, for the Shammaites won the dispute.]

[N]   [Indicating that the Shammaites in fact lost the dispute,] said R.
Abin, "[The Hillelites] had a further answer [to the arguments
of the Shammaites], as was taught by R. Hoshaya: Now if [in the
case of] clean [heave-offering, in which case] nonpriests who eat
it are subject to death, [this heave-offering] is neutralized [in unconsecrated produce], should it not also be the case [for unclean
heave-offering, for the eating of which] the priest [has trans-
gressed] a positive commandment, that the same [rule applies,
i.e., that this unclean heave-offering, is neutralized in clean
heave-offering?]" [See T. Ter. 6:4H–I. On the basis of this argument the Hillelites won the dispute with the Shammaites, such
that the latter were forced to concede to the Hillelite position, as
D, H, J–K and L have suggested.]

The exegetical issue, clearly stated at B, is answered through a
series of disjointed arguments, C–D, E–H + I + J–K, L, and
M + N.

5:5 [P: 5:2b]

[A]   *A seah of heave-offering which fell into a hundred [seahs of un-*
consecrated produce, and was thereby neutralized],

[B]   *and one lifted it out [i.e., took a new seah of heave-offering for*
the priest], and [the replacement heave-offering] fell into a dif-
ferent batch [of unconsecrated produce]—

[C]   R. Eliezer says, "[That which falls into the second batch] im-
       parts the status of heave-offering [to the produce with which it is
       mixed] as does true heave-offering."

[D]   But sages say, "It does not impart the status of heave-offering
       except in accordance with a calculation [of the percentage of the
       produce which is true heave-offering]."

Eliezer is consistent with his previous view. The heave-offering
which disappears into the unconsecrated produce is the same as
that which is lifted out. Sages, D, persist in stating that the
heave-offering taken out of the mixture contains the same proportion of true heave-offering that is contained in the larger
batch as a whole, that is, one one-hundredth. The Yerushalmi
addresses a single question left open by the Mishnah. This is how
the *seah* of produce removed from the mixture is to be treated.
There are two possibilities. We might deem the *seah* to be a mixture of 1/100 *seah* of heave-offering and 99/100 *seah* of unconsecrated produce. If this is the case, the addition of any small
quantity of unconsecrated produce would serve to neutralize the
heave-offering. The mixture then would contain one part heave-
offering in a hundred parts unconsecrated produce. Alternatively, the *seah* of the replacement offering might be treated not
as a mixture of heave-offering and unconsecrated produce, but
simply as though it were itself 1/100 *seah* heave-offering. It
would need to be mixed with a full *seah* of unconsecrated produce in order for that heave-offering to be neutralized. The
Yerushalmi questions which of these possible views underlies the
opinion of sages, M. Ter. 5:5D.

[I.A]   Said R. Yohanan, "*A seah of heave-offering which fell into a
        hundred [seahs] of unconsecrated produce [and one lifted it out
        of the batch to give to the priest; M. Ter. 5:5A–B]*—

[B]   "any small quantity of unconsecrated produce [which becomes
       mixed with it] nullifies [its status as heave-offering]." [To begin
       with it is only 1/100 true heave-offering. Any bit more unconse-
       crated produce is sufficient to neutralize the heave-offering in a
       ratio of one part heave-offering to slightly more than a hundred
       parts unconsecrated produce.]

[C]   Mishnah [Ter. 5:5D] contradicts the statement of R. Yohanan, [for: *Sages say, "Such heave-offering as is described at A] does not impart the status of heave-offering except in accordance with a calculation [of the percentage of true heave-offering it contains]."* [Sages state that if unconsecrated produce is mixed with the *seah* which is 1/100 heave-offering, that 1/100 *seah* heave-offering has the power to impart its own status to the unconsecrated produce. This is contrary to Yohanan, A–B, who says that the small quantity of heave-offering always is neutralized.]

[D]   [Developing Yohanan's view,] R. Yose in the name of R. Yohanan [said], "It was taught in the name of R. Yohanan only that [the *seah* of produce removed from the batch in which heave-offering was neutralized] does not ever impart its own status [to unconsecrated produce into which it falls (PM)].

[E]   "Now he said [that this is the case even if] there was [in the first mixture of heave-offering and unconsecrated produce] more heave-offering than unconsecrated produce, so long as [in the second mixture, of the replacement offering and other common food], there is more unconsecrated produce than the percentage of the mixture which is heave-offering.

[F]   "[Thus the heave-offering in the second mixture] is nullified [through being lost in] the larger quantity [of unconsecrated produce]."

Yohanan takes the view that the replacement offering is in two separate parts.[14] It is comprised of 1/100 *seah* heave-offering and 99/100 *seah* unconsecrated produce. Any small quantity of unconsecrated produce which is added to this mixture will cause the heave-offering to be neutralized, B. C states that sages take the opposite view. D–F appears to clarify Yohanan's view in light of C, with its point coming at F. D–F's larger meaning, however, is not at all clear. If the first mixture, E, contains more heave-offering than unconsecrated produce, that heave-offering is not neutralized. This is contrary to what E–F seems to assume.

[II.A]   Said R. Eleazar,[15] "[When sages, M. Ter. 5:5D, state that the *seah* of replacement offering imparts the status of heave-offering according to a calculation of how much true heave-offering it contains] they mean this applies only if [that *seah*] fell [all into the same batch of unconsecrated produce, so as to create] a single[16] mixture of heave-offering and unconsecrated produce." [But if half of the replacement offering falls into one batch, and the other half falls into a different batch, the heave-offering the replacement offering contains is neutralized.]

[B]   [The question is why sages hold the view ascribed to them at A.] Is it the opinion of R. Eleazar [who stands behind A] that [according to the sages] the unconsecrated produce on top [i.e., that unconsecrated produce which makes up the majority of the *seah* of replacement offering removed from the batch in which heave-offering was neutralized] and the unconsecrated produce below [in the batch into which that replacement offering falls] join together [to make up the quantity of unconsecrated produce needed to] neutralize [the small percentage of true heave-offering contained in the replacement offering]?

[C]   [No.] R. Eleazar reasons that [according to sages] the unconsecrated produce which is below [in the batch into which the replacement offering falls] remains distinct (so PM) [and does not combine with the unconsecrated produce contained in the replacement offering in order to neutralize the heave-offering. Therefore the unconsecrated produce below must itself contain insufficient food to neutralize the heave-offering located in the replacement offering. The unconsecrated produce with which the heave-offering already is mixed in the replacement offering does not count toward neutralizing that priestly gift.]

B–C outlines two possible interpretations of the sages' opinion, M. Ter. 5:5D. According to C, sages hold that the *seah* replacement offering removed from the mixture is an indivisible entity. The unconsecrated produce contained in that replacement offering does not join with other unconsecrated produce in order to neutralize the priestly gift. The replacement offering is treated as though it consists solely of 1/100 *seah* heave-offering. It is unclear how this understanding of the sages' view, or that given at B, is derived from A. The larger meaning of the unit thus remains obscure.

5:6 [P: 5:2c]

[E]   A seah of heave-offering which fell into less than a hundred
       [seahs of unconsecrated produce], and [that produce thereby]
       took on the status of heave-offering,

[F]   and [produce] fell from the mixture into a different batch—

[G]   R. Eliezer says, "[That portion of the mixture which falls into
       the second batch] imparts the status of heave-offering [to the
       produce with which it is mixed] as does true heave-offering."

[H]   But sages say, "A mixture of heave-offering and unconsecrated
       produce does not impart the status of heave-offering [to produce
       with which it is mixed] except in accordance with a calculation
       [of the quantity of true heave-offering contained in the mixture].

[I]   "And that which has been leavened [with heave-offering] does
       not impart the status of heave-offering to that which it leavens
       except in accordance with a calculation [of the quantity of leaven
       in the status of heave-offering in the mixture].

[J]   "And [water from an immersion pool which was made unfit by
       being mixed with] drawn water does not impart a status of inva-
       lidity to [other] immersion pools except in accordance with a
       calculation [of the percentage of drawn water it contains]."

Both the problem, E–F, and the possible answers, G versus H +
I–J, are the same as in the preceding pericope. The Yerushalmi's
first unit contains a dispute concerning the specific circumstances under which sages and Eliezer disagree. Unit **II** continues this examination of exactly what is at issue between the two
disputing parties.

[I.A]   Said R. Yose b. Hanina, "[The opinion of Eliezer, M. Ter. 5:6G,
         that produce which falls from a mixture of heave-offering and
         unconsecrated food is deemed to be true heave-offering], applies
         only if [the seah which fell was divided into five parts and these]
         fell into five [different batches of unconsecrated produce]. [We
         assume that the seah which fell from the mixture contains one-
         fifth of the seah of true heave-offering which was in the mixture.
         We now hold that this one-fifth seah heave-offering is found in

one of the five other batches. Not knowing which, we must treat all of the batches as though they contain a fifth *seah* of true heave-offering.]

[B]   "But if all [of the produce which fell from the original mixture] fell into a single batch [of unconsecrated produce], even R. Eliezer concurs [with sages, M. Ter. 5:6H, that the *seah* imparts the status of heave-offering to the produce with which it is mixed only in accordance with a calculation of the percentage of true heave-offering it contains]." [This is so because it is not likely that the whole *seah* is the true heave-offering which originally fell into the unconsecrated produce.]

[C]   [Disagreeing with A–B] R. Yohanan says, "Even if [the *seah* of produce from the first mixture of heave-offering and unconsecrated food] fell into a single batch, the dispute [between Eliezer and sages] stands."

Yose b. Hanina claims that there is only a narrow range of disagreement between Eliezer and sages, M. Ter. 5:6. Yohanan, C, states that this is not so. Neither Yose nor Yohanan indicates the reasoning which informs his position.

[II.A]   [The question is why Eliezer, M. Ter. 5:6G, holds that the second *seah* of produce, which falls from the mixture of unconsecrated produce and heave-offering, imparts to other food it falls into the status of heave-offering as though it were a true priestly gift.] Hilpai says, "[The reason is that] in the opinion of Eliezer, the unconsecrated produce [into which the second *seah* falls] is treated as though it were distinct [from the unconsecrated produce which is mixed with the heave-offering in that second *seah*]." [That is, the mixture of heave offering and unconsecrated produce which falls into the batch is deemed a single entity and distinct from the produce into which it falls. Within that *seah* it is not clear which produce is heave-offering and which is unconsecrated. Therefore the whole *seah* must be treated as heave-offering. The alternative, which Eliezer rejects, is to say that the unconsecrated produce in the second *seah* combines with the unconsecrated food into which that *seah* falls. All the unconsecrated produce thus joins together to neutralize the small amount of heave-offering. Eliezer holds the opposite, and therefore states that the *seah* which falls from the original mixture imparts the status of heave-offering as though it were a full *seah* of true heave-offering.]

[B] [17]   [How can this be Eliezer's view?] For R. Eleazer said [Y. Ter. 5:5 **II.**B], "In the opinion of rabbis, the unconsecrated produce at the bottom [i.e., into which the mixture of heave-offering and unconsecrated produce falls] is treated as distinct." [This is the same view which A attributes to Eliezer. How can the disputing parties have the same theory?]

[C]   [If indeed it is the case that all hold this view,] what accounts for the different opinions of R. Eliezer and rabbis [at M. Ter. 5:5-6]?

[D]   [Sages hold this view, reported at Y. Ter. 5:5 **II**, for the case of M. Ter. 5:5 alone. In that case the original heave-offering was neutralized in unconsecrated produce. The replacement offering then fell into other unconsecrated food. In that case sages hold that the unconsecrated produce in the replacement offering remains distinct from the unconsecrated produce into which it falls, for] there is a stringency which applies in the case of the *seah* [replacement offering] that is lifted out [of a batch of produce in which] a *seah* [of heave-offering was neutralized]. [Because of the stringency, that *seah* of replacement offering is not easily neutralized, as the sages' opinion, explained at Y. Ter. 5:5 **II**, holds. But sages do not hold that the unconsecrated produce in the second *seah* remains distinct from the other unconsecrated produce with which it is mixed in the case of M. Ter. 5:6, where the original heave-offering is not neutralized. There is no stringency in that case. For that case, only Eliezer holds the view attributed to him at A.]

[E]   Or perhaps [D's explanation is wrong and the sages hold the view ascribed to them at Y. Ter. 5:5 **II** both for the case of M. Ter. 5:5 and 5:6. If this is the case, then Eliezer, who holds in the case of M. Ter. 5:6 that the unconsecrated produce mixed with the heave-offering remains distinct, does not hold that it remains distinct in the case of M. Ter. 5:5. In this view he holds that the case of M. Ter. 5:5 is different from that of M. Ter. 5:6 because, in the former case, in which the heave-offering was neutralized], there is a leniency [which applies to the *seah* of replacement offering]. [In light of this leniency, at M. Ter. 5:5, Eliezer, unlike the sages, holds that the unconsecrated produce contained in the *seah* of replacement offering contributes to the neutralization of the heave-offering in that replacement offering. But at M. Ter. 5:6, where there is no leniency, Eliezer holds that the unconsecrated produce which is mixed with the heave-offering in the second *seah* remains distinct from other unconsecrated produce with which that *seah* becomes mixed, as A, above, claims.]

[F]   [E's claim that there is a leniency at M. Ter. 5:5 is] in line with [the statement of] R. Yohanan, who said [Y. Ter. 5:5 I.A–B], "*A seah of heave-offering which fell into a hundred [seahs] of unconsecrated produce [and one lifted it out of the batch to give to a priest; M. Ter. 5:5A–B]*—any small quantity [of unconsecrated produce which becomes mixed with it] nullifies [its status as heave-offering]."

The issue is whether or not unconsecrated produce with which heave-offering has been mixed later contributes to the neutralization of that same heave-offering. Eliezer, A, states that, in the case of M. Ter. 5:6, it does not. The unconsecrated produce previously mixed with heave-offering remains distinct from the second quantity of unconsecrated produce with which that heave-offering is mixed. B notes that for the case of M. Ter. 5:5 this same view is ascribed to sages, above at Y. Ter. 5:5 II. Since Eliezer and sages dispute the rule for the cases of M. Ter. 5:5–6, it is unclear how they can hold the same underlying theories. Two possible explanations appear, D and E + F. Both make essentially the same point, suggesting that the view ascribed to sages at Y. Ter. 5:5 II holds only for the sages' opinions at M. Ter. 5:5, and that the view attributed to Eliezer, here at A, applies only to the case of M. Ter. 5:6. This means that, contrary to what appeared to be the case, Eliezer and the sages do not have the same larger underlying theories.[18]

5:7 [P: 5:2d]

[A]   *A seah of heave-offering which fell into a hundred [seahs of unconsecrated produce, and so was neutralized]—*

[B]   *if one lifted it out [of the mixture to give to a priest] and a different [seah of heave-offering] fell [into the same produce],*

[C] *lifted out that [seah], and a different [seah of heave-offering] fell*
     [into the same produce]—

[D] *lo, this [i.e., the batch in which the mixtures occur] is permitted*
     [for consumption as unconsecrated produce],

[E] *until there [will have fallen into the batch] a greater quantity of*
     heave-offering than there [originally was] unconsecrated
     produce.

The Mishnah carries forward Eliezer's view. The produce the
householder removes from the batch comprises the heave-
offering which originally fell in. The batch still is composed of
one hundred *seahs* of unconsecrated produce and therefore neutralizes any other *seah* of heave-offering which should become
mixed with it. Unit **I** determines that one may not purposely
cause heave-offering to be mixed, one *seah* after another, with
the unconsecrated produce. The actions of a householder who in
this way attempts intentionally to violate the heave-offering's
holy status are null. The heave-offering retains the status of a
holy priestly gift and, moreover, imparts that status to the unconsecrated produce. Unit **II** turns to M. Ter. 5:7E, asking why
the rule of A–D applies only until the specific point established
by the Mishnah.

[**I.A**] It is taught: [If an individual purposely] allows many [*seahs* of]
     heave-offering [to fall, one at a time, into a single batch of un-
     consecrated produce, it is as if] he intentionally added [uncon-
     secrated produce to a batch in which heave-offering was mixed,
     so as to cause the neutralization of that heave-offering. In either
     case the actions of the householder who attempts intentionally to
     neutralize heave-offering are void. See M. Ter. 5:9I–K.]

[B] Yet [contrary to A's claim that the individual's intentional actions
     are null] we have learned [M. Miq. 7:2: *If an immersion pool]*
     contained forty seahs [of rain water] and one added [to it a seah
     of drawn water] and then removed a seah [of water, the pool] is
     deemed to remain fit, [for we hold that the same unfit water that
     was added to the pool later was removed].

[C] How many times [can this procedure be followed and the pool
     still be deemed valid]?

[D]   R. Isi in the name of R. Mana bar Tanhum [and] R. Abbahu in
       the name of R. Yohanan [say], "[The procedure may be per-
       formed] until [the point at which one would assume that] the
       majority of [the water in] the pool [is drawn water]."

[E]   [B–D implies that one purposely may add drawn water to the
       pool and then remove it, and that the desired result, mainte-
       nance of a valid immersion pool, is accomplished.] Yet here [at
       A] you say this, [i.e., the opposite, that if one purposely at-
       tempts to neutralize heave-offering a *seah* at a time, the action is
       void]!

[F]   [What accounts for the difference between the two rules?] There
       [as regards the immersion pool, the pool] contained sufficient
       [rain water to counteract the invalidating effect of more drawn
       water which would be placed in the pool, even if the original
       drawn water had not been removed (RiDBaZ)], and then one
       [anyway removed the original drawn water and] added [more
       drawn water] to it. [The pool therefore] remained fit.

[G]   But here [in the case of heave-offering] each *seah* of heave-offer-
       ing requires [its own] hundred *seahs* [of unconsecrated produce
       to neutralize it].

       A analyzes M. Ter. 5 : 7 in light of the rule of M. Ter. 5 : 9I–K,
       reaching the logical conclusion that the householder may not
       intentionally take actions to neutralize heave-offering. The prob-
       lem, B–E, is that this appears to contradict M. Miq. 7 : 2. The
       reason for the dissimilar rules is at F + G. F–G's response is odd,
       however, in that it ignores the original issue of the purposeful or
       unintentional character of the actions of the householder.

[II.A]   [Reference is to M. Ter. 5 : 7E: Once a greater quantity of heave-
          offering falls into the batch than there originally was unconse-
          crated produce, the heave-offering is not deemed neutralized.
          Rather, the batch must be treated as heave-offering.] Said R.
          Yose, "This means that even such a thing [as heave-offering]
          which, according to the Torah, is nullified [in mixtures with un-
          consecrated produce], calls up [produce in] its same status [which
          previously had been neutralized] so as to render forbidden [the
          batch in which the mixture occurs]." [19]

Yose states that the process of neutralization is reversible. Heave-offering that had lost its holy status regains its consecration at the point at which it is mixed with much holy produce. When this happens, all the heave-offering together imparts its own status to the unconsecrated produce with which it is mixed.

5:8 [P: 5:2e]

[F]   *A seah of heave-offering which fell into a hundred [seahs of un-consecrated produce, and so was neutralized], and which one had not lifted out [of the mixture] before a different [seah of heave-offering] fell [into that same batch]—*

[G]   *lo, this [i.e., the batch of produce] is forbidden [for consumption by nonpriests].*

[H]   *But R. Simeon permits.*

G holds that the batch contains two *seahs* of heave-offering and only one hundred *seahs* of unconsecrated produce. The mixture therefore must be treated as heave-offering. Simeon, H, claims that the first *seah* of heave-offering was neutralized when it fell into the unconsecrated produce. It therefore is deemed itself to be unconsecrated food. The second *seah* of heave-offering falls into a hundred and one *seahs* of unconsecrated produce and thus, like the first *seah* of heave-offering, is neutralized. The Yerushalmi begins by exploring the divergent theories of neutralization expressed by the Mishnah's disputing authorities. The second and final unit does not deal with issues raised here, such that it is impossible to account for its placement.

[I.A]   [The unit explains the different theories of neutralization which inform the views of Simeon, M. Ter. 5:8H, and the anonymous sages, M. Ter. 5:8F–G.] R. Simeon says, "[The replacement offering, taken from the mixture for a priest when a *seah* of heave-offering is neutralized] is sanctified at the point at which [the householder] knows [that the mixture has occurred]." [Thus the process of neutralization of the first *seah* already is complete when the second *seah* falls into the batch. This being the case, the second *seah* is neutralized as well.]

[B]   But rabbis [M. Ter. 5:8F–G] say, "[The replacement offering] is sanctified only when it [actually] is lifted out [of the mixture]." [Only at this point is the process of neutralization of the first *seah* of heave-offering complete. If a second *seah* of heave-offering falls into the batch before this point, we treat it as a case in which both *seahs* fell in at once. Together they impart to the unconsecrated produce the status of heave-offering.][20]

The positions of M. Ter. 5:8's authorities are explained, A versus B.

[II.A]   It is taught: [As for] a *seah* of [unclean (so RiDBaZ, GRA, PM)] heave-offering that fell into a hundred [*seahs* of unconsecrated produce and so was neutralized]—

[B]   [hoping to keep the *seah* of produce for himself at low cost, the householder] says to the priest, "Am I not obligated [simply] to give you the value [the unclean, and so inedible, heave-offering would have were it] wood? [Since unclean heave-offering may only be burned, surely this is the case. Therefore] take [from me] the value the [*seah* of heave-offering] would have were it wood, [and leave me the produce itself]."

[C]   [Unlike what the householder says, the priest knows that if the *seah* is removed from the clean unconsecrated produce, it may be eaten, so long as it is prepared in small bits (M. Ter. 5:2A + D–E). The heave-offering therefore is worth more than wood. The priest wishes to receive this full value. Therefore] the priest answers him, "[If this were a case in which] a *seah* of [unclean] heave-offering fell into less than a hundred [*seahs* of unconsecrated produce], would [the unclean heave-offering] not impart its own status to the batch? [Certainly it would.] Does wood impart its own status to a batch? [No, it does not. Therefore it clearly is unacceptable to treat unclean heave-offering as though it were wood, as you wish to do, B.]

[D]   [The meaning of this line is not clear:] "And will you not ultimately give [the *seah*] to[21] a different priest? Now will he pay him [i.e., you, the householder] the value [the *seah* would have were it wood]?"

[E]   [The problem created by the case at A may be summarized as
follows: When the unclean heave-offering was neutralized in the
clean unconsecrated produce, the heave-offering increased in
value. Before it could not be eaten by the priest; now it may be.
The householder says that the priest should not receive this increased value, which derives from the householder's produce.
He therefore still wishes to treat the heave-offering as though it
were unclean. The priest notes that the offering in all events belongs to the priest. The householder should give him the *seah* of
produce, or its full value, and not the much reduced value of
unclean heave-offering.] What should they do [in order to resolve the dispute]?

[F]   The householder gives the priest the value [of the original *seah*
of unclean heave-offering] as though it were wood.

[G]   And the rest [i.e., the increased value of the householder's produce caused by the presence of the extra *seah* of heave-offering]
they should divide.

[H]   [The same sort of compromise is suggested in the following case.]
A certain man knocked [his basket of low-valued] barley into [a
neighbor's basket of high-valued] wheat.

[I]   The case came before R. Judah bar Shalom and he said, "Let
[the neighbor] pay [the man] the value of [his lost] barley.

[J]   "[We also must take into account the fact that the mixture, now
owned entirely by the neighbor, will bring a higher price than
the barley and wheat would separately, for the whole mixture
may be sold at close to the value of high-priced wheat. There-
fore] let them divide the rest [i.e., the extra money which the
neighbor will receive when he sells the mixture]."

The issue is of a practical character, engendered by the Mishnah's discussion of the rules of neutralization. I see no particular
reason for its placement here. My translation and interpretation
follow RiDBaZ.

5:9 [P: 5:3]

[A]   *(1) A seah of [wheat in the status of] heave-offering which fell
into a hundred [seahs of unconsecrated wheat, and thereby was*

neutralized], and one ground it, [i.e., all of the wheat in the mixture], and it diminished [in quantity]—

[B]   just as the unconsecrated [wheat in the mixture] diminished [in quantity], so the heave-offering diminished [in quantity].

[C]   [The mixture therefore remains] permitted [for consumption by a nonpriest].

[D]   (II) A seah of [wheat in the status of] heave-offering which fell into less than a hundred [seahs of unconsecrated wheat, and thereby imparted its own status to the whole batch], and one ground it, [i.e., all of the wheat in the batch], and it increased [in quantity]—

[E]   just as the unconsecrated [wheat] increased [in quantity], so the [wheat in the status of] heave-offering increased [in quantity].

[F]   [The mixture therefore remains] forbidden [for consumption by a nonpriest].

[G]   If it is known that the unconsecrated wheat is of better quality than the [wheat in the status of] heave-offering—

[H]   [the mixture] becomes permitted [for consumption by a nonpriest, for the high-quality, unconsecrated wheat produces more flour than the low-quality heave-offering. Now there is sufficient unconsecrated produce in the mixture to neutralize the heave-offering.]

[I]   (III) A seah of heave-offering which fell into less than a hundred [seahs of unconsecrated produce], and afterwards [more] unconsecrated [produce] fell there [i.e., into the same batch]—

[J]   if [this happened] unintentionally, [the mixture becomes] permitted.

[K]   But if [it happened] intentionally, [the mixture remains] forbidden [for consumption by nonpriests].

B and E make the point. The milling equally affects the heave-offering and the unconsecrated produce. Only if it is known that this is not the case, G–H, does a different rule apply. I–K is cognate. As we have seen before, the householder may not take actions designed to neutralize heave-offering. Such intentional actions are void.

The Yerushalmi's discussion is striking in that it rejects the main points of the Mishnah's rules. Units **I–II** + **III,** first, claim that in a case such as that of A–C, the heave-offering remains neutralized even if it does not decrease in quantity, contrary to M. Ter. 5:9G–H. This is explained on the basis of facts and ideas unknown to the Mishnah. In this way the Yerushalmi does not directly reject what the Mishnah states, but, rather, adds its own set of mitigating concerns. Unit **IV** states that in the case described at G–H, the individual may intentionally take actions to neutralize the heave-offering. This contradicts the theory of I–K that actions designed to neutralize heave-offering are void. The Yerushalmi notes this fact and explains why the case at G–H is different. Unit **V** makes an obvious point regarding I–K. Its rule applies to other forbidden produce as well as to heave-offering. Unit **VI** concludes the chapter with a short homily on the obligations of a judge.

[**I.A**]   [The rule of M. Ter. 5:9] does not only apply if the heave-offering decreased in quantity [along with the unconsecrated produce.]

[**B**]   Rather, even if, [when ground], the unconsecrated produce decreased in quantity, and the heave-offering remained [in its same quantity, such that, by percentage, the batch now contains more than one percent heave-offering] the mixture is permitted [for consumption by a nonpriest].

The Yerushalmi contradicts what is explicit at M. Ter. 5:9G–H, claiming that we do not take account of the fact that the heave-offering and the unconsecrated produce react differently to being milled. As we shall see, PM solves the problem by reading Y. Ter. 5:9 **II,** which follows, as a continuation and explanation of this unit.[22] But the fact remains that this unit, as well as the following one, has a very different notion of the law from that presented at M. Ter. 5:9.

[**II.A**]   It is taught: The waste [left from the milling] of [grain in the status of] heave-offering does not join with [the flour in the status of] heave-offering in order [to make up the quantity of heave-offering which] renders forbidden [for consumption by nonpriests] unconsecrated [grain with which the heave-offering is mixed. That is, the refuse from the heave-offering is not deemed a consecrated food which has the power to impart its own status to unconsecrated grain.]

[B]   But the waste [left from the milling] of unconsecrated [grain] does join with the unconsecrated [flour to form the quantity of produce which] neutralizes heave-offering [with which it is mixed. This is because the refuse from the milling of grain is deemed edible.]

[C]²³   R. Bibi asked, "What is the law whether or not the waste [left from the milling of] heave-offering, [which we saw, A, is not itself deemed consecrated as a priestly gift], joins with unconsecrated grain so as to [form the quantity of produce which] neutralizes heave-offering?"

[D]   From that which R. Huna said—"The rinds of forbidden fruit, [which themselves are not deemed forbidden], join with permitted produce [in order to form the quantity of food needed to neutralize forbidden produce]"—this means that the refuse [left from the milling] of heave-offering joins with unconsecrated [grain to form the quantity of unconsecrated produce which] neutralizes heave-offering.

[E]   (Delete:) R. Huna says, "The rinds of forbidden produce neutralize that which is permitted."

The husks and other waste left from the milling of grain in the status of heave-offering are not deemed a consecrated priestly gift, A. But such waste is deemed unconsecrated food and so joins with other unconsecrated produce to create the quantity needed to neutralize the heave-offering in the mixture, as B–D states. This contradicts M. Ter. 5:9's notion that, when heave-offering and unconsecrated produce are ground, the ratio of one to the other remains the same, such that the mixture retains its previous status, permitted or forbidden. According to this unit, when the mixture is ground, the percentage of heave-offering will drop such that, in most cases, the offering would be neutralized. As PM notes, this unit explains Y. Ter. 5:9 I's insistence that, even if the quantity of what was heave-offering does not decrease along with that of the unconsecrated produce, the priestly gift is deemed to remain neutralized. The reason, this unit explains, is that less of what was heave-offering now is deemed consecrated. This notion is unknown to and, as I have said, contradicts, M. Ter. 5:9. Yet it makes sense in the generations after the formulation of Mishnah, when concern for the maintenance of the priestly caste was diminished. The Yerushalmi's rules greatly reduce the likelihood that the status of heave-offering will be imparted to the householder's unconsecrated produce.

[III.A] A *seah* of heave-offering which fell into a hundred [*seahs* of unconsecrated produce, and one lifted it out]—they do not remove the darnel which is in it [i.e., in the replacement offering].

[B] [If the heave-offering fell into] less than this [quantity of unconsecrated produce, and so imparted its own status to all of the produce in the batch]—they may remove the darnel which is in it [i.e., which is in the batch that must be treated as heave-offering. The householder may keep the darnel for himself. The rest must go to the priest.]

[C] [And so] a *log* of wine [in the status of heave-offering] that had been clarified, which fell into a hundred *logs* of [unconsecrated] wine which had not been clarified—they do not remove the lees which are in it [i.e., in the *log* of wine taken to replace the lost heave-offering wine].

[D] (Supply with PM and T.:) [If it fell into] less than this—they remove the lees which are in it [i.e., in the mixture of heave-offering and unconsecrated wine].

[E] A *log* of wine [in the status of heave-offering] which had not been clarified, which fell into a hundred *logs* of [unconsecrated] wine which had been clarified—they do not remove the lees which are in it [i.e., in the wine taken as a replacement offering; T. Ter. 6:10].

The householder's separation of a replacement offering constitutes a designation of that produce to be heave-offering. For this reason the householder may not take from that which he separates darnel (A) or lees (C, E). This is so even though these things are not edible and so are not normally made agricultural offerings. The designation is probative. B and D have the heave-offering impart its own status to the unconsecrated produce.

Now there has been no designation of the produce in the batch to be heave-offering. For this reason, the inedible produce in the batch is not deemed to take on the status of heave-offering. Accordingly it may be taken by the householder for his own use. These rules, cited directly from the Tosefta, are found here because the point they make is cognate to that of Y. Ter. 5:9 **II**, which preceded. Y. Ter. 5:9 **II** claims that what is not edible should not be deemed heave-offering. This pericope of the Tosefta does not however entirely support Y. Ter. 5:9 **II**'s contention. There the grain in the status of heave-offering had been designated to be heave-offering. Having been subject to that designation, the waste left from the milling should retain the status of a priestly gift. That fact, clear to this unit, is the opposite of what Y. Ter. 5:9 **II** claims.

[**IV.A**] [Y. refers to M. Ter. 5:9H: If the unconsecrated wheat is of better quality than the wheat in the status of heave-offering, when the mixture of the two is ground up, it becomes permitted for consumption by a nonpriest.] It is taught: Even de jure [i.e., intentionally] the individual may grind [the mixture of heave-offering and unconsecrated food], and [as a result the mixture] becomes permitted for consumption [by a nonpriest].

[B] This teaching [A] is [the opinion of] R. Yose.

[C] For *R. Yose says, "Even if one intentionally picks [the fruit of an orchard containing some saplings which are forbidden under the restriction of* Orlah, *or under the laws of Diverse Kinds, the forbidden produce within the batch of fruit he picks] is neutralized if it constitutes only one part within two hundred parts permitted fruit"* [M. Or. 1:6. Yose disputes the anonymous view at M. Or. 1:6, that the forbidden produce is not neutralized if the householder purposely picks it. Yose's view at M. Or. 1:6 is parallel to that expressed in A. He allows the householder purposely to perform some concrete action in order to neutralize forbidden food. The anonymous authorities of M. Or. 1:6 do not.]

[D] [In the following Zeira disagrees with B–C, claiming that the anonymous authorities of M. Or. 1:6, as well as Yose, agree with A.] Said R. Zeira, "[Householders intentionally may mill mixtures of heave-offering and unconsecrated produce], for it is usual for priests themselves to mill such mixtures in their homes."

[Since the priest is going to mill the mixture anyway, all agree that the householder may do so.]

[E] [In the understanding of Zeira, D,] for what case is there a difference [between the view of Yose and that of the anonymous sages of M. Or. 1:6]?

[F] For the case of [a mixture of permitted produce and produce subject to the restriction of Diverse Kinds].

[G] [24] In the opinion of R. Yose one may [intentionally] mill [such a mixture] and [this] renders it permitted [for consumption. It no longer is subject to the restriction of Diverse Kinds. This is comparable to what Yose holds at M. Or. 1:6.]

[H] In the opinion of [the anonymous] rabbis [of M. Or. 1:6], one may not [intentionally] mill [the mixture] in order to render it permitted [for consumption. As Zeira explains, these authorities hold only that one may mill a mixture of heave-offering and unconsecrated produce, for that is what the priest is going to do anyway. But one may not mill other mixtures of forbidden and permitted produce, for otherwise these would not be milled.]

The question is who stands behind the rule of A, that one purposely may mill a mixture of unconsecrated produce and heave-offering so as to cause the heave-offering to be neutralized. B–C claims it is the view of Yose alone. The parallel dispute at M. Or. 1:6 seems to prove this. Zeira disagrees, D, indicating why, in the case of the mixture with heave-offering, all authorities will agree that the householder purposely may cause the priestly gift to be neutralized. E–H stresses Zeira's point. The distinction drawn between the view of Yose and that of the anonymous sages, M. Or. 1:6, applies in all cases except for that given at A, in which there is a mixture of heave-offering and unconsecrated produce.

[V.A] R. Abbahu in the name of R. Yohanan [says], "[Any mixture of permitted and] forbidden [food] to which one unintentionally adds [more permitted produce, such that, as a result, there is sufficient permitted produce to neutralize the forbidden food— the mixture indeed] becomes permitted [for consumption].

[B]   "[But if the individual] intentionally [adds the permitted produce, the mixture remains] forbidden."

[C][25]   [Why need Yohanan state this?] Is this not indicated [explicitly]
in Mishnah [Ter. 5:9J–K]: *[If one adds produce] unintentionally, [the mixture becomes] permitted. [If one does so] intentionally, [the mixture remains] forbidden.*

[D]   [Yohanan needed to make his statement because] the Mishnaic
rule refers only to [mixtures of] heave-offering [and unconsecrated produce].

[E]   [Yohanan intended] to indicate that this applies as well in the
case of all other [sorts of forbidden] things.

Yohanan would not repeat in his own words what already is explicit in the Mishnah; so C. The distinctive point he wished to
make therefore must be found, D–E.

[VI.A]   R. Aha in the name of R. Yohanan [said], "Just as one is commanded to tell [others] a law which will be followed,[26] so he is
commanded not to tell [others] a law which [in all events] will
not be carried out."

[B]   Said R. Eleazar, "Just as it is forbidden to declare clean that
which is unclean, so it is forbidden to declare unclean that which
is clean."

[C]   Said R. Abba bar Jacob in the name of R. Yohanan, "If a question of law comes to you and you cannot determine whether [the
animal is only possibly unclean and so] to be left in a state of suspension [i.e., neither offered nor destroyed] or whether [it is certainly unclean and so] to be [destroyed through] burning, rush
to have it burned, rather than to leave it in a state of suspension.

[D]   "For there is nothing better loved in the Torah than bullocks
being burned and goats being burned [as sacrifices].

[E]   "[So] these [questionable offerings also should be destroyed]
through burning."

[F]   [Disagreeing,] R. Yose asked, "Do we adjudicate[27] a case in a
manner *not* in accordance with its commandment because some
[different] case *does* have that [particular] commandment?" [Yose's

point is that even though the Torah commands that certain clean animals should be burned as sacrifices, it does not imply that ones of questonable cleanness likewise should be burned. The cases are not comparable.]

The pericope collects three statements concerning the obligations of a judge, A, B, and C–E versus F.[28] These appear as a unit also at Y. Sot. 8:2 and Y. Hag. 1:8. C–E contradicts B, and is itself challenged at F.

6 Yerushalmi Terumot
Chapter Six

[A]   *[A nonpriest] who unintentionally eats heave-offering pays back the principal and an added fifth.*

[B]   *The same [rule applies to] (1) one who [unintentionally] eats [produce in the status of heave-offering], to (2) one who [unintentionally] drinks [liquids in the status of heave-offering], and to (3) one who [unintentionally] anoints [himself with oil in the status of heave-offering].*

[C]   *The same [rule applies to (4) one who unintentionally misappropriates] clean heave-offering, and to (5) [one who unintentionally misuses] unclean heave-offering.*

[D]   *He pays back [the principal and] added fifth, and [if he should eat the added fifth] a fifth of the added fifth.*

[E]   *He does not pay restitution with heave-offering; rather [he pays it with] unconsecrated produce, and this takes on the status of heave-offering.*

[F]   *And [since] the restitution is heave-offering [even] if the priest so wishes, he may not refuse [to take it].*

A nonpriest who unintentionally eats heave-offering compensates the priest by replacing the heave-offering with other produce. He also gives the priest an additional fifth of the heave-offering's quantity. This represents a fine in atonement for the offense of eating a holy thing. The same restitution, principal and added fifth, is required no matter how the nonpriest uses the heave-

offering (B). It must be paid whether the heave-offering was
clean or unclean (C). E–F describes the method of repayment.

The Yerushalmi's well-ordered discussion attacks each of the
Mishnah's points in turn. Units **I–II** refer to M. Ter. 6:1A, defining what quantity of produce constitutes an added fifth and
explaining what the Mishnah means by "unintentionally." Interpretation of B follows, unit **III**. The question is what acts of
consumption fall under the categories "eating" and "drinking,"
such that they obligate the nonpriest to the principal and added
fifth. Unit **IV** turns to M. Ter. 6:1C, which indicates that one
who eats unclean heave-offering must pay back clean produce.
What if one pays unclean produce as restitution anyway? Units
V–VI refer to E, explaining exactly what it means to say that the
produce paid as restitution takes on the status of heave-offering.
In what specific respects is it deemed to be a priestly gift? Units
VII–IX talk about cases in which a priest refuses to accept the
restitution, M. Ter. 6:1F. We find that in certain circumstances
the priest indeed may do so. Unit **X** concludes with a question
outside the parameters of the Mishnah's discussion, though none-
theless appropriate. The issue, taken from T. Ter., is to what
priest restitution must be paid, whether to any priest whose
heave-offering was eaten or only to a priest who is an associate
and trusted to maintain the offering's cleanness.

[**I.A**]   [44a] *One who unintentionally eats heave-offering. . . .* [M. Ter.
6:1A].

[**B**]   Scripture says, "And if a man eats of a holy thing unwittingly, he
shall add the fifth of its value [to it, and give the holy thing to
the priest"; Lev. 22:14].

[**C**]   [This means that] it [i.e., the principal] along with its fifth shall
constitute five parts [i.e., if the individual eats a *seah* of heave-
offering, he pays back a *seah* and a quarter, that is, five equal
parts of a quarter *seah* each].

To add "a fifth" of the heave-offering's value "to it" means "to
provide five parts" of produce where, previously, there were
four. This means that the nonpriest pays as restitution the quantity of heave-offering which he ate plus an additional twenty-five
percent.

[**II**.A]   [The unit refers to M. Ter. 7 : 1, which states that one who intentionally eats heave-offering pays the principal but not the added fifth.] Did not R. Abbahu in the name of R. Yohanan[1] say, "If one intentionally[2] ate forbidden fat, [for which he is subject to a sin offering, but, not knowing that this is the case], unintentionally [did not bring] the offering, they free him of culpability [for purposely eating the fat] and [instead] he receives the forty stripes [see Y. Ket. 3 : 1]; then he brings an offering [to repent for having omitted the first offering]."

[B]   [On the basis of A] also here [in the case of M. Ter. 7 : 1] let us say: If one intentionally [eats] heave-offering and unintentionally[3] does not pay the added fifth, let them free him [of culpability for purposely eating heave-offering and instead] inflict upon him the forty stripes; and let him [then] bring an added fifth, [as though he unintentionally had eaten the priestly gift].

[C]   [Explaining why B is not the case] said R. Zeira, "It is an ordinance of Scripture [that one brings the added fifth only for unintentionally eating heave-offering. For Scripture states], 'If a man eats of a holy thing *unwittingly*, [he shall add the fifth of its value to it and give the holy thing to the priest' (Lev. 22 : 14)].

[D]   "Now his [intentional] act of eating may be deemed unintentional only if he intentionally [ate the produce because he was] not certain [whether or not it was heave-offering. But if he had known] for certain [that it was heave-offering, he would] not intentionally [have eaten it]." [Only in such a case as is described here could intentional consumption of heave-offering be treated as unintentional, so as to fall under the rule of M. Ter. 6 : 1. In this case the added fifth will be paid. But in the case described at B, the consumption of the heave-offering must be deemed intentional, and, as at M. Ter. 7 : 1, the added fifth is not paid.]

[E]   Said R. Yose, "[D] leads us to conclude: One who would have refrained [from an act] if he had known [that it certainly was prohibited] is culpable as though he had acted unintentionally [and not intentionally]."

[F]   [The following tests E on an ambiguous case.] If one [who had eaten an olive's bulk of forbidden fat] said, "If I had known that [this forbidden fat comprised] a [full] olive's bulk [the minimum amount for the eating of which one is culpable], I would not have eaten it. But if I had known that it was only a half olive's bulk, I [still] would have eaten it"—[is the individual deemed to have eaten unintentionally or intentionally]?

[G]   Said R. Bun bar Hiyya, "It is as though he unintentionally ate a half olive's bulk [i.e., the second half, which he would not have eaten had he known it was forbidden] and intentionally [ate] a half olive's bulk [i.e., the first half, which he says he would have eaten even if he had known]." [According to Bun bar Hiyya, the man is culpable, for he ate the requisite quantity and part of his act of eating was intentional.]

[H]   Now does R. Bun bar Hiyya not understand matters as does R. Simeon b. Laqish? [He does not.]

[I]   For said R. Simeon b. Laqish, "[If] one ate a half olive's bulk [of forbidden fat] in a single act of inadvertence, he is not culpable, [for he ate less than the minimum quantity]."

[J]   And here [since the act of eating was in two distinct parts, it is as though] he ate two half olive's bulk, less some small amount. [Therefore Simeon b. Laqish holds that he is] not culpable.

[K]   [While] Simeon b. Laqish [disagrees in this case], he concedes [to Bun bar Hiyya that one is culpable for eating a half olive's bulk in the case of] objects from which individuals are forbidden to benefit, [e.g., foods used in idol worship].

[L][4]   And R. Simeon b. Laqish concedes [that one is culpable for eating a half olive's bulk] on the Day of Atonement.

[M]   And R. Simeon b. Laqish concedes [that one is culpable for eating a half olive's bulk if, at the time he eats it he intends] later on to finish [eating the amount that would render him culpable].

The pertinence of the unit to M. Ter. 6:1 is in the point made by Zeira, D, rephrased by Yose, E. One is deemed to have eaten heave-offering unintentionally even if he purposely ate what he *thought* might be a priestly gift. The act of eating is deemed unintentional so long as, at the time he consumed the food, the individual did not know *for certain* that it was heave-offering. Simeon b. Laqish and Bun bar Hiyya do not dispute this theory, F–J + K–M, but only its application in a specific case.

[**III**.A]   R. Abbahu in the name of R. Yohanan [says], "One who [intentionally] quaffs vinegar in the status of heave-offering receives the forty stripes [normally inflicted upon one who intentionally eats or drinks heave-offering]." [Quaffing vinegar is comparable to drinking any other liquid.]

[B]   R. Abbahu in the name of R. Yohanan [says],[5] "One who [intentionally] chews upon a stalk of wheat in the status of heave-offering receives the forty stripes [inflicted upon one who intentionally eats heave-offering]." [Chewing upon is comparable to eating.]

[C]   It is taught: One who [unintentionally] chews upon a stalk of wheat in the status of heave-offering repays [to the priest] the principal, but does not pay the added fifth,[6] [for chewing upon is not comparable to eating]. [The individual is not culpable for eating heave-offering and therefore does not pay the added fifth required by M. Ter. 6:1.]

[D][7]   [Contrary to C,] Rabbi says, "I say he pays [both] the principal and the added fifth." [Rabbi agrees with B, that chewing upon produce is comparable to eating it.]

[E]   R. Jeremiah in the name of R. Imi [says], "Sages [of C] concede to Rabbi [D] that in the case of one who, after bathing, quaffs vinegar in the status of heave-offering, he pays [both] the principal and added fifth.

[F]   "For [quaffing] vinegar revives the soul." [Quaffing vinegar thus is comparable to drinking other liquids. Sages disagree only concerning chewing upon wheat, which, they say, has no nutritional benefit and therefore is not like eating.]

The two separate parts of the pericope, A–B and C–D + E–F, ask whether or not all acts of consumption are deemed "eating" or "drinking" (M. Ter. 6:1B), such that a nonpriest who performs them is culpable for consuming heave-offering. E–F, the point of agreement between sages of C and Rabbi, D, explains the unit as a whole. All agree that an act of ingestion is deemed "eating" or "drinking" only if the individual derives nutritional benefit from it. If the nonpriest does not benefit from his actions, he cannot be deemed to have misused the priestly gift. C–D is a quibble over the facts of the matter, specifically, whether or not chewing on a stalk of wheat benefits the nonpriest.

[**IV.**A] It is taught: [If] one [unintentionally] ate unclean heave-offering, he must [anyway] make restitution with clean unconsecrated produce.

[B] But if he made restitution with unclean unconsecrated produce, he has fulfilled his obligation.

[C] R. Nathan says, "[Disputing B,] **Sumkos says, '[If he did it] unintentionally, that which he has done is done [and valid; the restitution takes on the status of heave-offering and serves to repay the priest]. [But if it was] intentional, that which he has done is not valid, [and the offender must go back and give clean produce to the priest'"**; T. Ter. 7:7C–D].

[D] [The following appears to contradict Sumkos. Yose, E, states that even if one intentionally gives unclean heave-offering instead of clean, it is valid.] There we have learned [M. Ter. 2:2]: *They may not separate unclean produce as heave-offering on behalf of clean produce.*

[E] It is taught in the name of R. Yose, "**If one separated unclean produce as heave-offering for clean produce, whether he did this unintentionally or intentionally, that which he has done is done [and valid]**"; T. Ter. 3:19A].

[F] The minority opinion in the present case [i.e., Yose] accords with the anonymous view there [at B, that one may give unclean heave-offering instead of clean].

[G] And the minority opinion there [i.e., Sumkos] accords with the anonymous position here [in M. Ter. 2:2, cited at D. These parties hold that one may not intentionally give unclean heave-offering instead of clean.]

The issue is whether or not unclean heave-offering may be put to those same purposes for which clean heave-offering is used. This is argued in two disputes, A–B versus C, for the case of restitution paid by a nonpriest who unintentionally eats heave-offering;[8] and D versus E, for the case of the householder's initial separation of heave-offering. The question of which position is authoritative is not answered. Instead, F–G correlates the opposing views expressed in the disputes.

[V.A]   [M. Ter. 6 : 1 states that the produce designated to replace heave-offering unintentionally eaten by a nonpriest takes on the status of heave-offering.] In what way?

[B]   R. Zeira in the name of R. Hanina [says], "Restitution [made for] heave-offering [unintentionally eaten by a nonpriest], lo, it is like heave-offering in all respects, except that, lo,[9] [if it is planted as seed], what grows from it is treated as unconsecrated produce.

[C]   "[By contrast] that which grows from [seed in the status of] heave-offering, lo, it is treated as unconsecrated produce in all respects, except that it is forbidden for [consumption by] nonpriests."[10]

[D]   Said R. Yose, "Both [of these rules, B and C] we have learned [explicitly] in the Mishnah.

[E]   "[We know from the Mishnah that] restitution [made for] heave-offering [which a nonpriest unintentionally eats], lo, it is like heave-offering in all respects, for we have learned: *[One who unintentionally eats heave-offering] does not pay restitution with heave-offering; rather [he pays it with] tithed, unconsecrated produce, and this takes on the status of heave-offering* [M. Ter. 6 : 1E].

[F]   "[We know that it is like heave-offering] except that [if it is planted as seed] what grows from it is unconsecrated, for we have learned: *That which grows from [seed in the status of] heave-offering has the status of heave-offering* [M. Ter. 9 : 4A].

[G]   "[Since the Mishnah states explicitly only that what grows from seed in the status of heave-offering is treated as heave-offering, this means] that what grows from the restitution [paid] for heave-offering [eaten by a nonpriest] is unconsecrated.

[H]   "[We know that] what grows from [seed in the status of] heave-offering, lo, it is like unconsecrated produce in all respects, for we have learned: *And [the field in which heave-offering is sown] is subject to [the laws of] gleanings, forgotten sheaves, and [produce growing in] the corner of a field. And poor Israelites and poor priests glean [in such a field*; M. Ter. 9 : 1–2H–I].

[I]   "[It is like unconsecrated produce in all respects,] except that it is forbidden for [consumption by] nonpriests, as we have learned: *And the poor Israelites sell their portion to the priests at the price of heave-offering; and the money which they receive is theirs [i.e., the poor Israelites"; M. Ter. 9 : 2J–K].

Zeira, B + C, states the meaning of M. Ter. 6:1E. Yose, D–I, shows how exegesis of the Mishnah yields the same understanding.

[VI.A] It is taught: Produce paid as restitution for heave-offering [unintentionally eaten by a nonpriest]—

[B] **they do not pay out from this produce the principal and added fifth [owed for a different batch of heave-offering unintentionally eaten by a nonpriest],**

[C] and [nonpriests] do not owe the principal and added fifth for [eating] this [produce].

[D] **And this produce is not[11] subject to the separation of dough offering.**

[E] **And hands [which have not been cleansed of their usual second-degree uncleanness], and one who has immersed on the self-same day [and awaits the setting of the sun, which marks the conclusion of the process of purification,] do not render [the restitution] unfit [for consumption],**

[F] **just as they [do not] render unconsecrated produce unfit [T. Ter. 8:2, with major variations].**

[G] And with this latter rule [E–F], even R. Simeon and R. Yose agree.[12] [See M. T.Y. 3:4. Simeon and Yose state that one who has immersed on the selfsame day renders invalid dough leavened with yeast in the status of heave-offering. The point here is that they do not hold that this applies in the case of dough leavened with yeast from restitution paid for heave-offering eaten by a nonpriest.]

The Yerushalmi's contribution is at G. Simeon and Yose, M. T.Y. 3:4, agree with what is stated anonymously in T. Ter. 8:2, cited in the Yerushalmi's version at A–F. They agree with the Tosefta that the restitution is not like true heave-offering.

[VII.A] *[Even] if the priest wishes,[13] he may not refuse [to take the restitution; M. Ter. 6:1F].*

[B] [This is the case] before [the nonpriest] designates [the restitution. That is, the priest may not tell the nonpriest that he is pardoned and need not pay the restitution. But once the nonpriest designates the restitution, the priest may refuse to take it.]

The Yerushalmi's interpretation of M. Ter. 6:1F appears at B. The implications of B's claim are discussed in the units which follow, Y. Ter. 6:1 **VIII** and **IX**.

[**VIII**.A] [M. Ter. 6:1D states that one who eats the added fifth must repay its value plus an added fifth.] If he designated [the added fifth, but before giving it to a priest] ate it—[is he subject to repaying both the principal and added fifth? This is] under dispute by Rabbi and R. Eleazar b. R. Simeon.

[B] For it is taught: "[If a man eats of a holy thing unwittingly, he shall add the fifth of its value to it] and shall give the holy thing to the priest" [Lev. 22:14].

[C][14] "[This means that] giving [the restitution to the priest] marks [the restitution's] sanctification [as heave-offering], so as to obligate one [who eats the restitution after this point to pay] the principal and added fifth.

[D] "But [simply] designating [the restitution] does not mark its sanctification [as heave-offering], so as to obligate one [who eats it at this point, before it has been given to a priest,] to pay the principal and added fifth"—the words of Rabbi.

[E] R. Eleazar b. R. Simeon [says], "Even [the simple act of] designating [the restitution] marks its sanctification [as heave-offering], so as to obligate one [who unintentionally eats it after this point to pay] the principal and added fifth [normally paid by a nonpriest] who eats heave-offering."

Rabbi, C–D, holds that Lev. 22:14 means that the restitution becomes a holy thing only at the point at which it is given to the priest. Eleazar b. Simeon offers the opposite interpretation: The restitution is holy at the time it is given to the priest. This means that the householder's designation marks its consecration as heave-offering. This view stands behind unit **VII**'s notion that, so long as the nonpriest designates the restitution, the priest need not

accept it. In light of his position here, Rabbi could not agree
with that rule.

[IX.A]   [If the priest] refused [to take the restitution paid by a nonpriest
who unintentionally ate heave-offering, telling the nonpriest to
keep the restitution for himself instead] and then [that non-
priest] ate [the restitution—what is the rule concerning his making payment for this produce which he ate? This is] under dispute between R. Yohanan and R. Simeon b. Laqish.

[B]   For they dispute [the following, parallel case: If a nonpriest]
stole heave-offering that belonged to the father of his mother
who was a priest [and the grandfather died, such that the nonpriest inherits the heave-offering, and he went ahead and unintentionally ate it]—

[C]   R. Yohanan says, "He makes restitution to [a member of] the
tribe [of priests and thereby requites himself of the original
theft]." [In the same way, the individual at A must make restitution to a priest. The fact that a priest had refused the first payment is not probative.]

[D]   But Resh Laqish says, "[Since the heave-offering belonged to the
nonpriest], he pays restitution to himself." [This produce paid
as restitution, which takes on the status of heave-offering, is
then sold to a priest, the only individual who rightly may eat it.
The same applies in the case at A. The nonpriest was given the
restitution by the priest. Therefore, if he eats it, he pays the
principal and added fifth to himself.]

[E]   Said R. Jonah, "This is how R. Simeon b. Laqish would answer
[the argument of] R. Yohanan: 'It is your opinion [C] that [the
nonpriest originally stole the heave-offering, such that] he makes
restitution to the tribe [of priests].

[F]   "'Yet [to the contrary] this we have learned: *[If a nonpriest] stole
heave-offering which was dedicated to the Temple and [uninten-
tionally] ate it, he pays two added fifths and the principal, [one
added fifth for eating heave-offering, and another for eating produce dedicated to the Temple; M. Ter. 6:4E–F].*

[G]   "'[If what you say is true, that a nonpriest is subject to an added
fifth just for having wrongly taken heave-offering, then, in M.
Ter. 6:4's case], he should pay three added fifths, [one for steal-

ing the heave-offering, one for eating the heave-offering, and one for eating produce dedicated to the Temple].'" [Since he need not pay three added fifths, it is clear that, contrary to what Yohanan says, the nonpriest's simply having taken heave-offering from a priest is not reason to state that he must make payment to a member of the tribe.]

[H] [Yohanan counters E–G's argument.] R. Yisa in the name of R. Yohanan [says], "[The reason that the individual at M. Ter. 6:4 need not pay three added fifths is that, for that case,] the Torah [explicitly] states that he is absolved of the theft." [This is through payment of a single added fifth, which he pays for unintentionally eating heave-offering. But in a different case, such as that at B, he must pay an added fifth just for stealing the produce.]

[I] R. Zeira said to R. Isi, "You (plural) state two matters in the name of R. Yohanan, but you (plural) do not indicate from where these [opinions are derived].

[J] "[The first is above at H:] Said R. Yohanan, 'One is absolved of the theft [through payment of one added fifth],' but you do not state how [Yohanan] derives this.

[K] "[The source of this is Lev. 22:14: 'And if a man eats of a holy thing unwittingly, he shall add the fifth of its value to it] and give the holy thing to the priest.'

[L] "[Scripture states explicitly that the man gives *the holy thing* to the priest. It is as though he returns the same holy thing that he originally took. This means that] once he has given it [i.e., the one added fifth] to the priest, he is absolved of the theft, [as though he never had taken the holy thing in the first place].

[M] [This second statement cited in the name of Yohanan without its scriptural source is irrelevant in the present context.] "You say in the name of R. Yohanan, 'In the same place that [the red heifer] is slaughtered, there it is burned,' but you do not state from which [scriptural passage this rule derives]."

[N] [Giving the source of this rule,] R. Eleazar in the name of R. Hoshaya [cited Num. 19:5], "'Along with its offal (*ʿl prŝh*) [the heifer] shall be burned.'"

[O] How should you understand this [verse]?

[P] R. Jeremiah in the name of R. Imi [said], "[It means]: in the place in which [the heifer] leaves (*PRŜ*) life, there it is burned."

[Q]   [We return to the issue of A–D.] R. Yohanan's view [at C] ac-
       cords with that of Rabbi [Y. Ter. 6:1 **VIII**.C–D, that the restitu-
       tion is not sanctified as heave-offering until it actually is given to
       the priest. Yohanan, C, therefore holds that the restitution must
       be given to a priest. Otherwise it is not valid. For this reason
       the nonpriest cannot keep it for himself, even if it rightly belongs
       to him.]

[R]   R. Simeon b. Laqish's view [D] accords with that of R. Eleazar
       b. R. Simeon [at Y. Ter. 6:1 **VIII**.E. Eleazar holds that the res-
       titution is sanctified as heave-offering as soon as it is designated.
       Simeon b. Laqish agrees; therefore he holds that it does not
       matter that restitution designated by the nonpriest, A or B, never
       is given to a priest.]

[S]   Said R. Bun bar Hiyya, "Is it not also possible that R. Simeon
       b. Laqish concurs with Rabbi, for [Rabbi holds that giving an
       object to the priest marks its sanctification] only in the case of
       something which [the nonpriest] is obligated to give the priest?

[T]   "But in the case of something that [the nonpriest] is not obli-
       gated to give the priest, [such as the restitution at A–B], even
       Rabbi concedes [that the designation of the thing (in this case,
       the restitution) marks its sanctification].

[U]   "For this is [stated explicitly in] the Mishnah [Bek. 1:6]: *One*
       [44b] *who sets aside the redemption lamb for the first born of an*
       ass [but has not yet given it to a priest] when [the ass] dies—R.
       Eliezer says, '[The person] is responsible for [the ass, and there-
       fore must pay the priest] the five selas, [as in the case of one who
       redeems] a [firstborn] son.' [The fact that the redemption lamb
       was already set aside is not probative. Until the lamb actually is
       given to the priest, the firstborn ass belongs to the householder.
       He remains responsible for it and must give the priest its value.]

[V]   *"But sages say, '[In these circumstances householders] are not*
       responsible for [the ass], except as they are responsible for the
       redemption of second tithe.' [In this case the householder has no
       responsibility. Once the redemption money is set aside, it is of
       no concern to the householder that the produce is lost. In the
       same manner, setting aside the lamb marks the end of the house-
       holder's responsibility for the firstborn ass.]

[W]   "R. Eliezer concedes in the case of firstborn of asses that [an
       Israelite] inherited from the estate of the father of his mother

who was a priest, that as soon as he sets aside [their redemption money], it becomes sanctified."

The priest refuses to take the added fifth that the nonpriest has designated to be restitution for heave-offering he unintentionally ate. The nonpriest keeps the added fifth and eats it. Now he is liable for another added fifth (M. Ter. 6:1D). To whom does he pay it? Yohanan, C, states that like all restitution paid for heave-offering unintentionally eaten by a nonpriest, this added fifth goes to a priest. Resh Laqish, D, takes seriously the fact that a priest had refused to accept the added fifth which the nonpriest ate. This means, he says, that the nonpriest himself owned the added fifth he ate. He therefore may keep the restitution as his own property, selling it to a priest. The remainder of the pericope is a discussion of this dispute, in three distinct parts. Jonah, E–G, and Yisa, H, have Yohanan and Resh Laqish dispute the issue between them. I–P intervenes, providing an excursus on the scriptural basis for two of Yohanan's rules, the one cited here as well as a second one, irrelevant to this context. I–P thus appears to be a fixed literary unit, brought as a whole to this context.[15] Q–T, finally, correlates the positions of Yohanan and Resh Laqish here with those of Rabbi and Eleazar b. Simeon, Y. Ter. 6:1 **VIII**. How U–W proves T is not at all clear.

[**X.A**]   [If] one [unintentionally] ate heave-offering belonging to [a priest who is] an associate [i.e., scrupulous about Levitical cleanness], he must pay restitution to a [priest who is an] associate [see T. Ter. 7:4L].

[B]   [If he unintentionally ate] heave-offering belonging to [a priest who is] an *Am Haares* [viz., who is not careful about cleanness], he must pay restitution to [a priest who is] an *Am Haares* [cf., T. Ter. 7:5M].

[C]   But he should not place [responsibility for the restitution's] cleanness in the hands of [a priest who is] an *Am Haares*!

[D]   What should he do [to resolve the problem introduced by C]?

[E]   He gives [restitution] for both sorts of [heave-offering, that which belonged to an associate and that which belonged to an *Am Haares*], to [a priest who is] an associate, and [the associate] takes the monetary equivalent of one of them and gives it to the priest who is an *Am Haares* [see T. Ter. 7:5N].

[F]   R. Bun bar Hiyya said in the presence of R. Simeon b. Laqish, "This [E] accords with the view of him who says that the designation [of the restitution] marks its sanctification [as heave-offering; see Y. Ter. 6:1 **VIII**].

[G]   "But in the view of the one who says that [the restitution] is sanctified [as heave-offering only] when it is given [to the priest], in this case [E], does [the restitution] not need to be accepted [by the priest to whom it is due]?" [It certainly does. Thus it is not clear how the associate can take the restitution due the *Am Haares*. In this view it would not be deemed a replacement for the heave-offering which was eaten unless it actually was given to the *Am Haares*.]

[H]   [Simeon b. Laqish] said to them, "This is a case in which [the replacement offering] is accepted [on behalf of the *Am Haares*] by another [i.e., by the priest who is an associate]."

The Yerushalmi's version of T. Ter. 7:5, A–E, is viewed (F–H) within the context of the dispute between Rabbi and Eleazar b. R. Simeon, Y. Ter. 6:1 **VIII**.

6:2 [P: 6:1b]

[A]   *The daughter of an Israelite who [unintentionally] ate heave-offering and afterwards was married to a priest [at which point she gains the right to eat the priestly gift]—*

[B]   *if [before she gained this right] she had eaten heave-offering of which a priest had not yet effected acquisition, she pays the principal and added fifth to herself.*

[C]   *But if she ate heave-offering of which a priest [already] had effected acquisition, she pays the principal to [its] owner [i.e., to the priest whose heave-offering she ate] and the added fifth to herself.*

[D]   *For they have said:*

[E]   *"One who unintentionally eats heave-offering pays the principal to the [heave-offering's] owner and the added fifth to whomever he wishes."*

Through marriage to a priest, an Israelite woman gains the right
to eat heave-offering. Even after she has this right, she must pay
restitution for heave-offering she unintentionally ate as a nonpriest. B–C explains how she does this, with E providing the
general principle. The Yerushalmi's one unit brings an additional
hypothetical circumstance to bear upon the case. In this way it develops the rule that, should the husband divorce the woman, she
may not keep for herself the added fifth she needs to designate.

[I.A]   [An Israelite woman unintentionally ate heave-offering and then
married a priest, M. Ter. 6:2. She must pay the principal to the
priest whose heave-offering she ate, but may keep the added fifth
for herself. If] she did not have time to pay restitution before
she was divorced [by her husband, the priest—what is the rule?
May she still keep the added fifth and sell it to a priest? Or since
she no longer has the right to heave-offering, must she give it to
a priest for free, as any other nonpriest would do?]

[B]   Come, see [what the answer is on the basis of the following, parallel case]:

[C]   If [at the time she was divorced] she had some [heave-offering of
the] tithe [which her husband, the priest, had given her], does
this [priestly gift] not remain hers [even after she is divorced? It
certainly does. She no longer may eat it, but she can sell it to a
priest. The same should be the case at A. The woman may keep
for herself the added fifth she owes.]

[D]   [No! C is wrong, for the cases are not comparable.] There [in the
case of heave-offering of the tithe, she may keep for herself the
tithe she was given because] the tithe makes up a concrete commodity [16] [which she acquired and which therefore belongs to her].

[E]   But here [in the case of the restitution], the heave-offering [17] [she
ate] is not a concrete commodity [which, through her act of eating, she acquired as her own possession. She never owned the
heave-offering. For this reason, when the priest divorces her, she
loses the right to keep any of the restitution paid for that heave-
offering.]

[F]   To what is the case [of heave-offering of the tithe which her husband, the priest, gave her] comparable?

[G]   [It is comparable to the case of] firstborn asses [that one inherited from a grandfather who was a priest. Under all circum-

stances the nonpriest may keep these for himself, Y. Ter. 6 : 1
IX.S – U. But the case of heave-offering unintentionally eaten before the woman was married to a priest is not comparable to
either of these cases, as E explained.]

A's question is answered at C versus D – E. The issue is which
paradigm applies to the added fifth the woman must pay. We
determine that it is not comparable to other sanctified produce
she owns, C. Rather, it is a holy thing she owes to others, D – E.

6 : 3 [P: 6 : 2a]

[A]   *"One who [unintentionally] gives his workers or guests heave-*
      offering to eat:

[B]   *"he pays the principal, and they pay the added fifth"—the words of*
      R. Meir.

[C]   *But sages say, "They pay [both] the principal and the added*
      fifth,

[D]   *"and he pays them the cost of their meal."*

The Mishnah asks whether the principal, like the added fifth, is
paid only by those who eat heave-offering or whether it also is
paid by people who in other ways benefit from the priestly gift.
Meir, A – B, takes the latter view. The householder used heave-
offering in place of his own food. He is responsible for the loss
of the offering and accordingly pays the principal to a priest.
Sages disagree. They hold that only a person who actually eats
heave-offering pays the principal. In this case, the workers who
ate it must pay. The householder is held only to his initial responsibility, the cost of the meal the workers ate. The Yerushalmi notes that the practical results of Meir's and the sages'
views are the same. The workers or guests pay the added fifth
and the householder repays the value of the produce they ate.
The Yerushalmi's problem thus is to determine why Meir and
the sages phrase their opinions differently when, in practical
terms, they do not disagree at all.

[I.A] Lo, [in a case such as that of M. Ter. 6:3] R. Meir states [that householders] pay [the principal], and rabbis, [i.e., sages, likewise] state[18] [that householders] pay [the principal, which they give to the workers].

[B] [Since in the view of both, the householder is responsible for the value of the meal which the workers ate,] what is the difference between their [views, such that Meir states the householder pays the principal directly to the priest while sages state that he pays it to the workers, who themselves pay it to the priest]?

[C] [Two answers are given, C–E and F–H.] Said R. Yohanan, "[The question of] who owns the food [which the workers ate is at issue] between them.

[D] "[For] R. Meir says, 'The householder owns the food [and accordingly is culpable for the principal].'

[E] "But rabbis say, 'The workers own the food, [for it was given to them by the householder. Therefore they must pay the principal.]'"

[F] R. Simeon b. Laqish says, "[Contrary to Yohanan, the sages and Meir agree that the meal belongs to the workers. They purchased it with their labor. Rather the issue] between them is who was responsible for preparing the food.

[G] "R. Meir says, 'The householder is responsible for preparing the food.' [He therefore should have been careful not to give the workers heave-offering. Since he was not careful, he is responsible for the principal.]

[H] "But rabbis say, 'The workers are responsible for preparing the food.'" [They should have been careful not to take and prepare heave-offering. Since they were not careful, they pay back the principal.]

[I] [In order to determine who is correct, Yohanan or Simeon b. Laqish, we examine M. Ter. 6:3D. Y. holds that Meir and sages agree that the householder pays the workers the value of their meal.] R. Abbahu in the name of R. Simeon b. Laqish [said], "Lo, to what is this comparable[19] [i.e., the fact that the householder is made to pay the workers for the meal which they ate]? To the case of one who sells something to his fellow, and it turns out that the thing was not his [to sell]. For [in such a case] he is obligated to return the purchase price to him." [In the same way,

at M. Ter. 6:3, the householder must pay the workers the value
of the meal they ate, but which was not rightly his to give them.]

[J]   If [this statement indeed] accords with [the view of] Simeon b.
Laqish, it makes sense. [For Simeon, G, holds that all agree
that, with their work, the employees purchased the food. Sages
and Meir therefore agree that, in accordance with I, the householder must give the workers the value of what they ate. Since
F–H and I are logical correlates, it appears as though Simeon b.
Laqish has correctly interpreted the dispute.]

[K]   [This shows that, by the same reasoning, Yohanan, B–E, has
not correctly understood the dispute.] But if [I] accords with
Yohanan—he said that the issue of who owns the food stands
behind the dispute[20] [of the sages and Meir. Rabbi's view, he
says, is that the workers own the food. There is no sale; accordingly, the householder is not liable to pay the workers the cost of
their meal. In view of this understanding,] how can you say this,
[that Meir and the sages agree that the householder must pay the
workers the price of their meal? In Yohanan's view you could not
state this. Therefore it appears that Yohanan's interpretation of
M. 6:3's dispute is unacceptable.]

[L]   [To the contrary, it is possible that Yohanan agrees with the view
of I. This is so if we claim that I] was stated only to accord with
[Yohanan's interpretation of the position of] R. Meir. [In Yohanan's view, Meir holds that the food belongs to the householder.
The workers buy it with their labor. The conclusion of I follows
logically.]

[M]   [The conclusion of I–L is that either Yohanan, B–E, or Simeon
b. Laqish, F–H, may correctly have understood M. Ter. 6:3's
dispute. We leave their interpretations of that dispute and turn
to a third one.] R. Abbahu in the name of R. Yose b. Hanina
[said], "[Sages and Meir agree both that the food belongs to the
workers and that the workers alone were responsible for preparing it. The issue] between them is the overall value of the meal
[which the workers ate].

[N]   "For [the householder] contracted with them to feed them unconsecrated produce [which has a high monetary value], but instead he fed them heave-offering [which has a low market value]."
[For this reason, the householder is made to pay the workers the
value of the meal they were supposed to have eaten.]

[O]   [M–N does not seem logical.] Now why should this matter [that the workers ate lower-priced food, for in all events they] have eaten [the consecrated produce, just as they would have eaten unconsecrated food. The difference in value seems irrelevant.]

[P]   [This notion that it does matter] accords with [the view of] one who says, '[As for] untithed produce [or other forbidden foods, such as heave-offering]—the soul of a person [who eats them] is shattered (*hth* [?]) because of them. [Therefore eating heave-offering is not comparable to eating the other foods which the householder was meant to give the workers. Accordingly, the householder must pay the workers the value of the meal they were supposed to have.]

The Yerushalmi suggests three different explanations of the dispute at M. Ter. 6:3: C–E, F–H, and M–N + O–P. I–L analyzes C–E and F–H.

6:4 [P: 6:2b]

[A]   *One who steals heave-offering, but does not eat it, pays as restitution twice the monetary equivalent of the heave-offering.*

[B]   *[If] he [unintentionally] ate it, he pays twice the principal and an added fifth [of one of the principals]:*

[C]   *[one] principal and the added fifth [he pays] out of unconsecrated produce,*

[D]   *and [the other] principal [he pays] in the monetary equivalent of heave-offering.*

[E]   *[If] he stole heave-offering which was dedicated [to the Temple] and [unintentionally] ate it—*

[F]   *he pays two added fifths and the principal.*

[G]   *For the [requirement of] payment of twofold restitution is not applicable in [the case of] items dedicated [to the Temple].*

Stealing carries its own fine, twice the value of that which was stolen (Ex. 22:9). This accounts for A. If the person steals and eats heave-offering, there are two sets of fines, B–D. For eating heave-offering, the offender pays a principal in unconsecrated food and an added fifth of that principal (M. Ter. 6:1). For stealing he further pays once the monetary value of the offering which, along with the principal already paid, constitutes the fine required by Ex. 22:9. E–F takes account of the fact that a second added fifth must be paid for eating produce which was dedicated to the Temple. But in the latter case twofold restitution does not apply, G. The Yerushalmi asks of this third case the most obvious questions. The heave-offering which was eaten belonged to the Temple. To whom is restitution made, to the Temple—which owned the produce—or to a priest, who will eat it? This issue is under dispute, units **I–II**. Unit **III** provides the scriptural basis for G.

[**I.A**]   [The question is to whom one who steals and eats heave-offering dedicated to the Temple pays the principal.] Said R. Yannai, "Mishnah refers to [two different] possibilities [i.e., sometimes the principal is given to the Temple and sometimes to an individual priest].

[B]   "[If the principal] consists of [at least] an olive's bulk [of produce, the minimum which is deemed worthy to be given to the Temple (PM)], but is not worth a *perutah* [PM: the minimum value which would meet the requirement of "giving" the holy thing to the priest (Lev. 22:14)], one pays it to the Temple.

[C]   "[If the principal] is worth a *perutah* but does not consist of an olive's bulk [of produce], he pays it to [a member of] the tribe [of priests]."

[D]   [If the principal] consists of an olive's bulk [of produce] and is worth a *perutah* [such that it may go either to the Temple or to a priest]—

[E]   Simeon bar Va in the name of R. Yohanan [says], "One pays it to the Temple."

[F]²¹   R. Yohanan says, "One pays it to [a member of] the tribe [of priests]."

The unit points to the ambiguous case, D, the adjudication of which is disputed, E versus F. But in the dispute, Yohanan is cited as the source of both views, a strange state of affairs.

[**II.A**]   [M. Ter. 6:4E–G describes a case in which two added fifths are paid. To whom are they paid, the Temple or a priest? Answering the question from Scripture,] said R. Zeira, "[The rule] is dictated by Scripture. [Lev. 22:14 states], 'If a man eats of a holy thing unwittingly, [he shall add the fifth of its value to it and give the holy thing to the priest.]'

[B]   "[This means that] to the same place to which the principal goes [i.e., to a priest], there the added fifth, [and, in this case, both added fifths], goes."

[C]   [Disagreeing] Kahana says, "He pays two added fifths: one [he pays] to [a member of] the tribe [of priests], and [the other] fifth [he pays] to the Temple."

Zeira's view, A–B, is based upon exegesis of Scripture. By contrast, Kahana is attentive to the Mishnah's own facts: two added fifths are paid. It therefore is reasonable that one will go to the Temple and one to a priest.

[**III.A**]   *For the [requirement of] payment of twofold restitution is not applicable in [the case of] items dedicated [to the Temple; M. Ter. 6:4G].*

[B]   [Why is this the case?] **As it is said, "[If a thief is found,] he shall pay double to his neighbor"** [Ex. 22:9].

[C]   **[He pays double for what he took from his neighbor,] but not for that which is consecrated, [which he stole from the Temple]** [T. Ter. 7:8B–D].

M. Ter. 6:4G's rule derives from Scripture.

6:5   [P: 6:2c]

[A]   *"They do not pay restitution with (1) gleanings, (2) forgotten sheaves, (3) [produce grown in] the corners [of a field, which is left for the poor], or (4) ownerless produce,*

[B]   *"and not with (5) first tithe from which heave-offering of the tithe has (some MSS.: not) been removed,*

[C]   *"and not with (6) second tithe or [produce] dedicated [to the Temple] which have (some MSS.: not) been redeemed,*

[D]   *"for a consecrated thing does not serve for the redemption of a consecrated thing"—the words of R. Meir.*

[E]   *But the sages permit [restitution to be made with] these things.*

Meir, A–D, holds that the payment of produce as restitution constitutes a designation of that produce to be heave-offering. It follows that produce paid as restitution must stand within a category of food that is subject to the separation of heave-offering. Only such produce may be designated a priestly gift. The things listed at A–D fall outside of this category and therefore may not be used as the principal and added fifth. According to the Yerushalmi's one unit, sages, E, agree to this principle (cf., Avery-Peck, p. 207). Sages differ from Meir only in that they note that some of the items in A–D once were subject to heave-offering. This was before they were designated tithes or set aside for the poor. Since they once were subject, sages hold that they still may be used as restitution. The issue, disputed by Simeon b. Laqish and Yohanan, is to which of A–D's items this applies. The Yerushalmi thus asks of the range of the dispute between Meir and the sages.

[**I.A**]   [The issue is with which items listed at M. Ter. 6:5A–D the sages, M. Ter. 6:5E, permit restitution to be paid, whether from all of them, or only from those listed at C and D: second tithe or produce dedicated to the Temple which have been redeemed, and first tithe from which heave-offering of the tithe has been removed.] R. Simeon b. Laqish said to them, "[Sages refer] to these last two items, [M. Ter. 6:5C–D alone].

[B]   "Why [do they state that these may be used as restitution]?

[C]   "For [at one time] they were subject to [the separation of] heave-offering and tithes, [i.e., before the produce was designated first or second tithe, or before it was dedicated to the Temple]." [Since at one time this produce could have been used as restitution, the sages say that it still may be used.]

[D]   [This challenges Simeon b. Laqish's reasoning.] Now, were gleanings, forgotten sheaves, and [produce grown in] the corner [of a field] not [once] subject to [the separation of] heave-offering and tithes, [just like the produce referred to at A–C? Certainly they were, before the householder left them as gleanings, forgot them, or designated them for the poor. By Simeon b. Laqish's reasoning, therefore, the sages should allow these things as well to be designated restitution.]

[E]   [D's reasoning is unacceptable for at M. Ter. 6:5A] we refer to produce which was forgotten before it was harvested[22] [i.e., before it became subject to heave-offering and tithes], and to produce [growing in] the corner [of a field] which, [as usual], was designated for the poor before it was harvested, [such that it too never became subject to heave-offering and tithes. Since these things never were subject to the separation of heave-offering, all agree that they may not be designated restitution for heave-offering eaten by a nonpriest. Simeon b. Laqish, A–C, is correct. Sages disagree only with M. Ter. 6:5B–C, not with M. 6:5A.]

[F]   [The following questions at what point in the harvest produce takes on the status of gleanings. It is primary at Y. Pe. 7:3. I translate and explain the full version found there, for as copied into Y. Ter. the material makes no sense. A–E's discussion continues below, at H. According to M. Pe. 7:3, a gleaning of grapes is a single grape that breaks off the cluster and falls to the ground during the harvest. A person who puts a basket beneath the vine to capture such grapes is deemed a robber of the poor. On this basis, Y. Pe. 7:3 concludes:] This means that a gleaning of grapes becomes sanctified [for the poor] at the point at which it falls [from the grape cluster, even before it reaches the ground. This accounts for the fact that a householder who captures such a grape in a basket has stolen from the poor. At the time it falls into the basket, the grape already belongs to the poor.]

[G][23]   This [i.e., F] does not serve to answer the question posed by Hilpai, for Hilpai asked, "What is the law whether or not gleanings [other than of grapes] are deemed sanctified [for the poor] at the point at which they are cut,[24] [but before they fall to the ground]?" [The issue is as follows: The gleaning falls from the harvester's hand, but instead of falling to the ground lands on some other object. Hilpai asks whether that piece of produce is deemed a gleaning, inasmuch as it fell from the harvester's hand, or not a gleaning, since it did not fall to the ground. At Y. Pe.

7:3 Samuel bar Abudimi states that the rule of M. Pe. 7:3,
referred to here at F, does not answer the question. The cases
are not comparable, for while at M. Pe. 7:3 the harvester purposely placed the basket beneath the cluster to prevent the grape-
gleaning from falling to the ground, in the case suggested by
Hilpai, the worker did not purposely prevent the produce from
falling to the ground. Thus an answer to Hilpai's question cannot
be provided on the basis of the information given at M. Pe. 7:3.]

[H]   [We turn back to discuss D, which states that the produce referred to at M. Ter. 6:5A never became subject to the separation
of heave-offering, since it was designated for the poor before it
was harvested. For the reason given here, this is unlikely.] R.
Yohanan said to him, [i.e., to Simeon b. Laqish, whose reasoning is recorded at A–C], "[It is not possible that M. Ter. 6:5A
refers to produce which was designated for the poor before it
was harvested, such that the produce never was subject to heave-
offering. We know that this is the case because], lo, we learn [in
the Mishnah that] gleanings, [i.e., produce the householder har-
vests and then drops, became potentially subject to tithes at the
point at which it was harvested. It then was removed from the
category of produce subject to tithes at the point at which it
dropped and became a gleaning for the poor.]

[I]   "You must reason that the produce growing in the corner of the
field which is left for the poor [to which M. refers] is like[25] the
gleanings [to which M. refers]." [Like the gleanings, the produce in the corner of the field was harvested by the householder,
such that potentially it was subject to heave-offering. Only afterwards did the householder designate it for the poor, at which
point it no longer could be designated heave-offering. But it once
had been subject to heave-offering. Therefore, in the view of the
sages, M. Ter. 6:5E, it still may be designated as restitution for
heave-offering unintentionally eaten by a nonpriest.]

[J]   [In light of H–I, we conclude with Yohanan's own understanding
of M. Ter. 6:5's dispute.] R. Yohanan said to him, "Concerning
all [of the items listed at M. Ter. 6:5A, the sages, M. Ter. 6:5E,
disagree]." [The sages hold that all of them may be designated as
the principal and added fifth.]

Simeon b. Laqish's view is stated, A, and supported, B–C +
D–E. Yohanan, H–I, disagrees. His own view is expressed at J.

As I indicate in the text, F–G intervenes. Presumably it is placed here because, like E, it concerns the point at which produce takes on the status of poor offerings. PM, however, reads it in light of E. He states that if we hold that the produce does not take on the status of a poor offering until it reaches the ground, it is deemed potentially subject to heave-offering from the time it is picked until that point. If this is the case, the gleaning may be used as restitution. This is Yohanan's point, H–I. The alternative is that the produce becomes a poor offering immediately upon being picked. If this is so, it may not be designated restitution, for it never was in the category of produce which becomes subject to heave-offering. While it is possible that this is what the redactor of the unit meant, it remains conjectural. It imposes upon Hilpai's statement a whole range of significance absent from its primary context in Y. Pe. 7:3. The relationship between F–G and the continuation of A–C's argument at H–I likewise is not clear.

6:6 [P: 6:3]

[A]   R. Eliezer says, "They pay restitution [for heave-offering un-intentionally eaten by a nonpriest] with [produce of] one kind on behalf of [produce] which is not of its same kind,

[B]   "with the stipulation that he must pay restitution with choicer [produce] for less choice [produce]."

[C]   But R. Aqiba says, "They pay restitution only with [produce of] one kind on behalf of [produce] which is of its same kind.

[D]   "Therefore:

[E]   "if he ate cucumbers [in the status of heave-offering grown on] the eve of the Sabbatical year, he waits for cucumbers [grown in] the year after the Sabbatical year and pays restitution with them."

[F]   On the basis of the same verse in accordance with which R. Eliezer rules leniently [A–B], R. Aqiba rules stringently [C–E].

[G]   For it is said, "[If a man eats of a holy thing unwittingly, he shall add the fifth of its value to it] and give the holy thing to the priest" [Lev. 22:14].

[H]   "[He may give to the priest] anything which is fit to be holy"— the words of R. Eliezer.

[I]   *But R. Aqiba says, "'And give the holy thing to the priest.' [He must give the priest] that holy thing which he ate."*

Eliezer's fundamental concern is that the priest receive his share from desirable produce. A nonpriest therefore may compensate the priest with a kind of food different from that which was eaten, so long as it is of better quality than that which was misappropriated. Aqiba, C, holds that the same requirements which apply to the initial designation of heave-offering apply as well to payment of the principal and added fifth. He simply follows M. Ter. 2:4–6. The consequences of Aqiba's view appear at E. Since produce of the Sabbatical year is not subject to the separation of heave-offering, it may not be used as restitution. If no produce from the sixth year of the kind he ate is available, the nonpriest is forced to wait for produce of that kind to appear in the first year of the seven-year cycle in order to pay the principal and added fifth. The Yerushalmi draws out the implications of Eliezer's and Aqiba's views for other particular cases, units I–III. At units IV–V it explains the meaning and implications of E.

[I.A]   [Eliezer, M. Ter. 6:6B, states that the householder should pay restitution with choicer produce on behalf of less choice produce.] How so?

[B]   [If] he ate a vegetable [in the status of heave-offering] and paid back dried figs,

[C]   **or ate dried figs [in the status of heave-offering] and paid back dates,**

[D]   **let a blessing be upon him** [T. Ter. 7:9D–E].

The Yerushalmi has its own version of T. Ter. 7:9.

[II.A]   If he ate first fruits, [which are the best of all produce and which are called by the title heave-offering (Dt. 12:6)], what should he pay as restitution, [so as to follow Eliezer's precept that one pays back choicer produce]?

[B]   [If the produce] he ate was grapes, let him pay wine as restitution. If he ate²⁶ olives, let him pay olive oil as restitution.

Produce that is already processed is deemed to be of enhanced
quality, B.

[III.A]   [PM: The following applies to the opinion of Aqiba, M. Ter.
6:6C, that one must pay as restitution the same sort of produce
that he ate. If] he ate dough offering, what is the rule whether or
not he may pay as restitution grain which has not yet reached
one third of its growth? [Perhaps this grain is deemed to be of
the same type as that which was eaten, since] produce that has
not yet reached a third of its growth is subject to [the separation
of] dough offering [so M. Hal. 1:3].

[B]   [If] one ate first fruits, what is the rule whether or not he may
pay restitution with unpicked produce? [Perhaps the unpicked
produce is deemed to be of the same sort as the first fruits] since
first fruits are designated while [the produce is as yet] unharvested [M. Bik. 2:4].

The issue is which different sorts of the same genus of produce
are deemed a single kind for the purpose of paying restitution.
The issue is familiar from M. Ter. 2:4–6. In the present instance, final rulings are not given, only suggestions.

[IV.A]   [M. Ter. 6:6E states that in order to pay restitution with produce
of the same kind as was eaten, one who eats cucumbers in the
status of heave-offering at the end of the sixth year of the Sabbatical cycle must wait until there are cucumbers of the first year
of the next cycle.] R. Abin in the name of our rabbis from there
[i.e., Babylonia] [said], "The implications [of M. Ter. 6:6E] are
that one may not pay restitution with produce grown outside of
the land [of Israel]." [If this were not the case, we would expect
that, during the seventh year, when produce grown in the land is
not available for use as restitution, produce from outside of the
land could be used.]

[B]   [No. A is not the necessary conclusion. Rather], you might say that they may use even [produce grown outside of the land of Israel] as restitution [for heave-offering unintentionally eaten by a nonpriest].

[C] [27]   [If this is the case, then the reason that M. Ter. 6:6E requires the individual to wait until the first year of the Sabbatical cycle, instead of saying that he should use imported produce, is that] the Mishnah, [i.e., this rule, was composed] before Rabbi had [passed the ordinance] permitting the importation of produce from outside of the land [of Israel] into the land [of Israel; see Y. Sheb. 6:4].

Once produce from outside of the land of Israel is imported into the land and is processed there, it becomes subject to the separation of heave-offering and tithes. It therefore may be used for restitution, as this analysis of M. Ter. 6:6E suggests.

[V.A]   Do not state that [M. Ter. 6:6E] applies to cucumbers only, since they are a type of produce that it is forbidden [to plant in the seventh year],

[B]   but that [in the case of other] produce that it is not forbidden [to plant in the seventh year], no, [i.e., do no claim that in the case of these other sorts of produce the rule of M. Ter. 6:6E does not apply, such that this other produce of the seventh year may be used as restitution].

[C]   For if you say that this is the case, [that certain produce of the seventh year may be used as the principal and added fifth], would [the nonpriest] not turn out to pay a debt (lit.: purchase a mattock) with funds, [in this case, produce,] of the seventh year? [He would. But this is forbidden. Therefore it is clear that in no case may produce of the seventh year be designated restitution for heave-offering unintentionally eaten by a nonpriest. M. Ter. 6:6E applies to all produce of the seventh year, not only to cucumbers.]

M. Ter. 6:6E suggests the case of cucumbers as an example. The same rule applies to other sorts of produce as well. No produce of the Sabbatical year may be used as restitution.

7 Yerushalmi Terumot
Chapter Seven

7:1

[A] *[A nonpriest] who intentionally eats heave-offering pays back the principal, but does not pay the added fifth.*

[B] *And that which is paid as restitution [retains the status of] unconsecrated produce.*

[C] *[Therefore] if the priest wished to refuse [it], he may refuse [it].*

For intentionally eating heave-offering the nonpriest is culpable for death (M. Ker. 1:5). Since he is liable for that punishment, he is not required to pay the fine of the added fifth. Nor may he designate heave-offering to replace that which he ate. Either act would constitute double punishment for a single crime. Instead the nonpriest simply gives the priest a quantity of produce equal to that which he took. This compensation does not take on the status of heave-offering. The priest therefore may refuse to accept it (C).

The issue of double punishment for a single sin engenders an extended Talmudic exposition. The Talmud discusses under what circumstances a person subject to death or stripes may also be punished by a fine. It wants to know also whether or not a person subject to execution at the hand of man, or extirpation by heaven, may be inflicted with stripes. These issues are debated throughout the long body of materials which follows. While thematically related to the central problem exposed by M. Ter. 7:1, the material on the whole is substantively unrelated. It is primary at M. Ket. 3:1, with the explanation of which it both begins, unit **I**, and ends, unit **IX**. Only unit **IV** is pertinent spe-

cifically to M. Ter. 7:1. As I said, the rest belongs here only
because of the direct relevance of its generative problematic.

[I.A]   [44c] *[A nonpriest] who intentionally eats heave-offering [pays
back the principal, but does not pay the added fifth; M. Ter. 7:1A].*

[B]   [Two Mishnaic passages appear contradictory.] There [at M.
Mak. 3:1] we have learned: *These receive the forty stripes: [one
who has connection with his sister, his father's sister, his mother's
sister, etc.].*

[C]   Yet [to the contrary] here [at M. Ket. 3:1] we have learned:
*These are girls [through the seduction of whom one incurs a
fine: (a list comparable to that of M. Mak. 3:1 ensues)].*

[D]   Here [at M. Mak. 3:1] you state that [such individuals] receive
the forty stripes, but there [at M. Ket. 3:1] you state that they
pay a fine! [What accounts for the divergent rules?]

[E]   Said R. Yohanan, "Mishnah refers to two different possibilities.

[F]   "If [others] warned him, [and he still went ahead and performed
the forbidden action], he receives the stripes [as at M. Mak. 3:1].

[G]   "[But] if they did not warn him [before he carried out the ac-
tion], he pays a fine [but does not receive stripes, M. Ket. 3:1]."

[H]   [Thus it is clear that] R. Yohanan reasons, "Wherever [one would
be culpable for] the payment of a fine as well as the punishment
of forty lashes, [and they warned him (so B. Ket. 32b)], he receives forty stripes, but does not pay the fine" (so Y. Ket. 3:1,
B. Ket. 32b, PM, and GRA, as required by the sense of F–G. Y.
Ter. reverses matters:[1] he pays the fine, but does not receive the
stripes).

[I]   [But contrary to H,] should he not both receive the forty stripes
and pay a fine?

[J]   [No. Here is how Yohanan knows that he is punished with stripes
alone. Dt. 25:2 states], "[A person is punished] in accordance
with his guilt (*rš'h*)."

[K]   [This means that] you obligate him to one punishment (*rš'h*),
but not to two punishments.

[L]   [Perhaps, then, for his one crime] he should pay a fine but not
receive the stripes?

[M] [M–N proves that L is not acceptable; but the logic of the proof is not entirely clear.] Scripture refers to one who is culpable for two sins.

[N] [Yet even though it refers to a case of two sins, Dt. 25:2 states:] "And the judge shall cause him to lie down and be beaten in his presence with a number of stripes in proportion to his offense." [In this severe case of two sins, flogging alone applies. It therefore is logical that flogging alone should be inflicted in the less serious case of a single sin.]

[O] [Simeon b. Laqish disagrees with Yohanan, G, who holds that if the sinner had not been warned, he pays a fine.] R. Simeon b. Laqish says, "Even if [witnesses] had not warned him [against commiting the act], he does not pay the fine [but rather receives stripes (PM)].

[P] "For if they had warned him, [but he went ahead and committed the crime, he would have been exempt from the fine and] would receive stripes." [PM: He is free from the fine if they warned him. Surely he is free from it if he had not been warned.]

[Q] Mishnah [Ket. 3:1] suggests a contradiction to the opinion of R. Simeon b. Laqish: *These are girls through [the seduction of] whom one incurs a fine.*

[R] Now if [witnesses] had warned the individual, would he not receive forty stripes? [He certainly would. Yet the Mishnah states that a fine also applies. Thus Simeon is wrong, O–P, for he states that if stripes are inflicted, a fine does not apply.]

[S] [Since Simeon b. Laqish's opinion, as explained at O–P, seems illogical, we must revise our notion of what Simeon said. How does he understand the relationship between the punishments of stripes and a fine?] R. Simeon b. Laqish reasoned in accordance with the opinion of R. Meir, for R. Meir states, "He [both] receives the stripes and pays a fine."

[T] [Explaining this position], R. Abbahu in the name of R. Simeon b. Laqish [said], "From the [case of] one who defames [a woman he has married by claiming that she was not a virgin], R. Meir deduced [that one may be both fined and inflicted with stripes].

[U] "[For Dt. 22:18 states that when that man is proven a perjurer, 'They shall whip him, and they shall fine him [a hundred *sheqels* in silver].'"

[V]   [Rejecting the analogy between the case of the defamer and other cases,] rabbis say, "The rule for the defamer is an exception,[2] and a rule which is itself an exception may not serve as a basis upon which to formulate other rules. [Therefore, unlike in the case of the defamer, in other cases, two punishments may not be inflicted.]

[W]   "[Here is how we know that the rule of the defamer is an exception.] For in all cases a man's own testimony may not serve to incriminate him. But in this case the man's own words, [which prove to be false], serve to incriminate him. [Therefore it is clear that this case is an exception to the general rule.]

[X]   "Therefore just as one does not use this [case of the defamer] as a basis for determining [that one's own words may serve to incriminate him] in other cases, so also one may not use it to learn about fines or the infliction of stripes."[3] [Rabbis thus hold that if there are stripes no fine may be imposed.]

[Y]   [To reject V–X we find a different case in which two punishments are inflicted.] But did not R. Abbahu in the name of R. Simeon b. Laqish say, "If one intentionally ate forbidden fat, [for which he is subject to a sin offering, but, not knowing that this is the case], unintentionally did not [bring] the offering, they free him of culpability [for purposely eating the fat] and [instead] he receives the forty stripes; then he brings an offering [to repent for having omitted the first offering]."

[Z]   [Now if it is possible to impose two punishments in that situation], then here [in the case of the individual referred to at M. Ket. 3:1 and M. Mak. 3:1] let him [both] receive the forty stripes and pay a fine!

[AA]   R. Bun bar Hiyya in the name of R. Samuel bar R. Isaac [explained why Y–Z is unacceptable and why, in the case of the individuals referred to at M. Ket. 3:1 and M. Mak. 3:1, only one punishment may be inflicted], "[In the case of] two punishments which are given into the hands of a court to decide [i.e., a fine and the forty stripes], you must select only one of them [to be administered in any given case. Both may not be inflicted.]

[BB]   "This excludes [from the limit of one punishment] cases which are given [for judgment] at the hands of heaven [i.e., such as that described at Y, in which a sacrifice is required]."

The explanation of two superficially contradictory rules, B–G, introduces the problem of the unit.[4] What happens in a case in which an individual is culpable for two punishments, a fine and stripes? H gives one answer, reasoned at I–N. Simeon b. Laqish gives his view, O–Q, which is rejected at R. Meir's position follows, S, with its own discussion, T–BB. Like Simeon's, Meir's view is proven unacceptable, AA. This means that the view of Yohanan alone stands. If a person should be culpable for both a fine and stripes, and had been warned against committing the offense, he receives the stripes but does not pay the fine.

[**II.A**]   All agree that a fine may not be inflicted along with the punishment of death.

[B]   [This is clear] because it is written [Lev. 24:17–18]: "He who kills a beast shall pay compensation." "He who kills a man shall be put to death."

[C]   Just as [in the case of] the one who kills a beast, they did not distinguish between one who unintentionally did so and one who intentionally did so but, rather, obligated[5] him to payment of a fine [even if he unintentionally did so],

[D]   so also [in the case of] one who kills a man, you should not distinguish between the case of one who unintentionally does so and one who intentionally does so but, rather, should exempt [from payment of a fine even the one who unintentionally does so. This is so even though the unintentional murderer is not executed.]

[E]   Concerning what do they [A] disagree?

[F]   Concerning whether or not one [who was not warned against committing a sin] pays a fine in a case in which he also receives the forty stripes.

[G]   R. Yohanan says, "No fine is paid by a person who is to be executed; but a fine is paid by a person who receives the forty stripes." [Cf., Y. Ter. 7:1 I.H. There the sinner had been warned.]

[H]   But R. Simeon b. Laqish says, "Just as one does not pay a fine if he is to be executed, so also [for an unintentional sin] he does not pay a fine if he is to receive the forty stripes." [Cf., Y. Ter. 7:1 I.S, which refers to an intentional sin.]

[I] [Explaining Simeon b. Laqish's view,] R. Imi the Babylonian said in the name of rabbis from there [i.e., Babylonia], "R. Simeon b. Laqish reasons [on the basis that in Scripture] the term 'guilty' appears twice.

[J] "One who is culpable for execution is called 'guilty.' [This is at Num. 35:31: 'You shall accept no ransom for the life of a murderer who is guilty of death.']

[K] "And one who is subject to stripes is called 'guilty.' [At Dt. 25:2: 'Then if the guilty man deserves to be beaten . . .']

[L] "Just as in the case of the guilty one who is mentioned as culpable for execution, so long as he is subject to execution he pays no fine,

[M] "likewise for the guilty one who is mentioned as receiving stripes, so long as he is subject to stripes, he pays no fine."

After the introduction, A–D, we have the views of Simeon b. Laqish and Yohanan on the punishment inflicted upon one who unintentionally transgresses (G versus H). Simeon's view is explained from Scripture, J–M. The unit follows logically from Y. Ter. 7:1I, which gave the views of these authorities for the case of an intentional sin. The only really interesting point is at D. The individual is exempt from a fine even though he will not be executed. The simple fact that the sin he committed is one to which, under certain circumstances, execution applies, renders a fine inapplicable. Monetary compensation is not levied in capital cases.

[III.A] [We turn back to the problem first posed at Y. Ter. 7:1 I.B–D, the apparent contradiction between M. Ket. 3:1 and M. Mak. 3:1.] Nathan bar Hoshaya [B. Ket. 32a: Ulla] says, "[There is no contradiction.] There [M. Ket. 3:1 requires a fine for sexual intercourse with his sister who is] a maiden, [i.e., a minor. But] here [at M. Mak. 3:1, which calls for inflicting stripes, reference is to a sister who is] a grown woman.

[B] "[In the case of] a maiden [who is violated], a fine is imposed, but not stripes (so Y. Ket. 3:1. Y. Ter. reads *mkr*).

[C]   "[In the case of] a grown woman, stripes are inflicted, since (*w*) a fine is not imposed (so Y. Ket. 3 : 1)."[6]

[D]   [C seems to be wrong.] But [in the case of the grown woman], is there not [a fine paid to compensate for] shame and loss of value [to a potential husband? Surely there is. Since this fine applies, stripes should not be inflicted, contrary to M. Mak. 3 : 1, explained at C.]

[E]   The rabbis of Caesarea say, "Solve the problem [posed at D by assuming] that [M. Mak. 3 : 1 refers to the case of a woman who was] seduced or who allowed him [to have intercourse with her]." [Since the woman yielded to the man, no money is paid for shame or loss of value. Since there is no fine, the man is subject to stripes, as C explains.

[F]   [On the basis of A–C it is clear that] Nathan bar Hoshaya reasoned, "Wherever a fine is to be paid and stripes are to be inflicted, one pays the fine but does not receive the stripes."

[G]   [Contrary to this] let him [both] pay the fine and receive the stripes!

[H]   [No. F is based on Dt. 25 : 2]: '[A person is punished] in accordance with his guilt (*rš‘h*).'

[I]   [This means that] you obligate him to one punishment (*rš‘h*), but not to two punishments.

[J][7]   Then let him receive stripes but not pay monetary compensation!

[K]   [This is unacceptable, as we learn] from the law for refuted false witnesses.

[L]   Just as refuted false witnesses pay a fine but do not receive stripes, so also in the present case [of one who has sexual intercourse with a sister], he pays the fine and does not receive the stripes, [as Nathan says, F].

[M]   [We have a further basis for F.] Said R. Nathan, "Nathan bar Hoshaya reasoned [from Dt. 25 : 2]: 'The judge shall cause him to lie down and be beaten in his presence with the number of stripes in proportion to his offense.'

[N]   "In the case of one who, by receiving stripes, atones for his guilt, [there is no fine].

[O]   "But this is not the case for one to whom, [after he received the

stripes, the judge would need] to say, 'Arise and pay [your fine].'"
[This person could not atone simply through stripes, for he still
must pay for the damage he caused. Yet, as we have seen, two punishments may not be inflicted. Therefore, he is made to pay the
fine, but does not receive the stripes, as Nathan explained, F.]

A–E gives Nathan bar Hoshaya's solution to the problem first
posed at Y. Ter. 7 : 1 **I.**B–D. F + G–O explains the theory which
underlies Nathan's explanation. The theory is supported on the
basis of Scripture, H–I and M–O.

[**IV.A**]   Mishnah [Ter. 6 : 1] is at variance with the view of R. Simeon b.
Laqish, [who holds, Y. Ter. 7 : 1 **II.**H, that even for an unintentional sin, against the performance of which the individual was
not warned, stripes are inflicted but monetary compensation is
not paid].

[B]   For [contrary to Simeon's view] have we not learned [M. Ter.
6 : 1]: *One who unintentionally eats heave-offering [pays back
the principal and an added fifth?* The sin was unintentional and
there was no prior warning. Yet contrary to Simeon, A, M. states
that the person must pay monetary compensation.]

[C]   [In order to understand M. Ter. 6 : 1, we must] interpret it as
following the view of R. Meir [Y. Ter. 7 : 1 I.S].

[D]   For R. Meir says, "[If the individual had been warned against
the sin, but performed the action anyway], he receives stripes
and pays monetary compensation." [If there was no warning,
compensation is paid, but stripes are not inflicted, as M. Ter. 6 : 1
assumes.]

[E]   Yet [contrary to D] so we have learned [M. Ter. 7 : 1]: *One who
intentionally eats heave-offering [pays back the principal but
does not pay the added fifth.* According to Meir, there should be
stripes as well as compensation. Whose view does M. Ter. 7 : 1
follow?]

[F]   [M. Ter. 7 : 1] accords well with the opinion of Nathan bar Hoshaya[8] [Y. Ter. 7 : 1 **III.**F], who said, "[Wherever a fine is to be
paid and stripes are to be inflicted], one pays the fine but does
not receive the stripes." [Therefore at M. Ter. 7 : 1 he pays the
principal but does not receive stripes.]

[G]   [You also may interpret M. Ter. 7:1 in line with] the opinion of
R. Yohanan, who said, "If [witnesses] warned [the potential sinner not to carry out the act, but he did so anyway], he receives
the stripes. But if [witnesses] did not warn him, he pays a fine
[and does not receive stripes]."

[H]   [In line with this view] interpret [M. Ter. 7:1] as referring to [a
nonpriest] who intentionally [ate heave-offering] without first
having been warned [against carrying out that action].

[I]   In the opinion of R. Simeon b. Laqish, it makes no difference
[whether the individual ate the heave-offering] intentionally or
unintentionally. [Stripes are inflicted. Compensation is not paid.]

[J]   [Likewise for Simeon] the same rule applies whether witnesses had
warned [the individual against his action] or whether they had not
warned him. [In either case he does not pay compensation.]

[K]   [The reason for I and J is that] R. Simeon b. Laqish reasoned in
line with the opinion of R. Meir, for R. Meir said, "[If the individual had been warned against the sin, but performed the action anyway], he receives stripes and pays monetary compensation" [see above, D].

[L]   Said R. Hanina in the presence of R. Mana, "It is possible that
R. Simeon b. Laqish holds that each of the Mishnaic pericopae
[with which we have been dealing] follows the view of R. Meir,
[such that along with the monetary compensation, stripes are
inflicted].

[M]   "[But can Simeon b. Laqish also argue that] Scripture is in line
with view of R. Meir?

[N]   "[Indeed, Scripture knows nothing of stripes in the case under
question.] For it is written [Lev. 22:14]: 'And if a man eats of a
holy thing unwittingly, [he shall add the fifth of its value to it
and give the holy thing to the priest].'" [Scripture imposes monetary compensation, but not stripes. According to Simeon b.
Laqish, who follows Meir, K, there should be both.]

[O]   [This explains that Simeon's (= Meir's) view does not contradict
Scripture. The case of one who eats heave-offering has its own
rule. It is an exception in which stripes and monetary compensation are not both inflicted.] For Simeon b. Laqish reasons that
the added fifth is [comparable to] a sacrifice [and not to a fine.
Since this is not monetary compensation, it does not carry along

with it stripes. The case of heave-offering therefore does not contradict Meir's principle that monetary compensation generally goes along with stripes.]

[P] [We now see that O is unacceptable.] Even if [Simeon] reasons that the added fifth is [comparable to] a sacrifice, is it so that the principal likewise is tantamount to a sacrifice?

[Q] Said R. Yudan bar Shalom, "[No, the principal is not comparable to a sacrifice.] Mishnah states that the principal is paid as a fine. [Since this is so, in Simeon's view there should be stripes as well.]

[R] "[The claim that the principal is a fine] is in line with what we have learned [M. Ter. 6:1]: *One may not pay restitution with produce in the status of heave-offering. Rather he pays it with unconsecrated produce from which tithes have been removed, and this produce takes on the status of heave-offering.*

[S] "Now, if he were allowed to pay compensation with produce such as that which he ate [i.e., heave-offering], it would be obvious [that this payment is not a fine. But, to the contrary, since he must pay with his own unconsecrated food, it is clear that the principal is paid as a fine.]

[T] "A Tannaitic teaching makes this same point, [that the principal is paid as a fine: If one unintentionally] ate unclean heave-offering, he must anyway pay restitution with clean unconsecrated produce. But if he paid it with unclean unconsecrated produce, he has fulfilled his obligation [cf., T. Ter. 7:2].

[U] "But does [the nonpriest] not owe [the priest] only the value [the heave-offering would have had were it] wood? [Since the heave-offering could not be eaten and should have been burned, this logically would be the case.]

[V] "[No. The nonpriest must repay the full value of the heave-offering.] This proves that the principal is paid as a fine.

[W] "Now just as you say that the principal is paid as a fine, so the added fifth is a fine." [It is not comparable to a sacrifice, contrary to what O proposed. We are left with the question of how Simeon, following Meir, explains the fact that stripes are not imposed.]

[X] [The explanation is as follows:] For Simeon b. Laqish follows his own particular view, in that Simeon b. Laqish said there [in an undisclosed source], "All was included under the general principle [provided by Ex. 20:16]: 'You shall not bear false witness against your neighbor.'

[Y]   "But the following [rule] was stated outside of the general principle [in order to explain it: 'If the witness is a false witness and has accused his brother falsely], then you shall do to him as he had meant to do to his fellow' [Dt. 19:18–19].

[Z]   "[This means that the false witness is] culpable for paying restitution.

[AA]   "[The same sort of reasoning explains why a nonpriest who eats heave-offering only pays restitution.] But here [in the case of heave-offering] all was included under the general rule [provided by Lev. 22:10]: 'An outsider shall not eat of a holy thing.'

[BB]   "[The following rule was stated] outside of the general principle [so as to explain it]: 'And if a man eats of a holy thing unwittingly, [he shall add the fifth of its value to it and give the holy thing to the priest', Lev. 22:14].

[CC]   "[This means that the individual is] subject to paying monetary compensation [and not to receiving stripes]."

The central issue is the basis for the view of Simeon b. Laqish. The problem for the exegete is to determine exactly which of Simeon b. Laqish's views is under discussion. One version, given previously at Y. Ter. 7:1 **II.H**, is assumed at A–J. But then we are told, K, that Simeon follows the quite different position of Meir. This view is primary at L–CC, which I interpret in light of K's contention that Simeon follows the view assigned to Meir. The other possibility, taken by PM, is that L–CC argues against the position attributed to Simeon b. Laqish at Y. Ter. 7:1 **II.H**. While this solves the problem of the apparent discontinuity between A–J and K–CC, it ignores what L states explicitly. I prefer to take seriously L, which refers to Simeon b. Laqish's ability to uphold Meir's view.

[V.A]   But has it not been taught [in a Tannaitic source]: Sages concede to R. Meir that a person who steals [and eats] forbidden fat which belongs to his fellow both receives stripes and pays monetary compensation?

[B]   For one who eats forbidden fat is subject to stripes, [and for stealing he pays a fine].

[C]⁹   But has it not been taught [in a Tannaitic source]: Sages concede to R. Meir that one who steals [and eats] heave-offering which belongs to his fellow [both] receives stripes and pays monetary compensation?

[D]   For one who eats heave-offering is subject to stripes, [and for stealing he pays a fine].

[E]   But has it not been taught [in a Tannaitic source]: Sages concede to R. Meir that one who muzzles his fellow's heifer [and uses it to thresh grain, an infringement of Dt. 25:4], receives stripes and pays a fine?

[F]   [He pays] six *qabs* for doing this with a heifer and four *qabs* for [so muzzling] an ass.¹⁰ [These are the quantities the animals presumably would have eaten during their work.]

[G]   For one who muzzles his heifer [while it is threshing] is subject to stripes.

[H]   Said R. Yose,¹¹ "This is also the case for those who are culpable for execution, [that they may need both to pay restitution and to receive stripes].

[I]   "[Here is a case in which that is so: If] one stole heave-offering which [a priest] had dedicated [to the Temple] and then [intentionally] ate it—[even though he is subject to death for intentional sacrilege], he [both] receives stripes [for intentionally eating heave-offering] and pays restitution.

[J]   "[He must pay restitution since] in all events he has misappropriated property [belonging to someone else]."

[K]   Said R. Mana in the presence of R. Yose, "From the preceding [we know that] one who has sexual intercourse with his sister, a minor (so Y. Ket. 3:1. Y. Ter. reads: an adult), should receive stripes and pay compensation.

[L]   "[This is logical since] one who has intercourse with his adult (so Y. Ket. 3:1) sister receives stripes." [For the younger one, therefore, we impose this punishment as well as the further one of a fine. It is a more severe crime.]

[M]   [Explaining why his own reasoning at K–L is unacceptable,] replied [44d] R. Mana, "[One who has intercourse with his younger sister does not receive both a fine and stripes, since for that sin] he becomes culpable both for extirpation and for paying compensation at one and the same time. [PM: He is subject to extirpation, a fine *and stripes*. Since we do not impose two earthly punishments for one sin, stripes alone are inflicted.]

[N]   "But [by contrast] there, [in the case of one who muzzles his fellow's heifer, he becomes culpable for the two punishments at different times, such that both may apply]. From the point at which he first muzzles the animal, he is subject to stripes. From this point onward, [while he threshes with the animal and refuses to allow it to eat,] he becomes culpable to pay a fine." [Comparable reasoning applies in the cases at A–B and C–D.]

[O]   [Zeira argues that Mana, M–N, is wrong.] R. Zeira replied in the presence of R. Mana, "[According to your reasoning,] if, on the Sabbath, one sets fire to the grain heap belonging to his fellow—from the point at which the first stalk burns he is subject to death [for profaning the Sabbath, and] from that point on, he is subject to pay compensation [for destroying his fellow's property].

[P]   "But do not say that this is the case, [for M. B.Q. 3:10 states explicitly that the man is not culpable for burning the fellow's stack, since he is already subject to death for profaning the Sabbath].

[Q]   "Rather, [if the man is to receive both punishments], for each stalk of grain [which is burned] he must be warned about the punishment of stripes, [which he will receive for profaning the Sabbath], and about the payment of compensation, [which he will have to make for destroying somebody else's property. Contrary to what Mana said, we do not deem the first stalk burned punishable with stripes and later ones with a fine.]

[R]   "And so here, [in the case of muzzling the fellow's cow, if he is to be subject both to stripes and a fine], for each act of muzzling the animal he must be warned concerning [the prohibition against muzzling], which renders him culpable for stripes, and concerning [his misuse of his neighbor's property], which renders him culpable for paying compensation." [If this is not done, he will be culpable only for one punishment, stripes.]

[S]   Said R. Yose b. R. Bun, "Two Amoraim [dispute the circumstances under which a person who muzzles an animal and threshes with it is not subject to stripes].

[T] "One says, '[If the individual muzzles an animal threshing] produce in the status of heave-offering or which is dedicated to the Temple [he is not subject to stripes].'

[U] "But the other says, '[If] he assigns an agent to muzzle the animal [on his behalf], the agent receives stripes, but he is exempt. [The designation of an agent to commit a sin is null. It is as though the agent muzzled the animal on his own behalf.]

[V] "'[We know this because Lev. 17:4 states]: "Bloodguilt shall be imputed to that man" [who slaughters an ox or lamb and does not offer it as a gift to the Lord before the tabernacle].

[W] "'[This means that each man is accountable for his own sin.] The one who sent him is not [accountable].'"

If there are two separate sins, A–B, C–D and E–G, all can agree with Meir (Y. Ter. 7:1 I.S) that both a fine and stripes apply. Yose, H, develops this notion, depicting a threefold sin, for which three appropriate punishments are inflicted. Mana, K–L, suggests a different case, claiming it too is parallel to those at A–G. This is debated by Mana, who argues against his own contention, and Zeira, who argues in its favor (M–N versus O–Q). Zeira's point is central. A single action does not comprise two different sins unless the individual had been warned separately concerning each of them. S–W suggests a secondary, and autonomous, consideration, pertinent to E–G.

[VI.A] [A, B, and C each present a circumstance under which we might deem a person who performs a single action to be culpable for two different sins.] (Read with Y. Ket. 3:1:) If [on Passover one ate leavened produce that turned out to be in the status of heave-offering, such that] he had unintentionally eaten heave-offering, but intentionally had eaten leaven;

[B] or [if a Nazirite drank wine that turned out to be in the status of heave-offering, such that he had] unintentionally drunk heave-offering, but intentionally drunk wine [which is forbidden of a Nazirite];

[C]   or [if, on the Day of Atonement, one ate food that turned out to be in the status of heave-offering, such that] he unintentionally had eaten heave-offering, but intentionally had broken the fast of the Day of Atonement—

[D]   if you claim that in each case there were two separate sins (*dbrym*), then it is clear [in your view that all will agree that the individual receives stripes and also pays compensation for the heave-offering wrongly eaten].

[E]   But if you hold that [the single act of eating renders the person culpable for] one sin (*dbr*) alone, [then in your view] R. Yohanan and R. Simeon b. Laqish will disagree [concerning the punishment. PM: Yohanan, Y. Ter. 7:1 I.H, will hold that stripes are inflicted, but compensation is not paid. Simeon b. Laqish, who follows Meir, Y. Ter. 7:1 I.S, will require both stripes and a fine.]

The issue is the same as at Y. Ter. 7:1 **IV,** whether or not we deem a single action to comprise two sins. While this question is posed, D–E, no criteria for answering it are suggested. Instead, we refer back to the positions of Yohanan and Simeon b. Laqish given at Y. Ter. 7:1 **I.**

[VII.A]   There we have learned [M. Meg. 1:5]: *There is no difference between the Sabbath and the Day of Atonement, except that [the punishment for] intentionally [breaking the rules of] this one [i.e., the Sabbath] is [execution] at the hand of man, and [the punishment for] intentionally [transgressing the rules] of that one [i.e., the Day of Atonement] is [death at the hand of heaven, through] extirpation.*

[B]   Thus as regards the payment of restitution, the [rules for] both are the same. [Since there is a death penalty, any restitution which normally would be paid need not be.]

[C]   Mishnah [Meg. 1:5] follows the opinion of R. Nehunia b. Haqqanah.

[D]   For it is taught: R. Nehunia b. Haqqanah says,[12] "The Day of Atonement is just like the Sabbath as regards [the obligation of one who transgresses the rules of either] to pay restitution, [just as B states]."

[E]   Now R. Simeon b. Manasia [expresses the same idea in a slightly different manner. He] says, "[The law for] those who are subject to extirpation [at the hand of heaven] is just like that for those who are subject to execution at the hand of an [earthly] court, [just as B states]."

[F]   [In] what [concrete case is the difference] between their [statements significant]?

[G]   R. Aha in the name of R. Abina says, "They differ concerning [whether or not one who rapes] a minor who is menstruating [is subject both to death and compensation]."

[H]   Said R. Mana, "They also differ concerning one who rapes his wife's sister."

[I]   [In either of these cases], in the opinion of R. Nehunia b. Haq-qanah, [the individual *is* culpable both for death and to pay compensation. This is as follows:] In the cases of both the Sabbath and the Day of Atonement, what was prohibited never can become permitted. But [as regards the menstruant or the sister of his wife, who at the time of the incidents were forbidden to him]—they may become permitted to him, [i.e., after the girl's period, or if his wife should die. These cases thus are unlike that of the Sabbath and Day of Atonement.] Therefore he pays compensation [as well as being culpable for death].

[J]   But R. Simeon b. Menasia says, "Extirpation is applicable in the case of [one who purposely transgresses] the Sabbath, and extirpation is applicable in the case of one who [transgresses] the Day of Atonement. Now in the case of this [sin, of raping his wife's sister or a menstruant,] extirpation also is applicable. [The cases all are comparable, and] therefore [the rapist, like the individual at A–B,] is exempt from paying compensation."

[K]   [We carry forward the discussion of the positions of Simeon b. Menasia and Nehunia b. Haqqanah.] R. Judah bar Pazzai asked, "[As for a punishment of] stripes [for transgressing a negative commandment] (Y. Ket. 3:2: *mkwt;* Y. Ter.: *lwwyn*) along with extirpation—do these Tannaim allow this?"

[L]   Said R. Yose, "The rabbis need [to know; i.e., sages are unclear on this issue]."

[M]   Said R. Jonah, "Why do they not establish the answer from this which R. Simeon b. Yohai taught, for R. Simeon b. Yohai taught:

R. Tarfon says, 'Extirpation is applicable in the case of [infringe-
ments of the] Sabbath, and extirpation is applicable in the case
of [infringement of] the Day of Atonement. (Read with Y. Ket.
3:1:) Just as in the case of the Sabbath, stripes and extirpation
may not both be inflicted, so in the case of the Day of Atonement, stripes and extirpation may not both be inflicted.'"

[N]   [We turn to question the views of different authorities.] Said
R. Mana in the presence of R. Yose, "Whether R. Simeon b.
Laqish [holds that stripes and extirpation both may be inflicted]
is in question.

[O]   "But the view of R. Yohanan [is clear]. (Read with Y. Ket. 3:1:)
If he allows stripes to be inflicted along with the death penalty,
all the more so will he not allow stripes to be inflicted along with
extirpation? [He certainly will.]

[P]¹³   "[The following proves that, while Yohanan allows stripes in
a case in which extirpation applies, the position of Simeon b.
Laqish is not clear. Yohanan and Simeon b. Laqish] disagree
[concerning the punishment inflicted in this case: As for] one
who, [on the same day,] slaughters an animal and its young,
[thereby transgressing Lev. 22:28,¹⁴ and who further performs
the slaughter] for purposes of idol worship [see M. Hul. 5:3]—

[Q]   "R. Yohanan says, '[If before the act of slaughtering] he had
been warned about [the prohibition against slaughtering to-
gether] "it and its young," he receives stripes.

[R]   "'[But if he had been warned instead] concerning [the prohibition against] idolatry, he is stoned to death.' [Even though under certain circumstances the sin is punishable by execution,
Yohanan holds that stripes may be inflicted (Q). If the sin was
punishable not by execution, but only by extirpation, certainly
he would hold that stripes are inflicted, as O suggested.]

[S]   "R. Simeon b. Laqish says, 'Even if he had been warned concerning [the prohibition against slaughtering together] "it and
its young," he does not receive stripes.

[T]   "'For if they had warned him concerning¹⁵ [the prohibition
against] idol worship, he would have been stoned to death.'"
[Since under a certain circumstance this sin is punishable by
execution, stripes may not be inflicted. But if the sin was punishable only by extirpation, and not execution, it is not clear
whether or not Simeon b. Laqish would allow stripes.]

[U]   [Arguing that matters are not so simple as Mana has presented them, N–T], (supply with Y. Ket. 3:1:) [Yose] said to him, "Even the position of R. Yohanan is not clear.

[V]   "[The case which you suggested as proof is not acceptable, for while] there [in that case] there are two separate sins (*dbrym*), [i.e., slaughtering 'it and its young,' and slaughtering for purposes of idolatry], here [we wish to find out about the applicability of stripes and extirpation in the case of only] one sin." [The fact that Yohanan allows both stripes and extirpation in the former case does not indicate that he will do so in the latter.]

The issue is no different from what has preceded, namely, the punishments which are applicable in the case of particular sins. A–J and K–M are really separate, since the latter does not depend on the former for sense. Yet the reference, K, to "these Tannaim" clearly indicates the redactor's own notion that these disparate materials constitute a single discussion. N–O, in turn, develops K–M's issue, with reference to the views of Yohanan and Simeon b. Laqish.

[VIII.A]   [The view of rabbis, Y. Ter. 7:1 I.V–X, is contrasted with that of Simeon b. Menasia and Nehunia b. Haqqanah. Rabbis hold that monetary compensation is not paid if stripes are to be inflicted. Simeon b. Menasia and Nehunia b. Haqqanah, Y. Ter. 7:1 VII.D–E and K–M, hold that if extirpation applies, restitution is not paid, and stripes may not be inflicted.] In the opinion of R. Simeon b. Laqish, in what case is the difference between the positions of those Tannaim [i.e., Simeon b. Menasia and Nehunia b. Haqqanah] and rabbis [significant]?

[B]   [They differ] concerning [the punishment inflicted upon those who are] culpable for transgressing a negative commandment but who are not subject to extirpation. [Simeon b. Menasia and Nehunia b. Haqqanah hold that such individuals pay compensation but do not receive stripes. Rabbis hold that they receive stripes but do not pay compensation (PM).]

[C]   Said R. Yudan, (read with Y. Ket. 3:1) "They differ concerning [the punishment] for one who has sexual intercourse with a *Mamzeret* [i.e., the daughter of a man and woman who could not legally marry each other]."

[D]   Said R. Hanania, "They differ concerning the case of one who, on a holiday, sets fire to a grain heap which belongs to his fellow."

[E]   [In each of these cases, C and D,] these Tannaim [i.e., Simeon b. Menasia and Nehunia b. Haqqanah] reason that, since the individuals are not subject to extirpation, they pay compensation.

[F]   But these rabbis reason that, since they are culpable for stripes, they do not pay compensation.

[G]   This proves that [M. Ket. 3:1], *these are girls [through the seduction of whom one incurs a fine: a Mamzeret]*, does not follow the position of rabbis. [We have seen, C + F, that in the case of intercourse with a *Mamzeret*, rabbis would inflict stripes, but would not impose a fine.]

[H]   (Read with Y. Ket. 3:1:) Said R. Mattenaya, "[It is possible to] interpret [M. Ket. 3:1] as being in line with the opinion of all authorities [including the rabbis. This is the case if M. Ket. refers to the case of] a *Mamzer* [i.e., son of an illicit union] who had intercourse with a *Mamzeret*." [In such a case stripes are not inflicted. Here rabbis can agree with the anonymous rule of M. Ket. 3:1 that a fine is paid.]

    Translated in Y. Ket. 3:1's version, the passage is clear. B – D + E–F answers the question posed at A. G gives the seemingly logical implication of F. H proves that this conclusion is not necessarily acceptable.

[IX.A]   [M. Ket. 3:1 states that a man who has intercourse with his (Y.: dead) brother's wife, a minor and still a virgin, is subject to a fine and extirpation. For the reason given here, this seems illogical.] Now [why should he be culpable for seducing] his [dead] brother's wife? [Since the maiden still is a virgin it is clear that the brother died childless. Therefore] is he not her Levir, [and responsible to sire children through her in order to carry on his brother's line]?

[B]   Said R. Mattenaya,[16] "[Explain why the punishments are inflicted by] interpreting [the passage to refer to a case of a brother] who [already] had children [by a previous marriage], who [then] betrothed a [new] wife [i.e., the virgin girl] and [subsequently] died.

[C]   "And [only afterwards] did his brother come and rape her."
[Since he had no role as a Levir, he is subject to punishment for
raping his brother's wife.]

M. Ket. 3:1 is explained, B–C.

7:2 [P: 7:2a]

[A]   *"The daughter of a priest who married an Israelite and afterwards [unintentionally] ate heave-offering pays the principal,
[for she ate what does not belong to her]. But [because she is of
priestly status] she does not pay the added fifth.*

[B]   *"And [if she commits adultery] her death is by burning, [as in
the case of all priestly women who commit adultery].*

[C]   *"[If] she married any person who is ineligible [for marriage to
priestly stock (see M. Yeb. 6:2), and then unintentionally ate
heave-offering],*

[D]   *"she pays the principal and added fifth, [for she no longer is
treated as a person of priestly status].*

[E]   *"And [if she commits adultery] her death is by strangling, [as in
the case of all Israelite women who commit adultery]"—the
words of R. Meir.*

[F]   *But sages say, "Both of these [women, A–B and C–E] pay the
principal but do not pay the added fifth,*

[G]   *"and [if they commit adultery] their death is by burning." [I.e.,
in all events the woman is treated as of priestly status.]*

The concern is the anomalous status of the daughter of a priest
who marries an Israelite. While such a woman is of priestly lineage, because of her marriage, she becomes an outcaste and loses
the right to eat holy things, which she had while living in her
father's house. The problem is whether in other respects the
woman still is treated as a person of priestly status, or whether
she is deemed an ordinary Israelite. The issue is disputed by
Meir, A–E, and the sages, F–G. Explanation of the views of
these authorities is the central focus of the Talmudic discussion
which follows (units **II** and **III**). Both views are shown to derive

from Scripture. In its first unit, the Yerushalmi answers the basic question of what sin the woman committed, B, E, and G. This is information which I have interpolated into the Mishnah, in brackets. The final unit (**IV**) examines the correlation between the principle of Meir here and that assigned to other authorities elsewhere in the tractate.

[**I.A**] The Mishnah [Ter. 7:2B, E, and G] means: If she committed adultery, her death is by burning.

The Yerushalmi renders explicit the meaning of M. Ter. 7:2B, E, and G.

[**II.A**] What is the scriptural basis for R. Meir's[17] [statement, M. Ter. 7:2A–E]?

[B] [The basis is Lev. 21:9]: "And the daughter of any priest], if she profanes herself by playing the harlot, [profanes her father; she shall be burned with fire]."

[C] [This applies to] any [daughter of a priest] who still is[18] fit to return to the house of her father [i.e., even if she had married an Israelite, M. Ter. 7:2B].

[D] [But] it excludes [from execution by fire] any [daughter of a priest] who is not fit to return to[19] the house of her father [i.e., because she married someone ineligible for marriage to priestly stock, M. Ter. 7:2E].

[E] [C seems illogical. If] she had married [an Israelite] who was fit for marriage to priestly stock and then committed adultery, is she fit to return to her father's house? [No, for she is subject to execution. C thus makes no sense. No woman who has committed adultery is fit to return to her father's house.]

[F] [In order to make sense of C we ask], what is [C's] point?

[G] [Scripture states] "If she profanes herself by playing the harlot."

[H] [This means that] one who profanes herself by playing the harlot [still is deemed fit to return to her father's house, such that, like all priestly women who commit adultery, her execution is by fire].

[I]   But [this is] not [the case if] she profaned herself through marriage [to someone ineligible for marriage to priestly stock. In
this case she is deemed unfit to return to her father's house,
such that, if she commits adultery, her execution is through
strangulation.]

The basis in Scripture for Meir's view, M. Ter. 7:2A–E, is given,
A–D, and explained, E–I.

[III.A]   What is the scriptural basis for the position of rabbis [M. Ter.
7:2F–G, that in all cases a woman of the priestly caste who marries a nonpriest is treated as of priestly status]?

[B]   [Lev. 21:9 states]: "And the daughter of any priest [if she profanes herself by playing the harlot, profanes her father, she shall
be burned with fire]."

[C]   [This means that] under all circumstances [the daughter of a
priest who commits adultery is executed through fire. This is
so even if she had married a person ineligible for marriage to
priestly stock, for she still is the daughter of a priest.]

[D]   On the basis [of C, we may conclude that the view of the sages,
M. Ter. 7:2F–G, applies] even if she was the issue of her priestly
father's illegitimate marriage,[20] [e.g., to a divorcee. Even though
neither he nor she retains priestly rights, she is "the daughter
of a priest." If she commits adultery, Lev. 21:9 applies.]

[E]   [C's conclusion is proven unacceptable.] Taught R. Hinena bar
Papa in the presence of R. Zeira, "According to R. Ishmael,
[Lev. 21:9's statement], 'She profanes her father,' [means that
the daughter of a priest] who profanes herself [through marriage
to a person ineligible for marriage to priestly stock still is under
the law of Lev. 21:9]. But one who is profaned through her
father's [marrying a divorcee or other woman ineligible for marriage to a priest] is not [deemed of priestly caste and is not subject to Lev. 21:9]." [If such a woman commits adultery, she is
not executed through fire.]

[F]   [Rejecting E,] said R. Hanina, "I know of a Beraita [in the
name] of R. Ishmael [in which he states], 'Even if she was the
issue of her priestly father's illegitimate marriage [she is deemed
the daughter of a priest and is subject to Lev. 21:9].'"

The unit is the functional parallel to the preceding one, which
explained Meir's view. The sages' view (M. Ter. 7:2F–G) is derived from Scripture, A–C, and its implications are argued, D–F.

[**IV.**A]   [According to Meir, M. Ter. 7:1A, a woman of questionable
priestly status who eats heave-offering pays back the principal
but not the added fifth. The problem is that this view is not
consistent with either of the possibilities suggested by Eliezer
and Joshua in M. Ter. 8:1, cited here.] But so we have learned:
*[The wife of a priest who was eating heave-offering, and they
came and told her, "Your husband has died," or "He has divorced you"* (such that, like the woman at M. 7:1 she no longer
had the right to eat heave-offering)]—

[B]   *R. Eliezer declares [her] subject to payment of the principal and
added fifth.*

[C]   *But R. Joshua exempts* [saying, presumably, that she need repay
nothing. Thus neither Eliezer nor Joshua can agree with Meir,
M. 7:2, who claims in a like circumstance that the woman pays
the principal but not the added fifth.]

[D][21]   [The following explains that C's conclusion is unacceptable. Contrary to it, Joshua and Meir are in agreement.] They reasoned:
Concerning what do [Eliezer and Joshua] disagree? [They dis-
agree] concerning [whether or not the woman need pay] the
added fifth.

[E]   But as for the principal, even R. Joshua agrees [that the woman
must pay it. The position of Meir, M. Ter. 7:2, thus is in agreement with that of Joshua, M. Ter. 8:1. The woman of questionable priestly status repays the principal but not the added fifth.]

[F]   [Here is a second way to prove that the views of Meir and Joshua
agree.] Concerning what do [Eliezer and Joshua] disagree? [They
disagree] concerning [heave-offering the woman] already had
eaten [before she was informed that her husband had died or
divorced her. In the case of such heave-offering Joshua says that
the woman pays no compensation, and Eliezer says that she pays
the principal and added fifth.]

[G]   But as for [heave-offering the woman eats] after [she knows that
her husband died or divorced her], even R. Joshua agrees that
she must pay the principal [but not the added fifth. Thus again
we see that he agrees with Meir, M. Ter. 7:2].

Meir's view, M. Ter. 7 : 1A, concurs with that of Joshua, M.
Ter. 8 : 1.

7 : 3 [P: 7 : 2b; M. Ter. 7 : 3–4]

[A]   *(1) One who gives his minor children or his slaves, whether they
are grown or minor, [heave-offering] to eat,*

[B]   *(2) one who eats heave-offering [separated from produce grown]
outside of the land [of Israel],*

[C]   *(3) and one who eats less than an olive's bulk of heave-offering*

[D]   *pays the principal but does not pay the added fifth.*

[E]   [That which is given as] restitution [retains the status of] unconsecrated produce.

[F]   [Therefore] if the priest wished to refuse [it], he may refuse [it].

[G]   *This is the general rule:*

[H]   *Anyone who pays the principal and added fifth—[that which is
given as] restitution [takes on the status of] heave-offering, and
[therefore, even] if the priest wished to refuse [it], he may not
refuse [it].*

[I]   *[But] anyone who pays the principal but does not pay the [added]
fifth—[that which is given as] restitution [retains the status of]
unconsecrated produce, [and, therefore], if the priest wished to
refuse [it], he may refuse [it].*

The pericope follows substantively from M. Ter. 7 : 1–2, suggesting three cases in which nonpriests who eat heave-offering pay
the principal but not the added fifth. M. Ter. 7 : 4 (which begins
here at G) concludes the unit of materials begun at M. Ter. 6 : 1.
It offers a general principle which coordinates and contrasts the
rules of M. Ter. 6 : 1–6 and M. Ter. 7 : 1–3.

For its part, the Yerushalmi ignores the theory of M. Ter. 7 : 3,
that in certain cases the added fifth need not be paid. Its concern
is with a secondary point. It wants to know how one person
(e.g., the slave) can make restitution for what was taken by a
different individual (e.g., the master). This question occupies
the Yerushalmi's one unit.

[I.A]   [If the master who fed his slave heave-offering, M. Ter. 7:3A] did not have time to pay [the principal, required by M. Ter. 7:3D] before the slave was set free, [the slave must himself pay the principal and added fifth (PM)], using [for payment] property which is his own, over which his master has no claim.

[B]   To what case is this comparable?

[C]   [To that of a certain] Reuben who stole from Simeon in order to pay Levi. [By giving the money to Levi], is [Reuben] released of responsibility for the theft? [This is comparable to A, where the householder stole from the priest to feed the slave. If the slave later pays compensation to the priest, is the householder relieved of responsibility for his actions?]

[D]   [The law for the case of Reuben, Simeon, and Levi] is under dispute by R. Hiyya the elder and R. Yannai.

[E]   For they dispute [the case of one who] stole [something] from one person's pouch and gave [what he stole] to someone else.

[F]   R. Eleazar in the name of R. Hiyya the elder [says], "[In order to pay back the person from whom the property was stolen,] they may take from the first person [i.e., the thief], but they may not reclaim [property] from the second [i.e., the one to whom the thief gave what he stole]." [The theory is that the thief alone is responsible for paying compensation. A person who receives stolen property has no responsibility to the one from whom it was stolen. Applied to the case of Reuben, Simeon and Levi, this theory states that, by paying Levi, Reuben is not released from responsibility for the original theft. Likewise in the case of heave-offering, the slave cannot pay compensation for heave-offering stolen by his former master. Hiyya the elder therefore cannot agree with A.]

[G]   [Contrary to F,] R. Yohanan in the name of R. Yannai [says], "They even may recover [stolen property] from the second person [i.e., the one to whom the thief gives it]." [According to this theory the person who receives stolen property is responsible to the original owner. In the case of Reuben, Simeon and Levi, Reuben is relieved of his responsibility for the theft if he gives what he stole to Levi *and* Levi then repays Simeon. In the same way, the slave who received heave-offering, A, may compensate the priest on behalf of the householder.]

[H]   [The Talmud states that Hiyya holds the opposite of what F claims.] Even Hiyya the elder agrees that should [Reuben, the thief,] give [what he stole] to Levi, that, by doing so, he is released of his responsibility for the theft.

A introduces C and the dispute between Hiyya and Yannai, F versus G. H, which revises F, hardly appears reasonable. It claims that simply by giving away that which he stole, the thief is absolved of his responsibility. This is not what A or G has argued. PM solves the problem by claiming that H means that while one cannot force a person who receives stolen goods to give them up, *if he does so* the thief is relieved of his responsibility for the original theft. This makes sense, but is not intrinsic to the specific wording of H.

7:4–5 [P: 7:3a; M. Ter. 7:5]

[A]   *Two bins, one [filled] with heave-offering, and the other [filled] with [less than a hundred seahs of] unconsecrated produce,*

[B]   *into one of which fell a seah of heave-offering,*

[C]   *but it is not known into which of them it fell—*

[D]   *lo, I say, "Into the [bin filled with] heave-offering it fell" [and so has not been mixed with unconsecrated produce].*

[E]   *[If] it is not known which [of the bins] is [filled] with heave-offering and which is [filled] with unconsecrated produce—*

[F]   *[if] a person ate [the produce in] one of them, he is exempt [from payment of the principal and added fifth, i.e., we assume that he ate unconsecrated produce].*

[G]   *And [as for] the second [bin]—he thereafter treats it as heave-offering.*

[H]   *"But [dough made from] it is subject to [the separation of] dough offering [since it might be unconsecrated produce]"—the words of R. Meir.*

[I]   *R. Yose exempts it [from the separation of dough offering, consistent with the theory of G].*

[J]   *[If] a different person ate [the produce in] the second [bin], he is exempt [from payment of the principal and added fifth, i.e., we assume that he ate unconsecrated produce].*

[K]   *[If] the same person ate [the produce in] both [of the bins], he*
pays restitution in accordance with [the quantity of produce in]
the smaller of the two [i.e., we assume that the smaller amount
of produce was heave-offering].

This pericope, along with those that follow at M. Ter. 7:6–7,
makes a single point. In a case in which we need not assume that
heave-offering was eaten by a nonpriest or in some other way
misused, we do not make that assumption. The point has its
simplest expression at A–D, with E then acting as superscription to three parallel cases which will follow: F–K in this pericope, and L–Q and R–Y in the following ones.

The Yerushalmi's one unit provides other cases which illustrate the Mishnah's principle and argues whether or not the law
for those particular instances indeed is what has been claimed. It
is unclear why, in V and L, this single discussion is broken into
two separately numbered pericopae, Y. 7:4 and 7:5. PM numbers this whole unit Y. 7:4.

[I.A]   [If there were two bins,] one containing unclean [unconsecrated
produce] and the other containing clean [unconsecrated produce,
and heave-offering fell into one of them but it is not known which],
I say, "It fell into the unclean [unconsecrated produce, such that
the clean produce has not been rendered unfit for consumption
by a nonpriest." Cf. T. Ter. 6:15–17.]

[B]   [If] one of the bins contained produce that was a mixture of
heave-offering and unconsecrated produce, which is treated as
heave-offering, and the other contained unconsecrated produce
that had not already been mixed with heave-offering, [and heave-
offering fell into one of them but it is not known into which], I
say "Into the produce which [already] is a mixture of heave-
offering and unconsecreated produce it fell."

[C]   [If] one of the bins contained a quantity of produce sufficient to
neutralize [the heave-offering] and one of them did not contain
produce sufficient to neutralize [the heave-offering, and heave-
offering fell into one of the bins but it is not known into which],
I say, "Into the bin which (PM:)[22] contains a sufficient quantity
of produce to neutralize the heave-offering it fell." [As at A–B,
we may claim that the status of clean unconsecrated produce was
not impaired through being mixed with heave-offering.]

[D][23]   R. Simeon b. Laqish in the name of Bar Qappara says, "This [i.e., C] is the case only if the other [bin, which does not contain sufficient produce to neutralize the heave-offering], does contain more[24] [produce than the quantity of heave-offering which might have fallen into it]." [In order to deem the heave-offering neutralized, Simeon b. Laqish requires that even if the heave-offering fell into the smaller quantity of unconsecrated produce, still it would have been nullified within that produce.]

[E]   R. Yohanan says, "[C applies] even if the second bin of produce does not contain more [unconsecrated food than the quantity of heave-offering which might have fallen into it]."

[F]   The views [assigned] to R. Simeon b. Laqish[25] [here and at Y. Ter. 4:8 V] are contradictory.

[G]   There [at Y. Ter. 4:8 V.B] he states, "The uncertainty [concerning whether or not heave-offering has been neutralized is adjudicated by claiming that the heave-offering] was voided [through being mixed] with a larger quantity [of unconsecrated produce]." [In this case, that larger quantity of unconsecrated produce is the bin which contains sufficient produce to neutralize the heave-offering.]

[H]   But here [at D] he says this, [i.e., the contrary, that the heave-offering is not neutralized unless the second bin as well contains a large quantity of unconsecrated produce].

[I]   [The reason for the contradiction is that] there [at Y. Ter. 4:8 Simeon b. Laqish's view is cited] in his own name, while here [at Y. Ter. 7:4 it is cited] in the name of Bar Qappara. [The implication is that Bar Qappara does not accurately represent Simeon's view (PM).]

[J]   The views [assigned] to R. Yohanan [here and at Y. Ter. 4:8 V] are contradictory.

[K]   There [at Y. Ter. 4:8 V.D] he says, [Is there proof [that the heave-offering is not mixed in the batch of produce]?" [No, there is not, and therefore we must deem the batch to have the status of heave-offering.]

[L]   But here [at E] he states this, [i.e., the contrary, that even though there is no proof that the heave-offering was not mixed in the smaller batch of unconsecrated produce, the heave-offering is deemed neutralized].

[M]   [The views assigned to Yohanan appear contradictory because] the present case [at Y. Ter. 7:4] is different [from the one at Y. Ter. 4:8]. For [in the present case] it is possible to attribute [the impairment in status to the batch which contains sufficient produce to neutralize the heave-offering. In the case at Y. Ter. 4:8 there is no second batch to which the impairment in status may be attributed. For that reason, Yohanan's position there is different from the one he holds here.]

A, B, and C give cases such as those found at M. Ter. 7:5. The point therefore is not new. Simeon b. Laqish and Yohanan, D–E, dispute the circumstances under which the rule given for the case at C applies. Finally, F–I and J–M, the views given here for each of these authorities are reconciled with positions cited in their names earlier in the tractate.

7:6 [P: 7:3b; PM: 7:5]

[L]   *[If the produce in] one of them [i.e., of the bins referred to at M. Ter. 7:5] fell into unconsecrated produce, it does not impart the status of heave-offering [to that produce].*

[M]   *And [as for] the second [bin]—he [thereafter] treats it like heave-offering.*

[N]   *"But [dough made from] it is subject to [the separation of] dough offering"—the words of R. Meir.*

[O]   *R. Yose exempts [it from the separation of dough offering].*

[P]   *[If the produce in the] second [bin] fell into a different batch [of unconsecrated produce], it does not impart the status of heave-offering [to that produce. That is, I still can say that the first bin contains the original heave-offering.]*

[Q]   *[If the produce in] both [of the bins] fell into a single batch [of unconsecrated produce], they impart the status of heave-offering [to that produce] in accordance with [the quantity of produce in] the smaller of the two [bins].*

As at M. Ter. 7:5, if we need not assume that heave-offering was misused, we do not do so. This accounts for L–M, P, and Q. Meir, N, states that because the dough might be made of uncon-

secrated produce, it is subject to the separation of dough offering. Yose, O, is consistent with M. The produce in the bin is to
be treated as heave-offering, such that dough made from it is not
subject to dough offering.

The Yerushalmi's three units present no surprises. The first
cites and explains cases comparable to the ones found in M. Ter.
7:6. It thus elucidates the larger legal issue which informs the
Mishnah. The second unit refers to dough offering, asking under
what circumstances produce of unknown status is subject to the
separation of that offering. Finally, we analyze M. Ter. 7:6P to
determine the authority who stands behind that rule and to pin-
point the principle which accounts for his particular position.

[I.A]   Two bins, one of unclean heave-offering and one of [a hundred *seahs* of] clean unconsecrated produce—

[B]   [if] a *seah* of unclean heave-offering fell into one of them, but
it is not known into which of them it fell,

[C]   lo, I say, "Into the [unclean] heave-offering it fell."

[D]   (Read with T.:) But the clean unconsecrated produce may not
be eaten in cleanness until they will ascertain that there is not
in each lump of dough so much as an egg's bulk [T. Ter. 6:16].

[E]   [If] a *seah* of clean heave-offering fell [into one of the two bins,
but it is not known which], I say, "Into the unclean[26] heave-
offering it fell."

[F]   But the [clean] unconsecrated produce must be eaten in small
bits, [which cannot impart uncleanness to each other or to the
person who eats them].

[G]   [If there were] two bins, one containing [45a] clean heave-offering
and the other containing clean[27] unconsecrated produce, and a
seah of clean heave-offering fell into one of them, but it is not
known into which of them it fell, I say, "Into the heave-offering
it fell."

[H]   But the [clean] unconsecrated produce must be eaten in small
bits, [which cannot impart uncleanness to each other or to the
person who eats them].

[I]   If a *seah* of unclean heave-offering fell [into one of them, but
it is not known into which], both of them are forbidden [for
consumption].

[J]   For what difference would it make [if we claimed that it fell into one and not the other]?

[K]   If [the unclean heave-offering] fell into the [clean] heave-offering, [the mixture is] forbidden.[28] [It may not be eaten by a priest, for it is unclean.]

[L]   If it fell into the [clean] unconsecrated produce, the mixture [likewise] is forbidden [for consumption. It may not be eaten by a nonpriest, for it is heave-offering. Yet a priest may not eat it, for it is unclean.]

[M]   Why [do we not simply say that the unclean heave-offering fell into the clean heave-offering, such that the clean unconsecrated produce will remain permitted for consumption]?

[N]   [The reason is that] what might be unclean is deemed certainly to be unclean. [Since the status of cleanness of the unconsecrated produce is in doubt, it must be deemed unclean.]

[O]   Only a doubt concerning whether or not unconsecrated produce was mixed with heave-offering may be adjudicated by deeming [the unconsecrated produce to remain] permitted. [All other cases of doubt are resolved stringently, by deeming the produce forbidden for consumption.]

Only I is new. It is explained at J–L + M–O, which gives the theory underlying the unit as a whole. If possible, we assume that heave-offering did not impart its own status to clean unconsecrated produce (O). We may not do this if the status of that food already is impaired, such that it could not be eaten (M + N). Since at I there is no choice but to state that the unconsecrated produce has been rendered unclean (N), we must also hold that it has been mixed with heave-offering.

[II.A]   [Reference is to M. Ter. 7:6N–O. Produce might have been mixed with heave-offering and so is treated as a priestly gift. Meir states that since it might be unconsecrated, dough made from it is subject to dough offering. Yose holds that it is not subject to that offering.] Said R. Yohanan, "[Dough made from produce] about which there is a doubt whether or not it was mixed with heave-offering is exempt from [the separation of] dough offering." [This same rule applies to produce which certainly was mixed with heave-offering, such that it took on the status of that offering, M. Hal. 1:4.]

[B]   "That concerning which there is a doubt whether or not it was mixed with heave-offering, but which is eaten as a mixture of heave-offering and unconsecrated produce, is subject to [the separation of] dough offering."

PM explains. In B's case there were two batches of produce, into one of which heave-offering fell. We assume it did not fall into the batch under question, such that this batch is deemed still to be unconsecrated. Only because of the doubt do we treat it as heave-offering (i.e., it is eaten by a priest). Under the assumption that it is unconsecrated, however, dough made from it is subject to the separation of dough offering. This is not the case at A. There the status of only one batch of unconsecrated produce is in doubt. Since there is no second batch to which to attribute the impairment in status, this batch must be treated in all respects like heave-offering. Dough made from it therefore is not subject to the separation of dough offering.

[III.A]   [M. Ter. 7:6P states that when the produce in the second bin into which heave-offering might have fallen itself is mixed with unconsecrated food, it does not impart the status of heave-offering to that food.] Said R. Yohanan, "This is [the opinion] of R. Judah. For there we have learned [M. Toh. 5:5: *Two paths, one of which was unclean and the other of which was clean—if a person walked down one of them and then prepared foods requiring preparation in cleanness, and then his fellow walked down the other and, afterwards, prepared foods requiring preparation in cleanness: R. Judah says]*, '*If they each asked individually whether or not the food they prepared is deemed clean, it is deemed clean. But if they asked [concerning the cleanness of the food] at one and the same time, [the food of both of them is deemed] unclean.'*

[B]²⁹   "R. Yose says, '*Either way [i.e., whether they asked together or separately] the food is deemed unclean.'*

[C]   "What is at issue [between Judah and Yose]?

[D]   "[Certainly they do not dispute the case in which the two people together ask concerning the cleanness of the food. For] if [it is a case] in which the two of them together ask [concerning the cleanness of the food, it is obvious that all of the food must be deemed] unclean. [It would be clear that one of the batches of food is unclean. Since we could not determine which, both would have to be deemed unclean.]

[E]   "[Likewise they do not dispute the case in which the two individuals come one after the other to ask whether the food they prepared is clean. For] if [it is a case] in which they came one after the other [to ask whether the food is deemed clean, it is obvious that it would indeed be deemed] clean. [The reason is that each of them individually can claim to have walked on the clean path.]

[F]   "Rather [since it is clear that Judah and Yose would not dispute the cases described at D–E], here is what they are [arguing] about:

[G]   "[They dispute the case] in which one [of the two people] comes to ask concerning [the cleanness of] his own [food] and that [prepared by] his fellow.

[H]   "R. Judah says, '[In such a case I] say to the person: Ask concerning your own [produce] and then go away' [i.e., the status of cleanness of your friend's produce is no concern of yours]. [Thus Judah treats the case as one in which the two individuals came one after the other. He deems all of the produce to be clean.]

[I]   "But R. Yose says, 'It is just like [a case in which] the two individuals asked at one and the same time, [and all of the food must be deemed unclean].'

[J]   "Now [the case] here [in M. Ter. 7:6P] is certainly comparable to one in which the two individuals asked [concerning the status of their produce] at one and the same time." [Yet according to M. Ter., both batches of produce are deemed to maintain their unconsecrated status. This follows the opinion of Judah, who holds that in all events we may treat each batch individually.]

Yohanan explains that M. Ter. 7:6P follows the opinion of Judah, M. Toh. 5:5, and not that of Yose. Judah reasons that each of the two related cases of doubt may be adjudicated independently. As a result, even though we know that one of the batches of produce has the status of heave-offering (in the case of M. Ter.) or is unclean (at M. Toh.), both are deemed to be unconsecrated or clean.

7:7 [P: 7:3c; PM: 7:6]

[R] *[If] he sowed [as seed the produce in] one of them [i.e., of the bins in one of which heave-offering was mixed, the crop which results] is exempt [from the laws of heave-offering. It is not treated as heave-offering. See M. Ter. 9:6.]*

[S] *And [as for] the second [bin]—he [thereafter] treats [the produce in] it as heave-offering.*

[T] *"But [dough made from] it is subject [to the separation of] dough offering"—the words of R. Meir.*

[U] *But R. Yose exempts [it from the separation of dough offering].*

[V] *[If] a different person sowed [as seed the produce in] the second [bin, the resultant crop] is exempt [from the laws of heave-offering].*

[W] *[If] one person sowed [the produce in] both [bins]—*

[X] *in the case of a kind [of produce] the seed of which disintegrates, [the crop] is permitted [for consumption as unconsecrated food. See M. Ter. 9:5–6.]*

[Y] *But in the case of a kind [of produce] the seed of which does not disintegrate, [the crop] is forbidden [for consumption as unconsecrated produce. Rather, it is treated as heave-offering.]*

All that has changed from before is at W + X–Y, which depends upon facts given at M. Ter. 9:5–6. If a seed disintegrates in the earth, what grows from it is deemed a new entity. Even if the seed was in the status of heave-offering, the crop which it produces is unconsecrated. This is not so if the seed is an integral part of the eventual crop. In such a case, the produce has the same status as the seed from which it grew.

Only the first of the Yerushalmi's two units is pertinent to this pericope. It asks under what specific conditions the rule of M. Ter. 7:7Y applies. This constitutes a close exegesis of the Mishnah's point. The second unit is primary at M. Ter. 9:5–6, for it contains a debate concerning the circumstances under which what grows from a seed which does not disintegrate indeed has the same status as that seed.

[I.A]   R. Zeira in the name of R. Hiyya bar Va [says], "The rule [of M. Ter. 7 : 7Y, which states that if both of the bins of seed are planted together, the crop which results has the status of heave-offering] applies [only] if he sowed [the produce in] the second [bin] before he had harvested [the crop which grew from the seed in] the first [bin].

[B]³⁰   "[But] if he sowed [the seed in] the second [bin] after³¹ he harvested [the crop which grew from] the first, [the two crops are not deemed to have the status of heave-offering, since] that which [already] has been harvested and produce which is yet to be harvested do not [join together to] constitute evidence [that all of the produce must be deemed heave-offering]."

The Yerushalmi defines what constitutes the planting together of the two separate bins of produce. As M. Ter. 7 : 7W says, only if the two suspect bins are planted together by a single person, might the crop which results have the status of heave-offering. The Yerushalmi thus provides a fine clarification of the Mishnah's point.

[II.A]   R. Hanina Toratha in the name of R. Yannai³² [says], "[As for] an onion in the status of heave-offering [which one planted], plucked, and then replanted—once the new growth is greater than that which originally was planted, it is deemed permitted [for consumption by a nonpriest]." [That is, the onion no longer has the status of heave-offering.]

[B]   R. Zeira replied, "[A is unacceptable] for have we not learned [at M. Ter. 9 : 6, paraphrased as follows: *That which grows from] a kind of seed which disintegrates is permitted [for consumption by nonpriests, even if the original seed was forbidden, e.g., because it was in the status of heave-offering].*

[C]   "*But in [the case of] a kind of seed which does not disintegrate— [that which grows from it is] forbidden*³³ [i.e., has the same status as the seed from which it grew]?

[D]   "[This means that] if it is a kind of seed which disintegrates, [that which grows from it] is permitted at the point at which the new growth is greater than that which originally was planted.

[E]   "But concomitantly, in the case of a kind of seed which does not
       disintegrate, [that which grows from it is] forbidden [i.e., has
       the same status as the original seed] even if the new growth be-
       comes greater than that which originally was planted." [A, which
       claims the opposite, thus is unacceptable.]

[F]   [In stating D–E] R. Zeira accords with his own view [cited else-
       where].

[G]   For R. Zeira said in the name of R. Yohanan, "[As for] an onion—
       subject to the restrictions of Mixed Kinds in a vineyard—which
       they picked and then replanted, even if it grows to several times
       [its original size] it [remains] forbidden [under the restrictions of
       Mixed Kinds].

[H]   "For that which grows from forbidden produce does not serve to
       neutralize that [same] forbidden produce [from which it grew]."

Contrary to Yannai, A, Zeira, B–E, claims that M. Ter. 9:6
means exactly what it says. What grows from forbidden seed is
forbidden, no matter how much larger than that original seed it
becomes. Zeira's reason appears at H. The forbidden produce
growing from the seed does not serve to neutralize the forbidden
status of that same seed.

8:1

[A] *(1) The wife [of a priest] who was eating heave-offering,*

[B] *[and] they came and told her, [Your husband] has died," or "[Your husband] has divorced you," [such that the woman no longer has the right to eat heave-offering];*

[C] *(2) and so [in the case of] a slave [of a priest] who was eating heave-offering,*

[D] *and they came and told him, "Your master has died," "He sold you to an Israelite," "He gave you [to an Israelite] as a gift," or, "He has made you a free man," [in any of which cases the slave no longer may eat heave-offering];*

[E] *(3) and so [in the case of] a priest who was eating heave-offering,*

[F] *and it became known that he is the son of a divorcee, or of a halusah [and therefore may not eat heave-offering]—*

[G] *R. Eliezer declares [all of these individuals] liable to payment of the principal and added fifth [of the heave-offering they unintentionally had eaten as nonpriests].*

[H] *But R. Joshua exempts.*

Eliezer deems it irrelevant that these people believed that they had the right to eat heave-offering. Objectively they did not have that right and therefore they must pay the principal and added fifth. This is the same law that applies to all nonpriests who unintentionally eat heave-offering. Joshua says that these individuals

are different from these others, for the former had no way of knowing that they should not eat the heave-offering. Since they acted under the assumption that they could eat heave-offering, when it
turns out that they should not have, they are not culpable.

The Yerushalmi's first issue is decidedly secondary. It asks
how it can be that a woman is divorced without her own knowing it. This is a question since, for the divorce to be valid, the
woman herself must receive the bill of divorce. After disposing
of this problem, we turn to Joshua's theory in exempting the
cited individuals from payment of the principal and added fifth,
M. Ter. 8:1H.

[I.A] [45b] *The wife [of a priest] who was eating heave-offering . . .*
[M. Ter. 8:1A].

[B] It makes sense to say that if [they told her], "Your husband has
died," [she is exempt from paying restitution for the heave-
offering]. [In this case she would have had no way of knowing that
he had died such that she had lost the right to eat the priestly gift.]

[C] [But if they told her], "He divorced you," [this makes no sense].
[Surely she would have received the bill of divorce and known
that she had lost the right to eat heave-offering. It should be
clear in this case that she is culpable for eating the offering. How
can Joshua suggest that she is not?]

[D] Rabbis say, "[His view] depends on an earlier Mishnaic teaching, which held that the daughter of an Israelite who was betrothed [to a priest] could eat heave-offering [= M. Ket. 5:2-3].

[E] "Now [in this case] her father could receive the bill of divorce
on her behalf, [such that she would lose the right to eat heave-
offering without knowing until later that this had happened]."

[F] R. Eliezer[1] says, "One might even say that [M. Ter. 8:1's reference to the woman who is divorced makes sense] according to
the later Mishnaic teaching, [which states that a woman who
marries a priest may not eat heave-offering until she actually has
entered the bridal chamber, M. Ket. 5:3, at which point her
father cannot receive the bill of divorce on her behalf].

[G] "[If this is the case,] explain [the fact that her divorce was completed without her knowing it by assuming] that [she assigned an

agent to accept the bill of divorce on her behalf], telling him, 'Accept my bill of divorce in such and such a place.'

[H]   "Now if it normally would have taken ten days to reach that place, but [the agent] found a fast horse and accepted her [bill of divorce] after only five days, [she would have been divorced five days earlier than she anticipated]." [The result would be that she might have eaten heave-offering even though she already had been divorced by the priest, just as M. Ter. 8:1 suggests might happen.]

[I]   Is not the view of [the Amora] R. Eliezer in accordance with the position of [the Tanna] R. Eleazar?[2]

[J]   For we have learned [M. Git. 6:4]: *[In a case in which a woman assigned an agent to, "Receive my bill of divorce for me in such and such a place," she continues to have the right to eat heave-offering until the messenger is assumed to have reached that place.]*

[K]   *R. Eleazar prohibits [her from eating heave-offering] forthwith.* [That is, she cannot wait until she believes him to have accepted the bill of divorce, but must desist from eating heave-offering as soon as he has left her sight. The reason is that Eleazar holds, M. Git. 6:3, that wherever or whenever the agent should accept the bill of divorce, it is valid. The problem arises when the woman does not desist and turns out to be divorced before she believed she would be.]

[L]   But does not R. Eleazar concede that if she said, "Receive my bill of divorce only in such and such a place," that she may continue to eat heave-offering until [the messenger with] the bill of divorce reaches that particular place? [If this is the case then Eleazar, M. Git. 6:4, cannot agree with H.]

[M]   Said R. Hanania, "[Eleazar agrees that] so long as she told him, 'Receive my bill of divorce in such and such a place,' it is as though she told him that it would not be a valid bill of divorce until after ten days, [i.e., the amount of time she assumes it will take the messenger to reach that place].

[N]   "As a result, [the heave-offering] which she ate in the meantime, she [believed she] was permitted to eat, [as H suggests]."

The problem is how the woman was divorced without knowing
it. Two possible reasons are suggested, D–E and F–H. At I–N
the second reason is shown to agree with the position of Eleazar,
M. Git. 6 : 4.

[**II.**A] [The question is why Joshua, M. Ter. 8 : 1H, exempts the individuals under consideration from payment of the principal and
added fifth.] R. Haggai asked the associates, "What is the basis
for [Joshua's] claim that one who eats [heave-offering] under the
assumption that he is permitted to do so is exempt [from payment of restitution]?

[B] "What is the difference between a case in which [the nonpriest]
thought that he ate unconsecrated produce, but it turned out to
be heave-offering, such that he is subject [to restitution],

[C] "and the present case, in which he believed that he had priestly
status, but turned out only to be an Israelite,[3] such that he should
be exempt [from the principal and added fifth]? [At both B and
C an individual who should not eat heave-offering unintentionally does so. How is the case at C different, such that for it Joshua
claims that the individual is exempt from restitution?]

[D] [Associates] said to him, "[Joshua bases his position] upon [the
rule for an individual who acts in accordance with] instructions
given by a court, [but later finds out that the court wrongly instructed him]." [Such an individual is not culpable for his actions, since he acted upon the decision of a court (M. Hor. 1 : 1).
Joshua holds that the case of M. Ter. 8 : 1 is comparable. The
individual did not unintentionally eat heave-offering because *he*
made the mistake of believing that what was consecrated was unconsecrated. Rather he acted in knowledge that what he ate was
heave-offering, but under the wrong assumption that he had the
right to eat it. This wrong assumption is comparable to his having
been told by a court that he could do what later turned out to be forbidden. As at M. Hor. 1 : 1, the individual is not culpable.]

[E] [Haggai] said to them, "I have another question.

[F.] "What difference is there between the case of one who believes
that it is a weekday [and so offers a sacrifice], but it turns out to
have been the Sabbath, in which case [Joshua holds that] the
person is culpable [for a sin offering],

[G]   "and the case of someone who believes that the offering [which he is sacrificing on the Sabbath] is a paschal lamb [such that his action would be permitted], but it turns out that it is a whole offering [which should not be sacrificed on the Sabbath]?" [In this case Joshua deems the individual] exempt [from a sin offering; M. Pes. 6:5.]

[H]   [Associates] said to him, "[Joshua determines the law of G] on the basis of [the rule for] one whose act of slaughter is permitted [because it was performed as a commanded action, i.e., a sacrifice (PM)]." [Since he thought the sacrifice was permitted, he is not culpable]."

[I]   [Haggai now points out the internal contradiction in the associates' explanation of Joshua's position.] He said to them, "I have another question.

[J]   "What is the difference between one who believes that [what he eats] is permitted fat, but it turns out that it is forbidden fat, in which case [Joshua holds that] he is culpable,

[K]   "and the case of someone who believes that his action is (read with PM, GRA:) permitted, but it turns out that it is forbidden,[4] in which case [according to your reasoning, Joshua always holds that] he is not culpable?" [There is no difference between the cases. It therefore is clear that the associates' reasoning, D, H, and in its most simple expression here at K, is unacceptable. It does not explain Joshua's view.]

[L]   [Unable to answer Haggai's question, J–K, the associates] did not respond to him at all.

[M]   [Haggai] said to them, "I will tell[5] you the basis [for Joshua's view].

[N]   "[The basis is Lev. 4:28:] 'When the sin which he has committed becomes known to him he shall bring [for his offering . . .]'

[O]   "[Joshua holds that this means]: One who repents when he becomes conscious of his sin is culpable [to bring an offering] for his unintentional sin.

[P]   "This excludes from culpability one who, [believing that his particular actions are permitted], would not stop what he was doing even though he knew [that to eat forbidden fat, or to offer the sacrifice on the Sabbath is a sin]." [Like the person who was told by the court what to do, this individual will not repent, for at the time of the action he believed that he had every right to perform it. Joshua holds that the rule of O does not apply to such an individual; he is not culpable at all.]

[Q]   R. Yose entered [the room in which] they [were discussing this issue, and the associates told him the argument which Haggai had proposed, J–K. They did not tell him Haggai's own answer, N–P.]

[R]   [Yose] said to them [i.e., the associates], "Why did you not answer [Haggai with Lev. 4:28]: 'When the sin which he has committed becomes known to him he shall bring [for his offering . . .]'?"

[S]   [Associates] said to him, "He [i.e., Haggai] posed the problem, and he himself solved it."

Haggai, I–K, proves that the associates' explanation of Joshua's position may be reduced to an absurdity. If the fact is simply that what the person thought was permitted turns out to be forbidden, then that individual should indeed be culpable for an unintentional sin, contrary to what Joshua says. Haggai claims, rather, that at issue for Joshua is not the person's assumption in performing an action, but his reaction when informed exactly what he ate. Believing that he has the right to eat heave-offering, the individual referred to at M. Ter. 8:1 would not stop eating. Such a person, says Joshua, may not be held culpable. He is different from an individual who, if told that he is eating heave-offering, immediately would stop doing so. Only this latter sort of individual is culpable for his actions. The unit concludes with an anecdote. Yose understood Joshua's position as well as did Haggai, and much better than did the associates.

8:2 [P: 8:1b; M. Ter. 8:1b]

[I]   *[If a priest] was standing and offering sacrifices at the altar, and it became known that he is the son of a divorcee or of a halusa—*

[J]   *R. Eliezer says, "All of the sacrifices which he [ever] had offered are invalid."*

[K]   *But R. Joshua declares [them] valid.*

[L]   *[If] it became known that he is blemished—his service [retroactively] is invalid.*

Joshua, K, holds that the service which the man performed under the assumption that he was a fit priest is valid. Just as in the first units of M. Ter. 8:1, Eliezer states that since objectively the man was not a qualified priest, his service retroactively is invalid. All can agree to the case of L. Aware of his physical defect, the person never could have perceived himself to be a legitimate priest. Thus there are no grounds upon which to deem his past service valid.

The Yerushalmi's first two units concentrate on Joshua's view, I + K, locating its source in Scripture and then drawing out its implications for a case in which the priest is in the middle of an act of sacrifice when he finds out that he is unfit. The final unit turns to a secondary question. If the priest who is found to be unfit is the high priest, there is a problem for those in exile because of manslaughter, Num. 35:22–28. The problem is addressed through a lengthy citation and analysis of T. Miq. 1:17–18.

[I.A]   R. Yohanan in the name of R. Yannai [said], "The following is one of the three [rabbinic] interpretations (so V, L, etc.; P: verses) that are clearly supported from [the actual text of] Scripture.

[B]   "[Dt. 26:3 states]: 'And you shall go to the priest who is in office at that time . . .'

[C]   "Is it possible that someone who is a priest now will not have priestly status at some later date? [To the contrary we should think that a person who turns out not to be a fit priest never was a fit priest.]

[D]   "[Answering C's question: Dt. 26:3] refers to [a priest] *who was standing and offering sacrifices at the altar and it became known that he is the son of a divorcee or of a* halusa, for [according to Joshua] his [past] service [at the altar] is valid [M. Ter. 8:1I + K]." [Thus, as Dt. 26:3 indicates, it is possible for someone to be a priest at one time, and not to be of priestly status at some later time. This accounts for Joshua's view at M. Ter. 8:1I–K.]

[E]   [A second scriptural basis for Joshua's position is given.] Said Rav, "[Joshua's view is based upon Moses' blessing of Levi, Dt. 33:11, which states, 'Bless, O Lord, his substance], and accept the work of his hands.'

[F]   "[This means that] as for anyone who is of the seed of Levi, his
       [past] service [at the altar] is valid."

[G]   [The interpretations of Rav, E–F, and Yohanan, D, are com-
       pared.] In the view of Rav, [Joshua holds that the past actions of
       a] priest [who turns out to be of impaired status] are valid only
       insofar as they concerned the offering of sacrifices. [But other
       aspects of the priestly duties which he performed are not valid,
       e.g., decisions concerning cleanness and uncleanness (PM). This
       is clear because according to Rav, the verse upon which Joshua's
       position is based refers only to the validity of the priest's service
       at the altar.]

[H]   But in the opinion of R. Yohanan, [Joshua's view that the past
       service of the priest is valid] applies to any [action of the] priest,
       [for Dt. 26 : 3 simply mentions a priest, without referring to a
       specific action].

[I]   In the view of Rav, [according to Joshua, the priest is deemed
       valid only insofar as to retain] holy things of the Temple [which
       had been given him before he turned out to be of impaired sta-
       tus. But he must return other holy things which he had been
       given, such as heave-offering.]

[J]   [But] in the opinion of R. Yohanan, [Joshua's view is that the
       priest who turns out to be invalid may retain] even[6] holy things
       of the country [i.e., those such as heave-offering and tithes which
       are designated outside of Temple].

[K]   In the opinion of Rav,[7] [Joshua's view applies] only during a pe-
       riod when the Temple exists, [for the verse on which his state-
       ment is based refers specifically to the validity of the priest's
       service at the Temple's altar].

[L]   [But] in the opinion of Yohanan, [Joshua's view applies] even
       now [that the Temple is not standing. For Dt. 26 : 3 refers to a
       priest who is in office 'at that time,' i.e., even a time at which the
       Temple does not exist.]

       Interpretations of two different verses of Scripture account for
       the position of Joshua, M. Ter. 8 : 1I + K. The implications of
       each interpretation are given, G–L. No attempt is made to show
       that one or the other provides the correct understanding of Joshua's

view. The issue here is the inner logic of Rav and Yohanan's interpretations of Scripture, not what Joshua actually would hold.

[**II.A**]   R. Jeremiah asked, "[Does the opinion of Joshua, that the past service of a priest who turns out not to be fit is valid, apply] even in these other cases [which follow]?

   [B]   "[Does Joshua hold that whatever he began to do as a fit priest, he may conclude doing even after he finds out that he is not fit, such that if] he had received [the blood of the offering, and at that point was informed that he is unfit] he [anyway may go ahead and] throw [it upon the altar], and that if he had taken the handful of meal offering [and at that point was told he is unfit] he [anyway] may offer it [upon the altar], and that [in the case of a bird offering, if] he had broken[8] its neck [and at that point found out that he is unfit, he anyway] may [go ahead and] sprinkle its blood?"

   [C]   [Claiming that Joshua holds that the priest may complete what he already has begun] R. Jacob bar Zibdi in the name of R. Isaac [said], "From what has been taught, they treated this case as comparable to that of *a sin offering which was stolen property—if this fact was not known to many [people], it still could effect atonement* [i.e., it is treated as a valid offering, M. Git. 5:5].

   [D]   "This means that [the priest] may receive [the blood, and even if it then turns out that he is unfit, may go ahead] and throw [it upon the altar]; he may take the handful of meal offering and then offer it [upon the altar]; he may break the neck [of the bird offering] and then sprinkle [the blood upon the altar]." [Joshua's position is that so long as many people do not know, the unfit priest may complete that which he began under the assumption that he was valid.]

The priest's right to complete what he began depends not upon his objective status, valid or disqualified, but whether or not the people in general will know that an unfit priest has served at the altar. If people will not know, then, out of respect to the altar, the unfit priest finishes what he validly began. His present actions, like his past service, are valid.

[**III.A**] [According to Num. 35:22–28, a person guilty of manslaughter goes into exile in a city of refuge. He must stay there until the high priest under whom he was judged guilty of manslaughter dies. According to M. Mak. 2:7, if at the time that judgment is passed there is no high priest in office, the person guilty of manslaughter must go into exile and never may return. The issue here is how we treat the case of a manslaughterer if the high priest under whom he was convicted turns out to be unfit. Is it as though that high priest had died, such that the guilty manslaughterer may return from exile, or is it like a case in which, at the time of the person's conviction, no high priest was in office, such that he never may return from exile?] R. Jacob bar Zibdi in the name of R. Isaac asked, "[If the high priest] *was standing and offering sacrifices at the altar, and it became known that he is the son of a divorcee or of a* halusah [M. Ter. 8:1I]—how do you adjudicate the case?

[B] "Is it like the case of [a high priest] who dies, such that a manslaughterer [convicted under that high priest's tenure] may return [from exile] to his own home?

[C] "Or [since this particular high priest never was fit] is it like the case of [a manslaughterer] whose judgment was passed [against him] when there was no high priest, such that he never may leave there [i.e., his place of refuge]?"

[D] Let us answer the question from this [T. Miq. 1:17]: **The water reservoir of Disqus in Yavneh was measured and found lacking [the forty *seahs* of water which comprise a valid immersion pool]. And R. Tarfon did declare clean [all of the things requiring preparation in purity which depended upon immersion in that particular pool]. But R. Aqiba declared [them all] unclean.**

[E] **Said R. Tarfon, "Since this immersion pool is in the assumption of being clean, it remains perpetually in this presumption of cleanness until it will be known for certain that it is made unclean."[9]**

[F][10] **Said R. Aqiba, "Since this immersion[11] pool is in the assumption of being unclean, it perpetually remains in the presumption of uncleanness until it will be known for sure that it is clean."**

[G]   [T. Miq. 1:18:] Said R. Tarfon, "To what is the matter to be likened? To one who was standing and offering [a sacrifice] at the altar and it became known that he is the son of a divorcee or the son of a *halusah*, for his [past] service is valid."

[H]¹²   Said R. Aqiba, "To what is the matter to be likened? To one who was standing and offering [a sacrifice] at the altar and it became known that he is disqualified by reason of a blemish, for his service is invalid [M. Ter. 8:1L]."

[I]   [T. Miq. 1:19:] Said R. Tarfon to him, "What is this, Aqiba? I draw an analogy to the son of a divorcee, but you draw an analogy to one disqualified by a blemish.

[J]   "Let us now see to what the matter is appropriately likened.

[K]   "If it is analogous to the son of a divorcee or to the son of a *halusah*, let us learn the law from the case of a son of a divorcee or the son of a *halusah*. If it is analogous to a blemished priest, let us learn the law from the case of the blemished priest."

[L]   Said R. Aqiba to him, "The unfitness affecting an immersion pool affects the immersion pool itself, and the unfit aspect of the blemished priest affects the blemished priest himself.

[M]   [T. Miq. 1:20:] "But let not the case of the son of a divorcee or the son of a *halusah* prove the matter, for his matter of unfitness derives from others [and not from himself].

[N]   "[Further] a ritual pool's unfitness [depends] on one only [i.e., the measurer] and the unfitness of a blemished priest [depends] on an individual only [i.e., the priest himself].

[O]   "But let not the son of a divorcee or the son of a *halusah* prove the matter, for the unfitness of this one must be established by a court."

[P]   They took a vote concerning the case and declared it unclean, [just as Aqiba had argued].

[Q]   Said R. Tarfon to R. Aqiba, "He who departs from you [i.e., from your teaching] is like one who departs from life."

[R]   [A conclusion is drawn from D–P to answer the question posed at A–C.] Said R. Yose, "This [i.e., O] means that [if] *he was standing and offering sacrifices at the altar and it became known that he is the son of a divorcee or of a* halusah [M. Ter. 8:1I], his service [at the altar] is deemed valid until he will be declared unfit by a court. [Thus he may complete his act of sacrifice. So long as a court has not made its declaration the priest is deemed fit. The implication is that the manslaughterer, A–C, was convicted during the tenure of a valid high priest. When a court finds the priest to be invalid, it is as though he has died, and the man returns from exile.]

[S]   "This [further] means that if [a priest] about whom there is a doubt whether or not he is clean or blemished[13] [performs a sacrifice], his service [at the altar] is valid.

[T]   "For you may deem [this possibly unclean or blemished priest] analogous to the son of a divorcee or the son of a *halusah* [who has not yet been declared unfit by a court]." [His service is valid until he is proven certainly to be unclean or blemished.]

[U]   But if you deem [the possibly unclean or possibly blemished priest] analogous to a [certainly] blemished priest, then his service [at the altar] is [immediately] invalid.

[V]   [U's alternative is shown to be correct. S–T is wrong.] Now [in the case of] an immersion pool, is there not a doubt [whether or not it is unclean]? [Certainly there is a doubt. Yet, as Aqiba argued, the pool anyway is deemed unclean. By analogy, if there is a question whether or not the priest is fit, his service should be invalid, as U has argued, contrary to S–T.]

[W]   [Another, unrelated, conclusion is drawn from O.] Said R. Hanina, "This means that all matters of impaired lineage must be determined by a court."

The question which sparks the long citation of T. Miq. 1:17–20, A–C, never is answered directly. Only the implications of R may be used to reason an answer to A–C's question. I have given these implications in brackets at R. I must assume that this is what the redactor of the pericope intended. Further implications of T. Miq. 1:17–20 follow, S–T + U–V and W. V's criticism of S–T is to the point. It notes that S–T is based upon a fact mentioned in T. Miq., that a court must decide upon the status of a priest of impaired lineage. In concentrating upon this fact, however, S–T ignores the larger theory proposed by Aqiba. What might be unclean must be deemed unclean. This means that the priest who might be unclean or blemished immediately is disqualified. His past service is invalid for as far back as the doubt existed, U–V.

8:3 [P: 8:1c; M. Ter. 8:2]

[M]   *And [in] all of these [cases given at M. Ter. 8:1A–F, if] they had heave-offering in their mouths [at the time they were notified that they were no longer fit to eat heave-offering]—*

[N]   *R. Eliezer says, "Let them swallow [it]."*

[O]   *But R. Joshua says, "Let them spit [it] out."*

[P]   *[If] they told someone [who had heave-offering in his mouth], "You have become unclean," or "The heave-offering has become unclean"—*

[Q]   *R. Eliezer says, "Let him swallow [it]."*

[R]   *But R. Joshua says, "Let him spit [it] out."*

[S]   *[If they told him], "You were unclean [at the time you began to eat the heave-offering," or, "The heave-offering was unclean,"*

[T]   *or [if] it became known that it [i.e., what he thought was heave-offering] is untithed produce, first tithe from which heave-offering [of the tithe] had not been taken, or second tithe or produce dedicated [to the Temple] which had not been redeemed,*

[U]   *or if he tasted a bedbug in his mouth—*

[V]   *lo, this one should spit it out.*

Joshua's view is consistent with what has preceded. As soon as the person knows that his actions are not permitted, he must stop doing them. Eliezer's view is that since the individual was permitted to begin the act, he may complete it. That this is Eliezer's position is proven by his agreement with Joshua at S–V. There it becomes clear that the individual should not even have begun to eat the produce. From the start it was unclean or otherwise forbidden. In such a case, even Eliezer has no basis on which to rule that the person may continue to eat.

The Yerushalmi's first unit correlates M. Ter. 8:2 with M. Ter.

8:1. It asks to which of M. 8:1A–F's cases does the dispute of
M. 8:2 apply. This entails an analysis of the theory behind Eliezer's view, a discussion which takes up the second half of this
first unit. Y. Ter. 8:3 **II–III** take up the more general issue suggested by the Mishnah. It discusses which sorts of foods people
may and may not eat.

[**I.A**]   Said R. Yohanan, "In which cases do [Eliezer and Joshua] disagree [concerning whether or not one who, while eating heave-
offering discovers that he should not be doing so, must spit out
what is in his mouth]?

[B]   "[They disagree] concerning the case of the woman [who is the
wife of a priest] and the slave [who belongs to a priest, M. Ter.
8:1A–D. [In these cases Eliezer holds that if the individuals
find out that they should not eat heave-offering, still they may
swallow what already is in their mouths. Joshua holds that they
must spit it out.]

[C]   "But in all other cases [i.e., that of the priest who discovers that
he is the son of a divorcee or a *halusah*], even R. Eliezer concedes [to Joshua, that the priest must spit out any heave-offering
which is in his mouth]."

[D]   Said R. Samuel bar R. Isaac, "The Mishnah itself indicates [that]
this [is so, i.e., that Eliezer concedes to Joshua in the case of the
priest].

[E]   "[M. Ter. 8:2T says]: *or [if] it became known that it [i.e., what
he thought was heave-offering] is untithed produce, first tithe
from which heave-offering of the tithe had not been removed,
second tithe or produce dedicated [to the Temple] which had not
been redeemed . . . [lo, this one should spit it out].*

[F]   "And R. Eliezer does not disagree, [stating that he may swallow it].

[G]   "[On the basis of this passage] what is the reasoning of R. Eliezer
[which allows him to say in certain cases that the individual may
swallow]?

[H]   "[This opinion applies] if [the individual] was permitted [to eat
the heave-offering] when he began [to eat it]." [As in the cases
cited at E, so for the priest who turns out to be the son of a

divorcee or of a *halusah,* the individual should not even have begun to eat. In all of these cases, therefore, Eliezer will agree with Joshua that heave-offering in the person's mouth must be spat out.]

[I]   [A different basis for Eliezer's view that the person may swallow is suggested.] It is taught: R. Nathan says, "It is not so that R. Eliezer holds [that they may swallow] because they were permitted [to eat heave-offering] when they began [to eat it].

[J]   "Rather, [the reason is] that R. Eliezer says, 'What is chewed up is comparable to that which already is swallowed. [Thus it makes no difference whether he swallows or spits out. Once the heave-offering is chewed up, the individual may just as well swallow it.]

[K]   "[This principle applies] even on the Sabbath, [such that if a person carried chewed up food in his mouth into the public domain, he is not culpable for carrying on the Sabbath],

[L][14]   "and even on Passover, [such that if he only chews the requisite volume of unleavened bread, but does not swallow it, he has fulfilled the obligation to eat unleavened bread],

[M]   "and even on the Day of Atonement, [such that a person who chews, but does not swallow, food is culpable for eating on that day],

[N]   "and [the principle applies] even to a Nazarite, [such that if the Nazirite chews, but does not swallow, grapes, he is culpable for breaking his vow of abstinence],

[O]   "and even to carrion, and even to improperly slaughtered meat, and even to [the meat of] unclean animals, and even to creeping things,[15] [such that a person who chews, but does not swallow, any of these forbidden foods still is culpable]."

Three distinct units have been juxtaposed at the redactional level to create a single discussion. The first unit, A–C, describes the limits of the dispute between Eliezer and Joshua, M. Ter. 8:2. To show that the Mishnah itself is clear on this matter, Samuel bar Isaac then suggests the theory which underlies Eliezer's view, D–H. Once this theory is suggested, I–J goes on to detail a second possible explanation of Eliezer's position. This explanation is unrelated to A–C. K–O goes with I–J. It details the implications of this latter understanding of Eliezer's view.

[**II.**A]   R. Hiyya in the name of R. Yohanan [says], "[As for] one who slaughters an animal and finds in its [stomach flesh from] an unclean animal—it is forbidden to eat [that unclean flesh].

[B]   "What is the scriptural basis [for this rule]?

[C]   " '[Flesh of a permitted] animal which is found in a [permitted] animal you may eat.' [16]

[D]   "But [Scripture does] not [say]: '[The flesh of] an unclean animal which is found in a [permitted] animal you may eat.' "

[E]   Said R. Jonah, "R. Hoshaya asked, 'What is the difference between [the case at A] and that of **mites found in lentils, gnats found in pods, or worms that are found in dates and dried figs,** [which one may eat, T. Ter. 7:11D]?'

[F]   "[The answer is that] there [in the case of insects, E] they are part of the fruit itself.

[G]   "But here [in the case of the unclean flesh, A] it is not part of the [permitted meat] itself."

[H]   As for the brine from pickled fish, [which contains fishblood]—before [the brine] has been strained, [the blood it contains is] permitted [for consumption. One may eat it along with the brine.]

[I]   But once it has been strained, [such that the blood is separate (PM)]—it is forbidden for consumption, [since one may not eat blood].

[J]   **Blood which is on a loaf [of bread]—he may scrape it off and eat it [i.e., the bread].**

[K]   **[If] it is discovered [already] between his teeth, he may eat it [i.e., the blood] and need not scruple [for having eaten blood; T. Ter. 7:11A–B].**

[L]   (Y. appears to be corrupt. Follow Jastrow, p. 378, s.v. *zbwzyn*.) Unclean mites, bees, and all unclean insects—

[M]   is it possible [that they should be deemed unclean] while they still are attached to a piece of fruit?

[N]   Scripture says, 'They are unclean' [see Lev. 11:20–23].

[O]   [This means that they are unclean] when they are animals unto themselves, but not when they are attached to fruit.

[P]   Is it possible [that they are deemed fit for consumption] even if they left [the piece of fruit] and then returned to it?

[Q]   Scripture says, 'They are unclean.'

[R]   [This means that they are unclean] even if they left [the piece of fruit] and then returned [to it].

[S]   R. Hiyya bar Ashi in the name of Rav [says], "Even if they [were attached to the piece of fruit] and moved to the edge [45c] of the food and then returned [to the center], lo, these are forbidden for consumption." [Once they move they are deemed autonomous creatures. The fact that they return to their original position does not change this.]

[T][17]   [Returning to the issue of A] Abba bar R. Huna in the name of R. Yohanan [says], "[As for] one who slaughters an animal and finds in it the flesh of a pig—[the pig] is permitted for consumption, [contrary to what A said]."

[U]   But R. Jonah said, "It is forbidden for consumption.

[V]   "What is the reason?

[W]   "[Scripture states]: The flesh of an 'animal' which is found in an animal you may eat.

[X]   "But you may not eat the flesh of an [unclean] bird which is found in an animal, and you may not eat the flesh of an unclean animal which is found in a [clean] animal."

If something which normally is forbidden is deemed an integral part of permitted food, it too may be eaten. This is illustrated at E–G (for the case of A–D), at H–I, J–K and L–S. T–X returns to the issue of A–D.

[III.A]   [M. Ter. 8:2U, which states that a person who tastes a bedbug in his mouth must spit out the food], does not mean that this applies only to a bedbug.

[B]   Rather [he must spit out] anything [the eating of] which brings a
person's soul to rest.

The bedbug, M. Ter. 8:2U, is only an example. The same rule
applies to other insects as well.

8:4 [P: 8:2; M. Ter. 8:3]

[W]   *[If] he was eating a cluster of grapes [as a chance meal, free of
liability to tithe] and entered from the garden into the courtyard
[at which point the grapes normally are subject to the separation
of tithes (M. Ma. 3:5-6)]—*

[X]   *R. Eliezer says, "Let him finish [eating the cluster without
tithing]."*

[Y]   *But R. Joshua says, "He may not finish it [unless he separates
tithes]."*

[Z]   *[If he was eating a cluster of grapes as a chance meal and] dusk
fell on the eve of the Sabbath [at which point the produce he is
eating is subject to the separation of tithes (M. Ma. 4:2)]—*

[AA]   *R. Eliezer says, "Let him finish [eating the cluster]."*

[BB]   *But R. Joshua says, "He may not finish it."*

The individual was permitted to begin eating the food without
separating tithes. For this reason, even if he enters a courtyard
or if Sabbath begins, he may finish eating it without tithing. So
Eliezer. Joshua's concern is the objective fact of the food's status.
Once it normally would be subject to tithes, the individual must
tithe before he eats it. This is the case even though he already
had begun eating without the obligation to tithe. The Yerushalmi
concentrates on Eliezer's view. In its first unit, it finds a correlation between that view and the position of Tarfon, M. Ma. 3:9.
In this way the Yerushalmi reads together two distinct pericopae
of the Mishnah in order to locate an overarching legal theory.
The second unit makes explicit the theory of Eliezer's view,
which I have given and which is implicit in the first unit. Nathan
rejects this understanding and, citing T. Ter., suggests a different way of interpreting Eliezer's view.

[I.A]   There we have learned [M. Ma. 3:9]: *"A grapevine which is planted in a courtyard—[the householder] takes the entire cluster of grapes [from the vine and eats it, without incurring the obligation to tithe]. And [this is] also [the case] with a pomegranate [picked from a tree growing in a courtyard], as well as for a melon [picked from a vine growing in a courtyard]"—the words of R. Tarfon.*

[B]   R. Zeira [and] R. Hiyya in the name of R. Yohanan say,[18] "[The view of] R. Tarfon is in agreement with [that of] R. Eliezer [M. Ter. 8:3X, who states that upon entering the courtyard with grapes, an individual need not tithe].

[C]   "[The reason that they agree is that like Eliezer in M. Ter.] R. Tarfon [in M. Ma.] says, 'They deem [the status of the food as regards tithes] at the conclusion [of the person's] eating it to be the same as its status at the beginning' [i.e., if the individual could eat some portion of the food without tithing, he may eat it all without incurring liability to tithe.]"

[D]   [A second explanation for the agreement between the two authorities is suggested.] R. Ila [and] R. Isa in the name of R. Yohanan say, "[The view of] R. Tarfon is in agreement with [that of] R. Eliezer.

[E]   "[The reason that they agree is that like Eliezer] R. Tarfon says, 'They deemed a single act of eating [any piece of fruit which normally] would require two or three [individual] acts of eating [i.e., because like a grape cluster the produce is segmented] to be comparable to a single act of eating.'" [This means that eating any small part of the piece of fruit is comparable to eating the whole thing. For Eliezer, we therefore need not distinguish between that which the individual eats before he enters the courtyard and what he eats afterwards. For Tarfon, concomitantly, there is no difference between the case of someone who picks individual grapes from a vine in a courtyard and one who picks the whole cluster.]

B–C and D–E each suggests the basis for the comparable positions of Eliezer, M. Ter. 8:3, and Tarfon, M. Ma. 3:9, cited at A. Each interpretation is given in the name of Yohanan. The underlying question facing the authorities of the pericope thus seems to have been why Yohanan held that Eliezer's and Tarfon's views were alike.

[II.A]   What is the reasoning of R. Eliezer [who states, M. Ter. 8:3, that the individual may finish eating without separating tithes]?

[B]   [He reasons that] since when he began [eating the produce he was] permitted [to do so without being obligated to tithe, he may also finish eating it without tithing].

[C]   [Disagreeing,] it is taught: **R. Nathan says,** "It is not that R. Eliezer said [that he may finish eating without tithing] because when he began [eating he was] permitted [to do so without being obligated to tithe].

[D]   "**Rather, [at M. Ter. 8:3] R. Eliezer [simply] says, 'The person may wait until the end of the Sabbath, or until he leaves the courtyard, and then may finish eating'**" [T. Ter. 8:10E].

C–D rejects B. According to Nathan, Eliezer's view is that the process by which food becomes subject to the separation of tithes is reversible. When the person leaves the courtyard, or the Sabbath ends, the produce reverts to its original status, so that it is again exempt from the separation of tithes.

8:5 [P: 8:3a; M. Ter. 8:4]

[A]   *Wine in the status of heave-offering which is left uncovered—let it be poured out [lest a snake drank from it and deposited in it venom].*

[B]   *And there is no need to state [that this is the law in the case] of unconsecrated [wine which is left uncovered].*

[C]   *Three [kinds of] liquids are forbidden [for consumption] on account of being left uncovered:*

[D]   *(1) water, (2) wine, and (3) milk.*

[E]   *But all other liquids are permitted [for consumption, even if they are left uncovered].*

[F]   *Remaining [uncovered for] how long renders them [i.e., the liquids listed at D] forbidden?*

[G]   *Long enough for a snake to leave a nearby [hiding-] place and drink [from them].*

The longest grouping of materials that we have so far encountered in the Yerushalmi is based upon what, in the Mishnah, is a very simple idea. If liquids are left uncovered, a snake might drink from them and thereby deposit venom in them. To prevent people from being poisoned, the Mishnah rules that people may not drink from liquids which have been left uncovered. In its twenty units, the Yerushalmi discusses every conceivable aspect of this rule. Through reports of several actual incidents, it highlights the importance of being careful not to drink liquids which might be contaminated by venom.

[I.A]   R. Jacob bar Aha [and] R. Simeon bar Ba in the name of R. Hanina [say], "Wine that was left uncovered must be spilled out, even if it is in the status of heave-offering.

[B][19]   "A stew that was prepared with water that had been left uncovered, even if [the food itself] is in the status of heave-offering, must be spilled out.

[C]   "And there is no need to say [that B] applies in the case of unconsecrated food [cooked with water which had been left uncovered]."

[D][20]   Said R. Yose, "The Mishnah [itself] has said this [i.e., what you report in your own name, C]: *Wine in the status of heave-offering which is left uncovered—let it be poured out. And there is no need to state [that this rule applies] in the case of unconsecrated [wine which is left uncovered*; M. Ter. 8:4A–B]."

[E]   [On a new topic] associates in the name of R. Yohanan [say], "Wine that was left uncovered—it is forbidden to retain[21] it [in one's possession, instead of spilling it out].

[F]   "And if one retained it and it turned to vinegar, it [still] is forbidden [for consumption].

[G]   "[Likewise] figs and grapes that were bitten [by snakes and that are forbidden for consumption, M. Ter. 8:6]—it is forbidden to retain them [in one's possession, lest someone eat them].

[H]   "But [by contrast to F] if one retained them and they dried out, they are permitted [for consumption, since the venom will have dried out].

[I][22]   In the town of R. Hiyya the elder they would perforate figs [with what appeared to be teeth marks], so that the associates would not eat them.

[J]   But R. Hiyya the elder would eat them, for in his opinion they were not forbidden [for consumption].

[K]   There was an incident [in which a person who ate these figs was poisoned], but even so [Hiyya] did not deem them forbidden.

[L]   [Contrary to Hiyya's ruling] is it not taught: **[If] one saw a bird peck at a fig, or a mouse gnaw at a watermelon, [even so the fruit] is forbidden. For I say, "Lest [the bird or mouse] ate at a place which already had been bitten [by a snake"; T. Ter. 7:17]?**

[M]   [K + L is explained.] Had the person [actually] guarded the produce [so as to know that before the bird or mouse gnawed at it, it contained no teeth marks of snakes]? [No, the person had not. This accounts for the fact that that produce is deemed forbidden. But in the case of the produce Hiyya the elder ate, it had been guarded, such that he knew for certain that the teeth marks did not derive from snakes. For this reason alone he did not deem that produce forbidden.]

The Yerushalmi presents a general catalog of rules pertinent to M. Ter. 8:4. The units are A–D, E–H and I–K + L–M.

[**II.A**]   R. Isaac bar Nahman in the name of R. Joshua b. Levi [says], "[Wine which is] sharp [in taste], or bitter, or sweet is not subject to the law of uncovered liquids."

[B]   [Carrying forward A] R. Simon in the name of R. Joshua b. Levi [says], "[Wine which is] sharp, bitter, or sweet is not subject to the law of uncovered liquids or to the restrictions that apply to wine which might have been used for a libation."

[C]   R. Simon holds that 'sharp [wine]' refers to spiced wine (*qwndytwn*), 'bitter [wine]' refers to absinthium (so Jastrow, p. 1195, s.v. *psyntytwn*), and 'sweet [wine]' refers to boiled wine.

[D]   R. Joshua bar Zidal had boiled wine which had been left unsupervised in the custody of a gentile.

[E]   He asked R. Yannai b. R. Ishmael [whether the wine was forbidden under the law of wine which might have been used for a libation].

[F]   [Yannai] said to him, "Thus said R. Simeon b. Laqish, 'Sweet [wine] is not subject to the law of uncovered liquids or to the restrictions which apply to wine that might have been used for a libation.'"

[G]   R. Yannai b. R. Ishmael [drank some sweet wine which had been left uncovered and] became sick.

[H]   R. Zeira, R. Hoshaya, R. Bun bar Kahana and R. Hanania, the associates of the rabbis, went up to visit him.

[I]   They saw R. Joshua bar Zidal sitting [there].

[J]   They said, "This one [i.e., R. Yannai b. R. Ishmael] knows a tradition [concerning the law].

[K]   "And this master [i.e., R. Joshua bar Zidal] knows a particular incident [which would indicate what the law should be].

[L]   "Come, let us ask him [what the law for sweet wine is]."

[M]   R. Yannai b. R. Ishmael said to them, "Thus said R. Simeon b. Laqish, 'Sweet [wine] is not subject to the laws of uncovered liquids or the restrictions which apply to wine that might have been used for a libation.'"

[N]   R. Zeira said to him, "Perhaps R. Simeon b. Laqish did not intend this rule to be applied in practice, but simply believed that it was a reasonable assumption [that such wine would not be drunk by snakes or used for a libation]?"

[O]   [Yannai b. R. Ishmael] replied to him, "No. [Simeon b. Laqish intended the rule] for actual practice, such that you may depend upon what he said [so as to drink sweet wine that was left uncovered or in the hands of a gentile]."

[P]   When they left [Yannai's house] R. Ila met R. Bun bar Kahana.

[Q]   [Ila] said to him, "How much you love a tradition [taught in the name of an Amora, such as follows at S–T],

[R]   "but is this [rule which follows] not taught in the Mishnah itself?

[S]   "For R. Hiyya taught: Why is boiled wine prepared by gentiles forbidden [under the restriction of wine which might have been used for a libation]? Because initially it was [regular] wine [and so forbidden under that restriction].

[T]²³   "Why is vinegar prepared by gentiles forbidden [under the laws of wine which might have been used for a libation]? Because it is produced from wine."

[U]   [Completing the thought begun at Q–R,] said R. Yose, "Mishnah says this explicitly [M. A.Z. 2:3]: *[These things that belong to gentiles are forbidden, and it is forbidden to have any benefit at all from them:] wine or vinegar of gentiles that at first was wine.*"

[V]   [We turn to a new discussion of the same issue.] R. Imi had visitors.

[W]   He said to them, "If boiled wine of mine was left uncovered, I would [not]²⁴ give it to you to drink."

[X]   R. Bibi said to him, "Bring some [boiled wine which was left uncovered], and I will drink [it]."

[Y]   [Imi] said, "Let anyone who wishes to die go to his own house and die."

[Z]   Bar Yudani left some of his spiced wine uncovered.

[AA]   He went and asked rabbis [whether it was permitted to drink it].

[BB]   They said, "It is forbidden."

[CC]   But did not R. Isaac bar Nahman in the name of R. Joshua b. Levi say [above, A], "[Wine which is] sharp [= spiced], bitter or sweet is not subject to the law of uncovered liquids"?

[DD]   [To solve the apparent contradiction between BB and CC] rabbis of Caesaria in the name of R. Hiyya bar Titus [say], "[If left uncovered, these types of wine are deemed permitted only] if one mixed into them one-third part ground frankincense [in two-thirds wine]." [This prevents snakes from drinking the wine.]

Certain types of wine, A, are not subject to the rule of M. Ter. 8:4. The rules for these wines, as well as stories in which they figure, are provided, A–C, D–O, P + Q–U, V–Y, and Z–DD. Within these distinct units, F does not answer D–E's question, an odd state of affairs.

[III.A]   They asked in the presence of R. Abbahu, "Boiled wine which is left uncovered—what is [the rule whether or not it is subject to the restriction of uncovered liquids]?"

[B]   He said to them, "R. Yohanan [did not know] whether sweet wine (*qrynh*) is subject [to that restriction]. Yet you ask me [such a question as A]? Is it not obvious that [the rule for] boiled wine likewise [should be in question]?"

[C]   [Abbahu] went in and asked R. Isaac[25] [about the rule for boiled wine (PM)].

[D]   He said, "It is forbidden [under the rule for uncovered liquids]."

[E]   [Once this was said], R. Abbahu recalled that R. Yohanan had [explicitly] said, "[Boiled wine is] forbidden [under the rule for uncovered liquids]."

The unit carries forward the issue of what sorts of wine are subject to the laws of uncovered liquids. The larger point which emerges, however, is a statement about Yohanan. Contrary to what Abbahu initially thinks, B, Yohanan did know the law, E.

[IV.A]   R. Jacob bar Aha [and] R. Imi in the name of R. Eleazar [say], "If a person continually enters and leaves [a house in which there is an open container of wine, the wine remains] permitted [for consumption, under the theory that it has been guarded such that a snake could not have drunk from it]."

[B]   The wine reservoir of Bar Netoza was left uncovered.

[C]   He went and asked R. Ba bar Mamel [whether the wine was forbidden under the rule of uncovered liquids].

[D]   [Ba bar Mamel] said to him, "If someone[26] was going in and out of the room, [the wine remains] permitted."

[E]   R. Jacob bar Aha [and] R. Imi in the name of R. Eleazar [say], "If someone slept [in the room with the wine], it [remains] permitted, [since snakes are afraid of the person sleeping there]."

[F]   [There was a dispute between] R. Hanania and R. Joshua b. Levi.

[G]   One said, "[If] a person sleeps [by the wine], it [remains] permitted."

[H]   But the other says, "[Even if] someone sleeps [by the wine reservoir, if it is uncovered], it is forbidden."

[I]   But it is not known which [authority] holds which opinion.

[J]   It is logical to say that R. Hanania holds that if a person sleeps [near the wine], it [remains] permitted.

[K]   For the position of R. Eleazar [as at E, above,] always is like that of R. Hanania.

[L]   [Moving the discussion to new grounds] R. Yose b. Saul told this story:

[M]   A certain woman loved to perform many good deeds, [but her husband hated such acts of charity]. One time a needy person came to her and she placed food before him. While he was eating, her husband came and chased him away. So she went and hid [the needy person] in the attic. [Then] she gave her husband food so that he could eat. [As he began eating] he fell deeply asleep. [While he slept] a serpent came and ate from [the food] which was before him. But [the person in the attic] saw [all of this]. When [the husband] awoke he got up and desired to eat that which was before him. [The person in the attic] began to speak with him [i.e., to warn him not to eat the food from which the snake had tasted].

[N]   [In light of this story can we say that if someone] sleeps [near the open wine that it remains] permitted? [Obviously not, for from the story it is clear that even if someone is sleeping nearby, a snake will eat food which is left open.]

[O]   [The conclusion based on the story is rejected. The situation described at M was unusual since that particular snake] was used to being in the house, [around those particular people]. [It therefore was not frightened by the sleeping man. In usual instances, however, snakes are frightened away, and therefore the uncovered wine or food remains permitted.]

[P]   [The story, M, raises a different issue.] Is [the woman] not rendered forbidden to her husband because she was alone [with the poor person up in the attic]?

[Q]   Since she is not suspected of this [i.e., shedding blood, as explained at R], she is not suspected of this [i.e., committing adultery].

[R]   [The fact that one who is not suspected of having shed blood likewise is not deemed an adulteress is proven by Ez. 23:45]: '[But righteous men shall pass judgment on them with the sentence of adulteresses, and with the sentence of women that shed blood]; because they are adulteresses, and blood is upon their hands.' [Thus if a woman does not have blood upon her hands, she need not be deemed an adulteress, even if she was alone with a man.]

From types of wine which are not subject to the law of uncovered liquids we move to circumstances in which uncovered wine is not subject to that law. A is illustrated by B–D. E serves as the basis for F–K. Its law is challenged by M + N, but is salvaged by O. P–R relates to M, but is not pertinent to the larger set of issues before us.

[V.A]   *M'SH B:* A butcher in Sepporis would give Israelites carrion and improperly slaughtered meat to eat. One time he drank wine on the Sabbath eve, went up to the roof, and fell off and died. [As he lay dead on the ground,] dogs licked up his blood.

[B]   They came and asked R. Hanina, "What is the rule whether or not we may lift him up away from the dogs, [and thereby carry on the Sabbath, which normally is forbidden]?"

[C]   [Hanina] answered them [with Ex. 22:31], "'You shall not eat any flesh that is torn by beasts in the field; you shall cast it to the dogs.'

[D]   "Now this person would steal [carrion] from dogs in order to feed Israelites."

[E]   [Concluding his reasoning, Hanina] said to them, "Let him rest [where he is], for [the dogs] are eating that which already belongs to them."

Perhaps we are to think that the wine the butcher drank, A, had been left uncovered, such that he was poisoned and therefore fell from the roof. Except for this provisional explanation, I see no reason, contextual or ideational, for the placement of this unit here.

[VI.A]   *M'SH B:* A certain pious man would gulp down wine which had been left uncovered. Once [after doing this] he suffered from a

[high] fever [which did not go away. As a result] they saw him on
the Day of Atonement sitting and expounding, with a glass of
water in his hand. [Even though this is forbidden on the Day
of Atonement, because of the fever, he needed to cool his brow
with the water. This was the price the pious man paid for ignoring the rules for uncovered liquids.]

[B]   A bottle of wine belonging to a certain man was left uncovered.
He went out on the eve of the great fast [i.e., the night before
the Day of Atonement] to spill it out. Someone saw him and said
to him, "Give [the wine] to me and I will drink it." He said to
him, "No. It has been left uncovered [and therefore is forbid-
den]." He said to him, "Give it to me [anyway], for the master
of [the coming fast day, i.e., God, who commanded that we prepare for the fast by eating and drinking] will stand [by me, to prevent my being injured by venom which might be in the wine]."

[C]   He had not even drunk the wine, [but only had tasted it], when
[already] he became sick.

Piety will not protect one from the danger of drinking wine
which contains snake venom. The point is made twice, in the
story at A and in the incident reported at B–C.

[VII.A]   [45D] R. Jeremiah in the name of B. Hiyya bar Ba [says], "All
[types of] venom cause sores to appear [on the skin]. But the
venom of a snake kills, [which other venoms do not do]."

[B]   (Supply from B. A.Z. 29b) R. Hiyya said, "One should not ask
[whether or not it is permitted to drink a liquid which was] left
uncovered."

[C]   R. Jeremiah asked R. Zeira [whether or not a particular bottle of
wine which had been left uncovered was forbidden].

[D]   [The Talmud interjects in amazement: Zeira is] the authority behind this tradition [B, yet Jeremiah] has asked him [whether or
not the uncovered wine is permitted]!

[E]   [The following story proves that, contrary to D, Zeira would be
a good person to ask concerning whether or not wine which has
been left uncovered is permitted.] R. Zeira was falling asleep as
he sat and ate. [As he fell asleep] he reached out and placed his

hand on the goblet [filled with wine]. He said to those [in the room with him], "Light the candle." They lit it and found a serpent which looked like a hair wrapped around [the goblet]. Zeira said [to the snake], "Evil one, [if] I had not been careful about you, [certainly I would have died]."

A and B–D + E describe the dangers of drinking wine which might contain snake venom. The point, E, is that the individual must be very careful, even in a circumstance under which one would not expect a snake to have the opportunity to deposit venom in wine.

[VIII.A] Said R. Imi, "We must be careful not to do those things about which people tend to be apprehensive.

[B] "[For instance] a person should not put coins in his mouth, [place] prepared foods under a bed, [insert] a piece of bread under his armpit, or leave a knife stuck in a radish or citron."

[C] Said R. Yose b. R. Bun, "All perspiration which derives from humans is a poison which causes death, except for sweat from the face."

[D] When they asked R. Jonathan [about B and Yose's claim, C], he said, "I am a surety upon your life [i.e., you can bet your life on it]."

[E] [R. Yannai explains why it is not reasonable to engage in activities, like those listed at B, which could prove dangerous.] Said R. Yannai, "[In doing these things] if one plucks [i.e., gains anything], he plucks [only] a piece of coal [i.e., nothing of value]. But if he loses, he loses a pearl [i.e., life itself]."

[F] [Simeon b. Laqish expresses the same idea as E.] Said R. Simeon b. Laqish, "If you were to sell yourself to *lanistae*, [who purchase men to participate in gladiatorial contests], you would sell yourself for a high price. But [if you unnecessarily endanger yourself] you are selling yourself for a trifle."

A–C provides a catalog of five folk health hints, to which even Jonathan subscribes, D. E + F makes the same point twice. It is silly to take one's life lightly.

[IX.A]   It is taught: **Water which has been left uncovered—one may not sprinkle his house with it [in order to lay down the dust], may not spill it out in the public way, may not give it to a gentile**[27] **to drink, and may not give to an animal owned by his fellow. But**[28] **he may water his own cattle with it.**

[B]   Water which has been left uncovered—**one may not mix plaster with it,** and may not use it to wash clothes, may not rinse pots and pans with it, and, there is no need to say, **may not wash his face, hands, or legs with it.**

[C]   **Others say, "They did not say [that one may not wash with it] except where he has a cut"** [T. Ter. 7:14A–F, with slight variation].

[D]   [The Talmud explains that there is no disagreement between B and C.] One's face is deemed to be like a cut, [such that one should not wash it with water which was left uncovered]. One's fingers and toes [likewise] are like cuts.

[E]   Water which has been left uncovered—one may not use it to prepare dough [see T. Ter. 7:13D–G].

[F]   **R. Nehemia says, "[If] one baked it, this is permitted, since the venom of a snake is destroyed in fire"** [T. Ter. 7:13H–I].

[G]   [Qualifying F] said R. Simon in the name of R. Joshua b. Levi, "[F applies] if [after being baked] the bread does not fall [i.e., fail to rise].

[H]   "But if it falls, it is forbidden, [since we attribute the dough's failure to rise to be a result of the venom it still contains]."

[I]   All agree that [even if] **water [which was left uncovered] is heated up, it [remains] forbidden** [T. Ter. 7:13P].

[J]   What is the difference between bread, [such that when it is cooked the venom is destroyed, F], and water, [such that even if it is heated, it remains forbidden, I]?

[K][29]   Here [in the case of the bread] the fire has full power ($šwlṭ$)

[L]   But here [in the case of water which is heated] the fire does not have full power.

[M]   Here [in the case of water being heated] the vessel separates [the water from the fire].

[N]   But here [in the case of bread being baked] there is no utensil to separate [the bread from the fire. In this case therefore the venom is burned up.]

[O]   [Samuel claims that heated water always is safe to drink, contrary to I.] Samuel says, "What will this evil creature [i.e., a snake] do to me? For I drink only water which has been heated."

[P]   [This explains that Samuel does not contradict I. He suggests a qualification. Samuel's] point is that if the water was cold and then was heated up, [so long as it is hot, it remains] permitted [see T. Ter. 7 : 13Q–R (PM)].

[Q]   [Hanina offers a further consideration.] Said R. Hanina,[30] "That evil one [i.e., the snake] is clear-minded [i.e., wise]. Therefore [the snake] does not drink water which had been warmed up but then cooled down."

[R]   This is to say: Hot water which cooled down is permitted [i.e., not subject to the restriction governing water which was left uncovered].

[S]   [Disagreeing with the preceding] R. Abbahu in the name of R. Yohanan [says], "Whether [the water had been heated and then cooled down] or [never had been heated], it is forbidden [under the rule for uncovered liquids]."

[T]   A Tannaitic teaching supports the position of R. Yohanan.

[U]   [T. Ter. 7 : 13Q–R reads]: **[As for] hot water [in an uncovered pot]—as long as it releases steam, it is not subject to [the law of uncovered liquids].**

[V]   [This means that], as for water which was left uncovered, even though one heated it up, [once it has cooled down], it is forbidden [under the rule for uncovered water].

We turn to the rules for water which has been left uncovered. The Yerushalmi cites and expands upon T. Ter., A–D + E–N. These latter materials, E–N, introduce O–V, in which Amoraim argue the same issue.

[X.A]   **Water used for pickling vegetables, water used in boiling foods, and water used in soaking lupines,[31] lo, it is permitted [i.e., not subject to the rule for uncovered liquids].**

[B]   **Water in which one soaked pickled vegetables, foods which
had been boiled or lupines, lo, this is forbidden [under the
rule for uncovered liquids].**

[C]   **[Water] in which one rinsed** grapes or **quince for a sick person is forbidden [under the rule for uncovered liquids;** T. Ter.
7:13J–N, with variations].

The Yerushalmi cites T. Ter. 7:13J–N. Once the water is used
for pickling, it no longer is deemed to be water. Consequently it
is not subject to the law of uncovered liquids, A. The processes
described at B–C do not change the liquid's status from that of
water. Therefore it still is subject to the law.

[**XI.A**]   [A container of wine covered with] *a wine strainer* [M. Ter.
8:7A]—

[B]   **R. Nehemiah**[32] says, "If the upper vat [into which the wine to
be strained is poured] was covered, even though the lower [vat,
into which the wine is being strained], is uncovered—[lo, this is
permitted]."

[C]   R. Judah says, "**If the bottom [vat, into which the wine is being strained] was covered [by the strainer], even though the
top [of the strainer, where the wine to be strained is poured],
was uncovered—[the wine] is not subject [to the rule of uncovered liquids;** T. Ter. 7:13A–B, attributed to Nehemiah].

[D]   "**For the venom of a snake is like a matted web, which remains
above, [trapped in the strainer]**"; T. Ter. 7:13C].

[E]   Said R. Eleazar, "[C–D applies] if he did not mix up [the wine in
the strainer]. But if he stirred it up, then [the wine which has been
strained into the lower vessel] is forbidden, [for the venom would
have been broken up so that it could pass through the strainer]."

The Yerushalmi offers an expanded version of T. Ter. 7:13. It
adds B, unknown to the Tosefta, and the clarification at E.

[**XII.A**]   **A bottle**[33] **in its case—[liquids in it remain] permitted** [T.:
forbidden].

[B]   **If [the bottle] is covered but not corked, [the liquid in it] is forbidden.**

[C]   **Corked but not covered—**

[D]   **if the cork sticks out [of the neck of the bottle, the liquid is] permitted** [= T. Ter. 7:16C–D + O–P].

[E]   [How far out of the bottle need the cork protrude?] Two Amoraim [dispute this question].

[F]   One says, "Far enough that the bottle can be lifted by its cork."

[G]   The other says, "[It must be so tight that] the whorl of a spindle [i.e., a very thin rod] cannot enter, [but one need not be able to lift the jar by its cork]."

[H]   Said R. Ba, "One who wishes to do well should both cork and cover [the bottle]."

The Yerushalmi answers a question left open by T. Ter. 7:16, E–G. H suggests a general consideration pertinent to C–D.

[XIII.A]   **An [open] bottle [filled with liquid] which they placed in a chest, a strong box or a cupboard,** and which they forgot about but then came back and found—**[the liquid] is forbidden.**

[B]   **[If] he checked [the storage places, to see that there were no snakes in them] and afterwards placed [the open vessel there—the liquid] is permitted** [T. Ter. 7:16A–B, with slight variations].

The Yerushalmi cites the Tosefta, adding the explanatory gloss at A.

[XIV.A]   An incident came before Rabbi in which an individual had seen [a snake] opening and closing [the top to a vessel].

[B]   [Rabbi] said, "Because of this [single] evil [snake, which is able to open covers], should we deem covers not to be an effective seal?" [No. This snake was an exception, and therefore we must continue to deem liquids in covered containers permitted for consumption.]

[C]   [Agreeing with Rabbi,] said R. Mana, "It does not make sense
to do more than to deem [the liquid uncovered in] that particular
case [34] forbidden." [Since snakes normally are not able to reclose
jars, there is no reason to assume that liquids in covered vessels
contain snake venom.]

Mana, C, repeats what Rabbi, B, already has said.

[XV.A]   [M. A.Z. 2:6 states that milk which a gentile milked when no
Israelite watched him is forbidden for consumption. The question here is why this is the case.] Said R. Jeremiah, "Milk which
a gentile milked—why is it forbidden?

[B]   "Because it is suspect of being mixed with milk from unclean
animals."

[C]   "[We know that the reason is suspicion that the milk derives
from unclean animals and not that the gentile may have left the
milk uncovered, because] we have learned [T. A.Z. 4:11P]: **An
Israelite may sit at the other side of his corral, and a gentile
may milk the [Israelite's] cows and bring the milk to him, and
he need not scruple.**" [In a case in which no unclean animals
are present, milk gotten by the gentile is permitted, even though
the Israelite did not watch the milking process. Thus it is clear
that milk of gentiles normally is forbidden because of the possibility that it derives from unclean animals, not because it might
have been left uncovered.]

[D]   [This disagrees with A–C.] Rabba in the name of R. Judah [and]
R. Simon in the name of R. Joshua b. Levi [say], "Milk which a
gentile milked—why is it forbidden?

[E]   "Because it is suspect of having been left uncovered."

[F]   But [if E is the case, then one need simply] let the milk sit out
[to turn into cheese. If there is venom in it, the venom should
float to the top and be visible.]

[G]   [Explaining why F is not viable,] said R. Samuel bar R. Isaac,
"[Even if no venom appeared on top of the cheese, it still would
have to be deemed forbidden] because of the venom which might
remain within the holes [in the cheese, and which would not be
visible at the surface]."

M. Ter. 8:4 states that milk which is left uncovered may not be
consumed. Is this the reason that M. A.Z. 2:6 holds that milk
which a gentile milked is forbidden? The Yerushalmi offers two
different answers, one in the name of Jeremiah, B–C, and the
other cited by Rabba and Simon, D–E. This second answer is
disputed, F versus G.

[XVI.A]   There are three types of venom, a venom which sinks [to the
bottom of liquid], a venom which floats, and a venom which remains [slightly below the surface of the liquid] like a web of mesh.

[B]   In the days of R. Jeremiah a reservoir [of wine] was left open in
the study hall.

[C]   The first ones drank from it and did not die.

[D]   [But the ones who drank from it] later on did die.

[E]   I [can explain this by] saying, "[The wine contained] the sort of
venom which sinks to the bottom."

[F]   [The point is made a second time.] Workers were in the field. A
jug of water was left uncovered. The first ones who drank from it
did not die. [But the ones who drank from it] after [them] died.

[G]   [To explain this] I can say, "[The water contained] the sort of
venom which sinks to the bottom."

[H]   A Tannaitic teaching makes the same point [T. Ter. 7:17, with
variations: As for] a jug [of wine] which was left uncovered,
and so **a watermelon at which [a mouse] gnawed,** and the first
group [of people] ate and drank [these things without being
harmed]—[even so] other people should not eat or drink [of
them].

[I]   [For] I can reason, "[The food contains] the sort of venom which
sinks to the bottom."

[J]   **[A jug] of wine which was left uncovered, and [later] ten men
drank from it [without being poisoned]—[even so] it is forbid-**
den for others to eat or drink after them.

[K]   [For] I can reason, "[The wine contains] the sort of venom which
sinks to the bottom."

A certain sort of venom sinks to the bottom of liquid, A. This claim is illustrated four times, B–E, F–G, H–I, and J–K.

[XVII.A]   **Five liquids [are not rendered forbidden] under the law of uncovered liquids: brine, vinegar, fish brine, oil, and honey.**

[B]   **R. Simeon prohibits** [for consumption] honey [which was left uncovered, contrary to A; T. Ter. 7:12. In T., Simeon rejects the whole list.]

[C]   Sages [of A] concede to R. Simeon that if one saw [a snake] bite at [honey, it is forbidden for consumption].

[D]   [That honey may contain venom is illustrated by the following.] R. Hinena bar Papa had a jar of honey in his hand. He had not even had time to ask [whether or not it was forbidden on account of having been left uncovered] when it shattered in his hand. [Presumably it did contain venom, which caused the vessel to break. This supports Simeon, B, who states that honey is subject to the rule for uncovered liquids.]

[E]   [To explain why covered jars are deemed impermeable to snakes,] Rav and Samuel, the two of them, say, "The earth has been given permission to split open, [such that a snake can enter the ground]. But vessels have not been given permission to split open, [such that a snake can get inside and then break out again without leaving a mark]."

[F]   R. Hiyya the elder and R. Simeon b. Rabbi were sitting in a house paved with marble (cf., Jastrow, p. 844, s.v. *mrmr*). They said, "Is it possible that [a snake] will appear in here?" [A snake] appeared. They said, "Blessed is he who chose sages [as sources for divine wisdom], for sages said, 'The earth has been given permission [by God] to split open [to allow a snake to pass]. But vessels have not been granted permission to split open [in that way].'"

The Tosefta's rule is enhanced, C, and illustrated, D. The illustration introduces E + F, on the larger question of snakes' ability to break through containers, just as they seemingly break through earth.

[**XVIII.**A]   R. Yannai was very afraid of [snakes], so he placed the legs of his bed in four vessels filled with water, [in order to prevent a snake from climbing onto the bed]. One time he reached out his hand and found [a snake] near him [in the bed].

[B]   He said, "Take [this snake] away from me, Lord who preserves the simple" [see Ps. 116:6].

It is likely that the previous unit, with its blessing, accounts for the presence of this one, in which God's name likewise is invoked, B.

[**XIX.**A]   How small a hole [in an otherwise sealed vessel renders the liquids it contains forbidden on account of the law of uncovered liquids]?

[B]   R. Jacob bar Aha [spoke] in the name of R. Hanina. He held out this, [i.e., his little finger and] said, "[Even if the hole is so small as] the tip of a child's finger [the liquids in the vessel are forbidden]."

[C]   [Answering the same question again,] R. Jacob bar Aha [and] R. Simeon bar Va in the name of R. Joshua b. Levi [say], "[Even if] it is so small that the tip of a finger of a one-day-old child will not fit into it.

[D]   "And even if [the opening is] smaller than this, it is possible [for the snake] to get in [to drink].

[E]   "[Yet in the case of these smaller holes, the liquid remains permitted,] for if [snakes are not certain that they] can leave [a vessel] they do not enter it [in order to drink]."

[F]   [A conclusion is drawn from E.] In the case of a vessel with many holes (*slp̄*), even if [the holes] are very small, [i.e., smaller than the tip of the finger of a day-old baby, the liquid contained in the vessel is] forbidden.

[G]   For [the snake] will enter through this [hole] and leave through a different one.

[H]   In the case of a satchel, no matter how high [off the ground] it is hung, [the liquids or foods it contains] are forbidden [as possibly containing snake venom].

[I]   For the snake climbs down [the rope from which the bag hangs and thereby gets to the food or drink].

A's question is answered, B and C–E. This introduces F–G, a direct conclusion from E. H–I is related in theme alone. Like F–G it portrays the snake's ability to enter a hard-to-reach place.

[**XX**.A]   [M. Ter. 8:4 says that liquids become forbidden if they are left uncovered long enough for a snake to leave a nearby hiding place and drink from them.] What constitutes 'nearby'?

[B]   Said R. Samuel, "[The distance] between the handle of the vessel and its mouth."

[C]   [But if the snake is really that close, will the individual] not see it, [such that, if no snake is seen, the liquid remains permitted]?

[D]   [Explaining why people have to be very careful,] said R. Hanina,[35] "A very small [kind of snake exists]. It is called a serpent and looks like a hair." [Since it is so small, one cannot trust in having seen it in order to be sure that it has not deposited venom in uncovered liquid.]

The Yerushalmi concludes these materials by referring to the last rule of M. Ter. 8:4. Samuel's answer to the question posed at A is explained, C + D.

8:6 [P: 8:3b; M. Ter. 8:5]

[A]   *[This is] the quantity of uncovered water [which is permitted for consumption]:*

[B]   *[any amount] such that the venom [of a snake] will be diluted in it [and not poison the water].*

[C]   *R. Yose says, "[Water] in [uncovered] vessels [becomes forbidden] in any quantity [i.e., no matter how large the vessel, water left uncovered in it is prohibited];*

[D]   *"and [as for water in pools in] the ground—[if there is more than] forty seahs [it is permitted]."*

The law of uncovered liquids does not apply if there is no danger
to life, B. Yose has a different theory. He equates venom with
uncleanness and reasons by analogy to immersion pools. If these
pools contain forty *seahs* of rainwater, they render cultically
clean objects which are rinsed in them. Yose claims that if this
same specification is met, D, the water neutralizes the effect of
the venom deposited in it. By contrast, water in a vessel, C,
never constitutes an immersion pool. It therefore always is subject to the law of uncovered liquids. The Yerushalmi examines
the Tosefta's material on this pericope (unit **I**) and then provides
a general consideration for the circumstances under which the
law of uncovered liquids applies (unit **II**).

[**I.A**]   It is taught [T. Ter. 7:14H + K + O–P]: **[In the case of] water [in a pool] in the ground, [if there are] forty** *seahs*, **[it is
permitted].**

[B]   **R. Nehemia says, "[There must be enough water] for a keg
made in Shihin to be filled from it."**

[C]³⁶   **[As for] wine—whether it is in the ground or in a vessel, it is
forbidden [on account of the law of uncovered liquids] in any
amount.**

[D]   [Another rule for wine follows.] **Wine—so long as it still is
[46a] fermenting, it is not subject to the law of uncovered
liquids.**

[E]   **How long [after its manufacture is wine deemed still to be]
fermenting?**

[F]   **Three days** [T. Ter. 7:15B–D].

[G]   [A further case for wine is reported.] **M⁽Ś́H W: A snake was
found [dead] next to a vat of wine. The incident was reported
to R. Judah [for him to rule on whether or not the wine was
prohibited], and he deemed it permitted** [T. Ter. 7:15A, with
minor variations. In T. the authority is Judah b. Baba.]

[H]   [T. Ter. 7:14L–N is cited, regarding water in a spring.] **[As for]
a spring—so long as it is running, [the water] is not subject to
the law of uncovered liquids.**

[I]   **Said R. Ishmael, the son of R. Yohanan b. Beroqah, "M⁽Ś́H
Š: R. Yohanan b. Nuri went down to [the home of] my father,**

R. Yohanan b. Beroqah, in Beth Shearim. He showed him a pond which contained only three logs of water.

[J]   "Now the rain was pouring down [into the pond]

[K]   "and [R. Yohanan b. Nuri] bent down and drank from it.

[L]   He said, 'Such [a pond] is not subject to the laws of uncovered liquids'" [T. Ter. 7:14L–N, with explanatory additions].

[M]   Now how much [rain must be falling such that the water in the pond is deemed permitted]?

[N]   R. Mana bar Tanhum in the name of R. Hanina [said], "[It must rain] so much as to fill up the grooves [which running water makes in mountain slopes]." [Cf., PM.]

[O]   [Giving a different answer,] R. Eleazar b. R. Yose in the name of Rav [said], "[It must rain] so much as to create [splatter marks which look like] goose feet."

[P]   [Carrying forward the preceding,] said R. Jacob bar Aha, "Once water [in ponds] in the fields has been rendered permitted [on account of the rain], water which [forms puddles] inside the house also is permitted."

An anthology of the Tosefta's materials is supplemented by the Yerushalmi's own discussion at M–O + P. The unit is topically relevant to M. Ter. 8:5's question of the circumstances under which uncovered liquids are subject to the restriction first introduced at M. Ter. 8:4.

[II.A]   R. Hoshaya taught, "[The rules for] uncovered [liquids] apply both in the land [of Israel] and outside of the land [of Israel],

[B]   "both in the sunny season, and in the rainy season."

These laws, legislated as a matter of safety, apply in all places, at all times.

8:7 [P: 8:3c; M. Ter. 8:6–7]

[A] *Figs, grapes, cucumbers, gourds, watermelons, and chatemelons
which have on them teeth marks [of snakes],*

[B] *even if they are in a jug (so Albeck),*

[C] *it is all the same whether they are large or small,*

[D] *it is all the same whether they are picked or unpicked,*

[E] *any [of them] which has moisture in it*

[F] *is forbidden.*

[G] *And [a beast which has been] bitten by a snake is forbidden [for
slaughter as food],*

[H] *as a danger to life.*

[A] *[A container of wine covered with] a wine strainer is forbidden
on account of the laws of uncovered [liquids].*

[B] *R. Nehemia permits [the latter].*

The same law that applies to liquids, M. Ter. 8:4–5, applies to
produce and meat, M. Ter. 8:6. Dry produce, self-evidently,
does not contain venom. M. Ter. 8:7A simply states that a wine
strainer does not prevent a snake from depositing venom in the
jug or vat which it covers. Nehemia disagrees.

The Yerushalmi begins by asking which Tannaitic authority
stands behind M. Ter. 8:6. Units II–IV refer to specific questions left open by the pericope: What if it is night and you cannot see your food? What is the law for fish and for specific sorts
of fruit? The final unit provides a perfect conclusion for all of
the Yerushalmi's materials on snakes. It proposes that if a person
pleases God, even the snake will serve and protect him.

[I.A] Said R. Yuda b. Pazzai, "Which authority stands behind the
rule that [produce which has on it] teeth marks [of snakes is
forbidden; M. Ter. 8:6A–F]?

[B] "It is Rabban Gamaliel, for *Rabban Gamaliel says, 'The serpent
also [renders invalid purification water from which it drinks], for
it vomits'* [M. Par. 9:3]." [The anonymous authority of M. Par.

9:3 does not hold that the snake vomits venom. That authority therefore would not hold that food which a snake has tasted is forbidden.]

[C]   [Jonah claims that the cases are not comparable and that even the anonymous authority of M. Par. 9:3 would agree to the rule of M. Ter. 8:6A–F.] Said R. Jonah, "What does the case of [M. Par. 9:3, the ordinance of which is a divine] commandment have to do with [the case of M. Ter. 8:6, which involves] teeth marks [of snakes, the rules for which are legislated because of a concrete danger to life]?

[D]   "And [in proof that the present rule does not derive from a divine ordinance, but from the need for great stringency] is it not taught: **[If] one saw a bird peck at a fig, or a mouse [gnaw] at a watermelon—[both of these] are forbidden [on account of the law of food with snake bites on it].**

[E]   **"For I say, 'Lest it ate at a place [on the fruit] which already had snake bites on it'"** [T. Ter. 7:17A–C. In light of this stringency, all authorities agree to M. Ter. 8:6A–F.]

[F]   [Supporting A–B] said R. Ba, "[M. Ter. 8:6 is the opinion of Gamaliel alone], for he says, 'A snake vomits.'"

[G]   [Jonah repeats what he said at C.] Said R. Jonah, "What does the case of [M. Par. 9:3, the ordinance of which is a divine] commandment have to do with [the case of M. Ter. 8:3, which involves] teeth marks [of snakes, the rules for which are legislated because of a concrete danger to life]?"

[H]   [A discussion primary at Y. Ber. 9:3 seems to prove that Jonah is wrong. That discussion claims the opposite of T. Ter. 7:17, cited above at D.] But [what of the rule for] meat which is improperly slaughtered?

[I]   For R. Ba in the name of rabbis from there [i.e., Babylonia] said, "[If] one properly slaughtered [an animal] and a pack of wolves snatched it, [if it later is recovered with teeth marks on it], it [still is deemed] fit [for consumption].

[J]   "For a pack of wolves is assumed to be fit."

[K]   But should we not be apprehensive, lest [the wolves] chewed [the meat, just as we assume in the case of the watermelon or fig, F, that a snake did so]?

[L]   [No, for that which is taken by] a pack of wolves is assumed to be fit [for consumption].

[M]   Yet, [to the contrary,] here [at D] you say this, [that we assume a snake had eaten the fruit to render it forbidden! If the issue is danger to life, in the case of the meat we should make the comparable assumption, that the wolves had rendered the meat forbidden. Since we do not do so, it appears that the possibility that a food is a concrete danger to life does not account for these rules. Therefore, as B states, only Gamaliel, stands behind the rule of M. Ter. 8:6A–F. There is no proof that other authorities should agree.]

[N]   [Here is the basis for Gamaliel's view. The case of T. Ter. 7:17, cited at D, like the case at M. Ter. 8:6, is special, for] in that case a stringency applies, for there is a danger to life.

[O]   Thus the rule for [produce which has on it] teeth marks [of snakes] is the opinion of Rabban Gamaliel [alone, just as B claimed].

The Yerushalmi proves that the rule of M. Ter. 8:6 is the position of Gamaliel, expressed as well at M. Par. 9:3. I have translated H–O as literally as possible. The exact nature of its argument is not clear. The material is odd, for what N–O gives as the reason for Gamaliel's view is the same reasoning which M rejects.

[II.A]   It is taught: R. Eliezer says, "A person may eat figs or grapes at night [when it is too dark to see whether or not they have teeth marks on them], and he need not be apprehensive.

[B]   "For it is said [in Scripture], 'The Lord preserves the simple' [Ps. 116:6]."

Ps. 116:6 proves that God preserves those who are not able to protect themselves, namely, by examining the food they are about to eat.

[III.A]   R. Jonah in the name of Rav [says], "A fish with teeth marks [on it] is forbidden."

[B]   R. Hezeqiah [and] R. Tabbi in the name of Rav [say], "A live fish [which is found with] teeth marks [on it] is forbidden.

[C]   "But if it is a pickled, [salted], fish [which is found to have teeth marks on it, it is permitted, for] the pickling process [causes the venom to] dissipate.

[D]   "[If one finds] a dead [fish with teeth marks], he may remove the place where the teeth marks are [and eat the rest of the fish]."

M. Ter. 8:6 gave the rule for an animal which was bitten by a snake. The Yerushalmi provides the rules for fish.

[**IV.**A]   R. Jacob bar Aha in the name of R. Hiyya bar Ba [says], "A watermelon [that has] teeth marks [on it], the core of which is liquified, [remains] forbidden."

[B]   A certain man was carrying a cucumber with teeth marks [on it]. He fed it to ten people and they [all] died.

[C]   [The reason was that] the spittle [of a snake, which was inside the moist cucumber], had passed [into the whole vegetable].

M. Ter. 8:6 states that only produce which is moist is subject to the restriction of food which has teeth marks on it. The Yerushalmi addresses the question of the law for a case when the produce is totally liquid, A. I assume that B + C is intended to illustrate A.

[V.A]   A certain man hated [to eat] lamb. One time he [unknowingly] was eating meat, and someone passed by and told him that it was lamb. He choked and died.

[B]   Ass drivers were lodging in an inn. They said, "Give us lentils [to eat]," and [the innkeepers] gave them it. They asked for a second helping and were given it. They said, "The first [lentils] were better than these." [Explaining,] they said [to the ass drivers], "[We did not wish to give you any more of the first batch since] we found the spinal column of a snake in it." [Upon hearing this the ass drivers] choked and died.

The same point is made twice, A and B. What you do not know will not hurt you. It is unclear why the pericope is placed here, since it has no substantive relationship to the present materials. Indeed, in theory it contradicts what is implicit in the preceding units and throughout this section of the Yerushalmi, that snake venom will hurt you, even if you do not know that it is there.

[**VI.A**] It is written [Prov. 16:7]: 'When a man's ways please the Lord, he makes even his enemies to be at peace with him.'

[B] R. Meir[37] says "[Scripture] refers to a dog, [which can be made a friend and helper of man]."

[C] But R. Joshua b. Levi says, "[Scripture] refers to the snake."

[D] [Showing that Meir is wrong, the following incident is reported.] Shepherds milked and [when they were not looking] a serpent came and drank of [the milk. Their] dog saw [this happen] and when [the shepherds] returned to drink [the milk], it started to bark at them. But they did not understand. In the end, they drank [the milk] and died. [Thus, contrary to Meir, B, the dog was not able to come to man's aid.]

[E] [This incident proves that, as Joshua b. Levi said, C, the snake comes to the aid of a person 'whose ways please the Lord.'] A certain man had ground garlic prepared in his house. A mountain snake came and ate of it while a snake that lived in the house watched. [When] the members of the household returned to eat some of the garlic, this [household snake] began to crumble dust upon them [i.e., upon the garlic], but the people did not understand. Therefore [the snake] threw itself into [the garlic, preventing the people from eating it. This proves that the snake can be at peace with humans, as Joshua b. Levi, C, interpreted Prov. 16:7.]

[F] [This indicates that, contrary to D, a dog can help people, as Meir suggested, B.] A certain man invited one of the rabbis [to eat at his house]. He seated his dog next to [that rabbi. The rabbi] said to him, "Have I disgraced you [in some way, such that you are so disrespectful as to seat me next to a dog?" The man] said to him, "Rabbi, [I do not intend to show you any disrespect. Rather] I am repaying [the dog's] own good character [by giving him the honor of sitting next to you. Here is why the dog deserves to be honored.] Marauders came into the village. One of them entered [my house] and attempted to take my wife captive. [To prevent this, the dog] bit [the captor's] testicles, [causing him to leave us alone]."

Even the snake will be a friend to the good person, E. Contrary to what D attempts to show, the same applies to the dog, F.

8:8 [P: 8:4a]

[A]   *A jug of [wine in the status of] heave-offering concerning which there arose a suspicion of uncleanness—*

[B]   *R. Eliezer says, "If it was lying in an exposed place, he should place it in a concealed place.*

[C]   *"And if it was uncovered, he should cover it."*

[D]   *R. Joshua says, "If it was lying in a concealed place, he should place it in an exposed place.*

[E]   *"And if it was covered, he should uncover it."*

[F]   *Rabban Gamaliel says, "Let him not do anything new with it [i.e., he must leave it as it is]."*

The heave-offering may not be destroyed, for it might be clean. This assumption, stated explicitly in the Yerushalmi's one unit, underlies the three positions here. Eliezer says that since we may not destroy the heave-offering, we must prevent it from becoming certainly unclean. This is the case even though a priest may not consume the possibly unclean offering. Joshua takes the opposite view. The individual may not destroy the heave-offering, but should do whatever he can to assure that it will be rendered certainly unclean. Then it may be burned. Gamaliel, F, rejects both of these alternatives. The individual need not protect what a priest in no event may eat. He may not, however, take actions designed to render unclean the holy heave-offering.

[I.A]   Said R. Yose b. R. Bun, "On the basis of the opinions of all three of them [i.e., the authorities of M. Ter. 8:8, it is clear that] it is forbidden to burn [holy produce] about which there is a doubt whether or not it is in a state of cleanness.

Yose b. R. Bun makes explicit the assumption which underlies the dispute at M. Ter. 8:8.

8:9 [P: 8:4b, M. Ter. 8:9–11]

[G]   *[As to] a jug [of wine in the status of heave-offering] which broke in the upper vat, and the lower [vat] is unclean—*

[H]   *R. Eliezer and R. Joshua agree that if he can save from it a fourth in a state of cleanness he should save [it].*

[I]   *But if not:*

[J]   *R. Eliezer says, "Let it go down [into the lower vat] and be made unclean.*

[K]   *"But let him not make it unclean with his hand [i.e., through his own actions]."*

[L]³⁸   *And so [in the case of] a jug of oil [in the status of heave-offering] which was spilled—*

[M]   *R. Eliezer and R. Joshua agree that if he can save from it a fourth in a state of cleanness, he should save [it].*

[N]   *But if not:*

[O]   *R. Eliezer says, "Let it run down and be soaked up [in the ground].*

[P]   *"But let him not soak it up with his hands, [an improper use of heave-offering]."*

[Q]³⁹   *But as regards both of these cases:*

[R]   *Said R. Joshua, "This is not heave-offering concerning which I am warned against rendering unclean.*

[S]   *"Rather, [it is heave-offering which a priest is warned] against eating."*

[T]   *And "not to render it unclean." How so? [I.e., in what case must the individual be careful not to render heave-offering unclean?]*

[U]   *[If] one was walking from place to place, and loaves [of bread] in the status of heave-offering were in his hand—*

[V]   *[if] a gentile said to him, "Give me one of them and I shall make it unclean, and if not, lo, I shall make all of them unclean"—*

[W]   *R. Eliezer says, "Let him make all of them unclean, but let [the Israelite] not give him one of them that he make it unclean."*

[X]   *R. Joshua says, "Let him place one of them before [the gentile], on a rock."*

Heave-offering has been spilled and is about to become unclean (G) or to be soaked up into the ground (L). The householder has no way of saving the priestly gift without himself rendering it unclean. As we should expect, Eliezer, J–K and O–P, states that the householder must let the heave-offering become unclean or be lost in the ground. He may himself do nothing improper with the offering. Joshua, R–S, takes the opposite view. He states that the issue here is the prevention of the consumption of unclean heave-offering by the priest. It therefore does not matter what the householder does. If he himself renders the heave-offering unclean, this will have the beneficial result of assuring that the priestly gift will be destroyed. Then it will not be available for a priest to consume accidentally. T + U–X is a replay of the disputes just described. Eliezer holds that the householder may not bear responsibility for the gentile's rendering a loaf of consecrated bread unclean. Should the gentile render all of the bread unclean, it is not the householder's fault. Joshua likewise is consistent with his previous position. Since the loaves all are about to be rendered unclean, the householder no longer is responsible for them. He may leave one loaf behind, where it certainly will be rendered unclean.

The Yerushalmi concentrates on Joshua's opinion, that under certain circumstances the householder is relieved of responsibility to protect heave-offering in cleanness. At this point he may even render it unclean himself. The Yerushalmi refers to M. Pes. 1:7, where Yose and Meir dispute under what conditions the householder himself may render heave-offering unclean. Their positions are correlated with that of Joshua, units **I–II** + **III**. The issue recurs in a redactional conclusion to Y. Ter. 8:9, unit **IX**. Units **IV–VI** + **VII** carry out the same sort of exercise, comparing Joshua's view to that of Simeon, M. Bek. 5:2. Only unit **VIII** turns to the view of Eliezer and to the specifics of the cases before us in M. Ter. 8:9–11.

[I.A]   [The position of Joshua at M. Ter. 8:8 + 9–11 is correlated with those of Meir and Yose, M. Pes. 1:7. Meir holds that at Passover people may burn clean leavened produce which is in the status of heave-offering together with unclean, leavened, heave-offering. This is the case even though, in doing so, the clean heave-offering will be rendered unclean. Yose says that they must be burned separately, so as not to render unclean the clean heave-offering.] Associates in the name of R. Eleazar [say], "[The law for] the first jug [of wine in the status of heave-offering, about which there is a suspicion of uncleanness, and which Joshua, M. Ter. 8:8, holds may not be burned,] accords with the view of R. Yose, [M. Pes. 1:7, who likewise states that one may not treat clean heave-offering as though it were unclean].

[B] "But [Joshua's position concerning] the second [jug of wine in the status of heave-offering, M. Ter. 8:9–11, that if the heave-offering is in all events going to be rendered unclean the person may himself render it unclean], accords with the view of R. Meir, [M. Pes. 1:7, that if heave-offering is going to be burned, it may be rendered unclean by the one who burns it]."

[C] [Explaining A–B,] associates say, "[Concerning] the first jug, [the view of Joshua] concurs with that of R. Yose, and R. Meir would not agree. [Meir, M. Pes. 1:7, would say that if the heave-offering may not be eaten anyway, then just as in the case of leavened produce in the status of heave-offering on Passover, the householder himself may render it unclean and burn it.]

[D] "But [concerning] the second [jug, the view of Joshua] concurs with that of R. Meir, and R. Yose would not agree. [Yose, M. Pes. 1:7, would not agree to the man's taking actions which would render heave-offering unclean. This is the case even though the heave-offering in all events will not be eaten by a priest.]

[E] [Suggesting that the reasoning of A–D is unacceptable,] R. Yose [an Amora] said to them [i.e., to the associates], "Look at what you are saying!

[F] "[You say that in the law for] the first jug, [the opinion of Joshua] accords with that of R. Yose, [but] that, according to R. Meir, [the heave-offering, concerning which there is a suspicion of uncleanness,] should be burned.

[G] "Yet [as we shall see below], R. Simeon [holds that in a case of suspicion of uncleanness, heave-offering] may be burned.

[H] "[Thus if matters are as you claim, that Meir also holds that in a case of suspicion, heave-offering may be burned], the opinions

of R. Meir and R. Simeon[40] [together] form a majority view over
the [minority] opinion of R. Yose.

[I]   "And [this being so, in a case of suspicion] they must burn [the
heave-offering].

[J]   "Yet [in practice this is not what happens]. For I saw that when
an actual case [of heave-offering about which there was a doubt
whether or not it was unclean] came before rabbis, they said,
'Leave [the heave-offering] in a state of suspension [i.e., it may
not be burned like unclean heave-offering, but may not be eaten
as though it were clean heave-offering].'" [From this case it is
clear that rabbis did not deem Meir's view, as well as Simeon's, to
be that in a case of suspicion heave-offering should be burned.
The argument of A–D therefore is unacceptable.]

[K]   Here is where we find that R. Simeon said [that in a case of
suspicion of uncleanness, heave-offering] is burned.

[L]   For we have learned [M. Pes. 1:7]: *R. Eliezer and R. Joshua
agree that [in the case of clean and unclean leavened produce in
the status of heave-offering, on Passover], they must burn each
of them separately.*

[M]   Now [concerning this] said R. Yohanan, "R. Simeon disagrees,
[holding that if heave-offering anyway may not be eaten, it may
be rendered unclean and then burned]."

[N]   [We go back to support the position of the associates, A–D.]
Now if you wish to say [as they do] that R. Meir never attributes
[to heave-offering] a status of suspension, [but rather that he always has such doubtful heave-offering burned, then the following will help to support your case.]

[O]   It is taught: **"Heave-offering which is in a suspended status of
cleanness and that which [certainly] is unclean do they burn
on the eve of Sabbath at sunset [i.e., before the start of Pas-
sover]"**—the words of R. Meir. But sages say, **"[They do this]
at their proper time, [i.e., burning each of them separately"**;
T. Pes. 3:10, with changes. Meir holds that the heave-offering
about which there is a suspicion of uncleanness may be treated
just like unclean heave-offering. This is what associates, A–D,
claimed Meir's position to be.]

[P]   [Zeira suggests a way to maintain both possible understandings
of Meir's view, that given at E–J and that of A–D + N–O. Only
under certain circumstances does Meir say doubtfully unclean

heave-offering should be burned.] Said R. Zeira in the presence
of R. Mana, "Interpret [Meir's view that heave-offering about
which there is a doubt whether or not it is unclean may be
burned] to apply [only] if [the individual] does (supply with Y.
Pes. 1:7: not) intend to ask [whether or not this particular batch
of heave-offering might be deemed clean]." [In this case, the
person himself has determined that the offering certainly is
unclean. Under this circumstance, Meir says that the priestly gift
may be burned as though it were unclean.]

[Q]   [Agreeing, Mana] said to him, "Thus said R. Yose, my teacher,
'All [heave-offering] in a suspended status of cleanness to which
we refer is [heave-offering] in a suspended status of cleanness
about which the individual does not intend to ask.

[R]   "'But [if] the individual intends to ask concerning [whether or
not] it [might be deemed clean], it is [deemed] clean.'

[S]   "[We know that this is so] for it is taught [T. Toh. 8:14C–D,
with slight variation]: **If he declared of [heave-offering of]
suspended status of cleanness, 'It is clean,' [or], 'It is unclean'** [41]
**[and did not intend to ask about it], lo, it is deemed unclean.
[But] if he said, 'Lo, I shall leave it until I shall inquire concerning it,' lo, this is deemed clean.''**

[T]   [Giving another explanation of why at T. Pes. 3:10 Meir allows
the heave-offering in a suspended status of cleanness to be
burned as though it certainly were unclean,] said R. Yose b. R.
Bun, "Interpret this as a case in which the suspicion of uncleanness arose just as the sun was setting. [In this case there would
be no time to do anything with the heave-offering except to burn
it with that which certainly was unclean.]

[U]   "[Now if this is so] you may not draw any conclusions [concerning
Meir's view] from this [particular case, since it is an exception
rather than a rule. This supports the view of Yose the Amora,
E–J, that Meir does not allow heave-offering concerning which
there is a suspicion of uncleanness to be burned as though it
certainly were unclean. Only in the special case cited at T does
he permit a householder to treat clean heave-offering as though
it were unclean.]

[V]   "Yet you say [above, C,] that [the law for] the first jug [about
which there is a suspicion of uncleanness and which Joshua says
may not be destroyed] accords with the view of R. Yose and that

R. Meir would not agree!" [As we just have seen, T–U, Meir
certainly does agree.]

[W]   [We move on to show that the rule for the second jug, above, D,
which Joshua says that the man may take actions to render
unclean, does not follow the view of Meir. This is contrary to
what A–D claimed.] And is it not taught: In what case does
[Joshua's] opinion apply, [that if the wine in the status of heave-
offering is in all events going to be rendered unclean, the householder himself may impart to it uncleanness]?

[X]   It applies in the case of a [lower] vat, [into which the heave-
offering is going to fall], which does not (so PM, as required by
the sense of the passage) contain sufficient [wine] to neutralize
the heave-offering [which will be mixed with it].

[Y]   But in the case of a [lower] vat which (delete: does not) contains
sufficient [wine] to neutralize [the heave-offering which is about
to fall into it, it is forbidden for the householder himself] to
render unclean any small quantity [of wine. The reason is that,
in this case, there is no gain to the householder who, in preventing the heave-offering from being mixed with his unconsecrated
wine, renders it unclean. In any event, the heave-offering will
not impart its own status to that unconsecrated wine.]

[Z]   Now if this were the view of R. Meir, whether or not there was
sufficient [unconsecrated wine] to neutralize [the heave-offering,
Meir would deem it] forbidden to render unclean any small
amount [42] [of the offering. That is, in no case would Meir allow
the person to render heave-offering unclean. This is in line with
what we just have seen, T–U. Meir does not allow the householder himself to impart uncleanness to that which still is clean.
He may do this only if there is no other choice, for instance, if a
doubt arose concerning the cleanness of heave-offering on the
eve of the Sabbath just before Passover.]

[AA]   [Now we see that D also is wrong in claiming that Yose cannot
agree with Joshua at M. Ter. 8:9.] And moreover, on the basis of
that which we have learned [M. Pes. 1:7, that in rejecting Meir's
claim that, at Passover, one may burn unclean heave-offering
with clean heave-offering,] R. Yose says, "That is not the inference [of the statement of Hanina, M. Pes. 1:6, that the
priests did not refrain from burning together sacrificial meat in
different levels of uncleanness." It is clear the Yose does agree

with Joshua, M. Ter. 8:9–11, that one may take actions which will render heave-offering unclean.]

[BB] For a person does not say, "That is not [the inference]," unless he agrees [in principle] with the previous [statement, upon which the inference is to be based. In this case that statement is that of Hanina, referred to at AA, that one may impart uncleanness to a holy thing which anyway will not be eaten. Yose agrees with this, as it applies to M. Ter. 8:9–11, but disagrees as it concerns the rules for burning heave-offering at Passover, M. Pes. 1:7. Thus the conclusion regarding Yose's opinion, D, is unacceptable.]

[CC] What is the reason [that Yose holds that burning together clean and unclean heave-offering at Passover (which he does not allow) is not comparable to rendering unclean heave-offering which is about to fall into unclean unconsecrated produce (which he does allow)]?

[DD] There [in the latter case of the heave-offering, M. Ter. 8:9–11,] the law has regard for the [potential loss of] property to Israelites. [Yose agrees that in order to prevent loss of their unconsecrated wine, Israelites may do whatever is required to prevent heave-offering from falling into it. This is so even if their actions will cause the heave-offering to be rendered unclean.]

[EE] [But as for] this case [of burning together clean and unclean heave-offering at Passover], what reason can you give [for allowing a person to do this? By burning them separately the individual incurs no loss, yet avoids purposely rendering unclean the clean heave-offering.]

[FF] [Contrary to EE there appears to be a monetary loss to an Israelite who, at Passover, burns separately clean and unclean leavened heave-offering.] Does the person not incur [a needless] expense, for he requires [a larger quantity of] wood in order to burn separately this [clean heave-offering] and this [unclean heave-offering? Since this is so, Yose should agree that, in the case described at BB, the person may himself render unclean the heave-offering by burning it with what is unclean.]

[GG] [This explains why the reasoning of FF is unacceptable. In Yose's view] the law is concerned with preventing a great loss, [such as would result from heave-offering's being mixed with a vat of unconsecrated wine; But] for a small loss [such as that entailed in

using slightly more wood for burning leaven at Passover] it was
not concerned. [Therefore Yose holds that for the case of M. Ter.
8:9–11 the individual may render the heave-offering unclean,
and so prevent a great monetary loss. Under the circumstance of
M. Pes. 1:7, however, he may not render the heave-offering unclean. Doing so would save only a small amount of money.]

[HH]   [Yose b. R. Bun claims that on the basis of Yose's statement,
"This is not the inference," M. Pes. 1:7, one may not reject the
reasoning concerning Yose's view at A–D, above. The weight of
this is to counter AA–GG, and to prove that, as A–D said, Yose
does not allow the householder himself to render heave-offering
unclean.] Said R. Yose b. R. Bun, "[In order to make sense of
A–D] interpret [Yose's statement, 'This is not the inference'] in
accordance with one who says, ['This is not the inference' is a
general rejection] of the opinion of R. Aqiba and R. Hanina, the
perfect of the priests. [They say, M. Pes. 1:6, that one may burn
together clean and unclean holy things. To the contrary, Yose
holds that one may not burn clean heave-offering with unclean,
nor himself render unclean clean heave-offering which is about
to be mixed with unclean unconsecrated produce.]

[II]   "[If this is what Yose's statement, 'This is not the inference,'
means], then you may not deduce from it anything [to claim that
Yose agrees with the position of Joshua, M. Ter. 8:9–11. For as
D above said, and contrary to AA–GG, Yose does not agree with
Joshua's view.]"

Two contrasting views of Joshua are identified and correlated
with positions held by Yose and Meir, M. Pes. 1:7. Joshua's
views are at M. Ter. 8:8 and 8:9–11. At M. Ter. 8:8 he holds
that the householder may not himself destroy heave-offering,
even though it already is unfit for consumption by a priest. (Y.
Ter. 8:8 I ascertained that this represents Joshua's view.) At M.
Ter. 8:9–11, by contrast, Joshua holds that, since the heave-
offering anyway is going to be lost (specifically: mixed with
unclean heave-offering or soaked up in the ground), the householder himself may render it unclean.

The Yerushalmi's point, A–D, is that Meir consistently holds
the position ascribed to Joshua at M. Ter. 8:9–11. The householder may himself render unclean heave-offering a priest anyway may not eat. This being the case, Meir does not agree with

the position Joshua takes at M. Ter. 8:8. A–D further states that, contrary to Meir, Yose consistently holds the view expressed by Joshua at M. Ter. 8:8. No matter what the circumstances, Yose holds that the householder himself may not impart uncleanness to heave-offering. Yose therefore will not agree with Joshua's view at M. Ter. 8:9–11.

The conclusion of A–D is that there is an inconsistency in Joshua's view and that Meir's and Yose's views each follow one aspect of Joshua's two-pronged position. The rest of the unit argues that this conclusion is unacceptable. Rather, as E–II proves, both Meir and Yose agree upon the view at A–D attributed to Yose alone, that the householder himself *never* may impart uncleanness to heave-offering. The force of this is to discredit the contrary view ascribed to Joshua at M. Ter. 8:9–11. The Yerushalmi shows that this view both contradicts what Joshua himself taught, M. Ter. 8:8, and explicitly was rejected by later authorities, Yose and Meir.

The Yerushalmi makes its point by proving that A–D correctly understands the view of Yose (shown at AA–II), but wrongly extrapolates Meir's view. This latter proof comes in two stages. E–V deals with Meir's view for the case of M. Ter. 8:8. It shows (V) that contrary to A–D, Meir *does* agree with Joshua and Yose that the householder may not destroy the doubtfully unclean heave-offering. W–Z takes up the second half of the analysis. It shows that, for the case of M. Ter. 8:9–11, Meir's view is the same as we now know it to be for M. Ter. 8:8. In all, Meir never allows a householder to impart uncleanness to heave-offering.[43] This is the case even if the heave-offering anyway will not be consumed by a priest. HH–II then shows that, contrary to AA–GG, A–D is correct in stating that, according to Yose, a householder never may render heave-offering unclean. The net result, as I said, is to show that Meir and Yose are unanimous in their rejection of the position of Joshua, M. Ter. 8:9–11. Contrary to the earlier authority, they do not take account of extenuating circumstances in order to determine that a householder is not responsible for maintaining heave-offering in cleanness. They hold, rather, that the individual always remains responsible.

[II.A]   [Just as in unit I, so here the position of Joshua, M. Ter. 8:8–11, is correlated with that of Meir and Yose, M. Pes. 1:7. In

M. Pes. Meir holds that at Passover people may burn clean leavened produce in the status of heave-offering together with unclean leavened produce in the status of heave-offering. This is so
even though the clean heave-offering thereby will be rendered
unclean. Yose says that they must be burned separately, so that
the person does not himself render unclean clean heave-offering.]
R. Ila and R. Zeira, the two of them, in the name of R. Yohanan
[say], "[The law for] the first jug [of wine in the status of heave-
offering, about which there is a suspicion of uncleanness, and
which Joshua, M. Ter. 8 : 8, holds may not be destroyed] accords
with the view of R. Yose [M. Pes. 1 : 7, who likewise states that
one may not treat clean heave-offering as though it were
unclean].

[B]   "And [Joshua's opinion concerning] the second [jug of wine in
the status of heave-offering, M. Ter. 8 : 9–11, that if the heave-
offering is in all events going to be rendered certainly unclean,
the person himself may impart uncleanness to it] accords with
[both] the opinion of R. Meir [M. Pes. 1 : 7, who holds that
heave-offering which is not going to be eaten anyway may be
rendered unclean] and that of R. Yose."

[C]   Said R. Zeira in the presence of R. Mana, "Does [Joshua's view
at M. Ter. 8 : 9–11, that the person himself may impart uncleanness to heave-offering] not contradict the view of R. (read with
Y. Pes. 1 : 8) Yose[44] [who holds, M. Pes. 1 : 7, that a person may
not impart uncleanness to heave-offering, even if it is going to be
destroyed anyway]?"

[D]   [Mana] said to him, "[If it is as you claim, C,] let us say that [the
opinion of Joshua, M. Ter. 8 : 9–11] does not accord with the
view of R. Meir [for the reason we shall see below], or with the
opinion of R. Yose.

[E]   "For we have found that in all cases R. Meir rules that holy produce for which the status [of cleanness] is suspended [i.e., in
doubt] is to be burned." [This opinion would not make sense if
Meir, like Joshua, holds that produce which will not be eaten by
a priest anyway may be rendered unclean. If that is what Meir
thought, he would not claim that produce in a suspended status
of cleanness should be burned. He would say that such produce
first should be rendered certainly unclean. Then the certainly
unclean heave-offering could be destroyed. Since, to the contrary, Meir holds simply that produce in a suspended status of

cleanness should be burned, it is clear that he does not agree
with Joshua that the householder may render this heave-offering
unclean.]

[F]   [Expanding upon E] said R. Mana, "I went to Caesarea and
heard Hezeqiah in the name of R. Jeremiah[45] [say], 'R. Meir
rules in all cases that [heave-offering] in a suspended status [of
cleanness] is to be burned.'

[G]   "Now I said to him, '[Did Meir hold this] for the case of [heave-
offering] which might have been rendered unclean [through contact with something deemed unclean] by the Torah?]

[H]   "[Jeremiah] said to me, 'Yes, [that is what I have heard. But even
so] I interpret [Meir's view to apply even if the heave-offering]
was rendered unclean through being in the dwelling of a gentile,
[the uncleanness of which was legislated by rabbinic authority
alone].'

[I]   "How do you know [that H is the case]?

[J]   "For it is taught [T. Ah. 18:7]: **On account of [having been
placed in] the dwelling of a gentile they suspend [the status of
holy things]. R. Yose b. R. Judah says, '[On this account] they
even burn [heave-offering].'"** [It is unclear how the statement in
the name of Yose b. R. Judah answers the question posed by I
concerning Meir's view, given by Jeremiah, H.][46]

What was proven at Y. Ter. 8:9 I is shown again. The main point
comes at E. Meir will not agree with Joshua, M. Ter. 8:9–11,
that a householder himself may impart uncleanness to heave-
offering which is about to become unclean. Contrary to B, Yose
likewise will not concede this claim, as C shows. While F–G
clearly supports E, the point of I–J is not clear, for the reason I
give in my interpolated comment there.

[III.A]   [At T. Pes. 3:10, cited at Y. Ter. 8:9 I.O, Meir holds that on the
eve of Sabbath, which is also the day preceding the eve of Passover, they burn leavened produce in the status of heave-offering
which is in a suspended status of cleanness together with certainly unclean heave-offering.] R. [46b] Huna in the name of R.
Jeremiah [said], "R. Meir [rules that] heave-offering in a sus-

pended status [of cleanness] may be burned on other days of the
year as well."

[B]   But it is taught [T. Pes. 3:10]: "**Heave-offering which is in a
suspended status [of cleanness], and that which certainly is
unclean do they burn [together] on the eve of Sabbath at sunset, [on the night before Passover]"—the words of R. Meir.
But sages say, "[They do this] at their proper time [i.e., burning each of them separately].**"

[C]   [If A is correct, then contrary to B, Meir should state that] they
may burn [the heave-offering in a suspended status of cleanness]
in the morning. [There should be no need to wait for Sabbath
eve to burn this heave-offering. Meir should allow the person to
burn it Friday morning.]

[D]   [To prove that A is correct] solve the problem [of why Meir states
specifically that the heave-offering may be burned on the eve of
Sabbath by assuming that this is] a case in which the person was
lazy and did not burn [the heave-offering in a suspended status of
cleanness in the morning, but rather waited until the last minute].
[Meir's point is that he may burn it *even* at this late hour.]

[E]⁴⁷   Know [for certain] that [D] is correct. For [at T. Pes. 1:7] do we
not learn [the rule not only for heave-offering in a suspended
status of cleanness, but also for] certainly unclean [heave-
offering]? [All agree that certainly unclean heave-offering may
be burned at any time.]

[F]   [Thus when Meir says that this unclean heave-offering is burned
on the eve of Sabbath] is it not clear that [he refers to the case of
a person who] became lazy and did not burn [the heave-offering
at some earlier time]? [Yes, this certainly is the case, proving that
A also is correct, as C + D has explained it.]

[G]   [Suggesting a different way to solve the contradiction between A
and B] said R. Abba Mari, the brother of R. Yose, "Solve the
problem [of the apparent contradiction between A and B by assuming that B refers to] a case in which the suspicion of uncleanness arose at that very moment, [just before the eve of Sabbath].

[H]   "[If this is the case] you cannot learn from that rule [of T. Pes.
3:10] anything [concerning Meir's view on when heave-offering
in a suspended status of cleanness may normally be burned]."

This unit is primary at Y. Pes. 1:8, for it draws out the implications of the view of Meir given at T. Pes. 3:10.[48]

[IV.A]   [At M. Bek. 5:2 Simeon says that if a firstling suffers from a congestion of blood, it may be bled, even though this will cause a blemish and render the firstling invalid for consumption as a holy thing. Simeon's reasoning is that, should it not be bled, the animal will die. Since in no event will it be consumed as a firstling, Simeon says that, through bleeding it, the man himself may render it invalid.] Said R. Yohanan, "R. Joshua [at M. Ter. 8:9–11] and R. Simeon [at M. Bek 5:2] both say the same thing [i.e., that if the holy thing in no event will serve its intended purpose, a person may himself take actions which will render it invalid]."

[B]   [Disagreeing] said R. Ila, "[As for] R. Simeon's view concerning firstlings, and R. Joshua's[49] position on heave-offering—this one [i.e., Simeon] does not agree with this one [i.e., Joshua], and this one [i.e., Joshua] does not agree with this one [i.e., Simeon]." [PM: Simeon need not agree with Joshua. In the case of which Simeon speaks, there is no certainty that bleeding the animal will cause a blemish. Simeon therefore allows the man to perform the bleeding. This is not the case for the householder with unclean hands who goes to sop up heave-offering. He certainly will render the heave-offering unclean. Therefore Simeon will not let him do it. Joshua, likewise, need not agree with Simeon. In the case of the heave-offering, M. Ter. 8:9–11, it is certain that if the householder does nothing, the offering will be lost. Joshua therefore allows the man himself to render it unclean. But in the case of the firstling, it is not known for certain that if it is not bled, it will die. Therefore, unlike Simeon, Joshua need not permit the man to bleed it. It thus appears that, contrary to A, Simeon and Joshua are not in agreement concerning the two cases in question.]

[C]   [Suggesting a mediating position,] said R. Zeira, "It makes sense to say that R. Simeon agrees to the view of R. Joshua [in M. Ter. 8:9–11], but that R. Joshua does not agree to the view of R. Simeon [at M. Bek. 5:2]." [The reasoning is as follows: In a case of doubt whether or not the holy thing anyway will be lost, Simeon allows the householder himself to invalidate it. In a case of certainty, such as that at M. Ter., surely he will allow the

householder to render the holy produce unclean, just as Joshua
does. The converse is not true. Joshua allows the individual to
render unclean such heave-offering as certainly will be ruined
anyway. He need not allow the householder to blemish a firstling
which might otherwise remain valid.]

[D]   [Questioning C] R. Bun bar Hiyya asked in the presence of
R. Zeira, "In your view R. Simeon concedes to the view of R.
Joshua.

[E]   "Yet have we not learned [M. Pes. 1:7: *R. Meir said, '. . . at
Passover people may burn clean heave-offering (which is leavened) together with unclean.'] . . . R. Eliezer and R. Joshua
agree that each should be burned by itself?*

[F]   "[Now if, as you say, Joshua's position is that whenever heave-
offering certainly is going to be wasted, the householder himself
may render it unclean, then contrary to E, Joshua should hold
that] he may burn the two [i.e., the clean and unclean heave-
offering] together." [Since this is not what Joshua says, it is clear
that Zeira misunderstood his position and has not proven that
Simeon agrees with what he says.]

[G]   [Zeira] replied to him [i.e., Bun bar Hiyya], "[The case referred
to at E is different since] there [the heave-offering still] is clean
[and fit to eat] according to the Torah.

[H]   "[That which is burned at Passover] is heave-offering still in its
natural [i.e., clean, edible] state. It is only you [i.e., rabbinic
authorities] who have ruled that it is to be burned [just before
the start of Passover]." [Yet at the time at which it is burned, it
still is good heave-offering and could be eaten. Therefore Joshua
does not allow the householder himself to render this heave-
offering unclean. This has nothing to do with the case of M. Ter.
8:9–11 or M. Bek. 5:2.]

[I]   [In order to counter Zeira's reply at H, Y. suggests that already at
the point at which heave-offering that is leavened is burned at
Passover, it is not fit to be eaten by a priest. If this is the case,
then, according to Zeira's understanding, C, even Joshua should
agree that the householder himself may render it unclean.] But
in all events has [this leavened heave-offering] not been rendered
invalid through [the householder's] lack of attentiveness [to it]?
[Once it became clear that no priest will eat this heave-offering,
the householder ceased to keep watch over it. When this oc-

curred the heave-offering was rendered invalid, as is shown by the following.]

[J]   And did not R. Yohanan say, "Inattention [renders heave-offering invalid] according to the Torah"? [D–F therefore is correct. The criticism of D–F, at G–H, is unfounded. As D–F states, C misunderstands the theory behind Joshua's position and as a result does not prove that Simeon agrees with Joshua, M. Ter. 8:9–11.]

[K]   [K–L is separate, reviewing theories heretofore suggested: As for] the second jug [of wine in the status of heave-offering, M. Ter. 8:9–11—Joshua agrees with] R. Meir, [who at M. Pes. 1:7 allows a person at Passover to render unclean heave-offering which he is about to burn. Joshua holds that according to the] Torah [one may not impart uncleanness to heave-offering, but that this rule is relaxed in the case in which the heave-offering already may not be consumed by a priest, i.e., that it is about to be mixed with unclean wine].

[L]   [As for a firstling which has suffered] a congestion of blood, [Joshua agrees with] R. Simeon [M. Bek. 5:2, that while] according to the Torah [one may not cause a blemish in a firstling, if the animal might otherwise die, this is permitted]. [This is the opposite of the conclusion I–J leaves us with.]

[M]   [Returning to the issue raised by I–J, we answer the question of why Joshua does not allow the householder at Passover to burn together the clean and unclean heave-offering which is leavened. As I has shown, that heave-offering already has been invalidated through the inattention of the householder. If, as C claims, Joshua's theory is that what already is invalid may be rendered unclean by the householder, then this should apply in this case as well. Zeira explains why it does not.] [Zeira, the authority behind C,] said to him [i.e., to Bun bar Hiyya, who brought up the issue of Joshua's view concerning the burning of heave-offering at Passover, D–F, "Contrary to the suggestion of I, the heave-offering that is leavened and which is to be burned at Passover is subject to the attentiveness of the householder.] He guards it so that it will not come into contact with other clean things [that are not to be destroyed before Passover]." [He must prevent the leavened heave-offering's being mixed with these other unleavened foods. Since that heave-offering has been watched, at the point that it is burned, it still is fit for consumption by a priest. This is the reason that Joshua, M. Pes. 1:7, does not allow the householder to render such heave-offering unclean, contrary to his view concerning the heave-offering at M. Ter. 8:8–11. The theory which Zeira originally proposed, C, thus stands. The criticism of C, at D–F + I–J, has here been shown to be unacceptable.]

[N] [M's explanation of why Joshua holds that, on Passover, clean heave-offering may not be burned with unclean is found unacceptable. The implication is that C rightly has been challenged by D–F + I–J.] Replied R. Isaac, the son of R. Hiyya the elder, "Imagine that it [i.e., the clean, leavened heave-offering already] had been placed upon the coals [to be burned]." [Now it already is turning to ashes and is unfit for consumption. Since this is the case, according to C, Joshua should hold that the householder may place with this now-burning, clean heave-offering other unclean heave-offering. Yet Joshua, M. Pes. 1:7 does not allow this. C therefore must be wrong.]

[O] [Zeira] said to him, "[Your understanding of the situation at M. Pes. 1:7 is correct. But Joshua's statement there pertains] only up to the point at which one actually places [the heave-offering in the fire]." [If the heave-offering already were on the fire, as N suggests, Joshua would agree that the householder may impart to it uncleanness. But before this point, as G–H + M have argued, he has good reason not to allow this and therefore does not. The net result is that C is correct. Contrary to D–F + I–J + N, M. Pes. 1:7 does not prove that C's understanding of Joshua's theory at M. Ter. 8:9–11 is unacceptable.]

C versus D–F provides the fulcrum of the pericope. Zeira, C, states that Joshua holds that whenever heave-offering certainly is going to be lost, the householder himself may impart to it uncleanness. Zeira notes that Simeon, M. Bek. 5:2, can agree with this. Simeon holds that even in a case in which the impending invalidity is only probable, the individual may take actions which certainly will render the holy thing invalid. On the contrary, however, Joshua need not agree with Simeon's view. For, as we saw, Joshua's view, M. Ter. 8:9–11, applies only in a case in which the heave-offering certainly will be lost, even if the householder himself does nothing.

The weight of Zeira's claim is that Joshua is not alone in holding that, under certain circumstances, a householder may impart
uncleanness to heave-offering. According to Zeira, Simeon agrees
with this. D–F attempts to prove the opposite, that Joshua is
alone in his view. In this way D–F's point is the same as that
already proposed and proven by Y. Ter. 8:8 **I**, where we saw that
neither Meir nor Yose could agree with Joshua. To prove this,
D–F points out that at M. Pes. 1:7 Joshua does not allow a
householder to impart uncleanness to heave-offering which, because it is leavened, must be destroyed before Passover. Since
this is the case, it appears that Joshua's view is not so reasoned as
Zeira, C, has claimed. If Zeira's understanding of Joshua's view
is incorrect, then it has not been proven that Simeon abides by
that view.

In the give and take which follows (G–H rejects D–F; I–J
counters G–H, but in turn is rejected by M; N challenges M,
but is shown unacceptable by O),[50] Zeira succeeds in proving
that the case of M. Pes. 1:7 is a singleton, in which an unusual
circumstance causes Joshua to depart from his otherwise consistent view. This view, that if heave-offering anyway will go to
waste the householder may himself render it unclean, is the same
as that which informs the view of Simeon, M. Bek. 5:2.

[V.A] Said R. Mana to R. Shimi, "You (plural) say that (read:) R. Simeon [M. Bek. 5:2, cited above, Y. Ter. 8:9 **IV**.A] agrees with the
view of R. Joshua [M. Ter. 8:9–11, in that both hold that if a
holy thing in all events will not be eaten, the householder himself may render it invalid].

[B] "[But this claim is not logical,] for even R. Joshua does not
[consistently abide by the theory which you have attributed to]
R. Joshua." [For instance, at M. Pes. 1:7 Joshua holds that at
Passover, even though leavened heave-offering is going to be
burned, that which is clean may not be rendered unclean.]

[C] [Shimi] said to him, "These Tannaitic authorities [have the following positions:] There [at M. Ter. 8:9–11] R. Meir's view [as
seen at M. Pes. 1:7] is evidenced in the position of R. Joshua.
[This was claimed above, Y. Ter. 8:9 **I**.B + D, but was dis-
proven in the ensuing discussion.]

[D] "But here [at M. Bek. 5:2] R. Simeon's view accords with that of
R. Joshua [M. Ter. 8:9–11, just as Zeira, Y. Ter. 8:9 **IV** has
proven]."

Mana, A–B, reopens the argument closed by Zeira at the conclusion of the preceding pericope. Zeira there proved that Simeon, M. Bek. 5:2, and Joshua, M. Ter. 8:9–11, have the same view. Shimi, here at D, reaches that same conclusion.

[VI.A]   There we have learned [M. Bek. 5:2: *"As for] a firstling which had a congestion of blood—even if it otherwise would die one may not bleed it"—the words of R. Judah. But sages say, "One should bleed it, so long as doing so will not cause a blemish. And if it did cause a blemish, by reason of this [the firstling] may not be slaughtered." R. Simeon says, "One may bleed it, even though this will cause a blemish."*

[B]   R. Abbahu in the name of R. Eliezer [said], "The opinion of R. Judah accords with that of (follow PM and read:) Rabban Gamaliel. [At M. Ter. 8:8, he holds that the householder may do nothing to change the status of cleanness of a jug of wine about which there is a doubt whether or not it already is unclean. Just like Judah at A, Gamaliel thus holds that even though the holy thing will go to waste, the person may do nothing himself to alter it.]

[C]   "And the opinion of rabbis [here at A] accords with that of R. Eliezer. [At M. Ter. 8:8, he says that the householder should attempt to protect that which might be invalid. So here the sages say that the person should bleed the firstling to prevent its possible death, but that this may not be done if it will in itself invalidate the animal.]

[D]   "And the view of R. Simeon [here at A] accords with that of R. Joshua." [At M. Ter. 8:8, he says that once the holy thing possibly is invalid, the householder may cause it to become certainly invalid. In the same way, Simeon here says that the individual may bleed the firstling, even though doing so will cause a blemish and invalidate it.]

[E]   [Developing D:] Now it is taught: R. Simeon[51] declares that one may bleed the animal, even if in doing so he purposely causes a blemish.

[F]   [This view of Simeon, E,] accords with the latter view of R. Joshua, [who, at M. Ter. 8:9–11, holds that once the holy thing is going to become invalid, the householder himself may take actions to render it invalid].

The positions of the three authorities cited at M. Bek. 5:2 correlate with those assigned to Gamaliel, Eliezer, and Joshua at M. Ter. 8:8. D versus E–F draws a clear distinction between the positions of Joshua at M. Ter. 8:8 and 8:9–11. Under certain circumstances, a householder may carry out actions which might render a holy thing invalid. So Joshua, M. Ter. 8:8, and Simeon, M. Bek. 5:2. Under more pressing conditions, M. Ter. 8:9–11, the householder even may purposely cause the holy thing to become invalid.

[VII.A]   R. Abbahu in the name of R. Simeon b. Laqish [said], "The scriptural basis for the view of R. Judah [M. Bek. 5:2, that one may not bleed a firstling which has suffered a congestion of blood] is [Dt. 12:16]: '[Only you shall not eat the blood]; you shall pour it out upon the earth like water.'

[B]   "[This means that God said], 'I did not permit you to do anything with its [i.e., an animal's] blood except to pour it out [during the act of slaughter.' But bleeding an animal is not permitted.]"

[C]   [Suggesting that Dt. 12:16 does not apply to sanctified animals,] R. Abba Mari the brother of R. Yose replied, "As regards beasts which are invalid for use in the sanctuary, it is written, '[Only you shall not eat the blood]; you shall pour it out upon the earth like water.'" [As B states, this proscribes the bleeding of unconsecrated animals. But it does not apply to sanctified ones.]

[D]   [Suggesting a wholly different point made by Dt. 12:16,] said R. Hiyya bar Abba,[52] "[Dt. 12:16] was stated [to teach a rule concerning] the power of a liquid to impart to dry foods susceptibility to uncleanness.

[E]   "[Its point is that] just as water [which is 'poured out'] renders [dry produce] susceptible to uncleanness, so blood [which is 'poured out'] renders [dry foods] susceptible to uncleanness."

[F]   [We turn to the scriptural basis for the views of sages and Simeon, cited above, Y. Ter. 8:9 **VI** A.] R. Abbahu in the name of R. Yohanan [said], "Both of them [derived their opinions through the interpretation] of the same verse [Lev. 22:21]. They explained: '[And when anyone offers a sacrifice of peace offerings to the Lord, to fulfill a vow or as a freewell offering, from the herd or from the flock], to be accepted it must be perfect; there shall be no blemish in it.'

[G]   "R. Simeon interprets this to mean [that] at a moment at which [the animal already] is acceptable [to God], one is not permitted to cause a blemish in it.

[H]   "But at a point at which it is not acceptable [to God, for instance, if it already has a congestion of blood], one is permitted to cause a blemish in it.

[I]   "But the sages say, '[The verse means that] even if [the animal already] is covered with blemishes, one is not permitted to cause it to have [another] blemish.'"

While primary at Y. Bek. 5:2, the unit is found here because of the previous reference to that pericope. It locates in Scripture the sources of the opinions of M. Bek. 5:2's authorities. F–I claims that different interpretations of the same verse led to the distinct views of Simeon and sages.

[VIII.A]   [M. Ter. 8:9–11 has a jug of heave-offering break by the upper vat, while the lower vat is unclean. Eliezer holds that the householder himself may take no actions which will render the heave-offering unclean. This view is explained.] R. Hama bar Uqba in the name of R. Yose bar Hanina [says], "[If the householder had] a vessel the inside of which was in a state of cleanness, but the outside of which was unclean, he may not [use the vessel and thereby risk] rendering unclean a small quantity[53] [of heave-offering] in order to save [in cleanness] a large quantity [of the heave-offering, even though it otherwise will run down into the lower vat]."

[B]   [But contrary to A] have we not learned [M. Ter. 8:9]: *R. Eliezer says]*, "*Let [the heave-offering] go down [into the lower vat] and be made unclean. But let him not render it unclean with his hands*"? [Contrary to A, Eliezer should allow the use of a vessel, even if it will impart uncleanness to some heave-offering. Eliezer only proscribes the use of one's hands to render heave-offering unclean.]

[C]   [To explain the view of Yose bar Hanina, A,] said R. Samuel bar Barkiya, "Interpret [Yose bar Hanina's statement] to refer to a case in which there were two vessels, [with either one of which the householder could have attempted to salvage some of the heave-offering in cleanness, and that] one of them had insides in a status of cleanness, but an unclean outside [as at A],[54] and that the other had unclean insides and (read:) unclean outsides. [Eliezer will not allow the individual to choose one of these vessels to prevent the heave-offering from going down in the lower vat, for he might accidentally take the wrong one and render all of the heave-offering unclean.]

[D] "But since the Mishnah itself (*mhdy;* so L, V; P reads *whry*) [speaks of the prohibition against rendering unclean the heave-offering with one's hands, Yose bar Hanina referred only to] one unclean vessel."[55]

[E] [Mana suggests that it is not necessary to interpret Yose bar Hanina's view through the addition of C. Rather, Mana says, Yose bar Hanina did not state A in reference to the case of M. Ter. 8:9 in particular. If this is so, then Yose bar Hanina's point is as given here.] Said R. Mana, "Interpret [Yose bar Hanina's statement, A,] to refer to a case in which [the heave-offering which has spilled is going to drain] into a clean vat. [In order to prevent this, the householder wishes to catch this heave-offering in a vessel the outside of which is unclean. Since the heave-offering is in no danger of becoming unclean by flowing into the other vat, Eliezer holds that the householder may not risk imparting to it uncleanness through use of this vessel.]

[F] "But the case [referred to] in the Mishnah [is different, for there the vat into which the wine is about to drain] is unclean." [In this case Yose bar Hanina agrees that Eliezer holds that one may risk rendering unclean some small quantity of heave-offering in order to save from uncleanness a large quantity. Eliezer only prohibits one to render the heave-offering unclean with his hands, as B suggests.]

[G] [E–F does not solve the problem posed by A–B], for have we not learned [M. Ter. 8:10L–P: Even if there is no unclean vat into which oil in the status of heave-offering is about to drain] R. Eliezer says, *"Let it run down and be soaked up [in the ground]. But let him not soak it up with his hands"*? [In E–F's understanding, since here the heave-offering is not going to be rendered unclean, the householder may not use a vessel the outside of which is unclean in order to salvage it. But this is the opposite of what Eliezer says. He states only that the person may not render it unclean with his hands, which implies that Eliezer *would* allow the use of a vessel. Yose bar Hanina therefore appears to be wrong when he states (A + E–F) that Eliezer's view is that, in such a case, the individual may not risk rendering the heave-offering unclean through use of the partially unclean vessel. From M. Ter. 8:10L–P it appears as though Eliezer does allow this.]

[H]   [To explain why Yose bar Hanina's claim does not apply here,] interpret [M. Ter. 8:10L–P] to be a case in which [the jug of oil] had rolled over to a field deemed unclean because of a plowed-up grave. [As the oil spills out there it is rendered unclean. Just as at F, therefore, Eliezer allows the individual to capture it in a vessel, even if in doing so he risks rendering it unclean himself. But if the wine were not about to be rendered unclean, Eliezer would not allow the use of an unclean vessel to scoop it up, just as Yose bar Hanina stated, A.]

The Yerushalmi interprets literally Eliezer's statement, M. Ter. 8:9–11, that even if heave-offering is about to become unclean, the householder may not render it unclean, "with his hands." Eliezer holds, the Yerushalmi says, that the individual may use a vessel, even if in doing so he risks imparting uncleanness to the heave-offering. This understanding of Eliezer's view, which is the basic assumption of the pericope, shows Yose bar Hanina's statement, A, to be unacceptable. The problem of the unit thus is to determine why, in the cited cases, Yose's interpretation of Eliezer's view does not apply. This analysis is in three parts, C–D, E–F, and G.

[**IX.A**]   [We return to the issue of Y. Ter. 8:9 **I.** Associates there, A–D, claim that Yose, M. Pes. 1:7, holds that in no circumstance may a householder render heave-offering unclean. Yose therefore agrees with Joshua, M. Ter. 8:8, that even if the cleanness of heave-offering is in doubt, the householder may not purposely render it unclean. But he disagrees with Joshua, M. Ter. 8:9, that if heave-offering is about to be rendered unclean anyway, the householder himself may render it unclean. An Amora, Yose, deemed the authority behind Y. Ter. 8:9 **I.**AA–BB, disagrees. He states that under certain circumstances Yose the Tanna will allow the householder himself to render heave-offering unclean. This is so, he says, in the case of M. Ter. 8:9. If the householder

there does not himself render the heave-offering unclean, he will
incur a substantial financial loss when the heave-offering drips
down into his vat of unclean, unconsecrated wine. The issue here
is for what sort of produce in the status of heave-offering associates and Yose, the Amora, hold that their interpretations apply.
The important facts are that unclean wine in the status of heave-
offering has no value. Unclean sanctified oil, to the contrary,
may be kindled in a lamp. We therefore should expect different
views concerning whether or not a householder himself may
render unclean each of these things.] In the opinion of the associates [that Yose never allows a householder to render heave-
offering unclean, even if it is about to be mixed with unclean,
unconsecrated food] both the first jug [referred to at M. Ter. 8:8
as being in a state of suspicion of uncleanness] and the second
jug[56] [referred to at M. Ter. 8:9, and which is about to be mixed
with unclean, unconsecrated produce]—[both of these jugs may
contain either oil or wine in the status of heave-offering. In both
cases Yose has the same view, that the householder may not
render consecrated produce unclean.]

[B]   [But] in the opinion of [the Amora] R. Yose [that under certain
circumstances Yose the Tanna allows the householder to impart
uncleanness to heave-offering, it makes a difference whether it
is] a jug of wine or a jug of oil. [Yose the Tanna allows him to
render unclean only wine in the status of heave-offering that is
about to be mixed with the householder's own unclean, unconsecrated wine. For if the householder does not stop the heave-
offering from being mixed with that unconsecrated produce, the
resulting mixture, in the status of unclean heave-offering, has no
value. The householder incurs a great financial loss. Yose, like
Joshua, allows him to prevent this by stopping the wine in the
status of heave-offering from running down into the lower vat,
even if in doing so he renders that heave-offering unclean. The
same reasoning does not apply if we deal with oil in the status of
heave-offering. The mixture of unclean oil in the status of heave-
offering would have value, for it may be kindled in a lamp. By
preventing this mixture from occurring, the householder therefore does not save himself from substantial financial loss. Under
such circumstances, Yose the Amora says, Yose the Tanna does
not allow the householder to render the heave-offering unclean
through his own actions.]

The conclusion of Y. Ter. 8:9 **I.AA–BB** is qualified. Those who claim there that Yose agrees with Joshua, M. Ter. 8:9, note that this agreement applies only in a case in which the householder stands to incur financial loss. The present unit adds that, for Yose to agree with Joshua, the potential financial loss must be substantial.

8:10 [P: 8:4c; M. Ter. 8:12]

[Y] *And so [in the case of] women to whom gentiles said, "Give [us] one of you that we may make her unclean, but if not, lo, we will make all of you unclean"—*

[Z] *let them make all of them unclean, but they should not hand over a single Israelite.*

Although stated anonymously, this is another example of the view Eliezer holds, M. Ter. 8:9–11. Despite the extenuating circumstances, the women may not take responsibility for the rape of one of their number. The Yerushalmi opens by asking under what circumstances the rule of M. Ter. 8:12 applies (units **I–II**). It goes on to speak in general about the obligation of Israelites to protect themselves from unruly gentiles (units **III–V**). This is accomplished through several stories involving specific rabbinic masters. In these stories Simeon b. Laqish emerges as a courageous advocate of fighting for one's rights. To the contrary, Yohanan is passive and willing to accept ill treatment at the hands of others.

[I.A] [The claim of M. Ter. 8:12, that Israelite women must allow gentiles to rape each of them, but may not hand over a single one of their number expressly for that purpose] makes no sense if one of them already had been rendered unclean [in this way].

[B] [The rule of M. Ter. 8:12 likewise] makes no sense if one of [the women was a Canaanite] slave.[57] [In either of these cases the woman who already is unfit should be handed over to the gentiles, rather than have the gentiles render unfit all of the women.]

If the woman is already of impaired status, she is turned over to be raped. This preserves the other women in their status of cleanness, with no loss (!) to the woman who has been handed over.

[II.A]   It is taught [T. Ter. 7 : 20]: **[As to] a group of men who were walking along and gentiles met them and said, "Give us one of your number that we may kill him, and if not, lo, we will kill all of you"—**

[B]   **let them kill all of them, but [58] let them not give over to them a single Israelite.**

[C]   **But if they singled one out,**

[D]   **such as they singled out Sheba the son of Bichri [2 Sam. 20]—**

[E]   **let them give him to them, that they not all be killed.**

[F]   Said R. Simeon b. Laqish,[59] "Now this [C–E] applies [only] if the man [already] is subject to execution,[60] as was Sheba the son of Bichri."

[G]   But R. Yohanan says, "[It applies] even if he is not subject to execution, as was Sheba the son of Bichri."

[H]   [Simeon b. Laqish's view is instantiated.] Ulla bar Qushab—[61] the government wanted him [for a sentence of death].

[I]   He fled and went to Lod [where he was] near R. Joshua b. Levi.

[J]   [The agents of the king] came and surrounded the town. They said, "If you do not give him to us, we will destroy the town."

[K]   R. Joshua b. Levi went to him [i.e., to Ulla] and convinced him [to give himself up]. So [Joshua b. Levi] turned him [i.e., Ulla] over to them [i.e., to the agents of the king].

[L]   Now [until then] Elijah (may his memory be for good!) had been accustomed to reveal himself to him [i.e., to Joshua b. Levi].

[M]   [When this stopped occurring, Joshua b. Levi] fasted several times. [As a result, Elijah] revealed himself to him.

[N]   [Elijah] said to him, "Should I reveal myself to informers [who deliver Jews into the hands of the government]?"

[O]   [Joshua b. Levi] said to him, "[I am no traitor.] Did I not [simply] carry out [a rule of] the law (*mšnh*) [i.e., T. Ter. 7:20, above, A–E]?"

[P]   [Elijah] said to him, "Is this indeed the law for pious ones (*hsydym*)?"

The point is the same as in the preceding unit. If there is good reason to turn over one person in particular, Israelites may do this. So A–E + F–K.[62] L–P takes the opposite view. Israelites should not turn other Israelites over to the government, as Elijah, P, indicates.

[III.A]   R. Imi was caught in a riot.

[B][63]   Said R. Jonathan, "[There is nothing that can be done except to] wrap up the dead one in his shroud."

[C]   Said R. Simeon b. Laqish, "[To the contrary], up to the point at which I am killed, I myself can kill. I will go and, through strength, will deliver him to safety."

[D]   [Simeon b. Laqish] went and calmed down [the men who were threatening Imi], and they turned [Imi] over to him.

[E]   [Simeon b. Laqish] said to them, "Come [with me] to the old man [i.e., Yohanan], so that he may bless [all of] you [for turning Imi over to me unharmed]."

[F]   They came to R. Yohanan. He said to them, "That which you wished to do to him [i.e., to Imi] will be done to you."

[G]   That group of people left [Yohanan's presence], but had not [even] arrived at Apipsiros (Jastrow, p. 104, s.v., *'pypsdws*, suggests reading: Palmyra) before all of them were gone [i.e., carried into captivity].

[H]   Zeir bar Hanina was caught in a riot.

[I]   R. Imi and R. Samuel went to calm [the people down] for his sake.

[J]   Zenobia, the queen [Jastrow: of Palmyra; PM: *king* of the rioting bandits], said to them, "[Why have you come to save him?] He teaches that your creator performs miracles for you." [Why do they not leave it to God to save him?]

[K]   While they were busy [speaking with Zenobia], a certain Sarqi [member of a nomadic tribe] entered carrying a sword. He said, "With this sword Bar Netsar [Jastrow, PM: name of a chief of robbers] killed his brother [PM: killed the brother of Zenobia]."

[L]   [In the ensuing disorder] Zeir bar Hanina escaped.

The doublet of stories develops the point of the preceding unit. Contrary to Jonathan, B, human daring can be successful. K–L tempers this conclusion. While humans must do what they can, it is God, presumably, who causes the distraction that allows Zeir to escape. I see no way to determine the correct referents at J and K.

[IV.A]   R. Yohanan (delete: said)[64] was robbed by the men of (?) Qanyah [a robber king].

[B]   [Yohanan] went to the meeting place [i.e., the house of study].

[C]   Now Simeon b. Laqish asked him question after question [concerning matters of law], but [Yohanan] did not reply.

[D][65]   [Simeon b. Laqish therefore] asked him, "What is the problem?"

[E]   [Yohanan] said, "All of the limbs [i.e., mental and physical functions of the body] depend upon the heart. And the heart [i.e., one's mood] depends upon the pocketbook."

[F]   [So Simeon b. Laqish] said, "What has happened [that has left you in such bad spirits]?"

[G]   [Yohanan] told him what had happened. He said, "I was robbed by the men of Qanyah."

[H]   [Simeon b. Laqish] said to him, "Show me the path on which [the robbers] left."

[I]   He showed it to him, [and Simeon went off in pursuit].

[J]   [Simeon b. Laqish] saw [the robbers] from a distance and began to chime out [against them].

[K]   They said, "Since it was R. Yohanan's [property which we took], take back half."

[L]   He said to them, "On your lives, I am taking it all back."

[M]   So he took back all [of Yohanan's property].

The rabbi's power prevails even over hoodlums. Yohanan, B–C, is wrong to sit in quiet acceptance.

[V.A]   Diocles the swineherd—the students of R. Judah the patriarch would make fun of him (*mḥwnyh*).

[B]   He became emperor [= Diocletian] and moved to Paneas.

[C]   He sent letters to the rabbis, [saying]: "You must be here [to see] me immediately after the end of the [coming] Sabbath."

[D]   He instructed the messenger [who was to deliver these orders], "Do not give them the letters until the eve [of Sabbath], just as the sun is setting." [Diocletian hoped to force the rabbis to miss the appointment, for they could not travel on the Sabbath. Then he could have revenge on them because of their previous treatment of him, A.]

[E]   The messenger came to them on the eve [of Sabbath] as the sun was setting.

[F]   [46c] [After receiving the message,] R. Yudan the Patriarch and R. Samuel bar Nahman were resting in the public baths in Tiberias. Antigris, [a certain spirit, appeared and] came to their side.

[G]   R. Yudan the patriarch wished to rebuke him [and chase him away].

[H]   R. Samuel bar[66] Nahman said to him [i.e., to Yudan], "Leave him be. He appears as a messenger of salvation."

[I]   [Antigris] said to them, "What is troubling the rabbis?"

[J]   They told him the story [and] he said to them, "[Finish] bathing [in honor of the Sabbath]. For your creator is going to perform miracles [for you]."

[K]   At the end of the Sabbath [Antigris] took them and placed them [in Paneas].

[L]   They told [the emperor], "Lo, the rabbis are outside!"

[M]   He said, "They shall not see my face until they have bathed."

[N]   [Diocletian] had the bath heated for seven days and nights, [so that the rabbis could not stand the heat].

[O]   [To make it possible for them to enter, Antigris] went in before them and overpowered (ʾnṣḥ) the heat.

[P]   [Afterwards] they went in and stood before [the king].

[Q]   He said to them, "Is it because your creator performs miracles for you that you despise the [Roman] Empire?"

[R]   They said to him, "Diocles the swineherd did we despise. But Diocletian the emperor we do not despise."

[S]   [Diocletian said to them],[67] "Even so, you should not rebuke [anyone], neither a young Roman, nor a young associate [of the rabbis, for you never know what greatness that individual will attain]."

In light of the preceding units, this too must be seen as a story of God's saving the day, through the spirit Antigris.[68] But the pericope is odd, for Diocletian is shown to be a man of greater understanding than the rabbis, R + S.

9:1 [P: 9:1a]

[A] *One who sows [as seed grain in the status of] heave-offering—*

[B] *if [he does this] unintentionally, he should plow up [the seed].*

[C] *But [if he does it] intentionally, he must let [it] grow.*

[D] *And if [the grain] reached a third of its growth—*

[E] *whether [he sowed it] unintentionally or intentionally, he must let [it] grow.*

[F] *But [in the case of] flax [in the status of heave-offering]—*

[G] *[even if he sowed it] intentionally, he must plough [it] up [and not allow it to grow at all].*

[H] *And [the crop which grows from heave-offering, C and E,] is subject to [the laws of] (1) gleanings, (2) forgotten sheaves, and (3) [produce growing in] the corner of a field.*

A crop grown from seed in the status of heave-offering itself is deemed a priestly gift. Cultivating such a crop therefore entails considerable loss to the householder, for this produce has a low market value. A householder who unintentionally plants heave-offering is allowed to plow up the seed, so as to avoid the loss. If he planted the heave-offering intentionally, however, he is not given the option to correct his wrong action, C. D–E and F–G augment A–C, giving us three rules in all. Each of these is the focus of one section of the Yerushalmi's tripartite discussion.

A–C is discussed at units **I–III**. Unit **IV** explains D–E, and unit **V** gives the point of F–G.

[**I.A**]   *One who sows [as seed grain in the status of] heave-offering—*
[if this is] unintentional, he should plow up [the seed. But if it is
intentional, he must leave the seed to grow; M. Ter. 9 : 1].

[B]   This makes sense only if the rules are reversed, [such that one who unintentionally planted heave-offering leaves it to grow, and one who intentionally does this is required to plow it up].

[C]   [For it makes sense to say that] they punish [the person who intentionally plants heave-offering by forcing him to plow up all of the seed such that] the whole crop will be lost. [To the contrary, if the individual unintentionally planted the seed in the status of heave-offering, he should be allowed to leave the crop to grow. This way he will at least derive from his work the low value of heave-offering, but not lose everything.]

The Yerushalmi correctly captures the point of the Mishnah's rule, to punish the individual who intentionally plants as seed produce in the status of heave-offering. But in order to accomplish this, the Yerushalmi claims that the Mishnah means exactly the opposite of what it says.

[**II.A**]   R. Samuel bar Abudimi asked, "What is the rule [whether or not a person] may be believed when he says, 'I intentionally [sowed seed in the status of heave-offering and therefore am allowed to leave it grow]'?"

[B]   And they said to him, "If it is a case in which it already was known [that the individual had planted seed in the status of heave-offering], no claim of his [is accepted. We may assume that he simply wishes to remedy his own situation.]

[C]   "But if, [the individual himself having said nothing at all, we would] not [know that he had planted seed in the status of heave-offering, then he is believed when he tells us both that he planted such seed and that he did so intentionally]. For [in this case], the mouth which [could have] prevented [people] from knowing

anything at all is the mouth which chose to inform [everyone of
the incident as a whole]."

The Yerushalmi applies to the case at hand the familiar theory of
testimony. If the individual already has been caught, B, we do
not accept statements of his intended to reduce his culpability.
We assume he is lying to make the best of the unpleasant circumstance in which he has been caught. This is not the case if
we depend upon the defendant for all the facts, C. If this individual had wanted to lie, he need not have said anything about
having planted seed in the status of heave-offering. When he
chooses to tell the truth in saying this much, we must assume
that he also tells the truth in anything else that he states. A better reading at A would have the individual claim unintentionally
to have sown the heave-offering seed, such that he has the right
to plow it up and prevent the future loss of a ripened crop. That
reading is not, however, supported by the available manuscript
evidence.

[**III.A**] R. Benjamin bar Zidal asked, "[If] he planted [as seed] vetches
in the status of heave-offering, [or if] he planted [as seed] heave-
offering separated from produce grown outside of the land [of
Israel—what is the rule whether or not that which grows from
these things likewise has the status of heave-offering]?"

[B] They said to him, "It is a [rabbinic] decree [that produce separated from vetches, or from produce grown outside of the land
of Israel is deemed to have the status of heave-offering]. And a
[rabbinic] decree [i.e., that what grows from produce in the
status of heave-offering is deemed heave-offering] does not apply
to [produce which is deemed heave-offering only because of] a
[rabbinic] decree."

The issue is the application of the rule of M. Ter. 9:1 in the case
of anomalous types of heave-offering. Vetches normally are used
as animal feed, such that they are not subject to heave-offering.
Produce grown outside of the land of Israel likewise is not subject to that offering. If such produce is designated heave-offering
anyway, it is deemed in certain respects to be a priestly gift. For

the reason given at B, however, the rule of M. Ter. 9:1 does not apply.

[**IV**.A]   [According to M. Ter. 9:1D–E, if a crop from seed in the status of heave-offering reaches a third of its growth, the householder may not plow it up and thereby destroy the produce.] This is to say that a status of consecration applies to this produce while it still is unpicked.

[B]   This [further] implies that if one separated [heave-offering] from produce which had not yet reached a third of its growth, [that which he separates] has not [thereby] been rendered sanctified [with the status of heave-offering].

Once it reaches a third of its growth, that which is growing in the ground is deemed heave-offering, such that it no longer may be plowed up. So M. Ter. 9:1D–E. From this it is clear that even that which is unpicked may take on a status of consecration (A). But this status applies only to produce, picked or unpicked, which already has reached a third of its growth (B).

[**V**.A]   *[In the case of flax in the status of heave-offering—even if he sowed it] intentionally, he must plow [it] up* [M. Ter. 9:1F–G].

[B]   [The reason for this is that] they inflicted a punishment such that he may not benefit from fiber [of the flax plant].

The seeds of flax are a food, from which linseed oil is derived. These may take on the status of heave-offering. The more valuable part of the plant, however, is used to make linen. This is not a food and therefore, even when grown from consecrated seed, remains unconsecrated. For this reason farmers who plant flax seed which has the status of heave-offering would be able to use the plant fibers for their own benefit, by making linen. In order to prevent this, B, they are required to plow up the plants.

9:2–3 [P: 9:1b; M. Ter. 9:2]

[I]   *And poor Israelites and poor priests glean [in a field planted with seed in the status of heave-offering].*

[J]   *And the poor Israelites sell their portion to the priests at the price of heave-offering.*

[K]   *And the money [which they receive] is theirs [i.e., the poor Israelites'].*

[L]   *R. Tarfon says, "Only poor priests should glean,*

[M]   *"lest they [i.e., the poor Israelites] forget and put [the produce they glean] in their mouths."*

[N]   *Said to him R. Aqiba, "If so, only clean [priests] should glean."*

Although deemed to have the status of heave-offering, a crop which grows from consecrated seed is subject to gifts for the poor (M. Ter. 9:1H). This pericope indicates how those gifts are collected. The problem is what poor Israelites are to do with their share, which they may not themselves consume. The answer appears at J–K versus L–M + N. The Yerushalmi notes that the view of J, that poor Israelites may glean in a field in which heave-offering is growing, applies even if the householder had accidentally left in that field sheaves that he himself had designated to be heave-offering (unit I). The second unit clarifies Tarfon's view, L–M, by indicating how it would apply in a different case, suggested by T. Toh. 8:4. The final unit simply repeats the statement of Aqiba, N. In V, L, and R this unit is marked 9:3. The reason for this is unclear.

[I.A]   R. Yose asked, "[If the householder] had set aside [as heave-offering] sheaves of his own [i.e., for a different field which he owned] and these became mixed up [with the forgotten sheaves in the field in which seed in the status of heave-offering had been planted—what is the rule?]

[B]   "Even so, [just as M. Ter. 9:2 states], *poor Israelites*[1] *and poor priests glean [in that field]."*

Poor Israelites are trusted to glean in a field in which heave-offering designated by the householder, and therefore exempt from poor tithes, is found.

[II.A]   It is taught [T. Toh. 8:4]: **The wife of an *Am Haares* may grind [grain] with the wife of an associate when [the wife of the *Am Haares*] is unclean, [for during this time she will be careful not to touch the associate's food]. But when she is clean, she should not grind [wheat with her].**

[B]   [This is because the wife of the *Am Haares*] believes that she is even cleaner than [the wife of the associate, such that she will go ahead and touch the food. Since she is not deemed clean at all, she must not be allowed to do this.]

[C]   Now in accordance with the position of R. Tarfon [M. Ter. 9:2L–M, that poor Israelites should not be allowed to glean in a field planted with seed in the status of heave-offering, lest they forget and eat some of the food], even if [the wife of the *Am Haares*] is unclean, she may not grind [grain with the wife of the associate], lest she forget and put [some of his clean food] into her mouth [and, by touching it, renders all of the food unclean].

C extrapolates the view Tarfon, M. Ter. 9:2L–M, would hold for the case of T. Toh. 8:4.

[III.A]   This is what the Mishnah [Ter. 9:2N] means: *If so, only clean [priests] should glean.*

This is exactly what Aqiba, M. Ter. 9:2N, states.[2]

9:4 [P: 9:1c; M. Ter. 9:3]

[O]   *And [the produce grown from seed in the status of heave-offering] is subject to (4) tithes and (5) poor man's tithe.*

[P]   *And poor Israelites and poor priests take [the poor man's tithe].*

[Q]   *And the poor Israelites sell their [portion] to the priests at the price of heave-offering;*

[R]   *and the money [which they receive] is theirs [i.e., the poor Israelites'].*

[S]   *He who threshes by hand [the produce grown in such a field] is praiseworthy.*

[T]   *But he who threshes [it] with cattle, how should he do this [so that the cattle do not eat the grain, which has the status of heave-offering]?*

[U]   *He hangs a feed bag from the neck of the beast and places in it [unconsecrated produce of] the same kind [as is being threshed].*

[V]   *It turns out that he does not muzzle the animal [prohibited by Dt. 25:4], but [also] does not feed it heave-offering.*

O–R makes the same point as M. Ter. 9:2. The issue of S–V is phrased at T. In threshing produce in the status of heave-offering, the householder must be careful to prevent the oxen from eating the consecrated food. Yet he also may not muzzle them (Dt. 25:4). The solution to this problem appears at U.

Units **I–II** make explicit the point of O. Unit **III** explains S. **IV** and **V** draw out the implications of T–U. These units are concluded by unit **VI**, which speaks in general about the meaning of Dt. 25:4, upon which T–U depends. Only P–R is given no attention by the Yerushalmi. This is because its same rule was discussed in the context of the preceding pericope, Y. Ter. 9:2–3.

[I.A]   This is what the Mishnah [Ter. 9:3] means: [Produce which grows from seed in the status of heave-offering] is subject to the separation of heave-offering, [first and second] tithe and poor man's tithe.

The Yerushalmi makes explicit exactly which offerings are referred to at M. Ter. 9:30.

[II.A]³   [As regards] a *litra* of onion in the status of first tithe which was planted [as seed] and, lo, there is in [the grown crop] about ten *litras* [of produce]—

[B]   lo, [the crop] is subject to the separation of [heave-offering and] tithes.

[C]   And [as regards] the first tithe which is in it [i.e., the first tithe which he separates from the grown crop], he [also] designates it heave-offering of the tithe for the [first tithe] that he originally planted.

[D]   [As regards] a *litra* of onions in the status of second tithe which was planted and, lo, there is in [the grown crop] about ten *litras* [of produce]—

[E]   [the crop] is subject to the separation of [heave-offering and] tithes.

[F]   And he goes and redeems the [second] tithe which he [originally] planted [T. Ter. 8:5–6].

The Yerushalmi cites T. Ter. 8:5–6 (with minor variations), adding no comment of its own. The material supplements M. Ter. 9:4C–E's law, which states that crops grown from seed in the status of first and second tithe do not have the status of those offerings. The Tosefta's point is that since the crop has no special status, the usual agricultural offerings must be separated from it. The householder also must designate the heave-offering of the tithe required of the original first tithe which he planted (C). For the case of second tithe, that original seed simply may be redeemed (F).

[III.A]   *He who threshes by hand [the produce grown from seed in the status of heave-offering] is praiseworthy* [M. Ter. 9:3S].

[B]   Than whom is he more praiseworthy?

[C]   [He is more praiseworthy] than one who threshes [this produce] with cattle.

The Yerushalmi makes explicit what already is obvious in the Mishnah.

[**IV.A**]   *But he who threshes [produce grown from seed in the status of*
heave-offering] with cattle, how should he do this? [He hangs a
feed bag from the neck of the beast and places in it unconse-
crated produce of the same kind as is being threshed; M. Ter.
9:3T–U].

[B]   It is taught [T. Ter. 8:3C–D]: **R. Simeon**[4] **says, "He places in**
[the feed bag] vetches, for they are of better quality than all
[other produce]."

[C]   Said R. Yose, "This indicates that [if] one did this [same thing]
in the case of [an animal threshing] unconsecrated produce, he
would not [thereby be deemed to] transgress [the rule of Dt. 25:4],
'You shall not muzzle [an ox when it treads out the grain].'"

[D][5]   [D–E is out of place in the present context. Discussion of C
continues at F–G.] One who [muzzles an ox being used to] tread
pulse or fenugreek does not [thereby] transgress the rule [of
Dt. 25:4], "You shall not muzzle an ox when it treads out the
grain."

[E]   But it [anyway] is forbidden to do this, for appearance sake.

[F]   [Yose's statement, C, is under dispute.] There are Tannaitic authorities who teach [as Yose does]: This applies [even] in the case
of threshing [of grain] which is permitted [for consumption by
nonpriests].

[G]   But [contrary to Yose] there are Tannaitic authorities who teach:
[One may use a feed bag on the animal only] in the case of threshing
[of grain] which is forbidden [i.e., of grain in the status of heave-
offering].

One may use a feedbag to prevent an ox from eating consecrated
produce it is threshing (A). Simeon explains that this is because
the householder is able to assure that the animal is not being
mistreated through use of the bag. On this basis Yose, C, claims
that the same method may be used while an ox threshes unconsecrated produce. All that matters is that the animal is not prevented from eating while it works. Anonymous Tannaitic authorities disagree concerning this issue, F–G. D–E breaks the
flow of the discussion and presumably is placed here only because of the verbal correspondence between C and D. Pulse and
fenugreek are not grains. They therefore do not fall under the
rule of Dt. 25:4.

[**V.A**] [M. Ter. 10:1 states that if a whole onion in the status of heave-offering is cooked with unconsecrated lentils, the lentils remain permitted for consumption by a nonpriest. But if the onion in the status of heave-offering is cut up, then, if it imparts its own taste to the lentils with which it is cooked, they are deemed to take on the consecrated status of heave-offering. Ba bar Mamel now explains the circumstances under which this applies.] Said R. Ba bar Mamel, "Mishnah speaks of a case in which [the whole onion] was placed [with the lentils] after the lentils already had cooked so much as to have the liquid in them dried out. The [mass of] lentils presses against [the onion in the status of heave-offering] so that it cannot impart [to them its flavor]. [In this case, the statement of M. Ter. 10:1 concerning the whole onion applies.]

[B] "But if one placed [the onion in the status of heave-offering with the lentils] before they [had cooked so much as to] release the liquid they contain—in this case, no." [In this situation even a whole onion will impart its taste to the lentils. Therefore the rule of M. Ter. 10:1 will not apply. The lentils that were cooked with the onion in the status of heave-offering will need to be treated themselves as heave-offering.]

[C] [The implication of A is stated.] Now, just as you state that the [mass of] lentils presses against [the onion] so that it cannot impart [to them its flavor], in the same way, lentils press against [46d] [the onion] so that it cannot absorb [their flavor].

[D] In what case does [C] apply?

[E] [In the case of] an unconsecrated onion that one cooked with lentils in the status of heave-offering—even so [the onion remains permitted since] the lentils press against it so that it cannot absorb [their flavor].

[F] [Another implication of A is given.] This is to say that [if the onion referred to at M. Ter. 10:1] is dry [the rule that it does not impart its own status of heave-offering to the lentils with which it is cooked applies].

[G] But if it is moist [then the lentils do not prevent it from imparting its taste to them, such that, even if the onion in the status of heave-offering is whole, it renders the lentils] forbidden [for consumption by nonpriests].

[H] In the case of an onion [in the status of heave-offering cooked] with [unconsecrated] leeks, whether [the onion] is moist or dry, whole or cut up, [it renders the leeks] forbidden [for consumption by nonpriests].

[I]   [The question is what constitutes "cutting up" the onion in the status of heave-offering.] If one removed the protuberance [on the blossom-end of the onion] it is as though [the onion] were cut up.

[J]   If there were two [or] three [whole onions cooked in one batch of lentils] it is as though [the lentils contained] a cut up [onion].

[K]   [If, as M. Ter. 10:1 states, a whole onion in the status of heave-offering may be cooked with unconsecrated lentils and not impart to them its own status], this is to say that [this applies] if the outer skin [of the onion] does not contain sufficient [pungency] to impart flavor [to the lentils].

[L]   But if [the outer skin] does have [sufficient pungency to impart the flavor of the onion to the lentils—what is the rule whether or not those lentils take on the status of heave-offering held by the onion with which they were cooked? To answer the question we must determine whether or not the outer skin of the onion, which normally is not eaten, is deemed to have the status of heave-offering. If it does not, then even if it imparts flavor to the lentils, they do not take on the status of a priestly gift. But if the outer skin is deemed heave-offering, then the lentils which it flavors will take on its status. The question of whether or not the outer skin of produce in the status of heave-offering is deemed to be heave-offering is answered through the following analysis.]

[M]   There are Tannaitic authorities who teach [that Dt. 25:4's rule against muzzling an ox that is treading out grain applies] only in [the case of an ox] treading out [grain which is] permitted [for consumption by nonpriests. These authorities state that if the grain is in the status of heave-offering, the householder may muzzle the ox which treads it.]

[N]   [But contrary to M], the Mishnah there [at M. Ter. 9:3] states that even in the case of the threshing of grain which is forbidden [for consumption by a nonpriest, the law against muzzling the animal applies].

[O]   For we have learned [M. Ter. 9:3U]: *He hangs a feed bag from the neck of the beast [and places in it unconsecrated produce of the same kind as is being threshed].* [The implication here is that the ox may not even be allowed to eat the *husks* of the grain in the status of heave-offering which it is threshing. That is why the householder must place other produce, of the same kind, in the feed bag. The reason the ox may not eat the husks from the heave-offering is that they too are deemed to have the status of a priestly gift. This means that at L as well, the skin of the onion is deemed to be heave-offering. If it imparts its flavor to lentils, they take on that sanctified status (so PM).]

The unit belongs with M. Ter. 10:1, where it is primary. It appears here because of M–N and O, which cite M. Ter. 9:3 and the discussion already begun in the preceding unit concerning that pericope. Each of the units of this longer pericope are discussed below, in their context within the Yerushalmi's treatment of M. Ter. 10:1.

[VI.A]   [Dt. 25:4's statement that 'You shall not muzzle an ox when it treads out the grain' applies to an ox which is] treading [the grain] but not to one which is threshing [it].

[B]   R. Eliezer b. Jacob says, "[One may not muzzle an ox] even if it is threshing [grain]."

[C]   [We turn to a new issue.] Said R. Abun, "R. Aqiba asked [the following question] of R. Simeon b. Yohai in order to test his knowledge: '[What is the rule] if an individual muzzled the animal outside [of the threshing area] and then brought it into [the threshing area]?' [Does this fall under the prohibition of Dt. 25:4, that you shall not muzzle an ox "*when* it treads out the grain"?]

[D]   "[Simeon b. Yohai] said to him, '[Lev. 10:9 states that the sons of Aaron may not drink wine or strong drink] "*when* you go into the tent of meeting."

[E]   "'[The term *when* here certainly does not mean that the priests may not drink wine after they come to the tent of meeting. Rather, it means they may not drink wine beforehand, i.e.,] "*since* you will be coming to the tent of meeting.'" [In the same way it is clear that the statement of Dt. 25:4, that one may not muzzle an ox *when* it is treading out the grain means that one may not muzzle an ox that is about to tread out grain.]

[F][6]   [Reaching the same conclusion as Simeon b. Yohai,] said R. Zeira, "[Dt. 25:4 states] 'You shall not muzzle an ox when it

treads out the grain.' [This means], 'You may not tread out grain
with an ox which is muzzled.'"

The exact meaning of Dt. 25:4 is disputed.

9:5 [P: 9:2a; M. Ter. 9:4]

[A]   *That which grows from [seed in the status of] heave-offering has
      the status of heave-offering.*

[B]   *And what grows from [the seed of produce] that grew from [seed
      in the status of] heave-offering is unconsecrated.*

[C]   *But [as regards] (1) produce which is subject to tithes, (2) first
      tithe, (3) after-growths of the seventh year [of the Sabbatical
      cycle], (4) heave-offering [separated from produce grown] out-
      side of the land of Israel, (5) mixtures of heave-offering and un-
      consecrated produce, and (6) first fruits—that which grows from
      them is common food [i.e., does not have the same status as the
      seed from which it grew].*

[D]   *That which grows from [seed] which is dedicated [to the Temple]
      or second tithe is unconsecrated.*

[E]   *And he redeems them [i.e., the seed] when they are sown.*

That which grows from heave-offering is consecrated and must
be eaten by a priest (A). Unlike true heave-offering, however, it
is subject to agricultural restrictions which apply to unconsecrated produce (M. Ter. 9:1–3). This crop, which thus does not
have the status of true heave-offering, does not itself produce a
consecrated crop (B). C applies this same logic to other types of
produce which, while subject to special restrictions, are not consecrated. D–E is a special case. While produce which is dedicated to the Temple or has the status of second tithe is consecrated, it may be redeemed. That which grows from it therefore
does not have a consecrated status. The Yerushalmi discusses
each of these three rules in turn. Unit **I** relates to B, unit **II**
interprets C, and units **III–IV** explain D.

[I.A]   [M. Ter. 9:4B states that what grows from seed of produce that itself grew from seed in the status of heave-offering is unconsecrated.] It is taught concerning this: In what case does this apply?

[B]   [It applies] *in the case of a kind of produce the seed of which disintegrates* [M. Ter. 9:5B; i.e., a case in which the seed is not an integral part of the produce which grows from it].

[C]   But in the case of a kind of produce the seed of which does not disintegrate, even that which grows from the seed of produce which, in turn, grew [from heave-offering] is forbidden [i.e., deemed to have the status of heave-offering].

The Yerushalmi coordinates the Mishnah's two different rules concerning the circumstances under which seed from heave-offering produces a crop which likewise is deemed to have the status of a priestly gift. To do this it applies the consideration of M. Ter. 9:5B to the rule of M. Ter. 9:4B.

[II.A]   *But [as regards] (1) produce which is subject to tithes,* the majority of which is unconsecrated, *(2) first tithe,* the majority of which is unconsecrated [i.e., all except for the heave-offering of the tithe which it contains], *(3) after-growths of the seventh year [of the Sabbatical cycle],* which are not commonly found,[7] *(4) heave-offering [separated from produce grown] outside of the land [of Israel],* which is not commonly found, *(5) mixtures of heave-offering and unconsecrated* produce, the majority of which is unconsecrated, and *(6) first fruits,*[8] which are not commonly found—[that which grows from all of these things is unconsecrated, M. Ter. 9:4C].

Each item in M. Ter. 9:4C is cited and explained.

[III.A]   *That which grows from [seed] which is dedicated [to the Temple] or [is in the status of] second tithe is unconsecrated. And he redeems them [i.e., the seed] when they are sown* [M. Ter. 9:4D–E].

[B]   R. Abbahu in the name of R. Yohanan [says], "[If the individual failed to redeem the seed when he sowed it, later, when the crop which results has been harvested] he redeems the whole storehouse [full of produce] for the value of that [one] original *seah* [of consecrated seed which he planted]."

The Yerushalmi emphasizes that what grows from produce dedicated to the Temple or in the status of second tithe is not consecrated. Only the original seed retains its holy status and needs to be redeemed.

[IV.A]   [Even though M. Ter. 9 : 4D–E includes under a single rule produce dedicated to the Temple and produce in the status of second tithe] there is a difference between [the laws for] produce dedicated [to the Temple] and that in the status of second tithe.

[B]   [In the case of produce grown from seed in the status of] second tithe, whether or not it is produce the seed of which disintegrates, it may be redeemed at the lowest going price;

[C]   except that if it is produce the seed of which disintegrates, it is redeemed at the current lowest price,

[D]   and in the case of produce the seed of which does not disintegrate, it is redeemed at the lowest going price of the time at which it was planted.

[E]   [Unlike this rule for second tithe, in the case of a crop grown from seed of] produce dedicated [to the Temple], whether it is a type of produce the seed of which disintegrates or a type of produce the seed of which does not disintegrate—its value is nothing other than the going price in the place and at the time [at which it is to be redeemed].

[F]   But in the case of a type of produce the seed of which disintegrates, he may redeem the whole storehouse [full of produce] at the value of that [one] *seah* [of consecrated seed] which he originally planted.

[G]   And in the case of a type of produce the seed of which does not disintegrate, [all of the crop is deemed consecrated such that] he must redeem all of the [produce in the] storehouse.

Produce which is dedicated to the Temple must be sold at the going price for such produce at the place and time of the sale,

E–G. This is not the case for produce in the status of second tithe, B–D. Like unit **I**, this pericope reads into M. Ter. 9:4 the consideration of M. Ter. 9:5B, whether or not the produce is a type the seed of which disintegrates.

9:6 [P: 9:2b; M. Ter. 9:5]

[A]   *[If there are] a hundred garden beds [planted] with [seed in the status of] heave-offering and one [planted] with unconsecrated [seed, but it is not known which contains the unconsecrated seed],*

[B]   *all are permitted [for consumption as unconsecrated food] in the case of a kind [of produce] the seed of which disintegrates.*

[C]   *But in the case of a kind the seed of which does not disintegrate,*

[D]   *even if there are a hundred beds [sown] with unconsecrated seed and one [planted] with heave-offering,*

[E]   *all of them are forbidden.*

According to the present pericope, the decisive factor for determining the status of consecration of a crop grown from heave-offering is the nature of the seed. If the seed is not an integral part of the produce which grows from it, that produce does not have the consecrated status of the seed. If, however, the seed is integral to the crop, the crop is sanctified. While we have seen that the Yerushalmi reads the two notions together (Y. Ter. 9:5 **I** and **IV**), the principle of this pericope does not agree with the law as stated at M. Ter. 9:1–4, which states that what grows from heave-offering is always consecrated.

The Yerushalmi first addresses the implications of A–B for other cases in which heave-offering might be neutralized. Unit **II** reads C–D in the same light. It asks of the relationship between this rule and previously discussed laws for neutralization, in particular, as interpreted by Yohanan.

[**I**.A]   [According to M. Ter. 9:5A–B, in the case of a kind of produce the seed of which disintegrates, even if one garden bed is planted with unconsecrated produce and one hundred are sown with heave-offering, all of the crop is permitted.] Said R. Yose, "This implies that if he had one hundred *seahs* of produce which had been taken [to replace heave-offering neutralized in a mixture of one part of that offering in] a hundred [parts unconsecrated produce] and [also had] one *seah* of unconsecrated produce, and these were mixed together [so that he did not know which *seah* was the unconsecrated produce, all are] permitted [as unconsecrated food]." [The reason is that we may deem each individual *seah* to be the unconsecrated food, just as we do with the garden beds, M. Ter. 9:5A–B.]

Yose points out the implications of M. Ter. 9:5A–B.

[**II.**A]   There [at Y. Ter. 5:5] said R. Yohanan, "[As for] the *seah* of heave-offering taken up [to replace the priestly gift neutralized in a mixture] with one hundred *seahs* of unconsecrated produce—any small quantity [of unconsecrated produce with which that *seah* of replacement heave-offering is mixed] voids its [status as heave-offering]."

[B]   [The implication of A is that] here [at M. Ter. 9:5C–D] if he picked [the produce in one of the garden beds] and any small quantity of unconsecrated produce fell into that [which he picked], the produce becomes permitted.

[C]   [The issue is whether or not Yohanan holds that, for the case of M. Ter. 9:5C–D, the householder purposely may cause the heave-offering to be neutralized. At Y. Ter. 5:9 Yohanan holds that he may mill a mixture of heave-offering and unconsecrated produce if he knows that, by doing so, he will increase the proportion of unconsecrated produce so as to neutralize the heave-offering. The implication is that] just as R. Yohanan says there, "He may mill [the mixture] so as to cause [the heave-offering] to become permitted [to a nonpriest]," so here [in the case of the garden beds] this is so [i.e., Yohanan holds here as well that the householder validly may take actions designed to neutralize the heave-offering].

[D]   [The cases of M. Ter. 5:9 and M. Ter. 9:5 are not comparable. Therefore the conclusion of C is unacceptable.] There [in the case of M. Ter. 5:9, once the mixture is milled, if the individ-

ual takes a replacement offering] some [small percentage of the
original heave-offering] and some [much larger quantity of unconsecrated produce] will come up in his hand. [In this case, the
heave-offering really does constitute only a small percentage of
the mixture. Yohanan therefore deems the heave-offering to be
neutralized.]

[E]   But here [in the case of the beds planted with heave-offering,
any one bed which the householder picks may contain] all of the
unconsecrated, untithed produce. [That is, the forbidden produce in the beds planted with heave-offering may all] come up in
his hand. [Contrary to C, Yohanan therefore does not allow the
householder purposely to neutralize this produce, which is fully
forbidden.]

[F]   [E applies] if he picked [the produce in] one of the [garden beds
alone]. But if he picked the produce in two of them, [we may
assume that] both this [i.e., heave-offering] and this [i.e., unconsecrated produce] came up in his hand. [Since in this case the
heave-offering already is only a percentage of a mixture with unconsecrated produce, as at D, Yohanan will allow the householder to take actions designed to neutralize that heave-offering.]

M. Ter. 9:5D–E is read as a problem of neutralization. A–B
claims that the produce in any one garden bed the householder
picks is comparable to the *seah* of produce which is removed
from a batch of a hundred *seahs* of unconsecrated produce in
which one *seah* of heave-offering was neutralized. Since the *seah*
which is removed from the mixture is not true heave-offering,
special considerations apply to it, as Yohanan, A, states. This
reading of M. Ter. 9:5, which greatly expands upon the Mishnah's interest in the pericope, leads logically to the discussion at
C–E + F.

9:7 [P: 9:2c; M. Ter. 9:6]

[A]   *Produce which is subject to the separation of tithes—*

[B]   *that which grows from it is permitted [for consumption as a
chance meal, in the case of] a kind [of produce] the seed of which
disintegrates.*

[C]   *But in [the case of] a kind the seed of which does not disintegrate—*

[D]   *[even] that which grows from [the seed of a crop] which grew
       from it is forbidden [for consumption as a chance meal, for like
       the seed, it is deemed subject to tithes].*

[E]   *What is a kind [of produce] the seed of which does not disintegrate?*

[F]   *[A kind] such as arum, garlic, or onions.*

[G]   *R. Judah says, "Garlic is like barley" [i.e., its seed disintegrates].*

M. Ter. 9:6 states for untithed produce the same principle M.
Ter. 9:5 gave for heave-offering. The Yerushalmi asks for how
many generations of crops from untithed seed does the produce
still maintain an untithed status. This is a direct response to D
here. The second and final unit supplements the discussion of
E–G, asking exactly what Judah, G, means to say.

[I.A]   [M. Ter. 9:6C–D states that in the case of a type of produce the
         seed of which does not disintegrate, if the original seed was from
         untithed food, then even that which grows from a crop which it-
         self grew from this seed is forbidden.] For how many [genera-
         tions of crops does this apply]?

[B]   R. Jacob bar Idi in the name of R. Yohanan [says], "Three gen-
       erations of crops are forbidden; [that is], up to the fourth gen-
       eration [of crops] is forbidden. But the fourth [generation itself]
       is permitted."

[C]   [Up to now we have spoken about seed which was subject to the
       separation of heave-offering and tithes. What if the seed was it-
       self in the status of heave-offering?] R. Samuel bar Abudimi
       asked in the presence of R. Mana, "For the case of [seed from
       produce in the status of] heave-offering, for how many [genera-
       tions are the crops forbidden]?"

[D]   He said to him, "They deem the fourth-generation crop [from seed
       in the status of heave-offering] to be just like the first-generation
       crop [from untithed seed].

[E]   [D is explained.] "Just as [in the case of] a first-generation crop
       of a type of produce the seed of which disintegrates, if [the seed
       has the status of] heave-offering [the crop is] forbidden, but if
       [the seed] was subject to tithes [the crop is] permitted,

[F]   "so [also] a fourth-generation crop from a type of produce the seed of which does not disintegrate, if [the seed is in the status of] heave-offering the crop is forbidden, but if [the seed] was subject to tithes [the crop is] permitted."

A–B answers the question left open by M. Ter. 9:6C–D. For how many generations are crops which grew from seed which had not been tithed themselves deemed untithed? C–F answers the same question for the case of produce in the status of heave-offering which is planted as seed.

[II.A]   What can you mention [as a type of produce the seed of which disintegrates]?

[B]   Said R. Yose b. R. Bun, "[A kind] such as lesbian figs."

[C]   [Judah, M. Ter. 9:6G, says that garlic is like barley in that its seed disintegrates.] R. Abbahu in the name of R. Yose b. Hanina [says], "[As for] garlic—[Judah holds that] if it is [the size of] barley, it is like [a type of produce] the seed of which disintegrates.

[D]   "If it is larger than this, it is like [a type of produce] the seed of which does not disintegrate."

[E]   [Rejecting C–D,] R. Yose b. R. Bun in the name of R. Yose b. Hanina [said], "[As for] garlic—[Judah holds that] it is like barley in all respects [i.e., no matter what size it is, its seed disintegrates]."

The Yerushalmi's discussion of M. Ter. 9:6F–G is clear as stated.

9:8 [P: 9:3; M. Ter. 9:7]

[H]   *One who weeds alongside a gentile [in a field of] leeks [grown from seed which has not been tithed]—*

[I]   *even though his [i.e., the gentile's] produce has the status of untithed produce,*

[J]   *[the Israelite] makes a chance meal of it [without tithing].*

[K]   *Saplings [from seed] in the status of heave-offering which became unclean—*

[L]   *if he planted them, they no longer render unclean [that with which they come into contact].*

[M]   *And [the fruit of the saplings] is forbidden for consumption [by nonpriests] until he [once] trims off that fruit, [which has the status of heave-offering].*

[N]   *R. Judah says, "Until he trims off [the fruit] and does so a second time [i.e., also trims off the next crop which grows]."*

The produce of the gentile was grown from untithed seed of a type which does not disintegrate. It therefore should not be available for consumption as a chance meal (M. Ter. 9:6). Since produce grown by a gentile is not subject to the separation of tithes, however, the restrictions which apply to the original seed are abrogated. Thus the Israelite is allowed to eat the produce as a chance meal. K–L is obvious. What is connected to the ground no longer conveys uncleanness. The issue at M–N is comparable to that of M. Ter. 9:4B, as discussed at Y. Ter. 9:5 I.

The Yerushalmi discusses each of the Mishnah's points in turn. We begin with the basis for the view of H–I, that produce grown by a gentile in the land of Israel is not subject to tithes. Unit II follows with the same rule, as applied to produce grown by a Samaritan. Unit III draws out the point of K–L by asking under what circumstances produce which once was unclean, but presently is both clean and in a consecrated status, may be eaten as a holy thing. The final unit interprets M. Ter. 9:7M–N.

[I.A]   R. Hiyya bar Ashi in the name of R. Abbahu in the name of R. Yohanan [says], "[The rule of M. Ter. 9:7H–J, that an Israelite may make a chance meal, without tithing, of produce grown by a gentile] is the position of R. Simeon." [At Y. Dem. 5:9, Simeon holds that produce grown on land owned by a gentile in the land of Israel is not subject to tithes.]

[B]   [A is unreasonable.] If this is the opinion of R. Simeon, [who holds that the produce is not subject to tithes at all], why [should the [Israelite need to eat it] as a chance meal? [If the produce is not subject to tithes, he may eat it] even as a regular meal, [which normally would be subject to the separation of tithes].

[C]   [This explains why B's argument is not acceptable.] Rather, since

R. Jeremiah [and] R. Hiyya in the name of R. Yohanan [say],
"R. Simeon concedes that [an Israelite who purchases produce
grown by a gentile] must separate the [required] tithes as a matter of law [established by the rabbis], therefore, you must say
[that the Israelites only may make a chance meal of this produce.
This being the case, as A suggested, M. Ter. 9:7H–J] is the
position of R. Simeon.

Simeon, Y. Dem. 5:9, stands behind the rule of M. Ter. 9:7H–J.
Produce grown by a gentile on the land of Israel is not subject
to tithes unless it is purchased by an Israelite. Because of this
anomalous character, an Israelite who eats the produce without
tithing may do so only in the form of a chance meal.

[II.A]   It is taught: One who weeds alongside a Samaritan [in the Samaritan's field]—it is permitted [for him to make a chance meal
of produce] about which there is a doubt [whether or not it grew
from seed of produce which had been tithed].

[B]   But if it is known for certain[9] [that the produce grew from seed
that was not tithed, the Israelite] may not [make a chance meal
of it].

[C]   Why [is A the case]?

[D]   For the status of doubt [concerning whether or not produce was
tithed] is voided when that produce is [growing] from the ground,

[E]   and that which grows from forbidden produce does not neutralize it. [The point of E is unclear.]

The rule of M. Ter. 9:7H–J is given for the case of a Samaritan,
instead of the Mishnah's gentile. A Samaritan is deemed in some
respects to be like an Israelite. Therefore if it is known for certain that his produce grew from untithed seed, it may not be
used for a chance meal without tithing, B. The same would apply to produce grown from untithed seed by an Israelite.

[III.A]   R. Abbahu in the name of R. Yohanan [says], "[As for] saplings
in the status of heave-offering which were rendered unclean [M.
Ter. 9:7K]—

[B]¹⁰   "[If when they were still unconsecrated they became unclean and he then] planted them and [only afterwards] designated them to be heave-offering [they now are deemed heave-offering and clean and may be eaten by a priest.]

[C]   "But if from the start [i.e., before they were rendered unclean] they had the status of heave-offering, [even though they subsequently are planted and rendered clean, the produce which grows from them may not be eaten by a priest, since] they already were removed [from the category of clean heave-offering which may be eaten by a priest]."

[D]   [The same exercise as at A–C is repeated.] R. Abbahu in the name of R. Yohanan [says], "[As for] water which becomes unclean—

[E]   "[If when it still was ordinary water it became unclean,] he may immerse it [in a pool, which renders water clean], and [afterwards] may designate it as the water [libation] of a festival [see M. Suk. 4:9–10].

[F]   "But if from the start [i.e., before the water became unclean] it had the status of a water [libation] for a festival, [even though one subsequently immersed it to render it clean, it may not be used for the libation since] it already was removed [from the category of water which may be put to that purpose]."

[G]   [The point of A–C and D–F is made again.] Said R. Abbahu in the name of R. Yohanan, "[As for] figs or grapes which became unclean—one may squeeze the juice out of them and designate [the juice] to be heave-offering. [The juice is deemed a new entity and not unclean.]

[H]   "But if [the figs or grapes] already had been designated heave-offering [at the point at which they became unclean, even if the person squeezes them, a priest may not drink the juice for] it already was removed [from the category of heave-offering which may be eaten by a priest]."

[I]   [Qualifying H,] R. Zeira [and] R. Yose in the name of R. Eleazar [say], "[If the produce already had been designated heave-offering and later became unclean,] the individual may squeeze [out the juice] in quantities of less than an egg's bulk [which neither receive nor impart uncleanness], and as a result the wine [or other juice which results] is fit [i.e., deemed clean] even for libations [at the altar]."

[J]   They say, "R. Simeon b. Laqish disagrees [with some aspect of what just has been said]."

[K]   [The question is] concerning what [does he disagree]?

[L]   [Does he disagree concerning the] lenient [rule at G, that one may press unclean figs or grapes and then designate the juice to be heave-offering],

[M]   or [does he disagree concerning the] stringent [rule at H, that if figs or grapes in the status of heave-offering are unclean, and one presses them, a priest still may not drink the juice]?

[N]   If you say that [he disagrees with the] lenient [rule of G], this makes sense. [If this is the case, Simeon b. Laqish's position simply is that the liquids inside of the figs or grapes were rendered unclean by that fruit. When the juice is squeezed out, it already is unclean and therefore is not fit for consumption by a priest.]

[O]   [But] if you say [that Simeon disagrees with the] stringent [rule of H, holding, to the contrary, that when juice is squeezed out of unclean produce in the status of heave-offering, it is deemed clean and may be eaten by a priest, it is impossible to explain this view].

[P]   For so we have learned [M. Ter. 9:7M: If unclean saplings in the status of heave-offering are planted, fruit which grows from them still] *is forbidden for consumption [by priests] until he trims off [the first crop] of fruit [from those saplings].* [Just as H claims, the normal process of purification (planting in the ground for the case of saplings, or squeezing out the juice, for the case of figs or grapes) does not render produce in the status of heave-offering permitted for consumption by a priest. Since the Mishnah itself states this explicitly, it is clear that Simeon b. Laqish does not disagree with it. His disagreement, referred to at J, therefore must be with G, as N suggests.]

The same exercise is repeated three times, A–C, D–F, and G–H. Once consecrated produce is unclean, it may not be consumed as a holy thing by a priest. Nor may it be put to the other uses reserved for consecrated produce. Even if it is rendered clean, it is not accorded the same status as a holy thing which never was unclean. I–P discusses G–H.

[IV.A] [Judah, M. Ter. 9:7N, states that produce from saplings in the status of heave-offering which are planted in the ground remains forbidden until the householder will have twice trimmed the sapling. What is to be trimmed?] R. Abbahu in the name of R. Yohanan [said], "This is what the Mishnah means: [The produce remains forbidden] until [the householder] trims off [the sapling's] leaves and does so a second time [after they once grow back]."

The Yerushalmi claims that M. Ter. 9:7M–N refers to trimming the leaves of saplings in the status of heave-offering which were planted. No reason for this suggestion is offered. It is more likely that the Mishnah refers to the harvesting of the tree's crop, parallel to the point made by M. Ter. 9:4B. The first (Judah: second) crop of a sanctified sapling has the status of heave-offering; subsequent crops do not.

10:1 [P: 10:1a]

[A] *[As regards] an onion [in the status of heave-offering] which one placed [i.e., cooked] among [unconsecrated] lentils—*

[B] *if [the onion] is whole, one is permitted [to eat the lentils as unconsecrated food].*

[C] *But if one cut up [the onion and then placed it among unconsecrated lentils]—*

[D] *[it is forbidden to eat the lentils as unconsecrated food] if [the onion] imparts [to them its] flavor.*

[E] *And [as regards] all other cooked foods—*

[F] *whether [the onion in the status of heave-offering] is whole or cut up,*

[G] *[it renders forbidden the unconsecrated food with which it is cooked] if it imparts [its] flavor [to that food].*

[H] *R. Judah permits [for consumption by a nonpriest] a pickled fish [which was cooked with an onion in the status of heave-offering],*

[I] *for the purpose [of the onion] is only to absorb the stench [of the fish and not to flavor the brine].*

Unconsecrated produce which is cooked with heave-offering may itself take on the status of a priestly gift. This may occur in either of two possible ways described here. The first, A–E, is that the heave-offering is made an integral part of the dish as a whole.

When this happens, all of the food must be treated like the heave-offering which is mixed with it. The other way in which unconsecrated produce takes on the status of heave-offering is that it is flavored by the priestly gift, E–G + H–I. Even if the actual produce in the status of heave-offering is removed, a nonpriest who eats the dish would benefit from the flavor of the heave-offering. To prevent this, the food is treated as heave-offering and eaten only by a priest.

The first five of the Yerushalmi's units deal with the circumstances under which the rule of M. Ter. 10:1A–D applies. They read into A–D the consideration known only at E–G, of whether or not the heave-offering imparts flavor to the unconsecrated produce. Units **VI–VII** then deal with the statement of Judah, M. Ter. 10:1H–I. E–G is not dealt with here as an autonomous unit. I assume that this is because the rest of the chapter as a whole deals with the rules for a case in which heave-offering imparts its flavor to unconsecrated food. This topic merely is introduced in the present pericope of the Mishnah.

[I.A]   *[As regards] an onion [in the status of heave-offering] which one placed [i.e., cooked] among [unconsecrated] lentils—[if the onion is whole, it is permitted to eat the lentils as unconsecrated food; M. Ter. 10:1A–B].*

[B]   R. Hezeqiah [and] R. Ahai in the name of R. Ba bar Mamel [say], "Mishnah speaks of a case in which [the whole onion] was placed [with the lentils] after the lentils already had cooked so much as to have the liquid in them dry out.

[C]   "[In this situation] the [mass of] lentils presses against [the onion in the status of heave-offering] so that it cannot absorb [its flavor]." [As a result, the lentils do not take on the status of heave-offering, as M. Ter. 10:1A–B says.]

[D]   [The implication of B–C is stated.] Now just as you state that the [mass of] lentils presses against [the onion] so that it cannot absorb [its flavor], in the same way, the lentils press against [the onion] so that it cannot impart [its flavor].

The Yerushalmi reads M. Ter. 10:1A–B in light of the consideration introduced at M. Ter. 10:1E–G. It sees the issue as being

whether or not the whole onion will impart its flavor to the lentils with which it is cooked.

[II.A]   The Mishnah [Ter. 10:1A–B] applies in the case of an unconsecrated onion which one placed with lentils in the status of heave-
offering.[1]

[B]   But in the case of an onion in the status of heave-offering which
one placed with unconsecrated lentils—in this case, no. [Namely,
in this case, even if the onion is whole, it imparts its flavor to the
lentils such that they take on the status of heave-offering.]

I do not know why the Yerushalmi makes this claim. M. Ter.
10:1 clearly assumes that the onion is heave-offering, as Judah's
opinion, M. Ter. 10:1H–I, proves.[2]

[III.A]   [If the onion referred to at M. Ter. 10:1A–B] is dry [the rule
that it does not impart its own status of heave-offering to the
lentils with which it is cooked applies].

[B]   But if it is moist [then the lentils do not prevent it from imparting to them its taste, such that, even if the onion in the status of
heave-offering is whole, it renders the lentils] forbidden [for consumption as unconsecrated food].

[C]   [M. Ter. 10:1A–D] applies in the case of an onion [in the status
of heave-offering].

[D]   But in the case of leeks [in the status of heave-offering], whether
they are moist or dry, whole or cut up, [they render] forbidden
[for consumption by nonpriests unconsecrated food with which
they are cooked].

Again the Yerushalmi imposes upon M. Ter. 10:1A–B the issue
of whether or not the heave-offering will impart flavor to the
unconsecrated lentils. The Yerushalmi holds that the lentils remain permitted so long as the heave-offering does not impart
flavor to them. Leeks, C–D, have a rule different from that for
onions. They are deemed always to impart flavor to the food
with which they are cooked.

[**IV.A**]   [The question is what constitutes "cutting up" the onion in the status of heave-offering which is going to be cooked with unconsecrated leeks, M. Ter. 10:1C.] If one removed the protuberance [on the blossom-end of the onion], it is as though the onion were cut up.

[B]   If there were two [or] three small [whole onions in the status of heave-offering cooked in one batch of unconsecrated lentils], it is as though [the lentils contained] a cut-up [onion].

The Yerushalmi interprets M. Ter. 10:1C.

[**V.A**]   [If, as M. Ter. 10:1A–B states, a whole onion in the status of heave-offering may be cooked with unconsecrated lentils and does not impart to them its own status], this is to say that [this applies] if the outer skin [of the onion] does not contain sufficient [pungency] to impart flavor[3] [to the lentils].

[B][4]   But if the outer skin does have sufficient [pungency] to impart flavor to the lentils, those unconsecrated lentils are rendered] forbidden [for consumption by a nonpriest].

The conclusion, B, assumes the discussion above, Y. Ter. 9:4 V.M–O, which proves that the skin of produce in the status of heave-offering has the same consecrated status as the edible part of the vegetable. For this reason the skin of the onion imparts the status of heave-offering to other foods which it flavors.

[**VI.A**]   There we have learned [M. M.S. 2:1]: *[As regards] fish which was cooked with leeks in the status of second tithe, such that it [i.e., the fish] became more valuable—the increase in value is assessed [as imparting to the fish the status of second tithe] in accordance with a reckoning [of what percentage of the fish's value may be attributed to the leeks in the status of second tithe].*

[B]   Said R. Hoshaya, "[This pericope of] the Mishnah [cited at A] is not in accordance with the view of R. Judah.

[C]   "For we have learned [M. Ter. 10:1H]: *R. Judah permits [for consumption by a nonpriest] pickled fish [which was cooked*

*with an onion in the status of heave-offering], for the purpose of
[the onion] is only to absorb the stench [of the fish, and not to
flavor the brine]."* [Contrary to A, Judah thus does not hold that
the fish takes on the status of the consecrated produce with which it
is cooked.]

[D]   [Suggesting another rule with which Judah cannot agree] rabbis
of Caesarea asked, "But this is what R. Abbahu said in the name
of R. Yohanan [Y. Naz. 6:1]: [In the case of] any forbidden thing
[which falls into permitted produce, they determine whether the
permitted produce is rendered forbidden by] imagining that [the
forbidden food] is an onion or a leek. [If an onion or leek of its
size would be sufficient to impart flavor to the food with which
it is mixed, then that food takes on the status of the forbidden
produce which fell into it.]

[E]   "This cannot be the opinion of R. Judah, [for Judah holds that
fish is not flavored by an onion which is cooked with it]."

Judah's statement at M. Ter. 10:1H is indicative of a larger theory he holds, that onions do not invariably flavor foods with
which they are cooked.

[VII.A]   [Judah, M. Ter. 10:1H, permits for consumption as unconsecrated food a pickled fish which was cooked with onions in the
status of heave-offering.] R. Judah concedes in the case of an
onion dedicated [to the Temple],⁵ and R. Judah concedes in the
case of an onion which had been used for purposes of idol worship. [In the case of either of such onions, Judah agrees that if
they are cooked with fish, they impart to that fish their own forbidden status.]

In certain cases the position of Judah, M. Ter. 10:1H, defined in
the preceding unit of the Yerushalmi, does not apply.

10:2 [P: 10:1b]

[A]   *[As regards] an apple [in the status of heave-offering] which one
chopped up and placed in [unconsecrated] dough,*

[B]   *and [as a result the dough] was leavened—*

[C]   *lo, this [i.e., the dough] is forbidden [for consumption by a nonpriest].*

[D]   *[As regards] barley [in the status of heave-offering] which fell into a well of water—*

[E]   *even though the water [in the well] was tainted [by the barley],*

[F]   *the water remains permitted [for consumption by a nonpriest].*

Two autonomous cases, A–C and D–F, illustrate the same issue as M. Ter. 10:1. At A–C the dough benefits from the leavening action of the apple in the status of heave-offering. Now it too must be deemed heave-offering and forbidden to nonpriests. The barley, D–F, ruins the flavor of the water. The person who drinks that water in no way benefits from the heave-offering. The water therefore retains its unconsecrated status. The Yerushalmi concentrates on T. Ter.'s pertinent materials. Yose disputes the rule of M. Ter. 10:2A–C. The Yerushalmi elaborates the point of disagreement and of agreement (unit **I**). Unit **II** speaks to the larger issue suggested by the contrast between A–C and D–F here. This is whether or not food the flavor of which has been spoiled by produce in the status of heave-offering indeed maintains its unconsecrated status, as D–F claims.

[I.A]   *[As regards] an apple [in the status of heave-offering] which one chopped up and placed in [unconsecrated] dough, and [as a result the dough] was leavened—lo, this [dough] is forbidden*[6] *[for consumption by a nonpriest; M. Ter. 10:2A–C].*

[B]   It is taught[7] [T. Ter. 8:9H]: R. Yose deems [the dough] permitted [i.e., not to have the status of heave-offering. Yose's claim in T. is that: **"that which is leavened by the apple is not deemed truly leavened."**]

[C]   R. Aha [and] R. Abbahu in the name of R. Yose b. R. Hanina [say], "Concerning what [do Yose and the anonymous rule of M. Ter. 10:2A–C] disagree?

[D]   "[They disagree] concerning a case in which [the dough] was leavened[8] by the juice [of the apple in the status of heave-offering].

[Unlike Yose, the anonymous authorities of M. Ter. 10:2A–C hold that this is a normal means of leavening dough. The dough is deemed truly leavened and therefore has the status of the heave-offering which served to leaven it.]

[E]   "But if [the dough] was leavened by the piece [of apple itself, all agree that this is not deemed true leavening of the dough, such that the dough remains] permitted [for consumption as unconsecrated food]."

[F]   [At M. Shab. 3:3, Yose disagrees with the anonymous view and states that on the Sabbath an individual may put an egg beside a kettle such that the egg will be cooked. At Y. Shab. 3:3, where the following is primary, Yose's view is explained on the basis of his position at T. Ter. 8:9H.] Just as R. Yose says there [at T. Ter. 8:9H], **"That which is leavened [by the apple in the status of heave-offering] is not deemed truly leavened, [such that it does not take on the status of heave-offering],"**

[G]   so he holds here [in the case of M. Shab. 3:3], "That which is cooked [through being placed next to the kettle] is not deemed truly cooked [and therefore is not forbidden for consumption on the Sabbath]."

A–E qualifies T. Ter. 8:9H. Yose and the anonymous rule of M. Ter. 10:2A–C disagree only if the unconsecrated dough was leavened by a piece of consecrated apple. In this case the Mishnah's authorities deem the dough forbidden. Since the piece of apple remains distinct from the dough, Yose holds that its leavening action is not comparable to that of normal leaven. The dough therefore remains unconsecrated.

While primary at Y. Shab. 3:3, the material at F–G is parallel. Eggs are not normally cooked by being placed next to a kettle. If this should occur on the Sabbath, Yose does not deem the eggs "cooked" in the usual sense of the word. He therefore permits them for consumption on the holy day.

[II.A]   **"It is all the same whether [heave-offering] imparts flavor [so as] to improve [the taste of food], or to spoil [it. In either case, the food to which the heave-offering imparted its flavor] is forbidden [for consumption by nonpriests]"—the words of R. Meir.**

[B]   R. Simeon says, "[If the heave-offering] improves [the taste of unconsecrated food, that food] is forbidden. [But if the heave-offering] spoils [its taste], it [remains] permitted [for consumption by a nonpriest"; T. Ter. 8:9I–L].

[C]   Said R. Simeon b. Laqish, "Concerning what case do they disagree?

[D]   "[They disagree] concerning a case in which [the heave-offering initially] improved [the flavor of the unconsecrated produce] but [later] spoiled the taste. [Meir takes into account the initial improvement, and he therefore states that the unconsecrated produce now has the status of heave-offering.]

[E]   "But [if the heave-offering initially] spoiled [the taste of the unconsecrated food] and later improved [it], R. Meir concedes [to Simeon, B, that the food does not take on the status of heave-offering]."

[F]   [Disagreeing with E] R. Yohanan[9] says "[According to Meir and Simeon] it makes no difference whether [the heave-offering first] spoils [the flavor of the unconsecrated produce] and later improves it, or whether it [initially] improves it but [ultimately] spoils it.

[G]   "Under dispute [between Meir and Simeon is simply a case in which at some point during the cooking, the heave-offering spoiled the flavor of the dish]." [It makes no difference whether this happened initially or later on.]

[H]   [The understandings of Simeon b. Laqish and Yohanan are applied in a concrete case, suggested by M. Ter. 10:2D–F.] There we have learned: *[As regards] barley [in the status of heave-offering] which fell into a well of water—even though the water [in the well] was tainted [by the barley], the water remains permitted [for consumption by a nonpriest].*

[I]   [In this case the flavor of the water was spoiled, and at no point was there any improvement in it. We therefore may question whether or not Meir, cited above at A, agrees that the water remains unconsecrated.] This [pericope of] Mishnah, what about it? [That is, is its rule under dispute by Simeon and Meir?]

[J]   R. Yohanan says, "It is under dispute." [Simeon, above at B, agrees with the rule of M. Ter. 10:2D–F, that the water remains permitted. Meir disagrees and holds that the tainted water must be treated as heave-offering. This is in line with his view above, A.]

[K]   R. Simeon b. Laqish said, "It is the opinion of both authorities." [In Simeon b. Laqish's understanding, D–E, Meir would
deem the water to have the status of heave-offering only if, before it was spoiled by the consecrated barley, it first improved in
flavor.]

[L]   [Yose bar R. Bun states that the dispute between Yohanan and
Simeon b. Laqish, J–K, is correctly reported.] R. Yose bar R.
Bun reported these traditions as follows, "R. Yohanan says, 'It is
under dispute.' R. Simeon b. Laqish says, 'It is the opinion of
both authorities.'"

The dispute between Meir and Simeon, A–B, is elaborated, C–G.
The basis for, or logic of, Simeon b. Laqish's and Yohanan's interpretations is not apparent. H–L goes ahead to apply their
understandings to a concrete case, that of M. Ter. 10:2D–F.

10:3 [P: 10:2a]

[A]   *One who scrapes hot bread [from the side of an oven] and places
it on top of a jug of wine in the status of heave-offering—*

[B]   *R. Meir deems [the bread] forbidden [for consumption by
nonpriests].*

[C]   *But R. Judah deems [it] permitted.*

[D]   *R. Yose deems [it] permitted in the case of bread made from
wheat,*

[E]   *but deems [it] forbidden in the case of bread made from barley,*

[F]   *for barley absorbs [the vapor of the forbidden wine].*

As understood by the Yerushalmi, the issue is whether or not the
hot bread will absorb the flavor of the wine.[10] Meir says that it
will, Judah that it will not. Yose holds that this depends upon
the sort of bread. The Yerushalmi examines each of these positions in turn. The first unit questions the type of jug the wine
must be in for Meir's view to apply. Unit **II** cites a story suggesting that Judah, C, is wrong. This story is shown to be inappro-
priate evidence. Finally, unit **III** asks how Yose will rule for a
case of bread made from both wheat and barley.

[I.A]   [Meir, M. Ter. 10:3A–B, states that if hot bread is placed on top
of a jug of wine in the status of heave-offering, it takes on the
consecrated status of the wine.] Said R. Zeira, "They asked in
the presence of R. Yannai, '[If] they placed [the bread] on top of
a sealed jug [of wine in the status of heave-offering], what [ac-
cording to Meir] is the rule [whether or not the bread takes on a
consecrated status]?'

[B]   "He said to them, 'Its [i.e., lightning's] crashing (*ry⁽w*) declares
concerning him [i.e., God]'" [Job 36:33]. [Yannai reads the
verse to mean: 'Its (i.e., A's) cognate (rule) (*ry⁽w*) declares concerning it (i.e., indicates the correct ruling).']

[C][11]   What is the meaning of 'Its crashing declares concerning him'?

[D]   Said R. Yose, "[The answer to the question at A] is in accordance with that which we have learned there [M. Mak. 3:2: *As
to] an [earthenware] vessel filled with produce which one placed
in liquid, or which was filled with liquid and [which one] placed
in [a container of] produce—[any produce which absorbs (liquid
through the sides of the vessel) is under the law, 'If water be put'
(i.e., it is thereby rendered susceptible to uncleanness)].*" [On
the basis of M. Mak. 3:2 it is clear that produce can absorb
liquid through a sealed vessel. This means that the hot bread
placed on top of the sealed jug of wine in the status of heave-
offering, A, may indeed take on the consecrated status of that
wine. The issue now is under what specific circumstances that
occurs.]

[E]   Just as you say there [in the case of M. Mak. 3:2] that its rule
applies [only] if the liquid [in which the vessel filled with fruit is
placed] actually touches the vessel, so here [in the case described
at A, the bread is deemed to absorb the consecrated wine within
the sealed jug only] if the loaf [of bread actually] touches the
sealed [top of the jug].

[F][12]   [Disagreeing with E,] said R. Mana, "Just as you say that the
rule [of M. Mak. 3:2] applies only if the liquid is touching the
vessel itself, so here [in the case described at A, if the bread is to
absorb the wine in the status of heave-offering] the loaf [of bread]
must be touching the (read:) vessel[13] itself."

[G]   [On the basis of Mana's] statement [F, it appears that Meir's view,
M. Ter. 10:3A–B, that the bread absorbs the wine, applies] even
if [the loaf of bread is] cold.[14]

[H]   [Supporting G,] said R. Ba, "There was an incident [in which] a cold [loaf of bread was placed on top of a jug containing wine in the status of heave-offering, and in this case Meir still ruled that the bread absorbed the wine and so took on the status of a priestly gift]."

[I]   Yet [at M. Ter. 10:3] we are taught [that Meir's view applies specifically to the case of] hot [bread placed upon consecrated wine]?! [Why does M. refer specifically to hot bread if its rule applies in the case of cold bread as well?]

[J]   Said R. Hisda, "[Hot bread must be mentioned explicitly], so that you do not [incorrectly] say, 'Since [in the case of hot bread] the vapor [which rises from the bread] prevents [the bread from absorbing the flavor of the wine, that bread remains] permitted.'"

[K]   [We turn back to the issue of M. Mak. 3:2.] What [liquids impart susceptibility to uncleanness by being absorbed through an earthenware vessel]?

[L]   R. Simeon b. Laqish says, "Water renders the produce [susceptible], but [other] liquids [are too heavy to be absorbed through the jar and therefore] do not render produce [susceptible to uncleanness].

[M]   "And this is not the view of R. Judah."

[N]   [M makes no sense. Just as L states, Judah, M. Ter. 10:3C, is explicit that wine is *not* absorbed through a vessel so as to impart its own status to a loaf of bread. This being the case, we must revise our notion of what Simeon b. Laqish said, L.] Rather, Simeon b. Laqish says, "Water [is absorbed through a jar so as to] render produce [susceptible to uncleanness. Indeed, so much water is absorbed into the earthenware that it greatly] reduces [the quantity of water into which the jar was placed].

[O]   "[Other] liquids, [such as wine, likewise are absorbed through a vessel so as to] render produce [susceptible to uncleanness. But these other liquids are absorbed in such small quantities that their own amount] is not reduced [through their being absorbed]."

[P]   [Just as M suggests, Judah, M. Ter. 10:3C, disagrees with Simeon b. Laqish's statement, for] R. Judah says, "Liquids [other than water are] not [absorbed into a vessel so as to] impart to produce [susceptibility to uncleanness] at all."

A–F and G–J discuss two issues concerning the view of Meir, M. Ter. 10:3A–B. The first is whether or not his position applies in the case of a corked jug. Next we discuss the case of a cold loaf of bread and why, in the Mishnah, Meir speaks specifically of hot bread. K–P, concerning the view of Judah, M. Ter. 10:3C (= M. Mak. 3:3), is tacked on as part of the discussion of M. Mak. 3:2, cited at A–F. The material is primary in the context of the Yerushalmi's discussion of that pericope of the Mishnah. Still, it is not out of place in the present location, for it introduces the discussion of Judah's position, M. Ter. 10:3C, which continues in the following unit of Y. Ter.

[**II.A**]   [The following story suggests that Judah, M. Ter. 10:3C, is wrong when he claims that bread which is placed on top of a jug of liquid does not absorb the flavor of that liquid.] Now here is what R. Yohanan said: "When we were walking with R. Hoshaya the elder to Caesarea to study Torah, we would place our batter-cakes on top of pressing pots [containing juice for] pickling, and [as a result, when we ate the bread] we would taste in it the flavor of the brine. Now this does not accord with the view of R. Judah, [who claims that the bread does not pick up the taste of the liquid in the vessel below it]."

[B]   [Contrary to A, the case described there does not contradict Judah's view] for [unlike at M. Ter. 10:3] they [actually] stuck [the batter-cakes into the upper rim of the pressing pots, so that they could absorb the liquid which was there. That is why the bread took on the taste of the brine.]

[C]   [But if B is the case, was this action of placing the bread into the brine] not forbidden as an act of stealing from the householder [who owned the pressing pots]?

[D]   [No, for] they would get the permission of the householder [to take a small amount of his brine].

The point is made at B. It is one thing to sop up liquid with bread. It is quite a different thing simply to place the bread on top of the jug of liquid. Only in the latter case would Judah, M. Ter. 10:3C, claim that the bread does not absorb the flavor of the liquid.

[III.A]   [Yose, M. Ter. 10:3D–F, states that bread made from wheat does not absorb the flavor of wine over which it is placed, but that bread made from barley does absorb. The question is what happens if the bread is composed part of wheat and part of barley. If it is] wheat on the bottom [of the loaf] and barley on the top— just as the wheat does not absorb [the wine], so the barley [which is not directly over the jug of wine] does not absorb [the flavor of the wine; the loaf remains permitted].

[B]   [If it is] barley on the bottom [of the loaf] and wheat on the top— just as the barley absorbs [the flavor of the wine], so [in this case we deem] the wheat to absorb [the flavor of the wine. Therefore the loaf is rendered forbidden.]

Whether or not the loaf will absorb the flavor of the wine is determined by the sort of flour which is at the bottom of the loaf.

10:4 [P: 10:2b]

[G]   *[As regards] an oven which one fired with cumin in the status of heave-offering and baked bread in it—*

[H]   *the bread remains permitted [for consumption by a nonpriest].*

[I]   *For the flavor of cumin is [not imparted to the bread], but [only] the smell of cumin.*

The point is at I. The burning cumin does not impart flavor to the bread, but only gives it the aroma of cumin. The Yerushalmi responds to this pericope by questioning the rule for roasting together in one oven permitted and forbidden meat. Unlike what one would assume on the basis of M. 10:4, the Yerushalmi proves that this is forbidden. This discussion is at units **I** and **III**. Unit **II** intervenes with material more properly placed with M. Ter. 10:2D–F. Perhaps this appears here because, like unit **I**, it contains a dispute between Rav and Samuel.

[I.A]   What is the rule whether or not one may roast together in the same oven two spits of meat, one of which holds properly slaughtered meat, and the other of which [47b] holds meat that is carrion? [Must the individual scruple that the taste of the carrion will render the properly slaughtered meat forbidden for consumption?]

[B]   R. Jeremiah says in the name of Rav, "It is forbidden."

[C]   But Samuel says in the name of Levi, "It is permitted."

[D]   A Tannaitic teaching contradicts the statement of Rav [B]: **They do not roast two Passover offerings in a single oven, because this creates confusion** [T. Pis. 5:11; i.e., one family might wind up eating the offering intended for the other family].

[E]   They stated [that it is forbidden to cook the offerings together] only because of [the possibility they would be] confused [with each other].

[F]   But they did not forbid this because of the mixing [of the flavors of the two pieces of meat. In the case of A, likewise, we need not be concerned that the taste of the carrion will render forbidden the properly slaughtered meat. This is as Samuel says, C, contrary to the statement of Jeremiah in the name of Rav, B.]

The pericope is relevant in a general way to the issue of M. Ter. 10:4.

[**II.**A]   Water in which savory [in the status of heave-offering] was steeped—

[B]   Rav says, "It is forbidden [to nonpriests, i.e., has the status of heave-offering]."

[C]   But Samuel says, "It is permitted [i.e., does not have the status of heave-offering]."

[D]   Samuel gave Rav water in which savory [in the status of heave-offering] had been steeped to drink.

The case is parallel to M. Ter. 10:2D–F. Rav holds that the savory improves the water and therefore imparts to it the status of heave-offering. Samuel takes the opposite view. D is enigmatic, since we are not told Rav's reaction.

[**III**.A]   [At Y. Ter. 10:4 **I**.A–B Rav states that one may not roast a piece
of permitted meat together with forbidden meat in one oven.
This unit indicates what Rav would do to cleanse an oven in
which forbidden meat had previously been cooked, so as to prepare it for use in roasting permitted meat.] As for this roasted
meat [15]—R. Hiyya bar Ashi in the name of Rav [said], "[To prepare an oven for use with such properly slaughtered meat] one
must heat [the oven up to a high temperature] using hardened
palm twigs."

This is how Rav would clean an oven so as to render it fit for
roasting properly slaughtered meat. The issue follows logically
from Rav's position at Y. Ter. 10:4 **I**.A–B.

10:5a [P: 10:3a; M. Ter. 10:5]

[A]   *[As regards] fenugreek which fell into a vat of [unconsecrated]
wine—*

[B]   *in [the case of fenugreek which is]—heave-offering or second
tithe,*

[C]   *if the seed [without the stalk] is sufficient to impart flavor [to the
wine, that wine is subject to the law of heave-offering or second
tithe].*

[D]   *But not [if the seed is not sufficient to impart flavor to the wine
without] the stalk.*

[E]   *In the case of [fenugreek which is produce of] (1) the seventh
year [of the Sabbatical cycle], (2) of a vineyard in which were
sown diverse kinds, or (3) [if it] is dedicated [to the Temple]—*

[F]   *If the seed and stalk [together] are sufficient to impart flavor [to
the wine, that wine is subject to the restrictions which applied to
the fenugreek].*

These rules follow from the fact that the seed of fenugreek is a
food, while the stalk is not. Only the seed, therefore, may take on
the status of an agricultural offering, A–D. At E–F, the stalks, like
the seed, are subject to all of the restrictions which apply to the
field as a whole. The rule of F follows. This latter rule attracts

the attention of the Yerushalmi. It recalls the consideration mentioned at Y. Ter. 10:2 **II**, and asks why the stalks, which spoil
the taste of the wine, should impart to that wine their own forbidden status.

[**I**.A]   [Reference is to M. Ter. 10:5E–F, which states that wine flavored by the stalks of consecrated fenugreek itself takes on a
consecrated status.] But does not the stalk [of the fenugreek]
spoil [the taste of the wine],[16] and then spoil it some more? [We
might expect that if a holy food spoils the taste of unconsecrated
wine, that the wine need not be deemed consecrated.]

[B]   [The Yerushalmi explains why the logical conclusion, given in
brackets at A, does not hold:] The Mishnah [Ter. 10:5E–F] follows the opinion of the one who says, "Even if [consecrated
produce] imparts taste so as to spoil [unconsecrated food, that
unconsecrated food is rendered] forbidden [under the restrictions which applied to the produce which flavored it. This is the
opinion of Meir, cited above, Y. Ter. 10:2 **II**.A.]

[C]   [B's reasoning is shown to be incomplete. M. Ter. 10:5E–F]
might even follow the view of one who says that [if consecrated
produce] imparts flavor so as to spoil [unconsecrated food, the
unconsecrated food remains] permitted. [This is the view of
Simeon, cited at Y. Ter. 10:2 **II**.B.]

[D]   In the present case, he [i.e., the authority of C] concedes that
the [wine] is rendered forbidden.

[E]   Why?

[F]   Anything into which fenugreek falls is improved.[17] [That is, even
if the stalk spoils the flavor, the seed improves it, such that on
the whole we deem the wine improved by the consecrated fenugreek (PM).]

The Yerushalmi reads into M. Ter. 10:5 the consideration of
whether the stalks of fenugreek improve or spoil the taste of wine.

10:5b [P: 10:3b; PM: 10:6; M. Ter. 10:6]

[G]   *One who had bundles of fenugreek grown in a vineyard in which
were sown diverse kinds—let them be burned.*

[H]   *[If] he had bundles of fenugreek which were subject to the separation of tithes—*

[I]   *he crushes [some of the stalks] and determines the quantity of seed which [all of the stalks together] contain*

[J]   *and separates [the tithes required] for [this quantity of] seed.*

[K]   *But he does not need to separate tithes for the stalks.*

[L]   *If he separated tithes [for the stalks],*

[M]   *he may not say, "I shall crush [all of the stalks] and shall take the stalks [for myself] and give the seed [to its proper recipients, priest and Levite]."*

[N]   *Rather, he must give [to the priest and Levite] the stalks along with the seed.*

The theory is the same as found at M. Ter. 10:5, which explains V, L, P, and R's presentation of the two pericopae as a single unit (my 10:5a–b). For convenience I have presented the two Mishnaic passages separately, followed by their respective Talmudic discussions. The Talmudic units themselves are numbered consecutively through Y. Ter. 10:5a and b.

Only L–M + N is new here. If the householder himself designates tithes for both the seed and stalks, his designation is valid. Having indicated that he deems the stalks to be food, he must give to the proper recipients the required quantity of them, as well as of the seed.

The Yerushalmi's concern is why the Mishnah refers to fenugreek bound up in bundles. It asks, unit **II**,[18] exactly what constitutes a "bundle" of fenugreek, and then questions why, for the case of other produce, the Mishnah does not speak of the separation of heave-offering and tithes from "bundles" (unit **III**).

[II.A]   [M. Ter. 10:6 refers to bundles of fenugreek.] Now how much [fenugreek] is in a bundle?

[B]   Twenty-five stalks.

[C]   Said R. Yohanan, "[For it to be deemed a bundle any] four of [the stalks must be fit to constitute] a bedtime [snack]."

The Yerushalmi defines the bundle referred to at M. Ter. 10:6.[19]

[III.A]   The implication of [M. Ter. 10:6's] rule is that[20] unless [fenu-
greek] is in bundles, it is exempt [from the separation of tithes].

[B]   On this basis, why is this not the case as well for stalks[21] of corn,
[that as soon as they are in bundles, they are subject to heave-
offering and tithes]?

[C]   [The case of corn is different, since] they do not[22] form [corn]
into bundles for this [same purpose as they do with fenugreek].
[The fenugreek will be stored and eaten in the form of bundles.
For corn, the bundles are simply a method of transporting the
produce to the threshing area.]

[D]   [To disprove C, a case of corn which is ready to be eaten as soon
as it is placed in bundles is suggested.] But do they not form
parched ears of corn [into bundles] for this [same purpose as
they do fenugreek, such that as soon as this is done, the parched
ears should be subject to heave-offering and tithes]?

[E]   [No, for unlike fenugreek, the parched ears of corn] were not
cultivated[23] for this purpose, [i.e., of being eaten parched. It is
only as an afterthought that the householder determines not to
thresh the corn.]

[F]   But [in the case of fenugreek] they [both] form it [into bundles]
for this purpose, [i.e., to eat it in that manner] and [from the
start] cultivated it to this purpose.

The storing of fenugreek in bundles marks the conclusion of the
processing of that produce. It therefore is the point at which the
fenugreek becomes subject to the separation of heave-offering
and tithes, just as M. Ter. 1:10 would lead us to expect. Being
formed into bundles does not necessarily mark the conclusion of
the processing of other sorts of produce.

10:6 [P: 10:4; PM: 10:7; M. Ter. 10:7]

[A]   *[As regards] unconsecrated olives which one pickled with olives
in the status of heave-offering—*

[B]   *[if it was] (1) crushed, unconsecrated [olives which were pickled]
with crushed [olives] in the status of heave-offering,*

[C]   *[or] (2) crushed, unconsecrated [olives which were pickled] with whole [olives] in the status of heave-offering,*

[D]   *(3) [or if they were pickled] in brine in the status of heave-offering—*

[E]   *it is forbidden [i.e., the unconsecrated olives are rendered forbidden for consumption by a nonpriest].*

[F]   *But [if] whole unconsecrated [olives are pickled] with crushed [olives] in the status of heave-offering—it is permitted.*

Crushed olives are assumed to be capable of receiving the flavor of the consecrated olives with which they are pickled. They therefore are deemed forbidden for consumption by a nonpriest (B, C). Whole olives, by contrast, are considered impervious to the flavor of the olives in the status of heave-offering and so retain their unconsecrated status (F). This distinction does not apply if the brine itself has the status of heave-offering (D). Brine always flavors the produce pickled in it.

The Yerushalmi's first unit makes explicit the distinction between the cases of B + C and F, as I just have described it. Unit **II** applies to this pericope the familiar question of whether or not we distinguish between cases in which the heave-offering improves the flavor of unconsecrated food and those in which it spoils that food's flavor.

[I.A]   Said R. Jonah, "[M. Ter. 10:7] indicates that crushed [olives] absorb [the liquids in which they are placed] and discharge[24] [that liquid again]. Then they absorb [the liquid] again.

[B]   "Whole olives absorb [the liquid in which they are placed] and then discharge it, but do not absorb it again."

Crushed olives ultimately absorb the flavor of that with which they are pickled (A), and whole olives do not (B). This accounts for the rules at M. Ter. 10:7B, C, and F. It is not clear why the Yerushalmi claims that all produce initially absorbs, but then discharges, the flavor of the food with which it is prepared.

[II.A]   [Does M. Ter. 10:7] imply that [if heave-offering imparts flavor
to unconsecrated food so as] neither to improve[25] nor spoil [the
unconsecrated food, that food anyway] is forbidden [i.e., takes
on the status of heave-offering? That is, is M. Ter. 10:7 an ambiguous case to which either Meir or Simeon, cited above, Y.
Ter. 10:2 II.A–B, can agree?]

[B]   [No.] The Mishnah follows the view of R. Simeon [alone]. For
**R. Simeon says, "[If heave-offering] imparts flavor so as to
spoil [unconsecrated food, that food anyway] is *forbidden*"** [T.
Ter. 8:9L. If heave-offering imparts its own status to produce
the flavor of which it ruins, certainly it imparts its own status to
produce the flavor of which it does not affect. Thus Simeon's
opinion stands behind the rule of M. Ter. 10:7A–E, which
states that food prepared with, but not flavored by, heave-
offering takes on the status of a priestly gift.]

[C]   [The problem is that, at B, the opinion of Simeon is cited incorrectly.] For, indeed, R. Simeon says, **"[If heave-offering] imparts flavor so as to spoil [unconsecrated food, that food re-
mains] *permitted.*"**[26]

[D]   [Apparently two contradictory positions are attributed to Simeon,
for indeed the view assigned to his name at B] accords with this
[statement in Simeon's name at M. Ter. 10:11C–D]: *R. Simeon
says, "[Unconsecrated] cabbage from an irrigated field which is
boiled with cabbage [in the status of heave-offering] from a rain-
watered field is forbidden [for consumption by nonpriests], since
it [i.e., the cabbage from the irrigated field] absorbs [the flavor
of the other cabbage]."*

The case of M. Ter. 10:7 is special, for in it there is no issue of
heave-offering's imparting flavor to unconsecrated food. All the
food is of the same kind. A points this out and asks which authority stands behind the Mishnah's rule that even in such a case
the unconsecrated produce takes on the status of heave-offering.
B claims that it is Simeon. C challenges this, stating that Simeon
is incorrectly cited. D provides a different statement of Simeon,
proving that he will agree to the rule of M. Ter. 10:7. The net result
is that contradictory positions have been assigned to Simeon (C
versus D), or that two different authorities have that same name.

10:7 [P: 10:5; PM: 10:8; M. Ter. 10:8–9]

[A]   *[As regards] unclean fish which one pickled with clean fish—*

[B]   *[in the case of fish pickled in] any keg which holds two seahs
[= 9600 zuz, weight of brine],*

[C]   *if [in that two seahs] it contains unclean fish of a weight of ten
zuz in Judean measure,*

[D]   *which equals five selas in Galilean measure,*

[E]   *the brine is forbidden [i.e., unclean].*

[F]   *R. Judah says, "[It is forbidden if there is] a quarter[-log, i.e.,
fifty zuz, of unclean fish] in two seahs."*

[G]   *R. Yose says, "[It is forbidden if the unclean fish is] one-sixteenth
[of the whole, i.e., 600 zuz]."*

[A]   *Unclean locusts which were pickled with clean locusts have not
invalidated [i.e., imparted uncleanness to] the brine [in which
they were pickled].*

[B]   *Testified R. Sadoq concerning the brine of unclean locusts, that it is
clean [i.e., that it does not impart susceptibility to uncleanness].*

What is the minimum quantity of forbidden food—here, unclean fish—which will flavor, and thereby render prohibited, the
food with which it is pickled? We have a tripartite dispute on the
matter, A–E + F + G. The three positions define progressively
greater quantities of unclean fish to be present in the brine before
that brine is rendered unclean. M. Ter. 10:9, which is lettered
independently of the foregoing, simply points out that locust brine
is not a liquid that imparts susceptibility to uncleanness.

Unit **I** describes the circumstances under which the rule of
M. Ter. 10:8 applies. Units **II–III** establish the specific proportions of the mixture which the anonymous rule, A–E, and Judah,
F, refer to as being unclean. The rule for cases of doubt concerning uncleanness concerns unit **IV** and marks the conclusion of
the Yerushalmi's discussion of M. Ter. 10:8. Unit **V** interprets
M. Ter. 10:9. It is not clear to me why this material was not
numbered separately in L which, as we have seen, fairly accurately preserves the division of pericopae familiar from MSS.
and editions of the Mishnah.

[I.A]   It is taught: R. Judah bar Pazzai of Bard'laya [says], "**[As re-gards] a clean unsalted fish which one pickled with an un-clean, salted fish—[the clean fish is rendered] forbidden**" [T. Ter. 9:2C, with slight variation].

[B]   But [to the contrary] is it not taught: R. Hiyya [says], "**He may wipe off [the clean fish] and it is permitted [i.e., clean;**" T. Ter. 9:2B]?

[C]   [How do we account for these two contradictory notions?] Said R. Mana, "The one who says [that the fish is] permitted refers to a case in which [the clean and unclean fish] were pickled at one and the same time. [In this case the pieces of fish both absorb the clean brine.]

[D]   "[By contrast] the one who says [that the fish is] forbidden[27] refers to a case in which [the clean and unclean fish] were pickled one after the other. [The clean fish is pickled second, in the brine in which unclean fish already was pickled.]

[E]   "You may know [for certain] that this [i.e., D] is the case, for so we have learned [M. Ter. 10:7D, concerning unconsecrated olives which are pickled with olives in the status of heave-offering]: *or [if they are pickled] in brine in the status of heave-offering—they are forbidden.*

[F]   "Does this not refer to a case in which [the consecrated and un-consecrated olives are pickled] one after the other?" [Surely it does, for it is the brine left over from the pickling of the olives in the status of heave-offering which imparts the status of heave-offering to the unconsecrated olives which are pickled after-wards. This is exactly the situation which Mana, D, claims ren-ders the clean fish unclean. On the basis of the Mishnah we therefore know that Mana's explanation of A–B is correct.]

The question is posed at C. Why does T. Ter. 9:2C (= M. Ter. 10:8) state that the fish is rendered unclean if, as T. Ter. 9:2B states, one simply may wipe off the unclean brine and then eat that pickled fish? Mana, C + D, claims that the answer to this question is reflected in the rule of M. Ter. 10:7D, cited here at E–F. If unclean food is pickled alone, it renders the brine un-clean. That brine imparts uncleanness to clean food later pickled in it. But if the clean and unclean foods are pickled at one and the same time, the clean food is not rendered unclean. Once it is removed from the brine, it need only be wiped off.

[II.A]   [M. Ter. 10 : 8A–C refers to the case of fish pickled in] *any keg which holds two seahs [= 9600 zuz of brine].*

[B]   How many [*logs*] are there in a *seah?*

[C]   Twenty-four *logs.*

[D]   And how many [*litras*] are in a *log?*

[E]   Two *litras.*

[F]   And how many [*zuz*] are in a *litra?*

[G]   One hundred *zuz.*

[H]   This means that each *zin* [i.e., ten *zuz* of unclean fish, referred to at M. Ter. 10 : 8C] equals one nine-hundred-and-sixtieth [of the two *seahs* of brine in the keg referred to at M. Ter. 10 : 8A].

[I][28]   R. Yose b. R. Bun instructed, "In the case of a mouse [which falls into food being cooked, it renders unclean in a mixture of so little as] one part [of mouse] to one thousand parts [other food]."

A–H establishes the percentage of the batch referred to by M. Ter. 10 : 8C. Yose b. R. Bun glosses, mentioning an unclean thing not referred to by the Mishnah.

[III.A]   [Judah, M. Ter. 10 : 8F, states that a mixture is rendered unclean if it contains a quarter-*log* of what is unclean in two *seahs* of food that is clean. The issue is what does he refer to as being clean or unclean, fish or brine.] R. Abbahu in the name of R. Yose b. R. Hanina [said], "[Judah refers to] a quarter-*log* of [unclean] brine in two *seahs* of [clean] brine.

[B]   "[Judah thus holds that it takes fifty *zuz* of what is unclean to render unclean two *seahs*. This is by contrast to M. Ter. 10 : 8C, which holds that even ten *zuz* of unclean food will render unclean two *seahs*. Why is Judah so lenient in determining the circumstances under which fish is rendered unclean?] For is it not the case that the brine of unclean fish is [itself] clean?" [Indeed, brine from unclean fish is not normally deemed unclean. Judah therefore states that only a large quantity of such brine renders unclean that with which it is mixed.]

[C]   [Exactly what percentage of the batch is ten *zuz?*] Said R. Abbahu, "Think of it as being close to [one part in] two hundred [i.e., fifty *zuz* in 9600 *zuz*, or exactly ¹⁄₁₉₂ of the batch]."

[D]   [Giving a different answer to the question posed at A,] R. Ila in the name of R. Simeon bar Hiyya [said], "[Judah refers to] a quarter-*log* of [unclean] brine in two *seahs* of [clean] fish along with its brine." [According to Simeon bar Hiyya, even if there is less than two *seahs* of clean brine to a quarter-*log* of unclean, Judah will deem the mixture to be clean. For Simeon says that Judah includes in the quantity of clean produce the volume of the clean fish itself. This is how he differs from the view of Abbahu at A.]

[E]   An incident [in which clean and unclean fish were pickled together] came before R. Ishaya, and he instructed [concerning whether or not the mixture was clean] in accordance with this [i.e., the view of Simeon bar Hiyya, D.]

[F]   A Tannaitic statement [likewise follows] this [view, represented at D–E, that we rule leniently in determining whether or not the brine in which unclean fish is pickled is itself unclean.] **To what case does this apply [i.e., that the brine is deemed unclean]? To the case in which one removes [the unclean fish from the brine] one piece at a time and places it before him. [If in this manner] he finds the specified measure [of unclean fish, the brine is deemed] unclean** (so T. Ter. 9:1I, and as required by the sense of this passage. Y. reads: permitted.)

[G]²⁹   **But if he removes [the unclean fish from the brine] one piece at a time and places them behind him, [the pieces of unclean fish are not deemed to join together for purposes of imparting uncleanness. This being the case,] even if he discovers [that the brine contains] more than the specified quantity [of unclean fish, the brine remains] permitted [i.e., clean;** T. Ter. 9:1H–L, with minor variations].

This is a dispute over the point made by Judah, M. Ter. 10:8F. Two different interpretations are given, A–C and D. D's view is supported by E and F–G.

[**IV.A**]   Through an accident a large keg [of foodstuffs; PM: edible lo-
cysts][30] [came under suspicion of being] unfit[31] [i.e., of containing unclean foods].

[B]   R. Haggai asked R. Ba bar Zabdah [whether or not the suspect
food is permitted for consumption].

[C]   He said to him, "Large quantities [of food] are not rendered
forbidden [through such matters of doubt].

[D]   R. Jacob bar Zibdi says, "R. Isaac asked, '[Is it really so that,
because of a matter of doubt, that which might be unclean is
deemed to be clean. No, it is not. This is proven by the case of a
writ of divorce on which the witnesses have the names of gentiles. If indeed these witnesses are gentiles, the writ is not valid.
But if we assume that the witnesses are Israelites with gentile
names, the writ is valid. According to C, in this case of doubt we
should take the latter alternative and deem the writ valid. But
this is not the law, for] these writs [of divorce]—are not the
names of unfit gentiles signed upon them? [Yes, and therefore,
even though there is a doubt, the writs are not valid.]

[E]   " 'Yet you said that, because of an accident [which leaves a question of doubt, we deem what might be invalid to be valid, A]?!' "
[The case of the writ of divorce proves the opposite. In a case of
doubt we rule stringently and deem the writs invalid. In the
same way the foodstuffs, A, must be deemed unclean.][32]

D–E challenges A–C. The unit is relevant here because it discusses a case in which there is a question of whether or not a
large quantity of food should be deemed unclean.[33] This is comparable to the case of the vat of fish and brine, M. Ter. 10:8.
Since in that case, however, there is no direct issue of doubt, it
does not appear that either of the positions taken here, A–C or
D–E, has direct relevance for our understanding of M. Ter. 10:8.

[**V.A**]   *Testified R. Sadoq concerning the brine of unclean locusts, that
it is clean* [M. Ter. 10:9B; M. Ed. 7:2].

[B]   What is the sense here of the word "clean"?

[C]   [It means] "clean" in that it does not impart susceptibility to
uncleanness.

[D] Yet as regards rendering unclean [that which already is susceptible to uncleanness]—any small amount [of unclean locust brine]
renders [foods] unclean.

The Yerushalmi explains M. Ter. 10:9B.

10:8 [P: 10:6a; PM: 10:9; M. Ter. 10:10–11a]

[A] *All [kinds of unconsecrated produce] which are pickled together
[with heave-offering remain] permitted [for consumption by
nonpriests],*

[B] *except [for unconsecrated produce pickled] with leeks [in the
status of heave-offering].*

[C] *(1) Unconsecrated leeks [which are pickled] with leeks in the
status of heave-offering,*

[D] *[or] (2) unconsecrated vegetables [which are pickled] with leeks
in the status of heave-offering*

[E] *are forbidden [for consumption by nonpriests].*

[F] *But unconsecrated leeks [which are pickled] with vegetables in
the status of heave-offering are permitted [for consumption by
nonpriests].*

[A] *R. Yose says, "All [kinds of unconsecrated produce] which are
boiled with beets [in the status of heave-offering] are forbidden
[for consumption by nonpriests],*

[B] *"since they [i.e., the beets] impart flavor [to that with which
they are cooked]."*

[C] *R. Simeon says, "[Unconsecrated] cabbage from an irrigated field
[which is boiled] with cabbage [in the status of heave-offering] from
a rain-watered field is forbidden [for consumption by nonpriests],*

[D] *"since it [i.e., the cabbage from the irrigated field] absorbs [the
flavor of the other cabbage]."*

[E] *R. Aqiba says, "All [kinds of permitted food] which are cooked
together [with forbidden food] are permitted [for consumption],*

[F] *"except [for that which is cooked] with [forbidden] meat."*

A holds that different types of produce which are pickled together do not flavor one another. Unconsecrated produce in the
mixture therefore does not take on the status of the heave-offering
that mixture contains. This is not what is assumed at M. Ter.
10:7. Yohanan, in unit **I**, resolves this contradiction by claiming
that M. Ter. 10:10A refers to produce which is being seethed,
not pickled. C states that leeks do not fall under A's rule. This
introduces C–E + F, on the laws for leeks. The Yerushalmi's
second unit takes up these rules, comparing them to the position
cited in Aqiba's name, M. Ter. 10:11E–F. Finally, the Yerushalmi
addresses the position of Simeon, M. Ter. 10:11C. The Yerushalmi states explicitly what I have added in brackets in the
translation, that the cabbage from the irrigated field absorbs the
flavor of the cabbage from the rain-watered field and not vice
versa.[34]

[**I**.A]   Said R. Yohanan, "[M. Ter. 10:10] does not refer to [consecrated
and unconsecrated produce which is] pickled [together], but
rather to that which is seethed [together].

[B]   "Pickling has the same effect [upon produce] as boiling." [Seething
indicates that the food has been cooked less than this.]

Yohanan solves the contradiction between M. Ter. 10:7 and M.
Ter. 10:10A by claiming that the latter refers to produce that is
seethed together, not pickled. He holds that, because of the
milder cooking action of seething, the heave-offering in the mixture does not impart its status to the unconsecrated produce. This
is not the case at M. Ter. 10:7 where, because of the pickling, the
heave-offering does impart its status to unconsecrated food.

[**II**.A]   R. Hanina of Toratha in the name of R. Hoshaya [said], "[As for
unconsecrated] leeks [which are pickled with consecrated] leeks,
[such that both the consecrated produce and the heave-offering]
are of the same kind—

[B]   "R. Aqiba deems [the unconsecrated leeks to remain] permitted
[for consumption by nonpriests. This is Aqiba's view at M. Ter.
10:11E.]

[C]   "But sages deem [the unconsecrated leeks to become] forbidden." [This equals the anonymous law of M. Ter. 10:10B.]

[D]   [Having spoken about leeks, we turn to the rule for meat.] R.
Isa in the name of R. Yohanan [says], "Sages concede to R. Aqiba
that in the case of [permitted] meat [cooked] with [its same kind
of forbidden] meat, [the permitted meat remains] permitted."
[This is the opposite of Aqiba's view, M. Ter. 10:11F, that forbidden meat imparts its own status to permitted meat with which
it is cooked. In the following, this troubles Zeira.]

[E]   Said R. Zeira to R. Isa, "Now if you had not stated this explicitly, we would not have thought that it was the case.

[F]   "For perhaps [Yohanan] actually stated [the rule as follows]: 'R.
Aqiba concedes to sages that in the case of [permitted] meat
[cooked] with [forbidden] meat, that the [permitted meat is ren-
dered] forbidden'?" [Thus Aqiba would be consistent with his
position at M. Ter. 10:11F.]

[G]   [Agreeing with Zeira] R. Abbahu came and in the name of R.
Yohanan [said], "R. Aqiba concedes to sages that in the case of
[permitted] meat [cooked] with [forbidden] meat, [the permitted
meat is rendered] forbidden."

[H]   R. Hinena[35] derived it [i.e., the understanding of Aqiba's view
given at F and G] from the latter [law, found at M. Ter. 10:11E–F]:
*R. Aqiba says, "All [kinds of permitted foods] which are cooked
together [with forbidden foods] are permitted [for consump-
tion], except [for that which is cooked] with [forbidden] meat,
[which is rendered forbidden]."*

[I]   [According to Hinena, this means that, in Aqiba's view] lo, [if
permitted] meat [is cooked] with [forbidden] meat, it is rendered
forbidden.

[J]   [If the view of Aqiba is so obvious on the basis of M. Ter.
10:11F] perhaps [Yohanan] actually said: "Sages concede to R.
Aqiba that in the case of [permitted] meat [cooked] with [forbid-
den] meat, [the permitted meat is rendered] forbidden."

[K]   [Agreeing with J,] R. Hanania [H–I] [and] R. Abbahu [G] in the
name of R. Yohanan [say], "Sages concede to R. Aqiba that in
the case of [permitted] meat [cooked] with [forbidden] meat,
[the permitted meat is rendered] forbidden."

The Yerushalmi takes a disproportionately large amount of space to repeat what Aqiba says explicitly at M. Ter. 10:11E–F. Contrary to M. Ter. 10:10B, Aqiba does not hold that consecrated leeks impart their status to other leeks with which they are prepared (A–C). But Aqiba does hold that forbidden meat imparts its own status to permitted foods with which it is cooked, M. Ter. 10:11F. This view is correctly reported five times, at F, G, H–I, J, and K. The issue of who concedes to whom, Aqiba to sages or sages to Aqiba, is clear as stated, J.

[**III.A**]   [Simeon, M. Ter. 10:11C–D, refers to cabbage from an irrigated field and cabbage from a rain-watered field. He states that if these are cooked together, one of them absorbs the flavor of the other. The issue is which absorbs the flavor of which.] Said R. Yose, "We used to reason that [the cabbage grown in the] rain-watered field absorbed [the flavor of the cabbage grown in the irrigated field. This is because the rain-watered field did not receive so much water as the irrigated field. The cabbage from the rain-watered field therefore would be drier than the other cabbage and thus more likely to absorb.]

[B]   "[But] from that which R. Huna [said, we discovered that we were wrong. Referring to a cabbage from a rain-watered field, he said], 'Take [for yourself] its trunk and give [as heave-offering (so Jastrow, p. 715, s.v. *lplwp'*)] its pulp [which is nice and moist].'

[C]   "This is to say that [the cabbage grown in] the irrigated field absorbs [the flavor of the moist, pulpy, cabbage grown in the rain-watered field]."

The Yerushalmi explains the statement of Simeon, M. Ter. 10:11C–D.

10:9 [P: 10:6b; PM: 10:9b; M. Ter. 10:11b]

[G]   *R. Yohanan b. Nuri says, "Liver renders [other food with which it is cooked] forbidden, but itself is not rendered forbidden,*

[H]   *"for it imparts [flavor], but does not absorb [flavor]."*

H explains G. The Yerushalmi addresses and answers the Mishnah's same issue, through an anecdote involving Zeira and Ba.

[I.A]   R. Jeremiah asked, "[Liver] which one seethed in forbidden fat—what is the rule [whether or not it is deemed forbidden for consumption]?"

[B]   R. Zeira never ate liver in his whole life.

[C]   R. Ba [prepared for him] seethed [liver] and gave it to him to eat.

[D]   But there are those who say that R. Ba pickled it and gave it to him to eat.

Presumably the liver, C, was seethed in forbidden fat, indicating that, in line with M. Ter. 10:11G, Ba did not deem the liver to take on the forbidden status of that fat. D suggests that C never happened. The implication is that, if liver were seethed in forbidden fat, contrary to M. Ter. 10:11G, it would be deemed forbidden.

10:10 [P: 10:6c; M. Ter. 10:12]

[A]   *[As regards] an egg which was spiced with forbidden spices [e.g., spices in the status of heave-offering]—*

[B]   *even its yolk is forbidden [for consumption].*

[C]   *since it [i.e., the yolk] absorbs [the flavor of the spices].*

[D]   *Liquid in which heave-offering has been boiled or pickled is forbidden to nonpriests.*

Two independent rules, A–C and D, follow the theory already familiar from the chapter. What is flavored by produce in the status of heave-offering, or by some forbidden food, itself becomes forbidden for consumption. The Yerushalmi's first unit gives the meaning of B. If the yolk is forbidden so is the egg white. Units **II–III** are only topically relevant, a compendium of rules concerning what sorts of eggs are forbidden or permitted for consumption. The final unit refers to D and the fact that, according to it, the liquid in which heave-offering is boiled or pickled is deemed a food, such that it may have the status of heave-offering.

[I.A]   *The yolk [of an egg prepared with forbidden spices] is forbidden, since it absorbs [the flavor of the spices; M. Ter. 10:12B–C].*

[B]   It is taught: Bar Qappara [says], "The yolk is forbidden, and all the more so the egg white."

The Yerushalmi interprets M. Ter. 10:12B: *even* its yolk is forbidden. The citation at A is not exact.

[II.A]   R. Isaac the elder in the name of R. Simeon b. Laqish [says], **"[As regards] eggs which one boiled and [later] found a baby bird in [one of] them—if it is of sufficient quantity to impart flavor [to all of the eggs, they are forbidden";** T. Ter. 9:5G–H].

[B]   R. Zeira, R. Simeon bar Abba in the name of R. Yohanan, R.[36] Adda bar Gershon, R. Birai [and] R. Levi bar Palta, a certain old man, in the name of Rabbi [said], "[If there are] sixty-one [eggs, one of which is found to have a baby bird in it, they all are] forbidden. But if there are sixty-two [eggs, one of which is forbidden, the others remain] permitted."

[C]   [Disagreeing,] R. Samuel bar Nahman in the name of R. Yohanan [said], "Our associate Adda testified before us concerning a case in which there were sixty [eggs, one of which was forbidden], and he said, '[If] someone brings me more than sixty [eggs, only one of which is forbidden], I will deem them all to be permitted.'" [Adda thus permits a mixture of one in sixty-one; B permits one in sixty-two.]

[D][37]   They said to Simeon bar Va,[38] "You say this [i.e., B, that Yohanan holds the eggs are forbidden in a mixture of one in sixty-one], but they say this [i.e., C, that a mixture of one in sixty-one is permitted]!" [What accounts for the difference between the two reports of Yohanan's view?]

[E]   [Simeon bar Va] said to them, "I [am reporting] that which I heard [from my teachers], and they [are reporting] what they heard [from their teachers]."

[F]   Simeon bar Va said in the presence of R. Hanina, "A case came before Rabban Gamaliel the son of Rabbi [concerning forty-five eggs one of which was discovered to be unfit]. He said to them [i.e., the petitioners], 'Father did not rule in a case of forty-seven[39] eggs, [one of which was unfit, that the mixture is permitted; yet you want] me to give such a decision in a case of forty-five[40] [eggs, one of which is unfit]!'" [I cannot do that. Rather, all the eggs are forbidden.]

[G]   [Giving a parallel case,] R. Hiyya in the name of R. Hanina [said], "A case [in which a forbidden egg was cooked with permitted eggs] came before Rabbi, and he said, 'Were there a total of fifty eggs?'" [If there were, then Rabbi would deem the eggs permitted for consumption. But if not, he deems all of the eggs forbidden for consumption.]

[H]   [We move ahead to describe the circumstances under which there is deemed sufficient food being cooked with the forbidden egg so as to prevent that egg from imparting its own forbidden status.] R. Hiyya in the name of R. Hanina [said], "Now the greens, and the [egg]shells and the water all join together [to create the quantity of food needed to neutralize the invalidating effect of the one forbidden egg]."

[I]   [Carrying forward H,] said R. Zeira, "[Even the volume of the] forbidden [egg is included] within [this required quantity]."

[J]   [Qualifying I,] said R. Huna, "The shell of the forbidden [egg] is added to the quantity of permitted produce."

[K]   R. Zeira [said], "This [i.e., H–I] is to say that [the rules for cases in which the clean eggs are not rendered forbidden] apply [only] if one boils them [i.e., all of the eggs] in their shells, such that all of the eggs will be boiled together.

[L][41]   "But if one boils [permitted] eggs out of their shells with a [forbidden] egg in its shell, or a [forbidden] egg out of its shell with [permitted] eggs in their shells; or if one places together a [forbidden] egg which is being boiled with [permitted] eggs that are not being boiled, or [permitted] eggs which are being boiled with a [forbidden] egg that is not being boiled, we need a different measure [by which to determine whether or not the forbidden egg has rendered the other eggs forbidden for consumption]."

The unit is a long discussion of T. Ter. 9:5G–H, cited at A. The issue is the number of permitted eggs which nullifies the flavor of one forbidden egg with which the eggs are cooked, B–G. H–L suggests further considerations for the circumstances under which the forbidden egg will or will not impart its status to the permitted ones.

[III.A]   **Abortive eggs are permitted for consumption [T. Ter. 9:5J].**

[B]   [This is proven by Job 21:10: 'The wicked's] bull breeds without aborting.' [Thus aborting has nothing to do with sin or, concomitantly, uncleanness.]

[C]   Eggs which have formed a membrane, lo, these are forbidden [for consumption].

[D]   **[As regards] spoiled eggs—let a hearty soul eat them [i.e., they are permitted].**

[E]   **If one found blood in them, he may throw out the blood [and eat the rest; T. Ter. 9:5K–L].**

[F]   [The following discusses the meaning of E.] R. Zeira went to visit R. Hiyya the son of R. Isaac of ʾAttush. He found him sitting. [Hiyya] said, "They did not teach [that the rest of the egg is forbidden] unless [he found the blood] on the yolk. But if he found it on the white of the egg, [he may remove the blood and the rest of the egg is] permitted."

[G]   [Hiyya] believed that he had received [this interpretation of E's rule] from his father.

[H]   [47c] [But proving that he was wrong,] R. Abbahu came and said in the name of R. Yohanan, "Whether the blood is found on the egg white or the yolk, [the egg is] forbidden." [This is contrary to T. Ter. 9:5L, cited at E.]

[I]   [Repeating Hiyya's understanding, F,] R. Halaphta b. Saul taught, "[If one found blood] on the yolk, [the egg is] forbidden. [If one found blood] on the egg white, [the egg is] permitted."

[J]   [Explaining the difference between the views of H and I,] said R. Zeira, "One who says [that if the blood is found on the yolk, the egg is] forbidden refers to a case in which [the blood] is found on the part of the yolk where germination sets in.

[K]   "[One who says that the egg is forbidden] even [if the blood is found] on the egg yolk [but also if it is found on the white], refers to a case [in which the blood] is found on the germinating point in the white of the egg, from which the baby bird is formed."

The Yerushalmi continues the discussion of types of eggs that are or are not forbidden for consumption. As in the preceding unit, the basis for the pericope is the materials found in the Tosefta which complement M. Ter. 10:12.

[IV.A]   There we have learned [M. Miq. 7:2]: *These [liquids] render [an immersion pool] invalid and do not serve to fill up its required measure [of forty seahs: drawn] water, whether it is clean or unclean, water in which food has been pickled or boiled, and unfermented grape-skin wine.*

[B]   [The problem is the inclusion in this list of water in which food was pickled or boiled. According to M. Ter. 10:12D if heave-offering is boiled or pickled in water, it imparts its own status to that water. This means that] here [at M. Ter. 10:12] you deem [water in which food was boiled or pickled itself] to be a food [such that it can take on the status of heave-offering] while [to the contrary] there [at M. Miq. 7:2] you deem it to be a liquid [such that it renders an immersion pool invalid. Foods do not render immersion pools invalid.]

[C]   [To explain the apparent contradiction,] said R. Mana, "Here [at M. Ter. 10:12] hard [types of produce were pickled or boiled in the water].

[D]   "[But to the contrary,] there [at M. Miq. 7:2 we refer to a case in which] soft [sorts of produce were pickled or boiled in the water].

[E]   "Here [at M. Ter. 10:12 reference is to a case] in which the food [still is in the liquid (PM)].

[F]   "There [at M. Miq. 7:2 reference is] to the liquid [alone]."

[G]   [Answering the question posed by B differently] said R. Yose b. R. Bun, "You might even say that in both cases [i.e., M. Ter. 10:12 and M. Miq. 7:2] reference is to hard produce, or that in both cases reference is to soft produce.

[H]   "[The real difference between the cases is that] the rule for liquids to which produce has imparted flavor applies if the produce
was heave-offering. [That which is flavored by heave-offering is
deemed to be a food and to have the status of heave-offering.]

[I]   "But [the rule for liquid to which produce] has imparted flavor
does not apply to [that which is being spilled into] an immersion
pool." [All that matters in the case of an immersion pool is that
it is a liquid. The fact that the liquid was flavored by produce is
irrelevant. As regards an immersion pool it is not deemed a food.]

The problem is succinctly phrased, B, and explained in two different ways, C–F and G–I.

11:1

[A] *They may not put cakes of pressed figs or dried figs [in the status of heave-offering] in fish brine [in order to flavor that brine],*

[B] *since this ruins them [i.e., the figs, for use as food].*

[C] *But they may put wine [in the status of heave-offering] in brine.*

[D] *And they may not perfume oil [in the status of heave-offering, for it may not thereafter be eaten].*

[E] *But they may make wine [in the status of heave-offering] into honied wine.*

[F] *They may not boil wine in the status of heave-offering,*

[G] *since this diminishes its [quantity].*

[H] *R. Judah permits [one to cook wine],*

[I] *for this improves it [i.e., the flavor of the wine].*

Food in the status of heave-offering must be eaten by a priest and therefore may not be processed in a way that renders it unavailable for consumption, A–B, D, and F–G. The heave-offering may be prepared with other foods so long as it will be eaten, C and E. Judah, H–I, rejects F–G, applying his theory familiar from M. Ter. 2:4, that the priest should be given produce of the best quality.

The Yerushalmi moves from the general theory of the pericope to the specifics of its rules. Unit I cites the Tosefta and discusses the larger notion which informs M. Ter. 11:1: Produce in the status of heave-offering must be used for its usual purpose, as a food, or, in certain cases, as a spice. Unit **II** determines which Tannaitic authority stands behind M. Ter. 11:1C. The final unit explains the meaning of "diminishes," here at G.

[**I.A**]   *They may not put cakes of pressed figs or dried figs [in the status of heave-offering] in fish brine* [M. Ter. 11:1A].

[B]   It is taught: **One may put a cake of pressed figs or dried figs [in the status of heave-offering] in fish brine in the same way that he adds spices.**

[C]   **He simply may not press them in order to squeeze out their juices.**

[D]   **In the case of spices [in the status of heave-offering] this is permitted [i.e., to squeeze them], since this is their normal use.**

[E]   **He ties up [in a bundle] spices [in the status of heave-offering], and puts them in this dish [which is cooking],** and then goes and puts them in this other dish [which is cooking]—

[F]   **When they are left without flavor, they are [thereafter] permitted [for consumption as unconsecrated food].**

[G]   **But if [they are] not [left without flavor] they [remain] forbidden [i.e., in the status of heave-offering;** T. Ter. 9:7A–G].

[H]   What is the difference between [the spices referred to at E–F] and dill?

[I]   For is it not taught: *Dill [in the status of heave-offering] which was used to flavor [the food in] a pot no longer is deemed to have the status of heave-offering and does not convey uncleanness as a food;* [M. Uqs. 3:4? This contradicts E–F, which states that a spice must completely lose its flavor, through use in several dishes, before it loses its status of heave-offering. According to M. Uq. 3:4, dill loses the status of heave-offering after its power to impart flavor is only slightly diminished.]

[J]   [The reason that dill has a lenient rule is that one would not have expected it to be deemed a food at all. By right, it never should have been deemed to have the status of heave-offering in the first place. Only by rabbinic authority is dill deemed a food, and therefore it has a lenient law, as M. Uqs. 3:4 indicates. These facts are explained in the following.] It is only your own [decision] that has deemed [dill to be a food].

[K]   Logic would indicate that [dill] never[1] would impart uncleanness as a food.

[L]   But just as [the rabbis] declared that [dill] would impart uncleanness as a food, so they declared that once it had imparted some of its flavor to [the food in] a pot, [its status as a food] is voided.

The Yerushalmi emphasizes the point central in M. Ter. 11:1. Produce in the status of heave-offering must be used in its normal fashion as a food. This being the case the priest may do anything he wants with the heave-offering, so long as it ultimately will be eaten (B–C). Since spices normally are used to flavor foods, they may be used for that purpose and need not be eaten. Once they no longer fulfill that purpose, they are deemed unconsecrated, E–G.

The Yerushalmi's own problem is stated at H–I. M. Uqs. 3:4 states that dill loses its consecrated status as soon as it is used a first time, even if it does not lose its flavor. The reason that dill does not have the same rule as other spices is indicated, J–L.

[II.A]   [M. Ter. 11:1C states that one may put wine in the status of heave-offering in fish brine.] R. Hiyya in the name of R. Yohanan [said], "This is the opinion of Rabbi."

[B]   For it is taught: [As regards placing] wine [in the status of heave-offering] in brine—Rabbi permits, but R. Eleazar b. R. Simeon prohibits [see T. Ter. 9:6B–C].

[C]   On the basis of these opinions, if one transgressed, [in Eleazar b. R. Simeon's view], and placed [wine in the status of heave-offering in unconsecrated brine]—

[D]   Rabbi would deem [the mixture] forbidden to nonpriests. [He holds that even when mixed with the brine, the wine maintains its status of heave-offering.]

[E]   But R. Eleazar b. R. Simeon would deem [the brine] permitted to nonpriests. [He holds that the brine ruins the wine. This is why he does not allow it to be mixed with brine in the first place. If it is anyway put in brine, the heave-offering-wine is ruined and loses its consecrated status. The brine therefore remains permitted for nonpriests.]

[F]   [We turn to a new issue, which develops E.] R. Mana b. R. Tanhum asked, "In accordance with the position of the one [i.e., Eleazar b. Simeon] who states that [when wine is mixed with brine, the wine is destroyed such that, even if the wine had the status of heave-offering, the brine remains] permitted to nonpriests, why did they deem brine of gentiles to be prohibited [for consumption by Israelites (M. A.Z. 2:4)?]" [The apparent reason is that gentiles flavor brine with their wine, which is forbidden. But if the brine destroys the wine, then logically the brine should remain permitted. How then does Eleazar b. Simeon explain the fact that brine of gentiles is forbidden?]

[G]   [Answering F's question,] R. Jeremiah in the name of R. Hiyya bar Va [said], "[The brine] is forbidden under the restrictions which pertain to anything cooked by a gentile." [Simply because it is cooked by a gentile, the brine is forbidden. The fact that it might contain wine is irrelevant.]

[H]   [Rejecting G's reasoning,] R. Yose replied, "But is it not taught: It is permitted [to purchase brine from a gentile who is] a professional [i.e., who does this for a living]; but it is prohibited [to purchase brine from a gentile who is] not a professional [see T. A.Z. 4:13F]?

[I]²   "[When we learn that] it is permitted [to purchase brine from] a professional, does this not mean that [it only is permitted to purchase brine] which is not (so PM, following Y. A.Z. 2:6) cooked?

[J]   "Now by this same reasoning, in the case of [a gentile] who is not a professional, it is forbidden [to purchase from him brine] *even* if it is not cooked!" [Contrary to G then, it is not the brine's having been cooked which renders it forbidden to Israelites. For even brine which has not been cooked may not be purchased from certain gentiles.]

[K]   [This carries forward H–J's argument.] And said R. Yohanan bar Mari, "Even one who holds that it is permitted [to purchase brine from a gentile who is] a professional [claims that] this applies only if [the Israelite] knows him [and therefore can trust him not to sell him brine which contains wine]." [Thus it is clear that the brine is forbidden because it contains wine, not because of its being cooked. G thus is not an acceptable answer to the question posed at F. How can Simeon b. Eleazar explain his view that wine in the status of heave-offering does not render unconsecrated brine forbidden to nonpriests, while it is the case that wine of gentiles does render forbidden fish brine prepared by gentiles?]

[L]   [The facts of the case, given at K, lead to the following understanding.] This is to say that, [according to Simeon b. Eleazar, an Israelite] is permitted to derive benefit from [wine in the status of] heave-offering [the consecrated status of which has been voided, e.g., when the wine was mixed with fish brine].

[M]   [47d] [But an Israelite] is not permitted to derive benefit from [wine used in] idol worship, [even after that wine has been ruined by being mixed with brine].

The unit is in three interrelated parts, A–B, C–E, and F–M. The first two deal directly with the rule of M. Ter. 11:1C and with its implications. F–M uses the material from A–B in order to interpret M. A.Z. 2:4.

[III.A]   [M. Ter. 11:1F–G states that one may not boil wine in the status of heave-offering because this diminishes it. The question is in what way boiling "diminishes" it.] R. Eleazar and R. Yohanan—

[B]   one states [that wine in the status of heave-offering may not be boiled] because it diminishes its quantity;

[C]   but the other says [that it may not be boiled] because this diminishes its [desirability to wine] drinkers.

[D]   And we do not know which [authority] holds which position.

[E]   [We may derive the answer] from Yohanan's statement [at Y. Ter. 2:5 I.C] that the positions of Judah [M. Ter. 11:1H–I and, in Y.'s view, M. Ter. 2:6C] are contradictory, and from Eleazar's statement [Y. Ter. 2:5 I.D–E] that they are not, [since] there [at M. Ter. 11:1H–I] the reference is to the priest and here [at M. Ter. 2:6C] the reference is to householders.

[F]   [Examination of these views shows that] it is R. Yohanan who holds that [by "diminishes" M. Ter. 11:1 means that boiling wine] diminishes its [desirability to wine] drinkers. [This is proven as follows: Yohanan holds that M. Ter. 11:1G means that boiling wine ruins (= diminishes) its flavor. In Yohanan's view, Judah's disputing opinion, M. Ter. 11:1H–I, must be that boiling wine *improves* its flavor. It is along this line of reasoning that Yohanan argues that Judah's opinion at M. Ter. 11:1H–I contradicts what he says at M. Ter. 2:6C, where the point clearly is that boiling wine *diminishes* its flavor. Eleazar, on the other hand, sees the issue at M. Ter. 11:1 as quantity. This is quite independent of the issue of M. Ter. 2:6C, which, as I said, clearly is flavor. Along these lines Eleazar sees no contradiction between the two views of Judah.]

[G]   [Agreeing with Yohanan's explanation of M. Ter. 11:1F–G,] Judah b. Bini [and] R. Imi in the name of R. Simeon b. Laqish [say], "[The meaning of M. Ter. 11:1G–H is] that [boiling wine] diminishes its [desirability to wine] drinkers."

The exegesis of M. Ter. 11:1G–H depends upon the discussion presented above at Y. Ter. 2:5 I.

11:2

[A]   *[As regards any of the following which have the status of heave-offering:] (1) honey made from dates, (2) wine made from apples, (3) vinegar made from winter grapes, or (4) any other fruit juice in the status of heave-offering—*

[B]   *R. Eliezer obligates [a nonpriest who unintentionally drinks any of these] to [payment of] the principal and added fifth.*

[C]   *But R. Joshua exempts.*

[D]   *And R. Eliezer declares [that these things render foods susceptible to] unclean[ness], under the laws of liquids.*

[E]   *Said R. Joshua, "Sages did not number seven liquids [which render foods susceptible to uncleanness] as do those who count spices [i.e., imprecisely].*

[F]   *"Rather, they said, 'Seven [kinds of] liquids [render foods susceptible to] unclean[ness], but all other liquids are clean [i.e., do not render foods susceptible to uncleanness (see M. Makh. 6:4)].'"*

The issue, A–C, is whether or not a nonpriest who unintentionally eats heave-offering which improperly was processed as fruit juice is obligated to pay restitution (see chapter 6). Eliezer holds that since the juice derived from heave-offering, the individual is culpable. Joshua takes account of the extenuating circumstances. The heave-offering should not have been made into juice (M. Ter. 11:1). The nonpriest therefore could not have known that it was heave-offering he was drinking. It follows for Joshua that he is exempt from restitution. D–F is independent. Eliezer and Joshua dispute whether or not fruit juices impart to foods which they moisten susceptibility to uncleanness.

The Yerushalmi covers in turn the dispute at A–C and then that of D–F. Each of these two sections begins with a discussion of the larger issue between Eliezer and Joshua, units I and III. This is followed in each case by an explanation of Eliezer's position, units II (based upon the Tosefta) and IV. Finally, Yohanan states explicitly the meaning of M. Makh. 6:4, referred to by Joshua, E–F. The point of this unit is to show that the understanding of Joshua, D–F, is correct and that Eliezer is wrong.

[I.A]³ They would reason, "[At M. Ter. 11:2A–C], concerning what do [Eliezer and Joshua] disagree?

[B]   "[Concerning whether or not a nonpriest who drinks fruit juices in the status of heave-offering is obligated to pay] the added fifth.

[C]   "But concerning the principal, even R. Joshua, [who holds that the added fifth need not be paid], concedes [that the principal must be paid]."

[D]   Concerning what do they disagree? [They disagree] concerning a case in which someone already [has processed produce in the status of heave-offering into fruit juice. Eliezer holds that the juice has the status of heave-offering; Joshua says that it does not.]

[E]   But [as for whether or not one may do this] de jure [see M. Ter. 11:3], even R. Joshua agrees [that one may not].

[F]   But [contrary to the claim of B–C] so we have learned: **Honey made from dates—R. Eliezer declares it subject to [the removal of] tithes.** But R. Joshua deems it exempt [T. Ter. 9:8A–B, which lacks Joshua's position. Joshua exempts fruit juice from the separation of tithes because he does not deem it to be a food.

This means that, contrary to C, he should not hold someone who drinks fruit juice made from produce in the status of heave-offering to be liable for the principal. Since it is not a food, the fruit juice cannot have the status of heave-offering.]

[G]   [Here is how Joshua can maintain the positions recorded in his name both at C and at F. His position] here [at C] applies in a case in which [the fruit juice] was made after [the produce] had become subject to tithes. [Like the produce from which it was made, the fruit juice is subject to tithes and, in a limited way, may take on the status of heave-offering.]

[H]   But here [at F, where Joshua does not deem the fruit juice to be subject to tithes at all, it is a case] in which [the fruit juice] was made before the produce became subject to the separation of tithes. [Since the produce from which the juice was made was not subject to tithes, the juice, which Joshua does not deem to be a food, likewise is not subject.]

A–C's interpretation of the dispute between Eliezer and Joshua reveals an apparent contradiction in the position of Joshua. This is explained at F–H. D–E is secondary, for it does not contribute to the unit as a whole. Still, its point is apposite, insomuch as it clarifies the positions of the disputing authorities.

[II.A]   **R. Eliezer agrees that if one tithed the dates [here, in the land of Israel, and turned them into honey] even in Apamaea, [a town in Syria], that the honey is permitted [for consumption without further tithing; T. Ter. 9:8E].**

[B]   This is to say that he separates heave-offering and tithes from the dates, on behalf of the honey, in accordance with the quantity of the dates [and not of the potential honey].

[C]   [B's conclusion is challenged. **Honey made from dates]—R. Eliezer declares it subject to [the removal of] tithes.**

[D][4]   It is taught" **R. Nathan says, "It is not that R. Eliezer deems [the honey] subject to [the separation of] tithes.**

[E]   **"Rather, R. Eliezer says that one may not eat of the** (read:) **honey unless he had tithed the dates [from which the honey was made";** T. Ter. 9:8A–D, with slight variations].

[F]   [Contrary to B] this is to say that he separates heave-offering and tithes from the dates on behalf of the honey in accordance with the quantity of dates and amount of honey [the dates will produce. This appears to be the case since, E, the tithing of dates serves to render the honey permitted for consumption.]

The unit is an exegesis of T. Ter. 9:8E, cited at A. B's conclusion is revised on the basis of T. Ter. 9:8A–D, at D–F.

[III.A]   *R. Eliezer declares [that the sorts of fruit juice listed at M. Ter. 11:2A render foods susceptible to] unclean[ness], under the law of liquids [M. Ter. 11:2D].*

[B]   It is taught: R. Nathan says, "It is not so that R. Eliezer deems [these fruit juices to render foods susceptible to] unclean[ness] under the law of liquids. [Like Joshua, M. Ter. 11:2E–F, he holds that they do not.]

[C]   "Concerning what do [Eliezer and the rule of M. Ter. 11:2E–F] disagree?

[D]   "Concerning a case in which a liquid [e.g., water] fell into [the fruit juice].

[E]   "For R. Eliezer declares that [the mixture renders foods susceptible to] unclean[ness] under the laws of liquids.

[F]   "But sages [= M. Ter. 11:2E–F] say, 'They rule [on whether or not the mixture is deemed a liquid] in accordance with what is in the majority, [fruit juice or water].'"

[G]   According to R. Nathan, R. Meir, R. Eliezer b. Jacob, and R. Eliezer, the three of them, all said the same thing [i.e., that a mixture of fruit juice and water imparts susceptibility to uncleanness].

[H]   [We know that] R. Meir [holds this view] for he said, "Fruit juice is (follow PM and delete: not) always nullified [by water which falls into it]." [See T. Makh. 1:7A, where Meir states: Fruit juice into which a drop of water of any amount has fallen imparts susceptibility to uncleanness.]

[I]   [We know that] R. Eliezer b. Jacob [holds this view] for it is taught: *R. Eliezer b. Jacob says, "Clean brine into which there*

fell any small amount of water is rendered unclean" [i.e., imparts susceptibility to uncleanness, M. Makh. 6:3].

[J]   And the opinion of R. Eliezer [already has been given] here
[at D–E.]

According to the Yerushalmi, Eliezer agrees with Joshua, M. Ter.
11:2E–F, that fruit juices do not render foods they moisten susceptible to uncleanness. They disagree only concerning fruit
juices which have been mixed with water. Eliezer says that these
are treated like water, such that they render foods susceptible
to uncleanness. Joshua holds that they still are fruit juices and
therefore do not render foods susceptible. The Yerushalmi's interpretation of the dispute is tendentious. It seeks to show that
Eliezer agrees with what is explicit at M. Makh. 6:4, that fruit
juices do not render foods susceptible to uncleanness. But it is
clear from M. Ter. 11:2 that Eliezer simply does not agree with
that rule.

[**IV.**A]   The [scriptural] basis for the view of R. Eliezer [M. Ter. 11:2D,
that fruit juices render foods which they wet down susceptible to
uncleanness] is [Lev. 11:34: 'Any food in it (i.e., an earthen
vessel) which may be eaten, upon which water may come, shall
be unclean]; and *all* drink [which may be drunk from every such
vessel shall be unclean].' [On the basis of the word 'all' Eliezer
states that these rules apply to fruit juices, just as to other liquids].

[B]   What is the [scriptural] basis for the view of rabbis [who, contrary to Eliezer, hold that fruit juices do not impart susceptibility to uncleanness]?

[C]   [The same verse, for it states, 'And all drink] which may be
drunk.' [Rabbis hold that since fruit juices are not normally
drunk, they do not fall under this rule.]

[D]   What [does Eliezer say in order to explain the words 'which may
be drunk']?

[E]   R. Eliezer follows the view of R. Ishmael, for R. Ishmael said,
"[If there is] a general statement [i.e., 'all drink'] and a defining
specification [i.e., 'which may be drunk'] all [matters of law] follow the general statement."

[F]   Indeed [Eliezer] goes even further than R. Ishmael, for [Eliezer] says, "Even if there is a general statement and a defining specification and then [Scripture] again repeats the general statement, all [matters of law] follow the general statement."

[G]   [Rejecting F,] R. Prigori of Caesarea [said], "R. Eliezer (read with GRA and PM:) accords with the view of R. Ishmael [as at E].

[H]   "But this is how R. Eliezer answers the argument of sages, [B + C]:

[I]   "'Just as [at Lev. 11:34] you have the statement, 'Any food which may be eaten,' which excludes [from the law] food which is rotten,

[J]   "'So I have the statement, 'All drink which may be drunk,' which excludes [from the law] liquids which are putrid, [but does not exclude fruit juices].'"

[K]   [Rejecting I–J,] they said to him, "Foods are not comparable to liquids. [Therefore the exclusionary phrase 'which may be drunk' for the case of liquids does not mean the same as the specification 'which may be eaten' for the case of foods. This is explained in the next line.]

[L]   "If you say for the case of foods [that the phrase 'which may be eaten' excludes that which is rotten], since rotten food is by nature unable to become unclean,

[M]   "can you make the same claim for the case of liquids [i.e., that the specification 'which may be drunk' excludes that which is putrid] when, in fact, putrid liquids are by nature still able to become unclean? [No, you cannot. The exclusionary phrase 'which are drunk' does not exclude liquid that is putrid, for liquids which are putrid both become unclean and render foods susceptible to uncleanness. Rather, the specification 'which are drunk' excludes from the law fruit juices, just as rabbis, C, said.]

[N]   "[Here is] a different argument [by which we can see that liquids and foods are not comparable].

[O]   "If you say for the case of foods [that the phrase 'which may be eaten' excludes that which is rotten], since foods which are [grown] specifically for consumption of people do not require the intention [of some particular person to eat them so as to become susceptible to uncleanness],

[P]   "can you make this same claim [i.e., that the phrase 'which may
       be drunk' excludes that which is putrid] for the case of liquids,
       inasmuch as [even those] liquids which are [prepared] specifi-
       cally for consumption by people must be subject to the intention
       [of a person who desires to drink them so as to become suscep-
       tible to uncleanness and concomitantly to impart such suscep-
       tibility]?" [No, the claim is unacceptable. As we saw at M, and
       as is assumed here at P, even putrid liquids become unclean and
       impart susceptibility to uncleanness. Therefore it is clear that
       the specification 'which may be drunk' does not exclude from the
       law putrid liquids, but rather fruit juices, just as rabbis said, C.]

[Q]   [This argues against the conclusion of O–P.] Now [is it the case
       that] since they require intention [so as to become susceptible to
       uncleanness as foods] that putrid liquids should by nature be
       deemed susceptible to uncleanness [and able to impart suscep-
       tibility to uncleanness, as claimed by M and P]?

[R]⁵   [No, rather] since they require intention [so as to be deemed a
       food and susceptible to uncleanness] putrid liquids should by
       nature be deemed insusceptible to uncleanness [and unable to
       impart susceptibility to uncleanness]. [Indeed, this is what the
       specification 'which may be drunk' tells us: Putrid liquids are
       not under the rule of Lev. 11:34. But that specification does not
       exclude from the law fruit juices. This is just as I–J argued. The
       challenge to this claim, K–M + N–Q, is proven unacceptable.]

[S]   [A new attempt is made to disprove I–J by showing that liquids
       and foods are not comparable.] Another matter:

[T]   They said to him [i.e., to Prigori, the authority behind I–J],
       "No. If you say for the case of foods [that the phrase 'which may
       be eaten' excludes that which is rotten], since foods normally fed
       to animals, which are given to people to eat, in no event are subject
       to that intention [to use them as food for humans, such that this
       animal feed never can become susceptible to uncleanness],

[U]⁶   "will you make this same claim [that the phrase 'which may be
       drunk' excludes liquids which are putrid] for the case of liquids,
       inasmuch as a liquid normally given to animals, which is drunk
       by a human, does come under [that person's] intention, [such
       that it is susceptible to uncleanness and concomitantly renders
       foods susceptible to uncleanness]?" [No, you cannot make that
       claim. Since the rules for foods and liquids are not the same, you

cannot claim that the exclusionary phrases cited for each mean the same things. The phrase 'which may be eaten' excludes from the law foods which are rotten. The phrase 'which may be drunk' does not exclude from the law liquids which are putrid, contrary to I-J. Rather, as rabbis say, C, it excludes from the law fruit juices.]

[V]   [This dispute concerning whether or not a rotten liquid is susceptible to uncleanness] is taught [in a Tannaitic tradition: **Lev. 11:34 states**] '**All drink [is susceptible to uncleanness].**'

[W]   **What does Scripture mean [by the specification]: 'which may be drunk'?**

[X]   **"This excludes [from the law] liquids which are putrid"—the words of R. Eliezer.**

[Y]   **They said to him, "[Putrid] liquids do not restrain fowl nor a cow [from drinking. Therefore this liquid still is under the law"; T. Toh. 9:12C-D, with variations].**

[Z]   [Z, BB, and DD list points upon which Eliezer and sages disagree.] Associates in the name of R. Eleazar [say], "R. Eliezer concedes to sages for the case of liquid which is putrid that it may be rendered unclean." [PM: he disagrees only in claiming that this liquid does not impart susceptibility to uncleanness. Sages say that it does.]

[AA]   [This is separate.] So we have learned [M. Toh. 9:3]: *Sap which exudes [from olives the preparation for consumption of which is complete]—R. Eliezer deems it clean [i.e., unable to impart susceptibility to uncleanness]. But sages deem it unclean [i.e., to be a liquid which imparts susceptibility to uncleanness].*

[BB]   [Claiming a different point of agreement between Eliezer and sages,] R. Ila in the name of R. Eleazar [said], "R. Eliezer concedes to sages concerning water from the Mediterranean Sea, that even if it is putrid, the Torah deemed it to be water [such that it imparts susceptibility to uncleanness].

[CC]   "[We know this because Gen. 1:10 states]: 'The waters that were gathered together [God] called seas.'"

[DD]   [Giving yet a final point of agreement] R. Jacob bar Zibdi in the name of R. Abbahu [said], "R. Eliezer concedes to sages that water in which beets were soaked and water in which [vegetables] were boiled does not impart susceptibility to uncleanness."

Ignoring the preceding unit, the Yerushalmi explains the scriptural basis for Eliezer's view that fruit juices impart susceptibility to uncleanness, A. Once the view of Joshua (= sages here), that the fruit juices do impart susceptibility to uncleanness, is derived from the same verse, B–C, an exegetical debate follows, D–Y. Finally Z + BB–DD lists certain liquids which Eliezer and sages agree impart to foods they moisten susceptibility to uncleanness. AA appears out of place, for it neither responds to Z nor belongs ideationally with Z, BB, and DD. The point of the prooftext, CC, is not clear.

[V.A]   [M. Makh. 6:4 lists seven liquids which render foods they wet down susceptible to uncleanness: dew, water, wine, oil, blood, milk, and bee's honey.] R. Yohanan in the name of R. Simeon b. Yohai [says], "If someone tells you that [the list of M. Makh. 6:4 is not exact and that actually there are] eight liquids [which impart susceptibility to uncleanness (e.g., that one may include honey from dates as well as honey from bees)], tell him, 'Lo, dew and water are actually the same thing, yet sages numbered them as two different things.' [This shows that the list really is exact and that one should not add to it different types of the same genus of liquid.]

[B]   "If [sages] had some further liquid [which they wished to include in M. Makh. 6:4's catalog], would they not have listed it [explicitly]?

[C]   [The same statement is repeated in a slightly different manner.] "Now if there was another [liquid they wished to include], would they not have included it [explicitly in M. Makh. 6:4's list]?"

This interpretation of M. Makh. 6:4 concurs with that of Joshua, M. Ter. 11:2E–F. Eliezer, M. Ter. 11:2D, cannot agree.

11:3 [P: 11:3a]

[A]   [Regarding produce in the status of heave-offering or second tithe:] they may not make (1) dates into honey, (2) apples into wine, (3) winter grapes into vinegar, nor, (4) [as regards] all other fruits, may they alter their natural condition if they are in the status of heave-offering or second tithe,

[B]   except [in the case of] olives and grapes.

[C]   They do not receive the forty stripes for [drinking liquids made from produce which is] from the first three years of growth of a vineyard or orchard [Lev. 19:23],

[D]   except for [drinking] that which is produced from olives or grapes.

[E]   And they may not bring first fruits [in the form of] liquids,

[F]   except for that which is produced from olives or grapes.

[G]   And no [fruit juice] imparts susceptibility to uncleanness under the law of liquids,

[H]   except for that [liquid] which is produce from olives or grapes.

[I]   And they may offer no [liquid] at the altar,

[J]   except for that [liquid] which is produced from olives or grapes.

The basis for the distinction between olives and grapes and all other fruits is the form in which each type of produce normally is eaten. Olives and grapes usually are made into oil and wine, and therefore, if in the status of heave-offering, must be processed in this manner. Other fruits normally are eaten fresh. For this reason, if such food is in the status of heave-offering, it must not be processed. The larger theory of the pericope thus is that produce or fruit that is processed in other than its normal way is not deemed a food. The rules of C–D, E–F, G–H, and I–J follow.

The Yerushalmi begins by addressing M. Ter. 11:3E–F, citing a Tannaitic tradition which states that fruit juices may be brought as first fruits. The Yerushalmi proves that this rule does not contradict the law of the Mishnah. The Yerushalmi's major unit on this pericope cites T. Ter. 9:9, which exposes a grey area in the law of M. Ter. 11:3A–B. The problem is what is to be done with unclean grapes or olives in the status of heave-offering. They themselves may be eaten by a priest, for they comprise less than the minimum quantity of food which imparts uncleanness. If they are processed, however, the resulting wine or oil will be unclean and therefore unusuable. At issue is whether, in such a case, we apply the rule that heave-offering should be processed as produce of its type normally is, or the rule which states that heave-offering must be eaten by the priest. This question generates four disputing sets of rules, one of Meir and three Ushan versions of a dispute on this issue between Eliezer and Joshua.

[I.A] R. Ila in the name of R. Eleazar [says], "This is what Mishnah [Ter. 11 : 3E–F] means: *They may not bring first fruits in the form of liquids, except for that which is produced from olives or grapes.*

[B] "[This means that] even after the householder [has produced the fruit juice and] has it [in his hand, ready to be brought as first fruit, he may not do so]." [Ila's point is that the rule of M. Ter. 11 : 3E–F applies post facto as well as de jure.]

[C] Yet [contrary to B] is it not taught: If one pressed [fruit in the status of] first fruits in order to bring it [to the Temple] as a liquid, from what [verse of Scripture] do we know that he may bring [the liquid]?

[D] Scripture [Dt. 26 : 2] states: '[You shall *take* some of the first of all the fruit of the ground, which] you *take* [from your land that the Lord your God gives you . . .]'? [The redundant use of the word "take" indicates that even if the first fruits are pressed into juice, they may be brought to the Temple.]

[E] [The reason for the apparent contradiction between B and C–D is given. The two statements apply to different cases. C–D applies if] from the beginning [the householder harvested the produce] for this purpose [i.e., to press the fruit into juice].

[F] But, [by contrast, B applies] if from the start he had not picked [the fruit] for this purpose, [but had designated it to be first fruits and only later determined to press that fruit for juice].

The apparent contradiction between A–B and C–D is explained, E–F. The point of the unit is to explain M. Ter. 11 : 3E–F, cited at A.

[II.A] **"[As regards] olives in the status of heave-offering—**

[B] **"[if they are] clean, let them be made into oil.**

[C] **"[If they are] unclean let them not be made into oil.**

[D]   "[As regards] grapes [in the status of heave-offering]—

[E]   "whether they are unclean or clean, let them not be made [into wine]"—the words of R. Meir.

[F]   R. Jacob says, (read following MSS. and editions of T.:) "R. Eliezer concedes to R. Joshua in [the case of] clean olives, that they should be made [into oil].

[G]   "Concerning what did they disagree?

[H]   "Concerning [the case of] unclean olives.

[I]   "For R. Eliezer says, 'Let them not be made [into oil],'

[J]   "and R. Joshua says, 'Let them be made [into oil],'

[K]   "'and clean grapes should be made [into wine], and unclean grapes should not be made [into wine].'"

[L]   Said R. Yudan, "R. Joshua concedes to R. Eliezer concerning [the case of] clean olives (T. adds: and grapes), that they should be made [into oil].

[M]   "Concerning what did they disagree?

[N]   "Concerning unclean [olives] (T.: and grapes).

[O]   "For R. Eliezer says, 'They should not be made [into oil],'

[P]   and R. Joshua says, 'They should be made [into oil].'

[Q]   "And [as for] grapes, whether they are clean or unclean, they should be made [into wine]." [This line is not found in T.]

[R]   Said Rabbi Yohanan,[7] "R. Eliezer and R. Joshua did not disagree concerning clean olives, that they should be made [into oil], and concerning unclean grapes, that they should not be made [into wine].

[S]   "Concerning what did they disagree?

[T]   "Concerning unclean olives and clean grapes.

[U]   "For R. Eliezer says, 'They should not be made [into oil or wine],'

[V]   "and R. Joshua says, 'They should be made [into oil and wine'"]; T. Ter. 9:9.

[W]   [We turn to an analysis of the positions just set out.] All of the authorities [i.e., Jacob, F–K, Yudan, L–P, and Rabbi, R–V] disagree with R. Meir for the case of clean grapes. [While Meir holds that they should not be made into wine, these others hold] that they should be made [into wine].

[X]   Now why[8] [does Meir] hold that [clean grapes in the status of heave-offering] should not be made [into wine]?

[Y]   [He holds that the grapes] are more valuable as a food than as a drink.

[Z]   All of the authorities [i.e., Meir, A–E, Jacob, F–K, and Rabbi, R–V] disagree with R. Yudan for the case of unclean grapes. [While in Yudan's view, Joshua holds that unclean grapes should be made into wine, all the other authorities state that there is agreement] that [unclean grapes in the status of heave-offering] should not be made [into wine].

[AA]   Now why [according to Yudan does Joshua hold that] one should make [unclean grapes in the status of heave-offering into wine? Since the unclean wine may not be drunk by the priest, we should not expect processing to be required.]

[BB]   [Joshua in all events wants the grapes processed] so that [the priest may] enjoy [use of] the shells and pomace. [When dried, these may be used by the priest as kindling.]

[CC]   [Concerning] unclean olives—Rabbi's [statement of Eliezer's view] and the position of Meir are in agreement. [Both hold that unclean olives in the status of heave-offering should not be pressed for oil.]

[DD]   [For the case of unclean olives] R. Jacob and R. Yudan agree. [Both hold that Eliezer states that these should not be made into oil, and that Joshua states they should be.]

[EE]   [Since there are so many different opinions concerning the rules for grapes and olives in the status of heave-offering], how do we rule in a concrete case?

[FF]   R. Zeira in the name of R. Eleazar [b. Pedat, Zeira's teacher, said], "[It is not clear] whether or not [we speak of a case in which the liquids] are mixed with foods." [Neither the point of this statement nor the manner in which it answers the question posed at EE is clear.]

[GG]   [The relationship between Zeira and Eleazar b. Pedat is described here. As for] R. Zeira—all [that he teaches] concerning [the rules of] heave-offering and purities, [he teaches as a] tradition in the name of R. Eleazar.

A chart indicates the areas of agreement and disagreement among the various authorities.[9] "+" stands for "may be made into wine or oil," and "−" means "may not be made into wine or oil."

	Meir (A–D)	Jacob (F–K)		Yudan (L–P)		Rabbi (R–V)	
		Eliezer	Joshua	Eliezer	Joshua	Eliezer	Joshua
clean olives	+	+	+	+	+	+	+
unclean olives	−	−	+	−	+	−	+
clean grapes	−	+	+	+	+	−	+
unclean grapes	−	−	−	−	+	−	−

There is in fact only a small range of disagreement as to the correct dispute between Eliezer and Joshua. All three Ushan renditions report the same dispute for cases concerning clean and unclean olives. Clean olives in the status of heave-offering should be made into oil, for this is their normal processing (so M. Ter. 11:3). Joshua holds that unclean olives as well should be made into oil, for this is the processing they normally undergo. Eliezer, by contrast, requires that the unclean olives be left unprocessed, so that the priest may eat them. Meir agrees, as CC–DD points out.

For the case of grapes in the status of heave-offering, matters are only slightly more complicated. We should expect that clean grapes in the status of heave-offering must be made into wine, just as the Mishnah indicated. As W states, only Meir (D–E) (and Rabbi's Eliezer, U) disagree with this. The Yerushalmi itself explains the view of Meir, X–Y, yet ignores the fact that Rabbi's Eliezer holds the same position. Meir deems grapes to be more valuable as a food than as wine. As regards unclean grapes, all of the versions have Eliezer remain consistent with his view concerning unclean olives. The unclean grapes should not be processed, for obvious reasons. Meir agrees. Regarding Joshua, as Z notes, only Yudan has him remain consistent with his position on unclean olives. He states that the unclean grapes should be processed into wine, even though the priest will not be able to drink that wine. AA–BB explains this view, indicating that Joshua wants the priest to be able to use the residue from the pressing of the grapes. For the case of unclean grapes, Jacob and Rabbi claim that Joshua reverts to the position of Eliezer. Since the wine would not be available for the consumption of the priest, the grapes should not be processed.

If Yerushalmi's own analysis of the positions in T. Ter. 9:9 thus is clear, the conclusion of its discussion, EE–GG, is not. While the question, EE, is important, the point of the answer, FF, is enigmatic.

11:4 [M. Ter. 11:4–5; P: 11:3b–11:4a]

[A]   *The stems of [fresh] figs, dried figs, pods, and carobs in the status of heave-offering are forbidden [for consumption] by nonpriests.*

[B]   *[As regards] the pits of produce in the status of heave-offering—*

[C]   *when he [i.e., the priest] keeps them, they are forbidden [for consumption by nonpriests].*

[D]   *But if he throws them out, they are permitted.*

[E]   *And so in the case of the bones of Holy Things [i.e., animal offerings]—*

[F]   *when he keeps them, they are forbidden [to nonpriests].*

[G]   *But if he throws them out, they are permitted.*

[H]   *Coarse bran [from grain in the status of heave-offering] is permitted [for consumption by nonpriests].*

[I]   *Fine bran from fresh [wheat in the status of heave-offering] is forbidden [to nonpriests].*

[J]   *But [fine bran] from old [wheat in the status of heave-offering] is permitted.*

[K]   *[The priest] may treat heave-offering just as he treats unconsecrated produce [i.e., he may throw out the parts he does not normally eat].*

[L]   *One who prepares fine flour [from wheat in the status of heave-offering], deriving a qab or two from each seah [of wheat], may not destroy the residue [which is edible].*

[M]   *Rather, he places it in a concealed place.*

Only food can have the status of heave-offering. Those parts of produce in the status of heave-offering that normally are not eaten therefore are not deemed consecrated as a priestly gift. They need not be eaten by a priest and, indeed, may be consumed by a nonpriest who wishes to eat them. The problem of the pericope is to establish criteria for determining what is food. According to A, H–J, and L–M there is an objective standard. B–C + D, its gloss at E–D + G, and K, by contrast, offer cases in which the priest's own attitude is determinative. What he saves for himself is deemed food and retains its consecrated status. What he throws out is considered inedible and does not have the status of heave-offering.

The Yerushalmi ignores the Mishnah's claim that, in certain cases, whether or not produce is deemed food depends upon the attitude of the priest. It concentrates solely on the question of what refuse from produce in the status of heave-offering is objectively edible, such that it too has a consecrated status. The tripartite discussion opens with an analysis of M. Ter. 11:4A–G. It asks under what circumstances refuse from produce in the status of heave-offering is edible. In its second section, the Yerushalmi cites T. Ter. 10:4 in order to explain what constitutes "fresh grain," M. Ter. 11:5I–J. Finally, at units **III–IV**, the Yerushalmi clarifies the theory of what constitutes edible refuse from food that stands behind M. Ter. 11:5L–M. The Yerushalmi thus addresses in turn each of the elements of the Mishnah's pericope.

[I.A]   Said R. Yohanan, "Mishnah [Ter. 11:4B–D] refers to the pits of pears and Crustumenian pears." [It states that if the priest keeps these, they are deemed heave-offering. But if he throws them out, they are unconsecrated. The reason (PM) is that some of the fruit remains stuck to the pit, such that the pit need not be deemed refuse.]

[B]   Said R. Eleazar, "You might even say that [M. Ter. 11:4B–D] refers to the pits [of all other fruit, even if small amounts of food do not remain stuck to them. Still, if these are kept by the priest, they are deemed to have the status of heave-offering, since they contain] juice which one is able to suck out."

[C]   [B's claim, that inedibles are deemed to maintain their consecrated status because of the juices they contain, is proven unacceptable.] But so we have learned: *And so in the case of the bones of Holy Things*—[if the priest keeps them, they retain their sanctified status; M. Ter. 11:4E–G].

[D]   Should you state [that these retain their holy status] because they are available for being sucked on?

[E]   No, [it is not because of the juices the bones contain. Rather, as we shall see at F, the bones are deemed sanctified because of] the cartilaginous tops of the forelegs. [This cartilage is edible, and it accounts for the fact that the bones are deemed a food.]

[F]   R. Abbahu came [and said] in the name of R. Yohanan, "Mishnah [Ter. 11:4E–G] refers to the cartilaginous tops of the forelegs." [The net result of this discussion is that Eleazar's claim, B, is unacceptable. Yohanan, A, is right. Food is deemed to retain the status of heave-offering, or some other level of sanctification, only if parts of it are edible. The fact that the priest might suck on it is not sufficient.]

Actual pieces of food that remain stuck to the pits of produce that has been eaten are considered edible refuse, A + C–F. Contrary to Eleazar, B, juice contained within the pits is not deemed edible refuse.

[II.A]   [*Fine bran from fresh (wheat in the status of heave-offering) is forbidden (to nonpriests). But (fine bran) from old (wheat in the status of heave-offering) is permitted* (M. Ter. 11:5I–J).]

[B]   (Read with T.:) **For how long is [fine bran from] fresh [wheat in the status of heave-offering] forbidden?**

[C]   **For as long as it is normal for people to thresh [at the threshing floor].**

[D]   **R. Aha says, "For thirty days [from the harvest]"** [T. Ter. 10:4A–E].

B–D's relevance to M. Ter. 11:5I–J is obvious. At B, the Yerushalmi's version reads: "Which [types of wheat] are deemed fresh?" While the point is clearly the same, the Tosefta's text makes better sense.

[III.A]   [One who prepares fine flour from grain in the status of heave-offering derives only a *qab* or two from each *seah* of wheat. The residue is deemed edible and so has the status of heave-offering. So M. Ter. 11:4L.] R. Abbahu in the name of R. Yohanan [said], "Indeed this is the correct measure [of how much fine flour is derived from wheat]."

[B]   But [to the contrary] is it not taught: One who prepares fine flour from grain need derive [from the grain only] as much [flour] as he desires. [The residue is deemed inedible refuse, which cannot have the status of heave-offering.]

[C]   And, [just as at B], one who cleans out [the husk of] a vegetable [to use the inside part alone] may clean out as much [or little] as he desires. [The remainder is deemed refuse.]

[D]   [How do we account for the contradiction between the rule of M. Ter. 11:4L, which states that the residue from the preparation of fine flour is a food, and B + C, which states that it is not?] R. Abbahu in the name of R. Yohanan [said], "[A] refers to a case in which he wishes to increase the quantity of heave-offering [he will give the priest]." [The householder who mills wheat in the status of heave-offering therefore deems even the refuse from the milling process to be a food.]

[E]   [Giving a different explanation,] R. Jeremiah [48a] in the name of R. Ila [said], "This [i.e., M. Ter. 11:4L] applies in years of famine. [In such years anything which can be eaten is deemed a food, even the residue from the milling process.]

[F]   "But this [i.e., B + C] applies in years of plenty." [In such years only the best of the produce is thought of as a food.]

The point is at E + F. The standard of what is edible depends upon the attitude of the society as a whole. Contrary to M. Ter. 11:5B–G, it is not determined by the desires of any particular priest who decides to keep or to throw out the refuse from what he eats.

[IV.A]   There we have learned [M. Ed. 3:3: *As for]* the entrails of melons and the outer leaves of [leafy] vegetables in the status of heave-offering—R. Dosa permits [these things to] nonpriests,

[claiming that they are refuse, not food]. But sages deem them
forbidden [to nonpriests, under the theory that they are foods].

[B]   R. Abbahu in the name of R. Yohanan [said], "They did not
teach [that this dispute applies] other than in the case of the
outer leaves of [leafy] vegetables grown by gardeners. [The gardeners clean their produce thoroughly. If the priest removes
more leaves from that which has been given to him as heave-
offering, these might be edible. Dosa claims that in all events
that which the priest removes is waste, and not consecrated.
Sages say that since the produce already was well cleaned, what
the priest later removes is food and is consecrated.]

[C]   "But in the case of the outer leaves of a [leafy] vegetable grown
by householders [i.e., on larger farms], even rabbis [i.e., sages]
concede [to Dosa that leaves which the priest cleans off of his
heave-offering are unconsecrated]." [The reason is that the farmers are not so careful as are gardeners about cleaning the refuse
off of produce. Therefore one may be certain that any leaves the
priest removes from heave-offering separated by a farmer are refuse, which does not have the status of heave-offering.]

[D]   [Suggesting a further qualification of M. Ed. 3:3, cited at A,]
R. Bun asked, "[The dispute of M. Ed. 3:3] makes no sense [ex-
cept (GRA, PM)] in the case of the great heave-offering, [which
householders separate for the priest. In this case the distinction
between the way gardeners, B, and farmers, C, prepare the produce they designate as heave-offering applies.]

[E]   "But in the case of heave-offering of the tithe, [which the Levite
separates from first tithe and gives to the priest, Dosa agrees
with sages that any leaves the priest subsequently removes are
forbidden to nonpriests]. [In this case the Levite receives produce
as it normally is prepared by the farmer or gardener. He goes ahead
and cleans thoroughly whatever he plans to designate heave-
offering of the tithe. As a result, heave-offering of the tithe which a
priest receives has no waste attached to it. Any leaves he should de-
tach must be deemed food and are consecrated.]

[F]   "[The larger theory which explains E is that] they may not pick
off more leaves [and deem them waste] once some leaves [have
been removed]. Nor may one cut off more of the stalk [and deem
it refuse] once some of the stalk [has been removed]."

While intended as an interpretation of M. Ed. 3:3, the unit is pertinent here because it advances the theory introduced in the preceding units. There is an objective standard of what is a food, such that it retains the consecrated status of heave-offering. B–C assumes that only certain of the outer leaves of leafy vegetables are waste. The rest of the vegetable is an edible food. Even those inside leaves that the priest determines to throw out as waste therefore retain the status of heave-offering. Beyond this, the unit simply points out that some farmers give the priest thoroughly cleaned produce, while others turn over vegetables that contain some waste. Depending upon which he receives, what the priest himself picks off will or will not be deemed edible. The qualification of E–F makes this same point in different terms.

11:5 [P: 11:4b; M. Ter. 11:6–8]

[A]   *[As to] a storage bin from which one emptied wheat in the status of heave-offering—*

[B]   *they do not obligate him to sit and pick up one at a time each kernel of wheat [that remains on the floor of the bin].*

[C]   *Rather, he may sweep [the bin] in his normal fashion and [then] may put unconsecrated [wheat in it].*

[D]   *And so [in the case of] a jug of oil [in the status of heave-offering] which was spilled—*

[E]   *they do not obligate him to sit and scoop [it] up with his hand.*

[F]   *Rather, he treats it as he treats unconsecrated [oil which spills; he may wipe it up with a rag, even though the rag will absorb some of the consecrated oil].*

[G]   *One who pours [wine or oil in the status of heave-offering] from one jar to another and [allows] three [last] drops to drip [from the jar he is emptying] may [then] put unconsecrated [wine or oil] in that [jar, without further wiping it out].*

[H]   *If [after three drops had fallen], he placed [the jar] on its side and [more oil or wine] drained [from it]—lo, this [wine or oil] is in the status of heave-offering.*

[I]   *And what quantity of heave-offering of the tithe [separated] from produce about which there is a doubt whether or not it previously was tithed need one take to the priest?*

[J]   *One eighth of an eighth log [= ⅟₆₄ log; less than this quantity is deemed insignificant and need not be given to the priest].*

The point, A–H, is that the priest's obligation to eat produce in the status of heave-offering is determined by whether or not people normally consider that produce to be food. If they do not—A–C, D–F, and G–H—the produce is deemed unconsecrated. H's qualification is obvious. By collecting what otherwise would not be deemed significant as food, the individual indicates that he desires the produce. This act is determinative, such that the wine or oil retains the status of heave-offering. I–J is thematically related. Small quantities of a priestly gift about which there is a doubt whether or not it has a sanctified status need not be given to a priest.

The Yerushalmi is attentive only to the last two of the Mishnah's rules, H and I–J. After explaining the underlying theory of H (units **I–II**), it turns to the Tosefta's complementary material. These outline in general terms a notion of what is edible and what is not (units **III–IV**). Unit **V** details the circumstances under which a householder need not give to the priest small quantities of heave-offering of the tithe, I–J.

[I.A]   There we have learned [M. B.B. 5:8: *A person who sells wine or oil must allow three last drops to drip from the measure. This belongs to the buyer. If after doing this the seller]* placed *[the measure] on its side and [more wine or oil] drained [from it]— lo, this [additional wine or oil which was in the measure] belongs to the seller.*

[B]   Said R. Yohanan, "This should not say, 'It belongs to the seller.' Rather, 'It belongs to the buyer.'

[C]   "[This is obvious] since here [at M. Ter. 11:8H] you state this [i.e., that additional wine or oil in the status of heave-offering which drips from a vessel from which three last drops already had drained has the status of heave-offering]." [This additional liquid which drains from the vessel has the same status as that which one poured out before the final three drips. In the same

way, the wine or oil which the seller collects after he has drained
the vessel should belong to the buyer, as Yohanan suggests, B.]

[D]   [Explaining why the case of the sale of wine or oil is different
from the transfer of wine or oil in the status of heave-offering]
said R. Isaac in the name of R. Eleazar, "[The wine which ultimately drains from the measure belongs to the seller, not the
buyer] because [the buyer already had] despaired [of gaining possession of any additional wine or oil which might have been in
the measure]." [The buyer's resignation gives the seller possession of what is left in the measure. By contrast, wine or oil in the
consecrated status of heave-offering belongs to the priest and
never reverts to Israelite ownership. Any small amount of it
which is collected in a vessel is deemed consecrated food and
must be turned over to a priest.]

The comparison between the rules of M. B.B. 5:8 and M. Ter.
11:8H leads to an understanding of each, D. A buyer leaves for
the seller any wine or oil which does not initially drip from the
measure. By contrast, heave-offering intrinsically belongs to the
priest. Even after the measure has been emptied in the usual
manner, any wine or oil in the status of heave-offering which is
collected must go to that individual.

[II.A]   [M. Ter. 11:8G states that once three last drops have drained
from a vessel which had contained wine or oil in the status of
heave-offering, the householder may immediately use the vessel
for unconsecrated wine or oil. He need not wipe out any wine or
oil in the status of heave-offering which still coats the sides of the
vessel.] Now does this same [rule] apply in the case of [other]
consecrated [wine or oil]?

[B]   R. Abbahu came [and said] in the name of R. Yohanan, "The
same [rule] applies even in the case of [other] consecrated [wine
or oil]."

[C]   [Qualifying B,] said R. Hoshaya, "They did not teach [that B is
the case] other than as regards such holy things as may be rendered permitted [for consumption by nonpriests through some
action of the householder. In such cases the householder simply
redeems any sanctified wine or oil which remains in the vessel

and then goes ahead and puts unconsecrated wine or oil in the container.]

[D] "But in the case of holy things that [the householder] has no way of rendering permitted [i.e., which are not subject to redemption], any small quantity [of consecrated wine or oil which remains after three last drops have drained] he must return [to the proper recipient, the priest]."

[E] [Referring to a specific example of C + D,] R. Bun bar Hiyya asked, "As for the *log* of oil brought by the leper [as part of the offering which marks his purification]—need he include [as part of the offering any oil which remains in the vessel after three last drops have dripped out], or need he not include [this remaining oil as part of the offering]?

[F] "If you state that he must include it, and he does not include it, he transgresses through having offered less [oil than the required *log*].

[G] "If you state that he need not include it, but he includes it anyway, he transgresses through offering more [than the required *log* of oil]."

[H] [Hinena states that the answer to E–G is obvious.] R. Hinena did not answer [the question posed by Bun bar Hiyya at all]. Rather [Hinena recalled], "Said R. Hoshaya [above, C], 'They did not teach [that consecrated oil or wine which collects in the container after three final drops had dripped out need not be treated as holy] except in the case of such holy things as may be rendered permitted [for consumption by nonpriests through some action of the householder]. But in the case of holy things which [the householder] has no way of rendering permitted [i.e., which are not subject to redemption], any small quantity [of consecrated wine or oil which remains after three last drops have drained] must be returned [to the proper recipient, the priest or altar].'

[I] "Now the *log* of oil brought by the leper—is it not a sort of holy thing which there is (read: no)[10] way of rendering permitted?

[J] "And you say [that any small quantity of such holy things] must be included [in the offering].

[K] "This means that [the leper] must go back and include [as part of his offering any oil which remains in the measure after three last drops have dripped out].

[L]   "And if he does not include [this additional oil,] he transgresses through having offered less [than the required *log*]."

The rule of M. Ter. 11:8G is generalized to apply to types of consecrated wine or oil other than heave-offering, A–B + C–D. This introduces E–G's question, answered at H–L.

[**III.A**]   [T. Ter. 8:16D states that one should not cook unconsecrated produce in a pot which previously had been used for food in the status of heave-offering. The following qualifies that rule.] It is taught: R. Hilaphta b. Saul [says], "[As for] a pot in which one had cooked food in the status of heave-offering—he may clean it three times in hot water, and this is sufficient." [Then he may go ahead and prepare unconsecrated produce in it.]

[B]   [Carrying forward A] said R. Ba, "But they do not derive the rule for [a pot in which] carrion [had been cooked] from this [rule for heave-offering]." [A pot in which carrion has been cooked may not be cleaned at all. It remains impure and never may be used for properly slaughtered meat.]

[C]   [Rejecting B,] R. Yose presented a problem in the presence of R. Ba. [Yose said, "A nonpriest who eats] heave-offering is subject to execution. But [one who eats] carrion has [simply transgressed] a negative commandment, [a relatively minor offense compared to that of eating heave-offering.

[D]   "Yet you say this, [that the laxity which applies in the case of heave-offering does not apply as well in the case of carrion]!" [Since the rules for carrion are generally less stringent, that makes no sense.]

[E]   [Explaining, Ba] said to him [i.e., to Yose], "[My view] follows the understanding of one who claims that [after the destruction of the Temple (PM) Israelites] accepted responsibility to separate heave-offering and tithes of their own accord." [This view holds that, according to the Torah, agricultural offerings need not be separated in the present era. Since it is simply the Israelites who determined to separate them anyway, certain leniencies apply. One such leniency is described at A. But the same lenient rule does not apply to carrion, the rules for which, all agree, are scriptural.]

[F]   [The claim of A is questioned.] R. Yosti bar Shonam asked in the presence of R. Mana, "We have learned: *[After three last drops of consecrated wine or oil have dripped from a vessel,] if one placed that vessel on its side and [more oil or wine] drained [from it]—lo, this [wine or oil] is in the status of heave-offering* [M. Ter. 11:8H].

[G]   "[M. Ter.'s theory is that the vessel absorbs some of the oil or wine in the status of heave-offering and later emits it.] Yet you state this, [above at A, that if one washes a pot in which produce in the status of heave-offering was cooked, all of the heave-offering is removed from that vessel such that unconsecrated food then may be cooked in it]!?" [This is contrary to the notion of M. Ter. 11:8H, that the container actually absorbs some consecrated food and that the food might later become mixed with unconsecrated food placed in the same vessel.]

[H]   [Explaining why the case described above at A is different, Mana] said to him, "In this case, [i.e., in which the householder washes the pot with [hot water], because of the heat [the pot] is thoroughly cleaned and [all of the food in the status of heave-offering] exudes [from it]." [This is different from the case of M. Ter. 11:8H, where the vessel is not cleaned out but simply allowed to drain.]

A introduces two distinct discussions, B–E and F–H. The unit belongs here because F–H depends upon M. Ter. 11:8H.

[IV.A]   [As regards] the lees of wine in the status of heave-offering—the first and second times [the priest strains water through them, the resultant liquid] is forbidden [to nonpriests]. But the third time, it is permitted [T. Ter. 10:12A–C].

[B]   In what case does this apply?

[C]   It applies in a case in which he[11] strained (*ntn*) water through them.

[D]   But if he did not strain water through them [but, rather, unconsecrated wine], even the third time [that he does this, the resultant liquid] is forbidden.

[E]   [As regards] lees of wine in the status of second tithe—the first time [that someone strains water through them, the resultant liquid is] forbidden [i.e., has the status of second tithe]. But the second time, [the resultant liquid] is permitted [i.e., unconsecrated].

[F]   R. Meir says, "The second time, [the liquid is forbidden] if [the wine lees] imparted to it flavor" [T. Ter. 10:12E–H].

[G]   R. Yohanan in the name of R. Simeon b. Yusdaq [said], "[As for lees from wine which is] dedicated [to the Temple]—[whether or not a liquid created by straining water through the lees is consecrated is determined] by a count [of the number of times water is strained through them]." [T. Ter. 10:12I–K: The first three times liquid is strained through lees dedicated to the Temple, the resultant liquid is consecrated. The fourth time is unconsecrated.]

[H]   [As regards] the chamber pot of a *zab*—the [water of the] first and second [washings of the pot] convey uncleanness. But the [water of the] third [rinsing] is clean (so T. Y.: first rinsing is unclean, second is clean).

[I]   Under what circumstances?

[J]   When one[12] put water in it [to rinse it].

[K]   But if one did not put water into it, [but rinsed it with clean urine]—even up to the tenth [rinsing], it conveys uncleanness [T. Ter. 10:13N–U].

The Tosefta's rules explore an ambiguity arising from the Mishnah's law that when consecrated produce no longer serves its purpose as a food, it loses its consecrated status. The problem is how to determine the point at which this occurs. The point, A, E + F, and G, is that we take into account the number of times people ordinarily use a given batch of lees to prepare a drink. For that same number of times, lees which have a consecrated status impart that status to the water which they flavor. The point at H is no different. B–D and I–K offer minor qualifications. Under the condition suggested by D, the consecrated lees never will cease to impart the flavor of wine to that with which they are mixed. So long as they impart flavor, they also impart their original consecrated status. The rule of K is the same. So long as the bedpan has the taint of urine, liquid rinsed in it is deemed unclean, as was the urine from a *zab* which the pan originally contained.

[V.A]   [According to M. Ter. 11:8I–J a householder who has ¹⁄₆₄ *log* of heave-offering of the tithe separated from produce about which there is a doubt whether or not it previously was tithed must give the offering to a priest. The following answers the question of what the householder should do with less than ¹⁄₆₄ *log*.] R. Yudan the son of the sister of R. Yose bar Hanina in the name of R. Yose bar Hanina [said], "[If he has] less than this [quantity], he places it in his lamp [and burns it]."

[B]   [A applies in the case of heave-offering of the tithe separated from a liquid, that is, wine or oil. We now are told the rule for solid foods.] R. Yannai in the name of R. Yudan [says], "(Read with GRA:) In the case of a [solid] food, [the householder must give the priest so much as] an egg's bulk [or more]."

[C]   [Further refinements of M. Ter. 11:8I–J follow.] (Read with GRA:) This rule [that small amounts of doubtful heave-offering of the tithe need not be given to a priest] applies in the case of unclean produce. But in the case of clean produce, no matter how small an amount [of heave-offering of the tithe the householder has collected], he must give it [to the priest. See T. Ter. 10:6E–H.]

[D]   This rule applies to heave-offering of the tithe separated from produce about which there is a doubt whether or not it previously was tithed. But in the case of produce which certainly was subject to the separation of heave-offering of the tithe, whether the offering is unclean or clean, of large quantity or small, one must give it [to the priest. See T. Ter. 10:6B–D.]

The rule of M. Ter. 11:8I–J applies only to unclean heave-offering of the tithe (C), separated from produce about which there is a doubt whether or not it was subject to the separation of that offering (D). If there is no doubt, or if the offering is clean, such that it may be eaten by the priest, the householder must turn over to that individual even very small quantities. In line with the larger theory of M. Ter. 11:6–8, the reason is that, if edible, even these small quantities that the householder collects are deemed foods. As indicated in brackets at C and D, the Yerushalmi derives this material from the Tosefta, which it paraphrases. A and B are clear as stated.

11:6 [P: 11:5a; M. Ter. 11:9]

[A]   *[As regards] vetches in the status of heave-offering—*

[B]   *[priests] may feed them to [their] cattle, animals, or fowl.*

[C]   *An Israelite who hired a cow from a priest may feed it vetches in the status of heave-offering.*

[D]   *But a priest who hired a cow from an Israelite,*

[E]   *even though he is responsible for feeding it,*

[F]   *may not feed it vetches in the status of heave-offering.*

[G]   *An Israelite who tended the cow of a priest in return for a share in the value of the animal may not feed it vetches in the status of heave-offering.*

[H]   *But a priest who tended the cow of an Israelite in return for a share in its value may feed it vetches in the status of heave-offering.*

Since vetches may be eaten by humans, they are subject to the separation of heave-offering. More commonly, however, they are used for fodder. In light of this customary usage, even if they are in the status of heave-offering they may be fed to the priest's animals, A–B. The only requirement is that the animal actually be the priest's property, C versus D–F. G–H introduces a case of joint ownership. In such a case the Israelite may not feed heave-offering to a cow owned by a priest. The Israelite himself ultimately will benefit, in the form of his share of the increased value of the animal. But the priest may feed heave-offering to an animal owned by an Israelite, under the theory that the priest receives as his share the benefit of that food. The Yerushalmi's two units look for the source of these rules in Scripture. Unit I covers M. Ter. 11:9G. Unit II refers to M. Ter. 11:9H.

[I.A]   What is the basis in Scripture for [the rule that] a cow belonging to a priest which is tended by an Israelite in return for a share in the value of the cow may not be fed [food] in the status of heave-offering [M. Ter. 11:9G]?

[B]   Scripture says, "If a priest buys a soul [i.e., slave] as his property for money, [the slave may eat of holy things; and those who are born in his house may eat of his food"; Lev. 22:11].

[C]   (Supply from *Sifra Emor, Parshata* 5:6:)[13] These individuals [i.e., slaves or members of the priestly household] may eat [the priest's consecrated] food, but cattle may not eat [his holy food].

[D]   [On the basis of Lev. 22:11] is it possible that [the priest] may not even give [his cattle] vetches [in the status of heave-offering]?

[E]   Scripture states, "A soul." [This means that while the priest may not give his cattle consecrated food which normally would be eaten by humans, he may give it consecrated vetches, which are not eaten by people (PM).]

[F]   [We attack D's question anew.] There are those who teach: Is it possible that [cattle belonging to a priest] may not be fed vetches and fenugreek [in the status of heave-offering]?

[G]   R. Hezeqiah, R. Jeremiah, [and] R. Hiyya in the name of R. Yohanan [say], "[While cattle belonging to a priest may eat consecrated vetches], there is no reference here to fenugreek [in the status of heave-offering. The priest's cattle may not eat such] fenugreek, [since it is subject to the separation of heave-offering] according to the Torah." [Unlike vetches, fenugreek normally is used for humans and not cattle. Therefore, if it is in the status of heave-offering it may not be fed to the priest's animals. Vetches normally are not eaten by people. Therefore even if they have the status of heave-offering, they may be fed to the priest's cattle.]

The rule of M. Ter. 11:9G is explained from Scripture, A–C + D–E. F–G likewise invokes Scripture, without citing a specific verse.

[II.A]   [According to M. Ter. 11:9H, a priest who tends the cow of an Israelite in return for a share in its value may feed it vetches in the status of heave-offering.] But is this [i.e., the contrary] not taught: What is the basis in Scripture [for the rule] that a priest who bought a slave [in partnership with an Israelite, such that] the Israelite owns even so little as one share in a thousand, may not give [the slave] produce in the status of heave-offering to eat?

[B]   [We know this because] Scripture states, "If a priest buys [a slave as his property for money, the slave may eat of holy things"; Lev. 22:11. Scripture implies that a slave who is not solely the property of the priest may not eat consecrated food. This is contrary to the rule of M. Ter. 11:9H, which states that a priest may feed vetches in the status of heave-offering to a cow of which he is not the sole owner.]

[C]   [Bar Qappara claims that at M. Ter. 11:9H the rule is reported incorrectly.] Bar Qappara taught, "The rule for both cases [i.e., that of the slave and that of the cow] is the same. Neither may be fed produce in the status of heave-offering."

M. Ter. 11:9H disagrees with Scripture, A–B. Bar Qappara claims that Scripture's rule is correct. On that basis he emends the Mishnah, C.

11:7 [P: 11:5b; M. Ter. 11:10]

[A]   *They kindle [unclean] oil [in the status of heave-offering] which is fit for burning in (1) synagogues, (2) houses of study, (3) dark alleyways and (4) for sick people,*

[B]   *in the presence of a priest.*

[C]   *[As regards] the daughter of an Israelite who married a priest but is accustomed to visit her father—*

[D]   *her father may kindle [oil in the status of heave-offering] in her presence.*

[E]   *"They kindle [oil in the status of heave-offering] in a house in which there is a wedding feast, but not in a house of mourning"—the words of R. Judah.*

[F]   *R. Yose says, "[They do so] in a house of mourning, but not at a wedding feast."*

[G]   *R. Meir prohibits in either case.*

[H]   *R. Simeon permits in either case.*

Unclean oil in the status of heave-offering may not be eaten by the priest. In line with M. Ter. 11:2, 3, and 9, it may be put to one of oil's other customary purposes, kindling in lamps. This may be done, A–B and C–D, so long as a priest will benefit from the light, even if nonpriests will enjoy it as well. The point of E–H is difficult to ascertain, since there is no apparent reason that the law for a house of mourning should differ from that of a wedding feast.

Units **I–II** treat the larger theory of A–B, asking to which of A's items the stringency of B applies, and whether or not a non-priest may burn oil in the status of heave-offering which he separated from his own produce, but never gave to a priest. We turn next to cases of ambiguity concerning the nonpriest's right to benefit from a lamp kindled with consecrated oil. Need the priest actually be present, or is it sufficient that he benefits indirectly from the Israelite's use of the heave-offering oil. This topic takes up units **III–IV**, which cite the Tosefta, and **V–VIII**, which make use of vignettes concerning specific rabbinic authorities. Unit **IX** gives the Yerushalmi's interpretation of the dispute at M. Ter. 11:10E–H. We conclude, unit **X**, with a further ambiguous case, the use of consecrated oil to light the lamps of Hanukah.

[I.A]   *They kindle [unclean] oil [in the status of heave-offering] which is fit for burning in (1) synagogues, (2) houses of study, [(3) dark alleyways, and (4) for sick people, in the presence of a priest; M. Ter. 11:10A–B].*

[B]   Simeon bar Ba in the name of R. Yohanan [said], "This is what Mishnah [Ter. 11:10A–B] means: [They kindle unclean oil in the status of heave-offering which is fit for burning] *for sick people, in the presence of a priest.*

[C]¹⁴   "Yet the Mishnah's first [three references—to burning oil in the status of heave-offering in synagogues, houses of study, and alleyways—mean that one may kindle heave-offering oil in those places] even if a priest is not present."

[D]   [B's idea is developed.] R. Hiyya taught, "[The obligation] to visit the sick has no set measure." [That is, one is obligated to do so continually, and doing so just once does not fulfill the responsibility.]

[E]   Said R. Hiyya bar Adda, "Mishnah [Ter. 11:10A] said this [explicitly]: [They kindle unclean oil in the status of heave-offering which is fit for burning] *for sick people, in the presence of a priest.*" [The implication is that the priest will come to visit several times. Each time that he comes, unclean oil in the status of heave-offering may be kindled (PM).]

The Yerushalmi's theory, B versus C, is that oil in the status of heave-offering may be kindled wherever it will serve the general public good, even if does not directly benefit a priest. D + E is tacked on because of its relevance to B.

[II.A]   [M. Ter. 11 : 10 states that Israelites may kindle unclean oil in the status of heave-offering in the presence of a priest. The question is under what circumstances this applies.] R. Jeremiah asked in the presence of R. Zeira, "Up to this point [we have assumed that M.'s rule applies] in the case of heave-offering [which the Israelite] inherited from the estate of the father of his mother, a priest,

[B]   "and that it applies as well in the case of heave-offering [that the Israelite himself separated] from his own crops [and never gave to a priest. Is this understanding correct?]"

[C]   [Zeira] said to him, "Who would claim that [the rule of M. Ter. 11 : 10A–B] applies in the case of heave-offering [that an Israelite separated] from his own crops [and never gave to a priest]?" [This is not the case, since the Israelite does not own that heave-offering. Rather, an Israelite may kindle in the presence of a priest only such oil in the status of heave-offering as he had inherited from his grandfather, a priest. This heave-offering belongs to the nonpriest, for use in the manner described by M. Ter. 11 : 10.]

[D]   R. Jonah [48b] and R. Yose [disputed this issue].

[E]   R. Jonah followed the view of R. Jeremiah, [B, who is uncertain whether or not an Israelite may kindle oil in the status of heave-offering that came from his own crops and never was given to a priest].

[F]   And R. Yose followed the view of R. Zeira, [C, who is certain that the Israelite may not kindle oil in the status of heave-offering which derived from his own crops and never was given to a priest].

[G]   [The issue now is whether or not a priest must be given posses-

sion even of such heave-offering as is unclean, in this case unclean oil which is fit for burning. Since this is the issue], the one
[i.e., Jonah and Jeremiah, E] who states [he is uncertain whether
or not the Israelite may kindle unclean oil in the status of] heave-
offering which derived from his own crops [and never was given
to a priest] might object to one who states that [the Israelite may
kindle oil in the status of] heave-offering which he inherited
from the father of his mother, a priest, [by asking why in such a
case] it is not necessary for [a priest] to take possession [of the
heave-offering which the Israelite inherited]. [Only the value of
that heave-offering belongs to the Israelite. He must sell the actual produce to a priest. The situation therefore is no different
from that of a householder who separates heave-offering from his
own crop and does not give it to a priest. In light of this it does
not appear logical to claim that the Israelite who inherits unclean
oil in the status of heave-offering may use it for kindling, but
that one who separated the unclean oil from his own produce
may not.]

[H]   [The one who is certain that the householder may not kindle
      unclean oil in the status of heave-offering that never was given to
      a priest] said to him [i.e., the authority behind G], "[In the case
      of the inherited heave-offering, the Israelite] acquires title [to the
      heave-offering] through someone else [i.e., the priestly grand-
      father who already had taken possession of the heave-offering]."
      [The Israelite therefore has the right of ownership over this
      heave-offering and may kindle it in a lamp. This is not the case
      for heave-offering that a householder separated but never gave
      to a priest. The nonpriest has no right to that heave-offering
      and therefore may not burn it in a lamp. Yose and Zeira, F, are
      correct.]

[I]   [The following examples, explained at N, illustrate the point of
      H. They show that if the nonpriest has acquired the right to
      heave-offering through a priest, the nonpriest may make use of
      that heave-offering oil. I follow T.'s version of the material, which
      is abbreviated in Y.][15] It is taught: **[As regards] an Israelite who
      was sitting in the shop of a priest—lo, this [priest] may fill for
      him a lamp with oil [in the status of heave-offering] that is fit
      for burning, [and the Israelite] may go up to the attic, or down
      to the cellar, in order to do what is needful to the priest, but
      not what is needful to the Israelite.**

[J] If [the Israelite] was a partner in the ownership of the store, this is permitted [i.e., the Israelite may use the heave-offering oil for his own needs, since this ultimately benefits the priest].

[K] And so [in the case of] a priest who was dining in the home of an Israelite—lo, this [priest] may kindle for him a lamp [filled] with oil [in the status of heave-offering] which is fit for burning.

[L] Even though the priest [later] got up and left, they do not obligate him to put out the lamp, until it goes out by itself [T. Ter. 10:9D–J].

[M] [The authorities of G object:] Has [the Israelite] acquired [the unclean oil in the status of heave-offering, such that he may make use of it to his own benefit]?

[N] [The authority of H explains that the case is parallel to that of heave-offering which a nonpriest inherits.] He said to them, "[Just as above at H, this is a case] in which [the Israelite] acquires title [to the heave-offering] through someone else [i.e., the priest who owns it and who filled the lamp for the Israelite]." [Under such circumstances, comparable to those of a nonpriest's inheriting heave-offering, that nonpriest may make use of the priestly gift in accord with the rules of M. Ter. 11:10. But if the nonpriest simply separated the offering from his produce and never gave it to a priest, that nonpriest has no control over the priestly gift. As Yose and Zeira say, F, the householder does not have the prerogative to make use of such heave-offering.]

M. Ter. 11:10 states that under certain circumstances a non-priest may kindle oil in the status of heave-offering. How does he come to possess the heave-offering with which he fills the lamp? Either he has inherited it from his grandfather, a priest (A), or he has separated it from his own produce but has never given it to a priest (B). The issue, phrased at G, is whether or not the nonpriest may make use of such oil that he has not given to the priest. The conclusion of the debate, H–N, is that he may not. Such oil is not his rightful possession and therefore he may in no event make use of it. He may only kindle oil that he has inherited, and so owns, or that belongs to a priest who has given him permission to use it.

[**III.A**]   (Delete this line, which is an incorrect transcription of T. Ter.
10:9L. The stich appears correctly at B.) It is taught: The daughter of an Israelite who enters [the home of a priest may kindle
oil in the status of heave-offering] to do what is needful to the
priest, but not [to do what is needful] to the Israelite.

[**B**]   It is taught: **The daughter of an Israelite who entered [to visit]**
(Y.: to kindle) **the daughter of a priest [and wishes to leave]—
[the priest's daughter] dips a wick in oil [in the status of heave-
offering] which is fit for burning and kindles it [for her;** T. Ter.
10:9L–M, with slight variations].

[**C**]   [The question is why the Israelite woman is allowed to benefit
from the consecrated oil. The priest himself neither is present
nor has given permission.] R. Huna in the name of the house of
R. Yannai [said], "This [rule] was [legislated] at a time at which
packs of wolves were [roaming the streets]. [Because of the danger of going out at night without a light, a court ordained that
even consecrated oil could be used in the lamp of the Israelite
woman, to scare off the wolves.]

[**D**]   "[Once this rule had been established, as a temporary measure,]
no court arose [with sufficient power] to rescind it.

[**E**]   [The rest of Huna's statement makes sense only in the context of
Y. Sheb. 4:2, where it is primary.] "Just as you state there, [i.e.,
here at B–C, that a lenient ruling remained in effect because] no
court arose which could nullify it, so you must state here [re-
garding the lenient rule referred to at Y. Sheb. 4:2, that it was
legislated as a temporary measure but remained in effect be-
cause] no court arose [which had the power] to nullify it."

T. Ter. 10:9L–M, cited at B, seems to contradict the principle
of M. Ter. 11:10, that oil in the status of heave-offering which is
kindled in a lamp must benefit a priest. C–D explains why the
Tosefta's particular circumstance was excepted from that rule. E
makes sense only in the context of Y. Sheb. 4:2.

[**IV.A**]   **[As regards] a priest's cattle which were being fed [in a barn]
by an Israelite, and so the garments of a priest which were
being woven by an Israelite—**

[B]   [the Israelite] may kindle on their account oil [in the status of heave-offering] which is fit for burning and need not scruple [T. Ter. 10:9A–C, with minor variations].

[C][16]   A priest who came to do business (T.: to eat) with an Israelite, and for this reason kindles oil [in the status of heave-offering] which was fit for burning—even though [the priest] gets up and leaves, they do not require him to put out the lamp, until it goes out by itself [T. Ter. 10:9H–J, with slight variations].

The two rules, A–B and C, repeat the point made by M. Ter. 11:10. As long as the oil in the status of heave-offering is used to the benefit of the priest, it is irrelevant that nonpriests likewise enjoy the light. These rules of the Tosefta add that this principle applies even if the priest benefits in a most tangential way, e.g., in cases in which he is not present (A–B), or if he should get up to go once he has made some use of the lamp (C).

[V.A]   R. Hanania bar Akbari was working with R. Hiyya of Sepphoris [who was a priest].

[B]   When [Hanania] was ready to leave him, [Hiyya] filled him a lamp with oil [in the status of heave-offering] which was fit for burning.

[C]   [Why was he permitted to do this?] Have we not said [that an Israelite may use a lamp filled with consecrated oil] to do what is needful to the priest, but not to do what is needful to the Israelite [T. Ter. 10:9F]?

[D]   [Answering C's question,] they said, "If [Hiyya] had not done this, [Hanania] would not have come [to help him at all]." [Therefore, filling Hanania's lamp was needful to Hiyya.]

[E]   [Developing D,] they reasoned, "When [Hanania] arrived at his own house, he would extinguish [the lamp filled with oil in the status of heave-offering, for at this point it no longer served Hiyya's purposes]."

[F]   [Explaining that this is not the case,] said R. Hinena, "Because [Hanania left the lamp burning,] he was wakeful and therefore arose early in the morning [in order to return to Hiyya to continue working]." [Thus even in Hanania's own house, the lamp filled with heave-offering oil benefited Hiyya the priest.]

We continue the previous unit's discussion of cases in which a priest benefits from a nonpriest's use of oil in the status of heave-offering. So long as the priest derives some benefit, that use is permitted.

[VI.A]   One evening [a nonpriest] asked R. Imi, "If I dip one wick in unconsecrated [oil, may I kindle many other lamps with oil in the status of heave-offering and claim that I only benefit from the one unconsecrated light]?"

[B]   [Imi] said to him, "[No, for it is as though the unconsecrated lamp] is nullified in the presence of [all of the] wicks [lit with oil in the status of heave-offering]."

[C]   In accordance with [the statement of Imi, B,] R. Judah b. Pazzai instructed the members [17] of the household of Nehemia.

In this case the nonpriest would benefit from the consecrated oil (B), but a priest would not. Such use of the oil is prohibited.

[VII.A]   [After visiting with a priest,] R. Imi [a nonpriest] dipped a wick [in oil in the status of heave-offering to use it to light his way home].

[B]   [Unlike Imi,] R. Ila did not dip a wick [in oil in the status of heave-offering to use on the walk home].

[C]   [Does this imply that] R. Ila does not have the same understanding as R. Imi [i.e., that under the circumstances described at A a nonpriest may make use of a lamp filled with oil in the status of heave-offering which is fit for burning]?

[D]   [No. Ila agrees with that rule, stated explicitly at T. Ter. 10:9K. Rather] R. Ila reasoned [that he should not take the consecrated oil] because this might constitute theft [of the consecrated produce from the priest. He feared this] because he had a certain servant who [was not careful with lamps and] would make improper use of the consecrated [oil].

The use of the oil at A is permitted, for it means that the priest will not have to provide his guest with unconsecrated oil that the priest would have to purchase. D explains why Ila did not take advantage of the opportunity to use the priest's consecrated oil.

[VIII.A]   Gamaliel Zuga asked R. Yosa, "What is the rule [whether or not a nonpriest may] add unconsecrated oil [to a lamp which a priest had filled for him with oil in the status of heave-offering]?" [By doing this the nonpriest would prolong his use of the consecrated oil.]

[B]   [Yosa] said to him, "R. Hoshaya did not teach [the answer to this question. He said only that] they do not obligate him [i.e., the priest who gave the individual the original consecrated oil] to find [the nonpriest, so as to put out the lamp]."

[C]   [Indicating that it is permitted to add unconsecrated oil to consecrated oil in a lamp,] said R. Abbahu, "Jonathan b. Akhmai taught me [the following: As regards] the daughter of a priest who had in her hand a lamp filled with oil [in the status of heave-offering] which was fit for burning, on the eve of Sabbath at the time of sunset—lo, this one may add any [small] amount of unconsecrated oil to the lamp and may kindle it [for the Sabbath"; T. Ter. 10:9M]. [By adding the unconsecrated oil the woman shows that she does not intend to transgress the law by burning sanctified oil on the Sabbath. In the same way the nonpriest, A, may indicate that he does not mean to misuse consecrated oil.]

[D]   R. Zeira said to him, "What sort of person [is Jonathan b. Akhmai, whom you cite]?"

[E]   [Abbahu] said to him, "He was an important person and well versed in our Mishnah."

[F]   R. Hiyya of Kephar Tehumin described him [i.e., Jonathan b. Akhmai] in the presence of Rav (PM: Rabbi), and he designated him to be a sage.

The point, C, is derived from T. Ter. 10:9M.

[**IX**.A]   *"They kindle [unclean oil in the status of heave-offering] in a house in which there is a wedding feast, but not in a house of mourning"—the words of R. Judah.*

[B]   *R. Yose says, "[They do so] in a house of mourning, but not at a wedding feast."*

[C]   *R. Meir prohibits in either case.*

[D]   *R. Simeon permits in either case* [M. Ter. 11:10E–H].

[E]   What is R. Judah's[18] reasoning, [above, A]?

[F]   [Y. claims that the issue is the likelihood that the nonpriests will dirty themselves with the consecrated oil, e.g., by adjusting or moving the lamp. This would constitute an improper waste of the heave-offering.] In a house in which there is a wedding feast, since the people are cleanly dressed, they will not busy themselves [adjusting or moving] it [i.e., the lamp]. [Since the people will do their best not to dirty themselves with the oil, Judah allows the kindling of heave-offering at a wedding feast.]

[G]   [But] in a house of mourning, since people wear dirty clothing, they might busy themselves [adjusting or moving the lamp]. [Since the mourners are likely to spill and thereby waste some of the oil, Judah does not allow the use of oil in the status of heave-offering in a house of mourning.]

[H]   What is the reasoning of R. Yose,[19] [above, B]?

[I]   In a house of mourning, since the people are low-spirited, they will not busy themselves with it [i.e., the lamp]. [Therefore Yose allows oil in the status of heave-offering to be kindled in a lamp in a house of mourning.]

[J][20]   [But] in a house in which there is a wedding feast, since the people are overly active, they are likely to play with [the lamp]. [Therefore Yose does not allow oil in the status of heave-offering to be kindled in a lamp at a wedding feast.]

[K][21]   What is the reasoning of R. Meir, [above, C]?

[L]   In a house of mourning, since people wear dirty clothing, they might busy themselves [adjusting or moving the lamp]. [Since the mourners therefore are likely to spill and waste some of the oil, Meir does not allow the use of consecrated oil in a house of mourning. This is just like Judah, G.]

[M]   In a house in which there is a wedding feast, since the people are
      overly active, they are likely to play with [the lamp]. [Just as at
      L they therefore might spill and waste some of the oil. Meir thus
      does not allow a lamp filled with consecrated oil to be kindled at
      a wedding feast (= Yose, J).]

[N]   What is the reasoning of R. Simeon, [above, D]?

[O]   In a house of mourning, since the people are low-spirited, they
      will not busy themselves with [the lamp]. [For this reason Simeon
      allows consecrated oil to be kindled in the house of mourning,
      just like Yose, I.]

[P][22] [And] in a house in which there is a wedding feast, since the
      people are cleanly dressed, they will not busy themselves [adjust-
      ing or moving] it [i.e., the lamp]. [Since the people will not dirty
      themselves with the oil, Simeon allows the use of consecrated oil
      at a wedding feast as well (= Judah, F).]

      The Yerushalmi's interpretation is plausible. Yet, since it has no
      grounding in the actual language or context of the Mishnah's
      dispute, it cannot be shown to represent the sense intended by
      M. Ter. 11:10E–H's forumlator.

[X.A] [The question is which of M. Ter. 11:10's four authorities the
      law follows.] Those of the house of R. Yannai say, "The law ac-
      cords with the view of R. Simeon [M. Ter. 11:10H, that unclean
      oil in the status of heave-offering may be kindled both at a wed-
      ding feast and in a house of mourning]."

[B]   R. Jacob bar Aha in the name of R. Yoshaya [likewise states],
      "The law accords with the view of R. Simeon."

[C]   R. Yose of Sidon (so Jastrow, s.v., ṣydwn) asked in the presence
      of R. Jeremiah, "[Why need we teach explicitly that the rule
      follows the view of Simeon.] For if [we had] not [heard it explic-
      itly], what would we have said? [In a dispute between] R. Meir
      and R. Simeon, does the law not accord with the position of R.
      Simeon?" [Certainly it does. Therefore there appears to be no
      reason to state this explicitly, A and B.]

[D]   [Answering this criticism of A + B, Jeremiah] said to him, "[Who
      the law follows must be stated explicitly since this issue was ar-

gued] previously [PM: by Yose and Judah. Only afterwards was
it disputed by Meir and Simeon.]

[E]   "And indeed R. Judah's [23] view incorporates aspects of both [the
view of Meir and Simeon], and R. Yose's view incorporates aspects of both [the view of Meir and Simeon].

[F]   "Now [if this is a dispute between] R. Judah and R. Yose, the
law accords with the view of R. Yose." [But the point, as A + B
indicates, is that M. Ter. 11:10E–H is not to be read as a dispute
between Yose and Judah, such that the law follows Yose's view.
Rather, it is a dispute between Meir and Simeon, such that the
rule follows the position of Simeon. To prevent the possible confusion, this had to be stated explicitly.]

The question, posed at A, is answered at B. C's criticism then is
rejected, D–F.

[XI.A]   What is the rule [whether or not an Israelite] may kindle [un-
clean] oil [in the status of heave-offering] which is fit for burning
[in the lamps used] on Hanukah? [On the one hand, the Israelite
is not permitted himself to benefit from the oil. Therefore we
might say that this is forbidden. On the other hand, the Hanukah lamps are lit as an obligation and not for the enjoyment of
the Israelite. We might therefore rule that he may use consecrated oil for this purpose.]

[B]   Those of the house of R. Yannai say, "They may kindle [unclean]
oil [in the status of heave-offering] which is fit for burning [in
the lamps used] on Hanukah."

[C]   Said R. Nissa, "I never knew my father, [since he died before I
was born. Yet] my mother used to say to me, 'Your father used to
say: Anyone who does not have unconsecrated oil [for use in the
Hanukah lamps] should kindle [unclean] oil [in the status of
heave-offering] which is fit for burning.'" [Since the oil is intended for the fulfillment of a commandment, and not for the
enjoyment of the Israelite, this is permitted.]

B answers A's question. C supports B's contention.

Notes

Introduction

1. The other offerings set aside by the Israelite are first tithe, for the Levite; second tithe, which the householder himself eats in Jerusalem; poor man's tithe, for the poor; and first fruits, waved before the altar in Jerusalem. If the Israelite makes dough, he further must separate dough offering which, like heave-offering, goes to a priest. The Levite, for his part, takes from his first tithe an offering for the priest. This is called heave-offering of the tithe. All of these offerings are mentioned frequently by Y. Ter. On the structure and content of the Mishnah's Order of Agriculture as a whole, see Avery-Peck, *Agriculture, passim,* and Neusner, *Mishnah,* pp. 79–86 and 126–32.

2. Further grounds for the Mishnah's identification and description of this priestly due is at Neh. 10:37a, which refers to offerings of "the first of our coarse grain, and our contributions (*trwmtynw*), the fruit of every tree, the wine and the oil." The issue of the biblical sources for the Mishnah's system of tithes, and heave-offering in particular, has been discussed by Sarason, *Demai,* pp. 6–8, and in that same author's article, "Tithing."

3. This concern for the process of sanctification has in the first place prompted Mishnah's framers to talk about heave-offering. This is clear from the fact that the Order of Agriculture devotes tractates only to those offerings that have a consecrated status. These are heave-offering, second tithe, dough offering, and first fruits. There is no tractate on first tithe, which is not holy. The inclusion of Tractate Peah, on unconsecrated poor taxes, is explained by the fact that the produce of which it speaks stands completely outside of the system of tithes. It is not subject to the separation of agricultural dues. This produce had to be defined if, in its other tractates, the Order of Agriculture was accurately to detail what produce is subject to and available for payment as the various dues (see, e.g., M. Ter. 1:5).

4. The rules that make these points are at M. Ter. 1:1–4:6. M. Ter. makes its point explicit by stating that deaf-mutes, imbeciles, and mi-

nors, who are deemed not to understand the implications of their actions, may not separate heave-offering. They do not have the requisite powers of intention.

5. This must be qualified. The Israelite's power to designate food to be holy applies only to produce which, because it was grown on God's land, is susceptible to sanctification. Note however that even produce grown on the land of Israel is not automatically subject to the separation of agricultural offerings. It becomes subject only in response to certain desires and intentions on the part of the Israelite himself. The centrality of the Israelite in the designation of heave-offering thus extends to the circumstances under which produce becomes subject to that offering in the first place. See Jaffee, pp. 4–5.

6. These rules are at M. Ter. 6:1–8:3. Note also the cases at M. Ter. 9:1–7, in which a nonpriest plants heave-offering as seed. If this is done intentionally, he must allow the seed to grow, producing a crop which, because it is consecrated, the nonpriest may not eat. If the seed was planted unintentionally, the Israelite may prevent it from growing by plowing it up. He is not allowed to make personal use of what is designated for the priest. But by the same token, he is not held culpable, and so punished through loss of a fully grown and ripened crop, for what he did unintentionally.

7. These cases are at M. Ter. 11:1–10.

8. The tractate's only attributions to authorities who lived before 70 C.E. are in three disputes assigned to the Houses of Hillel and Shammai. As I have argued (in Neusner, *Mishnah*, pp. 292–93), only one of these disputes appears to actually go back to the historical Houses. It therefore is clear that the vast majority of the work on Tractate Terumot was done after the destruction of the Temple and, later, after the Bar Kokhba revolt. The history of the laws in this tractate as well as in the rest of the Order of Agriculture is detailed in my *Agriculture*.

9. The numbering in the outline follows the enumeration of pericopae found in Y. Ter. and followed in the designation of Y.'s pericopae throughout this book.

10. On the way in which the Mishnah's own formulators used literary constructions such as disputes and strings of linquisitically parallel cases in order to highlight the points they wished to make, see Avery-Peck, pp. 23–24 and Neusner, *Purities*, vol. 21, pp. 165–96.

11. Y.'s materials are designated by the enumeration of pericopae found in the Leiden manuscript and *editio princeps* in addition to a roman numeral. The roman numeral indicates my division of Y.'s pericopae into their constituent units. This is explained in the following section of the introduction.

12. I have included under this heading, as well as in the following ones, units in which the Yerushalmi explains some pericope other than that which is under discussion in M. Ter. These normally are cases in

which the cited pericope contains a rule cognate to that of M. Ter. The Yerushalmi's explanation of it accordingly serves the same purpose as its explanations of materials from within M. Ter. itself.

13. Under this heading I include rules and statements which, while unknown in Tannaitic documents, are cited in the Yerushalmi in the name of Tannaitic authorities and/or are introduced with the formulaic term *tny.* I intend no judgment as to the true antiquity of these materials.

14. Although the rules are the same, the Tosefta is not cited and its language is not used. Therefore I have placed the unit in this category, instead of at **II**: 1.

15. Note that the principles that the Yerushalmi's authorities derive from several purportedly correlated rules are not normally those suggested by M. Ter. concerning the processes of the holy. See, e.g., Y. Ter. 7:1 ff., in which Y.'s masters determine which punishments, and how many of them, are applicable in cases of various offenses. While important to community leaders, this issue was not on the minds of those who formulated the Mishnaic material on the basis of which the Talmud draws its conclusions.

16. The majority of units which begin by suggesting that two rules or statements are contradictory ultimately prove that they are not. This normally is accomplished by showing that the situations referred to in the rules are not comparable. The net result of these exercises is to indicate the correct situations in which each of the cited rules or opinions is properly applied.

17. My exegesis of Y. Ter. depends primarily upon PM, with reference as well to GRA and the other commentators listed in the bibliography. I indicate the source of my explanations in brackets in the body of the translation or in the comments which follow each unit.

18. MSS. and editions do not divide Y.'s pericopae into their constituent elements. The delineation of these units thus is one central aspect of my interpretation of the Yerushalmi. In this I frequently disagree with PM, who often attempts to tie together several seemingly unrelated discussions. At points at which PM's reading is feasible, it is discussed in the notes or in my comments, where I also indicate my reason for choosing to read the materials as distinct units.

19. I have not distinguished between Y.'s use of Hebrew and Aramaic. To do so would have complicated the translation through the use of yet another type style. Yet the advantages of doing so are not clear, since linguistic or philological analysis ultimatey will depend upon the original text, not a translation. So far as I can determine, the distinction between Hebrew and Aramaic has no weight in the exegesis of the Yerushalmi's materials.

20. This has been shown by Jacob Neusner in his pioneering study of the history of the Mishnaic law. See his, "Redaction, Formulation and

Form: The Case of Mishnah," *Jewish Quarterly Review* 70 (1980): 1–22. These same methods inform my exegesis of M. Ter. in *The Priestly Gift in Mishnah* (see Avery-Peck in the bibligraphy).

21. Since Y. is so extremely abstruse, I fear that my greatest error has been in rendering the translation more intelligible than the text should allow. This is a particular problem in cases in which interpretation of a unit depends upon a conjectural textual emendation, often suggested by PM or GRA. I have clearly marked such textual corrections and have designated the explanations that depend upon them as provisional. Only when further work has been done on the character of Y.'s materials and the lower criticism of its text has been completed will it be possible to pass final judgment on the meaning of many of its materials.

22. In the case of extremely complicated material, or where there is more than one possible interpretation, I use the comments for exegetical issues as well as for the other purposes outlined here.

23. For complete bibliographical information on these MSS. and editions, see the bibliography. As the reader will soon see, R is highly corrupt and of little use in establishing the correct text of Y. Ter. Normally, it evidences the same text as is preserved in L. Points where it does not tend to be scribal errors.

24. On the following, see Neusner's foreword to the translation, found in vol. 34, *Horayot and Niddah*, p. vii.

25. Ibid.

Chapter One

1. R reads: And said R. Samuel b. Nahman, 'Derive . . .' There is no difference in meaning.

2. GRA supplies at this point: This excludes the deaf mute. No MS. or edition supports this emendation. It is precluded by the inclusion of the deaf-mute at E.

3. R reverses D and E, contrary to the order of the biblical verse being exposited. The purpose of the shift is to allow the individuals cited at D–F to occur in the same order as they do in M.

4. The attribution to Huna is written in the margin of L. It is found in V and R.

5. In translating "even," I render the correct reading of M. Git. 2:5A, found in standard printings of M. and preserved in R. In error L and V read: except.

6. The scribe of R has omitted the rest of this stich and thoroughly confused what follows, through U. It is likely that he copied out of order two lines of the text before him.

7. T is irrelevant to the point Yose is making regarding writs of divorce written by deaf-mutes, imbeciles, or minors. Moreover, it is repeated verbatim at V, where it is pertinent. It is possible that this stich

appears in L and V through scribal error. As for the reading of R, see n. 6, above.

8. R lacks this stich, possibly through haplography.

9. I follow R which, correctly, indicates the following to be a Tannaitic statement, but not a citation of Mishnah. On the interpretation of this passage, see Lieberman, *On the Yerushalmi*, p. 24.

10. PM interprets the unit by claiming that Yohanan, R, holds that even with supervision a deaf-mute, imbecile, or minor may not validly write a writ of divorce. This exegesis is not viable for in light of it, the continuation of the discussion, S–V, is not comprehensible. It moreover has Yohanan violate the clear meaning of M. Git. 2:5A.

11. This is in line with the point made by Samuel bar Nahman, Y. Ter. 1:1 I.E, regarding deaf-mutes and imbeciles. The independence of the two units, however, is indicated by the fact that they do not share the same operative language (Y. Ter. 1:1 I.E makes no reference to intention) and do not both refer to all three of M.'s set trio, the deaf-mute, imbecile, and minor. Only through the redactional juxtaposition of the two units is Samuel bar Nahman's statement made to introduce the basic supposition of Y. Ter. 1:1 II.

12. C is lacking from the text of L, as well as from R. It is found in V and in the margin of L. The lemma is not part of the Toseftan pericope cited at B and is irrelevant to the discussion which follows.

13. Y. Git. 7:1 has a slightly expanded version of this stich. The meaning is the same.

14. I translate J–K as it appears in P, V, and in the marginal correction of L. R makes the same point in slightly different language.

15. R has jumbled this lemma. I can make no sense of its reading.

16. R reads: Zeira. The scribe has reversed the first two letters of the correct attribution to Ezra.

17. The scribe of R has dropped the rest of P and all of Q, probably through homoeotelueton.

18. I read with V and the marginal gloss in L. Through haplography several words have dropped out of the body of L.

19. R reads: R. Benjamin in the name of R. Levi. It also lacks the second sentence of this stich, lost through haplography.

20. The second sentence here is added in the margin of L and is found in V and P.

21. This pericope appears verbatim at Y. Git. 7:1. Since the larger issue is whether or not a deaf-mute may give written instructions regarding the divorce of his wife, it clearly is primary in that context.

22. PM and R read: R. Hila (= Ila). Since Yose and Hila are of the same generation of Palestinian Amoraim (Strack, pp. 125–26), it is unlikely that Yose would transmit a tradition in Hila's name. The source of this error, at least in R, seems to be a misreading of the first word of Yose's reply, *l'*, as *hyl'*; that is, the name Hila. In R the rest of the stich likewise has been miscopied.

23. Cf., Y. Ter. 1:1 **VI**. For B., Kasowski, *Talmud*, lists thirteen examples of this form (s.v., *dl'*).

24. C through the middle of F is written in the margin of L. It is likely that it dropped out of the text through haplography.

25. R, V, and the marginal gloss in L read *gwndyqws qwrdyyqws*. These are alternate forms of the same word. I follow GRA, who emends to read simply *qwrdyyqws*.

26. GRA reads at G–H: What is the law regarding a delirious person? R. Yose said, 'I saw a case come before R. Jonah regarding . . .' None of the other extant sources corroborates this reading.

27. R lacks the final clause at I and reverses J–K. J must be deleted since it both contradicts K and is not found in T. Ter. 1:3, which is being cited here.

28. Here and in the following R and P read: Resh Laqish. There is no difference in meaning.

29. R lacks H.

30. R lacks this stich. L and P lack the citation of Num. 18:28, but have the exegesis. I translate V.

31. "R. Yose" through "agent of" is written in the margin of L and appears in V, R, and P.

32. R lacks all but the last two words of this lemma, probably a case of haplography.

33. L and V have the Levite state, "You have a *kor* of first tithe for me." The reading of P and R, which I translate, is more to the point.

34. V and L read: *'ylwpwsh*. R reads: *'lpsh*. P has: *'lypwsh*.

35. I translate *'ysh*, following V, L, and R. P has: *'ysy*.

36. This material has its primary location at Y. Ber. 2:4, for it analyzes the dispute between Yose and sages (M. Ber. 2:4) over whether or not the *Shema* must be heard by the person who recites it.

37. I translate L and V, which have the whole verse. P has the first clause and: etc. R simply records the first clause.

38. P is irrelevant to this point, placed here as the formal parallel of Q.

39. Through haplography the scribe of R has dropped the rest of this stich, up to the last word at C.

40. I translate *nhls* in accordance with R and standard editions of M. L, V, and P have *hls*.

41. My translation of B–E follows Y. Yeb. 13:3, the text preferred also by GRA and PM. All MSS. and editions of Y. Ter. reverse B–C and D–E. This is clearly wrong, since F continues E, and not C, as it is made to do in the version of the pericope found in Y. Ter. Y. Ter. also gives different authorities: Abba b. Kahana instead of Abin Kahana at B, and Judah instead of Yose, D. In rendering these names, I follow Y. Yeb.

42. This unit thus disagrees with Y. Ter. 1:1 concerning the primacy of proper intention for the valid separation of heave-offering.

43. R and P read: in the name of. The parallel at Y. Yeb. 13:3 has: R. Aha b. Hinena. I see no way to determine the correct reading.

44. Through scribal error, R lacks the rest of this stich.

45. In error, R reads: may not bring.

46. R lacks: may bring.

47. BB through the middle of CC is written in the margin of L. It dropped from the body of the text through haplography.

48. HH is written in the margin of L. It apparently was deleted from the body of the text through haplography.

49. Through dittography the scribe of R has miscopied this stich. Note that on pp. 217–18 of the facsimile edition of this MS. the obverse and reverse sides of the page have been switched. Page 218 belongs before p. 217.

50. Through dittography the scribe of R has written the beginning of the attribution twice.

51. R reads: Yose.

52. A is found in P, R, and L. It is lacking in V.

53. The word šyṭṭh is found in P, but is lacking in L, V, and R. There is no difference in meaning.

54. I translate P, which has the singular pronoun normally found in this formulaic clause in Mishnah. L and V have the plural.

55. I translate the correct reading, "blind person," preserved in R. V and P add after "blind person" the word "imbecile," a type of individual who does not belong in this context. The source of the error is L. In it the word "imbecile," written through scribal error, was corrected in between the lines to read "blind person." Both the wrong original reading and the correction entered the printed edition.

56. I follow V and P, as required by the sense of the passage. R has: less. L has been corrected in two different hands, once to read "more," and once to read: less.

57. Through a copyist's error, R lacks: of the tithe.

58. L, followed by V, and R read: weigh it according to a [fixed] weight. I cannot account for this clearly wrong, though well attested, reading. I translate the correct wording of this Toseftan pericope, recorded in P.

59. So L and V. R reads: Ila. It is the same person.

60. Through a printer's error, the last five lines of 40d are repeated at the top of 41a.

61. In treating this unit as distinct from the foregoing, I follow GRA. Cf., PM.

62. So L, V, GRA, and RiDBaZ. Cf., P and PM.

63. R lacks A, a copyist's error.

64. I follow the version of the pericope found in all MSS. of T., and required by the continuation here, at G–H. As PM notes, the version in Y. reverses the positions of Rabbi and Simeon b. Gamaliel, C–D.

65. Beginning here the rest of Y.'s first chapter is missing from R, possibly through scribal error. The text of R resumes with the first line of Y. chapter two.

Chapter Two

1. R has this stich but lacks all that follows up to Y. Ter. 2:1 **VII,** which again cites Yohanan's exegesis of Num. 18:27. It is possible that the scribe simply skipped all of the materials between the two similar passages, an extreme case of haplography.

2. J–N are written in the margin of L. It is likely that they dropped out of the text through haplography.

3. Alternatively: It is all the same whether [the tithe] is in Judah or Galilee.

4. "And," found in T. Ter. 3:19 and in P, is lacking in V and L.

5. So P. L and V read: Gerer.

6. L lacks "a portion of," found in V and P and required by the sense of the passage.

7. R reads: Hiyya b. Rabba. This is surely a scribal error, since in the same MS. the name appears correctly at E.

8. R lacks B–C.

9. I translate the correct reading of V, L, and R: *nwšk.* P reads: *nwšw.*

10. P, V, and L read "eggs," a scribal error originating in L.

11. So PM, as required by F.

12. R lacks the patronymic.

13. R reverses the words "clean" and "unclean," a scribal error.

14. The root ʿ*RM*, "to act subtly," or "to get around a law," occurs here. PM and QE both claim the meaning here is "to dunk in water," a meaning for the root ʿ*RM* that I find in no other passage in the Talmudic literature.

15. R reverses C and D. There is no difference in meaning.

16. Through scribal error R lacks: wetting down.

17. In R's rendition of this pericope, Samuel, A, simply states that whether the person tithes his produce on the Sabbath intentionally or unintentionally, he may not eat it. Yose, B–C, rejects this by citing M. Ter. 2:3. This version appears to have been created through scribal error.

18. The version in T., R and the text of L reads simply: he may not eat [the food]. The word "never" is added between the lines in L, from where it entered V and P. There is no difference in meaning.

19. R reads: the following.

20. Through homoeoteleuton L and R lack "the end of," required by the continuation of the line.

21. I is lacking in all sources for Y. Ter.

22. R lacks "three," a case of homoeoarchton.

23. R lacks: not.

24. "Dried figs" is written twice in L, an error repeated in V.

25. R inserts L here, and not where it belongs. This makes no sense.

26. It would make better sense to read here, as at U: swelled up. But there is no evidence for such a reading.

27. G–I is written in the margin of L.

Chapter Three

1. R lacks: and which one touched. This is a copyist's error.

2. L, V, and R have 'srw, "forbid," instead of 'mrw, which I translate following P, PM, and RiDBaZ. I cannot make sense of the other reading.

3. So P. L and V read: R. Ba bar Jacob bar Idi.

4. My translation follows P and R. Cf., L and V, which ask the same question in slightly different language.

5. Through homoeoarchton R lacks: all.

6. See Avery-Peck, pp. 137–38, 141–42.

7. R gives the full name: R. Simeon b. Laqish. There is no difference in meaning.

8. "Not" is found in P, V, and L but, correctly, is lacking in R.

9. At D and E, I follow the several MSS. and editions of Y., as is required by G. MSS. of T. reverse the opinions of Shammai and Hillel, D–E. See Lieberman, *TK*, I, p. 329.

10. R lacks "of olives," a copyist's error.

11. So L, V. R reads: just as. The point is the same.

12. The scribe of R has written the name "Resh Laqish" after the name "Zeira," as well as in its correct place in the attribution. This is an error.

13. M. Ter. 3:7 begins here.

14. This unit is lacking in R.

15. R lacks E–H, a case of haplography.

Chapter Four

1. I is missing from the text of L, but is added in the margin.

2. R lacks "one," a scribal error.

3. R lacks "hmrbh," probably a copyist's error.

4. Cf., PM, who reads this pericope as a continuation of Y. Ter. 4:1 II.

5. R lacks the end of this stich.

6. The scribe of R notes here that this material is primary in the first chapter of Y. Dem.

7. R lacks the rest of the stich, presumably a case of haplography.

8. R lacks this unit.

9. R lacks D–E, a case of haplography.

10. So GRA, T. Ter. 5:3, and as required by the sense of F. L, V, P, and R have: one-sixtieth.

11. P, V, and L read in error: one-fiftieth. The correct reading is noted by PM.

12. The name Isi occurs here as well as at the beginning of the following unit. This has led the scribe of R to drop the rest of this stich and to begin copying Y. Ter. 4:3 **VI,** which follows. Realizing the error, he went back, completed this unit, and then began Y. Ter. 4:3 **VI** afresh.

13. The original text of L reads "did not intend" and lacks "not" at B. This has been corrected between the lines. The corrected reading, which I translate, appears as well in V and R.

14. R concludes the line: that he [even] may separate as much again as he already has separated. This seems inferior to the reading of L, which does in fact explain Yohanan's position. Note also that the scribe of R has written both the end of C and the beginning of D twice.

15. In R this stich is garbled.

16. R lacks this unit.

17. R lacks A through the middle of D, a scribal error.

18. So V, L, and R. P lacks: R. Yohanan.

19. This lemma is written in the margin of L.

20. I translate V, L, and P. R (and the parallel at Y. Or. 2:1) lacks: not. Y. Or.'s reading is inferior, and makes it difficult to make sense of C–D + E.

21. So P, L, and R. V reads: Eliezer.

22. The language of B is ambiguous. Perhaps B rejects A through a *reductio ad absurdum:* It makes no sense to require two white figs to one black, for if you are going to do that, you might as well require three to one, [four to one, and so on]. Mana, D, then agrees with this rejection of A as logically untenable. It is not clear to me which of the possibilities is intended.

23. E–F thus should agree in principle with Kahana, Y. Ter. 4:8 **I.E–F.**

24. I follow RiDBaZ and GRA, who interpret the unit through reference to M. Hal. 1:4. PM claims that the material is primary to Y. Ter., but does not make clear sense of it.

25. L and R end the stich here. I translate V. The meaning is the same either way.

26. I can make sense of the passage only by following GRA's emendation of D and E, as indicated. All MSS. and editions have the opposite readings.

27. The attribution is added in the margin of L.

28. This whole stich is added in the margin of L.

29. See Lieberman, *TK,* I, pp. 369–70.

30. This line in T. is lacking in Y.

31. This line in T. is lacking in Y.

32. R lacks the second half of this lemma, as well as I and J.

33. See Lieberman, *TK*, I, pp. 369–70.

34. So P. V, L, and R lack this sentence. The point remains the same.

35. R adds: and R. Joshua b. Levi.

36. R lacks this line.

37. The scribe of R has garbled G–I.

Chapter Five

1. This word, necessary for the sense of the line, is lacking in L, V, and R. I have supplied it following P.

2. L, V: *m'lh t'lh*. P lacks the first word, R the second. The meaning is the same.

3. L and V reverse the order of B and C. I follow P and R, which juxtapose the view of Yohanan, D, with its explanation, E. But in all, the difference is minor.

4. R lacks: and place.

5. I translate L, V, and R. P's slightly different reading has the same meaning.

6. P reads "half *seah*," a printer's error.

7. P, V, and L read: one-sixth of every four *qabs*. R has: a sixth [of] four *qabs*. Without GRA's emendation, G–J appears to make no sense.

8. R has an open space, but lacks the word: six.

9. R lacks: not.

10. P lacks this first part of the attribution. It is found in L, V, and R.

11. At C–D I follow the wording of T. Y. makes the same point, in slightly different language.

12. R lacks "the House of Shammai," a case of haplography.

13. L and V read simply: to the House of Hillel. I follow P and R. The point is the same in either case, but emerges somewhat more clearly from P's wording.

14. According to GRA, Yohanan is giving his interpretation of the opinion of sages, M. Ter. 5:5D. The continuation of the unit, C + D–E, makes this unlikely.

15. The name Yohanan has been corrected between the lines of L to read Eleazar. That is the name found in P, V, and R.

16. So PM, V, and L. P and R read "different," that is, *'ḥr* instead of *'ḥd*.

17. R has an extra line: Said R. Mana in the presence of R. Yudan, "Now [how can] Hilpai say [that] in the opinion of R. Eliezer the unconsecrated produce below remains distinct?" The line does not alter the meaning of the pericope. Nor do the additional authorities cited in R affect dating of the passage. All are contemporaries in roughly the time of Yohanan.

18. As noted above, GRA holds that Yohanan, Y. Ter. 5:5 I.A–B, is suggesting his own particular interpretation of what sages mean at M. Ter. 5:5. Accordingly, GRA states that F asserts simply that B–E is spurious, based on Eliezer's incorrect understanding of sages' view. I follow PM's interpretation.

19. The scribe of R has garbled the end of the line.

20. My interpretation follows Sens, cited by MP. C.f., PM, as well as MP's own interpretation of the passage.

21. The end of this line through H is written in the margin of L.

22. While I believe that PM's solution to the problem is tenable, I have presented these units separately. This is because they share no formal or linguistic interdependencies and indeed are not connected by joining language. Y. Ter. 5:9 II, further, appears separately at Y. Or. 1:3.

23. Through haplography, C was left out of the body of the text of L. It and D (lined out in the body of the MS.) have been added in the margin. This does not appear to be the source of the redundant E, for that line is found in R, as well as in P, V, and in L, both before and after the correction.

24. This line is lacking in R, a case of haplography.

25. C is written in the margin of L. It is lacking entirely from R. The point would be the same without it.

26. R lacks this word, through scribal error.

27. The scribe of R appears to have garbled the beginning of this line.

28. PM explains that this unit is found here because of Eleazar's statement, B, that one should not declare permitted that which is forbidden and vice versa. PM states that this develops the point of M. Ter. 5:9 I–K, that one may not purposely cause heave-offering to be neutralized. The connection is hardly more than tenuous and does not explain the inclusion here of the whole unit.

Chapter Six

1. The parallel at Y. Ter. 7:1 reads: R. Simeon b. Laqish.

2. I follow the parallel at Y. Ter. 7:1. The version at Y. Ter. 6:1 reverses the words "intentionally" and "unintentionally" in this line.

3. One who intentionally eats heave-offering is not expected to pay the added fifth (M. Ter. 7:1). The word "unintentionally" therefore is somewhat misleading in this context. Presumably it is included on the basis of the parallel at A. The meaning of the stich in all events seems clear.

4. R lacks L, apparently a case of haplography.

5. Instead of the correct attribution, found in L, V, and P, R has: it is taught. It appears as though the scribe has copied this in from the line below.

6. R lacks the end of this stich.

7. Between C and D, R contains three garbled lines. The scribe apparently copied D–F with several errors and then went on to copy it a second time, correctly.

8. Cf., T. Ter. 7:7A–B, which notes that unclean heave-offering should not be used as restitution for clean heave-offering unintentionally eaten by a nonpriest. In that pericope Sumkos answers the question of what happens if a nonpriest nevertheless makes restitution for clean heave-offering with unclean produce. This is the opposite of the situation depicted in Y. It is unclear whether Y. knows a different version of T. or whether its editor simply has created a new superscription for Sumkos's statement. Such a new superscription would have been formed in order to create the parallel needed for the case of M. Ter. 2:2 and T. Ter. 3:19, cited here at D–E.

9. The scribe of R has added here: it is forbidden to nonpriests. This makes no sense and surely is a copyist's error.

10. R lacks: nonpriests. The point is the same.

11. T.'s reading, which lacks "not," is preferable. The point of B and C is that the restitution is comparable to unconsecrated food, not true heave-offering. Therefore if made into bread, it should be subject to dough offering.

12. R lacks: agree.

13. R lacks the verb, a scribal error.

14. At C–E, I follow Sifre *Emor pereq* 6:7, maintaining only Y.'s attribution to Rabbi. Sifre has Meir. In Y.'s version D and E are the same. This renders the unit senseless.

15. Note the variation in names, and possibly authorities, at H and I.

16. In R this term is garbled.

17. The scribe of R has repeated the beginning of this line twice.

18. R lacks this word.

19. R lacks this word.

20. R repeats the preceding statement a second time, in slightly different words. This appears to be a scribal error.

21. F is lacking in R.

22. I follow the emendation of PM and GRA: *qmt lqt*, parallel to *qmt py'h* in the next clause. Y. reads: *nšykt py'h*.

23. Unlike F, G is found in Y. Ter.

24. Because of a printer's error, P (in Y. Ter., not in the version at Y. Pe.) reads *nšykh* instead of *nšyrh*.

25. Like P, PM reads *py'h blqt* instead of the better attested *py'h klqt* (found in L, V, and R). Thus he translates: Would you say that the produce designated in the corner of the field for the poor consists of [the same produce which will be] gleanings? This forces PM to suggest an unnecessarily complicated interpretation of Yohanan's position.

26. Through scribal error, R reads: paid.

27. R lacks D, probably the result of haplography.

Chapter Seven

1. The incorrect reading is found in L, V, P, and R. All have the correct reading at L, indicating that the present phrasing is a scribal error, not an alternate version of the unit.

2. The scribe of R has garbled this clause.

3. The end of this line is written in the margin of L. It is likely that it was omitted from the text through haplography. R has completely garbled the stich.

4. The citation of M. Ter. 7:1A, here at A, is irrelevant to what follows.

5. So PM, following Y. Ket. 3:1. P, V, L, and R read: to exempt.

6. Y. Ter. reads: neither a fine nor stripes apply. This reading contradicts what is explicit at M. Mak. 3:1.

7. J is missing from P, but found in V, L, and R.

8. R has "bar," but lacks the patronym. This is a scribal error.

9. C–D is written in the margin of L.

10. At the end of this stich R adds: four *qabs* and three *qabs* for an ass. This is nonsensical, presumably the result of scribal error.

11. R reads: Said R. Abbahu, "R. Yose said . . ."

12. R lacks the rest of D–H, beginning again after the attribution at I. This is a clear case of haplography.

13. In Y. Ter., what I translate at U occurs here instead. I follow Y. Ket. and PM.

14. Through a copyist's error, R adds: he receives stripes. This most likely is a case of *lapsus linguim*.

15. In R the conclusion of this unit and the beginning of the following one are garbled.

16. The attribution, missing in P, V, and L, is found in R and in the parallel at Y. Ket. 3:1.

17. "For R. Meir" is added between the lines in L.

18. P, L, and R have "is not fit," and, at D, read "is fit." I can make no sense of that reading. The emendation is suggested by PM and GRA.

19. R reads: to leave. This is a dittograph for the word "excludes" in the preceding line of text.

20. I translate L, V, and the suggestion of PM: *hllh mknh*. P has *hllh mbnh*, the result of a printer's error. R has *hllh mkhnh*, which makes sense. But it appears to be a copyist's error, since at F the correct word, *mknh*, appears.

21. Through dittography, D–E was written twice in the body of L. The second occurrence has been deleted with a line.

22. P, V, L, and R read: does not contain. In light of the continuation at D–E, this makes no sense.

23. V and L number D–M as Y. Ter. 7:5. The basis for this division is unclear, since the unit, as given here, comprises a single discussion.

24. This word is lacking in R, a case of haplography.

25. The name is lacking in R.

26. "Unclean" appears between the lines in L.

27. V, L, P, and R have: unclean. I have corrected the text to read: clean. This reading is assumed by L and the reasoning at Q–R.

28. R lacks "forbidden," reading N–P as a single sentence. The meaning is the same.

29. B–E is written in the margin of L.

30. The beginning of B is written in the margin of L.

31. P, V, L, and R read: before. I follow PM's correction, required by the sense of the passage.

32. R lacks: Yannai.

33. This and the following three words have dropped out of the text of R, a case of haplography.

Chapter Eight

1. P: Eleazar. Reference is to an Amora.

2. So V, L, and R. MSS. of M. Git. 6:4 read: Eliezer.

3. P, V, L, and R reverse "Israelite" and "priest," an obvious error (PM).

4. P, V, L, and R reverse "permitted" and "forbidden," an error corrected by PM and GRA.

5. So PM.

6. Through scribal error R adds here: in the present time.

7. In error V and L read: Rabbis. PM suggests the necessary correction.

8. P, V, L, and R have *šwrp* for *ʿwrp*.

9. For "unclean," P, V, and L have: lacking [the requisite volume]. The difference in meaning is not significant. I follow T.'s version, which has the wording of E parallel to that of F.

10. Lacking in R.

11. In L this word has been changed between the lines to read: unclean thing. The point is the same.

12. H is lacking in R.

13. PM deletes: blemished. It is found in all MSS. and editions and, so far as I can determine, belongs in the present context.

14. R reverses K and L. It further adds after L: *ylyp ʾt bhwms*. I cannot make sense of that addition.

15. The scribe of R omitted the last two items here and went on to copy the attribution which heads the following pericope. Realizing his error, he supplied the last entries of the list and began the following unit anew.

16. I cannot locate the source in Scripture of this citation.

17. In the facsimile edition of R, the page numbered 236 belongs before that numbered 235.

18. The scribe of R omitted the attribution and went on to copy the rest of this stich. Realizing the error, he then copied the whole line correctly.

19. B–C is lacking in R.

20. D is written in the margin of L.

21. In error the scribe of R has written: to sprinkle it. The same error occurs at G for the word "retain."

22. R introduces the story with the formulaic: *Mᶜśh B.*

23. This line is lacking in R.

24. "Not" appears in L, but has been crossed out in a later hand. It is necessary to the sense of the passage.

25. R reads "Sadoq," a scribal error.

26. R lacks the rest of this stich, through the attribution at E.

27. R lacks the preceding clause.

28. R lacks the rest of the stich.

29. In R the order of K–L and M–N is reversed. There is no difference in meaning.

30. R repeats the attribution twice, a copyist's error.

31. R lacks the rest of A and all of B.

32. R reverses the attribution at B and C, thus citing C in Nehemiah's name, just as in T. It is impossible to know whether the reading of L, P, and V, which I translate, is a corruption, or whether some error (or intentional revision) has occurred in R.

33. R lacks this first word.

34. Three words are lacking from the text of L but are supplied in the margin. They dropped out of the body of the text through haplography.

35. R has: Hanania.

36. C is added in the margin of L.

37. So V, L, and R. P has: Rabbi.

38. M. Ter. 8:10 begins here.

39. M. Ter. 8:11 begins here.

40. In error R lacks the second name.

41. R lacks these three words, as in T.'s version. The point is the same.

42. R lacks: any small amount.

43. As T states, Meir allows the householder to impart uncleanness to heave-offering under one circumstance alone. This is the case described at M. Pes. 1:7, as interpreted at T. If on the eve of the Sabbath preceding Passover leavened produce in the status of heave-offering develops a doubt concerning whether or not it is unclean, Meir allows the householder to burn this heave-offering with other, certainly unclean, heave-offering. That case has its own special law, for, with the Sabbath and Passover coming, the individual has no choice but to quickly destroy this leavened heave-offering.

44. Y. Ter.: Meir.

45. In error R reverses the names Meir and Jeremiah.

46. GRA solves the problem by stating that the claim is that Meir agrees with Yose b. Judah, cited here. While this might be the point, it is not intrinsic to the language of J.

47. Follow Y. Pes. and PM.

48. Cf., GRA, who reads this unit as the continuation of the argument of the preceding pericope.

49. Through haplography, the scribe of R has dropped the rest of this sentence, through the next occurrence of the name Joshua, at C.

50. K–L is separate and probably does not belong here at all, as I indicate in my comment in the translation. A–B is an introduction to the main point which interests Y., the mediating position of Zeira, C, which serves as the basis for the whole discussion which follows, D–O.

51. On D–F, cf., PM.

52. R reads: Adda. This is an error.

53. *dbr.* R: *'th*, a nonexistent word.

54. R lacks the rest of this stich, a case of haplography.

55. In L the word "unclean" is added by a later hand, between the lines. Indeed, the point of this stich is not entirely clear, since even without it, C makes perfect sense. We would expect D to challenge C. Yet I find no way of reading it that way.

56. R lacks this word.

57. R adds that the slave woman is unclean. This is a scribal addition.

58. So T. for the preceding words. Y. has: even though they all are to be killed. There is no difference in meaning.

59. In error R reads simply: Resh.

60. Through haplography, the scribe of R skipped from here to the citation of Yohanan, at G.

61. R reads: Qushar.

62. Both parties in the dispute agree to the principle just expressed. They disagree over a quibble, specifically, how good a reason we must have in order to turn someone over. As in the upcoming material, Yohanan, G, is less willing to fight the government than is Simeon b. Laqish, F. Yohanan, therefore, states that the person may be turned over even if he is not wanted for a capital offense.

63. Through dittography the scribe of R has copied this stich twice.

64. The word is lacking in R, but through error appears in L, V, and P.

65. The scribe of R has garbled this stich and the beginning of E.

66. R has the beginning of the name twice, a case of haplography.

67. So GRA, and as required by the sense of the passage.

68. There is a linguistic connection with Y. Ter. 8:10 **III**, for Q here is reminiscent of the statement there of Zenabia. While this may account for the inclusion of the unit here, the logic behind the particular ordering of these pericopae remains unclear.

Chapter Nine

1. Through haplography R lacks: poor Israelites.
2. In V, L, and R this unit is marked 9:3. The reason is not clear. PM correctly numbers the unit as part of Y.'s discussion of M. Ter. 9:2.
3. The scribe of R has garbled the beginning of the pericope.
4. R reads: Ishmael. This is a common error in the MS.
5. Through scribal error, R lacks most of this stich and jumps to the recurrence of this material at Y. Ter. 9:3 V.M–N. The intervening discussion is missing.
6. The scribe of R has garbled this stich.
7. R lacks the end of the pericope.
8. In error the scribe of L wrote: after-growths of the seventh year. This has been corrected between the lines.
9. R lacks this word, a scribal error.
10. B–C is written in the margin of L. It dropped out of the text through haplography.

Chapter Ten

1. Through scribal error R lacks this word through the last word of B.
2. Maimonides, Bertinoro, and Albeck state that the point of the pericope is the same whether it is the lentils or the onions which have the status of heave-offering. These exegetes make this claim because, on the basis of Y. Ter. 10:1 **I**, they incorrectly read the issue as being whether or not the heave-offering imparts flavor to the unconsecrated food. They thus neither agree with the clear sense of M. nor with the interpretation of the pericope given here.
3. The scribe of R skipped to the next occurrence of the word "flavor," a case of haplography.
4. This is written in the margin of L.
5. The first part of this line appears twice in R, a case of haplography.
6. R lacks this word.
7. R lacks the rest of this stich.
8. Through haplography the scribe of R has skipped from here to the middle of E.
9. Yohanan's statement, which follows, is lacking in R. The scribe skipped to the citation of M., at H. Realizing the error, he copied F–G at the end of the pericope, concluding it with: etc.
10. Cf., Avery-Peck, pp. 273–74.
11. R lacks this stich.
12. R lacks this line, a case of haplography.
13. So PM, as required by the sense of the passage. P, V, and L read: sealed top. This is just as at E.

14. The scribe of R misread the word and wrote *bynwnyt* instead of *swnnt*. The same error occurs at H.

15. R reads *smyh* in place of *ṭwwyh*.

16. R lacks the conclusion of this line. The point is the same.

17. R lacks this final word of the stich.

18. The units within Y. Ter. 10:5a and Y. Ter. 10:5b are numbered consecutively. This is in accordance with L and V, which present Y.'s material to M. Ter. 10:5–6 as a single discussion.

19. R lacks this pericope, through the middle of A in the following unit.

20. R begins here.

21. The scribe of R has miscopied the word, writing *hm ṭwblyn* instead of *šblym*.

22. The scribe of R wrote *'m* instead of *'yn*.

23. The scribe of R has garbled the last word of this line and the beginning of the next.

24. R lacks this word.

25. R lacks this word, a result of haplography.

26. The scribe of R wrote this line once, incorrectly concluding with the word "forbidden." He then copied it a second time, correctly.

27. R lacks the rest of the unit, probably a case of haplography.

28. R lacks this stich. The scribe wrote its first word, "instructed," but then, through haplography, skipped to the following unit, which begins with an attribution to Yose b. R. Hanina.

29. G is lacking in R.

30. PM reads the unit as continuous with the following. I find no substantive basis for this claim. The parallel at Y. A.Z. 2:9, which does not include the following pericope, presents a serious challenge to PM's suggestion.

31. R lacks this word.

32. L adds here: Here also it is because it was an accident. These words, which make no sense in context, are crossed out in a later hand.

33. D–E depends upon a discussion found at Y. Git. 1:1. The whole unit is paralleled at Y. A.Z. 2:9. Y.Ter. is not the primary context of this material.

34. It is unclear why Y.'s discussion of M. Ter. 10:11 has been broken into two parts, with the interpretation of M. Ter. 10:11G–H coming in Y. Ter. 10:9. This is a rare instance in which the numbering in L and V does not follow the standard division of M.'s pericopae. It is especially surprising since M. Ter. 10:11A–F and M. Ter. 10:11G–H are parts of a single, unitary literary construction.

35. P: Hanania.

36. V and L add the name "Zeira" again at this point. R repeats the name: Simeon.

37. In R, D–E is garbled.

38. This is the same authority as Simeon bar Abba, at B.

39. In error R reads: forty-five.

40. The scribe of R copied this last clause twice. The second time he wrote: forty-seven. This apparently was an attempt to correct the error cited in the preceding note.

41. In R this line is somewhat garbled, the result of scribal error.

Chapter Eleven

1. R lacks this word.

2. Through haplography the scribe of R has deleted most of I–J.

3. In error the scribe of R began with D–E. He then went back and copied A–E correctly.

4. R lacks this stich, a case of haplography.

5. R is written in the margin of L.

6. R lacks this stich.

7. "Yohanan" is written in the margin of L. It appears in V, P, and R. In R, however, R–T is copied a second time, with the proper attribution to Rabbi.

8. The scribe of R wrote *l'* instead of *lmh*.

9. The chart describes the pericope in T.'s version. Y.'s slight variation is referred to in the body of the comment.

10. So PM, as required by the continuation of the discussion, J–L. Note that J and K are redundant.

11. R adds: did not. At C it lacks these words.

12. L, V, P, and R add "did not" and lack these words at K. I follow T.'s reading, as does PM.

13. So PM.

14. R lacks this line.

15. Y.'s version gives I's rule for the case described at J. At K it refers to a priest who goes to the house of an Israelite "to do business." Y. lacks I entirely.

16. The scribe of R abbreviated this stich, indicating that it had already appeared above (at Y. Ter. 11:10 **II**.K).

17. So P, R, and PM: *l'ylyn*. V and L read: *k'ylyn*.

18. In L the name Yose has been corrected between the lines to read: Judah. In error R reads: Yose. It has the same name at F.

19. In L the name Meir has been corrected between the lines to read: Yose.

20. R lacks this stich.

21. I–K is written in the margin of L. The original deletion of this material presumably accounts for the error in names mentioned in the preceding notes. The scribe of R has garbled I–K.

22. R lacks this line.

23. In error R has Jeremiah.

Transliterations

א	= ʾ	ל	= l
ב	= b	מ, ם	= m
ג	= g	נ, ן	= n
ד	= d	ס	= s
ה	= h	ע	= ʿ
ו	= w	פ, ף	= p
ז	= z	צ, ץ	= ṣ
ח	= ḥ	ק	= q
ט	= ṭ	ר	= r
י	= y	שׁ	= š
כ, ך	= k	שׂ	= ś
		ת	= t

Transliterations represent the consonantal structure of the Hebrew word, with no attempt made to vocalize. I do not distinguish between the spirantized and nonspirantized forms of *b, g, d, k, p,* and *t*. Verbal roots are indicated by capitalization, e.g., *TRM*. When, on occasion, a word is vocalized, the following notation is used:

a = *qamaṣ, pataḥ* i = *ḥiriq*
ei = *ṣere-yod* o = *ḥolem, ḥolem ḥaser,*
e = *ṣere, segol, vocal šewaʾ* *qamaṣ qaṭan*
u = *šuruq, qubbuṣ*

Quiescent *šewaʾ* is not represented. Proper names and commonly used words are reproduced in their most frequent English usage, e.g., Eleazar, Mishnah, etc.

Abbreviations, Bibliography, and Glossary

A: *Talmud Yerushalmi, Seder Ze-raim and Masekhet Sheqalim*, with commentary of Elijah b. Judah Loeb of Fulda (ca. 1650–1715). 2 vols. Amsterdam, 1710. Reprint. Jerusalem, 1971.

Ah.: Ahilot.

Am Haares: An Israelite who is not trusted to properly tithe his produce or to observe the rules of Levitical cleanness. The opposite of a *haber*.

Amah: A cubit (pl.: *amot*).

Ar.: Arakhin.

Avery-Peck: Alan J. [Avery-]Peck. *The Priestly Gift in Mishnah. A Study of Tractate Terumot*. Chico, 1981.

Avery-Peck, Agriculture: Alan J. Avery-Peck. *The Mishnaic Division of Agriculture: A History and Theology of Seder Zeraim*. Chico, 1985.

A.Z.: Abodah Zarah.

b.: *ben*, "son of."

B.: *Babli*, Babylonian Talmud.

B.B.: Baba Batra.

Bek.: Bekhorot.

Ber.: Berakhot.

Bes.: Besah.

Bik.: Bikkurim.

B.M.: Baba Mesia.

Bokser, "Guide": Baruch M. Bokser. "An Annotated Bibliographical Guide to the Study of the Palestinian Talmud," in Wolfgang Haase, ed. *ANRW* (II, 19, 2). Berlin and New York, 1979), pp. 139–256.

Bokser, *Judaism*: Baruch M. Bokser. *Post Mishnaic Judaism in Transition. Samuel on Berakhot and the Beginnings of Gemara*. Chico, 1980.

B.Q.: Baba Qamma.

Chron.: Chronicles.

Comm.: Commentary.

Dem.: Demai.

Demai: Produce about which there is a doubt whether or not the required heave-offering and tithes were removed.

Denar: A coin worth one-half of a *shekel*.

Diverse Kinds: Heterogeneous plants and animals. These may not be joined together through being planted in the same field,

551

harnessed together or crossbred (Lev. 19:19, Dt. 22:9–11).

Dt.: Deuteronomy.

Dupondium: A coin worth one-twelfth of a *shekel*.

Eccles.: Ecclesiastes.

Ed.: Eduyyot.

Eighteen Benedictions: The central prayer of the liturgy, recited three times daily, four times on Sabbath and festivals, and five times on the Day of Atonement.

Erub: A deposit of food which is used (1) to amalgamate several distinct domains or (2) to establish a temporary abode. As a result, on the Sabbath, individuals may cross the boundaries of the distinct domains or move beyond the usual range of 2,000 cubits permitted for movement on the holy day.

Erub.: Erubin.

Etrog: A citron, carried on the Festival of Boothes as the "fruit of goodly trees," mentioned at Lev. 23:40.

Ex.: Exodus.

Ezek.: Ezekiel.

Feliks: Yehudah Feliks. *Agriculture in Palestine in the Period of the Mishnah and Talmud* (Hebrew) Jerusalem and Tel Aviv, 1963.

Gen.: Genesis.

Ginzberg: Louis Ginzberg. *Yerushalmi Fragments from the Genizah. I. Text with various readings from the editio princeps.* New York, 1909. Reprint. New York and Hildesheim, 1970.

Git.: Gittin.

GRA: Elijah b. Solomon Zalman. "HaGaon Rabbi Eliyahu," or "Vilna Gaon." Lithuania, 1720–97. Mishnah and Talmud commentaries in standard editions.

Haas: Peter J. Haas. *A History of the Mishnaic Law of Agriculture. Tractate Maaser Sheni.* Chico, 1980.

Haber: A person who (1) separates all required agricultural offerings from food he grows or purchases and (2) who eats his food in a state of cultic cleanness. The opposite of an *Am Haares*.

Hag.: Hagigah.

Hal.: Hallah.

Halisah: The ceremony which severs the bond between a man and his brother's childless widow (see Dt. 27:7–9). "The rite of removing the shoe."

Hallel: A portion of the liturgy, consisting of Ps. 113–18, recited on festivals and new moons.

Halusah: A woman who has undergone the ceremony of *halisah*.

Homer: A unit of measure equal to about eleven bushels.

Hor.: Horayot.

Hul.: Hullin.

Is.: Isaiah.

Issar: A coin, valued at one-forty-eighth of a *shekel*.

Issaron: A measure of volume, equal to one-tenth of an *ephah*.

Jastrow: Marcus Jastrow. *A Dictionary of the Targumim, the Talmud Babli and Yerushalmi, and the Midrashic Literature.* 2 vols. New York. Reprint: 1950.

Jaffee: Martin S. Jaffee. *Mishnah's Theology of Tithing. A Study of Tractate Maaserot.* Chico, 1981.

Jer.: Jeremiah.

Josh.: Joshua.

Kasowski, *Talmud*: Chaim J. Kasowski. *Thesaurus Talmudis; concordantiae verborum quae in Talmude Babilonico reperuntur.* Jerusalem, 1954–

Kel.: Kelim.

Ker.: Keritot.

Kerem Rebai: A vineyard in its fourth year of growth, the produce of which is deemed sanctified (Lev. 19:24).

Ket.: Ketubot.

Ketubah: A marriage contract indicating the sum of money due to the wife upon her husband's death or once they are divorced.

Kil.: Kilayim.

Kor: A dry measure. The quantity of seed needed to plant 75,000 square cubits of land.

Krauss: Samuel Krauss. *Griechische und Lateinische Lehnwörter im Talmud, Midrasch, und Targum.* Berlin, 1899. Reprint. Hildsheim, 1964.

Lam.: Lamentations.

L: *The Palestinian Talmud. Leiden MS. Cod Scal. 3. A Facsimile of the original manuscript,* with an introduction by Saul Lieberman. 4 vols. Jerusalem, 1970.

Letekh: A measure of volume, equal to one and a half *ephah*.

Lev.: Leviticus.

Lieberman: Saul Lieberman. *Al Ha-Yerushalmi.* Jerusalem, 1929.

Lieberman, *Caesaria*: Saul Lieberman. *The Talmud of Caesaria. Jerushalmi Tractate Nezikin.* Supplement to *Tarbiz* II 4, in Hebrew. Jerusalem, 1931.

Lieberman, *TK*: Saul Lieberman. *Tosefta Ki-Fshuta: A Comprehensive Commentary on the Tosefta,* I. *Order Zeraim.* 2 vols. New York, 1955.

Lieberman, *YK*: Saul Lieberman. *Ha Yerushalmi Kiphshuto. A commentary based on manuscripts of the Yerushalmi and works of the Rishonim and Midrashim in Mss. and rare editions.* I, i *Sabbath, Erubin, Pesahim* (in Hebrew). Jerusalem, 1934.

Lit.: Literally.

Litra: A measure of volume, equal to $\frac{1}{144}$ of an *ephah*.

Log: $\frac{1}{72}$ of an *ephah*.

Lulab: The branches of palm, myrtle, and willow which are bound together and carried along with the *etrog* on the Festival of Boothes (see Lev. 23:40).

M.: Mishnah.

Ma.: Maaserot.

Maah: A coin, valued at one-twelfth of a *shekel*.

Mak.: Makkot.

Makh.: Makhshirin.

Mal.: Malachi.

Mamzer(et): The offspring of a man and woman who could not legally marry one another.

Maneh: A weight of gold or silver, equal to fifty *shekels*.

Marshall: J. Y. Marshall. *Manual of the Aramaic Language of the Pal-*

estinian Talmud. Grammar, vocalized text, translation, and vocabulary. Edited by J. Barton Turner, with an introduction by A. Mingana. Leiden, 1929.

Me.: Meilah.

Meg.: Megillah.

Melammed: E. Z. Melammed. *An Introduction to Talmudic Literature.* Jerusalem, 1973, in Hebrew.

Men.: Menahot.

Mid.: Middot.

Mil: Two thousand cubits.

Miq.: Miqvaot.

MP: *Mar'eh Hapannim.* Moses Margoliot (eighteenth century), supercommentary to the author's commentary to the Yerushalmi (*Penei Moshe;* see PM), in standard editions of Y.

M.Q.: Moed Qatan.

MS.: Manuscript (pl.: MSS.)

M.S.: Maaser Sheni.

M'SH B (W): A formulaic phrase used to introduce a legal precedent.

Naz.: Nazir.

Nazirite: One who has taken a vow neither to cut his hair, drink wine, nor contract corpse-uncleanness (see Num. 6:1–27).

Ned.: Nedarim.

Neg.: Negaim.

Neh.: Nehemiah.

Netin(ah): A descendant of the Gibeonites, designated at Josh. 9:27 as Temple slaves. They have impaired status within the Israelite community (see M. Qid. 4:1ff).

Neusner, *Appointed Times*: Jacob Neusner. *A History of the Mishnaic Law of Appointed Times.* 5 vols. Leiden: E. J. Brill, 1980–81.

Neusner, *Damages*: Jacob Neusner. *A History of the Mishnaic Law of Damages.* 4 vols. Leiden: E. J. Brill, 1982.

Neusner, *Holy Things:* Jacob Neusner. *A History of the Mishnaic Law of Holy Things.* 4 vols. Leiden, 1978–79.

Neusner, *Mishnah*: Jacob Neusner. *Judaism: The Evidence of the Mishnah.* Chicago, 1981.

Neusner, *Purities*: Jacob Neusner. *A History of the Mishnaic Law of Purities.* 22 vols. Leiden, 1974–77.

Neusner, *Tosefta*: Jacob Neusner. *The Tosefta Translated from the Hebrew.* 6 vols. New York, 1977–86.

Neusner, *Women*: Jacob Neusner. *A History of the Mishnaic Law of Women.* 4 vols. Leiden, 1979–80.

Nid.: Niddah.

Num.: Numbers.

NY: *Noam Yerushalmi.* Joshua Isaac Salonima. *Sefer Noam Yerushalmi. Vehu beur al hayyerushalmi.* 2 vols. Vilna, 1868. Reprint. Jerusalem, 1969.

Oh.: Ohalot.

Omer: The first sheaf of the season, which must be harvested and offered in the Temple as a meal offering. Only when this is done may the rest of the new grain be reaped (Lev. 23:10).

Or.: Orlah.

Orlah: Produce from an orchard in its first three years of growth that may not be eaten (Lev. 19:23).

P: *Talmud Yerushalmi*. Romm ed. and numerous reprints.

ʾP: A formulaic word used to introduce a named authority's expansion of a preceding rule.

Par.: Parah.

Pe.: Peah.

Peah: Produce that grows in the corner of the field and that must be left unharvested so it can be collected by the poor (see Lev. 19:9ff).

PM: *Penei Moshe*. Moses Margoliot (d. 1780), *Penei Moshe*. Commentary on Yerushalmi, found in standard editions. Amsterdam, 1754; Leghorn, 1770.

Perutah: A copper coin of small denomination.

Pes.: Pesahim.

Pondion: One-twenty-fourth of a *shekel*.

Prayer: The Eighteen Benedictions.

Prov.: Proverbs.

Ps.: Psalms.

Pundium: One-sixth of a *shekel*.

Qab: A measure of volume, equal to one-eighteenth of an *ephah*.

Qartob: A liquid or dry measure, equal to one-sixty-fourth of a *log*.

QE: *Qorban haʿedah*. Elijah b. Judah Loeb of Fulda, *Qorban haʿedah*. Commentary to the Yerushalmi. Dessau, 1743; Berlin, 1757, 1760–62. Reprinted in standard editions.

Qid.: Qiddushin.

Qin.: Qinnim.

R: *The Palestinian Talmud. Ms. Rome 133. A facsimile of the original manuscript.* Jerusalem, n.d.

R.: Rabbi.

Rabbinowitz: Louis I. Rabbinowitz. "Talmud, Jerusalem," *Encyclopaedia Judaica*. 15:772–79. Jerusalem, 1971.

Rabinovitz, STEI: Z. W. Rabinovitz. *Shaʿare Torath Eretz Israel. Notes and Comments on Yerushalmi.* Jerusalem, 1940; published by his son.

Ratner: B. Ratner. *Ahawath Zion we-Jeruscholaim. Varianten und Ergänzungen des Textes des Jerusalemitischen Talmuds nach alten Quellen und handschriftlichen Fragmenten ediert, mit kritischen Noten und Erlauterungen versehen.* 12 vols. III. *Terumot, Hallah* (1904). Vilna: Wittwe & Gebr. Romm et al., 1901–67.

R.H.: Rosh Hashanah.

RiDBaZ: David ibn Zimra (1479–1573), commentary to the Yerushalmi in standard editions.

Sam.: Samuel.

San.: Sanhedrin.

Sarason, Demai: Richard S. Sarason. *A History of the Mishnaic Law of Agriculture: A Study of Tractate Demai.* Leiden, 1979.

Sarason, "Tithing": Richard S. Sarason. "Mishnah and Scripture: Preliminary Observations on the Law of Tithing in *Seder Zeraʿim*," in W. S. Green, ed., *Approaches to Ancient Judaism. Vol. II.* Chico, 1980, pp. 81–96.

Schwab: Moise Schwab. *Le Talmud de Jerusalem. Traduit pour la premiere fois en francais.* Paris, reprint: 1960.

Seah: One third of an *ephah*.

Sens: Samson b. Abraham of Sens (France, late twelfth-early thirteenth centuries). Mishnah commentary in Romm edition of the Babylonian Talmud.

Shab.: Shabbat.

Shabu.: Shabuot.

Shekel: The chief coin of the Israelites, weighing between a quarter and a half of an ounce.

Shema: A section of the liturgy composed of Dt. 6:4–9, 11:13–21, and Num. 15:37–41. It is recited twice daily, morning and evening.

Sheq.: Sheqalim.

Sifra: *Sifra debe Rab, hu Sefer Torat Kohanim,* edited by Isaac Hirsch Weiss. Vienna, 1862. Reprint. New York, 1946.

Sirillo: Solomon b. Joseph Sirillo (Spain, Balkans, Palestine, died c. 1558). Commentary to the Yerushalmi, Order Zeraim. Jerusalem, 1934–67, *Terumot,* 1934.

Sot.: Sotah.

Strack: Hermann Strack. *Introduction to the Talmud and Midrash.* Reprint. Philadelphia, 1959.

Suk.: Sukkah.

S.Y.: Nahum Trebitsch. *Shalom Yerushalayim,* commentary to the Yerushalmi, Order Zeraim. Jerusalem, 1980.

T.: Tosefta.

Ta.: Taanit.

Tam.: Tamid.

Tebul yom: A person who has immersed in a ritual bath and awaits the setting of the sun, which marks the completion of the process of purification.

Tem.: Temurah.

Ter.: Terumot.

Terefah: Meat which is ruined in the process of ritual slaughter through some improper act of the slaughterer.

Terisit: A coin.

Toh.: Tohorot.

T.Y.: Tebul Yom.

Uqs.: Uqsin.

V: *Talmud Yerushalmi . . . Venezia.* (Reprint: no place, no date.) *Editio princeps* printed by Daniel Bomberg, 1523–24.

Y.: Yerushalmi, Talmud of the land of Israel.

Yad.: Yadayyim.

Yeb.: Yebamot.

Yom.: Yoma.

Y.T.: Yom Tob.

Zab.: Zabim.

Zab(ah): A person who has suffered a flux and is deemed unclean. (Pl.: *zabim, zabot*).

Zeb.: Zebahim.

Zech.: Zechariah.

Zuckermandel: M. S. Zuckermandel. *Tosephta. Based on the Erfurt and Vienna Codices with parallels and varients.* Reprint. Jerusalem, 1963.

Zuz: A coin, valued at a *denar* (i.e., one-half of a *shekel*). Pl.: *zuzim*.

Index of Biblical and Talmudic References

General Index